WESTERN CIVILIZATION

NINTH EDITION

Volume I: To 1715

Jackson J. Spielvogel
The Pennsylvania State University

CENGAGE
Learning·

Australia • Brazil • Mexico • Singapore • United Kingdom • United States

CENGAGE
Learning®

Western Civilization, Volume I: To 1715, Ninth Edition, Advantage Edition

Jackson J. Spielvogel

Product Manager: Brooke Barbier

Content Developer: Lauren Floyd

Product Assistant: Katie Coaster

Media Developer: Kate MacLean

Marketing Brand Manager: Melissa Larmon

Manufacturing Planner: Sandee Milewski

Art and Design Direction, Production Management, and Composition: PreMediaGlobal

Cover Image: A court festival. From the "Roman de Saint Graal," Ms. 527, fol. 1 recto. 15th c.e. Credit: Erich Lessing/ Art Resource, NY.

For product information and technology assistance, contact us at **Cengage Learning Customer & Sales Support, 1-800-354-9706.**

For permission to use material from this text or product, submit all requests online at **www.cengage.com/permissions.** Further permissions questions can be e-mailed to **permissionrequest@cengage.com.**

Library of Congress Control Number: 2014932039

Student Edition:

ISBN-13: 978-1-285-44846-6

ISBN-10: 1-285-44846-4

Cengage Learning
200 First Stamford Place, 4th Floor
Stamford, CT 06902
USA

Cengage Learning is a leading provider of customized learning solutions with office locations around the globe, including Singapore, the United Kingdom, Australia, Mexico, Brazil, and Japan. Locate your local office at **www.cengage.com/global**.

Cengage Learning products are represented in Canada by Nelson Education, Ltd.

To learn more about Cengage Learning Solutions, visit **www.cengage.com.**

Purchase any of our products at your local college store or at our preferred online store **www.cengagebrain.com.**

Printed in the United States of America
1 2 3 4 5 6 7 18 17 16 15 14

Brief Contents

Contents

Preface

DURING A VISIT to Great Britain, where he studied as a young man, Mohandas Gandhi, the leader of the effort to liberate India from British colonial rule, was asked what he thought of Western civilization. "I think it would be a good idea," he replied. Gandhi's response was as correct as it was clever. Western civilization has led to great problems as well as great accomplishments, but it remains a good idea. And any complete understanding of today's world must take into account the meaning of Western civilization and the role Western civilization has played in history. Despite modern progress, we still greatly reflect our religious traditions, our political systems and theories, our economic and social structures, and our cultural heritage. I have written this history of Western civilization to assist a new generation of students in learning more about the past that has helped create them and the world in which they live.

At the same time, for the ninth edition, as in the eighth, I have added new material on world history to show the impact other parts of the world have made on the West. Certainly, the ongoing struggle with terrorists since 2001 has made clear the intricate relationship between the West and the rest of the world. It is important then to show not only how Western civilization has affected the rest of the world but also how it has been influenced and even defined since its beginnings by contacts with other peoples around the world.

Another of my goals was to write a well-balanced work in which the political, economic, social, religious, intellectual, cultural, and military aspects of Western civilization have been integrated into a chronologically ordered synthesis. I have been especially aware of the need to integrate the latest research on social history and women's history into each chapter of the book rather than isolating it either in lengthy topical chapters, which confuse the student by interrupting the chronological narrative, or in separate sections that appear at periodic intervals between chapters.

Another purpose in writing this history of Western civilization has been to put the *story* back in history. That story is an exciting one; yet many textbooks fail to capture the imagination of their readers. Narrative history effectively transmits the knowledge of the past and is the form that best aids remembrance. At the same time, I have not overlooked the need for the kind of historical analysis that makes students aware that historians often disagree on their interpretations of the past.

FEATURES OF THE TEXT

To enliven the past and let readers see for themselves the materials that historians use to create their pictures of the past, I have included in each chapter **primary sources** (boxed documents) that are keyed to the discussion in the text. The documents include examples of the religious, artistic, intellectual, social, economic, and political aspects of Western life. Such varied sources as a Renaissance banquet menu, a student fight song in nineteenth-century Britain, letters exchanged between a woman and her fiancé on the battle front in World War I, the Declaration of the Rights of Woman and the Female Citizen in the French Revolution, and a debate in the Reformation era all reveal in a vivid fashion what Western civilization meant to the individual men and women who shaped it by their activities. I have added questions at the end of each source to help students in analyzing the documents.

Each chapter has **detailed chronologies** that reinforce the events discussed in the text and that appear at the end of each chapter. **Updated maps and extensive illustrations** serve to deepen the reader's understanding of the text. **Detailed map captions** are designed to enrich students' awareness of the importance of geography to history. To facilitate understanding of cultural movements, illustrations of artistic works discussed in the text are placed near the discussions. Throughout the text, illustration captions have been revised and expanded to further students' understanding of the past. **Chapter outlines** at the beginning of each chapter give students a useful overview and guide them to the main subjects of each chapter. A **guide to pronunciation** is now provided in the text in parentheses following the first mention of a complex name or term. **Chapter Notes** are now at the end of the book rather than at the end of each chapter.

NEW TO THIS EDITION

As preparation for the revision of *Western Civilization*, I reexamined the entire book and analyzed the comments and reviews of many colleagues who have found the book to be a useful instrument for introducing their students to the history of Western civilization. In making revisions for the ninth edition, I sought to build on the strengths of the first eight editions and, above all, to maintain the balance, synthesis, and narrative qualities that characterized those editions. To keep up with the ever-growing body of historical scholarship, new or revised material has been added throughout the book on the following topics:

Chapter 1 new historiographical subsection, "The Spread of Humans: Out of Africa or Multiregional?"; religion in Neolithic societies; Amenhotep II and Amenhotep III; health care in ancient Egypt; the role of ritual in ancient Egypt; new Opposing Viewpoints feature on "The Great Flood: Two Versions."

Chapter 2 new historiographical subsection, "Was There a United Kingdom of Israel?"; Zoroastrianism.

Chapter 3 Minoan Crete; the role of the phalanx and colonies in the rise of democracy in Greece; helots and women in Sparta; political systems in Sparta and Athens; the background of Themistocles; Sophocles; sports and violence in ancient Greece.

Chapter 4 new historiographical subsection, "The Legacy: Was Alexander Great?"; women in the Hellenistic world.

Chapter 5 origins of the Etruscans; Julius Caesar and Cleopatra VII.

Chapter 6 client kingdoms; new Images of Everyday Life feature on "Children in the Roman World"; early Christianity.

Chapter 7 Roman emperors and church councils; Pope Gregory the Great; the labor of women in Frankish society; new subsection on "The Growing Wealth of Monasteries"; Latin church fathers; Benedictine monastic vows; Synod of Whitby.

Chapter 8 the *missi dominici;* the role of aristocratic women; women in Byzantium; women in the Slavic world; women in the world of Islam; new historiographical subsection, "What Was the Significance of Charlemagne?"

Chapter 9 roles of peasant women; commercial capitalism; women in medieval cities; new document on "Goliardic Poetry: The Archpoet."

Chapter 10 new historiographical subsection, "What Were the Effects of the Crusades?"; vassalage.

Chapter 11 new organization of material on art and the Black Death: new subsection, "Art and the Black Death"; new subsection, "A New Art: Giotto"; foreign *condottieri* in Italy.

Chapter 12 new Images of Everyday Life feature on "Family and Marriage in Renaissance Italy"; new historio-graphical subsection, "Was There a Renaissance for Women?"; English civil wars in the fifteenth century.

Chapter 13 new historiographical subsection, "Catholic Reformation or Counter-Reformation?"; new document on "Queen Elizabeth I: 'I Have the Heart of a King.'"

Chapter 14 new document on "Marco Polo's *Travels*"; new subsection, "Disease in the New World"; the West Indies.

Chapter 15 new historiographical subsection, "Was There a Military Revolution?"; Judith Leyster; Rembrandt.

Chapter 16 Maria Merian; Galileo's telescope; new document on "Margaret Cavendish: The Education of Women."

The enthusiastic response to the primary sources (boxed documents) led me to evaluate the content of each document carefully and add new documents throughout the text, including new comparative documents in the feature called **Opposing Viewpoints**. This feature, which was introduced in the seventh edition, presents a comparison of two or three primary sources in order to facilitate student analysis of historical documents. Focus questions are included to help students evaluate the documents. **Images of Everyday Life,** which combines two illustrations with a lengthy caption to provide insight into various aspects of social life, has also been expanded and includes such new topics as "Children in the Roman World."

Also new to the ninth edition are **historiographical sections,** which examine how and why historians differ in their interpretation of specific topics. Examples include "Was There a United Kingdom of Israel?"; "Was There a Renaissance for Women?"; "Was There an Agricultural Revolution?; "The Retreat from Democracy: Did Europe Have Totalitarian States?"; and "Why Did the Soviet Union Collapse?"

Because courses in Western civilization at American and Canadian colleges and universities follow different chronological divisions, a one-volume edition and two two-volume edition are available to fit the needs of instructors. Teaching and learning ancillaries include the following.

SUPPLEMENTS

For the Instructor

MindTap[TM]*: The Personal Learning Experience*   MindTap for Spielvogel's *Western Civilization* (PAC: 9781285843124) is a personalized, online digital learning platform providing students with the *Western Civilization* content and related interactive assignments and app services while giving you a choice in the configuration of coursework and curriculum enhancement. Through a carefully designed chapter-based learning path, students can access the Making America ebook (Mind Tap Reader, see description below); Aplia[TM] assignments developed for the most important concepts in each chapter (see Aplia description below); brief quizzes; and a set of web applications known as MindApps to help you create the most engaging course for your students. The MindApps range from ReadSpeaker (which reads the text out loud to students) to Kaltura (allowing you to insert inline video and audio into your curriculum) to ConnectYard (allowing you to create digital "yards" through social media—all without "friending" your students). MindTap for Spielvogel's *Western Civilization* goes well beyond an eBook, a homework solution/digital supplement, a resource center website, or a Learning Management System. It is truly a Personal Learning Experience that allows you to synchronize the text reading and engaging assignments and quizzes. To learn more, ask your Cengage Learning sales representative to demo it for you—or go to www.Cengage.com/MindTap.

Aplia[TM] (PAC: 9781285736358)   Aplia is an online interactive learning solution that improves comprehension and outcomes by increasing student effort and engagement. Founded by a professor to enhance his own courses, Aplia provides automatically graded assignments with detailed, immediate explanations on every question. The interactive assignments have been developed to address the major concepts covered in *Western Civilization,* 9e and are designed to promote critical thinking and engage students more fully in learning. Question types include questions built around animated maps, primary sources such as newspaper extracts, or imagined scenarios, like engaging in a conversation with Benjamin Franklin or finding a diary and being asked to fill in some blanks; more in-depth primary source question sets address a major topic with a number of related primary sources and questions that promote deeper analysis of historical evidence. Many of the questions incorporate images, video clips, or audio clips. Students get immediate feedback on their work (not only what they got right or wrong, but why), and they can choose to see another set of related questions if they want more practice. A searchable eBook is available inside the course as well so that students can easily reference it as they work. Map-reading and writing tutorials are also available to get students off to a good start.

Aplia's simple-to-use course management interface allows instructors to post announcements, upload course materials, host student discussions, e-mail students, and manage the gradebook; a knowledgeable and friendly support team offers assistance and personalized support in customizing assignments to the instructor's course schedule. To learn more and view a demo for this book, visit www.aplia.com.

MindTap Reader for Western Civilization   MindTap Reader is an eBook specifically designed to address the ways students assimilate content and media assets. MindTap Reader combines thoughtful navigation ergonomics, advanced student annotation, note-taking, and search tools, and embedded media assets such as video and MP3 chapter summaries, primary source documents with critical thinking questions, and interactive (zoomable) maps. Students can use the eBook as their primary text or as a multimedia companion to their printed book. The MindTap Reader eBook is available within the MindTap and Aplia online offerings found at www.cengagebrain.com.

Online PowerLecture with Cognero®   (ISBN: 9781285455044) This PowerLecture is an all-in-one online multimedia resource for class preparation, presentation, and testing. Accessible through Cengage.com/login with your faculty account, you will find available for download: book-specific Microsoft® PowerPoint® presentations; a Test Bank in both Microsoft® Word® and Cognero® formats; an Instructor Manual; Microsoft® PowerPoint® Image Slides; and a JPEG Image Library.

Test Bank   The Test Bank offered in Microsoft® Word® and Cognero® formats contains multiple-choice and essay questions for each chapter. Cognero® is a flexible, online system that allows you to author, edit, and manage test bank content for *Western Civilization, 9e*. Create multiple test versions instantly and deliver through your LMS from your classroom, or wherever you may be, with no special installs or downloads required.

eInstructor's Resource Manual   Prepared by Jennifer McNabb of Western Illinois University. This manual has many features, including chapter outlines, suggested lecture topics, map exercises, discussion questions for the primary sources, relevant worldwide web sites/resources, and relevant video resources. Available on the instructor's companion website.

CourseReader   CourseReader is an online collection of primary and secondary sources that lets you create a customized electronic reader in minutes. With an easy-to-use interface and assessment tool, you can choose exactly what your students will be assigned—simply search or browse Cengage Learning s extensive document database to preview and select your customized collection of readings. In addition to print sources of all types (letters, diary entries, speeches, newspaper accounts, and more), the collection includes a growing number of images and video and audio clips.

Each primary source document includes a descriptive headnote that puts the reading into context. In addition, each document is further supported by both critical thinking and multiple-choice questions designed to reinforce key points. For more information, visit www.cengage.com/coursereader.

Cengagebrain.com   Save your students time and money. Direct them to www.cengagebrain.com for a choice in formats and savings and a better chance to succeed in your class. *Cengagebrain.com,* Cengage Learning's online store, is a single destination for more than 10,000 new textbooks, eTextbooks, eChapters, study tools, and audio supplements. Students have the freedom to purchase á la carte exactly what they need when they need it. Students can save 50 percent on the electronic textbook and can purchase an individual eChapter for as little as $1.99.

Custom Options   Nobody knows your students like you, so why not give them a text that is tailor-fit to their needs? Cengage Learning offers custom solutions for your course—whether it's making a small modification to *Western Civilization, 9e* to match your syllabus or combining multiple sources to create something truly unique. You can pick and choose chapters, include your own material, and add additional map exercises along with the *Rand McNally Atlas* to create a text that fits the way you teach. Ensure that your students get the most out of their textbook dollars by giving them exactly what they need. Contact your Cengage Learning representative to explore custom solutions for your course.

For the Student

Western Civilization Companion Website   This website for students features a wide assortment of resources to help students master the subject matter. The website, prepared by Ryan Swanson of George Mason University, includes a glossary, flashcards, interactive quizzing, chapter outlines, and audio chapter summaries.

eBook   This interactive multimedia eBook links out to rich media assets such as video and MP3 chapter summaries. Through this eBook, students can also access chapter outlines, focus questions, chronology and matching exercises, primary source documents with critical thinking questions, and interactive (zoomable) maps. Available at www.cengagebrain.com.

Doing History: Research and Writing in the Digital Age, 2e   (ISBN: 9781133587880) Prepared by Michael J. Galgano, J. Chris Arndt, and Raymond M. Hyser of James Madison University. Whether you're starting down the path as a history major or simply looking for a straightforward, systematic guide to writing a successful paper, you'll find this text to be an indispensable handbook to historical research. This text's "soup to nuts"approach to researching and writing about history addresses every step of the process, from locating your sources and gathering information, to writing clearly and making proper use of various citation styles to avoid plagiarism. You'll also learn how to make the most of every tool available to you— especially the technology that helps you conduct historical research efficiently and effectively. The second edition includes a special appendix linked to CourseReader (see above), where you can examine and interpret primary sources online.

The History Handbook, 2e   (ISBN: 9780495906766) Prepared by Carol Berkin of Baruch College, City University of New York, and Betty Anderson of Boston University. This book teaches students both basic and history-specific study skills such as how to take notes, get the most out of lectures and readings, read primary sources, research historical topics, and correctly cite sources. Substantially less expensive than comparable skill-building texts, *The History Handbook* also offers tips for Internet research and evaluating online sources. Additionally, students can purchase and download the *eAudio* version of *The History Handbook* or any of its eighteen individual units at www.cengagebrain.com to listen to on the go.

Writing for College History, 1e   (ISBN: 9780618306039) Prepared by Robert M. Frakes of Clarion University. This brief handbook for survey courses in American history, Western Civilization/ European history, and world civilization guides students through the various types of writing assignments they may encounter in a history class. Providing examples of student writing and candid assessments of student work, this text focuses on the rules and conventions of writing for the college history course.

The Modern Researcher, 6e   (ISBN: 9780495318705) Prepared by Jacques Barzun and Henry F. Graff of Columbia University. This classic introduction to the techniques of research and the art of expression is used widely in history courses, but is also appropriate for writing and research methods courses in other departments. Barzun and Graff thoroughly cover every aspect of research, from the selection of a topic through the gathering of materials, analysis, writing, revision, and publication of findings. They present the process not as a set of rules but through actual cases that put the subtleties of research in a useful context. Part One covers the principles and methods of research; Part Two covers writing, speaking, and getting one's work published.

Reader Program   Cengage Learning publishes a number of readers. Some contain exclusively primary sources, others are devoted to essays and secondary sources, and still others provide a combination of primary and secondary sources. All of these readers are designed to guide students through the process of historical inquiry. Visit www.cengage.com/history for a complete list of readers.

Rand McNally Historical Atlas of Western Civilization, 2e,   (ISBN: 9780618841943) This valuable resource features more than forty-five maps, including maps that highlight Classical Greece and Rome; maps documenting European civilization during the Renaissance; maps that follow events in Germany, Russia, and Italy leading up to World Wars I and II; maps that show the dissolution of communism in 1989; maps documenting language and religion in the Western world; and maps describing the unification and industrialization of Europe.

Document Exercise Workbook   (ISBN: V1: 9780534560836; V2: 9780534560843) Prepared by Donna Van Raaphorst of Cuyahoga Community College. A collection of exercises based around primary sources. Available in two volumes.

ACKNOWLEDGMENTS

I began to teach at age five in my family's grape arbor. By the age of ten, I wanted to know and understand everything in the world, so I set out to memorize our entire set of encyclopedia volumes. At seventeen, as editor of the high school yearbook, I chose "patterns" as its theme. With that as my early history, followed by many rich years of teaching, writing, and family nurturing, it seemed quite natural to accept the challenge of writing a history of Western civilization as I approached that period in life often described as the age of wisdom. Although I see this writing adventure as part of the natural unfolding of my life, I gratefully acknowledge that without the generosity of many others, it would not have been possible.

David Redles gave generously of his time and ideas, especially for Chapters 28, 29, and 30. Chris Colin provided research on the history of music, while Laurie Batitto, Alex Spencer, Stephen Maloney, Shaun Mason, Peter Angelos, and Fred Schooley offered valuable editorial assistance. I deeply appreciate the valuable technical assistance provided by Dayton Coles. I am deeply grateful to John Soares for his assistance in preparing the map captions and to Charmarie Blaisdell of Northeastern University for her detailed suggestions on women's history. Daniel Haxall of Kutztown University provided valuable assistance with materials on postwar art, popular culture, Postmodern art and thought, and the Digital Age. I am especially grateful to Kathryn Spielvogel for her work as editorial associate for

Chapters 15–30. I am also thankful to the thousands of students whose questions and responses have caused me to see many aspects of Western civilization in new ways.

My ability to undertake a project of this magnitude was in part due to the outstanding European history teachers that I had as both an undergraduate and a graduate student. These included Kent Forster (modern Europe) and Robert W. Green (early modern Europe) at The Pennsylvania State University and Franklin Pegues (medieval), Andreas Dorpalen (modern Germany), William MacDonald (ancient), and Harold J. Grimm (Renaissance and Reformation) at The Ohio State University. These teachers provided me with profound insights into Western civilization and also taught me by their examples that learning only becomes true understanding when it is accompanied by compassion, humility, and open-mindedness.

I would like to thank the many teachers and students who have used the first eight editions of my *Western Civilization*. Their enthusiastic response to a textbook that was intended to put the story back in history and capture the imagination of the reader has been very gratifying. I especially thank the many teachers and students who made the effort to contact me personally to share their enthusiasm. Thanks to Cengage's comprehensive review process, many historians were asked to evaluate my manuscript and review each edition. I am grateful for their innumerable suggestions over the course of all nine editions, which have greatly improved my work.

The editors at Cengage Wadsworth have been both helpful and congenial at all times. I especially wish to thank Clark Baxter, whose clever wit, wisdom, gentle prodding, and good friendship have added much depth to our working relationship. Margaret Beasley thoughtfully, wisely, efficiently, and pleasantly guided the overall development of the ninth edition. I also thank Brooke Barbier for her suggestions and valuable editorial insights. I also want to express my gratitude to John Orr, whose good humor, well-advised suggestions, and generous verbal support made the production process easier. Pat Lewis, a truly outstanding copy editor, continued to teach me much about the fine points of the English language. Abigail Baxter provided valuable assistance in suggesting illustrations and obtaining permissions for the illustrations.

Above all, I thank my family for their support. The gifts of love, laughter, and patience from my daughters, Jennifer and Kathryn; my sons, Eric and Christian; my daughters-in-law, Liz and Laurie; and my sons-in-law, Daniel and Eddie, were enormously appreciated. I also wish to acknowledge my grandchildren, Devyn, Bryn, Drew, Elena, Sean, Emma, and Jackson, who bring great joy to my life. My wife and best friend, Diane, contributed editorial assistance, wise counsel, good humor, and the loving support that made it possible for me to accomplish a project of this magnitude. I could not have written the book without her.

About the Author

JACKSON J. SPIELVOGEL is associate professor emeritus of history at The Pennsylvania State University. He received his Ph.D. from The Ohio State University, where he specialized in Reformation history under Harold J. Grimm. His articles and reviews have appeared in such journals as *Moreana, Journal of General Education, Catholic Historical Review, Archiv für Reformationsgeschichte,* and *American Historical Review.* He has also contributed chapters or articles to *The Social History of the Reformation, The Holy Roman Empire: A Dictionary Handbook,* the *Simon Wiesenthal Center Annual of Holocaust Studies,* and *Utopian Studies.* His work has been supported by fellowships from the Fulbright Foundation and the Foundation for Reformation Research. At Penn State, he helped inaugurate the Western civilization courses as well as a popular course on Nazi Germany. His book *Hitler and Nazi Germany* was published in 1987 (seventh edition, 2013). He is the coauthor (with William Duiker) of *World History,* first published in 1998 (seventh edition, 2013), and *The Essential World History* (seventh edition, 2014). Professor Spielvogel has won five major university-wide teaching awards. In 1988–1989, he held the Penn State Teaching Fellowship, the university's most prestigious teaching award. He won the Dean Arthur Ray Warnock Award for Outstanding Faculty Member in 1996 and the Schreyer Honors College Excellence in Teaching Award in 2000.

TO DIANE,
WHOSE LOVE AND SUPPORT MADE IT ALL POSSIBLE
J.J.S.

Introduction to Students of Western Civilization

CIVILIZATION, AS HISTORIANS define it, first emerged between five and six thousand years ago when people in different parts of the world began to live in organized communities with distinct political, military, economic, and social structures. Religious, intellectual, and artistic activities assumed important roles in these early societies. The focus of this book is on Western civilization, a civilization that many people identify with the continent of Europe.

DEFINING WESTERN CIVILIZATION

Western civilization itself has evolved considerably over the centuries. Although the concept of the West did not yet exist at the time of the Mesopotamians and Egyptians, their development of writing, law codes, and different roles based on gender all eventually influenced what became Western civilization. Although the Greeks did not conceive of Western civilization as a cultural entity, their artistic, intellectual, and political contributions were crucial to the foundations of Western civilization. The Romans produced a remarkable series of accomplishments that were fundamental to the development of Western civilization, a civilization that came to consist largely of lands in Europe conquered by the Romans, in which Roman cultural and political ideals were gradually spread. Nevertheless, people in these early civilizations viewed themselves as subjects of states or empires, not as members of Western civilization.

With the rise of Christianity during the Late Roman Empire, however, peoples in Europe began to identify themselves as part of a civilization different from others, such as that of Islam, leading to a concept of a Western civilization different from other civilizations. In the fifteenth century, Renaissance intellectuals began to identify this civilization not only with Christianity but also with the intellectual and political achievements of the ancient Greeks and Romans.

Important to the development of the idea of a distinct Western civilization were encounters with other peoples. Between 700 and 1500, encounters with the world of Islam helped define the West. But after 1500, as European ships began to move into other parts of the world, encounters with peoples in Asia, Africa, and the Americas not only had an impact on the civilizations found there but also affected how people in the West defined themselves. At the same time, as they set up colonies, Europeans began to transplant a sense of Western identity to other areas of the world, especially North America and parts of Latin America, that have come to be considered part of Western civilization.

As the concept of Western civilization has evolved over the centuries, so have the values and unique features associated with that civilization. Science played a crucial role in the development of modern Western civilization. The societies of the Greeks, Romans, and medieval Europeans were based largely on a belief in the existence of a spiritual order; a dramatic departure to a natural or material view of the universe occurred in the seventeenth-century Scientific Revolution. Science and technology have been important in the growth of today's modern and largely secular Western civilization, although antecedents to scientific development also existed in Greek and medieval thought and practice, and religion remains a component of the Western world today.

Many historians have viewed the concept of political liberty, belief in the fundamental value of every individual, and a rational outlook based on a system of logical, analytical thought as unique aspects of Western civilization. Of course, the West has also witnessed horrendous negations of liberty, individualism, and reason. Racism, slavery, violence, world wars, totalitarian regimes—these, too, form part of the complex story of what constitutes Western civilization.

THE DATING OF TIME

In our examination of Western civilization, we also need to be aware of the dating of time. In recording the past, historians try to determine the exact time when events occurred. World War II in Europe, for example, began on September 1, 1939, when Hitler sent German troops into Poland, and ended on May 7, 1945, when Germany surrendered. By using dates, historians can place events in order and try to determine the development of patterns over periods of time.

If someone asked you when you were born, you would reply with a number, such as 1996. In the United States, we would all accept that number without question because it is part of the dating system followed in the Western world (Europe and the Western Hemisphere). In this system, events are dated by counting backward or forward from the year 1. When the system was first devised, the year 1 was assumed to be the year of the birth of Jesus, and the abbreviations B.C. (before Christ) and A.D. (for the Latin words *anno Domini*, meaning "in the year of the Lord") were used to refer to the periods before and after the birth of Jesus, respectively. Historians now generally prefer to refer to the year 1 in nonreligious terms as the beginning of the "common era." The abbreviations B.C.E. (before the common era) and C.E. (common era) are used instead of B.C. and A.D., although the years are the same. Thus, an event that took place four hundred years before the year 1 would be dated 400 B.C.E. (before the common era)—or the date could be expressed as 400 B.C. Dates after the year 1 are labeled C.E. Thus, an event that took place two hundred years after the year 1 would be dated 200 C.E. (common era), or the date could be written A.D. 200. It can also be written simply as 200, just as you would not give your birth year as 1996 C.E., but simply as 1996. In keeping with the current usage by most historians, this book will use the abbreviations B.C.E. and C.E.

Historians also make use of other terms to refer to time. A *decade* is ten years, a *century* is one hundred years, and a *millennium* is one thousand years. Thus, "the fourth century B.C.E." refers to the fourth period of one hundred years counting backward from the year 1, the beginning of the common era. Since the first century B.C.E. would be the years 100 B.C.E. to 1 C.E., the fourth century B.C.E. would be the years 400 B.C.E. to 301 B.C.E. We could say, then, that an event in 350 B.C.E. took place in the fourth century B.C.E.

Similarly, "the fourth century C.E." refers to the fourth period of one hundred years after the beginning of the common era. Since the first period of one hundred years would be the years 1 to 100, the fourth period or fourth century would be the years 301 to 400. We could say, then, that an event in 350 took place in the fourth century. Likewise, the first millennium B.C.E. refers to the years 1000 B.C.E. to 1 C.E.; the second millennium C.E. refers to the years 1001 to 2000.

The dating of events can also vary from people to people. Most people in the Western world use the Western calendar, also known as the Gregorian calendar after Pope Gregory XIII, who refined it in 1582. The Hebrew calendar uses a different system in which the year 1 is the equivalent of the Western year 3760 B.C.E., considered to be the date of the creation of the world according to the Bible. Thus, the Western year 2014 is the year 5774 on the Hebrew calendar. The Islamic calendar begins year 1 on the day Muhammad fled Mecca, which is the year 622 on the Western calendar.

1

THE ANCIENT NEAR EAST: THE FIRST CIVILIZATIONS

© Essam Al-Sudani/AFP/Getty Images

Excavation of Warka showing the ruins of Uruk

CHAPTER OUTLINE

• The First Humans • The Emergence of Civilization • Civilization in Mesopotamia • Egyptian Civilization: "The Gift of the Nile" • On the Fringes of Civilization

THE FIRST HUMANS

Historians rely primarily on documents to create their pictures of the past, but no written records exist for the prehistory of humankind. In their absence, the story of early humanity depends on archaeological and, more recently, biological information, which anthropologists and archaeologists use to formulate theories about our early past. Although modern science has given us more precise methods for examining prehistory, much of our understanding of early humans still relies on conjecture.

The earliest humanlike creatures—known as **hominids**—existed in Africa as long as 3 to 4 million years ago. Known as Australopithecines (aw-stray-loh-PITH-uh-synz), they flourished in East and South Africa and were the first hominids to make simple stone tools.

Another stage in early human development occurred around 1.5 million years ago when *Homo erectus* ("upright human being") emerged. *Homo erectus* made use of larger and more varied tools and was the first hominid to leave Africa and move into both Europe and Asia.

The Emergence of *Homo sapiens* Around 250,000 years ago, a crucial stage in human development began with the emergence of *Homo sapiens* (HOH-moh SAY-pee-unz) ("wise human being"). The first anatomically modern humans, known as *Homo sapiens sapiens* ("wise, wise human being"), appeared in Africa between 200,000 and 150,000 years ago. Recent evidence indicates that they began to spread outside Africa around 70,000 years ago. Map 1.1 shows probable dates for different movements, although many of these are still controversial.

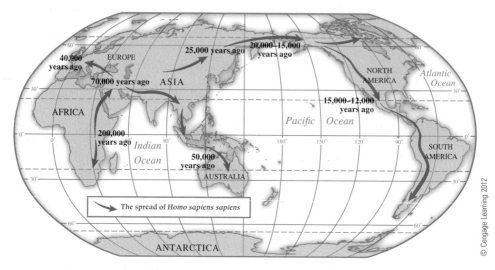

© Cengage Learning 2012

MAP 1.1 The Spread of *Homo sapiens sapiens*

Homo sapiens sapiens spread from Africa beginning about 70,000 years ago. Living and traveling in small groups, these anatomically modern humans were hunter-gatherers. Although groups of people advanced beyond their old hunting grounds at a rate of only 2 or 3 miles per generation, this was enough to populate the world in some tens of thousands of years.

These modern humans, who were our direct ancestors, soon encountered other hominids, such as the Neanderthals, whose remains were first found in the Neander valley in Germany. Neanderthal remains have since been found in both Europe and the western part of Asia and have been dated to between 200,000 and 30,000 B.C.E. Neanderthals relied on a variety of stone tools and were the first early people to bury their dead. By 30,000 B.C.E., *Homo sapiens sapiens* had replaced the Neanderthals, who had largely become extinct.

The Spread of Humans: Out of Africa or Multi-Regional?   The movements of the first modern humans were rarely sudden or rapid. Groups of people advanced beyond their old hunting grounds at a rate of only 2 or 3 miles per generation, but this was enough to populate the world in some tens of thousands of years. Some scholars, who advocate a multiregional theory, have suggested that advanced human creatures may have emerged independently in different parts of the world, rather than in Africa alone. But the latest genetic, archaeological, and climatic evidence strongly supports the out-of-Africa theory as the most likely explanation of human origin. In any case, by 10,000 B.C.E., members of the *Homo sapiens sapiens* species could be found throughout the world. By that time, it was the only human species left. All humans today, whether they are Europeans, Australian Aborigines, or Africans, belong to the same subspecies of human being.

The Hunter-Gatherers of the Old Stone Age   One of the basic distinguishing features of the human species is the ability to make tools. The earliest tools were made of stone, and so scholars refer to this early period of human history (c. 2,500,000–10,000 B.C.E.) as the **Paleolithic Age** (*paleolithic* is Greek for "old stone").

For hundreds of thousands of years, humans relied on gathering and hunting for their daily food. Paleolithic peoples had a close relationship with the world around them, and over time, they came to know which plants to eat and which animals to hunt. They did not know how to grow crops or raise animals, however. They gathered wild nuts, berries, fruits, and a variety of wild grains and green plants. Around the world, they hunted and consumed various animals, including buffalo, horses, bison, wild goats, and reindeer. In coastal areas, fish were a rich source of nourishment.

The gathering of wild plants and the hunting of animals no doubt led to certain patterns of living. Archaeologists and anthropologists have speculated that Paleolithic people lived in small bands of twenty or thirty people. They were nomadic, moving from place to place to follow animal migrations and vegetation cycles. Hunting depended on careful observation of animal behavior patterns and required a group effort for success. Over the years, tools became more refined and more useful. The invention of the spear, and later the bow and arrow, made hunting considerably easier. Harpoons and fishhooks made of bone increased the catch of fish.

Both men and women were responsible for finding food—the chief work of Paleolithic people. Since women bore and raised the children, they generally stayed close to the camps, but they played an important role in acquiring food by gathering berries, nuts, and grains. Men hunted wild animals, an activity that often took them far from camp. Because both men and women played important roles in providing for the band's survival, many scientists believe that a rough equality existed between men and women. Indeed, some speculate that both men and women made the decisions that affected the activities of the Paleolithic band.

Some groups of Paleolithic people found shelter in caves, but over time, they also created new types of shelter. Perhaps the most common was a simple structure of wood poles or sticks covered with animal hides. Where wood was scarce, Paleolithic hunter-gatherers might use the bones of mammoths to build frames that were then covered with animal hides. The systematic use of fire, which archaeologists believe began around 500,000 years ago, made it possible for the caves and human-made structures to have a source of light and heat. Fire also enabled early humans to cook their food, making it taste better, last longer, and, in the case of some plants, such as wild grain, easier to chew and digest.

The making of tools and the use of fire—two important technological innovations of Paleolithic peoples—remind us how crucial the ability to adapt was to human survival. But Paleolithic peoples did more than just survive. The cave paintings of large animals found in southwestern France and northern Spain bear witness to the cultural activity of Paleolithic peoples. A cave discovered in southern France in 1994—known as the Chauvet (shoh-VAY) cave after the leader of the expedition that found it—contains more than three hundred paintings of lions, oxen, owls, bears, and other animals. Most of these are animals that Paleolithic people did not hunt, which suggests to some scholars that the paintings were made for religious or even decorative purposes. The discoverers were overwhelmed by what they saw: "There was a moment of ecstasy.... They overflowed with joy and emotion in their turn.... These were moments of indescribable madness."[1]

The Neolithic Revolution (c. 10,000–4000 B.C.E.) The end of the last ice age around 10,000 B.C.E. was followed by what scholars call the **Neolithic Revolution,** a significant change in living patterns that occurred in the New Stone Age (*neolithic* is Greek for "new stone"). The name "New Stone Age" is misleading, however. Although Neolithic peoples made a new type of polished stone ax, this was not the major change that occurred after 10,000 B.C.E.

An Agricultural Revolution The biggest change was the shift from gathering plants and hunting animals for sustenance (food gathering) to producing food by systematic agriculture (food production). The planting of grains and vegetables provided a regular supply of food, while the domestication of animals, such as goats, cattle, pigs, and sheep, provided a steady source of meat, milk, and fibers such as wool for clothing. Larger animals could also be used as beasts of burden. The growing of crops and the taming of food-producing animals created a new relationship between humans and nature. Historians speak of this as an agricultural revolution. Revolutionary change is dramatic and requires great effort, but the ability to acquire food on a regular basis gave humans greater control over their environment. It also allowed them to give up their nomadic way of life and begin to live in settled communities.

Systematic agriculture probably developed independently between 8000 and 7000 B.C.E. in four different areas of the world. Different plants were cultivated in each area: wheat, barley, and lentils in the Near East; rice and millet in southern Asia; millet and yams in western Africa; and beans, potatoes, and corn (maize) in the Americas. The Neolithic agricultural revolution needed a favorable environment. In the Near East, the upland areas above the Fertile Crescent (present-day northern Iraq and southern Turkey) were initially more conducive to systematic farming than the river valleys. This region received the necessary rainfall and was the home of two wild plant (barley, wheat) and four wild animal (pigs, cows, goats, sheep) species that humans eventually domesticated.

Neolithic Farming Villages   The growing of crops on a regular basis gave rise to more permanent settlements, which historians refer to as Neolithic farming villages or towns. One of the oldest and most extensive agricultural villages was Çatal Hüyük (chaht-ul hoo-YOOK), located in modern-day Turkey. Its walls enclosed 32 acres, and its population probably reached six thousand during its high point from 6700 to 5700 B.C.E. People lived in simple mudbrick houses that were built so close to one another that there were few streets. To get to their homes, people had to walk along the rooftops and then enter the house through a hole in the roof.

Archaeologists have discovered twelve cultivated products in Çatal Hüyük, including fruits, nuts, and three kinds of wheat. Artisans made weapons and jewelry that were traded with neighboring peoples. Religious shrines housing figures of gods and goddesses have been found at Çatal Hüyük, as have a number of female statuettes. Molded with noticeably large breasts and buttocks, these "earth mothers" perhaps symbolically represented the fertility of both "mother earth" and human mothers. The shrines and the statues point to the important role of religious practices in the lives of these Neolithic people.

Consequences of the Neolithic Revolution   The Neolithic agricultural revolution had far-reaching consequences. Once people settled in villages or towns, they built houses for protection and other structures for the storage of goods. As organized communities stored food and accumulated material goods, they began to engage in trade. People also began to specialize in certain crafts, and a division of labor developed. Pottery was made from clay and baked in a fire to make it hard. The pots were used for cooking and to store grains. Woven baskets were also used for storage. Stone tools became refined as flint blades were developed to make sickles and hoes for use in the fields. Obsidian—a volcanic glass that was easily flaked—was also used to create very sharp tools. In the course of the Neolithic Age, many of the food plants still in use today began to be cultivated. Moreover, vegetable fibers from such plants as flax were used to make thread that was woven into cloth.

The change to systematic agriculture in the Neolithic Age also had consequences for the relationship between men and women. Men assumed the primary responsibility for working in the fields and herding animals, jobs that kept them away from the home. Although women also worked in the fields, many remained close to home, caring for the children, weaving cloth, and performing other household tasks. In time, as work outside the home was increasingly perceived as more important than work done at home, men came to play the more dominant role in human society, which gave rise to the practice of **patriarchy** (PAY-tree-ark-ee), or a society dominated by men, a basic pattern that would persist until our own times.

Other patterns set in the Neolithic Age also proved to be enduring elements of human history. Fixed dwellings, domesticated animals, regular farming, a division of labor, men holding power—all of these are part of the human story. Despite all our modern scientific and technological progress, human survival still depends on the growing and storing of food, an accomplishment of people in the Neolithic Age. The Neolithic Revolution was truly a turning point in human history.

Between 4000 and 3000 B.C.E., significant technical developments began to transform the Neolithic towns. The invention of writing enabled records to be kept, and the use of metals marked a new level of human control over the environment and its resources. Already before 4000 B.C.E., craftspeople had discovered that certain rocks could be heated to liquefy metals embedded in them. The metals could then be cast in molds to produce tools and weapons that were more refined than stone instruments. Although copper was the first metal to be used in producing tools, after 4000 B.C.E. craftspeople in western Asia discovered that combining copper and tin produced bronze, a much harder and more durable metal than copper. Its widespread use has led historians to call the period from around 3000 to 1200 B.C.E. the Bronze Age; thereafter, bronze was increasingly replaced by iron.

At first, Neolithic settlements were mere villages. But as their inhabitants mastered the art of farming, more complex human societies emerged. As wealth increased, these societies began to develop armies and to build walled cities. By the beginning of the Bronze Age, the concentration of larger numbers of people in the river valleys of Southwest Asia and Egypt was leading to a whole new pattern for human life.

THE EMERGENCE OF CIVILIZATION

As we have seen, early human beings formed small groups that developed a simple culture that enabled them to survive. As human societies grew and developed greater complexity, a new form of human existence—called civilization—came into being. A **civilization** is a complex culture in which large numbers of human beings share a variety of common elements. Historians have identified a number of basic characteristics of civilization. These include (1) an urban focus: cities became the centers of political, economic, social, cultural, and religious development; (2) a distinct religious structure: the gods were deemed crucial to the community's success, and professional priestly classes, as stewards of the gods' property, regulated relations with the gods; (3) new political and military structures: an organized government bureaucracy arose to meet the administrative demands of the growing population, and armies were organized to gain land and power and for defense; (4) a new social structure based on economic power: while kings and an upper class of priests, political leaders, and warriors dominated, there also existed a large group of free people (farmers, artisans, craftspeople) and at the very bottom, socially, a class of slaves; (5) the development of writing: kings, priests, merchants, and artisans used writing to keep records; and (6) new forms of significant artistic and intellectual activity: for example, monumental architectural structures, usually religious, occupied a prominent place in urban environments.

The civilizations that developed in Southwest Asia and Egypt, the forerunners of Western civilization, will be examined in detail in this chapter. But civilization also developed independently in other parts of the world. Between 3000 and 1500 B.C.E., the valleys of the Indus River in India supported a flourishing civilization that extended hundreds of miles from the Himalayas to the coast of the Arabian Sea. Two major cities—Harappa (huh-RAP-uh) and Mohenjo-Daro (moh-HEN-joh-DAH-roh)—were at the heart of this South Asian civilization. Many written records of the Indus valley civilization exist, but their language has not yet been deciphered. This Indus valley civilization carried on extensive trade with city-states in Southwest Asia.

Another river valley civilization emerged along the Yellow River in northern China about 4,000 years ago. Under the Shang (SHAHNG) dynasty of kings, which ruled from 1570 to 1045 B.C.E., this civilization contained impressive cities with huge outer walls, royal palaces, and large royal tombs. A system of irrigation enabled early Chinese civilization to maintain a prosperous farming society ruled by an aristocratic class whose major concern was war.

Scholars long believed that civilization emerged only in four areas, in the fertile river valleys of the Tigris and Euphrates, the Nile, the Indus, and the Yellow River— that is, in Southwest Asia, Egypt, India, and China. Recently, however, archaeologists have discovered two other early civilizations. One of these flourished in Central Asia (in what are now the republics of Turkmenistan and Uzbekistan) around 4,000 years ago. People in this civilization built mudbrick buildings, raised sheep and goats, had bronze tools, used a system of irrigation to grow wheat and barley, and had a writing system.

Another early civilization emerged in the Supe River valley of Peru. At the center of this civilization was the city of Caral, which flourished around 2600 B.C.E. It contained buildings for officials, apartment houses, and grand residences, all built of stone. The inhabitants of Caral also developed a system of irrigation by diverting a river more than a mile upstream into their fields.

Why early civilizations developed remains difficult to explain. One theory maintains that challenges forced human beings to make efforts that resulted in the rise of civilization. Some scholars have argued that material forces, such as the growth of food surpluses, made possible the specialization of labor and development of large communities with bureaucratic organization. But the area of the Fertile Crescent, in which civilization emerged in Southwest Asia (see Map 1.2), was not naturally conducive to agriculture. Abundant food could be produced only with a massive human effort to manage the water, an undertaking that required organization and led to civilized cities. Other historians have argued that non-material forces, primarily religious, provided the sense of unity and purpose that made such organized activities possible. Finally, some scholars doubt that we will ever discover the actual causes of early civilization.

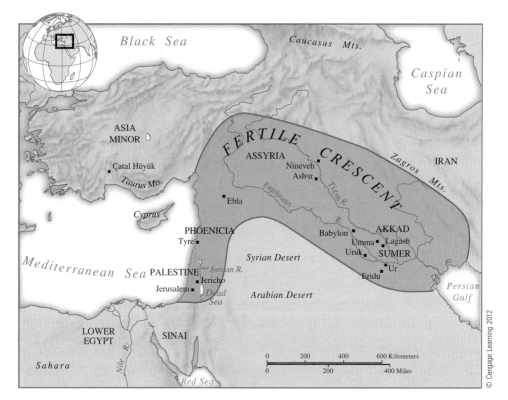

MAP 1.2 The Ancient Near East

The Fertile Crescent encompassed land with access to water. Employing flood management and irrigation systems, the peoples of the region established civilizations based on agriculture. These civilizations developed writing, law codes, and economic specialization.

CIVILIZATION IN MESOPOTAMIA

The Greeks spoke of the valley between the Tigris and Euphrates (yoo-FRAY-teez) Rivers in Southwest Asia as Mesopotamia (mess-uh-puh-TAY-mee-uh), the land "between the rivers." The region receives little rain, but the soil of the plain of southern Mesopotamia was enlarged and enriched over the years by layers of silt deposited by the two rivers. In late spring, the Tigris and Euphrates overflow their banks and deposit their fertile silt, but since this flooding depends on the melting of snows in the upland mountains where the rivers begin, it is unpredictable and sometimes catastrophic. In such circumstances, people could raise crops only by building a complex system of irrigation and drainage ditches to control the flow of the rivers. Large-scale irrigation made possible the expansion of agriculture in this region, and the abundant food provided the material base for the emergence of civilization in Mesopotamia.

The City-States of Ancient Mesopotamia   The creators of Mesopotamian civilization were the Sumerians (soo-MER-ee-unz or soo-MEER-ee-unz), a people whose origins remain unclear. By 3000 B.C.E., they had established a number of independent cities in southern Mesopotamia, including Eridu, Ur, Uruk, Umma, and Lagash. There is evidence that the Sumerians were not the first people in the region. A number of Sumerian agricultural and craft terms are not Sumerian in origin, indicating that the Sumerians adopted some aspects of preexisting settlements. As the Sumerian cities grew larger, they came to exercise political and economic control over the surrounding countryside, forming city-states. These city-states were the basic units of Sumerian civilization.

Sumerian Cities   Sumerian cities were surrounded by walls. Uruk, for example, occupied an area of approximately 1,000 acres encircled by a wall 6 miles long with defense towers located every 30 to 35 feet along the wall. City dwellings, built of sun-dried bricks, included both the small flats of peasants and the larger dwellings of the civic and priestly officials. Although Mesopotamia had little stone or wood for building purposes, it did have plenty of mud. Mudbricks, easily shaped by hand, were left to bake in the hot sun until they were hard enough to use for building. People in Mesopotamia were remarkably inventive with mudbricks, inventing the arch and constructing some of the largest brick buildings in the world.

The most prominent building in a Sumerian city was the temple, which was dedicated to the chief god or goddess of the city and often built atop a massive stepped tower called a **ziggurat** (ZIG-uh-rat). The Sumerians believed that gods and goddesses owned the cities, and much wealth was used to build temples as well as elaborate houses for the priests and priestesses who served the gods and supervised the temples and their property. The priests and priestesses had great power. In fact, historians believe that in the early stages of a few city-states, priests and priestesses may have played an important role in ruling. The Sumerians believed that the gods ruled the cities, making the state a **theocracy** (government by a divine authority). Actual ruling power, however, was primarily in the hands of worldly figures known as kings.

Kingship   Sumerians viewed kingship as divine in origin— kings, they believed, derived their power from the gods and were the agents of the gods. As one person said in a petition to his king: "You in your judgment, you are the son of Anu [god of the sky]; your commands, like the word of a god, cannot be reversed; your words, like rain pouring down from heaven, are without number."[2] Regardless of their origins, kings had power—they led armies, initiated legislation, supervised the building of public works, provided courts, and organized workers for the irrigation projects on which Mesopotamian agriculture depended. The army, the government bureaucracy, and the priests and priestesses all aided the kings in their rule. Befitting their power, Sumerian kings lived in large palaces with their wives and children.

Economy and Society   The economy of the Sumerian city-states was primarily agricultural, but commerce and industry became important as well. The people of Mesopotamia produced woolen textiles, pottery, and metalwork. Foreign trade, which was primarily a royal monopoly, could be extensive. Royal officials imported luxury items, such as copper and tin, aromatic woods, and fruit trees, in exchange for dried fish, wool, barley, wheat, and the goods produced by Mesopotamian metalworkers. Traders traveled by land to the eastern Mediterranean in the west and by sea to India in the east. The invention of the wheel around 3000 B.C.E. led to the development of carts with wheels that made the transport of goods easier.

Sumerian city-states probably contained four major social groups: elites, dependent commoners, free commoners, and slaves. Elites included royal and priestly officials and their families. Dependent commoners included the elites' clients who worked for the palace and temple estates. Free commoners worked as farmers, merchants, fishers, scribes, and craftspeople. Probably 90 percent or more of the population were farmers. They could exchange their crops for the goods of the artisans in free town markets. Slaves belonged to palace officials, who used them mostly in building projects; temple officials, who used mostly female slaves to weave cloth and grind grain; and rich landowners, who used them for farming and domestic work.

Empires in Ancient Mesopotamia   As the number of Sumerian city-states grew and the states expanded, new conflicts arose as city-state fought city-state for control of land and water. During the Early Dynastic Age (3000–2340 B.C.E.), the fortunes of various cities rose and fell over the centuries. The constant wars, with their burning and sacking of cities, left many Sumerians in deep despair, as is evident in this Sumerian poem from the city of Ur: "Ur is destroyed, bitter is its lament. The country's blood now fills its holes like hot bronze in a mold. Bodies dissolve like fat in the sun. Our temple is destroyed, the gods have abandoned us, like migrating birds. Smoke lies on our city like a shroud."[3]

The Akkadian Empire Located on the flat, open land of Mesopotamia, the Sumerian city-states were also vulnerable to invasion. To the north of the Sumerian city-states were the Akkadians (uh-KAY-dee-unz). We call them a Semitic people because of the language they spoke. Around 2340 B.C.E., Sargon, leader of the Akkadians, overran the Sumerian city-states and established a dynastic empire. Sargon used the former rulers of the conquered city-states as his governors. His power was based on the military, namely, his army of 5,400 men. Sargon's empire, including all of Mesopotamia as well as lands westward to the Mediterranean, inspired generations of Near Eastern leaders to emulate his accomplishment. Even in the first millennium B.C.E., Sargon was still remembered in chronicles as a king of Akkad who "had no rival or equal, spread his splendor over all the lands, and crossed the sea in the east. In his eleventh year, he conquered the western land to its furthest point, and brought it under his sole authority."[4]

One of Sargon's successors, his grandson Naram-Sin (c. 2260–2223 B.C.E.), continued the greatness of the Akkadian empire. Like his grandfather, Naram-Sin waged numerous military campaigns, which led him to an extreme level of self-glorification. He called himself "King of the Four Corners (of the Universe)" and took the extraordinary step of declaring himself a god. An inscription found in northern Iraq reads: "Naram-Sin, the strong one, king of Akkad, when the four corners (of the universe) together were hostile to him, he remained victorious in nine battles in a single year.... Because he had been able to preserve his city in the time of crisis, (the inhabitants of) his city asked ... that he be the god of their city Akkad, and built a temple for him in the midst of Akkad."[5] By the end of his reign, however, Naram-Sin was battling hill peoples who finally caused the fall of the Akkadian empire by 2150 B.C.E.

The Third Dynasty of Ur   The end of the Akkadian empire brought a return to independent city-states in Mesopotamia. Much confusion ensued, as is evident in the recorded Sumerian king list, which stated bluntly, "Who was king? Who was not king?" The confusion ended when Ur-Nammu established a new dynasty that reunified much of Mesopotamia with its capital at Ur. This Third Dynasty of Ur (c. 2112–2000 B.C.E.) witnessed a final flowering of Sumerian culture. The economy flourished, and new temples and canals were built. Each province was required to contribute goods to the central government.

Around 2000 B.C.E., however, invaders from Iran destroyed Ur and brought an end to the Third Dynasty. Even earlier, the Amorites, a large group of Semitic-speaking seminomads, described by Sumerian scribes as dressed in sheepskins, living in tents, and eating raw meat, had entered the region and done battle with kings of the Third Dynasty. The Amorites or Old Babylonians gradually settled down and over the next two hundred years established their influence throughout much of Mesopotamia. One of their kings, Hammurabi (ham-uh-RAH-bee), managed to establish power and create a new empire.

Hammurabi's Empire   Hammurabi (1792–1750 B.C.E.) had a well-disciplined army of foot soldiers who carried axes, spears, and copper or bronze daggers. He learned to divide his opponents and subdue them one by one. Using such methods, he gained control of Sumer and Akkad and reunified Mesopotamia almost to the old borders established by Sargon. After his conquests, Hammurabi called himself "the sun of Babylon, the king who made the four quarters of the world obedient," and established his capital at Babylon.

Hammurabi, the man of war, was also a man of peace. He followed in the footsteps of previous conquerors by assimilating Mesopotamian culture; as a result, Sumerian ways continued to exist despite the end of the Sumerians as a political entity. A collection of his letters, found by archaeologists, reveals that the king took a strong interest in state affairs. He built temples, defensive walls, and irrigation canals; encouraged trade; and brought about an economic revival. Indeed, Hammurabi saw himself as a shepherd to his people: "I am indeed the shepherd who brings peace, whose scepter is just. My benevolent shade was spread over my city. I held the people of the lands of Sumer and Akkad safely on my lap."[6] Hammurabi left his dynasty strong enough that it survived until the 1550s B.C.E., when the Kassites from the northeast took over.

The Code of Hammurabi   Hammurabi is best remembered for his law code, a collection of 282 laws. For centuries, laws had regulated people's relationships with one another in the lands of Mesopotamia, but only fragments of these earlier codes survive. Although many scholars today view Hammurabi's collection less as a code of laws and more as an attempt by Hammurabi to portray himself as the source of justice to his people, the code still gives us a glimpse of the Babylonian society of his time.

The Code of Hammurabi reveals a society with a system of strict justice. Penalties for criminal offenses were severe and varied according to the social class of the victim. A crime against a member of the upper class (a noble) was punished more severely than the same offense against a member of the lower class. Moreover, the principle of "an eye for an eye, a tooth for a tooth" was fundamental to this system of justice. This meant that punishments should fit the crime: "If a freeman has destroyed the eye of a member of the aristocracy, they shall destroy his eye." Hammurabi's code had an impact on legal ideas in Southwest Asia for hundreds of years, as the following verse from the Hebrew Bible (Leviticus 24:19–20) demonstrates: "If anyone injures his neighbor, whatever he has done must be done to him: fracture for fracture, eye for eye, tooth for tooth. As he has injured the other, so is he to be injured."

Hammurabi's code took the responsibilities of public officials very seriously. The governor of an area and city officials were expected to catch burglars. If they failed to do so, the officials in the district where the crime was committed had to replace the lost property. If the officials did not apprehend a murderer, they had to pay a fine to the relatives of the murdered person.

The law code also furthered the proper performance of work with what amounted to consumer protection laws. Builders were held responsible for the buildings they constructed. If a house collapsed, killing the owner, the builder was put to death. If the collapse caused the death of the son of the owner, the son of the builder was put to death. If the collapse destroyed goods, they had to be replaced and the house itself reconstructed at the builder's expense.

The number of laws in Hammurabi's code dedicated to land tenure and commerce reveal the importance of agriculture and trade in the Mesopotamian economy. Laws concerning land use and irrigation were especially strict, an indication of the danger of declining crop yields if the land was used incompetently. If landowners and tenants failed to keep dikes in good repair or to control water flow properly, thereby causing damage to others' crops, they were required to pay for the grain that was destroyed.

Commercial activity was carefully regulated. Rates of interest on loans were watched closely. If the lender raised the interest rate after a loan was made, he lost the entire amount of the loan. The Code of Hammurabi even specified the precise wages of laborers and artisans, such as brickmakers and jewelers.

The largest number of laws in the code focused on marriage and the family. Parents arranged marriages for their children. After marriage, the parties involved signed a marriage contract; without it, no one was considered legally married. The husband provided a bridal payment, and the woman's parents were responsible for a dowry to the new husband.

As in many patriarchal societies, women had far fewer privileges and rights in the married relationship than men. A woman's place was in the home, and failure

The Code of Hammurabi

Hammurabi's code is the most complete Mesopotamian law code, although not the earliest. It was inscribed on a stone stele (STEE-lee), or pillar, topped by a bas-relief picturing Hammurabi receiving the inspiration for the law code from the sun god Shamash, who was also the god of justice. As the following examples illustrate, the law code emphasized the principle of "an eye for an eye" and punishments that varied according to the victim's social status.

The Code of Hammurabi

25. If fire broke out in a freeman's house and a freeman, who went to extinguish it, cast his eye on the goods of the owner of the house and has appropriated the goods of the owner of the house, that freeman shall be thrown into that fire.

129. If the wife of a freeman has been caught while lying with another man, they shall bind them and throw them into the water. If the husband of the woman wishes to spare his wife, then the king in turn may spare his subject.

131. If a freeman's wife was accused by her husband, but she was not caught while lying with another man, she shall make affirmation by god and return to her house.

196. If a freeman has destroyed the eye of a member of the aristocracy, they shall destroy his eye.

198. If he has destroyed the eye of a commoner or broken the bone of a commoner, he shall pay one mina of silver.

199. If he has destroyed the eye of a freeman's slave or broken the bone of a freeman's slave, he shall pay one-half his value.

209. If a freeman struck another freeman's daughter and has caused her to have a miscarriage, he shall pay ten shekels of silver for her fetus.

210. If that woman has died, they shall put his daughter to death.

211. If by a blow he has caused a commoner's daughter to have a miscarriage, he shall pay five shekels of silver.

212. If that woman has died, he shall pay one-half mina of silver.

213. If he struck a freeman's female slave and has caused her to have a miscarriage, he shall pay two shekels of silver.

214. If that female slave has died, he shall pay one-third mina of silver.

Q *What do these laws from the Code of Hammurabi reveal about Mesopotamian society?*

Source: PRITCHARD, JAMES; ANCIENT NEAR EASTERN TEXTS RELATED TO THE OLD TESTAMENT—THIRD EDITION WITH SUPPLEMENT. © 1950, 1955, 1969, renewed 1978 by Princeton University Press. Reprinted by permission of Princeton University Press.

to fulfill her expected duties was grounds for divorce. If she was not able to bear children, her husband could divorce her, but he had to return the dowry to her family. If a wife tried to leave home to engage in business, thus neglecting her house, her husband could divorce her and did not have to repay the dowry. Furthermore, a wife who was a "gadabout, ... neglecting her house [and] humiliating her husband," could be drowned. We do know that in practice not all women remained at home. Some worked in the fields and others in business, where they were especially prominent in running taverns.

Women had some rights, however. A husband who divorced his wife without good reason had to return her dowry. A woman could seek a divorce and get her dowry back if her husband was unable to show that she had done anything wrong. In theory, a wife was guaranteed the use of her husband's legal property in the event of his death. A mother could also decide which of her sons would receive an inheritance.

Sexual relations were strictly regulated as well. Husbands, but not wives, were permitted sexual activity outside marriage. A wife and her lover caught committing adultery were pitched into the river, although if the husband pardoned his wife, the king could pardon the guilty man. Incest was strictly forbidden. If a father had incestuous relations with his daughter, he would be banished. Incest between a son and his mother resulted in both being burned.

Fathers ruled their children as well as their wives. Obedience was duly expected: "If a son has struck his father, they shall cut off his hand." If a son committed a serious offense, his father could disinherit him.

The Culture of Mesopotamia

A spiritual worldview was of fundamental importance to Mesopotamian culture. To the peoples of Mesopotamia, the gods were living realities who affected all aspects of life. It was crucial, therefore, that the correct hierarchies be observed. Leaders could prepare armies for war, but success really depended on a favorable relationship with the gods. This helps explain the importance of the priestly class and is the reason why even the kings took great care to dedicate offerings and monuments to the gods.

The Importance of Religion

One of the most famous accounts of the creation of the universe from the ancient Near East was the Babylonian creation epic known as the *Enumaelish*. The name comes from the first three words of the first two lines of the poem:

When on high the heavens were not yet named,
And below, the earth was not called by a name.

The *Enuma elish* tells how the god Marduk was endowed with absolute power by the other gods to do battle with Tiamat, a primordial goddess who personified the forces of watery chaos. Marduk defeats Tiamat in battle and proceeds to create the universe by dividing Tiamat in two, one part becoming the heavens and the other the earth with her breasts as mountains. From her eyes came the Tigris and Euphrates Rivers. The *Enuma elish* was recited during the New Year Festival celebrated in honor of Marduk in the city of Babylon, which the all-powerful god founded as an earthly residence for the gods after he created the universe.

The Mesopotamians viewed their city-states as earthly copies of a divine model and order. Each city-state was sacred because it was linked to a god or goddess. Hence, Nippur, the earliest center of Sumerian religion, was dedicated to Enlil

(EN-lil), the god of wind. Moreover, located at the heart of each major city-state was a temple complex. Occupying several acres, this sacred area consisted of a ziggurat with a temple at the top dedicated to the god or goddess who owned the city. The temple complex was the true center of the community. The main god or goddess dwelt there symbolically in the form of a statue, and the ceremony of dedication included a ritual that linked the statue to the god or goddess and thus supposedly harnessed the power of the deity for the city's benefit. Considerable wealth was poured into the construction of temples and other buildings used for the residences of priests and priestesses who served the gods. Although the gods literally owned the city, the temple complex used only part of the land and rented out the remainder. The temples dominated individual and commercial life, an indication of the close relationship between Mesopotamian religion and culture.

The physical environment had an obvious impact on the Mesopotamian view of the universe. Ferocious floods, heavy downpours, scorching winds, and oppressive humidity were all part of the Mesopotamian climate. These conditions and the resulting famines easily convinced Mesopotamians that this world was controlled by supernatural forces and that the days of human beings "are numbered; whatever he may do, he is but wind," as *The Epic of Gilgamesh* laments (see "Mesopotamian Literature" later in this chapter). In the presence of nature, Mesopotamians could easily feel helpless, as this poem relates:

> *The rampant flood which no man can oppose,*
> *Which shakes the heavens and causes earth to tremble,*
> *In an appalling blanket folds mother and child,*
> *Beats down the canebrake's full luxuriant greenery,*
> *And drowns the harvest in its time of ripeness.*[7]

The Mesopotamians discerned cosmic rhythms in the universe and accepted its order but perceived that it was not completely safe because of the presence of willful, powerful cosmic forces that they identified with gods and goddesses.

With its numerous gods and goddesses animating all aspects of the universe, Mesopotamian religion was **polytheistic.** The four most important deities were An, Enlil, Enki (EN-kee), and Ninhursaga (nin-HUR-sah-guh). An was the god of the sky and hence the most important force in the universe. Since his basic essence was authority, he was also viewed as the source or active principle of all authority, including the earthly power of rulers and fathers alike. In one myth, the gods address him thus:

> *What you have ordered comes true!*
> *The utterance of prince and lord is but what you have ordered, do agree*
>   *with.*
> *O An! your great command takes precedence, who could gainsay it?*
> *O father of the gods, your command, the very foundations of heaven*
>   *and earth, what god could spurn it?*[8]

Enlil, god of wind, was considered the second greatest power of the visible universe. In charge of the wind and thus an expression of the legitimate use of force, Enlil became the symbol of the proper use of force on earth as well. Enki was the god of the earth. Since the earth was the source of life-giving waters, Enki was also the god of rivers, wells, and canals. More generally, he represented the waters of creativity and was responsible for inventions and crafts. Ninhursaga began as a goddess associated with soil, mountains, and vegetation. Eventually, however, she was worshiped as a mother goddess, a "mother of all children," who manifested her power by giving birth to kings and conferring the royal insignia on them.

Human beings' relationship with their gods was based on subservience since, according to Sumerian myth, human beings were created to do the manual labor the gods were unwilling to do for themselves. Moreover, humans were insecure because they could never be sure what the gods would do. But humans did make attempts to circumvent or relieve their anxiety by discovering the intentions of the gods and by trying to influence them as well; these efforts gave rise to the development of the arts of **divination.**

Divination took a variety of forms. A common form, at least for kings and priests who could afford it, involved killing animals, such as sheep or goats, and examining their livers or other organs. Supposedly, features seen in the organs of the sacrificed animals foretold events to come. Thus, one handbook states that if the animal organ has shape x, the outcome of the military campaign will be y. Private individuals relied on cheaper divinatory techniques. These included interpreting shapes in the smoke from burning incense or the pattern formed when oil was poured into water. The Mesopotamian arts of divination arose out of the desire to discover the purposes of the gods and goddesses. If people could decipher the signs that foretold events, the events would be predictable and humans could act wisely.

Writing   The realization of writing's great potential was another aspect of Mesopotamian culture. The oldest Mesopotamian texts date to around 3000 B.C.E. and were written by the Sumerians, who used a **cuneiform** (kyoo-NEE-uh-form) ("wedge-shaped") system of writing. Using a reed stylus, they made wedge-shaped impressions on clay tablets, which were then baked or dried in the sun. Once dried, these tablets were virtually indestructible, and the several hundred thousand that have been found so far have provided a valuable source of information for modern scholars. Sumerian writing evolved from pictures of concrete objects to simplified and stylized signs, leading eventually to a phonetic system that made possible the written expression of abstract ideas. Sumerian was the chief spoken and written language of Mesopotamia in the third millennium B.C.E., but it was replaced in the second millennium by Akkadian.

Mesopotamian peoples used writing primarily for record keeping. The most common cuneiform tablets record transactions of daily life: tallies of cattle kept by cowherds for their owners, production figures, lists of taxes and wage payments, accounts, contracts, and court decisions dealing with business matters. There are also monumental texts, documents that were intended to last forever, such as inscriptions etched in stone on statues and royal buildings.

Still another category of cuneiform inscriptions includes a large body of basic texts produced for teaching purposes. Schools for scribes were in operation by 2500 B.C.E. They were necessary because considerable time was needed to master the cuneiform system of writing. The primary goal of scribal education was to produce professionally trained scribes for careers in the temples and palaces, the military, and government service. Pupils were male and primarily from wealthy families.

Mesopotamian Literature   Writing was important because it enabled a society to keep records and maintain knowledge of previous practices and events. Writing also made it possible for people to communicate ideas in new ways, which is especially evident in Mesopotamian literary works. The most famous piece of Mesopotamian literature was *The Epic of Gilgamesh,* an elaborate poem that records the exploits of a legendary king of Uruk. Gilgamesh (GILL-guh-mesh), wise, strong, and perfect in body, part man, part god, abused the citizens of Uruk:

> "Gilgamesh sounds the tocsin for his amusement," the people complained, "his arrogance has no bounds by day or night. No son is left with his father, for Gilgamesh takes them all, even the children.... His lust leaves no virgin to her lover, neither the warrior's daughter nor the wife of the noble."[9]

The citizens asked the gods to send a competitor to oppose Gilgamesh and keep him busy. The gods comply and send a hairy, barbaric beast named Enkidu whom Gilgamesh tries to weaken by sending a prostitute to seduce him. When Enkidu finally comes to Uruk, he and Gilgamesh engage in a fierce struggle that neither can win. The two become fast friends and set off in pursuit of heroic deeds. Ishtar (Sumerian Inanna), the goddess of love, attempts to seduce Gilgamesh, but he refuses her advances. In anger, she convinces her father Anu (Sumerian An) to send the Bull of Heaven to kill Gilgamesh and Enkidu. They manage to kill the bull instead, but the gods decide that in return one of them must die. When Enkidu

The Development of Cuneiform. *Pictured here is the cone of Uruinimgina, an example of cuneiform script from an early Sumerian dynasty. The inscription announces reductions in taxes.*

Louvre, Paris//© Réunion des Musées Nationaux/Art Resource, NY

dies, Gilgamesh experiences the pain of mortality and begins a search for the secret of immortality. He finds Utnapishtim, a man who had been granted "everlasting life" by the gods. Utnapishtim tells how he survived the Great Flood sent by the gods to destroy humankind. Regretting what they had done, the gods bestowed immortality on Utnapishtim, who now instructs Gilgamesh to dive to the bottom of a river and find a certain plant that gives the power to grow younger. Although Gilgamesh finds the plant, a snake snatches it away before he can eat it. Gilgamesh remains mortal. The desire for immortality, one of humankind's great searches, ends in frustration. "Everlasting life," as this Mesopotamian epic makes clear, is only for the gods.

Mathematics and Astronomy   People in Mesopotamia made outstanding developments in mathematics and astronomy. In math, the Sumerians devised a number system based on 60, using combinations of 6 and 10 for practical solutions. They used the processes of multiplication and division and compiled tables for the computation of interest. Geometry was used for practical purposes, such as measuring fields and building projects. In astronomy, the Sumerians made use of units of 60 and charted the chief heavenly constellations. Their calendar was based on twelve lunar months and was brought into harmony with the solar year by adding an extra month from time to time.

EGYPTIAN CIVILIZATION: "THE GIFT OF THE NILE"

Although contemporaneous with Mesopotamia, civilization in Egypt evolved along somewhat different lines. Of central importance to the development of Egyptian civilization was the Nile River. That the Egyptian people recognized its significance is apparent in this *Hymn to the Nile*: "The bringer of food, rich in provisions, creator of all good, lord of majesty, sweet of fragrance…. He who … fills the magazines, makes the granaries wide, and gives things to the poor. He who makes every beloved tree to grow."[10] Egypt, like Mesopotamia, was a river valley civilization.

The Impact of Geography   The Nile is a unique river, beginning in the heart of Africa and coursing northward for thousands of miles. It is the longest river in the world. Thanks to the Nile, an area several miles wide on both banks of the river was capable of producing abundant harvests. The "miracle" of the Nile was its annual flooding. The river rose in the summer from rains in Central Africa and the Ethiopian highlands, crested in Egypt in September and October, and left a deposit of silt that enriched the soil. The Egyptians called this fertile land, dark from the silt and the lush crops that grew on it, the "Black Land." Beyond these narrow strips of fertile fields lay the deserts (the "Red Land").

Unlike the floods of Mesopotamia's rivers, the flooding of the Nile was gradual and usually predictable, and the river itself was seen as life-enhancing, not life-threatening. Although a system of organized irrigation was still necessary, the small villages along the Nile could make the effort without the massive state intervention that was required in Mesopotamia. Egyptian civilization consequently tended to remain more rural, with many small population centers congregated along a narrow band on both sides of the Nile. About 100 miles before it empties

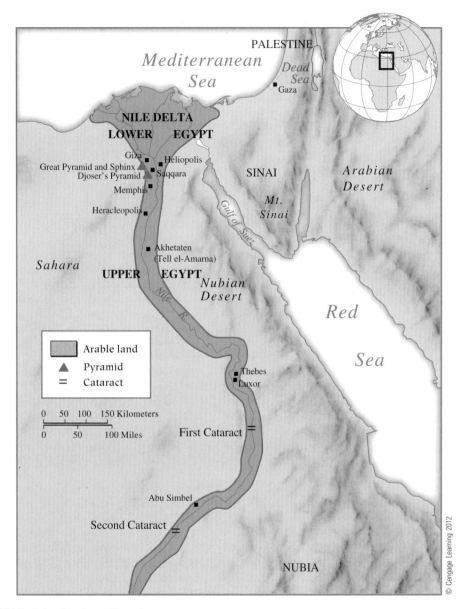

MAP 1.3 Ancient Egypt

Egyptian civilization centered on the life-giving water and flood silts of the Nile River, with most of the population living in Lower Egypt, where the river splits to form the Nile delta. Most of the pyramids, built during the Old Kingdom, are clustered at the entrance to the delta.

into the Mediterranean, the river splits into two major branches, forming the delta, a triangular-shaped territory called Lower Egypt to distinguish it from Upper Egypt, the land upstream to the south (see Map 1.3). Egypt's important cities developed at the tip of the delta. Even today, most of Egypt's people are crowded along the banks of the Nile River.

The Great Flood: Two Versions

Both the Mesopotamian *Epic of Gilgamesh* and the Hebrew Bible (Old Testament) include accounts of a great flood. In the first selection, taken from *The Epic of Gilgamesh*, Utnapishtim tells Gilgamesh the story of how he survived the flood unleashed by the gods to destroy humankind. Utnapishtim recounts how the god Ea advised him to build a boat and how he came to land the boat at the end of the flood. The second selection is the account of the great flood that appears in the book of Genesis in the Hebrew Bible. The biblical Noah appears to be a later version of the Mesopotamian Utnapishtim.

The Epic of Gilgamesh

"In those days the world teemed, the people multiplied, the world bellowed like a wild bull, and the great god was aroused by the clamor. Enlil heard the clamor and he said to the gods in council, 'The uproar of mankind is intolerable and sleep is no longer possible by reason of the babel.' So the gods agreed to exterminate mankind. Enlil did this, but Ea [Sumerian Enki, god of the waters] because of his oath warned me in a dream … 'tear down your house and build a boat, abandon possessions and look for life, despise worldly goods and save your soul alive. Tear down your house, I say, and build a boat.... Then take up into the boat the seed of all living creatures…' [Utnapishtim did as he was told, and then the destruction came.]

"For six days and six nights the winds blew, torrent and tempest and flood overwhelmed the world, tempest and flood raged together like warring hosts. When the seventh day dawned, the storm from the south subsided, the sea grew calm, the flood was stifled; I looked at the face of the world and there was silence, all mankind was turned to clay. The surface of the sea stretched as flat as a rooftop; I opened a hatch and the light fell on my face. Then I bowed low, I sat down and I wept, the tears streamed down my face, for on every side was the waste of water. I looked for land in vain, but fourteen leagues distant there appeared a mountain, and there the boat grounded; on the mountain of Nisir the boat held fast, she held fast and did not budge.

"… When the seventh day dawned, I loosed a dove and let her go. She flew away, but finding no resting-place she returned. Then I loosed a swallow, and she flew away but finding no resting-place she returned. I loosed a raven, she saw that the waters had retreated, she ate, she flew around, she cawed, and she did not come back. Then I threw everything open to the four winds, I made a sacrifice and poured out a libation on the mountain top."

The surpluses of food that Egyptian farmers grew in the fertile Nile valley made Egypt prosperous. But the Nile also served as a unifying factor in Egyptian history. In ancient times, the Nile was the fastest way to travel through the land, making both transportation and communication easier. Winds from the north pushed sailboats south, and the current of the Nile carried them north. Often when they headed downstream (north), people used long poles or paddles to propel their boats forward.

Unlike Mesopotamia, which was subject to constant invasion, Egypt was blessed by natural barriers that protected it from invasion and gave it a sense of

Genesis 6:11–15, 17–19; 7:24; 8:3, 13–21

Now the earth was corrupted in God's sight and was full of violence. God saw how corrupt the earth had become, for all the people on earth had corrupted their ways. So God said to Noah, "I am going to put an end to all people, for the earth is filled with violence because of them. I am surely going to destroy both them and the earth. So make yourself an ark of cypress wood: make rooms in it and coat it with pitch inside and out.... I am going to bring flood waters on the earth to destroy all life under the heavens, every creature that has the breath of life in it. Everything on earth will perish. But I will establish my covenant with you, and you will enter the ark—you and your sons and your wife and your sons' wives with you. You are to bring into the ark two of all living creatures, male and female, to keep them alive with you...."

The waters flooded the earth for a hundred and fifty days .... By the first day of the first month of Noah's six hundred and first year, the water had dried up from the earth. Noah then removed the covering from the ark and saw that the surface of the ground was dry.... Then God said to Noah, "Come out of the ark, you and your wife and your sons and their wives. Bring out every kind of living creature that is with you—the birds, the animals, and all the creatures that move along the ground—so they can multiply on the earth and be fruitful and increase in number upon it." So Noah came out, together with his sons and his wife and his son's wives ... [and all the animals]. Then Noah built an altar to the Lord and, taking some of all the clean animals and clean birds, he sacrificed burnt offerings on it. The Lord smelled the pleasing aroma and said in his heart. "Never again will I curse the ground because of man, even though every inclination of his heart is evil from childhood. And never again will I destroy all living creatures, as I have done."

Q *What does the selection from* The Epic of Gilgamesh *tell you about the relationship between the Mesopotamians and their gods? How might you explain the similarities and the differences between the Mesopotamian account and the flood story in Genesis?*

Sources: From THE EPIC OF GILGAMESH translated with an introduction by N. K. Sandars (Penguin Classics 1960, Third edition 1972). Copyright © N. K. Sandars, 1960, 1964, 1972. Reproduced by permission of Penguin Books Ltd. Scripture taken from the HOLY BIBLE, NEW INTERNATIONAL VERSION®. Copyright © 1973, 1978, 1984 Biblica. Used by permission of Zondervan. All rights reserved. The "NIV" and "New International Version" trademarks are registered in the United States Patent and Trademark Office by Biblica. Use of either trademark requires the permission of Biblica.

security. These barriers included the deserts to the west and east; the cataracts (rapids) on the southern part of the Nile, which made defense relatively easy; and the Mediterranean Sea to the north. These barriers, however, were effective only when they were combined with Egyptian fortifications at strategic locations. Nor did they prevent the development of trade. Indeed, there is evidence of very early trade between Egypt and Mesopotamia.

In essence, Egyptian geography and topography played important roles in the early history of the country. The regularity of the Nile floods and the relative isolation of the Egyptians created a sense of security that was accompanied by a feeling of changelessness. As the ancient Egyptians said, when the Nile floods each year, "the fields laugh and people's faces light up." Unlike people in Mesopotamia, Egyptians faced life with a spirit of confidence in the stability of things. Egyptian civilization was characterized by a remarkable degree of continuity over thousands of years.

The Old and Middle Kingdoms   The basic framework for the study of Egyptian history was provided by Manetho (MAN-uh-thoh), an Egyptian priest and historian who lived in the early third century B.C.E. He divided Egyptian history into thirty-one dynasties of kings. Using Manetho's and other lists of kings, modern historians have divided Egyptian history into three major periods known as the Old Kingdom, the Middle Kingdom, and the New Kingdom. These were periods of long-term stability characterized by strong monarchical authority, competent bureaucracy, freedom from invasion, much construction of temples and pyramids, and considerable intellectual and cultural activity. But between the periods of stability were intervals known as the Intermediate Periods, characterized by weak political structures and rivalry for leadership, invasions, a decline in building activity, and a restructuring of society.

The Old Kingdom   According to the Egyptians' own tradition, their land consisted initially of numerous populated areas ruled by tribal chieftains. Around 3100 B.C.E., during the Early Dynastic Period, the first Egyptian royal dynasty, under a king called Menes (MEE-neez), united both Upper and Lower Egypt into a single kingdom. Henceforth, the king would be called "King of Upper and Lower Egypt," and one of the royal crowns would be the Double Crown, combining the White Crown of Upper Egypt and the Red Crown of Lower Egypt. Just as the Nile united Upper and Lower Egypt physically, kingship united the two areas politically.

The Old Kingdom encompassed the fourth through eighth dynasties of Egyptian kings, lasting from around 2575 to 2125 B.C.E. It was an age of prosperity and splendor, made visible in the construction of the greatest and largest pyramids in Egypt's history. The capital of the Old Kingdom was located at Memphis, south of the delta.

Kingship was a divine institution in ancient Egypt and formed part of a universal cosmic scheme: "What is the king of Upper and Lower Egypt? He is a god by whose dealings one lives, the father and mother of all men, alone by himself, without an equal."[11] In obeying their king, subjects helped maintain the cosmic order. A breakdown in royal power could only mean that citizens were offending divinity and weakening the universal structure. Among the various titles of Egyptian kings, that of pharaoh (originally meaning "great house" or "palace") eventually came to be the most common.

Although they possessed absolute power, Egyptian kings were supposed to rule not arbitrarily but according to set principles. The chief principle was called *Ma'at* (muh-AHT), a spiritual precept that conveyed the idea of truth and justice, especially right order and harmony. To ancient Egyptians, this fundamental order and harmony had existed throughout the universe since the beginning of time.

Pharaohs were the divine instruments who maintained it and were themselves subject to it.

Although theoretically absolute in their power, in practice Egyptian kings did not rule alone. Initially, members of the king's family performed administrative tasks, but by the fourth dynasty, a bureaucracy with regular procedures had developed. Especially important was the office of vizier, "steward of the whole land." Directly responsible to the king, the vizier was in charge of the bureaucracy, with its numerous departments, including police, justice, river transport, and public works. Agriculture and the treasury were the most important departments. Agriculture was, of course, the backbone of Egyptian prosperity, and the treasury collected the taxes, which were paid in kind. A careful assessment of land and tenants was undertaken to establish the tax base.

For administrative purposes, Egypt was divided into provinces or nomes, as they were later called by the Greeks—twenty-two in Upper and twenty in Lower Egypt. A governor, called by the Greeks a nomarch, was head of each nome and was responsible to the king and vizier. Nomarchs, however, tended to build up large holdings of land and power within their nomes, creating a potential rivalry with the pharaohs.

The Middle Kingdom   A decline in centralized authority, a drought caused by low levels of the Nile and a decline in rainfall, and economic troubles brought about the collapse of the Old Kingdom, ushering in the First Intermediate Period (c. 2125–2010 B.C.E.). A so-called prophet named Nefer-Rohu (Neferti) described the scene:

> This land is so damaged that there is no one who is concerned with it, no one who speaks, no one who weeps.... The sun disk is covered over. It will not shine so that people may see.... The rivers of Egypt are empty, so that the water is crossed on foot. Men seek for water for the ships to sail on it... . This land is helter-skelter, and no one knows the result that will come about, which is hidden from speech, sight, or hearing.[12]

Eventually, a new royal dynasty managed to pacify all Egypt and inaugurated the Middle Kingdom, a new period of stability lasting from around 2010 to 1630 B.C.E.

Much of the Middle Kingdom's history centered around the twelfth dynasty founded by Amenemhet I, a vizier who established himself and his successors as pharaohs. Egyptians later portrayed the Middle Kingdom as a golden age, a clear indication of its stability. Several factors contributed to its vitality. The nome structure was reorganized. The boundaries of each nome were now settled precisely, and the obligations of the nomes to the state were clearly delineated. Nomarchs were confirmed as hereditary officeholders but with the understanding that their duties must be performed faithfully. These included the collection of taxes for the state and the recruitment of labor forces for royal projects, such as stone quarrying.

The Middle Kingdom was characterized by a new concern on the part of the pharaohs for the people. In the Old Kingdom, the pharaoh had been viewed as an inaccessible god-king. Now he was portrayed as the shepherd of his people with the responsibility to build public works and provide for the public welfare. As one pharaoh expressed it: "He [a particular god] created me as one who should do that which he had done, and to carry out that which he commanded should be done.

He appointed me herdsman of this land, for he knew who would keep it in order for him."[13]

As confirmation of its newfound strength, Egypt embarked on a period of expansion. Lower Nubia was conquered, and fortresses were built to protect the new southern frontier. The government also sent military expeditions into Canaan and Syria. Although they did not remain there, this campaign marks the beginning of Egyptian imperialism in those areas.

Society and Economy in Ancient Egypt   Egyptian society had a simple structure in the Old and Middle Kingdoms; basically, it was organized along hierarchical lines with the god-king at the top. The king was surrounded by an upper class of nobles and priests who participated in the elaborate rituals of life that surrounded the pharaoh. The members of this ruling class ran the government and managed their own landed estates, which provided much of their wealth.

Below the upper classes were merchants and artisans. Merchants engaged in active trade up and down the Nile as well as in town and village markets. Some merchants also engaged in international trade; they were sent by the king to Crete and Syria, where they obtained wood and other products. Expeditions traveled into Nubia for ivory and down the Red Sea to Punt for incense and spices. Egyptian artisans displayed unusually high standards of craftsmanship and physical beauty and produced an incredible variety of goods: stone dishes; beautifully painted boxes made of clay; wooden furniture, especially of Lebanon cedar; gold, silver, and copper tools and containers; paper and rope made of papyrus; and linen clothes.

The great majority of people in Egypt simply worked the land. In theory, the king owned all the land but granted portions of it to his subjects. Large sections were in the possession of nobles and the temple complexes. Most of the lower classes were serfs, common people who were bound to the land and cultivated the estates. They paid taxes in the form of crops to the king, nobles, and priests; lived in small villages or towns; and provided military service and labor for building projects.

The Culture of Egypt   Egypt produced a culture that dazzled and awed its later conquerors. The Egyptians' technical achievements alone, especially visible in the construction of the pyramids, demonstrated a measure of skill unique to the world of that time. To the Egyptians, all of these achievements were part of a cosmic order suffused with the presence of the divine.

Spiritual Life in Egyptian Society   The Egyptians had no word for religion because it was an inseparable element of the world order to which Egyptian society belonged. Egypt was part of the universal cosmic scheme, and the pharaoh was the divine being whose duty was to preserve Egypt's place within that divinely ordained cosmic order.

This perspective helps explain the importance of ritual in ancient Egypt. Through their rituals, Egyptians worked to maintain the cosmic order by appeasing the gods and goddesses who controlled the universe. An Egyptian ritual ceremony focused on an image of a deity and providing it with food and sustenance, thereby performing an act of ritual worship to appease the god. The pharaoh was at the heart of Egypt's ritual life. He supervised the sacred ceremonies that were performed in the temples, although in practice the pharaoh's religious deputies—the priests—carried out the daily ceremonies.

The Egyptians had a remarkable number of gods associated with heavenly bodies and natural forces, hardly unusual in view of the importance to Egypt's well-being of the sun, the river, and the fertile land along its banks. The sun was the source of life and hence worthy of worship. A sun cult developed, and the sun god took on different forms and names, depending on his specific function. He was worshiped as Atum in human form and as Re (or Ra), who had a human body but the head of a falcon. The pharaoh took the title "Son of Re" because he was regarded as the earthly embodiment of Re.

River and land deities included Osiris (oh-SY-russ) and Isis (Y-sis) with their child Horus, who was related to the Nile and to the sun as well. Osiris became especially important as a symbol of resurrection. A famous Egyptian myth told of the struggle between Osiris, who brought civilization to Egypt, and his evil brother Seth, who killed him, cut his body into fourteen parts, and tossed them into the Nile. Isis, the faithful wife of Osiris, found the pieces and, with help from other gods, restored Osiris to life. As a symbol of resurrection and as judge of the dead, Osiris took on an important role for the Egyptians. By identifying with Osiris, one could hope to gain new life, just as Osiris had done. The dead, embalmed and mummified, were placed in tombs (in the case of kings, in pyramidal tombs), given the name of Osiris, and by a process of magical identification became Osiris. Like Osiris, they would then be reborn. The flood of the Nile and the new life it brought to Egypt were symbolized by Isis gathering all of the parts of Osiris together and were celebrated each spring in the festival of the new land.

Later Egyptian spiritual practice began to emphasize morality by stressing the role of Osiris as judge of the dead. The dead were asked to give an account of their earthly deeds to show whether they deserved a reward. Other means were also employed to gain immortality. As seen in the *Book of the Dead* from the period of the New Kingdom, magical incantations were used to ensure a favorable journey to a happy afterlife. Specific instructions explained what to do when confronted by the judge of the dead. These instructions had two aspects. In the negative confession, the deceased gave a detailed list of what he had not done:

> I have not committed evil against men.
> I have not mistreated cattle....
> I have not blasphemed a god.....
> I have not done violence to a poor man....
> I have not made anyone sick....
> I have not killed....
> I have not caused anyone suffering....
> I have not had sexual relations with a boy.
> I have not defiled myself....
> I have not driven cattle away from their pasturage.[14]

Later the supplicant made a speech listing his good actions: "I have done that which men said and that with which gods are content…. I have given bread to the hungry, water to the thirsty, clothing to the naked, and a ferry-boat to him who was marooned. I have provided divine offerings for the gods and mortuary offerings for the dead."[15]

At first the Osiris cult was reserved for the very wealthy, who could afford to take expensive measures to preserve the body after death. During the Middle Kingdom, however, the cult became "democratized" and was extended to all Egyptians who aspired to an afterlife.

The Pyramids   One of the great achievements of Egyptian civilization, the building of pyramids, occurred during the Old Kingdom. Pyramids were not built in isolation but as part of a larger complex dedicated to the dead—in effect, a city of the dead. The area included a large pyramid for the king's burial, smaller pyramids for his family, and mastabas (MAS-tuh-buhs), rectangular structures with flat roofs, as tombs for the pharaoh's noble officials. The tombs were well prepared for their residents. The rooms were furnished and stocked with numerous supplies, including chairs, boats, chests, weapons, games, dishes, and a variety of foods. The Egyptians believed that human beings had two bodies, a physical one and a spiritual one, which they called the ka. If the physical body was properly preserved (that is, mummified) and the tomb furnished with all the various objects of regular life, the *ka* could return and continue its life despite the death of the physical body.

Osiris as Judge of the Dead. *According to the* **Book of the Dead,** *after making a denial of offenses (the "negative confession"), the deceased experienced the "weighing of the heart." Shown here is a judgment scene from the* **Book of the Dead** *of Hunefer, a royal scribe who died around 1285 B.C.E. Hunefer's heart is placed on one side of a balance scale; on the other side is the feather of Ma'at, the goddess of truth. For Hunefer, heart and feather are of equal weight, so the god Anubis ushers him into the presence of Osiris, seated on his throne at the right. A "Swallowing Monster," a hybrid creature combining crocodile, lion, and hippopotamus, stood ready at the scale to devour the deceased if he failed the test.*

To preserve the physical body after death, the Egyptians practiced mummification, a process of slowly drying a dead body to prevent it from rotting. Special workshops, run by priests, performed this procedure, primarily for the wealthy families who could afford it. According to Herodotus, an ancient Greek historian (see Chapter 3) who visited Egypt around 450 B.C.E., "The most refined method is as follows: first of all they draw out the brain through the nostrils with an iron hook.... Then they make an incision in the flank with a sharp Ethiopian stone through which they extract all the internal organs."[16] The liver, lungs, stomach, and intestines were then placed in four special jars that were put in the tomb with the mummy. The priests then covered the corpse with a natural salt that absorbed the body's water. Later, they filled the body with spices and wrapped it with layers of linen soaked in resin. At the end of the process, which took about seventy days, a lifelike mask was placed over the head and shoulders of the mummy, which was then sealed in a case and placed in its tomb.

Pyramids were tombs for the mummified bodies of pharaohs. The first pyramid was a step pyramid built at Saqqara in the third dynasty during the reign of King Djoser (ZHOH-sur). The architect Imhotep, a priest of Heliopolis, the center dedicated to the sun cult, was responsible for constructing the pyramid.

The first real pyramid, with each side filled in to make an even surface, was constructed around 2600 B.C.E. by King Snefru, who built three pyramids. But the largest and most magnificent of all was built under Snefru's son Khufu. Constructed at Giza around 2540 B.C.E., the famous Great Pyramid covers 13 acres, measures 756 feet at each side of its base, and stands 481 feet high. Its four sides are almost precisely oriented to the four points of the compass.

The building of the Great Pyramid was an enormous construction project that used limestone blocks as well as granite from Upper Egypt. Herodotus reported that it took 100,000 Egyptians twenty years to build the Great Pyramid. But Herodotus wrote two thousand years after the event, and considerable controversy and speculation still surround the construction of the Great Pyramid, especially in view of the precision with which it was built. The stone slabs on the outside of the pyramid, for example, fit so closely side by side that a hair cannot be pushed into the joints between them. The Great Pyramid still stands as a symbol of the power of Egyptian kings of the Old Kingdom. No later pyramid ever matched its size or splendor. But an Egyptian pyramid was not just the king's tomb; it was also an important symbol of royal power. It could be seen for miles away as a visible reminder of the glory and might of the ruler, a living god on earth.

Art and Writing   Commissioned by kings or nobles for use in temples and tombs, Egyptian art was largely functional. Wall paintings and statues of gods and kings in temples served a strictly spiritual purpose. They were an integral part of the performance of ritual, which was thought necessary to preserve the cosmic order and hence the well-being of Egypt. Likewise, the mural scenes and sculptured figures found in the tombs had a specific function. They were supposed to aid the journey of the deceased into the afterworld.

Egyptian art was also formulaic. Artists and sculptors were expected to observe a strict canon of proportions that determined both form and presentation. This canon gave Egyptian art a distinctive appearance for thousands of years. Especially characteristic was the convention of combining the profile, semiprofile, and frontal views of the human body in relief work and painting in order to represent each part of the body accurately. This fashion created an art that was highly stylized yet still allowed distinctive features to be portrayed.

Writing emerged in Egypt during the first two dynasties. It was the Greeks who later labeled Egyptian writing **hieroglyphics,** meaning "priest-carvings" or "sacred writings." Hieroglyphs (HY-uh-roh-glifs) were signs that depicted objects and had a sacred value at the same time. Although hieroglyphs were later simplified for writing purposes into two scripts, they never developed into an alphabet. Egyptian hieroglyphs were initially carved in stone, but later the two simplified scripts were written on papyrus, a paper made from the papyrus reed that grew along the Nile. Most of the ancient Egyptian literature that has come down to us was written on papyrus rolls and wooden tablets.

Disorder and a New Order: The New Kingdom   The Middle Kingdom came to an end in the midst of another period of instability. An incursion into the delta region by a people known as the Hyksos (HIK-sos) initiated this second age of disorder. The Hyksos, a Semitic-speaking people, infiltrated Egypt in the seventeenth century B.C.E. and came to dominate much of Egypt. The presence of the Hyksos was not entirely negative for Egypt, however. They taught the Egyptians how to use bronze to make agricultural tools and weapons. The Hyksos also introduced new aspects of warfare, including the horse-drawn war chariot, a heavier sword, and the compound bow. Eventually, the Egyptians made use of their new weapons to throw off Hyksos domination.

The Egyptian Empire   It was the pharaoh Ahmose I who managed to defeat and expel the Hyksos from Egypt. He reunited Egypt, founded the eighteenth dynasty, established the New Kingdom (c. 1539–1069 B.C.E.),and launched the Egyptians along a new militaristic and imperialistic path characterized by the development of a more professional army. No longer content to remain in isolation, Egypt now pursued an active political and diplomatic policy.

During the period of the New Kingdom, Egypt became the most powerful state in the ancient Near East (see Map 1.4). Thutmose (thoot-MOH-suh) I (c. 1493–1481 B.C.E.) expanded Egypt's border to the south by conquering the African kingdom of Nubia. The warrior Thutmose III (c. 1479–1425 B.C.E.) led seventeen military campaigns into Canaan and Phoenicia. The Egyptians occupied these lands but permitted local native princes to rule. Amenhotep (ah-mun-HOH-tep) II (c. 1426–1400 B.C.E.), the successor of Thutmose III, also campaigned in the Near East and not only solidified the Egyptian empire, but also increased Egypt's prosperity by bringing back enormous quantities of booty.

The new Egyptian imperial state reached its height during the reign of Amenhotep III (c. 1390–1353 B.C.E.), the great-grandson of Thutmose III. Caring little about military affairs and content to maintain the empire he had inherited, Amenhotep III spent much of his reign constructing magnificent new buildings and temples. Especially famous were the temple centers at Karnak and Luxor and the immense statues of Amenhotep III in front of the mortuary temples along the Nile.

MAP 1.4 The Egyptian and Hittite Empires

The Hittite empire was the dominant power north of Egypt for roughly two centuries. It assimilated important linguistic, political, and religious aspects of the peoples it conquered and thus helped transmit Mesopotamian culture to the eastern Mediterranean.

By the end of his reign, Amenhotep III faced a growing military challenge from a people known as the Hittites (see "The Hittite Empire" later in this chapter). His son, Amenhotep IV (c. 1353–1336 B.C.E.), proved even less able to deal with this threat, a failure that was due in large part to a religious upheaval that he had initiated in Egypt.

Akhenaten and Religious Change Amenhotep IV introduced the worship of Aten, god of the sun disk, as the supreme god and later in his reign as the only god. In the pharaoh's eyes, he and Aten had become co-rulers of Egypt. Changing his own name to Akhenaten (ah-kuh-NAH-tun) ("Servant of Aten"), the pharaoh closed the temples of other gods and especially endeavored to lessen the power of the priesthood dedicated to the god Amon-Re at Thebes. Akhenaten strove to reduce the priests' influence by replacing Thebes as the capital of Egypt with Akhetaten ("Horizon of Aten"), a new city located at modern Tell el-Amarna, 200 miles north of Thebes. The pharaoh decreed that Akhetaten, not Thebes, would be his final resting place: "If I die in any town of the north, the south, the west, or the east in these millions of years, let me be brought back so that I may be buried in Akhetaten."[17]

Akhenaten's attempt at religious change failed. It was too much to ask Egyptians to ignore their traditional ways and beliefs, especially since they saw the destruction of the old gods as subversive of the very cosmic order on which Egypt's survival and continuing prosperity depended. Moreover, the priests at Thebes were unalterably opposed to the changes, which diminished their influence and power. At the same time, Akhenaten's preoccupation with religion caused him to ignore foreign affairs and led to the loss of both Syria and Canaan. Akhenaten's changes were soon undone after his death by those who influenced his successor, the boy-pharaoh Tutankhamun (toot-ahng-KAH-muhn) (c.1332–1322 B.C.E.). Tutankhamun returned the government to Thebes and restored the old gods. The Aten experiment had failed to take hold, and the eighteenth dynasty itself came to an end with the rise to power of a military officer and vizier, Horemhab, who assumed the kingship in 1319 B.C.E.

The End of the Empire   The nineteenth dynasty managed to restore Egyptian power one more time. Under Ramesses (RAM-uh-seez) II (c. 1279–1213 B.C.E.), the Egyptians went on the offensive, and after an inconclusive struggle with the Hittites at the Battle of Kadesh, regained control of Canaan and restored Egypt as an imperial power. During his long sixty-seven-year reign, Ramesses II provided visible demonstrations of his power by constructing mammoth new temples, many of them adorned with colossal statues of himself.

Statues of Ramesses II at Abu Simbel. *After being driven out of Canaan and Syria by the Hittites, Egypt grew to power one final time under Ramesses II. He succeeded in reconquering Canaan but was unable to restore the boundaries of the previous empire. The massive Temple of Ramesses II, located at Abu Simbel, was carved out of a cliff of Nubian sandstone. The giant statues represent Ramesses II.*

After the death of Ramesses II, struggles for the throne weakened the government, and new invasions in the twelfth century by the "Sea Peoples," as the Egyptians called them, destroyed Egyptian power in Canaan and drove the Egyptians back within their old frontiers. The days of Egyptian empire were ended, and the New Kingdom itself expired with the twentieth dynasty in 1069 B.C.E. For the next thousand years, despite periodic revivals of strength, Egypt was dominated by Libyans, Nubians, Assyrians, Persians, and finally Macedonians after the conquest of Alexander the Great (see Chapter 4). In the first century B.C.E., Egypt became a province in Rome's mighty empire.

Daily Life in Ancient Egypt   Ancient Egyptians had a very positive attitude toward daily life on earth and followed the advice of the wisdom literature, which suggested that people marry young and establish a home and family. Monogamy was the general rule, although a husband was allowed to keep additional wives if his first wife was childless. Pharaohs were entitled to harems, though the queen was acknowledged as the Great Wife, with a status higher than that of the other wives. The husband was master in the house, but wives were very much respected and in charge of the household and education of the children. From a book of wise sayings (which the Egyptians called "instructions") came this advice:

> If you are a man of standing, you should found your household and love your wife at home as is fitting. Fill her belly; clothe her back. Ointment is the prescription for her body. Make her heart glad as long as you live. She is a profitable field for her lord. You should not contend with her at law, and keep her far from gaining control.... Let her heart be soothed through what may accrue to you; it means keeping her long in your house.[18]

Women's property and inheritances remained in their hands, even after marriage. Although most careers and public offices were closed to women, some women did operate businesses. Peasant women worked long hours in the fields and at numerous domestic tasks, especially weaving cloth. Upper-class women could function as priestesses, and a few queens even became pharaohs in their own right. Most famous was Hatshepsut (hat-SHEP-soot) in the New Kingdom. She initially served as regent for her stepson Thutmose III but assumed the throne for herself and remained in power until her death.

Hatshepsut's reign was a prosperous one, as is especially evident in her building activity. She is most famous for the temple dedicated to herself at Deir el Bahri (dayr ahl BAH-ree) on the west bank of the Nile at Thebes. As pharaoh, Hatshepsut sent out military expeditions, encouraged mining, fostered agriculture, and sent a trading expedition up the Nile. Hatshepsut's official statues sometimes show her clothed and bearded like a king. She was addressed as "His Majesty." That Hatshepsut was aware of her unusual position is evident from an inscription she had placed on one of her temples. It read: "Now my heart turns to and fro, in thinking what will the people say, they who shall see my monument in after years, and shall speak of what I have done."

Marriages were arranged by parents. The primary concerns were family and property, and the chief purpose of marriage was to produce children, especially sons. Daughters were not slighted, however. Numerous tomb paintings show the close and affectionate relationship parents had with both sons and daughters. Marriages could and did end in divorce, which was allowed, apparently with compensation for the wife. Adultery, however, was strictly prohibited, and punishments were severe, especially for women, who could have their noses cut off or be burned at the stake.

Under normal circumstances, Egypt was blessed by a material abundance that not only kept its entire population fed but also enabled its upper classes to lead a life of gracious leisure. These wealthy families had attractive homes located on walled estates. Much energy was devoted to the garden, which contained fruit trees and vegetables, as well as tree-lined paths and pools for the family's leisure time.

Tomb paintings indicate that the upper classes participated in numerous banquets where guests were lavishly fed and entertained (see Images of Everyday Life). Although some people obviously got drunk, a collection of "instructions" advises more circumspect behavior:

> If you are one of those sitting at the table of one greater than yourself, take what he may give, when it is set before your nose. You should gaze at what is before you....
> Let your face be cast down until he addresses you, and you should speak only when he addresses you. Laugh after he laughs, and it will be very pleasing to his heart and what you may do will be pleasing to the heart.[19]

The same collection of "instructions" warns that when one has been invited to a party, "beware of approaching the women. It does not go well with the place where that is done."[20]

Entertainment, especially music, was a regular feature of parties. The Egyptians used an astonishing variety of instruments: drums, tambourines, flutes, trumpets, and stringed instruments that were plucked rather than played with a bow. Singers, accompanying themselves on lute or harp, presented songs in praise of the host's generosity and of enjoying life.

Judging from the paintings in their tombs, the upper classes found myriad ways to entertain themselves as well. Fowling in the stands of papyrus reeds that grew along the riverbanks was a favorite pastime. So was hunting animals, but only for the men. Armed with bows and arrows, the hunters rode in chariots and used dogs to pursue antelope, gazelles, and other creatures. Indoor activities included board games among other things. The earliest known board games in the world have been found in Egyptian tombs. Many are made of wood decorated with ivory or ebony. The games played on them involved moving pieces on the boards according to the roll of the dice.

The gulf between the upper and lower classes of Egyptian society was especially evident in health care. While the elite had a healthy diet and could call on doctors and dentists for medical help, the peasants suffered from numerous debilitating diseases. The ailments of women, especially those related to fertility, pregnancy, and childbirth, attracted special attention from the medical world.

Regardless of class, most Egyptians believed that disease came from bad spirits or incorrect behavior. To protect themselves, people used magic spells and amulets that carried images of protective deities. Nevertheless, Egyptian records include lists of prescriptions for broken bones, wounds, stomach problems, rashes, and numerous other ailments.

ON THE FRINGES OF CIVILIZATION

Mesopotamia and Egypt have dominated our story of the beginnings of Western civilization, but significant developments were also taking place on the fringes of these civilizations. Farming had spread into the Balkan peninsula of Europe by 6500 B.C.E., and by 4000 B.C.E. it was well established in southern France, central Europe, and the coastal regions of the Mediterranean. Although migrating farmers from the Near East may have brought some farming techniques into Europe, historians now believe that the Neolithic peoples of Europe domesticated animals and began to farm largely on their own.

One outstanding feature of late Neolithic Europe was the building of megalithic structures. *Megalith* is Greek for "large stone." Radiocarbon dating, a technique that allows scientists to determine the age of objects, shows that the first megalithic structures were built around 4000 B.C.E., more than a thousand years before the great pyramids were built in Egypt. Between 3200 and 1500 B.C.E., standing stones placed in circles or lined up in rows were erected throughout the British Isles and northwestern France. Other megalithic constructions have been found as far north as Scandinavia and as far south as the islands of Corsica, Sardinia, and Malta. Some archaeologists have demonstrated that the stone circles were used as observatories to detect not only such simple astronomical phenomena as the midwinter and midsummer sunrises but also such sophisticated observations as the major and minor standstills of the moon.

By far the most famous of these megalithic constructions is Stonehenge in England. Stonehenge consists of a series of concentric rings of standing stones. Its construction sometime between 2100 and 1900 B.C.E. was no small accomplishment. The eighty bluestones used at Stonehenge weigh 4 tons each and were transported to the site from their original source 135 miles away. Like other megalithic structures, Stonehenge indicates a remarkable awareness of astronomy on the part of its builders, as well as an impressive coordination of workers.

The Impact of the Indo-Europeans   For many historians, both the details of construction and the purpose of the megalithic structures of Europe remain a mystery. Also puzzling is the role of the Indo-European people. The term *Indo-European* refers to people who used a language derived from a single parent tongue. Indo-European languages include Greek, Latin, Persian, Sanskrit, and the Germanic languages. It has been suggested that the original Indo-European-speaking peoples were based somewhere in the steppe region north of the Black Sea or in southwestern Asia, in modern Iran or Afghanistan. Although there had been earlier migrations, around 2000 B.C.E. they began major nomadic movements into Europe (including present-day Italy and Greece), India, and the Near East. The Indo-Europeans who moved into Asia Minor and Anatolia (modern Turkey) coalesced with the native peoples to form the first Hittite kingdom, known as the Old Kingdom (c. 1700–1400 B.C.E.), with its capital at Hattusas (Boğazköy in modern Turkey).

IMAGES OF EVERYDAY LIFE

The Egyptian Diet

The diet of the upper and lower classes in ancient Egypt varied considerably. Meat and fowl, including beef, goat, pork, goose, and pigeons, were on the tables of the rich. Although done for sport as well as food, hunting waterfowl in the stands of papyrus reeds that grew along the river's banks was a favorite pastime of the Egyptian upper classes. The image below left shows a hunting scene from

British Museum, London/© Werner Forman/Art Resource, NY

The Hittite Empire

The Hittites began to spread outward around 1600 B.C.E., but it was not until around two hundred years later that a new line of kings created the Hittite New Kingdom or Hittite empire. Especially notable was Suppiluliumas (suh-PIL-oo-LEE-uh-muss) I (c. 1370–1330 B.C.E.), one of the strongest rulers of the era, who established Hittite control from western Turkey to northern Syria. Suppiluliumas formed an alliance with the Egyptians and then conquered Syria. The Hittites were the first of the Indo-European peoples to make use of iron, enabling them to construct weapons that were stronger and cheaper to make because of the widespread availability of iron ore.

For the next hundred years, the Hittites were in conflict with Egypt until the Egyptian pharaoh Ramesses II made a remarkable nonaggression treaty that stabilized relations between Egypt and the Hittites. The end of Hittite power came in part from internal problems but also as a result of attacks by the Sea Peoples from the west around 1200 B.C.E. and by a group of aggressive tribespeople known as the Gasga, who raided Hittite cities. By 1190 B.C.E., Hittite power had come to an end.

During its heyday, however, the Hittite empire was one of the great powers in western Asia. The Hittite ruler, known as the "Great King," controlled the core areas of the kingdom, but in western and southern Anatolia and Syria, he allowed the eighteenth-dynasty tomb of Nebamun in Thebes. Nebamun, a nobleman, is seen standing in his boat using his throwstick to hunt birds. He holds three birds in his right hand while a cat retrieves two in its claws and holds the wings of another in its teeth. The basic diet of the poor consisted chiefly of bread, and the baking of bread was an important task in all households. The tomb painting below right from the eighteenth-dynasty tomb of Mennah shows two men carrying grain while slave girls fight over leftovers in the background.

Tombs of the Nobles, Thebes, Egypt/Erich Lessing/Art Resource, NY

local rulers to swear allegiance to him as his vassals. Constant squabbling over succession to the throne, however, tended to weaken the royal authority at times.

During its height, the Hittite empire also demonstrated an interesting ability to assimilate other cultures into its own. In language, literature, art, law, and religion, the Hittites borrowed much from Mesopotamia as well as from the native peoples they had subdued. Recent scholarship has stressed the important role of the Hittites in transmitting Mesopotamian culture, as they transformed it, to later Western civilizations in the Mediterranean area, especially to the Mycenaean Greeks (see Chapter 3).

CHRONOLOGIES

THE FIRST HUMANS

c. 2–4 million years ago	Australopithecines flourished
c. 100,000–1.5 million years ago	*Homo erectus* flourished
c. 200,000 B.C.	*Homo sapiens sapiens* emerged

THE BIRTH OF EARLY CIVILIZATIONS

c. 3100 B.C.	Egypt
c. 3000 B.C.	Mesopotamia and India
c. 2600 B.C.	Peru
c. 2000 B.C.	China and Central Asia

CHIEF EVENTS IN MESOPOTAMIAN HISTORY

c. 3000–2340 B.C.	Sumerian city-states: Early Dynastic Age
c. 2112–2000 B.C.	Third Dynasty of Ur
1792–1750 B.C.	Hammurabi's reign
c. 1550 B.C.	Invasion by Kassites

THE EGYPTIANS

c. 3100–2686 B.C.	Early Dynastic Period
c. 2686–2181 B.C.	Old Kingdom
c. 2180–2055 B.C.	First Intermediate Period
c. 2055–1650 B.C.	Middle Kingdom
c. 1650–1550 B.C.	Second Intermediate Period
c. 1550–1070 B.C.	New Kingdom
1070–30 B.C.	Postempire Egypt

2

THE ANCIENT NEAR EAST: PEOPLES AND EMPIRES

The judgment of Solomon as painted by Raphael in the sixteenth century

Vatican Palace, Vatican State//© Scala/Art Resource, NY

CHAPTER OUTLINE

- The Hebrews: "The Children of Israel" • The Neighbors of the Israelites
- The Assyrian Empire • The Neo-Babylonian Empire • The Persian Empire

THE HEBREWS: "THE CHILDREN OF ISRAEL"

The Hebrews were a Semitic-speaking people who had a tradition concerning their origins and history that was eventually written down as part of the Hebrew Bible, known to Christians as the Old Testament. Describing themselves originally as nomads organized into clans, the Hebrews' tradition states that they were descendants of the patriarch Abraham, who had migrated from Mesopotamia to the land of Canaan, where they became identified as the "Children of Israel." Again according to tradition, a drought in Canaan caused many Hebrews to migrate to Egypt, where they lived peacefully until they were enslaved by pharaohs who used them as laborers on building projects. These Hebrews remained in bondage until Moses led them eastward out of Egypt in the Exodus, which some historians have argued would have occurred in the first half of the thirteenth century B.C.E. According to the biblical account, the Hebrews then wandered for many years in the desert until they entered Canaan. Organized into twelve tribes, they became embroiled in conflict with the Philistines, a people who had settled in the coastal area of Canaan but were beginning to move inland.

Many scholars today doubt that the early books of the Hebrew Bible reflect the true history of the early Israelites. They argue that the early books of the Bible, written centuries after the events described, preserve only what the Israelites came to believe about themselves and that recent archaeological evidence often contradicts the details of the biblical account. Some of these scholars have even argued that the Israelites were not nomadic invaders but indigenous peoples in the Canaanite hill country. What is generally agreed, however, is that between 1200 and 1000 B.C.E., the Israelites emerged as a distinct group of people, possibly organized into tribes or a league of tribes.

Was There a United Kingdom of Israel? According to the Hebrew Bible, the Israelites established a united kingdom of Israel beginning with Saul (c. 1020–1000 B.C.E.), who supposedly achieved some success in the ongoing struggle with the Philistines. But after his death, a brief period of anarchy ensued until one of Saul's lieutenants, David (c. 1000–970 B.C.E.), reunited the Israelites, defeated the Philistines, and established control over all of Canaan. According to the biblical account, some of his conquests led to harsh treatment for the conquered people: "David also defeated the Moabites. He made them lie down on the ground and measured them off with a length of cord. Every two lengths of them were put to death, and the third length was allowed to live. So the Moabites became subject to David and brought tribute."[1] Among David's conquests was the city of Jerusalem, which he supposedly made into the capital of a united kingdom.

According to the biblical account, David's son Solomon (c. 970–930 B.C.E.) did even more to strengthen royal power. He expanded the political and military establishments and extended the trading activities of the Israelites. Solomon is portrayed as a great builder, who was responsible for the Temple in the city of Jerusalem. The Israelites viewed the Temple as the symbolic center of their religion and hence of the kingdom of Israel itself. Under Solomon, ancient Israel was supposedly at the height of its power (see Map 2.1).

MAP 2.1 The Israelites and Their Neighbors in the First Millennium B.C.

United under Saul, David, and Solomon, greater Israel split into two states—Israel and Judah—after the death of Solomon. With power divided, the Israelites could not resist invasions that dispersed many Jews from Canaan. Some, such as the "ten lost tribes," never returned. Others were sent to Babylon but were later allowed to return under the rule of the Persians.

The accuracy of this biblical account of the united kingdom of Israel under Saul, David, and Solomon has been recently challenged by a new generation of archaeologists and historians. Although they mostly accept Saul, David, and Solomon as historical figures, they portray them more as chief warlords than as kings. If a kingdom of Israel did exist during these years, it was not as powerful or as well organized as the Hebrew Bible says. Furthermore, they argue, there is no definitive archaeological evidence that Solomon built the Temple in Jerusalem.

The Kingdoms of Israel and Judah

There may or not have been a united kingdom of Israel, but after Solomon's death tensions between northern and southern tribes in Israel led to the establishment of two separate kingdoms—the kingdom of Israel, composed of the ten northern tribes, with its capital eventually at Samaria, and the southern kingdom of Judah, consisting of two tribes, with its capital at Jerusalem. The northern kingdom of Israel joined with some small Syrian states to temporarily stop the onslaught of the Assyrians (uh-SEER-ee-unz), who had consolidated their kingdom to the northeast (see "The Assyrian Empire" later in this chapter). But the power of the kingdom of Israel declined, and by the end of the ninth century, Israel was forced to pay tribute to Assyria. In the next century, Israel itself was destroyed. The Assyrians overran the kingdom, destroyed the capital of Samaria in 722 or 721 B.C.E., and deported many Israelites to other parts of the Assyrian Empire. These dispersed Israelites (the "ten lost tribes") merged with neighboring peoples and gradually lost their identity.

The southern kingdom of Judah was also forced to pay tribute to Assyria but managed to survive as an independent state as Assyrian power declined. A new enemy, however, appeared on the horizon. The Chaldeans (kal-DEE-unz) first demolished Assyria and then, under King Nebuchadnezzar (neb-uh-kud-NEZZ-ur) II, conquered Judah and completely destroyed Jerusalem in 586 B.C.E. Many upper-class people from Judah were deported to Babylonia. The memory of their exile is still evoked in the stirring words of Psalm 137:

> By the rivers of Babylon, we sat and wept when we remembered Zion....
> How can we sing the songs of the Lord while in a foreign land?
> If I forget you, O Jerusalem, may my right hand forget its skill
> May my tongue cling to the roof of my mouth if I do not remember you,
>   if I do not consider Jerusalem my highest joy.[2]

But the Babylonian captivity of the people of Judah did not last. A new set of conquerors, the Persians, destroyed the Chaldean kingdom but allowed the people of Judah to return to Jerusalem and rebuild their city and temple. The revived kingdom of Judah remained under Persian control until the conquests of Alexander the Great in the fourth century B.C.E. The people of Judah survived, eventually becoming known as the Jews and giving their name to Judaism, the religion of Yahweh (YAH-way), the Israelite God.

The Spiritual Dimensions of Israel

The spiritual perspective of the Israelites evolved over time. Early Israelites probably worshiped many gods, including nature spirits dwelling in trees and rocks. For some Israelites, Yahweh was the chief god of Israel, but many, including kings of Israel and Judah, worshiped other gods as well. It was among the Babylonian exiles in the sixth century B.C.E. that Yahweh—the God of Israel—came to be seen as the *only* God. After these exiles returned to Judah, their point of view eventually became dominant, and pure **monotheism**, or the belief that there is only one God for all peoples, came to be the major tenet of Judaism.

"I am the Lord Your God": Ruler of the World   According to the Jewish conception, there is but one God, whom the Jews called Yahweh. God is the creator of the world and everything in it. To the Jews, the gods of all other peoples were mere idols. The Jewish God ruled the world; he was subject to nothing. All peoples were his servants, whether they knew it or not. This God was also transcendent. He had created nature but was not in nature. The stars, moon, rivers, wind, and other natural phenomena were not divinities or suffused with divinity, as other peoples of the ancient Near East believed, but were God's handiwork. All of God's creations could be admired for their awesome beauty but not worshiped as gods.

This omnipotent creator of the universe was not removed from the life he had created, however, but was a just and good God who expected goodness from his people. If they did not obey his will, they would be punished. But he was also a God of mercy and love: "The Lord is gracious and compassionate, slow to anger and rich in love. The Lord is good to all; he has compassion on all he has made." [3] Despite the powerful dimensions of God as creator and sustainer of the universe, the Jewish message also emphasized that each person could have a personal relationship with this omnipotent being. As the psalmist sang: "My help comes from the Lord, the Maker of heaven and earth. He will not let your foot slip—he who watches over you will not slumber." [4]

The chief source of information about Israel's spiritual conceptions is the Hebrew Bible. Its purpose was to teach the essential beliefs about the God of Israel after the Babylonian captivity of the Jews and their dispersal. During and after the Babylonian exile, the Jews recorded many of their traditions in order to create and preserve their identity. These writings became the core of the Hebrew Bible. The first five books, known as the **Pentateuch** (PEN-tuh-took), which cover the time from the beginning of the world until the Israelites' arrival in Canaan, constitute the **Torah** (TOR-uh), or law code, governing the lives of worshipers and their relations to one another and to the non-Jewish population. The Hebrew Bible focuses on one basic theme: the necessity for the Jews to obey their God.

"You Only Have I Chosen": Covenant and Law   Three aspects of the Jewish religious tradition had special significance: the covenant, the law, and the prophets. The Israelites believed that during the Exodus from Egypt, when Moses supposedly led his people out of bondage into a land of plenty promised to them by Yahweh, a special event occurred that determined the Jewish experience for all time. According to tradition, God entered into a covenant or contract with the tribes of Israel, who believed that Yahweh had spoken to them through Moses. The Israelites promised to obey Yahweh and follow his law. In return, Yahweh promised to take special care of his people, "a peculiar treasure unto me above all people."

This covenant between Yahweh and his chosen people could be fulfilled, however, only by obedience to the law of God. Law became a crucial element of the Jewish world and had a number of different dimensions. In some instances, it set forth specific requirements, such as payments for offenses. Most important, since

The Covenant and the Law: The Book of Exodus

According to the biblical account, it was during the Exodus from Egypt that the Israelites supposedly made their covenant with Yahweh. They agreed to obey their God and follow his law. In return, Yahweh promised to take special care of his chosen people. These selections from the book of Exodus describe the making of the covenant and God's commandments to the Israelites.

Exodus 19:1–8

In the third month after the Israelites left Egypt—on the very day—they came to the Desert of Sinai. After they set out from Rephidim, they entered the Desert of Sinai, and Israel camped there in the desert in front of the mountain. Then Moses went up to God, and the Lord called to him from the mountain, and said, "This is what you are to say to the house of Jacob and what you are to tell the people of Israel: 'You yourselves have seen what I did to Egypt, and how I carried you on eagles' wings and brought you to myself. Now if you obey me fully and keep my covenant, then out of all nations you will be my treasured possession. Although the whole earth is mine, you will be for me a kingdom of priests and a holy nation.' These are the words you are to speak to the Israelites." So Moses went back and summoned the elders of the people and set before them all the words the Lord had commanded him to speak. The people all responded together, "We will do everything the Lord has said." So Moses brought their answer back to the Lord.

Exodus 20:1–17

And God spoke all these words, "I am the Lord your God, who brought you out of Egypt, out of the land of slavery. You shall

the major characteristic of God was his goodness, ethical concerns stood at the center of the law. Sometimes these took the form of specific standards of moral behavior: "You shall not murder. You shall not commit adultery. You shall not steal."[5] But these concerns were also expressed in decrees that regulated the economic, social, religious, and political life of the community, for God's laws of morality applied to all areas of life. These laws made no class distinctions and emphasized the protection of the poor, widows, orphans, and slaves.

The Prophets   The Israelites believed that certain religious leaders or holy men, called prophets, were sent by God to serve as his voice to his people. In the ninth century B.C.E., the prophets were particularly vociferous about the tendency of the Israelites to accept other gods, chiefly the fertility and earth gods of other peoples in Canaan. They warned of the terrible retribution that Yahweh would exact from the Israelites if they did not keep the covenant to remain faithful to him alone and just in their dealings with one another.

The golden age of prophecy began in the mid-eighth century and continued during the time when the people of Israel and Judah were threatened by Assyrian and Chaldean conquerors. These "men of God" went through the land warning the Israelites that they had failed to keep God's commandments and would be have no other gods before me. You shall not make for yourself an idol in the form of anything in heaven above or on the earth beneath or in the waters below. You shall not bow down to them or worship them; for I, the Lord your God, am a jealous God, punishing the children for the sin of the fathers to the third and fourth generation of those who hate me, but showing love to a thousand generations of those who love me and keep my commandments. You shall not misuse the name of the Lord your God, for the Lord will not hold anyone guiltless who misuses his name. Remember the Sabbath day by keeping it holy. Six days you shall labor and do all your work, but the seventh day is a Sabbath to the Lord your God. On it you shall not do any work, neither you, nor your son or daughter, nor your manservant or maidservant, nor your animals, nor the alien within your gates. For in six days the Lord made the heavens and the earth, the sea, and all that is in them, but he rested on the seventh day. Therefore the Lord blessed the Sabbath day and made it holy. Honor your father and your mother, so that you may live long in the land the Lord your God is giving you. You shall not murder. You shall not commit adultery. You shall not steal. You shall not give false testimony against your neighbor. You shall not covet your neighbor's house. You shall not covet your neighbor's wife, or his manservant or maidservant, his ox or donkey, or anything that belongs to your neighbor."

Q *What was the nature of the covenant between Yahweh and the Israelites? What was its moral significance for the Israelites? How does it differ from Hammurabi's code, and how might you explain those differences?*

Source: Scripture taken from the HOLY BIBLE, NEW INTERNATIONAL VERSION®. Copyright © 1973, 1978, 1984 Biblica. Used by permission of Zondervan. All rights reserved. The "NIV" and "New International Version" trademarks are registered in the United States Patent and Trademark Office by Biblica. Use of either trademark requires the permission of Biblica.

punished for breaking the covenant: "I will punish you for all your iniquities." Amos prophesied the fall of the northern kingdom of Israel to Assyria; twenty years later, Isaiah said the kingdom of Judah too would fall.

Out of the words of the prophets came new concepts that enriched the Jewish tradition and ultimately Western civilization, including a notion of universalism and a yearning for social justice. Although the Jews' religious practices gave them a sense of separateness from other peoples, the prophets transcended this by embracing a concern for all humanity. All nations would someday come to the God of Israel: "All the earth shall worship you." A universal community of all people under God would someday be established by Israel's effort. This vision encompassed the elimination of war and the establishment of peace for all the nations of the world. In the words of the prophet Isaiah: "He will judge between the nations and will settle disputes for many people. They will beat their swords into plowshares and their spears into pruning hooks. Nation will not take up sword against nation, nor will they train for war anymore."[6]

The prophets also cried out against social injustice. They condemned the rich for causing the poor to suffer, denounced luxuries as worthless, and threatened Israel with prophecies of dire punishments for these sins. God's command was to live justly, share with one's neighbors, care for the poor and the unfortunate, and act with compassion. When God's command was not followed, the social fabric of the community was threatened. These proclamations by Israel's prophets became a source for Western ideals of social justice, even if they have never been perfectly realized.

Although the prophets ultimately developed a sense of universalism, the demands of the Jewish religion—the need to obey their God—encouraged a separation between the Jews and their non-Jewish neighbors. Unlike most other peoples of the Near East, Jews could not simply be amalgamated into a community by accepting the gods of their conquerors and their neighbors. To remain faithful to the demands of their God, they might even have to refuse loyalty to political leaders.

The Social Structure of the Hebrews

Originally, the Israelites were organized along tribal lines, but by the time of the monarchy a new social structure had evolved as the Israelites settled in towns and villages, leaving them with conspicuous "divisions of the population."

Social Patterns   The "men of rank and influence" formed a special group of considerable importance in Hebrew society. This group included officials of the king, military officers, civil officials, and governors. Although simply servants to the kings, they held a privileged position in the society at large. The common people, sometimes called "people of the land," remained a body of free people having basic civil rights. Their livelihood came mostly from the land and from various crafts. These peasants and artisans sold their own produce and products directly to buyers in markets in their local town or village squares, thus avoiding the need for intermediaries or traders. There was no real merchant class in ancient Israel. Commerce was carried on by foreigners, such as the Phoenicians. Not until the **Diaspora** (dy-ASS-pur-uh), when Jews became scattered throughout the ancient world after their exile to Babylon, did they become merchants.

Family   The family was the central social institution in Hebrew life and consisted of individuals connected by common blood and a common living place. A family living in one house could comprise husband and wife, married sons and their wives, and their children. The Hebrew family was **patriarchal** (pay-tree-AR-kul). The husband-father was master of his wife and possessed absolute authority over his children, including the power of life and death.

Marriage and Women   Marriage was an important aspect of Hebrew family life. In ancient Israel, polygamy was an accepted form of marriage, especially for kings and wealthier citizens. Hebrew law limited kings to eighteen wives and citizens to four. In practice, only kings could afford a large harem. When others had more than one wife, it was usually because they desired more children; the first wife, for example, might be unable to have children or have produced only daughters.

Many Hebrews, however, believed that monogamy was the preferred form of marriage. Wives were honored for their faithfulness and dedication to their husbands. The book of Proverbs in the Hebrew Bible provides a picture of what Hebrews considered a perfect wife:

> *A wife of noble character who can find? She is worth far more than*
> *   rubies.*
> *Her husband has full confidence in her and lacks nothing of value.*
> *She brings him good, not harm, all the days of her life.*
> *She selects wool and flax and works with eager hands.*
> *She is like the merchant ships, bringing her food from afar.*
> *She gets up while it is still dark; she provides food for her family and*
> *   portions for her servant girls.*
> *She considers a field and buys it; out of her earnings she plants a*
> *   vineyard.*
> *She sets about her work vigorously; her arms are strong for her tasks....*
> *She speaks with wisdom, and faithful instruction is on her tongue.*
> *She watches over the affairs of her household, and does not eat the bread of*
> *   idleness.*
> *Her children arise and call her blessed; her husband also, and he praises her.*[7]

Women were greatly valued, but their work was obviously never done.

Although the Hebrew Bible, a male-edited work, reveals a society dominated by men, it also includes stories of women who played heroic roles in the early history of Israel. Deborah, for example, played a prominent role in the defeat of the Canaanites at Mount Tabor. After the same battle, Jael killed Sisera, the leader of the Canaanites. According to the Song of Deborah, "Most blessed of women be Jael, ... most blessed of tent-dwelling women.... Her hand reached for the tent peg, her right hand for the workman's hammer. She struck Sisera, she crushed his head, she shattered and pierced his temple. At her feet he sank, he fell; there he lay."[8]

But these accounts are not the norm. In the Hebrew Bible, women are mostly dependent on men. It should not surprise us, then, to learn that a married woman was subject to her husband's authority. A married woman left her parents' home, lived with her husband's family, and became a member of their clan. Her children also belonged to the husband's clan. Since boys and girls were married at a relatively young age, parents took the responsibility for matchmaking. Wives were expected to remain faithful to their husbands, an ideal that would later have an impact on Christian attitudes toward women.

The primary goal of marriage was to produce children. They were the "crown of man," and sons, in particular, were desired. Daughters would eventually leave the family house, but sons carried on the family line. Mothers were in charge of the early education of children, especially in regard to basic moral principles. As boys matured, their fathers took over responsibility for their education, which remained largely informal. This included religious instruction as well as general education for life. The rod was not spared as a matter of principle. Since trades were usually hereditary, fathers also provided their sons' occupational education. As one rabbi (a Jewish teacher) warned, "He who does not teach his son a useful trade is bringing him up to be a thief."[9] Additional education for boys came from priests, whose sacred mission was to instruct people in the Torah. The only education girls received was from their mothers, who taught them the basic fundamentals of how to be good wives, mothers, and housekeepers.

THE NEIGHBORS OF THE ISRAELITES

The Israelites were not the only people living in Canaan. The Philistines, who invaded from the sea, established five towns on the coastal plain of the region. They settled down as farmers and eventually came into conflict with the Israelites. The Phoenicians (fuh-NEE-shunz) had resided in Canaan for some time but now found themselves with a new independence. A Semitic-speaking people, the Phoenicians resided along the Mediterranean coast on a narrow band of land 120 miles long. They had rebuilt their major cities, Byblos (BIB-luhs), Tyre, and Sidon (SYD-un), after destruction by the Sea Peoples. Their newfound political independence helped the Phoenicians expand the trade that was already the foundation of their prosperity. In fact, Byblos had been the principal distribution center for Egyptian papyrus outside Egypt (the Greek word for book, *biblos*, is derived from the name Byblos).

All three chief cities of Phoenicia were seaports, but they also served as distribution centers for the lands to the east in Mesopotamia. The Phoenicians themselves produced a number of goods for foreign markets, including purple dye, glass, wine, and lumber from the famous cedars of Lebanon. In addition, the Phoenicians improved their ships and became great international sea traders. They charted new routes, not only in the Mediterranean but also in the Atlantic Ocean, where they sailed south along the west coast of Africa. The Phoenicians established a number of colonies in the western Mediterranean, including settlements in southern Spain, Sicily, and Sardinia. Most of the Phoenician colonies were trading stations, not permanent settlements. A major exception was Carthage, the Phoenicians' most famous colony, located on the North African coast.

Phoenician Plaque.
The Phoenicians, a Semitic-speaking people dwelling in ancient Canaan, became the predominant sea traders of the ancient Near East. Ivory was one of the favorite materials of Phoenician artists of the ninth and eighth centuries B.C.E. This ivory plaque is one of a pair in the classic Phoenician style. It shows a lioness killing a Nubian; in the background are lilies and papyrus flowers.

National Museum, Baghdad//Werner Forman/Art Resource, NY

Culturally, the Phoenicians are best known as transmitters. Instead of using pictographs or signs to represent whole words and syllables as the Mesopotamians and Egyptians did, the Phoenicians simplified their writing by using twenty-two different signs to represent the sounds of their speech. These twenty-two characters or letters could be used to spell out all the words in the Phoenician language. Although the Phoenicians were not the only people to invent an alphabet, theirs would have special significance because it was eventually passed on to the Greeks. From the Greek alphabet was derived the Roman alphabet that we still use today. The Phoenicians achieved much while independent, but they ultimately fell subject to the Assyrians, Chaldeans, and Persians.

THE ASSYRIAN EMPIRE

Independent states in Canaan flourished in the power void that followed the destruction of the Hittite kingdom and the weakening of the Egyptian empire. But this state of affairs did not last; new empires soon came to dominate vast stretches of the ancient Near East. The first of these empires emerged in Assyria, an area whose location on the upper Tigris River brought it into both cultural and political contact with southern Mesopotamia.

Although part of Mesopotamia, Assyria, with its hills and adequate, if not ample, rainfall, had a different terrain and climate. The Assyrians were a Semitic-speaking people; for much of their early history, they were vassals of foreign rulers, including Sargon of Akkad, the Third Dynasty of Ur, and the Babylonian King Hammurabi. From about 1650 to 1360 B.C.E., the Hurrian kingdom of Mitanni in northern Mesopotamia dominated Assyria. The Assyrians finally became independent when the Hittites destroyed Mitanni; we read in Hittite documents from about 1360 B.C.E. of the emergence of the "king of the land of Assyria." For the next 250 years, the Assyrians experienced alternating expansion and decline until the reassertion of Assyrian power under Tiglath-Pileser (TIG-lath-py-LEE-zur) I (1114–1076 B.C.E.), a brutal conqueror whose policy of deliberate terror set a pattern for later Assyrian rulers.

The Assyrian Empire created by Tiglath-Pileser was unable to maintain its strength after his death. A new phase of expansion did not begin until the ninth century with the conquests of Shalmaneser (shal-muh-NEE-zur) III (858–824 B.C.E.), who marched westward into Canaan and southward into Babylonia. Yet Assyrian power did not go unchallenged. The almost continuous warfare on these new frontiers did not end until the reigns of Tiglath-Pileser III (744–727 B.C.E.) and Sargon II (721–705 B.C.E.), who waged military campaigns almost every year, reestablishing control over Mesopotamia and completely subduing Canaan. The conquered territories were then incorporated into the empire as provinces. These two kings were also responsible for centralizing the system of government in order to increase the power of the king. By 700 B.C.E., the Assyrian Empire had reached the height of its power and included Mesopotamia, sections of Asia Minor, Syria, Canaan, and Egypt up to Thebes (see Map 2.2).

Ashurbanipal (ah-shur-BAH-nuh-pahl) (669–627 B.C.E.) was one of the strongest Assyrian rulers, but it was already becoming apparent during his reign that the Assyrian Empire was greatly overextended. Internal strife intensified as

MAP 2.2 The Assyrian and Neo-Babylonian Empires

The Assyrian Empire expanded in large part due to its brutal military methods. It maintained its rule through use of a common language and religion, along with extremely violent suppression of internal revolts. It was overthrown by Chaldeans in Babylonia, leading to the Neo-Babylonian Empire epitomized by Nebuchadnezzar.

powerful Assyrian nobles gained control of vast territories and waged their own private military campaigns. Moreover, subject peoples greatly resented Assyrian rule. The hatred that the Babylonians felt after the brutal Assyrian sack of the city of Babylon in 689 B.C.E., for example, led them to rebel during the reign of Ashurbanipal. Soon after Ashurbanipal's death, the Assyrian Empire began to disintegrate. The capital city of Nineveh fell to a coalition of Chaldeans and Medes (see "The Neo-Babylonian Empire" later in this chapter) in 612 B.C.E., and in 605 B.C.E., the Neo-Babylonian Empire took over the rest of the empire.

Organization of the Empire   At its height, the Assyrian Empire was ruled by kings whose power was considered absolute. Under their leadership, the empire became well organized. By eliminating governorships held by nobles on a hereditary basis and instituting a new hierarchy of local officials directly responsible to the king, the Assyrian kings gained greater control over the resources of the empire. The relationship between the king and his officials was based on personal loyalty. Loyalty to the king was also expected of all people in Assyria. According to King Ashurbanipal, when his father King Esarhaddon appointed him as his successor, he "convened the people of Assyria, great and small, from coast to coast, made them swear a loyalty oath by the gods and established a binding agreement to protect my future kingship over Assyria."[10]

The Assyrians also developed an efficient system of communication to administer their empire more effectively. They established a network of posting stages that used relays of horses (mules or donkeys in mountainous terrain) to carry messages throughout the empire. The system was so effective that a provincial governor anywhere in the empire (except Egypt) could send a question to the king in his palace and receive an answer within a week.

The Assyrian Military Machine

The ability of the Assyrians to conquer and maintain an empire derived from a combination of factors. Through years of practice, the Assyrians developed effective military leaders and fighters. They were able to enlist and deploy troops numbering in the hundreds of thousands, although most campaigns were not on such a large scale. In 845 B.C.E., Shalmaneser III led an army of 120,000 men across the Euphrates on a campaign. Size alone was not decisive, however. The Assyrian army was extremely well organized and disciplined. It included a standing army of infantry as its core, accompanied by cavalry and horse-drawn war chariots that were used as mobile platforms for shooting arrows. Moreover, the Assyrians had the advantage of having the first large armies equipped with iron weapons. The Hittites (see Chapter 1) had been the first to develop iron metallurgy, but iron came to be used extensively only after new methods for hardening it came into common use after 1000 B.C.E.

Another factor in the Assyrian army's success was its ability to use different kinds of military tactics. The army was capable of waging guerrilla warfare in the mountains and set battles on open ground as well as laying siege to cities. The Assyrians were especially renowned for their siege warfare. They would hammer a city's walls with heavy, wheeled siege towers and armored battering rams while sappers dug tunnels to undermine the walls' foundations and cause them to collapse. The besieging Assyrian armies learned to cut off supplies so effectively that if a city did not fall to them, the inhabitants could be starved into submission.

A final factor in the effectiveness of the Assyrian military machine was its ability to create a climate of terror as an instrument of warfare, a policy that one historian has called "calculated frightfulness." The aim of the Assyrians was to encourage their enemies to surrender quickly rather than face a series of atrocities. The Assyrians became famous for their terror tactics, although some historians believe they were no worse than other Near Eastern conquerors. As a matter of regular policy, the Assyrians laid waste to the land in which they were fighting, smashing dams, looting and destroying towns, setting crops on fire, and cutting down trees, particularly fruit trees. The Assyrians were especially known for their brutality toward their captives. King Ashurnasirpal (ah-shur-NAH-zur-pahl) II recorded this account of his treatment of prisoners:

> 3,000 of their combat troops I felled with weapons.... Many of the captives taken from them I burned in a fire. Many I took alive; from some of these I cut off their hands to

the wrist, from others I cut off their noses, ears, and fingers; I put out the eyes of many of the soldiers.... I burned their young men and women to death.

After conquering another city, the same king wrote: "I fixed up a pile of corpses in front of the city's gate. I flayed the nobles, as many as had rebelled, and spread their skins out on the piles.... I flayed many within my land and spread their skins out on the walls."[11] Note that this policy of extreme cruelty to prisoners was not used against all enemies but was reserved primarily for those who were already part of the empire and then rebelled against Assyrian rule.

Assyrian Society and Culture   Unlike the Hebrews, the Assyrians were not fearful of mixing with other peoples. In fact, the Assyrian policy of deporting many prisoners of newly conquered territories to Assyria created a polyglot society in which ethnic differences were not very important. It has been estimated that over a period of three centuries, between 4 and 5 million people were deported to Assyria, resulting in a population that was racially and linguistically mixed. What gave identity to the Assyrians themselves was their language, although even that was akin to that of their southern neighbors in Babylonia. Religion was also a cohesive force. Assyria was literally "the land of Ashur," a reference to its chief god. The king, as the human representative of the god Ashur, brought order to his people and served as a final unifying focus.

Agriculture formed the principal basis of Assyrian life. Assyria was a land of farming villages with relatively few significant cities, especially in comparison with southern Mesopotamia. Unlike the river valleys, where farming required the minute organization of large numbers of people to control irrigation, Assyrian farms received sufficient moisture from regular rainfall.

Trade was second to agriculture in economic importance. For internal trade, metals, such as gold, silver, copper, and bronze, were used as a medium of exchange. Various agricultural products also served as a form of payment or exchange. Because of their geographic location, the Assyrians served as intermediaries and participated in an international trade, importing timber, wine, and precious metals and stones while exporting textiles produced in palaces, temples, and private villas.

The culture of the Assyrian Empire was a hybrid. The Assyrians assimilated much of Mesopotamian civilization and saw themselves as guardians of Sumerian and Babylonian culture. Ashurbanipal, for example, amassed a large library at Nineveh that included the available works of Mesopotamian history. Assyrian religion also reflected this assimilation of other cultures. Although the Assyrians considered their own national god, Ashur, their chief deity, they recognized virtually all of the Mesopotamian gods and goddesses as well.

Among the best-known objects of Assyrian art are the relief sculptures found in the royal palaces in three of the Assyrian capital cities, Nimrud, Nineveh, and Khorsabad. These reliefs, which were begun in the ninth century and reached their high point in the reign of Ashurbanipal in the seventh century, depicted two different kinds of subject matter: ritual or ceremonial scenes revolving around the person of the king and scenes of hunting and war. The latter show realistic action scenes of the king and his warriors engaged in battle or hunting animals, especially lions.

These reliefs depict a strongly masculine world where discipline, brute force, and toughness are the enduring values, indeed, the very values of the Assyrian military monarchy.

THE NEO-BABYLONIAN EMPIRE

The Chaldeans, a Semitic-speaking people, had gained ascendancy in Babylonia by the seventh century and came to form the chief resistance to Assyrian control of Mesopotamia. The Chaldean king Nabopolassar (nab-uh-puh-LASS-ur) (626–605 B.C.E.), who joined forces with the Medes to capture the Assyrian capital Nineveh in 612 B.C.E., was responsible for establishing a new Babylonian monarchy. But it was his son Nebuchadnezzar II (605–562 B.C.E.) who achieved the final defeat of the Assyrian Empire. Under his rule, the Chaldeans defeated Egypt to gain control of Syria and Canaan, destroyed Jerusalem, carried the people of Judah into exile in Babylon, and in the process regained for Babylonia a position as the leading power in the ancient Near East (see Map 2.2).

During Nebuchadnezzar's reign, Babylonia was renowned for a prosperity based on lush agricultural lands, lucrative trade routes, and industries, especially textiles and metals. Nebuchadnezzar rebuilt Babylon as the center of his empire, giving it a reputation as one of the great cities of the ancient world. Babylon was surrounded by towering walls, 8 miles in length, encircled by a moat filled by the Euphrates River. The Ishtar Gate opened onto the Triumphal Way, which led to the sacred precincts of Marduk, the chief Babylonian god. Babylon was adorned with temples and palaces; most famous of all were the Hanging Gardens, renowned as one of the Seven Wonders of the ancient world. These were supposedly built to satisfy Nebuchadnezzar's wife, a princess from the land of Media, who missed the mountains of her homeland. A series of terraces led to a plateau, an artificial mountain, at the top of which grew the lush gardens irrigated by water piped to the top. According to the account of a first-century C.E. author, from a distance the gardens made a remarkable impression:

> On the top of the citadel are the hanging gardens, a wonder celebrated in the tales of the Greeks.... Columns of stone were set up to sustain the whole work, and on these was laid a floor of squared blocks, strong enough to hold the earth which is thrown upon it to a great depth, as well as the water with which they irrigate the soil; and the structure supports trees of such great size that the thickness of their trunks equals a measure of eight cubits [about 12 feet]. They tower to a height of fifty feet, and they yield as much fruit as if they were growing in their native soil.... To those who look upon the trees from a distance, real woods seem to be overhanging their native mountains.[12]

The splendor of the Neo-Babylonian Empire proved to be short-lived. Nabonidus (nab-uh-NY-duss) (555–539 B.C.E.) was the last king of the Chaldean dynasty. He had a great interest in history and encouraged scholars to collect Sumerian texts and study the Sumerian language. But his policies aroused considerable internal dissent. Among other things, Nabonidus neglected the cult of Marduk, instead worshiping the moon god, Sin. When Babylon fell to the Persian conqueror Cyrus in 539 B.C.E., the Babylonians welcomed him as a liberator.

Ishtar Gate of Babylon.
Nebuchadnezzar rebuilt Babylon as the center of his empire and adorned it with such architectural wonders as the Ishtar Gate, which was built of blue glazed bricks and opened onto the Triumphal Way. The bricks were made separately and then assembled on the gate walls. Figures of the dragon of Marduk (patron god of the city of Babylon, whose sacred animal was the dragon) and the bull of Adad (god of storms, whose sacred animal was the bull) alternate on the surfaces of the gate. Ishtar was the Babylonian goddess of war and sexual love. This picture shows the Ishtar Gate as it was rebuilt in the Pergamum Museum in Berlin.

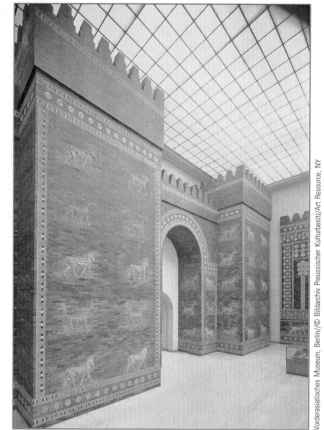

Vorderasiatisches Museum, Berlin//© Bildarchiv Preussischer Kulturbesitz/Art Resource, NY

THE PERSIAN EMPIRE

The Persians were an Indo-European-speaking people related to the Medes. Both peoples probably formed part of the great waves of Indo-European migrations into the Mediterranean, the Near East, and India. The Persians lived to the southeast of the Medes, who occupied the western Iranian plateau south of the Caspian Sea. Primarily nomadic, both Medes and Persians were organized in clans. Both peoples were led by petty kings assisted by a group of warriors who formed a class of nobles. Their populations also included both free and unfree people who worked the land, craftspeople, and slaves.

By 735 B.C.E., the Medes had begun to form a confederation of the various tribes, and around the beginning of the seventh century, they became unified under a monarchy. The Persians did likewise under the Achaemenid (ah-KEE-muh-nud) dynasty established in Persis in southern Iran. About fifty years later, the Persians were made subject to the Medes. The Medes now constituted a powerful state and joined the Babylonians in attacking the Assyrians. After the capture of Nineveh in 612 B.C.E., King Cyaxares (si-AK-suh-reez) established a Median empire, the first Iranian empire known to the ancient Near East.

Cyrus the Great   In 559 B.C.E., Cyrus became the leader of the Persians, united them under his rule, and went on the offensive against the Medes. By 550 B.C.E., he had established Persian control over Media, making it the first Persian **satrapy** (SAY-truh-pee), or province. Three years later, Cyrus defeated the prosperous Lydian kingdom in western Asia Minor, and Lydia became another Persian satrapy (see Map 2.3). Cyrus's forces then went on to conquer the Greek city-states that had been established on the Ionian coast of western Asia Minor. Cyrus then turned eastward, subduing the eastern part of the Iranian plateau, Sogdia, and even western India. His eastern frontiers secured, Cyrus entered Mesopotamia in 539 and captured Babylon. His treatment of Babylonia showed remarkable restraint and wisdom. Babylonia was made into a Persian province under a Persian **satrap** (SAY-trap), or governor, but many government officials were kept in their positions. Cyrus took the title "King of All, Great King, Mighty King, King of Babylon, King of the Land of Sumer and Akkad, King of the Four Rims (of the Earth), the Son of Cambyses the Great King, King of An-shan"[13] and insisted that he stood in the ancient, unbroken line of Babylonian kings. By appealing to the vanity of the Babylonians, he won their loyalty. Cyrus also issued an edict permitting the Jews, who had been brought to Babylon in the sixth century B.C.E., to return to Jerusalem with their sacred temple objects and to rebuild the Temple there as well.

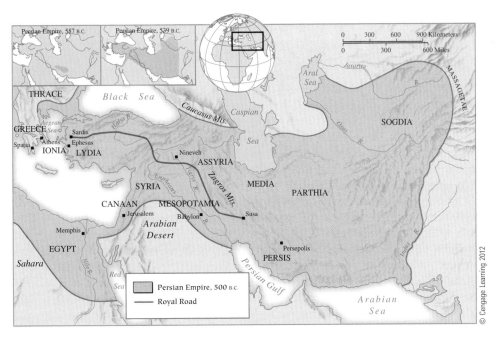

© Cengage Learning 2012

MAP 2.3 The Persian Empire at the Time of Darius

Cyrus the Great united the Persians and led them in successful conquest of much of the Near East. By the time of Darius, the Persian Empire was the largest the world had yet seen. The Persians allowed a high degree of religious toleration and gave some government positions to natives of conquered territories.

From 538 to 530 B.C.E., Cyrus consolidated his empire. Among other things, he constructed forts, especially in the northeast, to protect against nomadic incursions. It was there that he undertook his last campaign. In 530 B.C.E., he marched from Sogdia into the territory of the Massagetae, where he was killed in battle.

To his contemporaries, Cyrus the Great was deserving of his epithet. The Greek historian Herodotus recounted that the Persians viewed him as a "father," a ruler who was "gentle, and procured them all manner of goods."[14] Cyrus must have been an unusual ruler for his time, a man who demonstrated considerable wisdom and compassion in the conquest and organization of his empire. Cyrus obtained the favor of the priesthoods in his conquered lands by restoring temples and permitting religious toleration. He won approval by using not only Persians but also native peoples as government officials in their own states. He allowed Medes to be military commanders. Unlike the Assyrian rulers of an earlier empire, he had a reputation for mercy. Medes, Babylonians, and Jews all accepted him as their legitimate ruler. Some peoples portrayed him as a great leader and peacemaker. Indeed, a Hebrew prophet regarded him as the anointed one of God: "I am the Lord who says of Cyrus, 'He is my shepherd and will accomplish all that I please'; he will say of Jerusalem, 'Let it be rebuilt'; and of the temple, 'Let its foundations be laid.' This is what the Lord says to his anointed, to Cyrus, whose right hand I take hold of to subdue nations before him."[15] Cyrus had a genuine respect for ancient civilizations—in building his palaces, he made use of Assyrian, Babylonian, Egyptian, and Lydian practices. Indeed, Cyrus believed that he was creating a "world empire" that included peoples who had ancient and venerable traditions and institutions.

Expanding the Empire   Upon Cyrus's death in 530 B.C.E., his son Cambyses (kam-BY-seez) II assumed power as the Great King. Four years later, Cambyses undertook the invasion of Egypt, the only kingdom in the Near East not yet brought under Persian control. Aided by the Phoenician fleet, he defeated and captured the pharaoh and the Egyptian forces. Egypt was made into a satrapy with Memphis as its capital. In the summer of 525 B.C.E., Cambyses took the title of pharaoh.

After the death of Cambyses in 522, Darius (duh-RY-uss) emerged as Great King after a year of intense civil war. Once in charge, Darius (521–486 B.C.E.) turned to the task of strengthening the empire. He codified Egyptian law and built a canal to link the Red Sea and the Mediterranean. A campaign into western India led to the creation of a new Persian province that extended to the Indus River. Darius also moved into Europe proper, conquering Thrace and making the Macedonian king a vassal. In 499 B.C.E., the Ionian Greek cities in western Asia Minor rose in revolt and temporarily obtained their freedom. With aid from the Greek mainland, most notably from Athens, the Ionians then invaded Lydia and burned Sardis, center of the Lydian satrapy. This event led to Darius's involvement with the mainland Greeks. After reestablishing control of the Ionian Greek cities, Darius undertook an invasion of the Greek mainland, which culminated in the Athenian victory in the Battle of Marathon in 490 B.C.E. (see Chapter 3).

The Fall of Babylon

Under the Chaldeans, Babylon became the center of an empire and gained a reputation as one of the great cities of the ancient world. But the Neo-Babylonian Empire did not last, and Babylon fell to the Persian forces under King Cyrus in 539 B.C.E. In his history of the Persian wars, the ancient Greek historian Herodotus described how Cyrus supposedly captured Babylon.

Herodotus, *The Persian Wars*

Cyrus, with the first approach of the ensuing spring, marched forward against Babylon. The Babylonians, encamped without their walls, awaited his coming. A battle was fought at a short distance from the city, in which the Babylonians were defeated by the Persian king, whereupon they withdrew within their defenses. Here they shut themselves up, and made light of his siege, having laid in a store of provisions for many years in preparation against this attack; for when they saw Cyrus conquering nation after nation, they were convinced that he would never stop, and that their turn would come at last.

Cyrus was now reduced to great perplexity, as time went on and he made no progress against the place. In this distress, either someone made the suggestion to him, or he thought himself of a plan, which he proceeded to put in execution. He placed a portion of his army at the point where the river enters the city and another body at the back of the place where it issues forth, with orders to march into the town by the bed of the stream, as soon as the water became shallow enough: he then himself drew off with the unwarlike portion of his host, and made for the place where

Nitocris [supposedly a queen of Babylon] dug the basin for the river, where he did exactly what she had done formerly: he turned the Euphrates by a canal into the basin, which was then a marsh, on which the river sank to such an extent that the natural bed of the stream became fordable. Hereupon the Persians who had been left for the purpose at Babylon by the river-side, entered the stream, which had now sunk so as to reach about midway up a man's thigh, and thus got into the town. Had the Babylonians been apprised of what Cyrus was about, or had they noticed their danger, they would not have allowed the entrance of the Persians within the city, which was what ruined them utterly, but would have made fast all the streetgates which gave upon the river, and mounting upon the walls along both sides of the stream, would so have caught the enemy as it were in a trap. But, as it was, the Persians came upon them by surprise and so took the city. Owing to the vast size of the place, the inhabitants of the central parts (as the residents at Babylon declare) long after the outer portions of the town were taken, knew nothing of what had chanced, but as they were engaged in a festival, continued dancing and reveling until they learned of the capture but too certainly. Such, then, were the circumstances of the first taking of Babylon,

Q *Do you think this is a realistic account of the fall of Babylon? What image do you have of Cyrus from this account?*

Source: From THE PERSIAN WARS by Herodotus, translated by George Rawlinson, copyright 1942 by Random House, Inc. Used by permission of Modern Library, a division of Random House, Inc.

Governing the   By the reign of Darius, the Persians had created the largest
Empire   empire the world had yet seen. It not only included all the
old centers of power in the Near East, Egypt, Mesopotamia, and Assyria but also extended into Thrace and Asia Minor in the west and into India in the east.

For administrative purposes, the empire had been divided into approximately twenty satrapies. Each satrapy was ruled by a provincial governor or satrap, literally a "protector of the kingdom." Although Darius had not introduced the system of satrapies, he did see that it was organized more rationally. He created a sensible system for calculating the tribute that each satrapy owed to the central government and gave the satraps specific civil and military duties. They collected tributes, were responsible for justice and security, raised military levies, and normally commanded the military forces within their satrapies. In terms of real power, the satraps were miniature kings who established courts imitative of the Great King's.

From the time of Darius on, satraps were men of Persian descent. The major satrapies were given to princes of the king's family, and their positions became essentially hereditary. The minor satrapies were placed in the hands of Persian nobles. Their offices, too, tended to pass from father to son. The hereditary nature of the governors' offices made it necessary to provide some checks on their power. Consequently, some historians think that there were officials at the satrapal courts, such as secretaries and generals in charge of the garrison, who reported directly to the Great King, keeping him informed of what was going on within the various satrapal governments. It is also possible that an official known as the "king's eye" or "king's messenger" made annual inspections of each satrapy.

An efficient system of communication was crucial to sustaining the Persian Empire. Well-maintained roads facilitated the rapid transit of military and government personnel. One in particular, known as the Royal Road, stretched from Sardis, the center of Lydia in Asia Minor, to Susa, the chief capital of the Persian Empire (see Map 2.3). Like the Assyrians, the Persians established staging posts equipped with fresh horses for the king's messengers.

The Great King   In this vast administrative system, the Persian king occupied
an exalted position. Although not considered a god like the Egyptian pharaoh, he was nevertheless the elect one or regent of the Persian god Ahuramazda (see "Persian Religion" later in this chapter). All subjects were the king's servants, and he was the source of all justice, possessing the power of life and death over everyone. Persian kings resided largely in seclusion in a series of splendid palaces and were not easily accessible. Darius in particular was a palace builder on a grand scale. His description of the construction of a palace in the chief Persian capital of Susa demonstrated what a truly international empire Persia was:

> This is the ... palace which at Susa I built. From afar its ornamentation was brought.... The cedar timber was brought from a mountain named Lebanon; the Assyrians brought it to Babylon, and from Babylon the Carians and Ionians brought it to Susa. Teakwood was brought from Gandara and from Carmania. The gold which was used here was brought from Sardis and from Bactria. The stone—lapis lazuli and carnelian—was

Darius, the Great King. *Darius ruled the Persian Empire from 521 to 486 B.C.E. He is shown here on his throne in Persepolis, a new capital city that he built. In his right hand, Darius holds the royal staff. In his left hand, he grasps a lotus blossom with two buds, a symbol of royalty.*

brought from Sogdiana.... The silver and copper were brought from Egypt. The ornamentation with which the wall was adorned was brought from Ionia. The ivory was brought from Ethiopia, from India, and from Arachosia. The stone pillars were brought from ... Elam. The artisans who dressed the stone were Ionians and Sardians. The goldsmiths who wrought the gold were Medes and Egyptians.... Those who worked the baked brick [with figures] were Babylonians. The men who adorned the wall were Medes and Egyptians. At Susa here a splendid work was ordered; very splendid did it turn out.[16]

But Darius was unhappy with Susa. He did not really consider it his homeland, and it was oppressively hot in the summer months. He built another residence at Persepolis, a new capital located to the east of the old one and at a higher elevation.

The policies of Darius also tended to widen the gap between the king and his subjects. As the Great King himself said of all his subjects, "What was said to them by me, night and day it was done."[17] Over a period of time, the Great Kings in their greed came to hoard immense quantities of gold and silver in the various treasuries located in the capital cities. Both their hoarding of wealth and their later overtaxation of their subjects are seen as crucial factors in the ultimate weakening of the Persian Empire.

In its heyday, however, the empire stood supreme, and much of its power depended on the military. By the time of Darius, the Persian monarchs had created a standing army of professional soldiers. This army was truly international, composed of contingents from the various peoples who made up the empire. At its core was a cavalry force of 10,000 and an elite infantry force of 10,000 Medes and Persians known as the Immortals because they were never allowed to fall below 10,000 in number. When one was killed, he was immediately replaced. The Persians made effective use of their cavalry, especially for operating behind enemy lines and breaking up lines of communication. The Persian navy consisted of ships from subject states, including the Phoenicians, Egyptians, Anatolians, and Ionian Greeks.

Persian Religion   Of all the Persians' cultural contributions, the most original was their religion, **Zoroastrianism**. Zoroaster (ZOR-oh-asstur), or Zarathustra, was a semilegendary figure who, according to Persian tradition, was born in 660 b.c.e. After a period of wandering and solitude, he experienced revelations that caused him to be revered as a prophet of the "true religion." It is difficult to know what Zoroaster's original teachings were, since the sacred book of Zoroastrianism, the Zend Avesta, was not written down until the third century c.e. Scholars believe, however, that the earliest section of the Zend Avesta, known as the Yasna, consisting of seventeen hymns or *gathas*, contains the actual writings of Zoroaster. This enables us to piece together his message.

Like the Hebrews, Zoroaster taught a spiritual message of monotheism. To Zoroaster, the religion he preached was the only perfect one, and Ahuramazda (uh-HOOR-uh-MAHZ-duh) was the only God. Ahuramazda (the "Wise Lord") was the supreme deity who brought all things into being:

> *This I ask of You, O Ahuramazda; answer me well:*
> *Who at the Creation was the first father of Justice?—*
> *Who assigned their path to the sun and the stars?—*
> *Who decreed the waxing and waning of the moon, if it was not You?— ...*
> *Who has fixed the earth below, and the heaven above with its clouds that it*
>   *might not be moved?—*
> *Who has appointed the waters and the green things upon the earth?—*
> *Who has harnessed to the wind and the clouds their steeds?— ...*
> *Thus do I strive to recognize in You, O Wise One,*
> *Together with the Holy Spirit, the Creator of all things.*[18]

According to Zoroaster, Ahuramazda also possessed abstract qualities or states that all humans should aspire to, such as Good Thought, Right, and Piety. Although Ahuramazda was supreme, he was not unopposed. Right is opposed by the Lie, Truth by Falsehood, Life by Death. At the beginning of the world, the good spirit of Ahuramazda was opposed by the evil spirit (in later Zoroastrianism identified with Ahriman).

Humans also played a role in this cosmic struggle between good and evil. Ahuramazda, the creator, gave all humans free will and the power to choose between right and wrong. The good person chooses the right way of Ahuramazda. Zoroaster taught that there would be an end to the struggle between good and evil. Ahuramazda would eventually triumph, and at the last judgment at the end of the world, the final separation of good and evil would occur. Individuals, too, would be judged. Each soul faced a final evaluation of its actions. The soul of a person who had performed good deeds would achieve paradise; but if the deeds had been evil, the person would be thrown into an abyss of torment. Some historians believe that Zoroastrianism, with its emphasis on good and evil, heaven and hell, and a last judgment, had an impact on Christianity, a religion that eventually surpassed it in significance.

The spread of Zoroastrianism was due to its acceptance by the Great Kings of Persia. The inscriptions of Darius make clear that he believed Ahuramazda was the only God. Although Darius himself may have been a monotheist, dramatic changes in Zoroastrianism occurred over time. Before Zoroaster, Persian religion had focused on the worship of forces of nature, such as the sun, moon, fire, and wind, with the aid of priests known as Magi. As the kings and Magi propagated Zoroaster's teachings on Ahuramazda. Zoroastrianism lost its monotheistic emphasis, and the old nature worship resurfaced. Soon Persian religion had returned to polytheism, with Ahuramazda the chief of a number of gods of light. Mithra, the sun god, became a helper of Ahuramazda and later, in Roman times, the source of another religion. Persian kings were also very tolerant of other religions, and gods and goddesses of those religions tended to make their way into the Persian pantheon. Moreover, as frequently happens to the ideas of founders of religions, Zoroaster's teachings acquired concrete forms that he had never originally intended. The struggle between good and evil was taken beyond the abstractions of Zoroaster into a strong ethical dualism. The spirit of evil became an actual being who had to be warded off by the use of spells and incantations.

CHRONOLOGIES

THE ISRAELITES

c. 1020–1000 B.C.	Saul—first king
c. 1000–970 B.C.	King David
c. 970–930 B.C.	King Solomon
722 or 721 B.C.	Northern kingdom of Israel destroyed by Assyria
586 B.C.	Southern kingdom of Judah falls to Chaldeans; destruction of Jerusalem
538 B.C.	Return of exiles to Jerusalem

THE ASSYRIAN EMPIRE

1114–1076 B.C.	Tiglath-Pileser I
858–824 B.C.	Shalmaneser III
744–727 B.C.	Tiglath-Pileser III
721–705 B.C.	Sargon II
669–626 B.C.	Ashurbanipal
612 B.C.	Capture of Nineveh
605 B.C.	Assyrian Empire destroyed

THE CHALDEAN EMPIRE

600s B.C.	Ascendancy in Babylonia
625–605 B.C.	Nabopolassar establishes Neo-Babylonian monarchy
605–562 B.C.	Height of empire under King Nebuchadnezzar II
539 B.C.	Fall of Babylon

THE PERSIAN EMPIRE

600s B.C.	Unification of Persians
559–530 B.C.	Conquests of Cyrus the Great
530–522 B.C.	Cambyses II and conquest of Egypt
521–486 B.C.	Reign of Darius

3

THE CIVILIZATION OF THE GREEKS

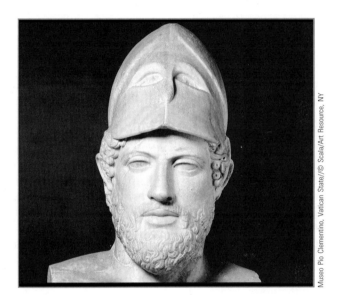

Museo Pio Clementino, Vatican State/© Scala/Art Resource, NY

A bust of Pericles

CHAPTER OUTLINE

• Early Greece • The Greeks in a Dark Age (c. 1100–c. 750 B.C.E.)
• The World of the Greek City-States (c. 750–c. 500 B.C.E.) • The High
Point of Greek Civilization: Classical Greece • Culture and Society of
Classical Greece

EARLY GREECE

Geography played an important role in the evolution of Greek history. Unlike the landmasses of Mesopotamia and Egypt, Greece occupied a small area, a mountainous peninsula that encompassed only 45,000 square miles of territory, about the size of the state of Louisiana. The mountains and the sea played especially significant roles in the development of Greek history. Much of Greece consists of small plains and river valleys surrounded by mountain ranges 8,000 to 10,000 feet high. The mountainous terrain had the effect of isolating Greeks from one another. Consequently, Greek communities tended to follow their own separate paths and develop their own way of life. Over a period of time, these communities became attached to their independence and were only too willing to fight one another to gain advantage. No doubt the small size of these independent Greek communities fostered participation in political affairs and unique cultural expressions, but the rivalry among these communities also led to the bitter warfare that ultimately devastated Greek society.

The sea also influenced the evolution of Greek society. Greece had a long seacoast, dotted by bays and inlets that provided numerous harbors. The Greeks also inhabited a number of islands to the west, the south, and particularly the east of the Greek mainland. It is no accident that the Greeks became seafarers who sailed out into the Aegean and Mediterranean Seas, first to make contact with the outside world and later to establish colonies that would spread Greek civilization throughout the Mediterranean region.

Topography helped determine the major territories into which Greece was ultimately divided. South of the Gulf of Corinth was the Peloponnesus (pel-uh-puh-NEE-suss), which was virtually an island (see Map 3.1). Consisting mostly of hills, mountains, and small valleys, the Peloponnesus was the location of Sparta, as well as the site of Olympia, where athletic games were held. Northeast of the Peloponnesus was the Attic peninsula (or Attica), the home of Athens, hemmed in by mountains to the north and west and surrounded by the sea to the south and east. Northwest of Attica was Boeotia (bee-OH-shuh) in central Greece, with its chief city of Thebes (THEEBZ). To the north of Boeotia was Thessaly, which contained the largest plains and became a great producer of grain and horses. To the north of Thessaly lay Macedonia, which was not of much importance in Greek history until 338 B.C.E., when a Macedonian king, Philip II, conquered the Greeks.

Minoan Crete   The earliest civilization in the Aegean region emerged on the large island of Crete, southeast of the Greek mainland. A Bronze Age civilization that used metals, especially bronze, in making weapons had been established there by 2800 B.C.E. This forgotten civilization was rediscovered at the turn of the twentieth century by the English archaeologist Arthur Evans, who named it "Minoan" (mih-NOH-uhn) after Minos (MY-nuss), a legendary king of Crete. In language and religion, the Minoans were not Greek, although they did have some influence on the peoples of the Greek mainland.

Evans's excavations on Crete led to the discovery of an enormous palace complex at Knossus (NOSS-suss), near modern Heraklion, that was most likely the center of a far-ranging "sea empire," probably largely commercial. We know

MAP 3.1 Ancient Greece (c. 750–338 B.C.E.)

Between 750 and 500 B.C.E., Greek civilization witnessed the emergence of the city-state as the central institution in Greek life and the Greeks' colonization of the Mediterranean and Black Seas. Classical Greece lasted from about 500 to 338 B.C.E. and encompassed the high points of Greek civilization in art, science, philosophy, and politics, as well as the Persian Wars and the Peloponnesian War.

from archaeological remains that the people of Minoan Crete were accustomed to sea travel and had made contact with the more advanced civilization of Egypt. Egyptian products have been found in Crete and Cretan products in Egypt. Minoan Cretans also made contact with and exerted influence on the Greek-speaking inhabitants of the Greek mainland.

The Minoan civilization reached its height between 2000 and 1450 B.C.E. The palace at Knossus, the royal seat of the kings, demonstrates the prosperity and power of this civilization. It was an elaborate structure built around a central courtyard and included numerous private living rooms for the royal family and workshops for making decorated vases, small sculptures, and jewelry. The complex even included bathrooms with elaborate drains. The rooms were decorated with frescoes in bright colors depicting sporting events and naturalistic scenes that have led some observers to conclude that the Cretans had a great love of nature. Storerooms in the palace held enormous jars of oil, wine, and grain, presumably paid as taxes to the king.

Eventually, however, the centers of Minoan civilization on Crete suffered a collapse. Many historians believe that a tsunami triggered by a powerful volcanic eruption on the island of Thera was responsible for destroying towns and ships on the north coast of Crete, while volcanic ash devastated the land. Although people began to rebuild, there is evidence that mainland Greeks known as the Mycenaeans invaded and pillaged many centers, including Knossus, which was destroyed around 1400 B.C.E.

The First Greek State: Mycenae The term *Mycenaean* (my-suh-NEE-un) is derived from Mycenae (my-SEE-nee), a remarkable fortified site first excavated by the amateur German archaeologist Heinrich Schliemann (HYN-rikh SHLEE-mahn). Mycenae was one center in a Mycenaean Greek civilization that flourished between 1600 and 1100 B.C.E. The Mycenaean Greeks were part of the Indo-European family of peoples (see Chapter 1) who spread from their original Central Asian location into southern and western Europe, India, and Iran. One group entered the territory of Greece from the north around 1900 B.C.E. and managed to gain control of the Greek mainland and develop a civilization.

Mycenaean civilization, which reached its high point between 1400 and 1200 B.C.E., consisted of a number of powerful monarchies centered in fortified palace complexes. Like Mycenae itself, the palaces were built on hills and surrounded by gigantic stone walls. The royal families lived within the walls of these complexes, while the civilian populations lived in scattered locations outside the walls.

These various centers of power probably formed a loose confederacy of independent states, with Mycenae being the strongest. According to tablets written in an early form of Greek script called Linear B, a Mycenaean king used the title of *wanax*. Next in importance to the king were commanders of the army, priests, and bureaucrats who kept careful records. The free citizenry included peasants, soldiers, and artisans, with the lowest rung of the social ladder consisting of serfs and slaves.

The Mycenaeans were above all a warrior people who prided themselves on their heroic deeds in battle. Archaeological evidence also indicates that the Mycenaean monarchies developed an extensive commercial network. Mycenaean pottery has been found throughout the Mediterranean basin, in Syria and Egypt to the east and Sicily and southern Italy to the west. But some scholars believe that the Mycenaeans, led by Mycenae itself, also spread outward militarily, conquering Crete and making it part of the Mycenaean world. Some of the Aegean islands also fell subject to Mycenaean control. The most famous of all the Mycenaeans' supposed military adventures has come down to us in the epic poetry of Homer (discussed in the next section). Did the Mycenaeans, led by Agamemnon, king of Mycenae, sack the city of Troy on the northwestern coast of Asia Minor around 1250 B.C.E.? Scholars have debated this question ever since Schliemann began his excavations in 1870. Some believe that Homer's account does have a basis in fact, although there is little archaeological evidence to support it.

A Mycenaean Death Mask. *This death mask of thin gold was one of several found by Heinrich Schliemann in his excavation of Grave Circle A at Mycenae. These masks are similar to the gold mummy masks used in Egyptian royal tombs. Schliemann claimed—incorrectly—that he had found the mask of Agamemnon, king of Mycenae in Homer's Iliad.*

National Archaeological Museum, Athens//© Erich Lessing/Art Resource, NY

By the late thirteenth century B.C.E., Mycenaean Greece was showing signs of serious trouble. Mycenae itself was torched around 1190 B.C.E., and other Mycenaean centers show similar patterns of destruction as new waves of Greek-speaking invaders moved into Greece from the north. By 1100 B.C.E., the Mycenaean culture was coming to an end, and the Greek world was entering a new period of considerable insecurity.

THE GREEKS IN A DARK AGE (C. 1100–C. 750 B.C.E.)

After the collapse of the Mycenaean civilization, Greece entered a difficult period in which population declined and food production dropped. Because of the difficult conditions and our lack of knowledge about the period, historians refer to it as the Dark Age. Not until 850 B.C.E. did farming revive. At the same time, some new developments were forming the basis for a revived Greece.

During the Dark Age, large numbers of Greeks left the mainland and migrated across the Aegean Sea to various islands and especially to the southwestern shore of Asia Minor, a strip of territory that came to be called Ionia (y-OH-nee-uh). Based on their dialect, the Greeks who resided there were called Ionians. Two other major groups of Greeks settled in established parts of Greece. The Aeolian (ee-OH-lee-un) Greeks, located in northern and central Greece, colonized the large island of Lesbos and the adjacent territory on the northwestern coast of Asia Minor. The Dorians (DOR-ee-unz) established themselves in southwestern Greece, especially in the Peloponnesus, as well as on some of the southern Aegean islands, including Crete and Rhodes.

Other important activities occurred in this Dark Age as well. Greece saw a revival of some trade and some economic activity besides agriculture. Iron replaced bronze in the construction of weapons, making them affordable for more people. And farming tools made of iron helped reverse the decline in food production. At some point in the eighth century B.C.E., the Greeks adopted the Phoenician alphabet to give themselves a new system of writing. By reducing all words to a combination of twenty-four letters, the Greeks made learning to read and write simpler. Finally, near the end of this Dark Age appeared the work of Homer, who has come to be viewed as one of the great poets of all time.

Homer and Homeric Greece   The *Iliad* and the *Odyssey*, the first great epic poems of early Greece, were based on stories that had been passed on from generation to generation. It is generally assumed that early in the eighth century B.C.E., Homer made use of these oral traditions to compose the *Iliad*, his epic of the Trojan War. The war was sparked by Paris, a prince of Troy. By kidnapping Helen, wife of the king of the Greek state of Sparta, he outraged all the Greeks. Under the leadership of the Spartan king's brother, Agamemnon of Mycenae, the Greeks attacked Troy. Ten years later, the Greeks finally won and sacked the city.

But the *Iliad* is not so much the story of the war itself as it is the tale of the Greek hero Achilles (uh-KIL-eez) and how the "wrath of Achilles" led to disaster. As is true of all great literature, the *Iliad* abounds in universal lessons. Underlying them all is the clear message, as one commentator has observed, that "men will still come and go like the generations of leaves in the forest; that [man] will still be weak, and the gods strong and incalculable; that the quality of a man matters more than his achievement; that violence and recklessness will still lead to disaster, and that this will fall on the innocent as well as on the guilty."[1]

The *Odyssey*, Homer's other masterpiece, is an epic romance that recounts the journeys of one of the Greek heroes, Odysseus (oh-DISS-ee-uss), after the fall of Troy, and his ultimate return to his wife. But there is a larger vision here as well: the testing of the heroic stature of Odysseus until, by both cunning and patience, he prevails. In the course of this testing, the underlying moral message is "that virtue is a better policy than vice."[2]

Although the *Iliad* and the *Odyssey* supposedly deal with the heroes of the Mycenaean age of the thirteenth century B.C.E., many scholars believe that they really describe the social conditions of the Dark Age. According to the Homeric view, Greece was a society based on agriculture in which a landed warrior-aristocracy controlled much wealth and exercised considerable power. Homer's world reflects the values of aristocratic heroes.

Homer's Enduring Importance   This, of course, explains the importance of Homer to later generations of Greeks. Homer did not record history; he made it. The Greeks regarded the *Iliad* and the *Odyssey* as authentic history as recorded by one poet, Homer. These masterpieces gave the Greeks an ideal past with a cast of heroes and came to be used as standard texts for the education of generations of Greek males. As one Athenian stated, "My father was anxious to see me develop into a good man ... and as a means to this end he compelled me to memorize all of Homer."[3] The values Homer

Homer's Ideal of Excellence

The *Iliad* and the *Odyssey*, epics that the Greeks believed were written by Homer, were used as basic texts for the education of Greeks for hundreds of years in antiquity. This passage from the *Iliad*, describing a conversation between Hector, prince of Troy, and his wife, Andromache (an-DRAHM-uh-kee), illustrates the Greek ideal of gaining honor through combat. At the end of the passage, Homer also reveals what became the Greek attitude toward women: women are supposed to spin and weave and take care of their households and their children.

Homer, *Iliad*

Hector looked at his son and smiled, but said nothing. Andromache, bursting into tears, went up to him and put her hand in his. "Hector," she said, "you are possessed. This bravery of yours will be your end. You do not think of your little boy or your unhappy wife, whom you will make a widow soon. Some day the Achaeans [Greeks] are bound to kill you in a massed attack. And when I lose you I might as well be dead.... I have no father, no mother, now.... I had seven brothers too at home. In one day all of them went down to Hades' House. The great Achilles of the swift feet killed them all....

"So you, Hector, are father and mother and brother to me, as well as my beloved husband. Have pity on me now; stay here on the tower; and do not make your boy an orphan and your wife a widow...."

"All that, my dear," said the great Hector of the glittering helmet, "is surely my concern. But if I hid myself like a coward and refused to fight, I could never face the Trojans and the Trojan ladies in their trailing gowns. Besides, it would go against the grain, for I have trained myself always, like a good soldier, to take my place in the front line and win glory for my father and myself...."

As he finished, glorious Hector held out his arms to take his boy. But the child shrank back with a cry to the bosom of his girdled nurse, alarmed by his father's appearance. He was frightened by the bronze of the helmet and the horsehair plume that he saw nodding grimly down at him. His father and his lady mother had to laugh. But noble Hector quickly took his helmet off and put the dazzling thing on the ground. Then he kissed his son, dandled him in his arms, and prayed to Zeus and the other gods: "Zeus, and you other gods, grant that this boy of mine may be, like me, pre-eminent in Troy; as strong and brave as I; a mighty king of Ilium. May people say, when he comes back from battle, 'Here is a better man than his father.' Let him bring home the bloodstained armor of the enemy he has killed, and make his mother happy."

Hector handed the boy to his wife, who took him to her fragrant breast. She was smiling through her tears, and when her husband saw this he was moved. He stroked her with his hand and said: "My dear, I beg you not to be too much distressed. No one is going to send me down to Hades before my proper time. But Fate is a thing that no man born of woman, coward or hero, can escape. Go home now, and attend to your own work, the loom and the spindle, and see that the maidservants get on with theirs. War is men's business; and this war is the business of every man in Ilium, myself above all."

Q *What important ideals for Greek men and women are revealed in this passage from the Iliad?*

Source: From THE ILIAD by Homer, translated by E. V. Rieu, Revised and updated by Peter Jones with D. C. H. Rieu, Edited with an introduction and notes by Peter Jones (Penguin Classics, 1950, Revised translation 2003). Copyright © the Estate of E. V. Rieu, 1946. Revised translation and Introduction and Notes copyright © Peter V. Jones, 2003. Reproduced by permission of Penguin Books Ltd.

taught were essentially the aristocratic values of courage and honor. A hero strives for excellence, which the Greeks called *arete* (ahr-ih-TAY). In the warrior-aristocratic world of Homer, *arete* is won in a struggle or contest. Through his willingness to fight, the hero protects his family and friends, preserves his own honor and that of his family, and earns his reputation.

In the Homeric world, aristocratic women, too, were expected to pursue excellence. Penelope, for example, the wife of Odysseus, the hero of the *Odyssey*, remains faithful to her husband and displays great courage and intelligence in preserving their household during her husband's long absence. Upon his return, Odysseus praises her for her excellence: "Madame, there is not a man in the wide world who could find fault with you. For your fame has reached heaven itself, like that of some perfect king, ruling a populous and mighty state with the fear of god in his heart, and upholding the right."[4] Homer gave the Greeks a model of heroism, honor, and nobility. But in time, as a new world of city-states emerged in Greece, new values of cooperation and community also transformed what the Greeks learned from Homer.

THE WORLD OF THE GREEK CITY-STATES (C. 750–C. 500 B.C.E.)

In the eighth century B.C.E., Greek civilization burst forth with new energies, beginning the period that historians have called the Archaic Age of Greece. Two major developments stand out in this era: the evolution of the *polis* (POH-liss), or city-state, as the central institution in Greek life and the Greeks' colonization of the Mediterranean and Black Seas.

The *Polis*   The Greek *polis* (plural, *poleis*) developed slowly during the Dark Age but by the eighth century B.C.E. had emerged as a unique and fundamental institution in Greek society. In a physical sense, the *polis* encompassed a town or city or even a village and its surrounding countryside. But each had a central place where the citizens of the *polis* could assemble for political, social, and religious activities. In some *poleis,* this central meeting point was a hill, which could serve as a place of refuge during an attack and later in some locales came to be the religious center where temples and public monuments were erected. Below this *acropolis* (uh-KROP-uh-liss) would be an *agora* (AG-er-uh), an open space that served both as a place where citizens could assemble and as a marketplace.

Poleis varied greatly in size, from a few square miles to a few hundred square miles. The larger ones were the product of consolidation. The territory of Attica, for example, had once had twelve *poleis* but eventually became a single *polis* (Athens) through a process of amalgamation. The population of Athens grew to about 250,000 by the fifth century B.C.E. Most *poleis* were much smaller, consisting of only a few hundred to several thousand people.

Although our word *politics* is derived from the Greek term *polis*, the *polis* itself was much more than just a political institution. It was, above all, a community of citizens in which all political, economic, social, cultural, and religious activities were focused. As a community, the *polis* consisted of citizens with political rights (adult males), citizens with no political rights (women and children), and noncitizens (slaves and resident aliens). All citizens of a *polis* possessed rights, but these rights were coupled with responsibilities. The Greek philosopher Aristotle argued that the citizen did not belong just to himself: "We must rather regard every citizen as belonging to the state." The unity of citizens was important and often meant that states would take an active role in directing the patterns of life. Nevertheless, the loyalty that citizens had to their *poleis* also had a negative side. *Poleis* distrusted one another, and the division of Greece into fiercely patriotic sovereign units helped bring about its ruin. Greece was not a united country but a geographic location. The cultural unity of the Greeks did not mean much politically.

A New Military System: the Greek Way of War   As the *polis* developed, so did a new military system. In earlier times, wars in Greece had been fought by aristocratic cavalry—nobles on horseback. These aristocrats, who were large landowners, also dominated the political life of their *poleis*. But by the end of the eighth century, a new military order came into being that was based on **hoplites** (HAHP-lyts), heavily armed infantrymen who wore bronze or leather helmets, breastplates, and greaves (shin guards). Each carried a round shield, a short sword, and a thrusting spear about 9 feet long. Hoplites advanced into battle as a unit, shoulder to shoulder, forming a **phalanx** (a rectangular formation) in tight order, usually eight ranks deep. As long as the hoplites kept their order, were not outflanked, and did not break, they either secured victory or, at the very least, suffered no harm. The phalanx was easily routed, however, if it broke its order. The safety of the phalanx thus depended on the solidarity and discipline of its members. As one seventh-century B.C.E. poet observed, a good hoplite was "a short man firmly placed upon his legs, with a courageous heart, not to be uprooted from the spot where he plants his legs."[5]

The hoplite force, which apparently developed first in the Peloponnesus, had political as well as military repercussions. The aristocratic cavalry was now outdated. Since each hoplite provided his own armor, men of property, both aristocrats and small farmers, made up the new phalanx. Those who could become hoplites and fight for the state could also challenge aristocratic control. Thus, the development of the hoplite and phalanx became an important factor in the rise of democracy in Greece.

In the new world of the Greek city-states, war became an integral part of the Greek way of life. The Greek philosopher Plato described war as "always existing by nature between every Greek city-state."[6] The Greeks created a tradition of warfare that became a prominent element of Western civilization. For example, the Greeks devised excellent weapons and body armor, making effective use of technological improvements. Greek armies included a wide number of citizen-soldiers, who gladly accepted the need for training and discipline, giving them an edge over their opponents' often far-larger armies of mercenaries. Moreover, the Greeks displayed a willingness to engage the enemy head-on, thus deciding a battle quickly and with as few casualties as possible. Finally, the Greeks demonstrated the effectiveness of heavy infantry in determining the outcome of a battle. All of these features of Greek warfare remained part of Western warfare for centuries.

Museo Nazionale di Villa Giulia, Rome//© Scala/Art Resource, NY

The Hoplite Forces. *The Greek hoplites were infantrymen equipped with large round shields and long thrusting spears. In battle, they advanced in tight phalanx formation and were dangerous opponents as long as this formation remained unbroken. This vase painting from the seventh century* B.C.E. *shows two groups of hoplite warriors engaged in battle. The piper on the left is leading another line of soldiers preparing to enter the fray.*

Colonization and the Growth of Trade

Greek expansion overseas was another major development of the Archaic Age. Between 750 and 550 B.C.E., large numbers of Greeks left their homeland to settle in distant lands. Poverty and land hunger created by the growing gulf between rich and poor, overpopulation, and the development of trade were all factors that led to the establishment of colonies. Some Greek colonies were simply trading posts or centers for the transshipment of goods to Greece. Most were larger settlements that included fertile agricultural land taken from the native populations in those areas. Each colony was founded as a *polis* and was usually independent of the mother *polis* (the *metropolis*) that had established it.

In the western Mediterranean, new Greek settlements were established along the coastline of southern Italy, including the cities of Tarentum (Taranto) and Neapolis (Naples) (see Map 3.2). So many Greek communities were established in southern Italy that the Romans later called it *Magna Graecia* (MAG-nuh GREE-shuh) ("Great Greece"). An important city was founded at Syracuse in eastern Sicily in 734 B.C.E. by the city-state of Corinth, one of the most active Greek states in establishing colonies. Greek settlements were also established in southern France at Massilia—modern Marseilles (mar-SAY)—in eastern Spain, and in northern Africa west of Egypt.

To the north, the Greeks set up colonies in Thrace, where they sought good agricultural lands to grow grains. Greeks also settled along the shores of the Black Sea and secured the approaches to it with cities on the Hellespont and Bosporus,

MAP 3.2   Greece and Its Colonies in the Archaic Age

Impelled by overpopulation and poverty, Greeks spread out from their homelands during the Archaic Age, establishing colonies in many parts of the Mediterranean. The colonies were independent city-states that traded with the older Greek city-states.

most notably Byzantium, site of the later Constantinople (Istanbul). A trading post was established in Egypt, giving the Greeks access to both the products and the advanced culture of the East.

The Effects of Colonization   The establishment of these settlements over such a wide area had important effects. For one thing, they contributed to the diffusion of Greek culture throughout the Mediterranean basin. The later Romans had their first contacts with the Greeks through the settlements in southern Italy. Furthermore, colonization helped the Greeks foster a greater sense of Greek identity. Before the eighth century, Greek communities were mostly isolated from one another, leaving many neighboring states on unfriendly terms. Once Greeks from different communities went abroad and encountered peoples with different languages and customs, they became more aware of their own linguistic and cultural similarities.

Colonization also led to increased trade and industry. The Greeks sent their pottery, wine, and olive oil to these areas; in return, they received grains and metals from the west and fish, timber, wheat, metals, and slaves from the Black Sea region. In many *poleis*, the expansion of trade and industry created a new group of rich men who perceived that the decisions of the *polis* could affect their businesses. They now desired new political privileges but found them impossible to gain because of the power of the ruling aristocrats. This desire for change soon led to political crisis in many Greek states.

Tyranny in the Greek *Polis* When the *polis* emerged as an important institution in Greece in the eighth century, monarchical power waned, and kings virtually disappeared in most Greek states or survived only as ceremonial figures with little or no real power. Instead, political power passed into the hands of local aristocracies. But increasing divisions between rich and poor and the aspirations of newly rising industrial and commercial groups in Greek *poleis* opened the door to the rise of **tyrants** in the seventh and sixth centuries B.C.E. They were not necessarily oppressive or wicked, as our word *tyrant* connotes. Greek tyrants were rulers who seized power by force and who were not subject to the law. Support for the tyrants came from the new rich, who made their money in trade and industry, as well as from poor peasants, who were in debt to landholding aristocrats. Both groups were opposed to the domination of political power by the aristocrats.

Tyrants usually achieved power by a local coup d'état and maintained it by using mercenary soldiers. Once in power, they built new marketplaces, temples, and walls that created jobs, glorified the city, and also enhanced their own popularity. Tyrants also favored the interests of merchants and traders by encouraging the founding of new colonies, developing new coinage, and establishing new systems of weights and measures. In many instances, they added to the prosperity of their cities. By their patronage of the arts, they encouraged cultural development.

The Example of Corinth   One of the most famous examples of tyranny can be found in Corinth (KOR-inth). During the eighth and early seventh centuries B.C.E., Corinth had become one of the most prosperous states in Greece under the rule of an oligarchy led by members of the Bacchiad family. Their violent activities, however, made them unpopular and led Cypselus (SIP-suh-luss), a member of the family, to overthrow the oligarchy and assume sole control of Corinth.

Cypselus was so well liked that he could rule without a bodyguard. During his tyranny, Corinth prospered by exporting vast quantities of pottery and founding new colonies to expand its trade empire. Cypselus's son, Periander, took control of Corinth after his father's death but ruled with such cruelty that shortly after he died in 585 B.C.E., his son, who succeeded him, was killed, and a new oligarchy soon ruled Corinth.

As in Corinth, tyranny elsewhere in Greece was largely extinguished by the end of the sixth century B.C.E. The children and grandchildren of tyrants, who tended to be corrupted by their inherited power and wealth, often became cruel and unjust rulers, making tyranny no longer seem such a desirable institution. Its very nature as a system outside the law seemed contradictory to the ideal of law in a Greek community. Tyranny did not last, but it played a significant role in the evolution of Greek history. The rule of narrow aristocratic oligarchies was destroyed. Once the tyrants were eliminated, the door was opened to the participation of more people in the affairs of the community. Although this trend culminated in the development of democracy in some communities, in other states expanded oligarchies of one kind or another managed to remain in power. Greek states exhibited considerable variety in their governmental structures; this can perhaps best be seen by examining the two most famous and most powerful Greek city-states, Sparta and Athens.

Sparta   The Greeks of Sparta and Athens spoke different dialects
and developed different political systems. The Spartans
sought stability and conformity and emphasized order. The Athenians
allowed for individual differences and stressed freedom. Although the two states
shared a common heritage, their differences grew so large in their own minds
that they were ultimately willing to engage in a life-and-death struggle to
support their separate realities. When they did so, the entire Greek world was
the real loser.

Located in the southeastern Peloponnesus, in an area known as Laconia
(luh-KOH-nee-uh), the Spartans had originally occupied four small villages
that eventually became unified into a single *polis* (a fifth soon joined the
others). This unification made Sparta a strong community in Laconia and
enabled the Spartans to conquer the neighboring Laconians. Many Laconians
became **perioikoi** (per-ee-EE-koh-ee), free inhabitants but not citizens who
were required to pay taxes and perform military service for Sparta. Other
Laconians became known as **helots** (HEL-uts) (derived from a Greek word for
"capture"). They were bound to the land and forced to work on farms and as
household servants for the Spartans.

When the land in Laconia proved unable to maintain the growing number of
Spartan citizens, the Spartans looked for land nearby and, beginning around
730 B.C.E., undertook the conquest of neighboring Messenia despite its larger size and
population. Messenia possessed a spacious, fertile plain ideal for growing grain. After
its conquest, which was not completed until the seventh century B.C.E., the Messenians
were made helots and forced to work for the Spartans. But the helots drastically
outnumbered the Spartan citizens (some estimates are ten to one) and constantly threatened to revolt. To ensure control over them, the Spartans made a conscious decision to
create a military state.

Sometime between 800 and 600 B.C.E., the Spartans instituted a series of
reforms that are associated with the name of the lawgiver Lycurgus (ly-KUR-guss).
Although historians are not sure that Lycurgus ever existed, there is no doubt about
the result of the reforms that were made: Sparta was transformed into a perpetual
military camp.

The New Sparta   The lives of Spartans were now rigidly organized. At birth, each
child was examined by state officials who decided whether it was fit to live. Those
judged unfit were exposed to the elements and left to die. Boys were taken from
their mothers at the age of seven and put under control of the state. They lived in
barracks, where they were subjected to harsh discipline to make them tough and
given an education that stressed military training and obedience to authority. At
twenty, Spartan males were enrolled in the army for regular military service.
Although allowed to marry, they continued to live in the barracks and ate their
meals in public dining halls with their fellow soldiers. Meals were simple; the
famous Spartan black broth consisted of a piece of pork boiled in blood, salt, and
vinegar, causing a visitor who ate in a public mess to remark that he now understood why Spartans were not afraid to die. At thirty, Spartan males were recognized as mature and allowed to vote in the assembly and live at home, but they
remained in the army until the age of sixty.

While their husbands remained in military barracks until age thirty, Spartan women lived at home. Because of this separation, Spartan women had greater freedom of movement. Permitted to own and inherit land, Spartan women had more power in the household than was common for women elsewhere in Greece and could even supervise large estates. They were encouraged to exercise and remain fit to bear and raise healthy children. Like the men, Spartan women engaged in athletic exercises in the nude. At solemn feasts, the young women would march naked in processions, and in the presence of the young men, they would sing songs about those who had showed special gallantry or cowardice on the battlefield. Many Spartan women upheld the strict Spartan values, expecting their husbands and sons to be brave in war. The story is told that as a Spartan mother was burying her son, an old woman came up to her and said, "You poor woman, what a misfortune." "No," replied the other, "because I bore him so that he might die for Sparta and that is what has happened, as I wished."[7] Another Spartan woman saw her son off to war by telling him to come back carrying his shield or carried on it.

The Spartan social structure was rigidly organized. At the summit were the *Spartiates* (spar-tee-AH-teez)—full Spartan citizens. Each Spartan citizen owned a piece of land, worked by the helots, to provide economic sustenance. With their material needs provided for them, Spartan citizens could dedicate themselves to their duties as a ruling class. Below the *Spartiates* were the *perioikoi*. Though free, they did not possess the privileges of citizenship and served as small merchants and artisans. They were subject to military duty, however. At the bottom of the social scale were the helots, perpetually bound to the land. They were assigned to the lands of the Spartan citizens. The helots farmed the land and gave their masters half of the produce. According to one seventh-century Spartan poet, helots worked "like donkeys exhausted under heavy loads." A secret police force lived among them and was permitted to kill any helot considered dangerous. To legalize this murder, the state officially declared war on the helots at the beginning of each year.

The Spartan State   The so-called Lycurgan reforms also reorganized the Spartan government, creating an **oligarchy**. Two kings from different families were primarily responsible for military affairs and served as the leaders of the Spartan army on its campaigns. Five men, known as the *ephors* (EFF-urz), were elected each year and were responsible for the education of youth and the conduct of all citizens. A council of elders, composed of the two kings and twenty-eight citizens over the age of sixty, decided what issues would be presented to an assembly of all male citizens. This assembly did not debate but only voted on the proposals put before it by the council of elders. The assembly also elected the council of elders and the *ephors*.

To make their new military state secure, the Spartans deliberately turned their backs on the outside world. Foreigners, who might bring in new ideas, were discouraged from visiting Sparta. Nor were Spartans, except for military reasons, encouraged to travel abroad where they might pick up new ideas. Trade and commerce were likewise minimized. Spartan citizens were discouraged from pursuing philosophy, literature, the arts, or any subject that might foster novel thoughts dangerous to the stability of the state. The art of war and ruling was the Spartan ideal. All other arts were frowned on.

In the sixth century, Sparta used its military might and the fear it inspired to gain greater control of the Peloponnesus by organizing an alliance of almost all the Peloponnesian states. Sparta's strength enabled it to dominate this Peloponnesian League and determine its policies. By 500 B.C.E., the Spartans had organized a powerful military state that maintained order and stability in the Peloponnesus. Raised from early childhood to believe that total loyalty to the Spartan state was the basic reason for existence, the Spartans viewed their strength as justification for their militaristic ideals and regimented society.

Athens   By 700 B.C.E., Athens had established a unified *polis* on the peninsula of Attica. Although early Athens had been ruled by a monarchy, by the seventh century B.C.E. it had fallen under the control of its aristocrats. They possessed the best land and controlled political and religious life by means of a council of nobles called the Areopagus (ar-ee-OP-uh-guss), assisted by a board of nine archons. Although there was an assembly of full citizens, it possessed few powers.

Near the end of the seventh century B.C.E., Athens faced political turmoil because of serious economic problems. Many Athenian farmers found themselves sold into slavery when they were unable to repay the loans they had borrowed from their aristocratic neighbors, pledging themselves as collateral. Over and over, there were cries to cancel the debts and give land to the poor. Athens seemed on the verge of civil war.

The Reforms of Solon   Hoping to avoid tyranny, the ruling Athenian aristocrats responded to this crisis by choosing Solon (SOH-lun), a reform-minded aristocrat, as sole archon in 594 B.C.E. and giving him full power to make reforms. Solon canceled all current land debts, outlawed new loans based on humans as collateral, and freed people who had fallen into slavery for debt. He refused, however, to carry out the redistribution of the land and hence failed to deal with the basic cause of the economic crisis.

Like his economic reforms, Solon's political measures were also a compromise. Though by no means eliminating the power of the aristocracy, they opened the door to the participation of new people, especially the nonaristocratic wealthy, in the government. Wealth instead of birth now qualified people for holding political office, thus creating upward political mobility. Solon divided all Athenian citizens into four classes on the basis of wealth. Only men in the first two classes (the wealthiest classes) could hold the archonship and be members of the Areopagus.

The Move to Tyranny   But Solon's reforms, though popular, did not solve Athens's problems. Aristocratic factions continued to vie for power, and the poorer peasants resented Solon's failure to institute land redistribution. Internal strife finally led to the very institution Solon had hoped to avoid—tyranny. Pisistratus (puh-SIS-truh-tuss), an aristocrat and a distant relative of Solon's, seized power in 560 B.C.E. and made himself a tyrant.

Pisistratus did not tamper very much with the constitution. The assembly, councils, and courts continued to function while he made sure that his supporters were elected as magistrates and council members. Pisistratus curried favor with the small farmers by offering land and loans to the needy. His ambitious building program, aimed at beautifying the city, also created jobs. Pursuing a foreign policy that aided Athenian trade, Pisistratus also maintained the support of the mercantile and industrial classes. Pisistratus's mild tyranny was popular with many Athenians, but they rebelled against his son and ended the tyranny in 510 B.C.E. Although the aristocrats attempted to reestablish an aristocratic oligarchy, Cleisthenes (KLYSS-thuh-neez), an aristocratic reformer, opposed this plan and, with the backing of the Athenian people, gained the upper hand in 508 B.C.E. The reforms of Cleisthenes now established the basis for Athenian democracy.

The Reforms of Cleisthenes A major aim of Cleisthenes's reforms was to weaken the power of traditional localities and regions, which had provided the foundation for aristocratic strength. He made the *demes*, the villages and townships of Attica, the basic units of political life. Cleisthenes enrolled all the citizens of the demes in ten new tribes, each of which contained inhabitants located in the country districts of Attica, the coastal areas, and Athens itself. The ten tribes thus contained a cross section of the population and reflected all of Attica, a move that gave local areas a basic role in the political structure. Each of the ten tribes chose fifty members by lot each year for a new Council of Five Hundred, which was responsible for the administration of both foreign and financial affairs and prepared the business that would be handled by the assembly. This assembly of all male citizens had final authority in the passing of laws after free and open debate; thus, Cleisthenes's reforms strengthened the central role of the assembly of citizens in the Athenian political system.

The reforms of Cleisthenes laid the foundations for Athenian democracy. More changes would come in the fifth century when the Athenians themselves would begin to use the word *democracy* (from the Greek words *demos*, "people," and *kratia*, "power"; thus, "power to the people") to describe their system. By 500 B.C.E., Athens was more united than it had been and was about to assume a more important role in Greek affairs.

Greek Culture in the Archaic Age The period after the Dark Age witnessed a revitalization of Greek life that is also evident in Greek art and literature. Some aspects of Archaic Greek culture, such as pottery and sculpture, were especially influenced by the East. Greek sculpture, particularly that of the Ionian Greek settlements in southwestern Asia Minor, demonstrates the impact of the considerably older Egyptian civilization. There we first see the life-size stone statues of young male nudes known as *kouros* (KOO-rohss) figures. The *kouros* bears considerable resemblance to Egyptian statues of the New Kingdom. The figures are not realistic but stiff, with a slight smile; one leg is advanced ahead of the other, and the arms are held rigidly at the sides of the body.

Greek literature of the seventh century is perhaps best known for its lyric poetry. The lyric is considerably shorter than epic poetry (such as Homer's) and focuses on personal emotions, usually the power of love and its impact on human lives. Later Greeks acknowledged Sappho as their greatest female lyric poet. Born in the seventh century, Sappho lived on the island of Lesbos in the Aegean Sea, where she taught music and poetry to her young charges. Many of her poems are love songs to her female students. Our word *lesbian* is derived from Sappho's island of Lesbos. Sappho, like many upper-class Greeks, accepted that homosexual and heterosexual feelings could exist in the same individual. Sappho was a wife and a mother who also wrote poems about love between men and between women.

Archaic Greece is also known for poets who reflected the lifestyles of both aristocrats and peasants. A wide gulf, however, separated the wealthy aristocrat with his large landed estates from the poor peasants and small farmers who eked out their existence as best they could. Hesiod (HEE-see-uhd), a poet from Boeotia in central Greece who lived around 700 B.C.E., wrote a lengthy epic poem titled *Works and Days*. Himself a farmer, Hesiod distrusted aristocrats and looked down on what he considered the aristocratic emphasis on pride and war. One of his aims was to show that the gods punished injustice and that the way to success was to work: "Famine and blight do not beset the just, who till their well-worked fields and feast. The earth supports them lavishly." Therefore:

> *... you must learn to organize your work*
> *So you may have full barns at harvest time.*
> *From working, men grow rich in flocks and gold*
> *And dearer to the deathless gods. In work*
> *There is no shame; shame is in idleness.*[8]

Works and Days is the first known paean to work in Western literature.

Theognis of Megara (THEE-og-niss of MEG-er-uh) described a way of life considerably different from Hesiod's. Theognis was an aristocrat who lived and wrote primarily in the sixth century B.C.E. As a result of revolutionary upheaval, he, like other aristocrats in sixth-century *poleis*, lost his position and probably his wealth. Sent into exile, he became a bitter man. In his poetry, he portrayed aristocrats as the only good people who are distinguished from others by their natural intelligence, virtue, honor, and moderation. The lower classes or common people were by nature bad and debased:

> *Only a fool does favors for the base;*
> *You'd do as well to sow the gray salt sea.*
> *No crop of corn would come up from the deep,*
> *No gratitude, no favors from the base.*
> *The scum are never sated. If you slip,*
> *Just once, their former friendship melts away.*
> *But put a gentleman once in your debt,*
> *You have a friend for life; he won't forget.*

Aristocrats, then, should associate only with other aristocrats: "Avoid low company, mix only with the better sort of men.... From them you will learn goodness. Men of little worth will spoil the natural beauty of your birth."[9] The poems of Theognis reveal the political views and biases of a typical sixth-century aristocrat.

THE HIGH POINT OF GREEK CIVILIZATION: CLASSICAL GREECE

Classical Greece is the name given to the period of Greek history from around 500 B.C.E. to the conquest of Greece by the Macedonian king Philip II in 338 B.C.E. It was a period of brilliant achievement, much of it associated with the flowering of democracy in Athens under the leadership of Pericles. Many of the lasting contributions of the Greeks occurred during this period. The age began with a mighty confrontation between the Greek states and the mammoth Persian Empire.

The Challenge of Persia   As Greek civilization expanded throughout the Mediterranean region, it was inevitable that it would come into contact with the Persian Empire to the east. In his play *The Persians*, the Greek playwright Aeschylus (ESS-kuh-luss) expressed what some Greeks perceived to be the essential difference between themselves and the Persians. The Persian queen, curious to find out more about the Athenians, asks: "Who commands them? Who is shepherd of their host?" The chorus responds: "They are slaves to none, nor are they subject."[10] Thus, at least some Greeks saw the struggle with the Persians as a contest between freedom and slavery. To the Greeks, a person was a citizen of the state, not a subject.

The Ionian Greek cities in southwestern Asia Minor had already fallen subject to the Persian Empire by the mid-sixth century B.C.E. (see Chapter 2). An unsuccessful revolt by the Ionian cities in 499, assisted by the Athenian navy, led the Persian ruler Darius to seek revenge by attacking the mainland Greeks in 490. Darius may also have wished to expand his empire westward.

The First Persian Attack The Persians sailed across the Aegean, captured Eretria (which had also aided the Ionian rebels) on the island of Euboea across from Attica, and then transferred their army to the plain of Marathon, only 26 miles from Athens (see Map 3.3). The Athenians, aided by the Plataeans (from a neighboring town in Boeotia), confronted the Persians without additional assistance. The two armies were quite different. The Persians, with their light-armed troops, were more mobile and flexible and relied heavily on missiles; the Greek hoplites were armed with heavy shields and relied on spear thrusts at close range. The Athenians and Plataeans were clearly outnumbered, but led by Miltiades (mil-TY-uh-deez), one of the Athenian leaders who insisted on attacking, the Greek hoplites charged across the plain of Marathon and crushed the Persian forces. The Persians did not mount another attack against mainland Greece for ten years.

In the meantime, Athens had acquired a new leader, Themistocles (thuh-MISS-tuh-kleez), a man lacking in aristocratic connections but strongly favored by Athenian merchants and highly skilled in speaking in the democratic assembly. Themistocles persuaded his fellow citizens to pursue a new military policy, namely, the development of a navy. The Athenians used a newly discovered vein of silver from Laurium to finance the construction of ships and new port facilities. By 480 B.C.E., Athens had produced a navy of about two hundred vessels, primarily triremes (TRY-reemz) (ships with three banks of oars).

MAP 3.3 The Persian Wars

The Athenians defeated Persia in 490 B.C.E. at Marathon. Athens later led a coalition of Greek city-states that decisively defeated Xerxes' navy at the Battle of Salamis in 480 B.C.E., leading Xerxes to withdraw most of his troops back to Asia.

A revolt in Egypt, compounded by the death of Darius in 486 B.C.E., kept the Persians from mounting another attack on Greece. Xerxes (ZURK-seez), the new Persian monarch, was bent on revenge and expansion, however. Some of the Greeks prepared by forming a defensive league under Spartan leadership, although many Greek states remained neutral; some even fought on the Persian side.

The Invasion of Xerxes The Persians under Xerxes mounted their invasion in 480 B.C.E. Their military forces were massive: close to 150,000 troops, almost seven hundred naval ships, and hundreds of supply ships to feed their large army. The Persians crossed the Hellespont by forming a bridge of ships and then moved through Thrace and Macedonia on their way into Greece. The Greek plan, as it evolved, was to fight a holding action at the pass of Thermopylae (thur-MAHP-uh-lee) along the main road from Thessaly into Boeotia, probably to give the Greek fleet of three hundred ships at Artemisium, off northern Euboea, the chance to fight the Persian fleet. The Greeks knew that the Persian army depended on the fleet for supplies. A Greek force numbering close to nine thousand, under the leadership of the Spartan king Leonidas (lee-AHN-ih-duss) and his contingent of three hundred Spartans, held off the Persian army at Thermopylae for two days. The Spartan troops were especially brave. When told that Persian arrows would darken the sky in battle, one Spartan warrior supposedly responded, "That is good news. We will fight in the shade!" Unfortunately for the Greeks, a traitor told the Persians of a mountain path they could use to outflank the Greek force. King Leonidas and the three hundred Spartans fought to the last man.

The Athenians, now threatened by the onslaught of the Persian forces, decided to abandon Athens and evacuated the population of Attica to the offshore island of Salamis (SAH-luh-miss). Meanwhile, the Greek fleet remained in the straits off Salamis while the Persians sacked Athens. The Peloponnesians wanted the Greeks to retreat to the Peloponnesus and the Greek ships to move to the isthmus as well. Themistocles's refusal and his threat to withdraw the Athenian ships altogether if a fight was not made forced the ships to remain and set up the naval Battle of Salamis. Although the Greeks were outnumbered, they managed to outmaneuver the Persian fleet (mostly Phoenicians and Ionians) and decisively defeated it. The Persians still had their army and much of their fleet intact, but Xerxes, frightened at the prospect of another Ionian revolt, returned to Asia but left a Persian force in Thessaly.

Early in 479 B.C.E., the Greeks formed the largest Greek army seen up to that time. The Athenians forced the Spartans to move north of the Peloponnesus and take on the Persians at Plataea (pluh-TEE-uh), northwest of Athens, where the Greek forces decisively defeated the Persian army. The remnants of the Persian forces retreated to Asia. At the same time, the Greeks destroyed much of the Persian fleet in a naval battle at Mycale (MIH-kuh-lee) in Ionia. The Greeks were overjoyed at their victory but remained cautious. Would the Persians try again?

The Greek Trireme.
The trireme became the standard warship of ancient Greece. Highly maneuverable, fast, and outfitted with metal prows, Greek triremes were especially effective at ramming enemy ships. The photo shows the Olympias, *a trireme reconstructed by the Greek navy.*

© AAAC/Topham/The Image Works

The Growth	After the defeat of the Persians, Athens stepped in to

The Growth of an Athenian Empire   After the defeat of the Persians, Athens stepped in to provide new leadership against the Persians by forming a confederation called the Delian League. Organized in the winter of 478–477 B.C.E., the Delian League was dominated by the Athenians from the beginning. Its main headquarters was the island of Delos (DEE-lahs), sacred to the Ionian Greeks, but its chief officials, including the treasurers and commanders of the fleet, were Athenians. Athens also provided most of the league's three hundred ships. Under the leadership of the Athenians, the Delian League pursued the attack against the Persian Empire. Virtually all of the Greek states in the Aegean were liberated from Persian control, and the Persian fleet and army were decisively defeated in 469 B.C.E. in southern Asia Minor. Arguing that the Persian threat was now over, some members of the Delian League wished to withdraw. Naxos did so in 470 and Thasos in 465 B.C.E. The Athenians responded vigorously. They attacked both states, destroyed their walls, took over their fleets, eliminated their liberty, and forced them to pay tribute. "No secession" became Athenian policy. The Delian League was rapidly becoming an instrument of Athenian imperialism and the nucleus of an Athenian empire.

The Age of Pericles   At home, Athenians favored the new imperial policy, especially in the 450s B.C.E., when an aristocrat named Pericles (PER-i-kleez) began to play an important political role. Under Pericles, Athens embarked on a policy of expanding democracy at home while severing its ties with Sparta and expanding its new empire abroad. This period of Athenian and Greek history, which historians have subsequently labeled the Age of Pericles, witnessed the height of Athenian power and the culmination of its brilliance as a civilization.

In the Age of Pericles, the Athenians became deeply attached to their democratic system. The sovereignty of the people was embodied in the assembly, which consisted of all male citizens over eighteen years of age. In the 440s, that was probably a group of about 43,000. Meetings of the assembly were held on the hillside of the Pnyx (NIKS), east of the Acropolis. Not all could attend, and the number present seldom exceeded 6,000, which was the capacity of the Pnyx. The assembly passed all laws and made final decisions on war and foreign policy. Although anyone could speak, usually only respected leaders did so, a feat that required considerable speaking ability in such a large crowd. The reforms of Cleisthenes had introduced the Council of Five Hundred, elected by lot from the ten tribes. It prepared the agenda for the assembly and made recommendations for action. Thus, the council served as a control on the assembly.

Routine administration of public affairs was handled by a large body of city magistrates, usually chosen by lot without regard to class and usually serving only one-year terms. This meant that many male citizens held public office at some time in their lives. A board of ten officials known as generals—*strategoi* (strah-tay-GOH-ee)—was elected by public vote to guide affairs of state, although their power depended on the respect they had attained. Generals were usually wealthy aristocrats, even though the people were free to select

Athenian Democracy: The Funeral Oration of Pericles

In his *History of the Peloponnesian War*, the Greek historian Thucydides presented his reconstruction of the eulogy given by Pericles in the winter of 431–430 B.C.E. to honor the Athenians killed in the first campaigns of the Great Peloponnesian War. It is a magnificent, idealized description of the Athenian democracy at its height.

Thucydides, *History of the Peloponnesian War*

Our constitution is called a democracy because power is in the hands not of a minority but of the whole people. When it is a question of settling private disputes, everyone is equal before the law; when it is a question of putting one person before another in positions of public responsibility, what counts is not membership of a particular class, but the actual ability which the man possesses. No one, so long as he has it in him to be of service to the state, is kept in political obscurity because of poverty. And, just as our political life is free and open, so is our day-to-day life in our relations with each other. We do not get into a state with our next-door neighbor if he enjoys himself in his own way, nor do we give him the kind of black looks which, though they do no real harm, still do hurt people's feeling. We are free and tolerant in our private lives; but in public affairs we keep to the law. This is because it commands our deep respect.

We give our obedience to those whom we put in positions of authority, and we obey the laws themselves, especially those which are for the protection of the oppressed, and those unwritten laws which it is an acknowledged shame to break.... Here each individual is interested not only in his own affairs but in the affairs of the state as well: even those who are mostly occupied with their own business are extremely well-informed on general politics—this is a peculiarity of ours: we do not say that a man who takes no interest in politics is a man who minds his own business; we say that he has no business here at all. We Athenians, in our own persons, take our decisions on policy or submit them to proper discussions: for we do not think that there is an incompatibility between words and deeds; the worst thing is to rush into action before the consequences have been properly debated.... Taking everything together then, I declare that our city is an education to Greece, and I declare that in my opinion each single one of our citizens, in all the manifold aspects of life, is able to show himself the rightful lord and owner of his own person and do this, moreover, with exceptional grace and exceptional versatility. And to show that this is no empty boasting for the present occasion, but real tangible fact, you have only to consider the power which our city possesses and which has been won by those very qualities which I have mentioned.

Q *In the eyes of Pericles, what are the ideals of Athenian democracy? In what ways does Pericles exaggerate his claims? Why would the Athenian passion for debate described by Pericles have been distasteful to the Spartans?*

Source: From THE HISTORY OF THE PELOPONNESIAN WAR by Thucydides, translated by Rex Warner, with an introduction and notes by M. I. Finley (Penguin Classics, 1954, Revised edition 1972). Translation copyright © Rex Warner, 1954. Introduction and Appendices copyright © 1972. Reproduced by permission of Penguin Books, Ltd.

otherwise. The generals could be reelected, enabling individual leaders to play an important political role. Pericles's frequent reelection (fifteen times) as one of the ten generals made him one of the leading politicians between 461 and 429 B.C.E.

All public officials were subject to scrutiny and could be deposed from office if they lost the people's confidence. After 488 B.C.E., the Athenians occasionally made use of a tactic called *ostracism*. Members of the assembly could write on a broken pottery fragment, or *ostrakon* (AHSS-truh-kahn), the name of the person they most disliked or considered most harmful to the *polis*. Frequently, this was someone whose policy, approved at first by the assembly, had failed. A person who received a majority (if at least six thousand votes were cast) was exiled for ten years, although the practical Athenians often recalled a man from exile if they needed him.

Pericles expanded the Athenians' involvement in democracy, which was by now what Athenians had come to call their form of government. Power was in the hands of the people: male citizens voted in the assemblies and served as jurors in the courts. Lower-class citizens were now eligible for public offices formerly closed to them. Pericles also introduced state pay for office-holders, including the widely held jury duty. This meant that even poor citizens could hold public office and afford to participate in public affairs. Nevertheless, although the Athenian system of government was unique in its time in that citizens had equal rights and the people were the government, aristocrats continued to hold the most important offices, and many people, including women, slaves, and foreigners residing in Athens, were not given the same political rights.

Athenian Imperialism The Athenian pursuit of democracy at home was coupled with increasing imperialism abroad as Athens attempted to create both a land empire in Greece and a maritime empire in the Aegean. As we have seen, after 470 B.C.E., Athenian policies had the effect of converting the voluntary allies of the Delian League into the involuntary subjects of an Athenian naval empire. After 462 B.C.E., Athens attempted to expand its empire on the Greek mainland as well. The creation of a land empire, however, overextended the Athenians and involved them in a series of skirmishes with Sparta and its allies known as the First Peloponnesian War (c. 460–445 B.C.E.). After a series of defeats in 445 B.C.E., the land empire of Athens disintegrated, and Athens agreed to a thirty years' peace with the Spartans in the following year. Athens consented to give up most of its land empire, and in return, Sparta recognized the existence of Athens's maritime empire.

While building its land empire, Athens continued its offensive against Persia and at the same time tightened its control over the Delian League. Citing the threat of the Persian fleet in the Aegean, the Athenians moved the treasury of the league from the island of Delos to Athens itself, possibly in 454 B.C.E. Members were, in effect, charged a fee (tribute) for the protection that Athens claimed to provide. Pericles also used the treasury money of the league, without the approval of its members, to build new temples in Athens, an arrogant reminder that the Delian League had become the Athenian empire. The pursuit of imperialism, both in Greece and abroad, took its toll, however. Pericles recognized the dangers of Athenian exhaustion and sought a lull. After peace was made with Sparta in 445 B.C.E., the Athenians had a breathing space in which to beautify Athens and enjoy the fruits of empire, but it was not long before all of Greece was plunged into a new and prolonged struggle.

The Great Peloponnesian War (431– 404 B.C.E.)   In his classic *History of the Peloponnesian War*, the great Greek historian Thucydides (thoo-SID-uh-deez) pointed out that the fundamental, long-range cause of the war that began in 431 B.C.E. was the fear that Athens and its empire inspired in Sparta. The Spartans were especially concerned that Athens would use its superior naval power to weaken Sparta's control of the Peloponnesian League. The immediate causes of the war involved conflicts between Corinth and Athens and between Athens and Megara. When these two allies of Sparta threatened to withdraw from the Peloponnesian League if Sparta did not back them, the Spartans sent an ultimatum to Athens: if the Athenians did not back down in their disputes with Corinth and Megara, it would mean war. The Athenians refused to compromise when Pericles convinced them that if they accepted Sparta's ultimatum, they would be admitting that Sparta was the dominant power in Greece.

At the beginning of the war in 431 B.C.E., both sides believed they had winning strategies. The Athenian plan was based on the navy. The citizens of Attica would be brought in behind the protective walls of Athens and the port of Piraeus (py-REE-uss *or* pih-RAY-uss), while the overseas empire and the navy would keep them supplied (see Map 3.4). Pericles knew perfectly well that the Spartans and their allies could beat the Athenians in pitched battles, which, of course, formed the focus of the Spartan strategy. The Spartans and their allies invaded Attica and ravaged the fields and orchards, hoping that the Athenians would send out their army to fight beyond the walls. But Pericles was convinced that Athens was secure behind its walls and retaliated by sending out naval excursions to ravage the seacoast of the Peloponnesus.

In the second year of the war, however, a plague devastated the crowded city of Athens and wiped out possibly one-third of the population. Pericles himself died the following year (429 B.C.E.), a severe loss to Athens. Dominance now passed to Cleon, leader of the war party, who was opposed by Nicias (NISS-ee-uss), head of a conservative faction that favored peace. Despite the losses from the plague, the Athenians fought on in a struggle that witnessed numerous instances of futile destruction. Cleon achieved some successes for the Athenians; Brasidas (BRASS-i-duss) came to be a dynamic general for the Spartans. At the Battle of Amphipolis (am-FIPP-oh-liss) in 422 B.C.E., both generals were killed, and the new Athenian leader, Nicias, negotiated the Peace of Nicias (421 B.C.E.). Although both parties agreed to keep the peace for fifty years, the truce did not solve the problems that had caused the war in the first place.

A second phase of the war began only six years after the fifty-year truce. This phase was initiated by Alcibiades (al-suh-BY-uh-deez), a nephew of Pericles. Elected

MAP 3.4   The Great Peloponnesian War (431–404 B.C.E.): Alliances and Battles

During much of the fifth century B.C.E., Athens sought to dominate Greece and the Aegean Sea. The Peloponnesian War ultimately saw Sparta and the Peloponnesian League defeat Athens and its allies, culminating in the destruction of Athens's navy and the dismantling of its empire in 404 B.C.E.

to the generalship in 420 B.C.E., he proved to be a poor choice because of his reck-lessness and self-seeking. In 415 B.C.E., he convinced the Athenians to invade the island of Sicily, arguing that its conquest would give the Athenians a strong source of support to carry on a lengthy war. But the expedition was ill-fated. Alcibiades himself was removed from the leadership of the expedition on a charge of profaning the religious mysteries. Rather than stand trial, he fled to Sparta and advised the Spartans on how to defeat Athens by getting help from Persia and assembling a navy with ships and money supplied by the Persians. The Spartans later followed his advice.

In the meantime, the Athenians pursued the Sicilian policy. A "great expe-dition" consisting of five thousand Athenian hoplites was sent out in 415 B.C.E. and reinforced two years later by an even larger army of Athenians and allies.

All was in vain. The Athenians failed to take Syracuse and were captured during their retreat. All of the Athenians were killed or sold into slavery. These heavy losses at Syracuse had immediate domestic repercussions. The democracy was weakened, and an aristocratic oligarchy was temporarily established (411–410 B.C.E.).

Despite the disaster, the Athenians refused to give up; they raised new armies and sent out new fleets. The final crushing blow, however, came in 405 B.C.E., when the Athenian fleet was destroyed at Aegospotami (ee-guh-SPAH-tuh-my) on the Hellespont. Athens was besieged and surrendered the next year. Its walls were torn down, the navy was disbanded, and the Athenian empire was dissolved. The great war was finally over.

The Decline of the Greek States (404–338 B.C.E.)   The next seventy years witnessed continuing warfare among the Greeks, with the leading roles shifting among Sparta, Athens, and a new Greek power, the city-state of Thebes. After the defeat of Athens in 404 B.C.E., the Spartans established their own control over Greece. The Athenian empire was no more. Oligarchies, headed by local ten-man boards in cooperation with Spartan garrisons, were placed in control of the states "liberated" from Athenian imperialism. But oligarchical control proved ineffective, especially in Athens, where the ruling oligarchical faction of thirty, set up by the Spartans, earned the nickname of "Thirty Tyrants" by executing about fifteen hundred of their democratic opponents. This led to a reaction in which the Athenians were able to reestablish their democracy in 403 B.C.E. They also rebuilt their navy and again became an important force in the Greek world.

To maintain its new leadership in Greek affairs, Sparta encouraged a Panhellenic crusade against the Persians as a common enemy. The Persians had taken advantage of the Greeks' internal struggle to reimpose their control over the Greek states in western Asia Minor. But the Persians had learned the lessons of Greek politics. They now offered financial support to Athens, Thebes, and other Greek states to oppose Spartan power within Greece itself, thus beginning a new war, the Corinthian War (395–386 B.C.E.). The war ended when the Greek states, weary of the struggles, accepted the King's Peace, dictated by the Great King of Persia.

The city-state of Thebes, in Boeotia north of Athens, now began to exert its influence. Under their leader Epaminondas (ih-PAM-uh-NAHN-duss), the Thebans dramatically defeated the Spartan army at the Battle of Leuctra (LOOK-tra) in 371 B.C.E. Spartan power declined, to be replaced by the ascendancy of the Thebans. But Theban power was short-lived. After the death of Epaminondas in the Battle of Mantinea (man-tuh-NEE-uh) in 362 B.C.E., the Thebans could no longer dominate Greek politics. And yet the Greek states continued their petty wars, seemingly oblivious to the growing danger to the north, where King Philip II of Macedonia was developing a unified state that would finally end the destructive fratricide of the Greek states by imposing Macedonian authority.

CULTURE AND SOCIETY OF CLASSICAL GREECE

Classical Greece saw a period of remarkable intellectual and cultural growth throughout the Greek world. Historians agree, however, that Periclean Athens was the most important center of Classical Greek culture.

The Writing of History   History as we know it, the systematic analysis of past events, was a Greek creation. Herodotus (huh-ROD-uh-tuss) (c. 484–c. 425 B.C.E.), was the author of *The Persian Wars*, a work commonly regarded as the first real history in Western civilization. The Greek word *historia* (from which we derive our word *history*) means "research" or "investigation," and it is in the opening line of Herodotus's work that we find the first recorded use of the word:

> Here are presented the researches (*historiae*) carried out by Herodotus of Halicarnassus. The purpose is to prevent the traces of human events from being erased by time, and to preserve the fame of the important and remarkable achievements produced by both Greeks and non-Greeks; among the matters covered is, in particular, the cause of the hostilities between Greeks and non-Greeks.[11]

The central theme of Herodotus's work is the conflict between the Greeks and the Persians, which he viewed as a struggle between Greek freedom and Persian despotism. Herodotus traveled widely for his information and was dependent for his sources on what we today would call oral history. Although he was a master storyteller and sometimes included considerable fanciful material, Herodotus was also capable of exhibiting a critical attitude toward the materials he used. Regardless of its weaknesses, Herodotus's history is an important source of information on the Persians and our chief source on the Persian Wars themselves.

Thucydides Thucydides (c. 460–c. 400 B.C.E.) was a far better historian; in fact, modern historians consider him the greatest of the ancient world. Thucydides was an Athenian and a participant in the Peloponnesian War. He had been elected a general, but a defeat in battle led the Athenian assembly to send him into exile. In *History of the Peloponnesian War*, he described his activities:

> I lived through the whole of it, being of an age to understand what was happening, and I put my mind to the subject so as to get an accurate view of it. It happened, too, that I was banished from my country for twenty years after my command at Amphipolis [422 B.C.E.]; I saw what was being done on both sides, particularly on the Peloponnesian side, because of my exile, and this leisure gave me rather exceptional facilities for looking into things.[12]

Unlike Herodotus, Thucydides was not concerned with underlying divine forces or gods as explanatory causal factors in history. He saw war and politics in purely rational terms, as the activities of human beings. He examined the long-range and immediate causes of the Peloponnesian War in a clear, methodical, objective fashion. Thucydides placed much emphasis on accuracy and the precision of his facts. As he stated:

> And with regard to my factual reporting of the events of the war I have made it a principle not to write down the first story that came my way, and not even to be guided by my own general impressions; either I was present myself at the events which I have described or else I heard of them from eyewitnesses whose reports I have checked with as much thoroughness as possible.[13]

Thucydides also provided remarkable insight into the human condition. He believed that human nature was a constant: "It will be enough for me, however, if these words of mine are judged useful by those who want to understand clearly the events which happened in the past and which (human nature being what it is) will, at some time or other and in much the same ways, be repeated in the future."[14] He was not so naive as to believe in an exact repetition of events but felt that political situations recur in similar fashion and that the study of history is of great value in understanding the present.

Greek Drama   Drama as we know it was created by the Greeks and was clearly intended to do more than entertain. It was used to educate citizens and was supported by the state for that reason. Plays were presented in outdoor theaters as part of religious festivals. The form of Greek plays remained rather stable. Three male actors who wore masks acted all the parts. A chorus, also male, spoke the important lines that explained what was going on. Action was very limited because the emphasis was on the story and its meaning.

Aeschylus   The first Greek dramas were tragedies, plays based on the suffering of a hero and usually ending in disaster. Aeschylus (525–456 B.C.E.) is the first tragedian whose plays are known to us. Although he wrote ninety tragedies, only seven have survived. As was customary in Greek tragedy, his plots are simple. The entire drama focuses on a single tragic event and its meaning. Greek tragedies were sometimes presented in a trilogy (a set of three plays) built around a common theme. The only complete trilogy we possess, called the *Oresteia* (uh-res-TY-uh), was composed by Aeschylus. The theme of this trilogy is derived from Homer. Agamemnon, the king of Mycenae, returns a hero after the defeat of Troy. His wife, Clytemnestra, avenges the sacrificial death of her daughter Iphigenia by murdering Agamemnon, who had been responsible for Iphigenia's death. In the second play of the trilogy, Agamemnon's son Orestes (uh-RES-teez) avenges his father by killing his mother. Orestes is now pursued by the avenging Furies, who torment him for killing his mother. Evil acts breed evil acts, and suffering is one's lot, suggests Aeschylus. But Orestes is put on trial and acquitted by Athena, the patron goddess of Athens. Personal vendetta has been eliminated, and law has prevailed.

Sophocles   The most successful writer of Greek tragedies was the Athenian playwright Sophocles (SAHF-uh-kleez) (c. 496–406 B.C.E.), whose background included holding some important public offices in Athens. He won many first prizes in festival competitions for best tragedy, although only 7 of his 123 plays have survived. His most famous play is *Oedipus the King*. The oracle of Apollo foretells that a man (Oedipus) will kill his own father and marry his mother. Despite all attempts at prevention, the tragic events occur. Although it appears that Oedipus suffered the fate determined by the gods, Oedipus also accepts that he himself as a free man must bear responsibility for his actions: "It was Apollo, friends, Apollo, that brought this bitter bitterness, my sorrows to completion. But the hand that struck me was none but my own."[15]

In Sophocles's play *Antigone*, Antigone (an-TIG-uh-nee), the daughter of Oedipus, is caught in a terrible dilemma. Her brother Polynices (pol-uh-NY-seez) has died in an attempt to seize the throne of Thebes, and now the king of Thebes, Antigone's uncle Cleon, has forbidden his burial as a traitor to the state. Should Antigone adhere to her principles and fulfill her obligation to the gods by burying her brother or face death by defying the authority of the state? In the confrontation between Cleon and Antigone, Sophocles bears witness to the complexity of human existence.

Euripides The third outstanding Athenian tragedian, Euripides (uoo-RIP-i-deez) (c. 485–406 B.C.E.), moved beyond his predecessors in creating more realistic characters. His plots also became more complex, reflecting a greater interest in real-life situations. Perhaps the greatest of all his plays is *The Bacchae*, which deals with the introduction of the hysterical rites associated with Dionysus (dy-uh-NY-suss), god of wine. Euripides is often seen as a skeptic who questioned traditional moral and religious values. Euripides was also critical of the traditional view that war was glorious. He portrayed war as brutal and expressed deep compassion for the women and children who suffered from it.

Greek tragedies dealt with universal themes that are still relevant in our day. They probed such problems as the nature of good and evil, the conflict between spiritual values and the demands of the state or family, the rights of the individual, the nature of divine forces, and the nature of human beings. Over and over again, the tragic lesson was repeated: humans were free and yet could operate only within limitations imposed by the gods. The real task was to cultivate the balance and moderation that led to awareness of one's true position. But the pride in human accomplishment and independence is real. As the chorus chants in Sophocles's *Antigone*: "Is there anything more wonderful on earth, our marvelous planet, than the miracle of man?"[16]

Greek Comedy Greek comedy developed later than tragedy. The plays of Aristophanes (ar-is-STAH-fuh-neez) (c. 450–c. 385 B.C.E.), who used both grotesque masks and obscene jokes to entertain the Athenian audience, are examples of Old Comedy, which was used to attack or savagely satirize both politicians and intellectuals. In *The Clouds*, for example, Aristophanes characterizes the philosopher Socrates as the operator of a thought factory where people could learn deceitful ways to handle other people. Later plays give up the element of personal attack and focus on contemporary issues. Of special importance to Aristophanes was his opposition to the Peloponnesian War. *Lysistrata*, performed in 411 B.C.E., at a time when Athens was in serious danger of defeat, has a comic but effective message against the war.

The Arts: The Classical Ideal
The artistic standards established by the Greeks of the Classical period have largely dominated the arts of the Western world. Classical Greek art did not aim at experimentation for experiment's sake but was concerned with expressing eternally true ideals. Its subject matter was basically the human being, expressed harmoniously as an object of great beauty. The Classical style, based on the ideals of reason, moderation, symmetry, balance, and harmony in all things, was meant to civilize the emotions.

In architecture, the most important form was the temple dedicated to a god or goddess. Since Greek religious ceremonies were held at altars in the open air, temples were not used to enclose the faithful, as modern churches are. At the center of Greek temples were walled rooms that housed the statues of deities

© Adam Crowley/Photodisc/Getty Images

The Parthenon. *The arts in Classical Greece were designed to express the eternal ideals of reason, moderation, symmetry, balance, and harmony. In architecture, the most important form was the temple, and the classic example of this kind of architecture is the Parthenon, built between 447 and 432 B.C.E. Located on the Acropolis in Athens, the Parthenon was dedicated to Athena, the patron goddess of the city, but it also served as a shining example of the power and wealth of the Athenian empire.*

and treasuries in which gifts to the gods and goddesses were safeguarded. These central rooms were surrounded by a screen of columns that make Greek temples open structures rather than closed ones. The columns were originally made of wood but changed to limestone in the seventh century and to marble in the fifth century B.C.E. The most significant formal element in Greek temples was the shape and size of the columns in combination with the features above and below the column.

Some of the finest examples of Classical Greek architecture were built in fifth-century Athens. The development of Athenian architecture was aided tremendously by the massive rebuilding program funded from the treasury of the Delian League and instituted almost a half-century after the Persians destroyed Athens in the Persian Wars. Especially important was a series of constructions on the Acropolis begun in 448 B.C.E., which included a monumental entrance gate, a temple to Athena Nike (the Bringer of Victory), and the Erechtheum, a multilevel temple. These temples honored the gods and heroes who protected Athens.

The most famous building, regarded as the greatest example of the Classical Greek temple, was the Parthenon, built between 447 and 432 B.C.E. and consecrated to Athena, the patron goddess of Athens. The Parthenon typifies the principles of Classical architecture: the search for calm, clarity, and freedom from superfluous detail. The individual parts of the temple were constructed in accordance with certain mathematical ratios found in nature. The architects' concern with these laws of proportion is paralleled by the attempt of Greek philosophers to understand the general laws of nature.

Greek sculpture also developed a Classical style that differed significantly from the artificial stiffness of the *kouros* figure of the Archaic Period. Statues of the male nude, the favorite subject of Greek sculptors, now exhibited more relaxed attitudes; their faces were self-assured, their bodies flexible and smooth-muscled. Although the figures possessed natural features that made them lifelike, Greek sculptors sought to achieve not realism but a standard of ideal beauty. Polyclitus (pahl-ee-KLY-tuss), a fifth-century sculptor, wrote a treatise (now lost) on a canon of proportions that he illustrated in a work known as the *Doryphoros* (doh-RIF-uh-rohss). His theory maintained that the use of ideal proportions, based on mathematical ratios found in nature, could produce an ideal human form, beautiful in its perfected and refined features. This search for ideal beauty was the dominant feature of the Classical standard in sculpture.

The Greek Love of Wisdom   *Philosophy* is a Greek word that literally means "love of wisdom." Early Greek philosophers were concerned with the development of critical or rational thought about the nature of the universe and the place of divine forces and souls in it.

Much of early Greek philosophy focused on the attempt to explain the universe on the basis of unifying principles. Thales of Miletus (THAY-leez of my-LEE-tuss), an Ionian Greek who lived around 600 B.C.E., postulated the unity of the universe. All things were linked by water as the basic substance. Another Ionian Greek, Pythagoras (puh-THAG-uh-russ) (c. 580–c. 490 B.C.E.), taught that the essence of the universe could be found in music and number. These early Greek philosophers may have eliminated the role of the gods as they were portrayed in Greek myths, but they did not eliminate divinity itself from the world, tending instead to identify it with the underlying, unchanging forces that govern the universe.

Many Greeks, however, were simply not interested in speculations on the nature of the universe. The **Sophists** (SAHF-ists) were a group of philosophical teachers in the fifth century who rejected such speculation as foolish; they argued that understanding the universe was beyond the reach of the human mind. It was more important for individuals to improve themselves, so the only worthwhile object of study was human behavior. The Sophists were wandering scholars who sold their services as professional teachers to the young men of Greece, especially those of Athens. The Sophists stressed the importance of **rhetoric** (the art of persuasive speaking) in winning debates and swaying an audience, a skill that was especially valuable in democratic Athens. To the Sophists, there was no absolute right or wrong—what was right for one individual might be wrong for another. True wisdom consisted of being able to perceive one's own good and to pursue its acquisition. Many people, however, viewed the Sophists as a threat to the traditional values of society and especially dangerous to the values of young people.

In Classical Greece, Athens became the foremost intellectual and artistic center. Its reputation is perhaps strongest of all in philosophy. After all, Socrates, Plato, and Aristotle raised basic questions that have been debated for more than two thousand years; these are still largely the same philosophical questions we wrestle with today.

Socrates   Socrates (SAHK-ruh-teez) (469–399 B.C.E.) left no writings, but we know about him from his pupils, especially his most famous one, Plato. By occupation, Socrates was a stonemason, but his true love was philosophy. He taught a number of pupils, but not for pay, because he believed that the goal of education was only to improve the individual. He made use of a teaching method that is still known by his name. The **Socratic method** employs a question-and-answer technique to lead pupils to see things for themselves using their own reason. Socrates believed that all real knowledge is within each person; only critical examination was needed to call it forth. This was the real task of philosophy, since "the unexamined life is not worth living."

Socrates's questioning of authority and public demonstrations of others' lack of knowledge led him into trouble. Athens had had a tradition of free thought and inquiry, but its defeat in the Peloponnesian War created an environment intolerant of open debate and soul-searching. Socrates was accused and convicted of corrupting the youth of Athens by his teaching, and an Athenian jury sentenced him to death.

Plato   One of Socrates's disciples was Plato (PLAY-toh) (c. 429–347 B.C.E.), considered by many scholars the greatest philosopher of Western civilization. Unlike his master Socrates, who wrote nothing, Plato wrote a great deal. He was fascinated with the question of reality: How do we know what is real?

According to Plato, a higher world of eternal, unchanging Ideas or Forms has always existed. To know these Forms is to know truth. These ideal Forms constitute reality and can be apprehended only by a trained mind, which, of course, is the goal of philosophy. The objects that we perceive with our senses are simply reflections of the ideal Forms. Hence, they are shadows, while reality is found in the Forms themselves.

Plato's ideas of government were set out in a dialogue titled *The Republic*. Based on his experience in Athens, Plato had come to distrust the workings of democracy. It was obvious to him that individuals could not attain an ethical life unless they lived in a just and rational state. This insight led him to construct an ideal state in which the population was divided into three basic groups. At the top was an upper class, a ruling elite, the famous philosopher-kings: "Unless either philosophers become kings in their countries or those who are now called kings and rulers come to be sufficiently inspired with a genuine desire for wisdom; unless, that is to say, political power and philosophy meet together ... there can be no rest from troubles ... for states, nor yet, as I believe, for all mankind."[17] The second group consisted of the courageous; they would be the warriors who protected the society. All the rest made up the masses, essentially people driven not by wisdom or courage but by desire. They would be the producers of society—the artisans, tradesmen, and farmers.

In Plato's ideal state, each group fulfilled its assigned role, creating a society that functioned harmoniously. The needs of the community, rather than the happiness of the individual, were Plato's concern, and he focused on the need for the guardians or rulers, above all, to be removed from any concerns for wealth or prestige so that they could strive for what was best for the community. To rid the guardians of these desires, Plato urged that they live together, forgoing both private property and family life. Plato believed that women, too, could be rulers; in this he departed radically from the actual practices of the Greek states.

Aristotle   Plato established a school at Athens known as the Academy. One of his pupils, who studied there for twenty years, was Aristotle (AR-iss-tot-ul) (384–322 B.C.E.), who later became a tutor to Alexander the Great. Aristotle did not accept Plato's theory of ideal Forms. He believed that by examining individual objects, we can perceive their form and arrive at universal principles, but they do not exist as a separate higher world of reality beyond material things; rather they are a part of things themselves. Aristotle's interests, then, lay in analyzing and classifying things based on thorough research and investigation. His interests were wide-ranging, and he wrote treatises on an enormous number of subjects: ethics, logic, politics, poetry, astronomy, geology, biology, and physics.

Like Plato, Aristotle wished for an effective form of government that would rationally direct human affairs. Unlike Plato, he did not seek an ideal state based on the embodiment of an ideal Form of justice; he tried to find the best form of government by a rational examination of existing governments. For his *Politics*, Aristotle examined the constitutions of 158 states and arrived at general categories for organizing governments. He identified three good forms of government: monarchy, aristocracy, and constitutional government. But based on his examination, he warned that monarchy can easily turn into tyranny, aristocracy into oligarchy, and constitutional government into radical democracy or anarchy. He favored constitutional government as the best form for most people.

Aristotle's philosophical and political ideas played an enormous role in the development of Western thought during the Middle Ages (see Chapter 9). So did his ideas on women. Aristotle believed that marriage was meant to provide mutual comfort between man and woman and contributed to the overall happiness of a community: "The community needs both male and female excellences or it can only be half-blessed." Nevertheless, Aristotle maintained that women were biologically inferior to men: "A woman is, as it were, an infertile male. She is female in fact on account of a kind of inadequacy." Therefore, according to Aristotle, women must be subordinated to men, not only in the community but also in marriage: "The association between husband and wife is clearly an aristocracy. The man rules by virtue of merit, and in the sphere that is his by right; but he hands over to his wife such matters as are suitable for her."[18]

Greek Religion   Greek religion was intricately connected to every aspect of daily life; it was both social and practical. Public festivals, which originated from religious practices, served specific functions: boys were prepared to be warriors, girls to be mothers. Since religion was related to every aspect of life, citizens had to have a proper attitude toward the gods. Religion was a civic cult necessary for the well-being of the state. Temples dedicated to a god or goddess were the major buildings of Greek society.

Homer gave an account of the gods that provided a definite structure to Greek religion. Over a period of time, most Greeks came to accept a common religion based on twelve chief gods who supposedly lived on Mount Olympus, the highest mountain in Greece. Among the twelve were Zeus (ZOOSS), the chief deity and father of the gods; Athena, goddess of wisdom and crafts; Apollo, god of the sun and poetry; Aphrodite (af-fruh-DY-tee), goddess of love; and Poseidon (puh-SY-duhn), brother of Zeus and god of the seas and earthquakes.

The twelve Olympian gods were common to all Greeks, who thus shared a basic polytheistic religion. Each *polis* usually singled out one of the twelve Olympians as a guardian deity of its community. Athena was the patron goddess of Athens, for example. Because it was desirable to have the gods look favorably on one's activities, ritual assumed enormous proportions in Greek religion. Prayers were often combined with gifts to the gods based on the principle "I give so that you, the gods, will give in return." Ritual meant sacrifices, whether of animals or agricultural products. Animal victims were burned on an altar in front of a temple or on a small altar in front of a home.

As another practical side of Greek religion, Greeks wanted to know the will of the gods. The most famous method of divining the will of the gods was the use of the *oracle*, a sacred shrine dedicated to a god or goddess who revealed the future. The most famous was the oracle of Apollo at Delphi, located on the side of Mount Parnassus, overlooking the Gulf of Corinth. At Delphi, a priestess listened to questions while in a state of ecstasy that was believed to be induced by Apollo. The priests interpreted her responses and gave them in verse form to the person asking the questions. Both representatives of states and individuals traveled to Delphi to consult the oracle of Apollo. States might inquire whether they should undertake a military expedition; individuals might raise such questions as "Heracleidas asks the god whether he will have off-spring from the wife he has now." Responses were often enigmatic and could be interpreted in more than one way. Croesus (KREE-suss), the king of Lydia in Asia Minor who was known for his incredible wealth, sent messengers to the oracle at Delphi, asking whether he should go to war with the Persians. The oracle replied that if Croesus attacked the Persians, a mighty empire would be destroyed. Overjoyed to hear these words, Croesus made war on the Persians but was crushed by his enemy. A mighty empire was indeed destroyed —Croesus's own.

Festivals also developed as a way to honor the gods and goddesses. Some of these (the Panhellenic celebrations) were important to all Greeks and were held at special locations, such as those dedicated to the worship of Zeus at Olympia, to Poseidon at the Isthmus of Corinth, and to Apollo at Delphi. The great festivals incorporated numerous events in honor of the gods, including athletic competitions to which all Greeks were invited.

According to tradition, such athletic games were first held at the Olympic festival in 776 B.C.E. and then held every four years thereafter to honor Zeus. Initially, the Olympic contests consisted of foot races and wrestling, but later boxing, javelin throwing, and various other contests were added. Competitions were always between individuals, not groups. The Greeks regarded winning athletes as great heroes and often rewarded them with parades, as well as money and free rent for life.

Olympic games were not without danger to the participants. Athletes competed in the nude, and rules were rather relaxed. Wrestlers, for example, were allowed to gouge the eyes of their competitors and even pick them up and drop them head first onto a hard surface. Boxers wrapped their hands and forearms with heavy leather thongs to make their blows more damaging. Occasionally, athletes were killed during the games. Given the animosity that often existed between city-states in ancient Greece, the deaths were not always accidental.

Life in Classical Athens   The Greek city-state was, above all, a male community: only adult male citizens took part in public life. In Athens, this meant the exclusion of women, slaves, and foreign residents, or roughly 85 percent of the total population of Attica. In the fifth century, Athens had the largest population of all the Greek city-states. There were probably 150,000 citizens, of whom about 43,000 were adult males who exercised political power. Resident foreigners, known as **metics**, numbered about 35,000 and received the protection of the laws, but they were also subject to some of the responsibilities of citizens, namely, military service and the funding of festivals. The remaining social group, the slaves, numbered around 100,000.

Slavery and the Economy   Slavery was a common institution in the ancient world. Economic necessity dictated the desirability of owning at least one slave, although the very poor in Athens did not own any. A soldier on campaign usually took along one slave to carry his armor. The really wealthy might own large numbers of slaves, but those who did usually employed them in industry. Most often slaves in Athens performed domestic tasks as cooks and maids or worked in the fields. Few peasants could afford more than one or two. Other slaves worked as unskilled or skilled laborers. Slaves who worked in public construction were paid the same as metics or citizens.

The Athenian economy was largely agricultural but highly diversified. Athenian farmers grew grains, vegetables, and fruit for local consumption; cultivated vines and olives for wine and olive oil, which were exportable products; and raised sheep and goats for wool and milk products. Given the size of the population in Attica and the lack of abundant fertile land, Athens had to import between 50 and 80 percent of its grain, a staple in the Athenian diet. Trade was thus very important to the Athenian economy. The building of the port at Piraeus and the Long Walls (a series of defensive walls 41 miles long connecting Athens and Piraeus) created the physical conditions that made Athens the leading trade center in the fifth-century Greek world.

Athens did not have large numbers of artisans, but those it had were important to the economy. Athens was the chief producer of high-quality painted pottery in the fifth century. Other crafts had moved beyond the small workshop into the factory through the use of slave labor.

A Simple Lifestyle   The Athenian lifestyle was basically simple. Athenian houses were furnished with necessities bought from artisans, such as beds, couches, tables, chests, pottery, stools, baskets, and cooking utensils. Wives and slaves made clothes and blankets at home. The Athenian diet was rather plain. Basic foods included barley, wheat, millet, lentils, grapes, figs, olives, almonds, bread made at home, vegetables, eggs, fish, cheese, and chicken. Olive oil was widely used, not only for eating but also for lighting lamps and for rubbing on the body after washing and exercise. Owners of country houses kept animals for reasons other than their flesh: oxen for plowing, sheep for wool, and goats for milk and cheese. Meat was consumed only on special occasions, such as festivals, when animals were sacrificed, cooked, and then eaten.

Family and Relationships   The family was an important institution in ancient Athens. It was composed of husband, wife, and children (a nuclear family), although other dependent relatives and slaves were regarded as part of the family because of its economic unity. The family's primary social function was to produce new citizens. Strict laws of the fifth century had stipulated that a citizen must be the offspring of a legally acknowledged marriage between two Athenian citizens.

Women were citizens who could participate in most religious cults and festivals but were otherwise excluded from public life. They could not own property beyond personal items and always had a male guardian: if unmarried, a father or male relative; if married, a husband; if widowed, a son or male relative.

The function of the Athenian woman as wife was very clear. Her foremost obligation was to bear children, especially male children who would preserve the family line. The marriage formula that Athenians used put it succinctly: "I give this woman for the procreation of legitimate children." A wife was also expected to take care of her family and her house, either doing the household work herself or supervising the slaves who did the actual work.

Women were kept under strict control. Since they were married at fourteen or fifteen, they were taught about their responsibilities at an early age. Although many managed to learn to read and play musical instruments, they were often cut off from any formal education. And women were expected to remain at home out of sight unless they attended funerals or festivals. If they left the house, they were to be accompanied.

Women in Athens served males in other ways as well. Prostitution flourished in Classical Athens. Most female prostitutes were slaves in brothels run as a business or trade by an Athenian citizen. Another class of prostitutes in Athenian society occupied a more favorable position; these more refined courtesans were known as **hetairai** (huh-TY-ree), literally "female companions." Usually ex-slaves or foreigners, these women were more sophisticated than ordinary prostitutes and were known for their intellectual and musical achievements as well as their physical ones. Athenian males continued the aristocratic practice of the *symposium*, a sophisticated drinking party, where *hetairai* were often present. Symposia were held in the men's dining rooms, and wives were not present. *Hetairai* danced, played musical instruments, and provided entertainment, including sex. Some *hetairai* achieved fortune and considerable renown. Aspasia was the most famous. A friend of Socrates and known for her learning, she was the mistress of Pericles and eventually became his wife.

Male homosexuality was also a prominent feature of Classical Athens. It was widely practiced and tolerated. Athenian law disenfranchised a citizen who had prostituted his body to another male, but nothing was done to males who engaged in homosexual love with male prostitutes or other adult males for love or pleasure. The law did not eliminate male prostitution but ensured that male prostitutes would be foreigners, not Athenian citizens.

The Greek homosexual ideal was a relationship between a mature man and a young male. It is likely that this was primarily an aristocratic ideal. While the relationship was frequently physical, the Greeks also viewed it as educational. The older male (the "lover") won the love of his "beloved" by his value as a teacher

Women in Athens and Sparta

In Classical Athens, a woman's place was in the home. She had two major responsibilities as a wife—bearing and raising children and managing the household. In the first selection, from a dialogue on estate management, Xenophon (ZEN-uh-fuhn) relates the instructions of an Athenian to his new wife. Although women in Sparta had the same responsibilities as women in Athens, they assumed somewhat different roles as a result of the Spartan lifestyle. The second, third, and fourth selections demonstrate these differences as seen in the accounts of three ancient Greek writers.

Xenophon, *Oeconomicus*

[Ischomachus addresses his new wife:] For it seems to me, dear, that the gods with great discernment have coupled together male and female, as they are called, chiefly in order that they may form a perfect partnership in mutual service. For, in the first place that the various species of living creatures may not fail, they are joined in wedlock for the production of children. Secondly, offspring to support them in old age is provided by this union, to human beings, at any rate. Thirdly, human beings live not in the open air, like beasts, but obviously need shelter. Nevertheless, those who mean to win stores to fill the covered place, have need of someone to work at the open-air occupations; since plowing, sowing, planting and grazing are all such open-air employments; and these supply the needful food.... For he made the man's body and

mind more capable of enduring cold and heat, and journeys and campaigns; and therefore imposed on him the outdoor tasks. To the woman, since he had made her body less capable of such endurance, I take it that God has assigned the indoor tasks. And knowing that he had created in the woman and had imposed on her the nourishment of the infants, he meted out to her a larger portion of affection for newborn babes than to the man....

Your duty will be to remain indoors and send out those servants whose work is outside, and superintend those who are to work indoors, and to receive the incomings, and distribute so much of them as must be spent, and watch over so much as is to be kept in store, and take care that the sum laid by for a year be not spent in a month. And when wool is brought to you, you must see that cloaks are made for those that want them. You must see too that the dry corn is in good condition for making food. One of the duties that fall to you, however, will perhaps seem rather thankless: you will have to see that any servant who is ill is cared for.

Xenophon, *Constitution of the Spartans*

First, to begin at the beginning, I will start with the begetting of children. Elsewhere those girls who are going to have children and are considered to have been well brought up are nourished with the plainest diet which is practicable and the smallest amount of luxury good possible; wine is certainly not allowed them at all, or only if well diluted. Just as the majority of craftsmen are sedentary, the other Greeks expect their girls to sit quietly and work wool. But how can one expect girls brought up like this to give birth to healthy babies? Lycurgus considered slave girls quite adequate to produce clothing, and thought that for free women the most important job was to bear children. In the first place, therefore, he prescribed physical training for the female sex no less than for the male; and next, just as for men, he arranged competitions of racing and strength for women also, thinking that if both parents were strong their children would be more robust.

Aristotle, *Politics*

Now, this license of the [Spartan] women, from the earliest times, was to be expected. For the men were absent from home for long periods of time on military expeditions.... And nearly two-fifths of the whole country is in the hands of women, both because there have been numerous heiresses, and because large dowries are customary. And yet it would have been better to have regulated them, and given none at all or small or even moderate ones. But at present it is possible for a man to give an inheritance to whomever he chooses.

Plutarch, *Lycurgus*

Since Lycurgus regarded education as the most important and finest duty of the legislator, he began at the earliest stage by looking at matters relating to marriages and births.... For he exercised the girls' bodies with races and wrestling and discus and javelin throwing, so that the embryos formed in them would have a strong start in strong bodies and develop better, and they would undergo their pregnancies with vigor and would cope well and easily with childbirth. He got rid of daintiness and sheltered upbringing and effeminacy of all kinds, by accustoming the girls no less than the young men to walking naked in processions and dancing and singing at certain festivals, when young men were present and watching.... The nudity of the girls had nothing disgraceful in it for modesty was present and immorality absent, but rather it made them accustomed to simplicity and enthusiastic as to physical fitness, and gave the female sex a taste of noble spirit, in as much as they too had a share in valor and ambition.

Q *In what ways were the lifestyles of Athenian and Spartan women the same? In what ways were they different? How did the Athenian and Spartan views of the world shape their conceptions of gender and gender roles, and why were those conceptions different?*

Sources: Xenophon, *Oeconomicus*. Reprinted by permission of the publishers and the Trustees of the Loeb Classical Library from *Xenophon, Memorabilia and Oeconomicus*, Loeb Classical Library Vol. IV, translated by E.C. Marchant and O.J. Todd, Cambridge, Mass.: Harvard University Press, Copyright © 1930, by the President and Fellows of Harvard College. The Loeb Classical Library is a registered trademark of the President and Fellows of Harvard College. Xenophon, *Constitution of the Spartans*, Aristotle, *Politics*, and Plutarch, *Lycurgus*. From *Ancient Greece: Social and Historical Documents from Archaic Times to the Death of Socrates*. Edited by Matthew Dillon and Lynda Garland. London: Routledge, 1994, pp. 393–95. Copyright © 1994 Mathew Dillon and Lynda Garland.

and by the devotion he demonstrated in training his charge. In a sense, this love relationship was seen as a way of initiating young males into the male world of political and military dominance. The Greeks did not feel that the coexistence of homosexual and heterosexual predilections created any special problems for individuals or their society.

CHRONOLOGIES

ARCHAIC GREECE: SPARTA

c. 730–710 B.C.	Conquest of Messenia
c. 560–550 B.C.	Beginning of Peloponnesian League

ARCHAIC GREECE: ATHENS

594–593 B.C.	Solon's reforms
c. 560–556 and 546–527 B.C.	Tyranny of Pisistratus
510 B.C.	Deposition of Hippias—end of tyranny
c. 508–501 B.C.	Cleisthenes' reforms

THE PERSIAN WARS

By 540s B.C.	Persian control of Greek cities in south-western Asia Minor
499–494 B.C.	Rebellion of Greek cities in Asia Minor
490 B.C.	Battle of Marathon
480–479 B.C.	Xerxes invades Greece
480 B.C.	Battles of Thermopylae and Salamis
479 B.C.	Battles of Plataea and Mycale

THE GREAT PELOPONNESIAN WAR

431 B.C.	Invasion of Attica
422 B.C.	Battle of Amphipolis
415–413 B.C.	Athenian invasion of Sicily
405 B.C.	Battle of Aegospotami
404 B.C.	Surrender of Athens

4

THE HELLENISTIC WORLD

Roman statuette of Alexander the Great wearing a helmet

Louvre, Paris//© Réunion des Musées Nationaux/Art Resource, NY

CHAPTER OUTLINE

• Macedonia and the Conquests of Alexander • The World of the Hellenistic Kingdoms • Hellenistic Society • Culture in the Hellenistic World • Religion in the Hellenistic World

MACEDONIA AND THE CONQUESTS OF ALEXANDER

While the Greek city-states were continuing their fratricidal warfare, to their north a new and ultimately powerful kingdom was emerging in its own right. The Macedonians were probably not Greek; scholars are still unsure whether the Macedonian language was an archaic dialect of Greek or an altogether separate language. The Greeks certainly viewed the Macedonians as barbarians but did allow them to participate as "Greeks" in the Olympic games beginning in the fifth century B.C.E.

Unlike the Greeks, the Macedonians were mostly rural folk and were organized in tribes, not city-states. Not until the end of the fifth century B.C.E., during the reign of King Archelaus (c. 413–399 B.C.E.) did Macedonia emerge as an important kingdom. But his reign was followed by decades of repeated foreign invasions and internal strife until King Philip II (359–336 B.C.E.) took control and turned Macedonia into the chief power of the Greek world.

Philip and the Conquest of Greece   Philip had spent three years as a hostage in Thebes, where he had gained a great admiration for Greek culture and absorbed the latest Greek military developments. Philip understood the importance of having an efficient army if Macedonia was to be a strong state. He used Macedonian countrymen, sturdy peasants and shepherds, as the core of his phalanx of infantrymen. From the gold mines of Mount Pangaeus, he obtained the wealth to pay these soldiers and establish a standing professional army that could fight year round.

Philip also instituted military reforms that transformed Macedonia into a major military power. He created a new phalanx of infantrymen who were more lightly armed than Greek hoplites; each carried a smaller shield and a shorter sword. Instead, the Macedonian infantryman's chief weapon was a long thrusting spear—18 feet in length, or twice as long as the Greek hoplite's spear. In this way, Macedonian infantrymen could impale an opposing hoplite force before the hoplites could even reach them. The Macedonian phalanx was supported by strong cavalry contingents that helped to break the opposing line of battle and create disorder in the enemy's ranks. Philip also recognized the value of technological improvements in warfare and created a group of engineers to design new catapults to destroy an enemy's fortifications. Finally, Philip strengthened the bonds between the army and its leaders. Even the king shared directly in the dangers of battle, as is evident from his many wounds. Philip's new army defeated the Illyrians to the west and the Thracians to the north and east and was then drawn into the Greeks' interstate conflicts.

The Greeks had mixed reactions to Philip's growing strength. Many Athenians, especially the orator Demosthenes (duh-MAHSS-thuh-neez), came to have a strong distrust of the Macedonian leader's intentions. Demosthenes delivered a series of orations, known as the *Philippics*, in which he portrayed Philip as ruthless, deceitful, treacherous, and barbaric and called on the Athenians to oppose him. Other Athenians, such as Isocrates (eye-SAHK-ruh-teez), a teacher of rhetoric, viewed Philip as a savior who would rescue the Greeks from themselves by uniting them and organizing the entire Greek world in a crusade against the common enemy, the Persians.

Demosthenes's repeated calls for action, combined with Philip's rapid expansion, finally spurred Athens into action. Allied with Thebes and some smaller states, Athens fought the Macedonians at the Battle of Chaeronea (ker-uh-NEE-uh), near Thebes, in 338 B.C.E. The Macedonian army crushed the Greek allies, and Philip was now free to consolidate his control over the Greek peninsula. While Thebes was punished severely, Athens was treated leniently out of respect for its past and expected cooperation in the future. The Greek states were joined together in an alliance that we call the Corinthian League because they met at Corinth. All members took an oath of loyalty: "I swear by Zeus, Earth, Sun, Poseidon, Athena, Ares, and all the gods and goddesses. I will abide by the peace, and I will not break the agreements with Philip the Macedonian, nor will I take up arms with hostile intent against any one of those who abide by the oaths either by land or by sea."[1]

Though based on the principle of self-governing, independent states, the league did have an army and a council. Philip of Macedon was recognized as *hegemon* (HEJ-uh-mun) (leader) of the league and its army. Although Philip allowed the Greek city-states autonomy in domestic affairs, he retained the general direction of their foreign affairs. Many Greeks still objected to being subject to the less civilized master from the north, but Philip insisted that the Greek states end their bitter rivalries and cooperate with him in a war against Persia.

Before Philip could undertake his invasion of Asia, however, he was assassinated, leaving the task to his son Alexander. Although Alexander justly deserves credit for the destruction of the Persian Empire, it was Philip who paved the way for the conquest. He had unified Macedonia, created a powerful military machine, and subdued the Greeks.

Alexander the Great

Alexander was only twenty when he became king of Macedonia. In the next twelve years, he achieved so much that he has ever since been called Alexander the Great. The illustrious conqueror was in many ways groomed for kingship by his father, who had taken Alexander along on military campaigns and at the important Battle of Chaeronea had given him control of the cavalry. After his father's assassination, Alexander moved quickly to assert his authority, securing the Macedonian frontiers and smothering a rebellion in Greece by sacking the city of Thebes, killing most of its male inhabitants, and selling the women and children into slavery. He then turned to his father's dream, the invasion of the Persian Empire.

Alexander's Conquests   There is no doubt that Alexander was taking a chance in attacking the Persian Empire. Although weakened in some respects, it was still a strong state. Alexander's fleet was inferior to the Persian navy, which drew its ships from the Phoenicians and other coastal peoples of western Asia, and his finances were shaky at best. His army would have to live off the countryside and win quick victories to gain the resources needed to continue the struggle. In the spring of 334 B.C.E., Alexander entered Asia Minor with an army of some 37,000 men. About half were Macedonians, the rest Greeks and other allies. The cavalry, which would play an important role as a strike force, numbered about five thousand. Architects, engineers, historians, and scientists accompanied the army, a clear indication of Alexander's grand vision and positive expectations at the beginning of his campaign.

His first confrontation with the Persians, at the Granicus River in 334 B.C.E. (see Map 4.1), nearly cost him his life but resulted in a major victory. By the following spring, the entire western half of Asia Minor was in Alexander's hands, and the Ionian Greek cities of southwestern Asia Minor had been "liberated" from the Persian oppressor. Not all of them wished to be liberated, however, and many regarded Alexander simply as their new master.

Meanwhile, the Persian king, Darius III, mobilized his forces to stop Alexander's army. Although the Persian troops outnumbered Alexander's, the Battle of Issus (ISS-uss) was fought on a narrow field that canceled the advantage of superior numbers and resulted in another Macedonian success. (The Persian cause was not helped when Darius made a spectacular exit from the battlefield before it was even clear who would be victorious.) After his victory at Issus in 333 B.C.E., Alexander laid siege to the port cities of Tyre and Gaza to prevent Persian control of the sea. The siege of Tyre provides an example of Alexander's military and engineering skills. Tyre stood on an island just off the coast. Lacking adequate naval resources to attack the city from the sea,

© Cengage Learning 2012

MAP 4.1 The Conquests of Alexander the Great

In just twelve years, Alexander the Great conquered vast territories. Dominating lands from west of the Nile to east of the Indus, he brought the Persian Empire, Egypt, and much of the Middle East under his control and laid the foundations for the Hellenistic world.

Alexander built a causeway from the coast to the city, a project that took six months but enabled him to use his siege machines against the city. After seven months, Tyre finally fell to Alexander's forces. Six thousand of the inhabitants were killed and 30,000 sold into slavery.

Egypt surrendered without a fight, and by the winter of 332 B.C.E., Syria, Palestine, and Egypt were under Alexander's domination. He took the traditional title of pharaoh of Egypt and was hailed as the "son of Amon," to the Greeks the equivalent of being called the son of Zeus. Alexander also built the first of a series of cities named after him (Alexandria) as the Greek administrative capital of Egypt. It became (and remains today) one of the most important cities in the Mediterranean world.

In the meantime, Darius indicated his willingness to make a peace settlement, offering to cede all land west of the Euphrates River to Alexander. Alexander refused and renewed the offensive. He moved now into the territory of the ancient Mesopotamian kingdoms and fought a decisive battle with the Persians at Gaugamela (gaw-guh-MEE-luh) in the summer of 331 B.C.E. At Gaugamela, Alexander's men were clearly outnumbered by the Persian forces, which had established the battle site on a broad, open plain where their war chariots could maneuver to best advantage. Alexander was able to break through the center of the Persian line with his heavy cavalry, followed by the infantry. The battle turned into a rout, although Darius managed to escape. After his victory, Alexander entered Babylon and then proceeded to the Persian capitals at Susa and Persepolis, where he acquired the Persian treasuries and took possession of vast quantities of gold and silver.

By 330 B.C.E., Alexander was again on the march. After Darius was killed by one of his own men, Alexander took the title and office of the Great King of the Persians. But he was not content to rest with the spoils of the Persian Empire. Over the next three years, he moved east and northeast, as far as modern Pakistan. By the summer of 327 B.C.E., he had entered India, which at that time was divided into a number of warring states. In 326 B.C.E., Alexander and his armies arrived in the plains of northwestern India. At the Battle of the Hydaspes (hy-DAS-peez) River, Alexander won a brutally fought battle. When Alexander made clear his determination to march east to conquer more of India, his soldiers, weary of campaigning year after year, mutinied and refused to go further. Alexander surrendered to their demands and agreed to return, leading his troops through southern Persia across the Gedrosian Desert, where they suffered heavy losses from appalling desert conditions. Alexander and the remnants of his army went to Susa and then Babylon, where he planned more campaigns. But in June 323 B.C.E., weakened from wounds, fever, and probably excessive alcohol, he died at the young age of thirty-two.

Alexander's Military Success   Historians, both ancient and modern, generally agree that Alexander was an outstanding military leader. How do they explain his success? For one thing, Alexander demonstrated superb tactical skills. His success in his numerous battles was based to a large extent on his ability to assess the topography of the battlefield and make plans that took advantage of the strengths and weaknesses of his enemy's forces as well as his own. Within hours after arriving at a potential battlefield, Alexander was able to plan troop formations and tactics appropriate to the landscape on which he was fighting. Then, too, if something went wrong after the battle began, he was quick to adapt to changing circumstances.

Alexander pushed his troops mercilessly, often catching his enemy by surprise as a result of a quick march. But he also maintained a personal interest in his troops and for the most part, until the campaign in India, kept their intense loyalty. His willingness to lead by personal example inspired his troops, although it often led to risks that endangered his own life. He did not hesitate to lead cavalry attacks into the ranks of his enemies. In India, he was injured when he led his troops up a ladder in their assault on the Mallians. He was, in fact, wounded eight times in battle.

Alexander also paid attention to details. All aspects of his campaigns were well organized, from obtaining supplies and reinforcements to doing advanced planning for excursions into little known territories. As the number of Macedonian troops declined from deaths in battle or from being assigned to occupy new conquests, Alexander recruited Persian troops. He also took advantage of his father's technical developments and made good use of siege warfare.

But there is also an uglier side to Alexander's military greatness. Did he become accustomed, as some historians have recently argued, to killing his enemies on a scale that far outstripped what was usual in Greek and Macedonian warfare?

The Legacy: Was Alexander Great?   Alexander is one of the most puzzling significant figures in history. Historians relying on the same sources give vastly different pictures of him. For some, his military ability, extensive conquests, and creation of a new empire alone justify calling him Alexander the Great. Other historians also praise Alexander's love of Greek culture and his intellectual brilliance, especially in matters of warfare. In the lands that he conquered, Alexander attempted to fuse the Macedonians, Greeks, and Persians into a new ruling class. Did he do this because he was an idealistic visionary who believed in a concept of universal humanity, as some suggest? Or was he merely trying to bolster his power and create an autocratic monarchy?

Those historians who see Alexander as aspiring to autocratic monarchy present a very different portrait of him as a ruthless Machiavellian. One has titled his biography *Alexander the Great Failure*. These critics ask whether a man who slaughtered indigenous peoples, who risked the lives of his soldiers for his own selfish reasons, whose fierce temper led him to kill his friends, and whose neglect of administrative duties weakened his kingdom can really be called great.

But how did Alexander view himself? We know that he sought to imitate Achilles, the warrior-hero of Homer's *Iliad*. Alexander kept a copy of the *Iliad*—and a dagger—under his pillow. He also claimed to be descended from Heracles, the Greek hero who came to be worshiped as a god. No doubt Alexander aspired to divine honors; as pharaoh of Egypt, he became a living god according to Egyptian tradition and at one point even sent instructions to the Greek cities to "vote him a god."

Regardless of his ideals, motives, or views about himself, one fact stands out: Alexander created a new age, the Hellenistic era. The word *Hellenistic* is derived from a Greek word meaning "to imitate Greeks." It is an appropriate way to describe an age that saw the extension of the Greek language and ideas to the non-Greek world of the ancient Near East. Alexander's destruction of the Persian monarchy had extended Greco-Macedonian rule over an enormous area. It created opportunities for Greek engineers, intellectuals, merchants, soldiers, and administrators. While the Greeks on the mainland might remain committed to the ideals of their city-states, those who followed Alexander and his successors participated in a new political unity based on the principle of monarchy. Alexander had transformed his army from a Macedonian force into an international one, owing loyalty only to himself. His successors used force to establish military monarchies that dominated the Hellenistic world after his death. Autocratic power, based on military strength and pretensions of divine rule, became a regular feature of those Hellenistic monarchies and was part of Alexander's political legacy to the Hellenistic world. His vision of empire no doubt inspired the Romans, who were, of course, Alexander's real heirs.

But Alexander also left a cultural legacy. As a result of his conquests, Greek language, art, architecture, and literature spread throughout the Near East. The urban centers of the Hellenistic Age, many founded by Alexander and his successors, became springboards for the diffusion of Greek culture. Alexander had established a number of cities and military colonies named Alexandria to guard strategic points and supervise wide areas. Most of the settlers were Greek mercenaries. It has been estimated that in the course of his campaigns, Alexander summoned some 60,000 to 65,000 additional mercenaries from Greece, at least 36,000 of whom took up residence in the garrisons and new cities. While the Greeks spread their culture in the Near East, they were also inevitably influenced by eastern ways. Thus, Alexander's legacy became one of the hallmarks of the Hellenistic world: the clash and fusion of different cultures.

THE WORLD OF THE HELLENISTIC KINGDOMS

The united empire that Alexander created by his conquests disintegrated after his death. All too soon, Macedonian military leaders were engaged in a struggle for power. By 301 B.C.E., any hope of unity was dead.

Hellenistic Monarchies   Eventually, four Hellenistic kingdoms emerged as the successors to Alexander: Macedonia under the Antigonid (an-TIG-uh-nid) dynasty, Syria and the east under the Seleucids (suh-LOO-sids), the Attalid (AT-uh-lid) kingdom of Pergamum (PURR-guh-mum), and Egypt under the Ptolemies (TAHL-uh-meez) (see Map 4.2).

Antigonid Kingdom of Macedonia   In Macedonia, the struggles for power led to the extermination of Alexander the Great's dynasty. Not until 276 B.C.E. did Antigonus Gonatus (an-TIG-oh-nuss guh-NAH-tuss), the grandson of one of Alexander's generals, succeed in establishing the Antigonid dynasty as rulers of Macedonia. The Antigonids viewed control of Greece as essential to their power but did not see outright conquest as necessary. Macedonia was, of course, also important to the Greeks. As one ancient commentator noted, "It is in the interest

MAP 4.2 The World of the Hellenistic Kingdoms

Alexander died unexpectedly at the age of thirty-two and did not designate a successor. Upon his death, his generals struggled for power, eventually establishing four monarchies that spread Hellenistic culture and fostered trade and economic development.

of the Greeks that the Macedonian dominion should be humbled for long, but by no means that it should be destroyed. For in that case … [the Macedonians] would very soon experience the lawless violence of the Thracians and Gauls, as they had on more than one occasion."[2] But the Greeks, like the Macedonians, eventually fell subject to Roman power.

Seleucid Kingdom   Another Hellenistic monarchy was founded by the general Seleucus (suh-LOO-kuss), who established the Seleucid dynasty of Syria. This was the largest of the Hellenistic kingdoms and controlled much of the old Persian Empire from Turkey in the west to India in the east, although the Seleucids found it increasingly difficult to maintain control of the eastern territories. In fact, an Indian ruler named Chandragupta Maurya (chun-druh-GOOP-tuh MOWR-yuh) (324–301 B.C.E.) created a new Indian state, the Mauryan Empire, and drove out the Seleucid forces. His grandson Asoka (uh-SOH-kuh) (269–232 B.C.E.) extended the empire to include most of India and is considered the greatest ruler in India's history. Asoka, a pious Buddhist, sought to convert the remaining Greek communities in northwestern India to his religion and even sent Buddhist missionaries to Greek rulers.

The Seleucid rulers maintained relations with the Mauryan Empire. Trade was fostered, especially in such luxuries as spices and jewels. Seleucus also sent Greek and Macedonian ambassadors to the Mauryan court. Best known of these was

Megasthenes (muh-GAS-thuh-neez), whose report on the people of India remained one of the West's best sources of information on India until the Middle Ages.

Kingdom of Pergamum   A third Hellenistic kingdom came into being by freeing itself from the Seleucids. This was the kingdom of Pergamum in western Asia Minor under the Attalid dynasty. It was Pergamum that brought the Romans into the area by seeking their aid first against the Antigonids and then against the Seleucids. This led to the Roman defeat of Antiochus (an-TY-uh-kuss) III, probably the strongest of the Seleucid monarchs, in 191 B.C.E. The Seleucids declined thereafter until their small remaining territory was made a Roman province in 63 B.C.E. Seventy years before that, the last of the Attalid dynasty had bequeathed his kingdom to Rome in his will.

Ptolemaic Kingdom of Egypt   The fourth Hellenistic monarchy was Egypt, which had come under the control of Ptolemy (TAHL-uh-mee), another Macedonian general. Named governor of Egypt after Alexander's death, Ptolemy had established himself as king by 305 B.C.E., creating the Ptolemaic (tahl-uh-MAY-ik) dynasty of pharaohs. Hellenistic Egypt lasted longer than all the other Hellenistic monarchies; it was not until the reign of Cleopatra VII, who allied herself with the wrong side in the Roman civil wars (see Chapter 5), that Egypt fell to the Romans in 30 B.C.E.

The Threat from the Celts   The Celts, also known as the Gauls, were a people who had occupied large areas of Europe north of the Alps during the Early Iron Age (c. 800–500 B.C.E.), especially the region to the south and west of the Rhine River, west of the Alps, and north of the Pyrenees (a region known as Gaul).

At the end of the fifth century B.C.E., possibly as a result of overpopulation, Celtic peoples began to migrate south and east. One group sacked the city of Rome in 390 B.C.E. (see Chapter 5). After the death of Alexander the Great, other groups of Celts began to threaten the Hellenistic world. Celts attacked Macedonia early in the third century B.C.E., as one ancient writer reported: "When the defeated Macedonians had fixed themselves within the walls of their cities, the victorious Brennus ravaged the fields of the whole of Macedonia with no one to oppose him."[3] Brennus also led a group of 30,000 Celts into Greece itself and caused considerable damage before being defeated in 278 B.C.E.

Other groups of Celts later attacked Asia Minor, where Attalus I bested them in 230 B.C.E. After his victory, Attalus gained control of much of Asia Minor and declared himself king of Pergamum. As a result of these attacks, the Celts, or Gauls, came to be feared everywhere in the Hellenistic world.

Political and Military Institutions   The Hellenistic monarchies created a semblance of stability for several centuries, even though Hellenistic kings refused to accept the new status quo and periodically engaged in wars to alter it. At the same time, an underlying strain always existed between the new Greco-Macedonian ruling class and the native populations. Together, these factors created a certain degree of tension that was

A Gaul and His Wife: Monument to the Victory of a Hellenistic King. *This statue of a Gaulish chieftain and his wife is a Roman copy of a bronze original that was part of a larger monument erected around 230–220 B.C.E. to commemorate the victory of Attalus I of Pergamum over the Gauls, a victory that gave Pergamum control over much of Asia Minor. In this scene, the defeated Gaulish leader plunges a sword into his chest just after he has killed his wife to prevent her from being sold into slavery.*

Palazzo Altemps, Rome © Araldo de Luca/CORBIS

never truly ended until the vibrant Roman state to the west stepped in and imposed a new order.

The Hellenistic kingdoms shared a common political system that represented a break with their Greek past. To the Greeks, monarchy was an institution for barbarians, associated in their minds with people like the Persians. Although they retained democratic forms of government in their cities, the Greeks of the Hellenistic world were forced to accept monarchy as a new fact of political life.

Although Alexander the Great had apparently planned to fuse Greeks and easterners, Hellenistic monarchs relied primarily on Greeks and Macedonians to form the new ruling class. In the Seleucid kingdom, for example, historians have estimated that only 2.5 percent of the people in authority were non-Greek, and most of them were commanders of local military units. Those who did advance to important administrative posts had learned Greek (all government business was transacted in Greek) and had become Hellenized in a cultural sense. The policy of excluding non-Greeks from leadership positions was due not to the incompetence of the natives but to the determination of the Greek ruling class to maintain its privileged position. It was the Greco-Macedonian ruling class that provided the only unity in the Hellenistic world.

Since the Hellenistic monarchs created and maintained their kingdoms by military force, warfare continued to be an integral part of the Hellenistic world. The phalanx—still composed of heavily armed infantry with 18-foot-long spears—and cavalry continued to form the core of the Hellenistic forces. But Hellenistic

Greek War Elephants. *Some of the armies in the Hellenistic world made use of elephants obtained from North Africa and India. Pictured on this Italian plate is a Greek war elephant that was brought to the Mediterranean by one of Alexander's successors. The battle fortress on the back of the elephant was a Greek innovation.*

Museo Nazionale di Villa Giulia, Rome/© Scala/Art Resource, NY

warfare also saw some innovations. Most noticeable were the elephants, "the tanks of ancient warfare," which were especially prominent in the armies of the Seleucids, who procured theirs from India, and the Ptolemies, who obtained them from North Africa. But even more important, since armies quickly learned tricks that neutralized the elephants, was the development of new siege machinery, especially the catapult and siege towers. In Classical times, cities with good walls were virtually impregnable; Alexander and later Hellenistic rulers could capture cities by using their new equipment.

Hellenistic Cities

Cities played an especially important role in the Hellenistic kingdoms. Throughout his conquests, Alexander had founded a series of new cities and military settlements, and Hellenistic kings did likewise. The new population centers varied considerably in size and importance. Military settlements were meant to maintain order and might consist of only a few hundred men heavily dependent on the king. But there were also new independent cities with thousands of inhabitants. Alexandria in Egypt was the largest city in the Mediterranean region by the first century B.C.E. Seleucus was especially active in founding new cities, according to one ancient writer: "The other kings have exulted in destroying existing cities; he, on the other hand, arranged to build cities which did not yet exist. He established so many ... that they were enough to carry the names of towns in Macedonia as well as the names of those in his family.... One can go to Phoenicia to see his cities; one can go to Syria and see even more."[4]

Hellenistic rulers encouraged this massive spread of Greek colonists to the Near East because of their intrinsic value to the new monarchies. Greeks (and Macedonians) provided not only a recruiting ground for the army but also a pool of civilian administrators and workers who would contribute to economic development. Even architects, engineers, dramatists, and actors were in demand in the new Greek cities. Many Greeks and Macedonians were quick to see the advantages of moving to the new urban centers and gladly sought their fortunes in the Near East. Greeks of all backgrounds joined the exodus until around 250 B.C.E., when the outpouring began to slow significantly.

Within the Hellenistic cities, the culture was primarily Greek. The political institutions of the cities were modeled after those of the Greek *polis*. Greeks of the Classical period would easily have recognized the councils, magistracies, assemblies, and codes of law. The physical layout of the new cities was likewise modeled on those of the Greek homeland. Using the traditional rectilinear grid, cities were laid out with temples, altars, and stone amphitheaters.

Many of the new urban centers were completely dominated by Greeks, while the native populations remained cut off from all civic institutions. The Greeks commissioned purely Greek sculpture, read literature of the Classical period, and had separate law courts for themselves. Complaints from resentful natives have been recorded. Not only was it difficult for easterners to enter the ranks of the ruling class, but those who did so had to become thoroughly Hellenized. This often required alienation from one's own culture.

The Greeks' belief in their own cultural superiority provided an easy rationalization for their political dominance of the eastern cities. But Greek control of the new cities was also necessary because the kings frequently used the cities as instruments of government, enabling them to rule considerable territory without an extensive bureaucracy. At the same time, for security reasons, the Greeks needed the support of the kings. After all, the Hellenistic cities were islands of Greek culture in a sea of non-Greeks. The relationship between rulers and cities, therefore, was a symbiotic one that bore serious consequences for the cities.

In their political system, religious practices, and architecture, the Greeks tried to re-create the *poleis* of their homeland in their new cities. But it was no longer possible to do so. The new cities were not autonomous entities and soon found themselves dependent on the power of the Hellenistic monarchies. Although the kings did not rule the cities directly, they restricted the cities' freedom in other ways. City administrators knew they could not conduct an independent foreign policy and did not try to do so. The kings also demanded tribute, which could be a heavy burden.

The Greek cities of the era were the chief agents for the spread of Hellenistic culture in the Near East, as far, in fact, as modern Afghanistan and India. These Greek cities were also remarkably vibrant despite their subordination to the Hellenistic monarchies and persisted in being a focal point for the loyalty of their citizens.

Economic Trends in the Hellenistic World   Agriculture was still of primary importance to both the native populations and the new Greek cities of the Hellenistic world. The Greek cities continued their old agrarian patterns. A well-defined body of citizens owned land and worked it with the assistance of slaves. But their farms were isolated units in a vast area of land ultimately owned by the king or assigned to large estate owners and worked by native peasants dwelling in villages. Overall, then, neither agricultural patterns nor methods of production underwent significant changes.

Few new products or manufacturing methods were introduced in the Hellenistic period, but the centers of manufacturing shifted significantly. Industry spread from Greece to the east—especially to Asia Minor, Rhodes, and Egypt. New textile centers were set up at Pergamum, and glass and silver crafts were developed in Syria. Leading all cities in manufacturing was Alexandria in Egypt, which became the center for the production of parchment, textiles, linens, oil, metalwork, and glass.

Commerce expanded considerably in the Hellenistic era. Indeed, trading contacts linked much of the Hellenistic world. The decline in the number of political barriers encouraged more commercial traffic. Although Hellenistic monarchs still fought wars, the conquests of Alexander and the policies of his successors made possible greater trade between east and west. Two major trade routes connected the east with the Mediterranean. The central route was the major one and led by sea from India to the Persian Gulf, up the Tigris River to Seleucia on the Tigris, which replaced Babylon as the center for water-borne traffic from the Persian Gulf and overland caravan routes as well. Overland routes from Seleucia then led to Antioch and Ephesus. A southern route wound its way from India by sea but went around Arabia and up the Red Sea to Petra or later Berenice (ber-uh-NY-see). Caravan routes then led overland to Coptos on the Nile, thence to Alexandria and the Mediterranean.

An incredible variety of products were traded: gold and silver from Spain; iron from northern Armenia; salt from Asia Minor; timber from Macedonia; purple dye from Tyre; ebony, gems, ivory, and spices from India; frankincense (used on altars) from Arabia; slaves from Thrace, Syria, and Asia Minor; fine wines from Syria and western Asia Minor; olive oil from Athens; and numerous exquisite foodstuffs, such as the famous prunes of Damascus. The greatest trade, however, was in the basic staple of life—grain. The great exporting areas were Egypt, Sicily, and the Black Sea region, while Rhodes and Delos served as the major depots for the international grain trade.

HELLENISTIC SOCIETY

One of the noticeable features of social life in the Hellenistic world was the emergence of new opportunities for women—at least for upper-class women. No doubt this was related to the changes in Hellenistic society itself, since the subordination of the cities to the kings altered the way men related to their *polis* and to each other. Some historians maintain that the visible role of Hellenistic queens may also have contributed to a new model for upper-class women.

New Opportunities for Women   The creation of the Hellenistic monarchies, which represented a considerable departure from the world of the city-state, gave new scope to the role played by the monarchs' wives, the Hellenistic queens. In Macedonia, a pattern of alliances between mothers and sons provided openings for women to take an active role in politics, especially in political intrigue. In Egypt, opportunities for royal women were even greater after the Ptolemaic rulers adopted the Egyptian custom of kings marrying their own sisters. Of the first eight Ptolemaic rulers, four wed their sisters. Ptolemy II and his sister-wife Arsinoë (ahr-SIN-oh-ee) II were both worshiped as gods in their lifetimes. Arsinoë played an energetic role in government and was involved in the expansion of the Egyptian navy. She was also the first Egyptian queen whose portrait appeared on coins with her husband. Hellenistic queens also showed an intense interest in culture. They wrote poems, collected art, and corresponded with intellectuals.

The development of the kingdom as the focus of political life in the Hellenistic era also resulted in fewer restrictions on women. In many cities, for example, women of all classes had a new freedom of movement. The most notable gains, especially for upper-class women, came in the economic area. Documents show increasing numbers of women involved in managing slaves, selling property, and making loans. Even then, legal contracts made by women had to include their official male guardians, although often these men were listed only to satisfy legal requirements and no longer played an important role. In Sparta, women were allowed to own land and manage their own economic affairs. As their husbands were often absent or had died in war, many Spartan women became wealthy; females owned 40 percent of the privately held land in Sparta.

Spartan women, however, were an exception, especially on the Greek mainland. Women in Athens, for example, still remained highly restricted and supervised. Although a few philosophers welcomed female participation in men's affairs, many philosophers rejected equality between men and women and asserted that the traditional roles of wives and mothers were most satisfying for women. In her treatise "On Chastity," Phintys (FIN-tiss) wrote that "serving as generals, public officials, and statesmen is appropriate for men," but "keeping house, remaining within, and taking care of husbands belongs to women."[5]

But the opinions of philosophers did not prevent upper-class women from making gains in areas other than the economic sphere. New possibilities for females arose when women in some parts of the Hellenistic world were allowed to pursue education in the fields of literature, music, and even athletics. Education, then, provided new opportunities for women: female poets appeared again in the third century B.C.E., and there are instances of women involved in both scholarly and artistic pursuits.

Some wealthy aristocratic women even became politically active and participated in running their cities. In the second century B.C.E., a number of cities passed decrees honoring women for their service to the community. Cyme, in Asia Minor, for example, paid homage to Archippe for her enormous financial contributions. In return, some women were given political rights and in a few instances were allowed to hold office as city magistrates. Some cities even erected statues of women in public squares. But often this generosity had an economic motive. When Phile of Priene was made a magistrate of her city, it was probably with the understanding that she would donate funds for public works. Once in office, she built an aqueduct and a reservoir for the community.

Improvements in the position of females were largely limited to upper-class women. Although peasant women faced fewer restrictions, they experienced no real benefit as they were still subject to a lifetime of hard work. A large group of women condemned to the practice of prostitution faced an even harsher reality. Inscriptional evidence indicates that small families were common in the Hellenistic world; boys were preferred, and rarely was more than one daughter raised. Unwanted girl babies were often exposed to the elements and left to die. Some of these infants were gathered up by eager entrepreneurs and raised to be slave prostitutes. Only the most beautiful and luckiest prostitutes came to be the companions (the *hetairai*) of upper-class men.

The Role of Slavery

The Hellenistic world witnessed the migration of large numbers of people from one area to another. Greeks and Macedonians went into the Hellenistic kingdoms of the east as administrators, mercenaries, engineers, scholars, artists, teachers, and merchants. Moreover, significantly large numbers of non-Greeks moved around for economic and military purposes. But the largest number of uprooted people were slaves. Slavery was viewed as a normal part of life in the Hellenistic world and in antiquity in general.

Slaves were obtained from four chief sources: the children of slaves; children who were sold by their parents or abandoned to perish; persons kidnapped by pirates; and, perhaps the largest source of all, prisoners of war. Delos, a major trading center, could handle 10,000 slaves a day in its markets. Although slaves came from everywhere, Thracians and Syrians were the most numerous. Slaves varied in price; Macedonians, Thracians, and Italians drew the highest prices.

Slaves were put to work in numerous ways in the Hellenistic world. States employed slaves as servants for government officials and in government-run industries such as weaving. Most slaves were used in domestic service, farming, and mines, but the situation could vary from state to state. Egypt had no slave class in the countryside, nor was there much domestic slavery outside Alexandria. But the Egyptians did use slave labor in state-run textile factories and made especially brutal use of them in mining operations. Women were also sold as slaves to be concubines for Greek and Macedonian soldiers and civilians.

The effects of slavery could also be important. The employment of large numbers of slaves in the Hellenistic kingdoms contributed to the Hellenizing process. Slaves working in homes, farms, or factories had opportunities to absorb Greek ways. This is especially evident in the case of the slave-wives of Hellenistic soldiers.

The Transformation of Education

In the Hellenistic world, education underwent a significant transformation. In the Classical period of Greek history, education had been left largely to private enterprise. Greek cities now began to supervise education in new ways. The Greek **gymnasium**, which had been primarily an athletic institution, evolved into a secondary school. The curriculum centered on music, physical exercise, and literature, especially the poetry of Homer. Wealthy individuals often provided the money for the schools and also

Treatment of Slaves in the Egyptian Gold Mines

Slavery was a common practice throughout antiquity. In both Classical Greece and the Hellenistic world, the worst-treated slaves were those who worked in the mines. The Egyptians were especially notorious for their treatment of slaves in the gold mines in Nubia, described in this account by Diodorus of Sicily, who lived in the first century B.C.E. His account was based on the now lost work of the second-century writer Agatharchides.

Diodorus of Sicily, *Library of History*

And those who have been condemned in this way—and they are a great multitude and are all bound in chains—work at their task unceasingly both by day and throughout the entire night, enjoying no respite and being carefully cut off from any means of escape; since guards of foreign soldiers who speak a language different from theirs stand watch over them, so that not a man, either by conversation or by some contact of a friendly nature, is able to corrupt one of his keepers.... And the entire operations are in charge of a skilled worker who distinguishes the stone and points it out to the laborers; and of those who are assigned to this unfortunate task the physically strongest break the quartz-rock with iron hammers, applying no skill to the task but only force, and cutting tunnels through the stone, not in a straight line but wherever the seam of gleaming rock may lead. Now these men, working in darkness as they do because of the bending and winding of the passages, carry lamps bound on their foreheads; and since much of the time they change the position of their bodies to follow the particular character of the stone they throw the blocks, as they cut them out, on the ground, and at this task they labor without ceasing beneath the sternness and blows of an overseer.

specified how it should be spent. An inscription from the city of Teos in Asia Minor specified that Polythroos "gave 34,000 drachmas ... for there to be appointed each year ... three grammar-masters to teach the boys and the girls;... for two gymnastics-masters to be appointed,... for a lyre—or harp—player to be appointed ... [to] teach music and lyre—or harp—playing to the children."[6]

The school in Teos was unusual, however, in that education was ordinarily for upper-class male children. An official known as the *gymnasiarch* served as the head of a gymnasium. This was a civic position of considerable prestige. He was not paid and was expected to provide money for sacrifices, competitions, entertainment, and even school repairs. Many cities passed decrees awarding praise and a "gold crown" to the gymnasiarch for his "munificence toward the people." The educational year culminated with various musical, academic, and athletic contests in which students competed for the honor of having their names inscribed on a victory column.

Hellenistic kings also served as patrons of gymnasia, recognizing their importance in training youths who might serve later as administrators of the state.

The boys there who have not yet come to maturity, entering through the tunnels into the galleries formed by the removal of the rock, laboriously gather up the rock as it is cast down piece by piece and carry it out into the open to the place outside the entrance. Then those who are above thirty years of age take this quarried stone from them and with iron pestles pound a specified amount of it in stone mortars, until they have worked it down to a smaller size. Thereupon the women and older men receive from them the rock of this size and cast it into mills of which a number stand there in a row, and taking their places in groups of two or three at the spoke or handle of each mill they grind it until they have worked down the amount given them to the consistency of the finest flour. And since no opportunity is afforded any of them to care for his body and they have no garment to cover their shame, no man can look upon the unfortunate wretches without feeling pity for them because of the exceeding hardships they suffer. For no leniency or respite of any kind is given to any man who is sick, or maimed or aged, or in the case of a woman for her weakness, but all without exception are compelled by blows to persevere in their labors, until through ill-treatment they die in the midst of their tortures. Consequently the poor unfortunates believe, because their punishment is so excessively severe, that the future will always be more terrible than the present and therefore look forward to death as more to be desired than life.

Q *Compare the treatment of slaves in the Egyptian gold mines with the treatment of slaves in Classical Athens. What does your comparison reveal about the nature of slavery in the Greek world?*

Source: Reprinted by permission of the publishers and the Trustees of the Loeb Classical Library from Diodorus Siculus, Loeb Classical Library Vol. 1, trans. by C. H. Oldfather, Cambridge, Mass.: Harvard University Press, Copyright © 1933 by the President and Fellows of Harvard College. The Loeb Classical Library is a registered trademark of the President and Fellows of Harvard College.

The institution of the gymnasium played a significant role in the diffusion of Greek culture throughout the Hellenistic world. Whether an upper-class Greek youth lived on the Greek mainland, in Alexandria, or in another city in the east, he could imbibe Greek culture and maintain that sense of superiority that characterized the Greek overlords of the Hellenistic kingdoms.

CULTURE IN THE HELLENISTIC WORLD

Although the Hellenistic kingdoms encompassed vast areas and many diverse peoples, the Greeks provided a sense of unity as a result of the diffusion of Greek culture throughout the Hellenistic world. The Hellenistic era was a period of considerable cultural accomplishment in many fields—literature, art, science, medicine, and philosophy. Although these achievements occurred throughout the Hellenistic world, certain centers, especially the great Hellenistic cities of Alexandria and Pergamum, stood out. In both cities, cultural developments were encouraged by the rulers themselves. Rich Hellenistic kings had considerable resources with which to patronize culture.

The Ptolemies in Egypt made Alexandria an especially important cultural center. The library became the largest in ancient times, with more than half a million scrolls. The museum (literally, "temple of the Muses") created a favorable environment for scholarly research. As a result, Alexandria became home to scholars of all kinds—poets, writers, philosophers, and scientists.

New Directions in Literature   The Hellenistic Age produced an enormous quantity of literature, most of which has not survived. Hellenistic monarchs, who held literary talent in high esteem, subsidized writers on a grand scale. The Ptolemaic rulers of Egypt were particularly lavish. The combination of their largess and the famous library drew a host of scholars and authors to Alexandria, including a circle of poets. Theocritus (thee-AHK-ruh-tuss) (c. 315–250 B.C.E.), originally a native of the island of Sicily, wrote 'little poems" or idylls dealing with erotic themes, lovers' complaints, and above all, pastoral themes expressing his love of nature and his appreciation of nature's beauty.

In the Hellenistic era, Athens remained the theatrical center of the Greek world. Though little tragedy was produced, a new kind of comedy developed that completely rejected political themes and sought only to entertain and amuse. The Athenian playwright Menander (muh-NAN-dur) (c. 342–291 B.C.E.) was perhaps the best representative of New Comedy. Plots were simple: typically, a hero falls in love with a not-really-so-bad prostitute who turns out eventually to be the long-lost daughter of a rich neighbor. The hero marries her, and they live happily ever after.

The Hellenistic period saw a great outpouring of historical and biographical literature. The chief historian of the Hellenistic Age was Polybius (puh-LIB-ee-uss) (c. 203–c. 120 B.C.E.), a Greek who lived for some years in Rome. Many historians regard him as second only to Thucydides among Greek historians. His major work consisted of forty books narrating the history of the "inhabited Mediterranean world" from 221 to 146 B.C.E. Only the first five books are extant, although long extracts from the other books survive. His history focuses on the growth of Rome from a city-state to a vast empire. It is apparent that Polybius understood the significance of the Romans' achievement. He followed Thucydides in seeking rational motives for historical events. He also approached his sources critically and used firsthand accounts.

Hellenistic Art   In addition to being patrons of literary talent, the Hellenistic monarchs were eager to spend their money to beautify and adorn the cities in their states. The founding of new cities and the rebuilding of old ones provided numerous opportunities for Greek architects and sculptors. The structures of the Greek homeland—gymnasia, baths, theaters, and temples—lined the streets of these cities. Most noticeable in the construction of temples was the use of the more ornate Corinthian order (see Chapter 3), which became especially popular during the Hellenistic era.

Drunken Old Woman. *Hellenistic sculptors no longer tried to capture ideal beauty in their sculpture, a quest that characterized Greek classicism, but moved toward a more emotional and realistic art. This statue of a drunken old woman is typical of this new trend in art. Old and haggard, mired in poverty, she struggles just to go on living.*

Musei Capitolini, Rome///© Araldo de Luca/CORBIS

Both Hellenistic kings and rich citizens commissioned sculptures. The kings erected thousands of statues, many paid for by their subjects, in towns and cities all over the Hellenistic world. Hellenistic sculptors traveled widely, attracted by the material rewards offered by wealthy patrons. While maintaining the technical skill of the Classical period, Hellenistic sculptors moved away from the idealism of fifth-century classicism to a more emotional and realistic art, seen in numerous statues of old women, drunks, and little children at play. They also placed a new emphasis on the female nude.

Alexander's incursion into the western part of India also resulted in some Greek cultural influences there, especially during the Hellenistic era. During the first century B.C.E., Indian sculptors began to create statues of the Buddha. The impact of Greek statues is especially evident in the Buddhist statues created in Gandhara, which today is part of Pakistan.

A Golden Age of Science and Medicine

The Hellenistic era witnessed a more conscious separation of science from philosophy. In Classical Greece, what we would call the physical and life sciences had been divisions of philosophical inquiry. Nevertheless, the Greeks, by the time of Aristotle, had already established an important principle of scientific investigation—empirical research, or systematic observation, as the basis for generalization. In the Hellenistic Age, the sciences tended to be studied in their own right.

One of the traditional areas of Greek science was astronomy, and two Alexandrian scholars continued this exploration. Aristarchus (ar-iss-TAR-kuss) of Samos (c. 310–230 B.C.E.) developed a *heliocentric* view of the universe, contending that the sun and the fixed stars remain stationary while the earth rotates around the sun in a circular orbit. He also argued that the earth rotates around its own axis. This view was not widely accepted, however, and most scholars clung to the earlier *geocentric* view of the Greeks, which held that the earth was at the center of the universe. Another astronomer, Eratosthenes (er-uh-TAHSS-thuh-neez) (c. 275–194 B.C.E.), determined that the earth was round and calculated the earth's circumference at 24,675 miles, an estimate that was within 200 miles of the actual figure.

A third Alexandrian scholar was Euclid (YOO-klid), who lived around 300 B.C.E. He established a school in Alexandria but is primarily known for his work titled *Elements*. This was a systematic organization of the fundamental elements of geometry as they had already been worked out; it became the standard textbook of plane geometry and was used up to modern times.

Archimedes   The most famous scientist of the Hellenistic period, Archimedes (ahr-kuh-MEE-deez) (287–212 B.C.E.), came from the western Mediterranean region. Archimedes was especially important for his work on the geometry of spheres and cylinders, for establishing the value of the mathematical constant pi, and for creating the science of hydrostatics. Archimedes was also a practical inventor. He may have devised the so-called Archimedean screw used to pump water out of mines and to lift irrigation water, as well as a compound pulley for transporting heavy weights. During the Roman siege of his native city of Syracuse, he constructed a number of devices to thwart the attackers. According to Plutarch's account, the Romans became so frightened "that if they did but see a little rope or a piece of wood from the wall, instantly crying out, that there it was again, Archimedes was about to let fly some engine at them, they turned their backs and fled."[7]

Archimedes's accomplishments inspired a wealth of semilegendary stories. Supposedly, he discovered specific gravity by observing the water he displaced in his bath and became so excited by his realization that he jumped out of the water and ran home naked, shouting, "Eureka!" ("I have found it!"). He is said to have emphasized the importance of levers by proclaiming to the king of Syracuse: "Give me a lever and a place to stand on, and I will move the earth." The king was so impressed that he encouraged Archimedes to lower his sights and build defensive weapons instead.

Medicine   The scientific foundations of medicine also made considerable strides in the Hellenistic period. This represents a continuation from the fifth century when Hippocrates (hih-PAH-kruh-teez), a contemporary of Socrates, is credited with having been the "first to separate medicine from philosophy" by stressing natural explanations and natural cures for disease. Herophilus (huh-ROF-uh-luss) and Erasistratus (er-uh-SIS-truh-tuss), both well-known physicians, were active in Alexandria in the first half of the third century B.C.E. Both were interested in anatomy and used dissection and vivisection (the dissection of living bodies) to expand their knowledge, or so the Roman author Celsus claimed:

> Moreover, as pains, and also various kinds of diseases, arise in the more internal parts, they hold that no one can apply remedies for these who is ignorant about the parts themselves; hence it becomes necessary to lay open the bodies of the dead and to scrutinize their viscera and intestines. They hold that Herophilus and Erasistratus did this in the best way by far, when they laid open men while alive—criminals received out of prison from the kings—and while these were still breathing, observed parts which beforehand nature had concealed, their position, color, shape, size, arrangement, hardness, softness, smoothness, relation, processes and depressions of each, and whether any part is inserted into or is received into another.[8]

Herophilus added significantly to the understanding of the brain, eye, liver, and the reproductive and nervous systems. Erasistratus made discoveries in the process of digestion.

It would be misleading, however, to think of medicine in the Hellenistic world only in terms of scientific advances. Alongside these developments, a wide range of alternative methods of healing continued to exist. These included magical practices, such as the use of amulets to cast off evil spirits, herbal remedies, and the healing powers of deities, especially those of Asclepius (uh-SKLEE-pee-uss), the god of healing.

Philosophy: New Schools of Thought

While Alexandria and Pergamum became the renowned cultural centers of the Hellenistic world, Athens remained the prime center for philosophy and continued to attract the most illustrious philosophers from the Greek world who established schools there. New schools of philosophical thought—the Epicureans and Stoics—reinforced Athens's reputation as a philosophical center.

Epicureanism Epicurus (ep-i-KYOOR-uss) (341–270 B.C.E.), the founder of **Epicureanism** (ep-i-kyoo-REE-uh-ni-zum), established a school in Athens near the end of the fourth century B.C.E. Epicurus's famous belief in a doctrine of "pleasure" began with his view of the world. Although he did not deny the existence of the gods, he did not believe they played any active role in the world. The universe ran on its own. This left human beings free to follow self-interest as a basic motivating force. Happiness was the goal of life, and the means to achieve it was the pursuit of pleasure, the only true good. But the pursuit of pleasure was not meant in a physical, hedonistic sense:

> When, therefore, we maintain that pleasure is the end, we do not mean the pleasures of profligates and those that consist in sensuality, as is supposed by some who are either ignorant or disagree with us or do not understand, but freedom from pain in the body and from trouble in the mind. For it is not continuous drinkings and revelings, nor the satisfaction of lusts, nor the enjoyment of fish and other luxuries of the wealthy table, which produce a pleasant life, but sober

The Stoic Ideal of Harmony with God

The Stoic Cleanthes (klee-AN-theez) (331–232 B.C.E.) succeeded Zeno as head of this school of philosophy. One historian of Hellenistic civilization has called this work by Cleanthes the greatest religious hymn in Greek literature. Certainly, it demonstrates that Stoicism, unlike Epicureanism, did have an underlying spiritual foundation. This poem has been compared to the great psalms of the Hebrews.

Cleanthes, *Hymn to Zeus*

Nothing occurs on the earth apart from you, O God,
nor in the heavenly regions nor on the sea,
except what bad men do in their folly;
but you know to make the odd even,
and to harmonize what is dissonant; to you the alien is akin.

And so you have wrought together
into one all things that are good and bad,
So that there arises one eternal logos [rationale] of all things,
Which all bad mortals shun and ignore,
Unhappy wretches, ever seeking the possession of good things
They neither see nor hear the universal law of God,
By obeying which they might enjoy a happy life.

Q Based on Cleanthes's poem, what are some of the beliefs of the Stoics? How do they differ from the beliefs of the Epicureans?

Source: From *Hellenistic Philosophy: Stoics, Epicureans, Sceptics*, Second Edition, A. A. Long. Copyright © 1986 by A. A. Long. Reprinted by permission of the University of California Press.

reasoning, searching out the motives for all choice and avoidance, and banishing mere opinions, to which are due the greatest disturbance of the spirit.

Pleasure was not satisfying one's desire in an active, gluttonous fashion but rather freedom from emotional turmoil and freedom from worry—the freedom that came from a mind at rest. To achieve this passive pleasure, one had to free oneself from public activity: "We must release ourselves from the prison of affairs and politics." They were too strenuous to give peace of mind. But this was not a renunciation of all social life, for to Epicurus, a life could be complete only when it was centered on the basic ideal of friendship: "Of all the things which wisdom acquires to produce the blessedness of the complete life, far the greatest is the possession of friendship."[9] Epicurus's own life in Athens was an embodiment of his teachings. He and his friends created their own private community where they could pursue their ideal of true happiness.

Stoicism Epicureanism was eventually overshadowed by another school of thought known as **Stoicism** (STOH-i-siz-um), which became the most popular philosophy of the Hellenistic world and persisted in the Roman Empire as well. It was the product of a teacher named Zeno (335–263 B.C.E.), who came to Athens and began to teach in a public colonnade known as the Painted Portico (the *Stoa Poikile*—hence the name Stoicism). Like Epicureanism,

Stoicism was concerned with how individuals find happiness. But Stoics took a radically different approach. To them, happiness, the supreme good, could be found only in virtue, which meant essentially living in harmony with divine will: "And this very thing constitutes the virtue of the happy man and the smooth current of life, when all actions promote the harmony of the spirit dwelling in the individual man with the will of him who orders the universe." [10] One achieved happiness by choosing to follow divine will through the free exercise of one's own will. To the Stoics, divine will was the same as the will of nature, since nature was simply a manifestation or expression of the gods. "Living according to nature," therefore, meant following divine will or the natural laws that the gods established to run the universe.

Virtuous living, then, was living in accordance with the laws of nature or submitting to divine will. This led to the acceptance of whatever one received in life, since divine will for us was by its very nature good. By accepting divine law, people mastered themselves and gained inner peace. Life's problems could not disturb such individuals, and they could bear whatever life offered (hence our word *stoic*).

Unlike Epicureans, Stoics did not believe in the need to separate oneself from the world and politics. Public service was regarded as noble. The real Stoic was a good citizen and could even be a good government official. Because Stoics believed that a divine principle was present throughout the universe, each human being also contained a divine spark. This led to a belief in the oneness of humanity. The world constituted a single society of equal human beings. Although humans were not equal in the outer world, the divine spark in each meant that all were free to follow divine will (what was best for each individual). All persons, then, even slaves, though unfree in body, were equal at the level of the soul.

Epicureanism and especially Stoicism appealed to large numbers of people in the Hellenistic world. Both of these philosophies focused primarily on the problem of human happiness. Their popularity would suggest a fundamental change in the character of the Greek lifestyle. In the Classical Greek world, the happiness of individuals and the meaning of life were closely associated with the life of the *polis*. One found fulfillment within the community. In the Hellenistic kingdoms, although the *polis* continued to exist, the sense that one could find satisfaction and fulfillment through life in the *polis* had weakened. As a result, individuals sought new philosophies that offered personal happiness. At the same time, in the cosmopolitan world of the Hellenistic states, with their mixtures of peoples, a new openness to thoughts of universality could also emerge. For some people, Stoicism embodied this larger sense of community. The appeal of new philosophies in the Hellenistic era can also be explained by the apparent decline in certain aspects of traditional religion.

RELIGION IN THE HELLENISTIC WORLD

When the Greeks spread throughout the Near East, they took their gods with them. Hellenistic cities increased the number of public festivals and celebrated them with great magnificence. But as time went on, there was a noticeable decline in the vitality of the traditional Greek Olympian religion. The civic cults based on the traditional gods no longer seemed sufficient to satisfy people's emotional needs.

This left Greeks receptive to the numerous religious cults of the eastern world. The Greeks were always tolerant of other existing religious institutions. Hence, in the Hellenistic cities of the Near East, the traditional civic cults of their own gods and foreign cults existed side by side. Alexandria had cults of the traditional Greek gods, Egyptian deities such as Isis and Horus, the Babylonian Astarte, and the Syrian Atargatis.

But for many people, the search for personal meaning remained unfulfilled. Among educated Greeks, the philosophies of Epicureanism and especially Stoicism offered help. Another source of solace came in the form of **mystery religions**.

Mystery Religions

Mystery cults, with their secret initiations and promises of individual salvation, were not new to the Greek world. But the Greeks of the Hellenistic era were also strongly influenced by eastern mystery cults, such as those of Egypt, which offered a distinct advantage over the Greek mystery religions. The latter had usually been connected to specific locations (such as Eleusis), which meant that a would-be initiate had to undertake a pilgrimage in order to participate in the rites. In contrast, the eastern mystery religions were readily available since temples to their gods and goddesses were located throughout the Greek cities of the east.

All of the mystery religions were based on the same fundamental premises. Individuals could pursue a path to salvation and achieve eternal life by being initiated into a union with a savior god or goddess who had died and risen again. The ritual of initiation, by which the seeker identified with the god or goddess, was no doubt a highly emotional experience.

The Egyptian cult of Isis was one of the most popular mystery religions. The cult of Isis was very ancient but became truly universal in Hellenistic times. Isis was the goddess of women, marriage, and children, as one of her hymns states: "I am she whom women call goddess. I ordained that women should be loved by men: I brought wife and husband together, and invented the marriage contract. I ordained that women should bear children."[11] Isis was also portrayed as the giver of civilization who had brought laws and letters to all humankind. The cult of Isis offered a precious commodity to its initiates—the promise of eternal life. In many ways, the mystery religions of the Hellenistic era helped pave the way for Christianity.

The Jews in the Hellenistic World

In observing the similarities among their gods and goddesses, Greeks and easterners tended to assume that the deities were the same beings with different names, giving rise to a process of **syncretism**. But a special position in the Hellenistic world was occupied by the Jews, whose monotheistic religion was exclusive and did not permit this kind of fusion of spiritual beings.

The Jewish province of Judaea was ruled by the Ptolemies until it fell under the control of the Seleucids by 200 B.C.E. In the reign of the Seleucid king Antiochus IV (175–163 B.C.E.), conflict erupted in Judaea. Hellenistic monarchs were generally tolerant of all religions, but problems with Rome prompted Antiochus to try to impose more cultural and religious unity in Judaea. When he sent troops to Jerusalem and seized the Temple, he sparked a Jewish uprising led by Judas Maccabaeus (JOO-dus mak-uh-BEE-uss). In 164 B.C.E., the rebels succeeded in recapturing the Temple, a joyous event that has been celebrated every year since in the Jewish holiday of Hanukkah (HAH-nuh-kuh) (Hebrew for "re-dedication"). Although the conflict in Judaea continued, the Seleucids ultimately made concessions and allowed the Jews considerable freedom.

But since the Diaspora (see Chapter 2), large numbers of Jews no longer lived in Judaea. There was a large Jewish population in Egypt, particularly in Alexandria, as well as Jewish settlements throughout the cities of Asia Minor and Syria. In each city, Jews generally set up a synagogue and formed a private association for worship as other foreigners did. Some city authorities also allowed the Jews to form a political corporation that gave them greater rights than other resident aliens. Most important, they gained the privilege to live by their own laws and their own judicial system. The Jews were not really interested in citizenship in the cities in which they resided because full citizenship meant worship of the city's gods, anathema to Jews who believed only in Yahweh.

CHRONOLOGY

MACEDONIA AND THE CONQUESTS OF ALEXANDER

359–336 B.C.	Reign of Philip II
338 B.C.	Battle of Chaeronea; Philip II conquers Greece
336–323 B.C.	Reign of Alexander the Great
334 B.C.	Alexander invades Asia; Battle of Granicus River
333 B.C.	Battle of Issus
331 B.C.	Battle of Gaugamela
330 B.C.	Fall of Persepolis, the Persian capital
327 B.C.	Alexander enters India
326 B.C.	Battle of Hydaspes River
323 B.C.	Death of Alexander

5

THE ROMAN REPUBLIC

*Horatius defending the bridge as envisioned by Tommaso Laureti,
a sixteenth-century Italian painter*

Musei Capitolini, Rome//© Giraudon/The Bridgeman Art Library

CHAPTER OUTLINE

- The Emergence of Rome • The Roman Republic (c. 509–264 B.C.E.)
- The Roman Conquest of the Mediterranean (264–133 B.C.E.) • Society and
Culture in the Roman Republic • The Decline and Fall of the Roman Republic
(133–31 B.C.E.)

The Emergence of Rome

Not much is known about the prehistoric peoples who lived in Italy. We do know that Indo-European peoples moved into Italy during the second half of the second millennium B.C.E. By the first millennium B.C.E., other peoples had also settled in Italy, the two most notable being the Greeks and the Etruscans (ih-TRUSS-kunz). Before examining these peoples, however, we need to consider the influence geography had on the historical development of the peoples on the Italian peninsula.

Geography of the Italian Peninsula

Geography had a major impact on Roman history. Italy is a narrow peninsula extending about 750 miles from north to south but averaging only about 120 miles across (see Map 5.1).

The Apennine Mountains traverse the peninsula from north to south, forming a ridge down the middle that divides west from east. Nevertheless, Italy has some fairly large fertile plains ideal for farming. Most important were the Po valley in the north, probably the most fertile agricultural area; the plain of Latium (LAY-shee-um), on which Rome was located; and Campania (kam-PAH-nyuh) to the south of Latium. To the east of the Italian peninsula is the Adriatic Sea, and to the west, the Tyrrhenian Sea and the large islands of Corsica and Sardinia. Sicily lies just west of the toe of the boot-shaped peninsula.

Although the Apennines bisect Italy, they are less rugged than the mountain ranges of Greece and so did not divide the peninsula into many small isolated communities. Italy also possessed considerably more productive farmland than Greece, enabling it to support a large population. Rome's location was favorable from a geographic point of view. Located 18 miles inland on the Tiber River, Rome had access to the sea but was far enough inland to be safe from pirates. Built on seven hills, it was easily defended, and because it was situated where the Tiber could be readily forded, Rome became a natural crossing point for north-south traffic in western Italy. All in all, Rome had a good central location in Italy from which to expand.

Moreover, the Italian peninsula juts into the Mediterranean Sea, making it an important crossroads between the western and eastern Mediterranean. Once Rome had unified Italy, involvement in Mediterranean affairs was natural. And after the Romans had conquered their Mediterranean empire, Italy's central location made their task of governing that empire considerably easier.

The Greeks

The Greeks arrived on the Italian peninsula in large numbers during the age of Greek colonization (750–550 B.C.E.; see Chapter 3). Initially, the Greeks settled in southern Italy. They founded Cumae on the Bay of Naples, Naples itself, and Tarentum and then crept around the coast and up the peninsula as far as Brindisi. They also occupied the eastern two-thirds of Sicily. In establishing their colonies, the Greeks planned permanent communities, secured the coastal plains for agriculture, and built walled cities with harbors to carry on trade. Ultimately, the Greeks had considerable influence on Rome. They cultivated the olive and the vine, passed on their alphabetic system of writing, and provided artistic and cultural models through their sculpture, architecture, and literature. Indeed, many historians view Roman culture as a continuation of Greek culture. While Greek influence initially touched Rome indirectly through the

MAP 5.1 Ancient Italy

Ancient Italy was home to several groups. Both the Etruscans in the north and the Greeks in the south had a major influence on the development of Rome.

Etruscans, the Romans' conquest of southern Italy and Sicily brought them into direct contact with the Greeks.

The Etruscans   The initial development of Rome was influenced most by a people known as the Etruscans, who had settled north of Rome in Etruria (ih-TROOR-ee-uh). They were a city-dwelling people who established their towns in commanding positions and fortified them with walls. Numerous inscriptions in tombs show that the Etruscans adopted alphabetic writing from the Greeks before 600 B.C.E.

The origins of the Etruscans are not clear, but many historians believe that recent DNA analysis has confirmed the theory of the ancient Greek historian Herodotus (see Chapter 3) that the Etruscans emigrated from the region of Lydia (now western Turkey). After 650 B.C.E., the Etruscans expanded in Italy and became the dominant cultural and economic force in a number of areas. To the north, they moved into north-central Italy. To the south, according to Roman tradition and archaeological evidence, they controlled Rome and possibly all of Latium. From Latium they moved south into Campania, founded a settlement at Capua, and came into direct contact with Greek colonists in southern Italy. In the sixth century B.C.E., the Etruscans were at the height of their power. But by 480 B.C.E., their power had begun to decline, and by 400 B.C.E., they were again limited to Etruria itself. Later they were invaded by the Gauls and then conquered by the Romans. But by then the Etruscans had already made an impact. By transforming villages into towns and cities, they brought urbanization to northern and central Italy (the Greeks brought urbanization to southern Italy). Rome was, of course, the Etruscans' most famous creation.

Early Rome: Impact of the Etruscans

According to Roman legend, Rome was founded by the twin brothers Romulus and Remus in 753 B.C.E. Of course, the Romans invented this story to provide a noble ancestry for their city. Archaeologists have found, however, that by the eighth century there was a settlement consisting of huts on the tops of Rome's hills. The early Romans, basically a pastoral people, spoke Latin, which, like Greek, belongs to the Indo-European family of languages (see Table 1.2 in Chapter 1). The Roman historical tradition also maintained that early Rome (753–509 B.C.E.) had been under the control of seven kings and that two of the last three had been Etruscans. Some historians believe that the king list may have some historical accuracy. What is certain is that Rome did fall under the influence of the Etruscans for about one hundred years during the period of the kings.

By the beginning of the sixth century, under Etruscan influence, Rome began to emerge as a city. The Etruscans were responsible for an outstanding building program. They constructed the first roadbed of the chief street through Rome—the Sacred Way—before 575 B.C.E. and oversaw the development of temples, markets, shops, streets, and houses. By 509 B.C.E., supposedly when the monarchy was overthrown, a new Rome had emerged, essentially a product of the fusion of Etruscan and native Roman elements. After Rome had expanded over its seven hills and the valleys in between, the Servian Wall was built in the fourth century B.C.E. to surround the city.

The Etruscans had an impact on Roman civilization in numerous ways, both large and small. The Romans adopted Etruscan dress—the toga and short cloak. The insignia of the Etruscan kings became the insignia of Roman magistrates. Most impressive was the *fasces* (FAS-eez), an ax surrounded by a bundle of rods used as a symbol for the power to scourge and execute, hence to rule. The Romans were also indebted to the Etruscans for the alphabet. The Latin alphabet was a modification of the Etruscan one derived from the Greeks.

The Romans traditionally associated the end of both monarchy and Etruscan domination with the rape of Lucretia, a Roman noblewoman of great virtue.

Raped by a son of the king, Lucretia told her father, husband, and their friends what had happened and then committed suicide "rather than be an example of unchastity to other wives," as an ancient Roman historian put it. Lucretia became the model Roman woman: a faithful wife and a pure and courageous woman who chose death rather than be seen as lacking in virtue. In revenge, the Roman nobles drove the king and his family from Rome and established a republican form of government, which ushered in the era of the Republic. According to the Romans of the late Republic, all this occurred in 509 B.C.E. Though interesting, the story has little historical foundation. It is more likely that the overthrow of the monarchy was accomplished by nobles who experienced a loss of power because of the shift from cavalry to heavy-armed infantry during the reign of Servius Tullius (SUR-vee-uss TUHL-ee-uss), the next-to-last king. The overthrow was not a patriotic uprising but an attempt by Roman nobles to maintain their position of power. Some scholars have even argued that the continuation of Etruscan influence at Rome into the fifth century necessitates dating the beginning of the Roman Republic to around 475 B.C.E., but most historians remain committed to a date close to the traditional 509 B.C.E.

THE ROMAN REPUBLIC (C. 509–264 B.C.E.)

The transition from monarchy to republican government was not easy. Rome felt threatened by enemies from every direction and in meeting these threats embarked on a course of military expansion that led to the conquest of the entire Italian peninsula. During this period of expansion in Italy, the Roman Republic developed political institutions that were in many ways determined by the social divisions that existed within the community.

The Roman State   In politics and law, as in conquest, the Romans took a practical approach and fashioned political institutions in response to problems as they arose. Hence, it is important to remember that the political institutions we will discuss evolved over a period of centuries.

Political Institutions   The Romans had a clear concept of executive authority, embodied in their word **imperium** (im-PEE-ree-um), or "the right to command." Invested with *imperium*, the chief magistrates of the Roman state exercised a supreme power that was circumscribed only by extraneous means—officials held office for a limited term and could be tried for offenses committed in office once their term ended.

The chief executive officers of the Roman Republic who possessed *imperium* were the consuls and praetors. Two **consuls** (KAHN-sulls), chosen annually, administered the government and led the Roman army into battle. In 366 B.C.E., a new office, that of the **praetor** (PREE-tur), was created. The praetor also possessed *imperium* and could govern Rome when the consuls were away from the city and could also lead armies. The praetor's primary function, however, was the execution of justice. He was in charge of the civil law as it applied to Roman citizens. In 242 B.C.E., reflecting Rome's growth, another praetor was added to judge cases in which one or both parties were noncitizens.

As Rome expanded into the Mediterranean, additional praetors were established to govern the newly conquered provinces (two in 227, two more in 197 B.C.E.). But as the number of provinces continued to grow, the Romans devised a new system in which ex-consuls and ex-praetors who had served their one-year terms were given the title of *proconsul* and *propraetor*, respectively, and sent out as provincial governors. This demonstrates once again the Romans' practical solution to an immediate problem. It was reasonable to assume that officials with governmental experience would make good provincial administrators, although this was not always true in practice due to the opportunities for financial corruption in the provinces.

Periodically, the Republic also created an extraordinary executive. In an emergency, the consuls would resign, and a **dictator** with unlimited power would be chosen to run the state. This office was supposed to last only for the duration of the emergency, the usual limit being six months. The Roman state also had administrative officials with specialized duties. **Quaestors** (KWES-turs) assisted consuls and praetors in the administration of financial affairs. **Aediles** (EE-dylz) supervised the public games and watched over the grain supply of the city, a major problem for a rapidly growing urban community that came to rely on imported grain to feed its population.

The Roman **senate** came to hold an especially important position in the Republic. The senate or council of elders was a select group of about three hundred men who served for life. The senate was not a legislative body and could only advise the magistrates. The advice of the senate was not taken lightly, however, and by the third century B.C.E. had virtually the force of law. No doubt the prestige of the senate's members furthered this development. But it also helped that the senate met continuously, while the chief magistrates changed annually and the popular assemblies operated slowly and met only periodically.

The Roman Republic possessed a number of popular assemblies. By far the most important was the **centuriate assembly**, essentially the Roman army functioning in its political role. Organized by classes based on wealth, it was structured in such a way that the wealthiest citizens always had a majority. The centuriate assembly elected the chief magistrates and passed laws. It is important to remember, however, that the Romans passed few statutory laws and simply left much governance to magisterial authority. As a result of the struggle between the orders, another assembly, the council of the plebs, came into being in 471 B.C.E. (see "The Struggle of the Orders" below).

The government of the Roman Republic, then, consisted of three major elements. Two consuls and later other elected officials served as magistrates and ran the state. An assembly of adult males (the centuriate assembly), controlled by the wealthiest citizens, elected these officials, while the senate, a small group of large landowners, advised them. Thus, the Roman state was an aristocratic republic controlled by a relatively small group of privileged people.

Social Organization   The family was the basis of Roman society. At its head was the ***paterfamilias*** (pay-tur-fuh-MEEL-yus), who theoretically had unlimited power over his family. When a father died, his sons became heads of their own families. Families were often grouped into social units known as *gentes* (GEN-tayz) or clans, descended from the same ancestor and bearing the same family name.

In the early Republic, a Roman citizen had two names, but three names became more common later in the Republic. Each man had a *praenomen* (pree-NOH-mun), or forename, which was his personal name. There were only a limited number of personal names, such as Gaius or Marcus, and these were usually abbreviated in writing (C. for Gaius, from the earlier spelling Caius, or M. for Marcus). The *praenomen* was followed by the *nomen* (NOH-mun), which was the name of the group of families or clan (*gens*) to which the person belonged. Thus, the full name of the politician and writer Cicero was Marcus Tullius Cicero, Tullius referring to the clan Tullia. The third name, in this case Cicero, was the *cognomen* (kahg-NOH-mun), which was an extra personal name, sometimes even a nickname by which the person was known. Eventually, the *cognomen* became a hereditary family name, enabling people to identify different branches of the same clan. Women usually had one name, the feminine form of the father's *nomen*. Thus, the daughter of Marcus Tullius Cicero was called Tullia. Names were important to the Romans because they signified a person's place in Roman society.

Closely associated with clan and family was the practice of clientage. Clients constituted a dependent class; they were people who did not have the means to protect themselves or their families without the assistance of a patron. The patron, usually a wealthy member of the upper classes, gave protection and especially legal assistance to his clients. In return, clients provided their patrons with certain services, such as field labor, military assistance, and, especially important in the Republic, votes in the assemblies.

The most noticeable element in the social organization of early Rome was the division between two groups—the **patricians** and the **plebeians** (pleh-BEE-unz). The patrician class in Rome consisted of families who were descended from the original senators appointed during the period of the kings. Their initial prominence was probably due to their wealth as great landowners. Thus, the patricians consti- tuted an aristocratic governing class. They alone could be consuls, other magistrates, and senators. Through their patronage of large numbers of dependent clients, they could control the centuriate assembly and many other facets of Roman life.

The plebeians constituted the considerably larger group of "independent, un- privileged, poorer and vulnerable men" as well as nonpatrician large landowners, less wealthy landholders, artisans, merchants, and small farmers. Although they were citizens, the plebeians did not possess the same rights as the patricians, and at the beginning of the fifth century B.C.E., they began a struggle to rectify that situation.

The Struggle of the Orders   Two major problems that existed in the fifth century probably fueled the struggle between the patricians and the plebeians. Both patri- cians and plebeians could vote, but only the patricians could be elected to govern- mental offices. Both had the right to make legal contracts and marriages, but intermarriage between patricians and plebeians was forbidden. The wealthy ple- beians wanted political equality with the patricians, namely, the right to hold office, and social equality in the form of the right of intermarriage.

The plebeians' first success came in 494 B.C.E., when they withdrew physically from the state. The patricians, realizing that they could not defend Rome by them- selves, were forced to compromise. Two new officials known as **tribunes of the plebs** were instituted (later the number was raised to five and then ten). These tribunes were given the power to protect plebeians against arrest by patrician magistrates. Moreover, after a new popular assembly for plebeians only, called the **council of the plebs**, was created in 471 B.C.E., the tribunes became responsible for convoking it and placing proposals before it. If adopted, these measures became *plebiscita* (pleb-i-SEE-tuh) ("it is the opinion of the plebs"), but they were binding only on the plebeians, not on the patricians. Nevertheless, the council of the plebs gave the plebeians considerable political leverage.

The next step for the plebeians involved the law. The plebeians came to realize that if they were to increase their power, they needed knowledge of the law and the legal and governmental procedures carefully guarded by the patricians. Due to plebeian pressure, a special commission of ten officials was created with the task of regularizing and publishing the laws. This action resulted in the publication in 450 B.C.E. of the Twelve Tables of Law, which included the legal procedures for going to court; provisions on family, women, and divorce; regulations concerning private property; rules governing relationships and injuries to others; and a provision prohibiting intermarriage between patricians and plebeians.

This publication of the laws led to further agitation from the plebeians between 450 and 445 since they could now see how disadvantaged they were. In particular, they demanded the right of intermarriage and admission to the chief magistracies, especially the consulship. In 445 B.C.E., the Canuleian law allowed patricians and plebeians to intermarry. Once this was permitted, the division between the two groups became less important, and the solidarity of the patrician class against plebeian gains began to falter. In the fourth century B.C.E., the consulship was opened to plebeians.

The chief landmark in Roman constitutional history—and the climax of the struggle between the orders—came in 287 B.C.E. with the Hortensian law. Henceforth all *plebiscita* passed by the plebeian assembly had the force of law and were binding on the entire community, both plebeians and patricians. Moreover, unlike the laws passed by the centuriate assembly, these *plebiscita* did not need the approval of the senate.

The struggle between the orders, then, had a significant impact on the development of the Roman constitution. Plebeians could hold the highest offices of state, they could intermarry with the patricians, and they could help pass laws binding on the entire Roman community. Although the struggle had been long, the Romans had handled it by compromise, not violent revolution. Theoretically, by 287 B.C.E. all Roman citizens were equal under the law, and all could strive for political office. But in reality, as a result of the right of intermarriage, a select number of wealthy patrician and plebeian families formed a new senatorial aristocracy called the *nobiles* (no-BEE-layz), which came to dominate the political offices. The Roman Republic had not become a democracy.

The Roman Conquest of Italy   At the beginning of the Republic, Rome was surrounded by enemies, including the Etruscans to the north and the Sabines (SAY-bynz), Volscians (VOL-shunz), and Aequi (EYE-kwee *or* EE-kwy) to the east and south. The Latin communities on the plain of Latium posed an even more immediate threat. If we are to believe Livy (LIV-ee), one of the chief ancient sources for the history of the early Roman

The Twelve Tables

The Twelve Tables were the first formal codification of Roman laws and customs. The code was inscribed on bronze plaques, which were eventually destroyed. These selections are taken from reconstructions of the code preserved in the works of later writers.

Selections from the Twelve Tables

Table III: Execution; Law of Debt

When a debt has been acknowledged, or judgment about the matter has been pronounced in court, thirty days must be the legitimate time of grace. After that, the debtor may be arrested by laying on of hands. Bring him into court. If he does not satisfy the judgment, or no one in court offers himself as surety in his behalf, the creditor may take the defaulter with him. He may bind him either in stocks or in fetters....

Unless they make a settlement, debtors shall be held in bond for sixty days. During that time they shall be brought before the praetor's court in the meeting place on three successive market days, and the amount for which they are judged liable shall be announced; on the third market day they shall suffer capital punishment or be delivered up for sale abroad, across the Tiber.

Table IV: Rights of Head of Family

Quickly kill ... a dreadfully deformed child.

If a father three times surrenders a son for sale, the son shall be free from the father.

A child born ten months after the father's death will not be admitted into legal inheritance.

Table V: Guardianship; Succession

Females shall remain in guardianship even when they have attained their majority.

If a man is raving mad, rightful authority over his person and chattels shall belong to his agnates [nearest male relatives] or to his clansmen.

A spendthrift is forbidden to exercise administration over his own goods.... A person who, being insane or a spendthrift, is prohibited from administering his own goods shall be under trusteeship of agnates.

Table VII: Rights Concerning Land

Branches of a tree may be lopped off all round to a height of more than 15 feet.... Should a tree on a neighbor's farm be bent crooked by a wind and lean over your farm, action may be taken for removal of that tree.

It is permitted to gather up fruit falling down on another man's farm.

Table VIII: Torts or Delicts

If any person has sung or composed against another person a song such as was causing slander or insult to another, he shall be clubbed to death.

If a person has maimed another's limb, let there be retaliation in kind unless he makes agreement for settlement with him.

Any person who destroys by burning any building or heap of corn deposited alongside a house shall be bound, scourged, and put to death by burning at the stake, provided that he has committed the said misdeed with malice aforethought, but if he shall have committed it by accident, that is, by negligence, it is ordained that he repair the damage, or, if he be too poor to be competent for such punishment, he shall receive a lighter chastisement.

Table IX: Public Law

The penalty shall be capital punishment for a judge or arbiter legally appointed who has been found guilty of receiving a bribe for giving a decision.

Table XI: Supplementary Laws

Intermarriage shall not take place between plebeians and patricians.

Q *What do the selections from the Twelve Tables reveal about Roman society? In what ways do these points of law differ from those found in the Code of Hammurabi? In what ways are they similar?*

Source: From *Roman Civilization*, Vol. I, Naphtali Lewis and Meyer Reinhold. Copyright © 1955 Columbia University Press. Reprinted by permission of the publisher.

Republic, Rome was engaged in almost continuous warfare with its neighbors for the next hundred years.

In his account of these years, Livy provided a detailed narrative of Roman efforts. Many of Livy's stories were legendary in character and indeed were modeled on events in Greek history. But Livy, writing in the first century B.C.E., used these stories to teach Romans the moral values and virtues that had made Rome great. These included tenacity, duty, courage, and especially discipline. Indeed, Livy recounted stories of military leaders who executed their own sons for leaving their place in battle, a serious offense because the success of the hoplite infantry depended on maintaining a precise order. These stories had little basis in fact, but like the story of George Washington and the cherry tree in American history, they provided mythic images to reinforce Roman patriotism.

By 338 B.C.E., Rome had crushed the Latin states in Latium. During the next fifty years, the Romans waged a fierce struggle with the Samnites (SAM-nyts), a hill people from the central Apennines, some of whom had settled in Campania, south of Rome. The conquest of the Samnites gave Rome considerable control over a large part of Italy and also brought it into direct contact with the Greek

© Jon Arnold Images (Walter Bibikow)/Alamy

Roman Roads in Italy. *The Romans built a remarkable system of roads. After laying a foundation with gravel, which allowed for drainage, the Roman builders placed flagstones, closely fitted together. Unlike other peoples who built similar kinds of roads, the Romans did not follow the contours of the land but made their roads as straight as possible to facilitate communications and transportation, especially for military purposes. Seen here is a view of the Via Appia (Appian Way), built in 312 B.C. under the leadership of the censor and consul Appius Claudius (Roman roads were often named after the great Roman families who encouraged their construction). The Via Appia was meant to make it easy for Roman armies to march from Rome to the newly conquered city of Capua, a distance of 152 miles.*

communities of southern Italy. Soon the Romans were involved in hostilities with some of these Greek cities. The Greek communities were primarily commercial cities and had no standing armies. They were accustomed to hiring mercenaries to fight their battles for them. Consequently, they bought the aid of King Pyrrhus (PEER-uss) of Epirus (approximately modern-day Epirus in Greece), who crossed the Adriatic with 20,000 troops and defeated the Romans twice. In both battles, however, Pyrrhus experienced heavy losses, leading him to comment that "another such victory, and we shall be lost"—hence our phrase "Pyrrhic (PEER-ik) victory." After a diversion to Sicily, Pyrrhus came back for one more battle with the Romans and this time was decisively defeated. By 267 B.C.E., the Romans had completed their conquest of southern Italy. After crushing the remaining Etruscan states to the north, Rome had conquered all of Italy, except the extreme north, by 264 B.C.E.

To rule Italy, the Romans devised the Roman confederation in 338 B.C.E. Under this system, Rome allowed some peoples—especially the Latins—to have full Roman citizenship. Most of the remaining communities were made allies. They remained free to run their own local affairs but were required to provide soldiers for Rome. Moreover, the Romans made it clear that loyal allies could improve their status and even aspire to becoming Roman citizens. Thus, the Romans had found a way to give conquered states a stake in Rome's success.

In the course of their expansion throughout Italy, the Romans pursued consistent policies that help explain their success. The Romans excelled at making the correct diplomatic decisions; they were superb diplomats. Though firm and even cruel when necessary—rebellions were crushed without mercy—they were also shrewd in extending their citizenship and allowing autonomy in domestic affairs. Once at war, the Romans were not only good soldiers but also persistent ones. The loss of an army or a fleet did not cause them to quit but spurred them on to build new armies and new fleets. Finally, the Romans had a practical sense of strategy. As they conquered, they settled Romans and Latins in new communities outside Latium. By 264 B.C.E., the Romans had established colonies—fortified towns—at all strategic locations. By building roads to these settlements and connecting them, the Romans assured themselves of an impressive military and communications network that enabled them to rule effectively and efficiently. By insisting on military service from the allies in the Roman confederation, Rome essentially mobilized the entire military manpower of all Italy for its wars.

THE ROMAN CONQUEST OF THE MEDITERRANEAN (264–133 B.C.E.)

After their conquest of the Italian peninsula, the Romans found themselves face to face with a formidable Mediterranean power—Carthage (KAR-thij). Founded around 800 B.C.E. by Phoenicians from Tyre, Carthage was located in a favorable position for commanding Mediterranean trade routes and had become an important commercial center (see Map 5.2).

In the sixth century B.C.E., Carthage was governed by two judges, who were elected annually. They were usually men of wealth from prominent families.

MAP 5.2 Roman Conquests in the Mediterranean, 264–133 B.C.

Separately elected generals led the military forces, which consisted primarily of mercenaries recruited from different parts of the western Mediterranean. There was also a senate composed of several hundred prominent men chosen for life. Ordinary citizens had little power, although a group of 104 judges examined the activities of officials and generals and prevented anyone from either group from establishing a tyranny.

Carthage gradually became a strong military state. By the third century B.C.E., its empire included the coast of North Africa, southern Spain, Sardinia, Corsica, and western Sicily. With its monopoly of western Mediterranean trade, Carthage was the largest and richest state in the area. The presence of Carthaginians (kar-thuh-JIN-ee-unz) in Sicily made the Romans apprehensive about Carthaginian encroachment on the Italian coast. In 264 B.C.E., mutual suspicions drove the two powers into a lengthy struggle for control of the western Mediterranean.

The Struggle with Carthage   The First Punic (PYOO-nik) War (264–241 B.C.E.)—the Latin word for Phoenician was *Punicus*—began when the Romans decided to intervene in a struggle between two Sicilian cities and sent an army to Sicily. The Carthaginians, who considered Sicily within their own sphere of influence, regarded this as a just cause for war. In going to war, both sides determined on the conquest of Sicily. The Romans realized that the war would be long and drawn out if they could not supplement their land operations with a navy and promptly developed a substantial fleet. The Carthaginians, however, had difficulty finding mercenaries to continue the fight. After a long struggle in which both sides lost battles in North Africa and Sicily, a Roman fleet defeated the Carthaginian navy off Sicily in 242 B.C.E., and the war quickly came to an end. In 241 B.C.E. Carthage gave up all rights to Sicily and had to pay an indemnity. Three years later, Rome took advantage of Carthage's problems with its mercenaries to seize the islands of Sardinia and Corsica. This act so angered the Carthaginians that, according to one story, their leading general, Hamilcar Barca, made his nine-year-old son swear that he would hate Rome ever after. The son's name was Hannibal (HAN-uh-bul).

Hannibal and the Second Punic War   Between the wars, Carthage made an unexpected recovery under the leadership of the general who had been briefly successful in Sicily in the First Punic War, Hamilcar Barca. Hamilcar extended Carthage's domains in Spain to compensate for the territory lost to Rome. A major goal in creating the Spanish empire was to get manpower for Carthage. Hamilcar and his successors proceeded to build up a formidable land army in the event of a second war with Rome because they realized that Carthage's success depended on defeating Rome on land. In 221 B.C.E., Hamilcar's son Hannibal, now twenty-five, took over the direction of Carthaginian policy. Within three years, Rome and Carthage were again at war.

Carthage and Rome had agreed to divide Spain into respective spheres of influence. Although Saguntum was located in the Carthaginian sphere, Rome made an alliance with the city and encouraged its inhabitants in anti-Carthaginian activities. Thoroughly provoked by the Roman action, Hannibal attacked Saguntum, and the Romans declared war on Carthage in 218 B.C.E. This time the Carthaginian strategy aimed at bringing the war home to the Romans and defeating them in their own backyard. In an amazing march, Hannibal crossed the Alps with an army of 30,000 to 40,000 men and 6,000 horses and elephants and advanced into northern Italy. The Alps took a toll on the Carthaginian army, and most of the elephants did not survive the trip. After defeating the Romans at the Trebia River, Hannibal added thousands of Gauls to his army and proceeded into central Italy. At Lake Trasimene in Etruria, he again defeated the Romans. In desperation, the Romans elected as consul Quintus Fabius Maximus, who became known as the "Delayer" because of his tactics of following and delaying Hannibal's army without risking a pitched battle. Hannibal hoped to destroy the Roman confederation and win Italian cities away from Rome. The policy failed; virtually all remained loyal to Rome.

In 216 B.C.E., the Romans decided to meet Hannibal head-on. It was a serious mistake. At Cannae (KAN-nye *or* KAN-ee), Hannibal's forces devastated a Roman army, killing as many as 40,000 soldiers. At last, some of the southern Italian cities rebelled against Roman rule and went over to Hannibal. Rome seemed on the brink of disaster but refused to give up and raised yet another army.

Rome gradually recovered. Although Hannibal remained free to roam in Italy, he had neither the men nor the equipment to lay siege to the major cities, including Rome itself. The Romans began to reconquer some of the rebellious Italian cities. More important, the Romans pursued a Spanish strategy that aimed at undermining the Carthaginian empire in Spain. Publius Cornelius Scipio, later known as Scipio Africanus (SIP-ee-oh af-ree-KAY-nuss) the Elder, was given command of the

Roman forces in Spain. A brilliant general who learned from Hannibal's tactics, he had pushed the Carthaginians out of Spain by 206 B.C.E.

The Romans then took the war directly to Carthage. Late in 204 B.C.E., Scipio led a Roman army from Sicily into North Africa and forced the Carthaginians to recall Hannibal from Italy. At the Battle of Zama (ZAH-muh) in 202 B.C.E., Scipio decisively defeated Hannibal and the Carthaginian forces, and the war was over. Eventually, Hannibal left Carthage and went to help Antiochus, the ruler of the Seleucid kingdom, in his struggle with Rome. After Antiochus made peace with the Romans, Hannibal fled to Bithynia, near the Black Sea. Pursued by the Romans, Hannibal killed himself saying, "Let us free Rome of her dread of one old man."

By the peace treaty signed in 201 by the Carthaginians and Romans, Carthage lost Spain, agreed to pay an indemnity, and promised not to go to war without Rome's permission. Spain, like Sicily, Corsica, and Sardinia earlier, was made into a Roman province. Rome had become the dominant power in the western Mediterranean.

The Destruction of Carthage   But some Romans wanted even more. A number of prominent Romans, especially the conservative politician Cato, advocated the complete destruction of Carthage. Cato ended every speech he made to the senate with the words, "And I think Carthage must be destroyed." When the Carthaginians technically broke their peace treaty with Rome by going to war against one of Rome's North African allies that had been encroaching on Carthage's home territory, the Romans declared war. Led by Scipio Aemilianus (SIP-ee-oh ee-mil-ee-AY-nuss) Africanus the Younger, Roman forces undertook their third and last war with Carthage (149–146 B.C.E.). This time, Carthage was no match for the Romans, who seized the opportunity to carry out the final destruction of Carthage. The territory of Carthage was made a province called Africa.

The Eastern Mediterranean   During the Punic Wars, Rome had become acutely aware of the Hellenistic states of the eastern Mediterranean when the king of Macedonia made an alliance with Hannibal after the Roman defeat at Cannae. But the Romans were preoccupied with the Carthaginians, and it was not until after the defeat of Carthage that Rome became involved in the world of Hellenistic politics as an advocate for the freedom of the Greek states. This support of the Greeks brought the Romans into conflict with both Macedonia and the kingdom of the Seleucids. Roman military victories and diplomatic negotiations rearranged the territorial boundaries of the Hellenistic kingdoms and achieved the freedom of the Greek states in 196 B.C.E. For fifty years, Rome tried to be a power broker in the affairs of the Greeks without direct control of their lands. When the effort failed, the Romans changed their policy.

Macedonia was made a Roman province in 148 B.C.E., and when some of the Greek states rose in revolt against Rome's restrictive policies, Rome acted decisively. The city of Corinth, leader of the revolt, was destroyed in 146 B.C.E. to teach the Greeks a lesson, and Greece was placed under the control of the Roman governor of Macedonia. Thirteen years later, in 133 B.C.E., the king of Pergamum deeded his kingdom to Rome, giving Rome its first province in Asia. Rome was now master of the Mediterranean Sea.

The Nature of Roman Imperialism

Rome's empire was built in three stages: the conquest of Italy, the conflict with Carthage and expansion into the western Mediterranean, and the involvement with and domination of the Hellenistic kingdoms in the eastern Mediterranean. The Romans did not have a master plan for the creation of an empire. Much of their expansion was opportunistic; once involved in a situation that threatened their security, the Romans did not hesitate to act. And the more they expanded, the more threats to their security appeared on the horizon, involving them in yet more conflicts. Indeed, the Romans liked to portray themselves as declaring war only for defensive reasons or to protect allies. That is only part of the story, however. It is likely, as some historians have suggested, that at some point a group of Roman aristocratic leaders emerged who favored expansion both for the glory it offered and for the economic benefits it provided. Certainly, by the second century B.C.E., aristocratic senators perceived new opportunities for lucrative foreign commands, enormous spoils of war, and an abundant supply of slave labor for their growing landed estates. By that same time, as the destruction of Corinth and Carthage indicates, Roman imperialism had become more arrogant and brutal as well. Rome's foreign success also had enormous repercussions for the internal development of the Roman Republic.

Evolution of the Roman Army

By the fourth century B.C.E., the Roman army consisted of four legions, each made up of 4,000 to 5,000 men; each legion had about 300 cavalry and the rest infantry. The infantry consisted of three lines of battle. The *hastati* (hahs-TAH-tee) (spearmen), made up of the youngest recruits, formed the front line; they were armed with heavy spears and short swords, and protected by a large oval shield, helmet, breastplate, and greaves (shin guards). The *principes* (PRIN-kih-payz *or* PRIN-sih-peez) (chief men), armed and protected like the *hastati*, formed the second line. The third line of battle was formed by the *triarii* (trih-AR-ee-ee) (third-rank men), who knelt behind the first two lines, ready to move up and fill any gaps. A fourth group of troops, poor citizens who wore cloaks but no armor and were lightly armed, functioned as skirmishers who usually returned to the rear lines after their initial contact with the enemy to form backup reserves.

In the early Republic, the army was recruited from citizens between the ages of eighteen and forty-six who had the resources to equip themselves for battle. Since most of them were farmers, they enrolled only for a year, campaigned during the summer months, and returned home in time for the fall harvest. Later, during the Punic Wars of the third century B.C.E., the period of service had to be extended, although this was resisted by farmers whose livelihoods could be severely harmed by a long absence. Nevertheless, after the disastrous Battle of Cannae in 216 B.C.E., the Romans were forced to recruit larger armies, and the number of legions rose to twenty-five.

The ancient historian Polybius believed that one of the reasons the Romans were so successful militarily was that in the early centuries of the Republic the Roman army was basically a citizen army led by the Republic's elected magistrates. An army of citizens defending their homeland would be braver and fight harder than hired mercenaries. Roman military success may also have been due to the aggressive behavior of the Roman military leaders, although this could be detrimental at sea. According to Polybius,

> The Romans, to speak generally, rely on force in all their enterprises, and think it is incumbent on them to carry out their projects in spite of all, and that nothing is impossible when they have once decided on it. They owe their success in many cases to this spirit, but sometimes they conspicuously fail by reason of it and especially at sea. For on land they are attacking men and the works of man and are usually successful, as there they are employing force against forces of the same nature.... But when they come to encounter the sea and the atmosphere and choose to fight them by force they meet with signal defeats.[1]

Major changes in the military would not come until the first century B.C.E. with the military reforms of Marius (see "Marius and the New Roman Army" later in this chapter).

SOCIETY AND CULTURE IN THE ROMAN REPUBLIC

One of the most noticeable aspects of Roman society and culture is the impact of the Greeks. The Romans had experienced Greek influence early on through the Greek cities in southern Italy. By the end of the third century B.C.E., however, Greek civilization played an ever-increasing role in Roman culture. Greek ambassadors, merchants, and artists traveled to Rome and spread Greek thought and practices. After their conquest of the Hellenistic kingdoms, Roman military commanders shipped Greek manuscripts and art back to Rome. Roman households used multitudes of educated Greek slaves. Greek models affected virtually every area of Roman life, from literature and philosophy to religion and education. Wealthy Romans hired Greek tutors and sent their sons to Athens to study. As the Roman poet Horace said, "Captive Greece took captive her rude conqueror." Greek thought captivated the less sophisticated Roman minds, and the Romans became willing transmitters of Greek culture—not, however, without some resistance from Romans who had nothing but contempt for Greek politics and feared the end of old Roman values. Even those who favored Greek culture blamed the Greeks for Rome's new vices, including luxury and homosexual practices.

Roman Religion   Every aspect of Roman society was permeated with religion. The official state religion focused on the worship of a pantheon of gods and goddesses, including Juno, the patron goddess of women; Minerva, the goddess of craftspeople; Mars, the god of war; and Jupiter Optimus Maximus (JOO-puh-tur AHP-tuh-muss MAK-suh-muss) ("best and greatest"), who became the patron deity of Rome and assumed a central place in the religious life of the city. As Rome developed and came into contact with other peoples and gods, the community simply adopted new deities. Hence, the Greek Hermes became the Roman Mercury, and the Greek Demeter, Ceres. Eventually, a complete amalgamation of Greek and Roman religion occurred, giving the Romans and the Greeks essentially the same "Greco-Roman" religion.

The Importance of Ritual   Roman religion focused on the worship of the gods for a very practical reason—human beings were thought to be totally dependent on them. The exact performance of ritual was crucial to establishing a right relationship with the gods. What was true for individuals was also valid for the state: it also had to observe correct ritual in order to receive its reward. Consequently, accurate performance of ritual was important, and the Romans established a college of priests or *pontiffs* to carry out that responsibility. Initially three in number, by the first century B.C.E., they had increased to sixteen. At the head of the pontiffs was the *pontifex maximus* (PAHN-ti-feks MAK-suh-muss) (chief pontiff), a powerful figure who controlled the state religion. First, Julius Caesar and later all emperors until 381 C.E. held this position. The *pontifex maximus* also chose six girls between the ages of six and ten to serve as Vestal Virgins.

The pontiffs were in charge of what the Romans called the divine law, maintaining the right relationship between the state and the gods. The pontiffs performed all public religious acts and supervised magistrates in the correct ritual for public political acts. If the rituals were performed correctly, the Romans would obtain the "peace of the gods." The Romans' success in creating an empire was no doubt taken as confirmation of divine favor. As Cicero, the first-century B.C.E. politician and writer, claimed, "We have overcome all the nations of the world, because we have realized that the world is directed and governed by the gods."[2]

The Use of Omens   In addition to the college of pontiffs, a college of *augurs* (AW-gurz) existed whose responsibility was to interpret the *auspices* (AWSS-puh-sizz)—signs or warnings that the gods gave to men through such phenomena as unusual changes in the weather or the migratory pattern of birds. Before every important act of state, a magistrate with *imperium* took the auspices to make sure the gods approved. The Romans attributed great importance to this— if the omens were unfavorable, the act was invalid or the planned action was not auspicious. As Cicero later commented, the augurs had "the highest and most important authority in the State" because "no act of any magistrate at home or in the field can have any validity for any person without their authority."[3] Auspices were taken by observing the flights of birds, lightning and other natural phenomena, and the behavior of certain animals.

Household Cults   Just as the state had an official cult, so did families. Because the family was regarded as a small state within the state, it had its own household cults, which included Janus, the spirit of the doorway; Vesta, the goddess of the hearth; and the Penates (puh-NAY-teez), the spirits of the storehouse. Here, too, proper ritual was important, and it was the responsibility of the *paterfamilias* as head of the family to ensure that the religious obligations were properly fulfilled.

One of the most important ceremonies involved purification. In his manual *On Agriculture*, Marcus Cato the Elder spelled out the proper ritual for purification of a landed estate. The ceremony included these words, addressed to Mars, the god of vegetation as well as war:

> Father Mars, I beg and entreat you to be of good will and favorable to me and to our house and household, for which purpose I have ordered the swine-sheep-bull procession to be led around my land and fields and farm. And [I beg] that you will check, thrust back, and avert diseases seen and unseen, crop failure and crop destruction, sudden losses and storms, and that you will permit the annual crops, the grain crops, the

The Vestal Virgins

The Vestal Virgins guarded the fire on the state hearth in the temple of Vesta (goddess of the hearth) in Rome. To the Romans, the extinguishing of the fire was a warning of the destruction of the city. It was also a sign that a Vestal Virgin had lost her virginity, an act that was punished harshly, as is explained in this selection from the historian Dionysius of Halicarnassus, a Greek who lived in Rome and published his *Roman Antiquities* near the end of the first century B.C.E.

Dionysius of Halicarnassus, *Roman Antiquities*

Originally there were four virgins who served the goddess Vesta. They were chosen by the king in accordance with the regulations which Numa established. Because of the numerous sacred duties which they perform, their number was increased to six, and six it has remained up to our own time. The virgins live in the sanctuary of the goddess, and no one can be prevented from entering there in the day if he so wishes, but it is forbidden for any man to stay there at night.

The priestesses remain pure and unmarried for 30 years, offering sacrifices, and performing other religious rituals in accordance with the law. They learn these rituals in the first ten years, and for the second ten years they perform them, and during the remaining ten years they must teach them to their successors. When the 30 years have been completed, nothing prohibits those who want to from putting aside their headbands and other insignia of their service and getting married. But only a few have done that, and their lives for their remaining years were neither enviable nor very happy. Therefore, taking what has happened to those unhappy few as a warning, the rest of the virgins remain in service to the goddess until their deaths, at which

time another virgin is appointed by the priests to take the place of the one who has died.

They receive many splendid honors from the city, and therefore they do not want children or marriage. And anyway, there are heavy penalties for misbehavior. Misdeeds are investigated and punished by priests according to the law. They whip those who have committed some lesser offense, but those who have lost their virginity are sentenced to a shameful and pitiful death. While they are still alive they are carried in a funeral procession. Their friends and relatives join the procession and mourn for them as though for someone deceased. They are taken as far as the Colline gate, and interred (alive) in an underground cell which has been built within the walls of the gate. They are dressed in funeral clothes but they receive no monument or funeral offering or any of the other rites which are customary at funerals.

There are said to be many clues which indicate that a priestess who is performing a holy ritual is no longer a virgin, but the principal clue is that the fire goes out, something which the Romans fear more than all catastrophes, since they believe that whatever was the cause of the fire going out, it warns of the destruction of the city. They reintroduce the fire with many rituals of atonement.

Q *What was the importance of the Vestal Virgins? Why were any violations of the rules treated with such harsh punishments?*

Source: Reprinted by permission of the publishers and the Trustees of the Loeb Classical Library from *Dionysius,* vol. 1, Loeb Classical Library Vol. 319, translated by Earnest Cary, Cambridge, Mass.: Harvard University Press, Copyright © 1937 by the President and Fellows of Harvard College. The Loeb Classical Library is a registered trademark of the President and Fellows of Harvard College.

Temple of Portunus.
The Romans considered the proper worship of the gods an important key to success. Typical of Roman religious architecture was the small urban temple located in the midst of a crowded commercial center. Pictured here is a rectangular temple built in Rome in the late second or early first century B.C.E. and dedicated to Portunus, the god of harbors. The temple was located in the cattle market close to the Tiber River.

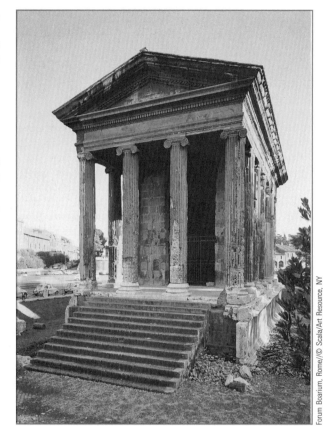

Forum Boarium, Rome//© Scala/Art Resource, NY

vineyards, and tree and vine slips to grow and turn out well. And [that you] keep safe the shepherds and the flocks and give good health and strength to me and to our house and household: with these purposes in view … receive the honor of this suckling swine-sheep-bull sacrifice.[4]

Proper observance of the ritual was so crucial that any error necessitated a repetition of the entire ritual.

Religious Festivals Religious festivals were an important part of Roman religious practice. There were two kinds: public festivals ordained and paid for by the state and private festivals celebrated by individuals and families. By the mid-second century B.C.E., six public festivals were celebrated annually, each lasting several days.

The practice of holding games also grew out of religious festivals. The games were inaugurated in honor of Jupiter Optimus Maximus but had become annual events by 366 B.C.E. In the late Republic, both the number of games and the number of days they lasted were increased. Originally, the games consisted of chariot racing in the Circus Maximus; later, animal hunts and theatrical performances were added. In the empire, gladiatorial contests would become the primary focus (see Chapter 6).

Education: The Importance of Rhetoric   The Romans did not possess a system of public education. In the early Republic, the family provided training in the various skills needed by a Roman citizen. Boys were expected to master the basic elements of farming, develop the physical skills needed to be good soldiers, learn the traditions of the state through the legends of heroic Roman ancestors, and become acquainted with public affairs. Girls were supposed to learn the skills needed to be good wives and mothers. Every upper-class Roman boy or girl was expected to learn to read.

Through contact with the Greek world, Roman education took on new ideals in the third and second centuries B.C.E. The wealthy classes wanted their children exposed to Greek studies and were especially attracted to the training in **rhetoric** and philosophy that would prepare their sons for a successful public career. For upper-class males, rhetoric—the art of persuasive speaking—was an especially important part of their education. To pursue a public career, they needed to learn good speaking skills that would enable them to win elections and lawsuits in the courts. By winning lawsuits, a person could make a name for himself and build political support.

Since knowledge of Greek was a crucial ingredient in education, schools taught by professional teachers emerged to supply this need. Those who could afford to might provide Greek tutors for their children, but less well endowed families could turn to private schools where most of the instructors were educated slaves or freedmen, usually of Greek origin. After several years of primary instruction, whose aim was simply to teach the basics of reading, writing, and arithmetic, the pupil went to a secondary school run by a *grammaticus*, or grammarian. These schools had a standard curriculum based on the liberal arts: literature, dialectic (logic), arithmetic, geometry, astronomy, and music. The core of the liberal arts and the curriculum, however, was Greek literature. As a result, by the second and first centuries B.C.E., educated Romans had become increasingly bilingual.

The Growth of Slavery   Slavery was a common institution throughout the ancient world, but no people possessed more slaves or relied so much on slave labor as the Romans eventually did. Before the third century B.C.E., a small Roman farmer might possess one or two slaves who would help farm his few acres and perform domestic chores. These slaves would most likely be from Italy and be regarded as part of the family household. Only the very rich would have large numbers of slaves.

The Roman conquest of the Mediterranean brought a drastic change in the use of slaves. Large numbers of foreign slaves were transported back to Italy. Thus, the chief source of slaves during the Republic was from capture in war, followed by piracy. Of course, the children of slaves also became slaves. Although some Roman generals brought back slaves to be sold to benefit the public treasury, ambitious generals of the first century, such as Pompey and Caesar, made personal fortunes by treating slaves captured by their armies as private property.

Slaves were used in many ways in Roman society. The rich, of course, owned the most and the best. In the late Republic, it became a badge of prestige to be attended by many slaves. Greeks were in much demand as tutors, musicians, doctors, and artists. Roman businessmen would employ them as shop assistants or artisans. Slaves were also used as farm laborers; huge gangs of slaves living in pitiful conditions worked the large landed estates known as **latifundia** (lat-ih-FOON-dee-uh). Cato the Elder argued that it was cheaper to work slaves to death and then replace them than to treat them well. Many slaves of all nationalities were used as menial household workers, such as cooks, valets, waiters, cleaners, and gardeners. Contractors used slave labor to build roads, aqueducts, and other public facilities. The total number of slaves is difficult to judge—estimates range from one-fourth to one-half the number of free people.

It is also difficult to generalize about the treatment of Roman slaves. There are numerous instances of humane treatment by masters and situations when slaves even protected their owners from danger out of gratitude and esteem. But slaves were also subject to severe punishments, torture, abuse, and hard labor that drove some to run away or even revolt against their owners. The Republic had stringent laws against aiding a runaway slave. The murder of a master by a slave usually meant the execution of all the other household slaves. Near the end of the second century B.C.E., large-scale slave revolts occurred in Sicily, where enormous gangs of slaves were subjected to horrible working conditions on large landed estates. Slaves were branded, beaten, fed inadequately, worked in chains, and housed at night in underground prisons. One revolt of 70,000 slaves lasted three years (135–132 B.C.E.) before it was crushed, and the great revolt on Sicily (104–101 B.C.E.) involved most of the island and required a Roman army of 17,000 men to suppress. The most famous revolt on the Italian peninsula occurred in 73 B.C.E. Led by a Thracian gladiator named Spartacus (SPAR-tuh-kuss), the revolt broke out in southern Italy and involved 70,000 slaves. Spartacus managed to defeat several Roman armies before he was finally trapped and killed in southern Italy in 71 B.C.E. Six thousand of his followers were crucified, the traditional form of execution for slaves.

The Roman Family

At the heart of the Roman social structure stood the family, headed by the *paterfamilias*—the dominant male. The household also included the wife, sons with their wives and children, unmarried daughters, and slaves. A family was virtually a small state within the state, and the power of the *paterfamilias* paralleled that of the state magistrates over citizens. He held absolute authority over his children; he could sell them or have them put to death. Like the Greeks, Roman males believed that the weakness of the female sex necessitated male guardians. The *paterfamilias* exercised that authority; on his death, sons or the nearest male relatives assumed the role of guardians. By the late Republic, however, although the rights of male guardians remained legally in effect, many upper-class women had found numerous ways to circumvent the power of their guardians.

Marriage Fathers arranged the marriages of daughters, although there are instances of mothers and daughters influencing the choice. In the Republic, women married *cum manu* (koom MAH-noo), "with legal control" passing from father to husband. By the mid-first century B.C.E., the dominant practice had changed to *sine manu* (SEE-nay MAH-noo), "without legal control," which meant that married daughters officially remained within the father's legal power. Since the fathers of most married women were dead, not being in the "legal control" of a husband made possible independent property rights that forceful women could translate into considerable power within the household and outside it. Traditionally, Roman marriages were intended to be for life, but divorce was introduced in the third century and became relatively easy to obtain since either party could initiate it and no one needed to prove the breakdown of the marriage. Divorce became especially prevalent in the first century B.C.E.—a period of political turmoil—when marriages were used to cement political alliances.

Some upper-class parents provided education for their daughters. Some girls had private tutors, and others may have gone to primary schools. But at the age when boys were entering secondary schools, girls were pushed into marriage. The legal minimum age was twelve; fourteen was a more common age in practice. Although some Roman doctors warned that early pregnancies could be dangerous to young girls, early marriages persisted due to the desire to benefit from dowries as soon as possible and the reality of early mortality. A good example is Tullia, Cicero's beloved daughter. She was married at sixteen, widowed at twenty-two, remarried one year later, divorced at twenty-eight, remarried at twenty-nine, and divorced at thirty-three. She died at thirty-four, not unusual for females in Roman society.

Upper-Class Women   In contrast to upper-class Athenian women, upper-class Roman women were not segregated from males in the home. Wives were appreciated as enjoyable company and were at the center of household social life. Women talked to visitors and were free to shop, visit friends, and go to games, temples, and theaters. Nevertheless, they were not allowed to participate in public life, although there are examples of women exerting considerable political influence through their husbands. In fact, while upper-class men served the government abroad or in the military, they depended on their wives and mothers to manage their estates and protect their political interests.

The Evolution of Roman Law   One of Rome's chief gifts to the Mediterranean world of its day and to succeeding generations of Western civilization was its development of law. The Twelve Tables of 450 B.C.E. were the first codification of Roman law, and although inappropriate for later times, they were never officially abrogated and were still memorized by schoolboys in the first century B.C.E. Civil law, or *ius civile* (YOOSS see-VEE-lay), derived from the Twelve Tables proved inadequate for later Roman needs, however, and gave way to corrections and additions by the praetors. On taking office, a praetor issued an edict listing his guidelines for dealing with different kinds of legal cases. The praetors were knowledgeable in law, but they also relied on Roman jurists—amateur law experts—for advice in preparing their edicts. The interpretations of the jurists, often embodied in the edicts of the praetors, created a body of legal principles.

In 242 B.C.E., the Romans appointed a second praetor who was responsible for examining suits between a Roman and a non-Roman as well as between two non-Romans. The Romans found that although some of their rules of law could be used

Roman Woman.
*Roman women,
especially those of the
upper class, had more
freedom than women in
Classical Athens despite
the persistent male belief
that women required
guardianship. This
depiction of a Roman
woman pouring water
from a pitcher is from a
fresco on the wall of the
Villa of the Mysteries in
Pompeii dating from the
first century B.C.E.*

SuperStock/Getty Images

in these cases, special rules were often needed. These rules gave rise to a body of law known as the *ius gentium* (YOOSS GEN-tee-um)—the law of nations—defined by the Romans as "that part of the law which we apply both to ourselves and to foreigners." But the influence of Greek philosophy, primarily Stoicism, led Romans in the late Republic to develop the idea of *ius naturale* (YOOSS nah-too-RAH-lay)—natural law—or universal divine law derived from right reason. The Romans came to view their law of nations as derived from or identical to this natural law, thus giving Roman jurists a philosophical justification for systematizing Roman law according to basic principles.

**The
Development
of Literature**

The Romans produced little literature before the third century B.C.E., and the Latin literature that emerged in that century was strongly influenced by Greek models. The demand for plays at public festivals eventually led to a growing number of native playwrights. One of the best known was Plautus (PLAW-tuss)

(c. 254–184 B.C.E.), who used plots from Greek New Comedy (see Chapter 4) for his own plays. The actors wore Greek costumes and Greek masks and portrayed the same stock characters: dirty old men, clever slaves, prostitutes, and young men in love, whose pains are recounted in this brief excerpt:

> Not the throes of all mankind
> Equal my distracted mind.
> I strain and I toss
> On a passionate cross:
> Love's goad makes me reel,
> I whirl on Love's wheel,
> In a swoon of despair
> Hurried here, hurried there—
> Torn asunder, I am blind
> With a cloud upon my mind.[5]

Though indebted to the Greeks, Plautus managed to infuse his plays with his own earthy Latin quality, incorporating elements that appealed to the Romans: drunkenness, gluttony, and womanizing. Plautus wrote for the masses and became very popular in Rome.

A second playwright of distinction was Terence (185–159 B.C.E.), who was born in Carthage and brought to Rome as a slave by a Roman senator who freed him. Terence also used plots from Greek New Comedy, but his plays contained less slapstick than those of Plautus. Terence was more concerned with the subtle portrayal of character and the artistry of his language. His refined Latin style appealed more to a cultivated audience than to the masses. In the prologue to *The Brothers*, he stated: "The author ... takes it as a high compliment if he can win the approval of men who themselves find favor with you all and with the general public, men whose services in war, in peace, and in your private affairs, are given at the right moment, without ostentation, to be available for each one of you."[6] Terence wrote for Rome's aristocracy.

Latin prose developed later than poetry and playwriting and was often the product of Rome's ruling elite. These upper classes were interested in history as a means of exalting their ideals and in oratory because it could be an important instrument for effective statecraft. Hence, their emphasis in writing prose was on creating works of a practical value. This is a prominent feature of the oldest existing work of Latin prose, Cato the Elder's treatise *On Agriculture*. In effect, this was a technical manual reminiscent of the practical handbooks produced in the Hellenistic world.

Despite their attraction to the Greek world, Romans were generally repelled by much of Greek philosophy with the exception of Stoicism. The latter's emphasis on virtuous conduct and performance of duty (see Chapter 4) fit well with Roman ideals and the practical bent of the Roman character.

Roman Art

The Romans were also dependent on the Greeks for artistic inspiration. During the third and second centuries B.C.E., they adopted many features of the Hellenistic style of art (see Chapter 4). The Romans excelled in architecture, a highly practical art. In addition to their justly famous highways, they built sturdy bridges and aqueducts that made use of the arch. They also developed the technique of using concrete in construction projects, which enabled them to erect giant amphitheaters, public baths, and the high-rise tenement buildings that housed Rome's exploding population in the late second and first centuries B.C.E.

The Romans developed a taste for Greek statues, which they placed not only in public buildings but in their homes as well. When demand outstripped the supply of original works, reproductions of Greek statues became fashionable. The Romans' own portrait sculpture was characterized by an intense realism that included even unattractive physical details.

Values and Attitudes   The Romans were by nature a conservative people. They were very concerned about maintaining the *mos maiorum* (MOHSS my-YOR-um), the customs or traditions of their ancestors. The Romans emphasized parental authority and, above all, their obligations to the state. The highest virtue was *pietas* (PY-ih-tass *or* PEE-ih-tass)—the dutiful execution of one's obligations to one's fellow citizens, to the gods, and to the state.

By the second century B.C.E., however, the creation of an empire had begun to weaken the old values. The Romans began to focus more on affluence, status, and material possessions. Emphasis shifted toward individualism and away from collective well-being, the old public spirit that had served Rome so well. Romans who worried about the decline of the old values blamed it on different causes. Some felt that after the destruction of Carthage, the Romans no longer had any strong enemies to challenge them. Others believed that the Romans had simply been overwhelmed by the affluence created by the new empire. And finally, there were those who blamed everything on the Greeks for importing ideas and practices baneful to the Romans.

Of course, Romans responded differently to the changes brought by the creation of an empire. Two examples from the second century demonstrate this well. Marcus Cato the Elder (234–149 B.C.E.) was a Roman praetor, consul, and member of the ruling class. Cato scorned the "Greeklings"—people who followed Greek ways and read Greek philosophy and literature. He wrote to his son:

> I shall speak about those Greek fellows in their proper place, son Marcus, and point out the results of my inquiries at Athens, and convince you what benefit comes from dipping into their literature, and not making a close study of it. They are a quite worthless people, and an intractable one, and you must consider my words prophetic. When that race gives us its literature it will corrupt all things.[7]

But Cato was not stupid. He not only learned Greek himself but also allowed his own son to study in Athens. He knew only too well that, like it or not, Greek was becoming a necessity for Roman political life.

Scipio Aemilianus (185–129 B.C.E.) was a member of a patrician family and a brilliant general who easily achieved the top offices of the Roman state. Scipio was also concerned about the traditional Roman values, but he was much more inclined to accept Rome's growing urbanization as it became the center of the Mediterranean world and was consequently more open to the Greeks as well. He was an admirer of

Greek philosophy and literature. While desirous of maintaining old Roman virtues, Scipio was well aware that the acquisition of an empire had created a new world with new demands and values.

THE DECLINE AND FALL OF THE ROMAN REPUBLIC (133–31 B.C.E.)

By the mid-second century B.C.E., Roman domination of the Mediterranean Sea was well established. Yet the process of building an empire had weakened and threatened the internal stability of Rome. This internal instability characterizes the period of Roman history from 133 until 31 B.C.E., when Octavian defeated Mark Antony and stood supreme over the Roman world. By that time, the constitution of the Roman Republic was in shambles.

Background: Social, Economic, and Political Problems   By the second century B.C.E., the senate had become the effective governing body of the Roman state. It had achieved this position through its own initiative—not through law, but by custom. As always, it comprised some three hundred men drawn primarily from the landed aristocracy who remained senators for life and held the chief magistracies of the Republic. During the wars of the third and second centuries, the senate came to exercise enormous power. It directed the wars and took control of both foreign and domestic policy, including financial affairs. The advice of the senate to the consuls had come to have the force of law.

Moreover, the magistracies and senate were increasingly controlled by a relatively select circle of wealthy and powerful families—both patrician and plebeian—called the **nobiles** ("nobles"). The *nobiles* were essentially the men whose families were elected to the more important political offices of the Republic. In the hundred years from 233 to 133 B.C.E., 80 percent of the consuls came from twenty-six families; 50 percent came from only ten families. Hence, the *nobiles* constituted a governing oligarchy that managed, through landed wealth, patronage, and intimidation, to maintain its hold over the magistracies and senate and thus guide the destiny of Rome while running the state in its own interests. When a new man—a *novus homo* (NOH-vuss HOH-moh)—did win a consulship, he and his descendants became members of this select oligarchy.

Division of the Aristocrats   By the end of the second century B.C.E., two types of aristocratic leaders, called the **optimates** (ahp-tuh-MAH-tayz) ("the best men") and the **populares** (PAWP-oo-lahr-ayss) ("favoring the people"), became prominent. These were not political parties or even individual cliques but leaders who followed two different approaches to politics. *Optimates* and *populares* were terms of political rhetoric that were used by individuals within the aristocracy against fellow aristocratic rivals to distinguish one set of tactics from another. The *optimates* tended to be the *nobiles* who controlled the senate and wished to maintain their oligarchical privileges, while the *populares* were usually other ambitious aristocrats who used the people's assemblies, especially the council of the plebs, as instruments to break the domination of the *optimates*. The conflicts between these aristocratic leaders and their supporters engulfed the first century B.C.E. in political turmoil.

Role of the Equestrians   Another social group in Rome also became entangled in this political turmoil—the *equites* (EK-wuh-teez) or **equestrians,** so called because they had once formed Rome's cavalry. Many equestrians had become extremely wealthy through a variety of means, often related to the creation of the empire. Some, for example, were private contractors who derived their wealth from government contracts for the collection of taxes, the outfitting of armies, and the construction of fleets and public works. In 218 B.C.E., the senate enacted a law that forbade senators to bid for state contracts or engage in commerce. The law effectively barred the equestrians from high office because they would have to give up their livelihoods to serve in the senate. By the end of the second century B.C.E., the equestrians were seeking real political power commensurate with their financial stake in the empire. They would play an important role in the political turmoil that brought an end to the Republic.

The Land Problem   Of course, equestrians and aristocrats together formed only a tiny minority of the Roman people. The backbone of the Roman state and army had traditionally been the small farmers who tilled their little plots of land and made up the chief source of recruits for the army. But economic changes that began in the period of the Punic Wars increasingly undermined the position of that group. This occurred for several reasons. Their lands had been severely damaged during the Second Punic War when Hannibal invaded Italy. Moreover, in order to win the wars, Rome had to increase the term of military service to six years. The Roman army was never meant to serve in distant wars but was called out for the "war season," after which the soldiers returned to their farms. Now when the soldiers returned home after many years of service abroad, they found their farms so deteriorated that they chose to sell out instead of remaining on the land. Landed aristocrats had been able to develop large estates (*latifundia*) by taking over state-owned land and by buying out small peasant owners. These large estates relied on slave and tenant labor and frequently concentrated on cash crops, such as grapes for wine, olives, and sheep for wool, which small farmers could not afford to do. Thus, the rise of *latifundia* contributed to the decline in the number of small citizen farmers. Since the latter group traditionally formed the basis of the Roman army— Rome conscripted only people with a financial stake in the community—the number of men available for military service declined. Many of the newly landless families stayed in the countryside, finding agricultural work as best they could. Some of them, however, drifted to the cities, especially Rome, where they formed a large class of day laborers who possessed no property. This new urban proletariat formed a highly unstable mass with the potential to create much trouble in depressed times.

The Reforms of Tiberius and Gaius Gracchus   Tiberius Gracchus (ty-BEER-ee-uss GRAK-us) (163–133 B.C.E.) was a member of the *nobiles* who ruled Rome. Although concerned with the immediate problem of a shortage of military recruits, Tiberius believed that the underlying cause of Rome's problems was the decline of the small farmers. Tiberius was not a revolutionary, and his proposals for reform, drafted with the help of several prominent senators, were essentially conservative; he was looking back to what had constituted the foundation of Rome's greatness.

Tiberius Gracchus was elected one of the tribunes of the plebs for 133 B.C.E. Without consulting the senate, where he knew his rivals would oppose his proposal, Tiberius took his legislation directly to the council of the plebs, which passed his land reform bill. It authorized the government to reclaim public land held by large landowners and to distribute it to landless Romans. Many senators, themselves large landowners whose estates included large tracts of public land, were furious, and a group of them took the law into their own hands and assassinated Tiberius.

The efforts of Tiberius Gracchus were continued by his brother Gaius (GY-uss) (153–121 B.C.E.), who was elected tribune for both 123 and 122 B.C.E. Like Tiberius, Gaius pushed for the rapid distribution of land to displaced farmers, but he also broadened his reform program to appeal to more people disenchanted with the current senatorial leadership. To win the support of the *equites*, he replaced the senators on the jury courts that tried provincial governors accused of extortion with members of the equestrian order and opened the new province of Asia to equestrian tax collectors. Thus, Gaius gave the *equites* two instruments of public power: control over the jury courts that often tried provincial governors and control over provincial taxation. Fellow senators, hostile to Gaius's reforms and fearful of his growing popularity, made use of a constitutional innovation, a "final decree of the senate," which encouraged the consuls to "do everything possible to prevent any misfortune befalling the Republic." As a result, Gaius and many of his followers were killed in 121 B.C.E. The attempts of the Gracchus brothers to bring reforms had opened the door to more instability and further violence.

Marius and the New Roman Army   In the closing years of the second century B.C.E., a series of military disasters gave rise to a fresh outburst of popular anger against the old leaders of the senate and resulted in the rise of Marius (MAR-ee-uss) (157–86 B.C.E.). Military defeats in northern Africa under a senate-appointed general encouraged Marius—a "new man" from the equestrian order—to run for the consulship with "Win the War" as his campaign slogan. Marius won and became a consul for 107 B.C.E. The council of the plebs then voted to give Marius command of the army in Africa, a definite encroachment on the senate's right to conduct wars. Generals no longer needed to be loyal to the senate.

Marius brought the war in northern Africa to a successful conclusion in 105 B.C.E. and was then called on to defeat the Celtic tribes (or Gauls, as the Romans called them), who threatened an invasion of Italy. Marius was made consul for five years, from 104 to 100 B.C.E., raised a new army, and decisively defeated the Celts, leaving him in a position of personal ascendancy in Rome.

In raising a new army, Marius initiated military reforms that proved to have drastic consequences. The Roman army had traditionally been a conscript army of small landholders—basically a citizen army, as described earlier. Marius recruited volunteers from both the urban and the rural proletariat who possessed no property. These volunteers, who were now trained more thoroughly, swore an oath of loyalty to the general, not the senate, and thus inaugurated a professional-type army that might no longer be subject to the state. Moreover, to recruit these men, a general would promise them land, so generals had to play politics to get legislation passed that would provide the land for their veterans. Marius left a powerful legacy. He had created a new system of military recruitment that placed much power in the hands of the individual generals.

The Role of Sulla

After almost a decade of relative quiet, the Roman Republic was threatened with another crisis—the Italian or Social War (90–88 B.C.E.). This war resulted from Rome's unwillingness to deal constructively with the complaints of its Italian allies. These allies had fought loyally on Rome's side but felt they had not shared sufficiently in the lands and bonuses given to Roman veterans. In 90 B.C.E., the Italians rebelled and formed their own confederation. Two years of bitter fighting left Italy devastated and took an enormous number of lives. The Romans managed to end the rebellion but only by granting full rights of Roman citizenship to all free Italians. "Rome was now Italy, and Italy Rome." [8] The influx of new voters into the popular assemblies drastically altered the voting power structure in favor of the *populares*, who had earlier favored enfranchisement of the Italians.

During this war, a new figure came to prominence—Lucius Cornelius Sulla (138–78 B.C.E.), a member of the *nobiles*. Sulla (SULL-uh) had been made a consul for 88 B.C.E. and been given command by the senate of a war in Asia Minor. But when the council of the plebs, contradicting the senate's wishes, transferred command of this war to Marius, a civil war ensued between the forces of Marius and Sulla. Sulla won and seized Rome itself in 82 B.C.E. He forced the senate to grant him the title of dictator to "reconstitute the Republic." After conducting a reign of terror to wipe out all opposition, Sulla revised the constitution to restore power to the senate. He eliminated most of the powers of the popular assemblies and the tribunes of the plebs and restored the senators to the jury courts. He also enlarged the senate by adding men of the equestrian order. In 79 B.C.E., believing that he had restored the traditional Republic governed by a powerful senate, he resigned his office of dictator, retired, and soon died, leaving a power vacuum. But his real legacy was quite different from what he had intended. His example of using an army to seize power would prove most attractive to ambitious men.

The Death of the Republic

For the next fifty years, Roman history would be characterized by two important features: the jostling for power by a number of powerful individuals and the civil wars generated by their conflicts.

The Rise of Pompey Not long after Sulla's attempts to revive senatorial power, the senate made two extraordinary military appointments that raised to prominence two very strong personalities—Crassus (KRASS-uss) (c. 112–53 B.C.E.) and Pompey (PAHM-pee) (106–48 B.C.E.). Crassus had fought for Sulla and had also become extremely rich—it was said that he "owned most of Rome." In 73 B.C.E., the senate gave Crassus a military command against the slave rebellion led by Spartacus, which he successfully completed. Pompey had also fought for Sulla and was given an important military command in Spain in 77 B.C.E. When he returned six years later, he was hailed as a military hero.

Despite their jealousy, Pompey and Crassus joined forces and were elected consuls for 70 B.C.E. Although both men had been supporters of Sulla, they undid his work. They restored the power of the tribunes and helped put *equites* back on the jury courts, thereby reviving the *populares* as a path to political power.

With their power reestablished by this action, friendly plebeian tribunes now proposed legislation that gave two important military commands to Pompey. In 67 B.C.E., he cleared the Mediterranean Sea of the pirates who were harassing Roman commerce. After this success, he was put in charge of the campaign against Mithridates (mih-thruh-DAY-teez), who thought he could take advantage of Rome's internal troubles to pursue his plans of conquest in Asia Minor. Pompey defeated Mithridates and reorganized the east, winning immense success and prestige as well as enormous wealth. When he returned to Rome, he disbanded his army, expecting that the senate would automatically ratify his eastern settlement and give land to his veterans. But new forces and new personalities had risen to prominence during his absence, and his requests encountered complications.

The Role of Cicero   Marcus Tullius Cicero (106–43 B.C.E.) was one of these new personalities. A *novus homo* ("new man") from the equestrian order and the first of his family to achieve the consulship, Cicero (SIS-uh-roh) made a name for himself as a lawyer, using his outstanding oratorical skills to defend people accused of crimes and to prosecute others, including a corrupt provincial governor. He became consul in 63 B.C.E. and upheld the interests of the senate. Cicero was one of the few prominent politicians who attempted to analyze the problems of the Republic systematically. He believed in a "concord of the orders," meaning the cooperation of the equestrians and senators. In effect, Cicero harked back to the days of collective rule, a time when political leaders were motivated to work together for the good of the Roman state. But collective rule was no longer meaningful to ambitious men seeking personal power. Cicero himself had few military skills and could not command an army. He realized that the senate needed the support of a powerful general if the concord of the orders was to be made a reality. In 62 B.C.E., he saw Pompey as that man. But a number of senators felt that Pompey had become too powerful, and they now refused to grant his wishes after his return from the east. These same senators treated Julius Caesar in a similar fashion when he returned from Spain. That turned out to be a big mistake.

The Struggle Between Pompey and Caesar   Julius Caesar (100–44 B.C.E.) had been a spokesman for the *populares* from the beginning of his political career, an alliance that ran in the family—Marius was his uncle by marriage. Caesar pursued political power by appealing to many of the same groups who had supported Marius. After serving as aedile and praetor, he sought a military

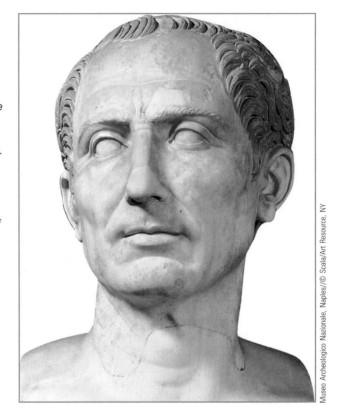

Caesar. *Conqueror of Gaul and member of the First Triumvirate, Julius Caesar is perhaps the best-known figure of the late Republic. Caesar became dictator of Rome in 47 B.C.E. and after his victories in the civil war was made dictator for life. Some members of the senate who resented his power assassinated him in 44 B.C.E. Pictured is a marble copy of a bust of Caesar.*

Museo Archeologico Nazionale, Naples//© Scala/Art Resource, NY

command and was sent to Spain. He returned from Spain in 60 B.C.E. and requested a special dispensation so that he could both celebrate a triumph with his troops and run for the consulship, which would place him in the highest rank within the senate. Rival senators blocked his request. Consequently, Caesar joined with two fellow senators, Crassus and Pompey, who were also being stymied by the senate. Historians call their coalition the First Triumvirate. Though others had made political deals before, the combined wealth and power of these three men was enormous, enabling them to dominate the political scene. Caesar was elected consul for 59 B.C.E. and used the popular assemblies to achieve the basic aims of the triumvirs: Pompey received his eastern settlement and lands for his veterans; equestrian allies of Crassus were given a reduction on tax contracts for which they had overbid; and Caesar was granted a special military command in Gaul (modern France, Belgium, and parts of the Netherlands) for five years.

Caesar did so well in Gaul that Crassus and Pompey realized anew the value of military command. They became consuls again for 55 B.C.E. and garnered more benefits for the coalition: Caesar was given a five-year extension in Gaul; Crassus, a command in Syria; and Pompey, one in Spain. When Crassus was killed in battle in 53 B.C.E., his death left two powerful men with armies in direct competition. Caesar had used his time in Gaul to gain fame and military experience. He had waged numerous campaigns, costing the lives of hundreds of thousands of men, women, and children, according to estimates. As a military leader, Caesar had always been willing to face great personal danger. One ancient writer said that Caesar's soldiers were astonished that:

> he should undergo toils beyond his body's apparent power of endurance ... because he was of a spare habit, had soft and white skin, suffered from epileptic fits.... Nevertheless, he did not make his feeble health an excuse for soft living, but rather his military service a cure for his feeble health, since by wearisome journeys, simple diet, continuously sleeping in the open air, and enduring hardships he fought off his trouble and kept his body strong against its attacks.[9]

Caesar's wars had also enabled him to amass enough booty and slaves to pay off all of the debts he had accumulated in gaining political offices. Moreover, he now had an army of seasoned veterans who were loyal to him. No doubt most senators would have preferred both Pompey and Caesar to lay down their commands and give up their armies. Since both refused, the leading senators fastened on Pompey as the less harmful to their cause and voted for Caesar to lay down his command and return as a private citizen to Rome. Such a step was intolerable to Caesar, as it would leave him totally vulnerable to his enemies. He chose to keep his army and moved into Italy by crossing the Rubicon, the river that formed the southern boundary of his province, on January 10, 49 B.C.E. (The phrase "crossing the Rubicon" is still used today to mean being unable to turn back.) According to his ancient biographer Suetonius, Caesar said to his troops, "Even now we could turn back; but once we cross that tiny bridge, then everything will depend on armed force."[10]

Pompey and his followers fled to Greece, where they raised a new army. Meanwhile it took Caesar until the end of 49 to raise a fleet and ship his troops to Greece. The next spring, at the Battle of Pharsalus (far-SAY-luss), Caesar's veterans carried the day against Pompey's forces. The defeated Pompey fled to Egypt, where the king had Pompey killed. The war continued, however, since some of the senators on his side had recruited new troops. After victories in North Africa and Spain, Caesar returned triumphant to Rome in 45 B.C.E.

No doubt Caesar realized that the old order of unfettered political competition could not be saved. He was unwilling to take the title of king, which was intensely disliked by the Roman upper classes, but he had no intention of giving up his control. Caesar had officially been made dictator in 47 B.C.E., and in 44 B.C.E. he was made dictator for life. He continued to hold elections for offices but saw to it that his supporters chose the people he recommended. As Rome's new ruler, he quickly instituted a number of ambitious reforms, although he seems not to have had any long-term vision for governing Rome but was only responding to immediate issues. He increased the senate to nine hundred members by filling it with many of his followers. He granted citizenship to a number of people in the provinces who had provided assistance to him. By establishing colonies of Roman citizens in North Africa, Gaul, and Spain, he initiated a process of Romanization in those areas. He tried to reorganize the administrative structures of cities in Italy in order to create some sense of rational order in their government.

The Assassination of Julius Caesar

When it became apparent that Julius Caesar had no intention of restoring the Republic as they conceived it, about sixty senators, many of them his friends or pardoned enemies, formed a conspiracy to assassinate the dictator. It was led by Gaius Cassius and Marcus Brutus, who naively imagined that this act would restore the traditional Republic. The conspirators set the Ides of March (March 15) of 44 B.C.E. as the date for the assassination. Caesar was in the midst of preparations for a campaign in the eastern part of the empire. Although warned about a plot against his life, he chose to disregard it. This account of Caesar's death is taken from his biography by the Greek writer Plutarch.

Plutarch, *Life of Caesar*

Fate, however, is to all appearance more unavoidable than unexpected. For many strange prodigies and apparitions are said to have been observed shortly before this event.... One finds it also related by many that a soothsayer bade him [Caesar] prepare for some great danger on the Ides of March. When this day was come, Caesar, as he went to the senate, met this soothsayer, and said to him mockingly, "The Ides of March are come," who answered him calmly, "Yes, they are come, but they are not past...."

All these things might happen by chance. But the place which was destined for the scene of this murder, in which the senate met that day, was the same in which Pompey's statue stood, and was one of the edifices which Pompey had raised and dedicated with his theater to the use of the public, plainly showing that there was something of a supernatural influence which guided the action and ordered it to that particular place. Cassius, just before the act, is said to have looked toward Pompey's statue, and silently implored his assistance.... When Caesar entered, the senate stood up to show their respect to him, and of Brutus's confederates, some came about his chair and stood behind it, others met him, pretending to add their petitions to those of Tillius Cimber, in behalf of his brother, who was in exile; and they followed him with their joint applications till he came to his seat. When he sat down, he refused to comply with their requests, and upon their urging

Caesar was a generous victor and pardoned many of the republican leaders who had opposed him, allowing them to return to Rome. He also replaced the Roman calendar with the Egyptian solar year of 365 days (this so-called Julian calendar, with later changes made in 1582, became the basis of our modern calendar). He planned much more in the way of building projects and military adventures in the east but was not able to carry them out. In 44 B.C.E., a group of leading senators who resented his curtailment of their power, assassinated him, believing that the old republican system would now return. In truth, however, they had set the stage for another civil war that delivered the death blow to the Republic.

The Final Struggle: Octavian Versus Antony   A new struggle for power soon ensued. Caesar's heir and adopted son, his grandnephew Octavian (ahk-TAY-vee-un), though only nineteen, took command of some of Caesar's legions.

him further began to reproach them severely for their demand, when Tillius, laying hold of his robe with both his hands, pulled it down from his neck, which was the signal for the assault. Casca gave him the first cut in the neck, which was not mortal nor dangerous, as coming from one who at the beginning of such a bold action was probably very much disturbed; Caesar immediately turned about, and laid his hand upon the dagger and kept hold of it. And both of them at the same time cried out, he that received the blow, in Latin, "Vile Casca, what does this mean?" and he that gave it, in Greek to his brother, "Brother, help!" Upon this first onset, those who were not privy to the design were astonished, and their horror and amazement at what they saw were so great that they dared not fly nor assist Caesar, nor so much as speak a word. But those who came prepared for the business enclosed him on every side, with their naked daggers in their hands. Which way soever he turned he met with blows, and saw their swords leveled at his face and eyes, and was encompassed like a wild beast in the toils on every side. For it had been agreed they should each of them make a thrust at him, and flesh themselves with his blood: for which reason Brutus also gave him one stab in the groin. Some say that he fought and resisted all the rest, shifting his body to avoid the blows, and calling out for help, but that when he saw Brutus's sword drawn, he covered his face with his robe and submitted, letting himself fall, whether it were by chance or that he was pushed in that direction by his murderers, at the foot of the pedestal on which Pompey's statue stood, and which was thus wetted with his blood. So that Pompey himself seemed to have presided, as it were, over the revenge done upon his adversary, who lay here at his feet, and breathed out his soul through his multitude of wounds, for they say he received three-and-twenty. And the conspirators themselves were many of them wounded by each other while they all leveled their blows at the same person.

Q *What does this account of Caesar's assassination reveal about the character of Julius Caesar? Based on this selection, what lessons did Classical historians intend their readers to take from their accounts of great and dramatic political events?*

Source: From *The Lives of the Noble Grecians and Romans* by Plutarch, translated by John Dryden and edited by Arthur H. Clough.

After forcing the senate to name him consul, he joined forces with Mark Antony, Caesar's ally and assistant, and Marcus Lepidus, who had been commander of Caesar's cavalry. Together, the three formed the Second Triumvirate, which was legally empowered to rule Rome. Their first act was to restore Sulla's policy of proscription, as described by the ancient historian Appian:

> As soon as they were on their own, the three drew up a list of those who were to die. They put on the list, both then and later, those of whom they were suspicious because of their ability, as well as their personal enemies, trading with each other for the lives of their own relations and friends. They decreed death and confiscation of property for about 300 senators and 2,000 equestrians, among them their own brothers and uncles, as well as senior officers serving under them who had had cause to offend them or their own colleagues.[11]

In addition to proscribing their enemies at home (Cicero was one of those killed), the three commanders pursued Caesar's assassins, who had in the meantime raised an army, and defeated them at Philippi in Macedonia. Lepidus was soon shunted aside, and Octavian and Antony then divided the Roman world between them—Octavian taking the west and Antony the east. To seal their bargain, Antony married Octavia, Octavian's sister.

But the empire of the Romans, large as it was, was still too small for two masters, and Octavian and Antony eventually came into conflict. Antony abandoned Octavia and allied himself with the Egyptian queen Cleopatra VII. Julius Caesar had succumbed to her beauty when he went to Egypt in 48 in pursuit of Pompey. Her son by Caesar, known as Caesarion ("little Caesar") was made co-regent of Egypt. Like Caesar before him, Antony also fell deeply in love with Cleopatra, fathering three children with her and giving her lands in the eastern Mediterranean. Octavian began a propaganda campaign, accusing Antony of catering to Cleopatra and giving away Roman territory to this "whore of the east." Finally, at the Battle of Actium in Greece in 31 B.C.E., Octavian's forces smashed the army and navy of Antony and Cleopatra. Both fled to Egypt, where, according to the Roman historian Florus, they committed suicide a year later:

> Antony was the first to commit suicide, by the sword. Cleopatra threw herself at Octavian's feet, and tried her best to attract his gaze: in vain, for his self-control was impervious to her beauty. It was not her life she was after, for that had already been granted, but a portion of her kingdom. When she realized this was hopeless and that she had been earmarked to feature in Octavian's triumph in Rome, she took advantage of her guard's carelessness to get herself into the mausoleum, as the royal tomb is called. Once there, she put on the royal robes which she was accustomed to wear, and lay down in a richly perfumed coffin beside her Antony. Then she applied poisonous snakes to her veins and passed into death as though into a sleep.[12]

Octavian, at the age of thirty-two, stood supreme over the Roman world (see Map 5.3). The civil wars had ended. And so had the Republic.

Literature in the Late Republic   The last century of the Roman Republic witnessed the completion of the union of Greek and Roman culture in a truly Greco-Roman civilization. Greek was now the language not just of Greece but of the entire Hellenistic world of the eastern Mediterranean, which Rome had conquered, and educated, upper-class Romans spoke it fluently. The influence of Greece would continue to be felt in the development of Latin literature.

In the last century of the Republic, the Romans began to produce a new poetry, less dependent on epic themes and more inclined to personal expression. Latin poets now took to using various Greek forms to express their own feelings about people, social and political life, and love. The finest example is the work of Catullus (kuh-TULL-uss) (c. 87–54 B.C.E.), the best lyric poet Rome produced and one of the greatest in world literature.

MAP 5.3   Roman Dominions in the Late Republic, 31 B.C.

Catullus   Like most of the great Roman writers of the first century B.C.E., Catullus was not from Rome. He grew up in northern Italy but came to Rome, where he joined a group of carefree, youthful aristocrats. He became a master at adapting and refining Greek forms of poetry to express emotions. He wrote a variety of poems on, among other themes, political figures, social customs, the use of language, the death of his brother, and the travails of love. Catullus became infatuated with Clodia, the promiscuous sister of a tribune and wife of a provincial governor, and addressed a number of poems to her (he called her Lesbia), describing his passionate love and hatred for her (Clodia had many other lovers besides Catullus):

> You used to say that you wished to know only Catullus,
>   Lesbia, and wouldn't take even Jove before me!
> I didn't regard you just as my mistress then: I cherished you
>   as a father does his sons or his daughters' husbands.

Now that I know you, I burn for you even more fiercely,
  though I regard you as almost utterly worthless.
How can that be, you ask? It's because such cruelty forces
  lust to assume the shrunken place of affection.[13]

The ability of Catullus to express in simple fashion his intense feelings and curiosity about himself and his world had a noticeable impact on later Latin poets.

Lucretius   Another important poet of the late Republic was Lucretius (loo-KREE-shus) (c. 94–55 B.C.E.), who followed an old Greek tradition of expounding philosophy in the form of poetry. Although Stoicism was the Greek school of philosophy that the Romans found most congenial, the philosophy of Epicurus also enjoyed a period of intense popularity between 60 and 40 B.C.E. Lucretius's lengthy poem *On the Nature of the Universe* played a role in furthering that philosophy. In this work, Lucretius attempted to set out poetically Epicurus's idea that the world and all its creatures had been created by an accidental combination of atoms and not by the operation of divine forces. Two themes are repeated: divine forces have no effect on us, and death is of no real consequence because the soul, like the body, is material and after death also dissolves into atoms. Lucretius was especially adept at using vivid imagery. Describing the movement of atoms in the void, he wrote:

Consider the rays of the sun that are always stealing
Into the shade of a house to pour their light.
There in the void you'll notice many and sundry
Dust flecks that mingle among the rays themselves,
Stirring up in a sort of ceaseless strife
Skirmishes, wars, realigning their squadrons, never
Stopping for breath, assailed by alliance, secession;
From this you can project how atoms are
Constantly tossed along the gulf of space.[14]

If the gods and death are of no significance, how then are we to lead our lives? Lucretius's Epicurean argument that a simple life free of political worries was the highest good ran counter to Roman ideals but had an obvious appeal to Romans sick of the civil discord of the first century B.C.E.

Cicero   The development of Roman prose was greatly aided by the practice of oratory. Romans had great respect for oratory, for the ability to persuade people in public debate often led to success in politics. Oratory was brought to perfection in a literary fashion by Cicero, the best exemplar of the literary and intellectual interests of the elite of the late Republic and, indeed, the greatest prose writer of that period. For Cicero, oratory was not simply skillful speaking. An orator was a statesman, a man who achieved his highest goal by pursuing an active life in public affairs.

Later, when the turmoil of the late Republic forced him into semiretirement politically, Cicero turned his attention to writing philosophical treatises. He performed a valuable service for Roman society by popularizing and making understandable the works of Greek philosophers. In his philosophical works, Cicero, more than anyone else, transmitted the Classical intellectual heritage to the Western world. Cicero's original contributions to Western thought came in the field of politics. His works *On the Laws* and *On the Republic* provided fresh insights into political thought, including the need for a mixed constitution: "A moderate and well-balanced form of government which is a combination of the three simple good forms (monarchy, aristocracy, and democracy) is preferable even to monarchy."[15] Centuries later his emphasis on the need to pursue an active life to benefit and improve humankind would greatly influence the Italian Renaissance.

Sallust Rome's upper classes continued to have a strong interest in history. The best-known historian of the late Republic is Sallust (86–35 B.C.E.), who established an approach to historical studies that influenced later Roman historians. Sallust, who served as governor of the province of Africa, was on Caesar's side in the civil war and after Caesar's death went into retirement and turned to the writing of history. His two extant works are *War with Jugurtha*, which discusses Rome's war with an African king from 111 to 105 B.C.E., and *War with Catiline*, an account of the conspiracy of the disaffected aristocrat Catiline. Sallust modeled his style after that of the Greek historian Thucydides, whose historical work experienced a sudden wave of popularity in the 50s and 40s B.C.E. Sallust's works expressed his belief that the most important causative factor in Roman history was the moral degeneration of Roman society, which he attributed to the lack of a strong enemy after Carthage and the corrupting influence of the Greeks.

Caesar Brief mention should also be made of the historical writing of Julius Caesar. Most famous is his *Commentaries on the Gallic War*, an account of his conquest of Gaul between 58 and 51 B.C.E. The work was published in 51 B.C.E., at a time when Caesar was afraid that his political enemies would take advantage of his absence from Rome. Although the *Commentaries* served a partisan purpose by defending his actions in Gaul, Caesar presented his material in straightforward, concise prose. He referred to himself in the third person and, as the following passage indicates, was not averse to extolling his own bravery:

> Caesar saw that the situation was critical, and there was no reserve to throw in. He snatched a shield from a soldier in the rear—he had not brought one himself—and moved to the front line; he called upon the centurions by name, encouraged the men to advance, and directed them to open their lines out to give freer play to their swords. His coming inspired the men with hope and gave them new heart. Even in a desperate situation each man was anxious to do his utmost when his general was looking on, and the enemy's onset was somewhat slowed down.[16]

Caesar's work reminds us that some of the best prose of the late Republic was written by politicians who were concerned with enhancing their own position in a world of civil conflict.

CHRONOLOGIES

THE ROMAN CONQUEST OF ITALY	
340–338 B.C.	Latin revolt
338 B.C.	Creation of the Roman confederation
343–290 B.C.	Samnite Wars
281–267 B.C.	Pyrrhic War

THE ROMAN CONQUEST OF THE MEDITERRANEAN	
264–241 B.C.	First Punic War
218–201 B.C.	Second Punic War
149–146 B.C.	Third Punic War
148 B.C.	Incorporation of Macedonia as a Roman province
146 B.C.	Destruction of Carthage

THE DECLINE AND FALL OF THE ROMAN REPUBLIC	
133 B.C.	Reforms of Tiberius Gracchus
123–122 B.C.	Reforms of Gaius Gracchus
104–100 B.C.	Marius: Consecutive consulships
82–79 B.C.	Sulla as dictator
60 B.C.	First Triumvirate (Caesar, Pompey, Crassus)
53 B.C.	Crassus killed by Parthians
48 B.C.	Battle of Pharsalus; Pompey killed in Egypt
47–44 B.C.	Caesar as dictator
44 B.C.	Assassination of Caesar
43 B.C.	Second Triumvirate; Cicero killed
31 B.C.	Octavian defeats Antony at Actium

6

THE ROMAN EMPIRE

A second-century Roman marble bust of Hadrian

Galleria degli Uffizi, Florence//© Alinari/The Bridgeman Art Library

CHAPTER OUTLINE

• The Age of Augustus (31 B.C.E.–14 C.E.) • The Early Empire (14–180)
• Roman Culture and Society in the Early Empire • Transformation of the
Roman World: Crises in the Third Century • Transformation of the Roman
World: The Rise of Christianity

166 | Chapter 6

The Achievements of Augustus

This excerpt is taken from a text written by Augustus and inscribed on a bronze tablet at Rome. Copies of the text in stone were displayed in many provincial capitals. Called "the most famous ancient inscription," the *Res Gestae* (RAYS GES-ty *or* REEZ JES-tee) of Augustus summarizes his accomplishments in three major areas: his offices, his private expenditures on behalf of the state, and his exploits in war and peace. Though factual in approach, it is a highly subjective account.

Augustus, *Res Gestae*

Below is a copy of the accomplishments of the deified Augustus by which he brought the whole world under the empire of the Roman people, and of the moneys expended by him on the state and the Roman people, as inscribed on two bronze pillars set up in Rome.

1. At the age of nineteen, on my own initiative and at my own expense, I raised an army by means of which I liberated the Republic, which was oppressed by the tyranny of a faction [Mark Antony and his supporters]....

2. Those who assassinated my father [Julius Caesar, his adoptive father] I drove into exile, avenging their crime by due process of law; and afterwards when they waged war against the state, I conquered them twice on the battlefield.

3. I waged many wars throughout the whole world by land and by sea, both civil and foreign, and when victorious I spared all citizens who sought pardon....

5. The dictatorship offered to me ... by the people and the senate, both in my absence and in my presence, I refused to accept....

17. Four times I came to the assistance of the treasury with my own money, transferring to those in charge of the treasury 150,000,000 sesterces. And in the consulship of Marcus

THE AGE OF AUGUSTUS (31 B.C.E.–14 C.E.)

In 27 B.C.E., Octavian proclaimed the "restoration of the Republic." He understood that only traditional republican forms would satisfy the senatorial aristocracy. At the same time, Octavian was aware that the Republic could not be fully restored and managed to arrive at a compromise that worked, at least during his lifetime. In 27 B.C.E., the senate awarded him the title of Augustus—"the revered one." He preferred the title *princeps* (PRIN-keps *or* PRIN-seps), meaning chief citizen or first among equals. The system of rule that Augustus established is sometimes called the **principate**, conveying the idea of a constitutional monarch as coruler with the senate. But while Augustus worked to maintain this appearance, in reality, power was heavily weighted in favor of the *princeps*.

The New Order   In the new constitutional order that Augustus created, the basic governmental structure consisted of the *princeps* (Augustus) and an aristocratic senate. Augustus retained the senate as the chief deliberative body of the Roman state. Its decrees, screened in advance by the *princeps*, now had the effect of law. The title of *princeps*—first citizen of the state—carried no power in itself, but

Lepidus and Lucius Arruntius I transferred out of my own patrimony 170,000,000 sesterces to the soldiers' bonus fund, which was established on my advice for the purpose of providing bonuses for soldiers who had completed twenty or more years of service....

22. I gave a gladiatorial show three times in my own name, and five times in the names of my sons or grandsons; at these shows about 10,000 fought....

25. I brought peace to the sea by suppressing the pirates. In that war I turned over to their masters for punishment nearly 30,000 slaves who had run away from their owners and taken up arms against the state....

26. I extended the frontiers of all the provinces of the Roman people on whose boundaries were peoples not subject to our empire....

27. I added Egypt to the empire of the Roman people....

28. I established colonies of soldiers in Africa, Sicily, Macedonia, in both

Spanish provinces, in Achaea, Asia, Syria, Narbonese Gaul, and Pisidia. Italy, moreover, has twenty-eight colonies established by me, which in my lifetime have grown to be famous and populous....

35. When I held my thirteenth consulship, the senate, the equestrian order, and the entire Roman people gave me the title of "father of the country" and decreed that this title should be inscribed in the vestibule of my house, in the Julian senate house, and in the Augustan Forum.... At the time I wrote this document I was in my seventy-sixth year.

Q *What were the achievements of Augustus? To what extent did these accomplishments create the "job" of being emperor? In what sense could this document be called a piece of propaganda?*

Source: From *Roman Civilization*, Vol. I, Naphtali Lewis and Meyer Renhold. Copyright © 1955 Columbia University Press. Reprinted by permission of the publisher.

each year until 23 B.C.E., Augustus held the office of consul, which gave him *imperium*, or the right to command (see Chapter 5). When Augustus gave up the consulship in 23 B.C.E., he was granted *maius imperium* (MY-yoos im-PEE-ree-um)—greater *imperium* than all others. The consulship was now unnecessary. Moreover, very probably in 23 B.C.E., Augustus was given the power of a tribune without actually holding the office itself; this power enabled him to propose laws and veto any item of public business. Although officials continued to be elected, Augustus's authority ensured that his candidates for office usually won. This situation caused participation in elections to decline. Consequently, the popular assemblies, shorn of any real role in elections and increasingly overshadowed by the senate's decrees, gradually declined in importance.

Augustus proved highly popular. As the Roman historian Tacitus commented, "Indeed, he attracted everybody's goodwill by the enjoyable gift of peace.... Opposition did not exist."[1] The ending of the civil wars had greatly bolstered Augustus's popularity. At the same time, his continuing control of the army, while making possible the Roman peace, was a crucial source of his power.

The Army

As a result of the civil wars of the first century B.C.E., the Roman army had increased in size and had become more

Louvre (Hervé Lewandowski), Paris/© RMN-Grand Palais/Art Resource, NY

The Praetorian Guard. *Augustus was responsible for setting up the praetorian guard as an imperial bodyguard of elite troops. Pictured in this second-century relief are members of the praetorian guard. Their body armor resembled that of the legionaries, although the cohort serving in the palace wore togas.*

professional with legionaries who served a longer term. Under the empire, the shift to a professional army was completed when early emperors created a bureaucracy that could train and administer such an army. The peace of the Roman Empire depended on the army, and so did the security of the *princeps*. Though primarily responsible for guarding the frontiers of the empire, the army was also used to maintain domestic order within the provinces. Moreover, the army played an important social role. It was an agent of upward mobility for both officers and recruits and provided impetus for **Romanization** wherever the legions were stationed. The colonies of veterans established by Augustus throughout the empire proved especially valuable in Romanizing the provinces.

Augustus maintained a standing army of twenty-eight legions. Since each legion at full strength numbered 5,400 soldiers, the Roman Empire had an army of about 150,000 men, certainly not large either by modern standards or in terms of the size of the empire itself (the population of the empire was probably close to 50 million). Roman legionaries served twenty years and were recruited only from the citizenry and, under Augustus, largely from Italy. Augustus also maintained a large contingent of auxiliary forces enlisted from the subject peoples. They served as both light-armed troops and cavalry and were commanded by Roman officers as well as tribal leaders. During the principate of Augustus, the **auxiliaries** numbered around 130,000. They were recruited only from noncitizens, served for twenty-four years, and along with their families received citizenship after their terms of service.

Augustus was also responsible for establishing the **praetorian guard**. These "nine cohorts of elite troops," roughly nine thousand men, had the important task of guarding the person of the *princeps*. They were recruited from Roman citizens in Italy and served for sixteen years. Eventually, the praetorian guard would play an important role in making and deposing emperors.

The role of the *princeps* as military commander gave rise to a title by which this ruler eventually came to be known. When victorious, a military commander was acclaimed by his troops as *imperator* (im-puh-RAH-tur). Augustus was so acclaimed on a number of occasions. *Imperator* is our word *emperor*. Although such a title was applied to Augustus and his successors, Augustus still preferred to use the title *princeps*.

Roman Provinces and Frontiers

Augustus inaugurated a new system for governing the provinces. Under the Republic, the senate had appointed the provincial governors. Now certain provinces were allotted to the *princeps*, who assigned deputies known as legates to govern them. These legates were from the senatorial class and held office as long as the emperor chose. The senate continued to designate the governors of the remaining provinces, but the authority of Augustus gave him the power to overrule the senatorial governors and thus to establish a unified imperial policy.

Since a governor had relatively few administrative officials to assist him, effective government of the provinces necessitated considerable cooperation from local authorities. By supporting the power of local elites—the upper classes—in return for their cooperation, Roman policy encouraged a substantial degree of self-government and local autonomy in the cities. By fostering municipal life, Rome essentially made cities and city-states the basic units of imperial administration. City councils of leading citizens made for stable local government, and leading city officials were rewarded for their administrative services with Roman citizenship.

Frontier Policy Augustus added more territory to the Roman Empire than any other single Roman. In the east, instead of creating new provinces, Augustus established client kingdoms, continuing a policy that had begun in the early second century B.C.E. with the conquest of Greece and parts of the Near East; this policy enabled him to minimize the Roman military presence in the east so that he could use his forces elsewhere. Augustus expended his greatest military efforts along the northern frontiers of the Roman Empire. He conquered the central and maritime Alps and then expanded Roman control of the Balkan peninsula up to the Danube River.

The extension of Roman power to the Danube now opened the door for Augustus's major military project—expansion into Germany. After 15 B.C.E., Roman forces advanced across the Rhine, and by 9 B.C.E. they had reached the Elbe River in eastern Germany. In 6 C.E., the Romans began another advance between the Elbe and the Danube but encountered a series of difficulties, including the great catastrophe of 9 C.E. when three Roman legions under Varus were massacred in the Teutoburg Forest by a coalition of German tribes led by Arminius, a German tribal leader who had served in the Roman auxiliary forces and had even received Roman citizenship. Roman historians blamed Varus for the disaster: "He [Varus] entertained the notion that the Germans were a people who were men only in voice and limbs.... With this purpose in mind, he entered the heart of Germany as though he were going among a people enjoying the blessings of peace."[2] The defeat severely dampened Augustus's enthusiasm for continued expansion in central Europe. Thereafter, the Romans were content to use the Rhine as the frontier between the Roman province of Gaul and the German tribes to the east. In fact, the difficulties had convinced Augustus that "the empire should not be extended beyond its present frontiers."[3] His defeats in Germany taught Augustus that Rome's power was limited. They also left him devastated; for months afterward he would beat his head against a door and shout, "Varus, give me back my legions!"

Augustan Society   Society in the Early Roman Empire was characterized by a system of social stratification, inherited from the Republic, in which Roman citizens were divided into three basic classes: the senatorial, equestrian, and lower classes.

The Social Order   Augustus had accepted the senatorial order as a ruling class for the empire. Senators filled the chief magistracies of the Roman government, held the most important military posts, and governed the provinces. One needed to possess property worth 1 million sesterces (an unskilled laborer in Rome received 3 sesterces a day; a Roman legionary, 900 sesterces a year in pay) to belong to the senatorial order. When Augustus took charge, the senate had more than a thousand members. Augustus revised the senatorial list and reduced its size to six hundred but also added new men from wealthy families throughout Italy. Overall, Augustus was successful in winning the support of the senatorial class for his new order.

The equestrian order was expanded under Augustus and given a share of power in the new imperial state. The order was open to all Roman citizens of good standing who possessed property valued at 400,000 sesterces. They could now hold military and governmental offices, but the positions open to them were less important than those held by the senatorial order. At the end of his career, an equestrian might be rewarded by membership in the senatorial order.

Citizens not of the senatorial or equestrian orders belonged to the lower classes, who made up the overwhelming majority of the free citizens. The diminution of the power of the Roman assemblies ended whatever political power they may have possessed earlier in the Republic. Many of these people were provided with free grain and public spectacles to keep them from creating disturbances. Nevertheless, by gaining wealth and serving as lower officers in the Roman legions, it was sometimes possible for them to advance to the equestrian order.

Augustus's Reforms Augustus was very concerned about certain aspects of Rome's social health. He believed that the civil strife of the first century B.C.E. had sapped the strength of public religion, which he considered the cornerstone of a strong state. Therefore, he restored traditional priesthoods that had fallen into disuse in the late Republic, rebuilt many ruined temples and shrines, and constructed new ones to honor the Roman gods.

Augustus also instituted a new religious cult to strengthen the empire. Since the Roman state was intimately tied to Roman religion, an imperial cult served as a unifying instrument for the Roman world. Augustus did not claim to be a god, but he did permit the construction of temples to his deified adoptive father, Julius Caesar. Augustus also permitted the building of temples to Augustus and Roma, the personification of the Roman state. The worship of Augustus and Roma became the foundation of the imperial cult. Its development was furthered when Augustus was acclaimed as a god upon his death.

Augustus's belief that Roman morals had been corrupted during the late Republic led him to initiate social legislation to arrest the decline. He thought that increased luxury had undermined traditional Roman frugality and simplicity and caused a decline in morals, evidenced by easy divorce, a falling birthrate among the upper classes, and lax behavior manifested in hedonistic parties and the love affairs of prominent Romans with fashionable women and elegant boys.

Through his new social legislation, Augustus hoped to restore respectability to the upper classes and reverse the declining birthrate as well. Expenditures for feasts were limited, and other laws made adultery a criminal offense. In fact, Augustus exiled his own daughter Julia for adultery. Augustus also revised the tax laws to penalize bachelors, widowers, and married persons who had fewer than three children.

A Golden Age of Latin Literature The high point of Latin literature was reached in the time of Augustus. The literary accomplishments of the Augustan Age were such that the period has been called the golden age of Latin literature.

Virgil The most distinguished poet of the Augustan Age was Virgil (VUR-jul) (70–19 B.C.E.). The son of a small landholder in northern Italy, he welcomed the rule of Augustus and wrote his greatest work in the emperor's honor. Virgil's masterpiece was *The Aeneid*, an epic poem clearly meant to rival the work of Homer. The poem makes an explicit connection between Troy and Rome. Aeneas (ih-NEE-uss), the son of Anchises of Troy, survives the destruction of Troy and eventually settles in Latium; thus, Roman civilization is linked to Greek history. The character of Aeneas is portrayed in terms that remind us of the ideal Roman—his virtues are duty, piety, and faithfulness. Virgil's overall purpose was to show that Aeneas had fulfilled his mission to establish the Romans in Italy and thereby start Rome on its divine mission to rule the world:

> Let others fashion from bronze more lifelike, breathing images—
> For so they shall—and evoke living faces from marble;
> Others excel as orators, others track with their instruments
> The planets circling in heaven and predict when stars will appear.

But, Romans, never forget that government is your medium!
Be this your art:—to practice men in the habit of peace,
Generosity to the conquered, and firmness against aggressors.[4]

As Virgil expressed it, ruling was Rome's gift.

Horace   Another prominent Augustan poet was Horace (HOR-uss) (65–8 B.C.E.), a friend of Virgil. Horace was a very sophisticated writer whose overriding concern seems to have been to point out to his contemporaries the "follies and vices of his age." In the *Satires*, a medley of poems on a variety of subjects, Horace is revealed as a detached observer of human weaknesses. He directed his attacks against movements, not living people, and took on such subjects as sexual immorality, greed, and job dissatisfaction ("How does it happen, Maecenas, that no man alone is content with his lot?"[5]). Horace mostly laughs at the weaknesses of humankind and calls for forbearance: "Supposing my friend has got liquored and wetted my couch.... Is he for such a lapse to be deemed less dear as a friend, or because when hungry he snatched up before me a chicken from my side of the dish?"[6] In his final work, the *Epistles*, Horace used another Greek form—the imaginary letter in verse—to provide a portrait of the things he held most dear: a simple life, good friends, and his beloved countryside.

Ovid   Ovid (AH-vid) (43 B.C.E.–18 C.E.) was the last of the great poets of the golden age. He belonged to a privileged group of Roman youths who liked to ridicule old Roman values. In keeping with the spirit of this group, Ovid wrote a frivolous series of love poems known as the *Amores*. Intended to entertain and shock, they achieved their goal. Ovid's most popular work was the *Metamorphoses*, a series of fifteen complex mythological tales involving transformations of shapes, such as the change of chaos into order. A storehouse of mythological information, the *Metamorphoses* inspired many Western painters, sculptors, and writers, including Shakespeare.

Another of Ovid's works was *The Art of Love*. This was essentially a takeoff on didactic poems. Whereas authors of earlier didactic poems had written guides to farming, hunting, or some such subject, Ovid's work was a handbook on the seduction of women. *The Art of Love* appeared to applaud the loose sexual morals of the Roman upper classes at a time when Augustus was trying to clean them up. The *princeps* was not pleased. Ovid chose to ignore the wishes of Augustus and paid a price for it. In 8 C.E., Ovid was implicated in a sexual scandal, possibly involving the emperor's daughter Julia. He was banished to a small town on the coast of the Black Sea and died in exile.

Livy   The most famous Latin prose work of the golden age was written by the historian Livy (LIV-ee) (59 B.C.E.–17 C.E.). Livy's masterpiece was a history of Rome from the foundation of the city to 9 B.C.E., written in 142 books, although only 35 of them have survived. Livy perceived history in terms of moral lessons. He stated in the preface:

The study of history is the best medicine for a sick mind; for in history you have a record of the infinite variety of human experience plainly set out for all to see; and in that record you can find for yourself and your country both examples and warnings: fine things to take as models, base things, rotten through and through, to avoid.[7]

For Livy, human character was the determining factor in history.

Livy's history celebrated Rome's greatness. He built scene upon scene that not only revealed the character of the chief figures but also demonstrated the virtues that had made Rome great. Of course, he had serious weaknesses as a historian. He was not always concerned about the factual accuracy of his stories and was not overly critical of his sources. But he did tell a good tale, and his work remained the standard history of Rome for centuries.

Significance of the Augustan Age
The Augustan Age was a lengthy one. Augustus died in 14 C.E. after dominating the Roman world for forty-five years. He had created a new order while placating the old by restoring and maintaining traditional values, a fitting combination for a leader whose favorite maxim was "Make haste slowly." By the time of his death, his new order was so well established that few Romans agitated for an alternative. Indeed, as the Roman historian Tacitus (TASS-i-tuss) pointed out, "Actium had been won before the younger men were born. Even most of the older generation had come into a world of civil wars. Practically no one had ever seen truly Republican government.... Political equality was a thing of the past; all eyes watched for imperial commands."[8] The Republic was now only a memory and, given its last century of warfare, an unpleasant one at that. The new order was here to stay.

THE EARLY EMPIRE (14–180)

There was no serious opposition to Augustus's choice of successor, his stepson Tiberius (ty-BEER-ee-uss). By designating a family member as *princeps*, Augustus established the Julio-Claudian dynasty; the next four rulers were related either to his own family or to that of his wife, Livia.

The Julio-Claudians (14–68)
The Julio-Claudian rulers varied greatly in ability. Tiberius (14–37) was a competent general and an able administrator who tried initially to involve the senate in government. Caligula (kuh-LIG-yuh-luh) (37–41) was a grandnephew of Tiberius and the great-grandson of Augustus. He exhibited tyrannical behavior and was extremely erratic. Claudius (KLAW-dee-uss) (41–54) had been mistreated by his family because of a physical disability due to partial paralysis, but he was intelligent, well educated, and competent. He was followed by Nero (NEE-roh) (54–68), who was only sixteen when he came to power. Nero's interest in the arts caused him to neglect affairs of state, especially the military, and that proved to be his undoing.

Several major tendencies emerged during the reigns of the four Julio-Claudians. In general, more and more of the responsibilities that Augustus had given to the senate tended to be taken over by the emperors. Moreover, an imperial bureaucracy was instituted under Claudius. He rationalized the central government by developing bureaucratic departments with talented freedmen as their chiefs. This practice further undermined the authority of the senators, who had previously shared in these responsibilities.

As the Julio-Claudian successors of Augustus began to behave openly like real rulers rather than "first citizens of the state," the opportunity for arbitrary and corrupt acts increased. Caligula, who became mentally unbalanced, wanted to be hailed as a god and neglected affairs of state while indulging his passions. Nero freely eliminated people he wanted out of the way, including his own mother, whom he had murdered. Without troops, the senators proved unable to oppose these excesses. Only the praetorian guard established by Augustus seemed capable of interfering with these rulers but did so in a manner that did not bode well for future stability. Caligula proved so unpredictable that the officers of the praetorian guard hatched a plot and assassinated him before he had ruled for four complete years. Afterward, they chose Claudius, uncle of Caligula, as the next emperor and forced the senate to confirm their act, thereby demonstrating the power of the military units stationed around Rome.

The downfall of the Julio-Claudian dynasty came during the reign of Nero. His early reign had been quite successful. The young emperor worked hard and with the assistance of his childhood tutor, the philosopher Seneca (SEN-uh-kuh), gave the empire a sound government. But Nero soon tired of his duties and began to pursue other interests, including singing, acting, horse racing, and sexual excesses. After Seneca resigned his position in disgust in 62, Nero's rule deteriorated. His obsession with singing and acting in public was greeted with contempt by the senatorial class. At the same time, he aroused animosity by executing a number of prominent figures, including a popular general, on charges of treason. His actions finally led to a conspiracy, not by the praetorian guard, but by the Roman legions themselves. In 68, Galba (GAHL-buh), governor of one of the Spanish provinces, rose in revolt and secured the principate for himself. Nero, abandoned by his guards, committed suicide by stabbing himself in the throat after uttering his final words, "What an artist the world is losing in me."

The Flavians (69–96)

Galba, however, was not readily accepted by the other provincial armies, which led to civil wars in 69, known as the year of the four emperors. Finally, Vespasian (vess-PAY-zhun), commander of the legions in the east, established himself as sole ruler and his family as a new dynasty known as the Flavians. The significance of the year 69 was summed up precisely by the Roman historian Tacitus when he stated that "a well-hidden secret of the principate had been revealed: it was possible, it seemed, for an emperor to be chosen outside Rome"[9]—chosen, of course, by members of the Roman army.

The accession of Vespasian to the imperial power demonstrated that it was no longer necessary to be descended from an ancient aristocratic family to be emperor. In fact, the family of Vespasian (69–79) was from the equestrian order. Once in control, he managed to reestablish the economy on a sound basis after the extravagances of Nero and the destruction wrought by the civil wars of 69. More important, Vespasian had no compunctions whatever about establishing the principle of dynastic succession for the principate. He was followed by his sons Titus (TY-tuss) (79–81) and Domitian (doh-MISH-un) (81–96). The Flavians, especially Domitian, dropped the pretense of the word *princeps* and began to use the title of *imperator* (emperor) freely. The emperor was rapidly becoming an absolute monarch.

The Five "Good Emperors" (96–180)   Many historians see the **Pax Romana** (PAKS *or* PAHKS ro-MAH-nuh) (the "Roman peace") and the prosperity it engendered as the chief benefits of Roman rule during the first and second centuries C.E. These benefits were especially noticeable during the reigns of the five so-called **good emperors**. These rulers treated the ruling classes with respect, cooperated with the senate, ended arbitrary executions, maintained peace in the empire, and supported domestic policies generally beneficial to the empire. Though absolute monarchs, they were known for their tolerance and diplomacy.

The first of the five good emperors was Nerva (NUR-vuh) (96–98), chosen by the senate after the assassination of Domitian. By chance, Nerva and his next three successors had no sons and had to resort to adoption to obtain heirs. According to one Roman historian, "Nerva, therefore, finding himself held in such contempt by reason of his old age, ascended the Capitol and said in a loud voice: 'May good success attend the Roman senate and people and myself: I hereby adopt Marcus Ulpius Nerva Trajan.'"[10] Trajan (TRAY-jun) (98–117) was a capable man who was also acceptable to the army, an increasingly important requirement. He had been born in Spain to an old Roman family and was the first emperor born outside Italy.

Trajan was succeeded by his second cousin Hadrian (117–138), who spent years inspecting the provinces and restoring the military forces to good order. Hadrian adopted as his successor Antoninus Pius (an-tuh-NY-nuss PY-uss) (138–161), who achieved a reputation as the most beneficent of the five good emperors. It was said of him that "one should behave in all things like a pupil of Antoninus: his energy on behalf of what was done in accord with reason, his equability everywhere, his serene expression, his sweetness, his disdain of glory, his ambition to grasp affairs."[11] Unlike Hadrian, who traveled extensively in the provinces, Antoninus Pius stayed in Rome and made even greater use of the senate. He in turn adopted Marcus Aurelius (MAR-kuss aw-REE-lee-uss) (161–180), who has been viewed as a philosopher-king of the sort Plato envisioned (see Chapter 3). Highly influenced by Stoicism, Marcus Aurelius wrote his *Meditations*, reflecting on the ideal of Stoic duty as a religious concept.

Under the five good emperors, the powers of the emperor continued to expand at the expense of the senate. Increasingly, imperial officials appointed and directed by the emperor took over the running of the government. The five good emperors also extended the scope of imperial administration to areas previously untouched by the imperial government. Trajan established a program that provided state funds to assist poor parents in raising and educating their children. He was not motivated simply by benevolence, as he believed that such assistance would materially aid in creating a larger pool of young men in Italy eligible for military service.

The five good emperors were widely praised by their subjects for their extensive building programs. Trajan and Hadrian were especially active in constructing public works—aqueducts, bridges, roads, and harbor facilities—throughout the provinces and in Rome. Trajan built a new forum in Rome to provide a setting for his celebrated victory column. Hadrian's Pantheon, a temple of "all the gods," is one of the grandest ancient buildings surviving in Rome.

The Roman Empire at Its Height: Frontiers and Provinces

At its height in the second century, the Roman Empire (see Map 6.1) covered about 3.5 million square miles and had a population, like that of Han China, estimated at more than 50 million. While the emperors and the imperial administration provided a degree of unity, considerable leeway was given to local customs, and the privileges of Roman citizenship were extended to many people throughout the empire. In 212 c.e., the emperor Caracalla (kar-uh-KAL-uh) completed the process by giving Roman citizenship to every free inhabitant of the empire. Since only citizens paid inheritance taxes, the emperor's gesture added an important source of revenue for the empire. Latin was the language of the western part of the empire, while Greek was used in the east.

MAP 6.1 The Roman Empire from Augustus through Trajan (14–117)

Augustus and later emperors continued the expansion of the Roman Empire, adding more resources but also increasing the tasks of administration and keeping the peace. Compare this map with Map 5.3.

Although Roman culture spread to all parts of the empire, there were limits to Romanization since local languages persisted and many of the empire's residents spoke neither Latin nor Greek.

Roman Frontiers   With the exception of Claudius's annexation of Britain, the first-century successors of Augustus had largely followed his advice to curb expansion and remain within the natural frontiers of the empire—the ocean to the west, the rivers in the north, and the desert in the east and south.

Although Trajan broke with Augustus's policy of defensive imperialism by extending Roman rule into Dacia (modern Romania), Mesopotamia, and the Sinai peninsula, his conquests represent the high-water mark of Roman expansion. His successors recognized that the empire was overextended and pursued a policy of retrenchment. Hadrian withdrew Roman forces from much of Mesopotamia. Although he retained Dacia and Arabia, he went on the defensive in his frontier policy, reinforcing the fortifications along a line connecting the Rhine and Danube Rivers and building a defensive wall 80 miles long across northern Britain. By the end of the second century, the vulnerability of the empire had become apparent. Frontiers were stabilized, and the Roman forces were established in permanent bases behind the frontiers. But when one frontier was attacked, troops had to be drawn from other frontiers, leaving them vulnerable. The empire lacked a real strategic reserve, and its weakness would become ever more apparent.

The Army and Romanization   The Roman army was the primary instrument for the defense of the Roman frontiers. In 14 C.E., it numbered twenty-eight legions but had increased to thirty by the time of Trajan. The auxiliaries were increased correspondingly, creating a Roman army of about 400,000 by the end of the second century. Since legionaries had to be Roman citizens, most recruits in Augustus's time were from Italy. Over the course of the first century, however, the Italians' reluctance to serve in the military led to the recruitment of citizens from the provinces. By 100 C.E., only one in five legionaries was Italian.

In addition to defense and protection, the Roman army also served as an important instrument for Romanizing the provinces. Roman military camps became centers for the spread of the Latin language and Roman institutions and ways of thought and conduct. The presence of large numbers of troops and their dependent women and slaves encouraged the development of trade and local production to meet the army's need for supplies. Urban centers developed around army bases or nearby colonies. Many cities along the Rhine had their roots in legionary bases or auxiliary forts. The city of Cologne, for example, grew out of the military colony the Romans called Colonia Agrippinensis. Since many veterans, when they retired, chose to remain in the new towns, establishing families and new businesses, the towns served to pass on Roman culture and attitudes to the people in the provinces.

Cities and Romanization   The administration and cultural life of the Roman Empire depended greatly on cities and towns. A provincial governor's staff was not large, so it was left to local city officials to act as Roman agents in carrying out many government functions, especially those related to taxes. Most towns and cities were not large by modern standards. The largest was Rome, but there were also some large cities in the east: Alexandria in Egypt numbered over 300,000 inhabitants, Ephesus in Asia Minor had 200,000, and Antioch in Syria had around 150,000. In the west, cities were usually small, with only a few thousand inhabitants. Cities were important in the spread of Roman culture, law, and the Latin language. They were also uniform in physical appearance, with similar temples, markets, amphitheaters, and other public buildings.

Magistrates and town councillors chosen from the ranks of the wealthy upper classes directed municipal administration. Although these municipal offices were unsalaried, wealthy citizens were eager to hold them because they conferred prestige and power at the local level as well as Roman citizenship. Roman municipal policy effectively tied the upper classes to Roman rule and ensured that these classes would retain control over the rest of the population.

The Romanization of the provinces was reflected in significant changes in the governing classes of the empire. In the course of the first century, there was a noticeable decline in the number of senators from Italian families. By the end of the second century, Italian senators made up less than half the total. Increasingly, the Roman senate was being recruited from wealthy provincial equestrian families. The provinces also provided many of the legionaries for the Roman army and, beginning with Trajan, supplied many of the emperors.

The extent and speed of Romanization varied widely in different areas of the empire, however. In the western areas where Greeks and Phoenicians had established cities centuries earlier, such as Spain, Africa, and parts of Gaul, Romanization occurred quickly. Temples, aqueducts, amphitheaters, and the Latin language all became a regular part of life in these areas.

The process of Romanization was less developed in other parts of the empire, especially in Asia, where towns and cities had their own traditions free of Roman influence. Their common language was Greek, not Latin, and many people outside the urban areas spoke neither Latin nor Greek. Even more important than geography in determining the degree of Romanization, however, was class status. By 200 C.E., the upper classes everywhere in the empire had become Romanized, sharing a common culture as well as similar economic and social interests.

Roman Law and Romanization   As Roman citizenship spread in the cities, the new citizens became subject to Roman law, which in itself became an important instrument in the process of Romanization. The Early Empire experienced great progress in the study and codification of law. The second and third centuries C.E. witnessed the "classical age of Roman law," a period in which a number of great jurists classified and compiled basic legal principles that have proved valuable to the Western world. Most jurists emphasized the emperor as the source of law: "What has pleased the emperor has the force of law."

During the classical age of Roman law, the identification of the law of nations with natural law led to a concept of natural rights. According to the jurist Ulpian (d. 228), natural rights implied that all men are born equal and should therefore be equal before the law. In practice, however, the principle was not applied.

The Romans did, however, establish standards of justice, applicable to all people, that included principles that we would immediately recognize. A person was considered innocent until proved otherwise. People accused of wrongdoing were allowed to defend themselves before a judge. A judge was expected to weigh evidence carefully before arriving at a decision. These principles lived on in Western civilization long after the fall of the Roman Empire.

For Roman citizens, Roman law provided a uniform system of principles by which they conducted their affairs and led their lives. After Roman citizenship was extended to all free persons in the empire in 212 C.E., Roman law became an even more significant factor in binding the entire empire together.

Prosperity in the Early Empire

The Early Empire was a period of considerable prosperity. Internal peace resulted in unprecedented levels of trade (see Map 6.2). Merchants from all over the empire came to the chief Italian ports of Puteoli on the Bay of Naples and Ostia at the mouth of the Tiber. The importation of large quantities of grain to feed the populace of Rome and an incredible quantity of luxury items for the wealthy upper

MAP 6.2   Trade Routes and Products in the Roman Empire, c. 200

Although still primarily an agrarian economy, the Roman Empire provided the single currency and stable conditions necessary for an expansion of trade in various commodities and products. An extensive system of roads and shipping routes also facilitated trade.

© Cengage Learning 2012

classes in the west led to a steady drain of gold and silver coins from Italy and the west to the eastern part of the empire.

Long-distance trade beyond the Roman frontiers also flourished during the Early Empire. Developments in both the Roman and Chinese empires helped foster the growth of this trade. Although both empires built roads chiefly for military purposes, the roads also facilitated trade. Moreover, by creating large empires, the Romans and Chinese not only established internal stability but also pacified bordering territories, thus reducing the threat that bandits posed to traders. As a result, merchants developed a network of trade routes that brought these two great empires into commercial contact. Most important was the overland Silk Road, a regular caravan route between West and East.

The Silk Road received its name from the Chinese export of silk cloth, which became a popular craze among Roman elites, leading to a vast outpouring of silver from Rome to China and provoking the Roman emperor Tiberius to grumble that "the ladies and their baubles are transferring our money to foreigners." The silk trade also stimulated a degree of mutual curiosity between the two great civilizations, but not much mutual knowledge or understanding. So far as is known, no personal or diplomatic contacts between the two civilizations ever took place. But two great empires at the extremes of the Eurasian supercontinent had for the first time been linked together in a commercial relationship.

The increased trade helped stimulate manufacturing. The cities of the east still produced the items made in Hellenistic times (see Chapter 4). The first two centuries of the empire also witnessed the high point of industrial development in Italy. Some industries became concentrated in certain areas, such as bronze work in Capua and pottery in Arretium in Etruria. Other industries, such as brickmaking, were pursued in rural areas on large landed estates. Much industrial production remained small-scale and was done by individual artisans, usually freedmen or slaves. In the course of the first century, Italian centers of industry experienced increasing competition from the provinces.

Despite the extensive trade and commerce, agriculture remained the chief occupation of most people and the underlying basis of Roman prosperity. While the large landed estates called *latifundia* still dominated agriculture, especially in southern and central Italy, small peasant farms persisted, particularly in Etruria and the Po valley. Although large estates concentrating on sheep and cattle raising used slave labor, the lands of some *latifundia* were worked by free tenant farmers called **coloni** (kuh-LOH-nee). The *colonus* was essentially a sharecropper who paid rent in labor, produce, or sometimes cash.

In considering the prosperity of the Roman world, it is important to remember the enormous gulf between rich and poor underlying it. The development of towns and cities, so important to the creation of any civilization, is based to a large degree on the agricultural surpluses of the countryside. In ancient times, the margin of surplus produced by each farmer was relatively small. Therefore, the upper classes and urban populations had to be supported by the labor of a large number of agricultural producers who never found it easy to produce much more than enough for themselves. In lean years, when there were no surpluses, the townspeople often took what they wanted, leaving little for the peasants.

ROMAN CULTURE AND SOCIETY IN THE EARLY EMPIRE

The shift from Republic to empire not only transformed the Roman political world, but also affected its cultural and social life. Intellectuals found ways to accommodate the autocratic rule of emperors while Roman architects created massive buildings befitting an empire. Gladiatorial games and slavery increased dramatically in the Early Empire, while upper-class women acquired greater independence.

The Silver Age of Latin Literature   In the history of Latin literature, the century and a half after Augustus is often labeled the "silver age" to indicate that the literary efforts of the period, while good, were not equal to the high standards of the Augustan "golden age." The popularity of rhetorical training encouraged the use of clever literary expressions, often at the expense of original and meaningful content. A good example of this trend can be found in the works of Seneca.

Seneca   Educated in Rome, Seneca (c. 4 B.C.E.–65 C.E.) became strongly attached to the philosophy of Stoicism (see Chapter 4). After serving as tutor to Nero, he helped run the government during the first five years of Nero's reign. Seneca began to withdraw from politics after Nero took a more active role in government. In 65, he was charged with involvement in a conspiracy against Nero and committed suicide at Nero's command.

In letters written to a young friend, Seneca expressed the basic tenets of Stoicism: living according to nature, accepting events dispassionately as part of the divine plan, and a universal love for all humanity. Thus, "the first thing philosophy promises us is the feeling of fellowship, of belonging to mankind and being members of a community.... Philosophy calls for simple living, not for doing penance, and the simple way of life need not be a crude one."[12] Viewed in retrospect, Seneca displays some glaring inconsistencies. While preaching the virtues of simplicity, he amassed a fortune and was ruthless at times in protecting it. His letters show humanity, benevolence, and fortitude, but his sentiments are often undermined by an attempt to be clever with words.

Tacitus   The greatest historian of the silver age was Tacitus (c. 56–120). His main works included the *Annals* and the *Histories*, which presented a narrative account of Roman history from the reign of Tiberius through the assassination of Domitian in 96. Tacitus believed that history had a moral purpose: "It seems to me a historian's foremost duty to ensure that merit is recorded, and to confront evil deeds and words with the fear of posterity's denunciations."[13] As a member of the senatorial class, Tacitus was disgusted with the abuses of power perpetrated by the emperors and was determined that the "evil deeds" of wicked men would not be forgotten. Many historians believe he went too far in projecting the evils of his own day back into his account of the past. Tacitus's work *Germania* is especially important as a source of information about the early Germans. But it too is colored by his attempt to show the Germans as noble savages in contrast to the decadent Roman upper classes.

Juvenal   The best poet of the silver age was Juvenal (JOO-vuh-nul) (c. 55–c. 128), who wrote five books of satires in which he pilloried the manners and vices of his generation. He attacked the affectations of Roman women, the abuse of slaves, the excesses of emperors, the eastern and Greek immigrants, his own poverty, and the inequities of Roman society. For example: "They demand that the teacher shall mold these tender minds.... 'See to it,' you're told, and when the school year's ended, you'll get as much as a jockey makes from a single race."[14] But Juvenal was not a reformer. Though he attacked many vices, he offered no basic critique of his society.

Art in the   The Romans contributed little that was original to painting
Early Empire   and sculpture. Much work was done by Greek artists and
                        craftspeople who adhered to the Roman desire for realism
and attention to details. Wall paintings and frescoes in the houses of the rich realistically depicted landscapes, portraits, and scenes from mythological stories.

In architecture, the Romans continued to imitate Greek styles and made use of colonnades, rectangular structures, and post-and-lintel construction. But the Romans were innovative in their own way. They made considerable use of curvilinear forms: the arch, vault, and dome. The Romans were the first people in antiquity to use concrete on a massive scale. By combining concrete and curvilinear forms, they were able to construct massive buildings—public baths, such as those of

© Nik Wheeler/CORBIS

Roman Aqueduct. *The engineering skills of the Romans enabled them to build massive constructions, including aqueducts such as this one in southern France, known as the Pont du Gard. The Pont du Gard is a three-story bridge built of blocks of stone without cement; at the top was a channel that carried water. Nîmes received its water from a source 30 miles away. Since gravity kept the water flowing, the channels holding the water had to have a gradual decline from the source of the water to its final destination. The Pont du Gard, which crosses the Gardon River outside Nîmes, was built to the exact height needed to maintain the flow of water into the city.*

Caracalla, and amphitheaters, the most famous of which was the Colosseum in Rome. These large buildings were made possible by Roman engineering skills. These same skills were put to use in constructing roads (the Romans built a network of 50,000 miles of roads throughout their empire), aqueducts (in Rome, almost a dozen aqueducts kept the population supplied with water), and bridges.

Imperial Rome   At the center of the colossal Roman Empire was the ancient city of Rome (see Map 6.3). Truly a capital city, Rome had the largest population of any city in the empire. It is estimated that its population was close to one million by the time of Augustus. For anyone with ambitions, Rome was the place to be. A magnet to many people, Rome was extremely cosmopolitan. Nationalities from all over the empire resided there, with entire neighborhoods inhabited by specific groups, such as Greeks and Syrians.

Rome was no doubt an overcrowded and noisy city. Because of the congestion, carts and wagons were banned from the streets during the day, but their noisy traffic at night often made sleep difficult. Evening pedestrian travel was dangerous. Although Augustus had organized a police force, lone travelers might be assaulted, robbed, or soaked by filth thrown out of the upper-story windows of Rome's massive apartment buildings.

MAP 6.3 Imperial Rome

A large, overcrowded, and dirty city, Rome was the political, economic, social, and cultural hub of the Roman Empire. Squalid and desperate living conditions for the poor contrasted dramatically with the city's magnificent architectural works.

An enormous gulf existed between rich and poor in the city of Rome. While the rich had comfortable villas, the poor lived in apartment blocks called *insulae*, which might be six stories high. Constructed of concrete, they were often poorly built and prone to collapse. The use of wooden beams in the floors and movable stoves, torches, candles, and lamps for heat and light created a constant danger of fire. Once started, fires were extremely difficult to put out. The famous conflagration of 64, which Nero was unjustly accused of starting, devastated a large part of the city. Besides the hazards of collapse and fire, living conditions were miserable. High rents forced entire families into one room. In the absence of plumbing and central heating, conditions were so uncomfortable that poorer Romans spent most of their time outdoors in the streets.

Fortunately for these people, Rome boasted public buildings unequaled anywhere in the empire. Its temples, forums, markets, baths, theaters, triumphal arches, governmental buildings, and amphitheaters gave parts of the city an appearance of grandeur and magnificence.

Though the center of a great empire, Rome was also a great parasite. Beginning with Augustus, the emperors accepted responsibility for providing food for the urban populace, with about 200,000 people receiving free grain. But even the free grain did not relieve the grim conditions of the poor. Early in the second century C.E., a Roman doctor claimed that rickets was common among the city's children.

In addition to food, entertainment was provided on a grand scale for the inhabitants of Rome. The poet Juvenal said of the Roman masses: "Nowadays, with no vote to sell, their motto is 'Couldn't care less.' Time was when their vote elected generals, heads of state, commanders of legions: but now they've pulled in their horns, there's only two things that concern them: Bread and Circuses."[15] The emperor and other state officials provided public spectacles as part of the great festivals—most of them religious in origin—celebrated by the state. More than one hundred days a year were given over to these public holidays. The festivals included three major types of entertainment. At the Circus Maximus, horse and chariot races attracted hundreds of thousands, while dramatic and other performances were held in theaters. But the most famous of all the public spectacles were the gladiatorial shows.

The Gladiatorial Shows   The gladiatorial shows were an integral part of Roman society. They took place in amphitheaters; the first permanent one was constructed in Rome in 29 B.C.E. Perhaps the most famous was the Flavian amphitheater, called the Colosseum, constructed in Rome under Vespasian and his son Titus to seat 50,000 spectators. Amphitheaters were constructed throughout the empire. They varied in size, with capacities ranging from a few thousand to tens of thousands. Considerable resources and ingenuity went into building them, especially in the arrangements for moving wild beasts efficiently into the arena. In most cities and towns, amphitheaters came to be the biggest buildings, rivaled only by the circuses for races and the public baths. As we shall see repeatedly in the course of Western civilization, where a society invests its money gives an idea of its priorities. Since the amphitheater was the primary location for the gladiatorial games, it is fair to say that public slaughter was an important part of Roman culture.

Gladiatorial games were held from dawn to dusk. Their main features were contests to the death between trained fighters. Most gladiators were slaves or condemned criminals who were trained for combat in special gladiatorial schools.

Gladiatorial games included other forms of entertainment as well. Criminals of all ages and both sexes were sent into the arena without weapons to face certain death from wild animals who would tear them to pieces. Numerous kinds of animal contests were also held: wild beasts against each other, such as bears against buffalo; staged hunts with men shooting safely from behind iron bars; and gladiators in the arena with bulls, tigers, and lions. Reportedly, five thousand beasts were killed in one day of games when the emperor Titus inaugurated the Colosseum in 80 C.E. Enormous resources were invested in capturing and shipping wild animals for slaughter, and whole species were hunted to extinction in parts of the empire.

These bloodthirsty spectacles were extremely popular with the Roman people. Tacitus reported, "Few indeed are to be found who talk of any other subjects in their homes, and whenever we enter a classroom, what else is the conversation of the youths."[16] But the gladiatorial games served a purpose beyond mere entertainment. Like the other forms of public entertainment, the games fulfilled both a political and a social function. Certainly, the games served to divert the idle masses from political unrest. It was said of the emperor Trajan that he understood that although the distribution of grain and money satisfied the individual, spectacles were necessary for the "contentment of the masses."

Disaster in Southern Italy

Gladiatorial spectacles were contrived by humans, but the Roman Empire also experienced some horrific natural spectacles. One of the greatest was the eruption of Mount Vesuvius (vuh-SOO-vee-uss) on August 24, 79. Although known to be a volcano, Vesuvius was thought to be extinct, its hillsides green with flourishing vineyards. Its eruption threw up thousands of tons of lava and ash. Toxic fumes killed many people, and the nearby city of Pompeii (pahm-PAY) was quickly buried under volcanic ash. To the west, Herculaneum and other communities around the Bay of Naples were submerged beneath a mud flow. Not for another 1,700 years were systematic excavations begun on the buried towns. The examination of their preserved remains has enabled archaeologists to reconstruct the everyday life and art of these Roman towns. Their discovery in the eighteenth century was an important force in stimulating both scholarly and public interest in Classical antiquity and helped give rise to the Neoclassical style of that century.

The Art of Medicine

Although early Romans had no professional physicians, they did possess an art of medicine. Early Roman medicine was essentially herbal. The *paterfamilias* would prepare various remedies to heal wounds and cure illnesses. Knowledge of the healing properties of plants was passed down from generation to generation. This traditional approach to medicine continued in the Early Empire.

As in other areas of Roman life, Greek influence was also felt in medicine. At the end of the third century B.C.E., scientific medicine entered the Roman world through professional practitioners from the Hellenistic world. Doctors became fashionable in Rome, although prejudice against them was never completely abandoned. Many were Greek slaves who belonged to the households of large aristocratic families. The first public doctors in Rome were attached to the Roman army. Military practices were then extended to imperial officials and their families in the provinces and included the establishment of public hospitals. Gladiatorial schools had their own resident doctors as well. In fact, one of the most famous physicians, the Greek Galen (129–199), emerged from the ranks of gladiatorial doctors to become court physician to the emperor Marcus Aurelius. Roman scientific medicine also witnessed the development of numerous specialists. For example, Alcon, the famous surgeon of the Flavian age, specialized in bone diseases and hernia operations.

Slaves and Their Masters   The number of slaves had increased dramatically in the Roman Republic as the empire expanded through warfare. Consequently, slaves were highly visible in the Early Empire. Slaves filled the residences of the rich. Possessing a large number of slaves was a status symbol; a single household might include dozens of slaves, serving as hairdressers, footmen, messengers, accountants, secretaries, carpenters, plumbers, librarians, goldsmiths, and doctors as well as ordinary domestic servants. The reliance on slaves, especially as skilled craftspeople, undoubtedly created unemployment among the free population. Some slaves worked at high-status jobs as architects and managers of businesses, while some imperial slaves held positions in the government bureaucracy. Slaves were also used on landed estates.

But the number of slaves probably peaked in the Early Empire. The defensive imperial policies pursued after Augustus led to a decline in the supply of slaves from foreign conquest. Manumission also contributed to the decline in the number of slaves. It had been customary in Rome for "good masters" to free their slaves, especially well-educated ones or good workers. Although freedmen became Roman citizens, they did not receive full rights of citizenship. They could vote but not run for office.

Many authors have commented on the supposed advance in humanitarian attitudes toward slaves in the Early Empire, especially in the second century. They argue that the philosophy of Stoicism, with its emphasis on the universality of humanity, had an influence in this direction. Seneca stressed the need for kindness to slaves. Very likely, however, the practical Romans were as much, if not more, concerned about the usefulness of their slaves as about any humanitarian attitudes. New laws in the second century moralized more than they actually improved the condition of slaves. Hadrian, for example, forbade the sale of slaves for immoral or gladiatorial purposes, but such laws had little impact on how masters actually treated their slaves. Despite the changes, there were still instances of slaves murdering their owners, and many Romans continued to live in fear of their slaves.

The Upper-Class Roman Family   By the second century C.E., significant changes were occurring in the Roman family (see Images of Everyday Life). The foundations of the authority of the *paterfamilias* over his family, which had already begun to weaken in the late Republic, were further undermined. The *paterfamilias* no longer had absolute authority over

Children in the Roman World

Like the Greeks, the Romans did not always raise all the children born into their families. Not only were deformed children exposed to die, but infant mortality rates were high—as many as half of all infants did not survive into adulthood. Nevertheless, upper-class families did take good care of their surviving children. The statue of a young boy shown in the illustration at the top reflects this concern. He is wearing a bulla, a golden amulet given to male children on the day they were named, nine days after birth, to protect them against evil spirits. Boys were encouraged to engage in athletic games at a very young age. The second illustration, a scene from a third-century sarcophagus, shows an idealized version of an upper-class child's life: he is depicted being breast-fed by his mother, being held by his father, playing in a small chariot pulled by a goat, and reciting to his father. The father was largely responsible for providing for the education of his children. Roman boys learned reading and writing, moral principles and family values, law, and physical training to prepare them to be soldiers. Girls learned at home what they needed to know to be good wives and mothers.

The end of childhood for Roman males came at the age of sixteen, when the young man gave up his bulla, exchanged his purple-edged toga for a plain white toga—the toga of manhood—and soon after began his career. For Roman girls, childhood ended at age fourteen, the common age of marriage. Lower-class children were put to work in their teens and were often apprenticed to a craftperson at age twelve. Slave children were expected to work when they were five.

Louvre, Paris//Gianni Dagli Orti/The Art Archive at Art Resource, NY

M·CORNELIO·M·F·PALESTATIO· · · · ·FECER·

Louvre, Paris//DeAgostini/SuperStock

his children; he could no longer sell them into slavery or have them put to death. Moreover, the husband's absolute authority over his wife also disappeared, a process that had begun in the late Republic. In the Early Empire, the idea of male guardianship continued to weaken significantly, and by the late second century, it had become a mere formality.

Upper-class Roman women in the Early Empire had considerable freedom and independence. They had acquired the right to own, inherit, and dispose of property. Upper-class women could attend races, the theater, and events in the amphitheater, although in the latter two places they were forced to sit in separate female sections. Moreover, ladies of rank were still accompanied by maids and companions when they went out. Some women operated businesses, such as shipping firms. Women still could not participate in politics, but the Early Empire saw a number of important women who influenced politics through their husbands or sons, including Livia, the wife of Augustus; Agrippina, the mother of Nero; and Plotina, the wife of Trajan.

At the end of the first century and beginning of the second, there was a noticeable decline in the number of children among the upper classes, a trend that had already begun in the late Republic. Especially evident was an increase in childless marriages. Despite imperial laws aimed at increasing the number of children, the low birthrate persisted. Not only did **infanticide** continue to be practiced, but upper-class Romans also used contraception and abortion to limit their families. There were numerous techniques for contraception. Though highly touted, amulets, magical formulas, and potions to induce temporary sterility proved ineffective, as did the rhythm method, since Roman medical writers believed that a woman was most fertile just when menstruation was ending. A more dependable practice involved the use of oils, ointments, and soft wool to obstruct the opening of the uterus. Contraceptive techniques for males were also advocated. An early version of a condom used the bladder of a goat, but it was prohibitively expensive. Although the medical sources do not mention it, the Romans may also have used the ubiquitous coitus interruptus. Abortion was practiced, using drugs or surgical instruments. Ovid chastises Corinna: "Ah, women, why will you thrust and pierce with the instrument, and give dire poisons to your children yet unborn?"[17]

Women also faced great dangers in childbirth. They gave birth at home with the assistance of a midwife and a few female relatives. Fathers-to-be and other males were not present. Although exact numbers are not available, we do know that many upper-class women between the ages of sixteen and thirty-five died in childbirth. Prominent women who died in childbirth or soon after due to complications include Cicero's daughter Tullia and Caesar's daughter Julia.

TRANSFORMATION OF THE ROMAN WORLD: CRISES IN THE THIRD CENTURY

During the reign of Marcus Aurelius, the last of the five good emperors, a number of natural catastrophes struck Rome. Floods of the Tiber, famine, and plague brought back from the east by the army led to considerable loss of population and a shortage of military manpower. To many Romans, these natural disasters seemed to portend an ominous future for Rome. New problems arose soon after the death of Marcus Aurelius.

Political and Military Woes Unlike the first four good emperors, who chose capable successors by adopting competent men as their sons, Marcus Aurelius allowed his own son, Commodus (KAHM-uh-duss) (180–192), to become emperor. A cruel man, Commodus was a poor choice, and his assassination led to a brief renewal of civil war until Septimius Severus (sep-TIM-ee-uss se-VEER-uss) (193–211), who was born in North Africa and spoke Latin with an accent, used his legions to seize power. On his deathbed, Septimius Severus advised his sons, "Live in harmony, make the soldiers rich, and don't give a damn for anything else." His advice set the tone for the new dynasty he established. The Severan rulers (193–235) began to create a military monarchy. The army was expanded, soldiers' pay was increased, and military officers were appointed to important government positions. A new stability seemed at hand, but the increased power of the military led new military leaders to aspire to become

Antikensammlung, Berlin//© Bildarchiv Preussischer Kulturbesitz/Art Resource, NY

Septimius Severus and His Family. *This portrait, which was painted on wood about 200 c.e. and found in Egypt, is the only existing painted likeness of a Roman emperor. The emperor is portrayed with gray hair and beard in memory of Marcus Aurelius. To legitimize his authority, Septimius Severus had himself adopted into the Antonine dynasty, calling himself the son of Marcus Aurelius. The emperor stands next to his wife with their two sons in front of them. The face of his son Geta has been blotted out, no doubt by order of the other son standing next to him, Caracalla, who had his brother killed when he succeeded to the throne.*

emperor, and the military monarchy of the Severan rulers degenerated into military anarchy.

For the next fifty years (235–284), the empire was mired in the chaos of continual civil war. Contenders for the imperial throne found that bribing soldiers was an effective way to become emperor. In these five decades, there were twenty-seven emperors, only four of whom did not meet a violent end. At the same time, the empire was beset by a series of invasions, no doubt encouraged by the internal turmoil. In the east, the Sassanid Persians made inroads into Roman territory. A fitting symbol of Rome's crisis was the capture of the Roman emperor himself, Valerian (253–260), by the Persians and his death in captivity, an event unprecedented in Roman history. Valerian's body was displayed in the chief towns of Persia. Germanic tribes also poured into the empire. The Goths overran the Balkans and moved into Greece and Asia Minor. The Franks advanced into Gaul and Spain. Not until the reign of Aurelian (aw-REEL-yun) (270–275) were most of the boundaries restored. Although he abandoned the Danubian province of Dacia, Aurelian reconquered Gaul and reestablished order in the east and along the Danube. He also built a new defensive wall around Rome to defend the city against invaders. Grateful citizens hailed him as "restorer of the world."

As civil wars and invasions wore down the central government, provinces began to break away from the empire. A military commander named Postumus seized control of Gaul and then gained the support of Britain and Spain. He defended his "Gallic empire" until he was killed by his own soldiers in 269. In the east, Zenobia (zuh-NOH-bee-uh), the wife of the ruler of Syria, seized power after his death and then in 270 extended her control over Egypt and much of Asia Minor. In 272, Emperor Aurelian ended this threat to imperial power by defeating Zenobia and her forces in Syria.

Economic and Social Crises   Invasions, civil wars, and a recurrence of the plague came close to causing a near collapse of the Roman Empire in the third century. The population declined drastically, possibly by as much as one-third. There was a significant decline in trade and small industry. The manpower shortage created by the plague affected both military recruiting and the economy. Farm production deteriorated as fields were ravaged by barbarians and even more often by the defending Roman armies. Many farmers complained that Roman commanders and their soldiers were confiscating produce and livestock. Provincial governors seemed powerless to stop these depredations, and some even joined in the frenzy.

The monetary system began to show signs of collapse as a result of debased coinage and the onset of serious inflation. Gold coins disappeared from circulation, and silver coins were diluted. The standard coin, the denarius, was now worth less than half of its first-century value. After further decline, it was replaced by new coins of even less value. Goods began to replace money as a medium of exchange.

Armies were needed more than ever, but financial strains made it difficult to enlist and pay the necessary soldiers. Short of cash, the imperial government paid its soldiers with produce, causing bitter resentment. Whereas in the second century the Roman army had been recruited among the inhabitants of frontier provinces, by the mid-third century, the state had to rely on hiring barbarians to fight under Roman commanders. These soldiers had no understanding of Roman traditions and no real attachment to either the empire or the emperors. By the end of the third century, a new form of political structure would emerge (see Chapter 7).

TRANSFORMATION OF THE ROMAN WORLD: THE RISE OF CHRISTIANITY

The advent of Christianity marks a fundamental break with the dominant values of the Greco-Roman world. Christian views of God, human beings, and the world were quite different from those of the Greeks and Romans. Nevertheless, to understand the rise of Christianity, we must first examine both the religious environment of the Roman world and the Jewish background from which Christianity emerged.

The Religious World of the Roman Empire Augustus had taken a number of steps to revive the Roman state religion, which had declined during the turmoil of the late Republic. The official state religion focused on the worship of a pantheon of Greco-Roman gods and goddesses, including Jupiter, Juno, Minerva, and Mars. Observance of proper ritual by state priests theoretically brought the Romans into proper relationship with the gods and guaranteed security, peace, and prosperity. The polytheistic Romans were extremely tolerant of other religions. The Romans allowed the worship of native gods and goddesses throughout their provinces and even adopted some of the local gods. In addition, the imperial cult of Roma and Augustus was developed to bolster support for the emperors. After Augustus, deceased emperors deified by the Roman senate were included in the official imperial cult.

The desire for a more emotional spiritual experience led many people to the mystery religions of the Hellenistic east, which flooded into the western Roman world during the Early Empire. The mystery religions offered secret teachings that supposedly brought special benefits. They promised their followers advantages unavailable through Roman religion: an entry into a higher world of reality and the promise of a future life superior to the present one. They also featured elaborate rituals with deep emotional appeal. By participating in their ceremonies and performing their rites, an adherent could achieve communion with spiritual beings and undergo purification that opened the door to life after death.

Many mystery cults were vying for the attention of the Roman world. The cults of Cybele or the Great Mother and the Egyptian Isis had many followers, especially among the urban poor who gained little from the prosperity of the Early Empire. The cult of Isis, an Egyptian mother goddess, had become especially widespread throughout the empire by the first century C.E. Isis, seen in her role as the loving mother of Horus, appealed especially to women. Initiation into the cult of Isis came with a promise of immortality after death.

Perhaps the most important mystery cult was Mithraism. Mithra was the chief agent of Ahuramazda, the supreme god of light in Persian Zoroastrianism (see Chapter 2). In the Roman world, Mithra came to be identified with the sun god and was known by his Roman title of the Unconquered Sun. Mithraism had spread rapidly in Rome and the western provinces by the second century C.E. and was especially favored by soldiers, who viewed Mithra as their patron deity. It was a religion for men only and featured an initiation ceremony in which devotees were baptized in the blood of a sacrificed bull. Mithraists paid homage to the sun on the first day of the week (Sunday), commemorated the sun's birthday around December 25, and celebrated ceremonial meals.

The Jewish Background   Christianity emerged out of Judaism, and so it is to the Jewish political-religious world that we must turn to find the beginnings of Christianity. In Hellenistic times, the Jewish people had enjoyed considerable independence under their Seleucid rulers (see Chapter 4). Roman involvement with the Jews began in 63 B.C.E., and by 6 C.E., Judaea had been made a province and placed under the direction of a Roman procurator. But unrest continued, augmented by divisions among the Jews themselves. The Sadducees favored a rigid adherence to Hebrew law, rejected the possibility of personal immortality, and favored cooperation with the Romans. The Pharisees adhered strictly to Jewish ritual and, although they wanted Judaea to be free from Roman control, did not advocate violent means to achieve this goal. The Essenes were a Jewish sect that lived in a religious community near the Dead Sea. As revealed in the Dead Sea Scrolls, a collection of documents first discovered in 1947, the Essenes, like many other Jews, awaited a Messiah who would save Israel from oppression, usher in the kingdom of God, and establish a paradise on earth. A fourth group, the Zealots, were militant extremists who advocated the violent overthrow of Roman rule. A Jewish revolt in 66 C.E. was crushed by the Romans four years later. The Jewish Temple in Jerusalem was destroyed, and Roman power once more stood supreme in Judaea.

The Origins of Christianity   Jesus of Nazareth (c. 6 B.C.E.–30 C.E.) was a Palestinian Jew who grew up in Galilee, an important center of the militant Zealots. He began his itinerant public preaching as a young adult amid the confusion and conflict in Judaea. Jesus's message was basically simple. He reassured his fellow Jews that he did not plan to undermine their traditional religion: "Do not think that I have come to abolish the Law or the Prophets; I have not come to abolish them but to fulfill them."[18] According to Jesus, what was important was not strict adherence to the letter of the law and attention to rules and prohibitions but the transformation of the inner person: "So in everything, do to others what you would have them do to you, for this sums up the Law and the Prophets."[19] God's command was simply to love God and one another: "Love the Lord your God with all your heart and with all your soul and with all your mind and with all your strength. The second is this: Love your neighbor as yourself."[20] In the Sermon on the Mount, Jesus presented the ethical concepts—humility, charity, and brotherly love—that would form the basis for the value system of medieval Western civilization. As we have seen, these were not the values of Classical Greco-Roman civilization.

Although some Jews welcomed Jesus as the Messiah who would save Israel from oppression and establish God's kingdom on earth, Jesus spoke of a heavenly

Christian Ideals: The Sermon on the Mount

Christianity was simply one of many religions competing for attention in the Roman Empire during the first and second centuries. The rise of Christianity marked a fundamental break with the value system of the upper-class elites who dominated the world of Classical antiquity. As these excerpts from the Sermon on the Mount in the Gospel of Matthew illustrate, Christians emphasized humility, charity, brotherly love, and a belief in the inner being and a spiritual kingdom superior to this material world. These values and principles were not those of Classical Greco-Roman civilization as exemplified in the words and deeds of its leaders.

The Gospel According to Matthew

Now when he saw the crowds, he went up on a mountainside and sat down. His disciples came to him, and he began to teach them saying:

> Blessed are the poor in spirit: for theirs is the kingdom of heaven.
> Blessed are those who mourn: for they will be comforted.
> Blessed are the meek: for they will inherit the earth.
> Blessed are those who hunger and thirst for righteousness: for they will be filled.
> Blessed are the merciful: for they will be shown mercy.
> Blessed are the pure in heart: for they will see God.
> Blessed are the peacemakers: for they will be called sons of God.
> Blessed are those who are persecuted because of righteousness: for theirs is the kingdom of heaven....

You have heard that it was said, "Eye for eye, and tooth for tooth." But I tell you, Do not resist an evil person. If someone strikes you on the right cheek, turn to him the other also....

You have heard that it was said, "Love your neighbor, and hate your enemy." But I tell you, Love your enemies and pray for those who persecute you....

Do not store up for yourselves treasures on earth, where moth and rust destroy, and where thieves break in and steal. But store up for yourselves treasures in heaven, where moth and rust do not destroy, and where thieves do not break in and steal. For where your treasure is, there your heart will be also....

No one can serve two masters. Either he will hate the one and love the other, or he will be devoted to the one and despise the other. You cannot serve both God and Money.

Therefore I tell you, do not worry about your life, what you will eat or drink; or about your body, what you will wear. Is not life more important than food, and the body more important than clothes? Look at the birds of the air; they do not sow or reap to store away in barns, and yet your heavenly Father feeds them. Are you not much more valuable than they?... So do not worry, saying, What shall we eat? or What shall we drink? or What shall we wear? For the pagans run after all these things, and your heavenly Father knows that you need them. But seek first his kingdom and his righteousness, and all these things will be given to you as well.

Q What were the ideals of early Christianity? How do they differ from the values and principles of Classical Greco-Roman civilization?

Source: Scripture taken from the HOLY BIBLE, NEW INTERNATIONAL VERSION®. Copyright © 1973, 1978, 1984 Biblica. Used by permission of Zondervan. All rights reserved. The "NIV" and "New International Version" trademarks are registered in the United States Patent and Trademark Office by Biblica. Use of either trademark requires the permission of Biblica.

kingdom, not an earthly one: "My kingdom is not of this world."[21] Consequently, he disappointed the radicals. At the same time, conservative religious leaders believed Jesus was another false Messiah who was undermining respect for traditional Jewish religion. To the Roman authorities of Palestine and their local allies, Jesus was a potential revolutionary who might transform Jewish expectations of a messianic kingdom into a revolt against Rome. Therefore, Jesus found himself denounced on many sides and was given over to the Roman authorities. The procurator Pontius Pilate ordered his crucifixion. But that did not solve the problem. A few loyal disciples of Jesus spread the story, common to mystery cults (see Chapter 4), that he had overcome death, been resurrected, and then ascended into heaven. The belief in Jesus's resurrection became an important tenet of Christian doctrine. Jesus was now hailed by his followers as the "anointed one" (*Christ* in Greek), the Messiah who would return and usher in the kingdom of God on earth.

The Importance of Paul   Christianity began, then, as a religious movement within Judaism and was viewed that way by Roman authorities for many decades. Although tradition holds that one of Jesus's disciples, Peter, founded the Christian church at Rome, the most important figure in early Christianity after Jesus was Paul of Tarsus (c. 5–c. 67). Paul reached out to non-Jews and transformed Christianity from a Jewish sect into a broader religious movement.

Called the "second founder of Christianity," Paul was a Jewish Roman citizen who had been strongly influenced by Hellenistic Greek culture. He believed that the message of Jesus should be preached not only to Jews but to Gentiles (non-Jews) as well. Paul was responsible for founding Christian communities throughout Asia Minor and along the shores of the Aegean.

It was Paul who provided a universal foundation for the spread of Jesus's ideas. He taught that Jesus was, in effect, a savior-god, the son of God, who had come to earth to save all humans, who were basically sinners as a result of Adam's original sin of disobedience against God. By his death, Jesus had atoned for the sins of all humans and made it possible for all men and women to experience a new beginning with the potential for individual salvation. By accepting Jesus as their savior, they, too, could be saved.

The Spread of Christianity   At first, Christianity spread slowly. Although the teachings of early Christianity were mostly disseminated by the preaching of convinced Christians, written materials also appeared. Paul had written a series of letters, or epistles, outlining Christian beliefs for different Christian communities. Some of Jesus's disciples may also have preserved some of the sayings of the master in writing and would have passed on personal memories that became the basis of the written gospels—the "good news" concerning Jesus of Matthew, Mark, Luke, and John—which eventually became the authoritative record of Jesus's life and teachings and formed the core of the New Testament. Controversy over the legitimate gospels, however, continued well into the fourth century. Recently, some scholars have argued that other gospels, such as that of Thomas, were rejected because they deviated from the beliefs about Jesus held by the emerging church leaders. In the first few centuries after Jesus's death, who was a Christian and what Christianity was remained open to discussion.

Although Jerusalem was the first center of Christianity, its destruction by the Romans in 70 C.E. left individual Christian churches with considerable independence. By 100, Christian churches had been established in most of the major cities of the east and in some places in the western part of the empire. Many early Christians came from the ranks of Hellenized Jews and the Greek-speaking populations of the east. But in the second and third centuries, an increasing number of followers were Latin-speaking people. A Latin translation of the Greek New Testament that appeared soon after 200 aided this process.

Early Christian Communities   Early Christian groups met in private homes in the evening to share a common meal called an *agape* (ah-GAH-pay) or love feast and to celebrate what became known as the sacrament of the **Eucharist** (YOO-kuh-rist) or Lord's Supper—the communal celebration of Jesus's Last Supper:

> While they were eating, Jesus took bread, gave thanks and broke it, and gave it to the disciples, saying, Take and eat; this is my body. Then he took the cup, gave thanks, and offered it to them, saying, Drink from it, all of you. This is my blood of the covenant, which is poured out for many for the forgiveness of sins.[22]

Early Christian communities were loosely organized, with both men and women playing significant roles. Some women held important positions, often as preachers. Local churches were under the leadership of boards of elders (*presbyters*), but by the beginning of the second century, officials known as *bishops* came to exercise considerable authority over the presbyters. These bishops based their superior position on apostolic succession—as the successors to Jesus's original twelve apostles (disciples), they were living representatives of Jesus's power. As Ignatius of Antioch wrote in 107, "It is clear that we must regard a bishop as the Lord Himself.... Your clergy ... are attuned to their bishop like the strings of a harp, and the result is a hymn of praise to Jesus Christ from minds that are in unison."[23] Bishops were invariably men, a clear indication that by the second century C.E., most Christian communities were following the views of Paul that Christian women should be subject to Christian men.

Although some of the fundamental values of Christianity differed markedly from those of the Greco-Roman world, the Romans initially did not pay much attention to the Christians, whom they regarded at first as simply another sect of Judaism. The structure of the Roman Empire itself aided the growth of Christianity. Christian missionaries, including some of Jesus's original twelve apostles, used Roman roads to travel throughout the empire spreading their "good news."

The Changing Roman View of Christianity   As the popular appeal of Christianity grew, the Roman attitude toward it began to change. As we have seen, the Romans were tolerant of other religions except when they threatened public order or public morals. Many Romans came to view Christians as harmful to the order of the Roman state. These views were often based on misperceptions. The celebration of the Lord's Supper, for example, led to rumors that Christians practiced horrible crimes, such as the ritualistic murder of children. Although we know these rumors are untrue, some Romans believed them and used them to incite people against the Christians during times of crisis. Moreover, because Christians held their meetings in secret and seemed to be connected to Christian groups in distant areas, the government could view them as potentially dangerous to the state.

Some Romans felt that Christians were overly exclusive and hence harmful to the community and public order. The Christians did not recognize other gods and therefore abstained from public festivals honoring the popular deities. Finally, Christians refused to participate in the worship of the state gods and the imperial cult. Since the Romans regarded these as important to the state, the Christians' refusal seemed to undermine the security of the state and hence constituted an act of treason, punishable by death. It was also proof of atheism (disbelief in the gods) and subject to punishment on those grounds. But to the Christians, who believed there was only one real God, the worship of state gods and the emperors was idolatry and would endanger their own salvation.

Roman persecution of Christians in the first and second centuries was never systematic but only sporadic and local. Persecution began during the reign of Nero. After the fire that destroyed much of Rome, the emperor used the Christians as scapegoats, accusing them of arson and hatred of the human race and subjecting them to cruel deaths in Rome. In the second century, Christians were often ignored as harmless. By the end of the reigns of the five good emperors, Christians still represented a small minority, but one of considerable strength. That strength lay in their conviction of the rightness of their path, a conviction that had been reinforced by the willingness of the first Christians to become martyrs for their faith.

Christian Martyrs   From its beginning, Christianity was characterized by the willingness of many of its followers to accept death for their faith. In 177, a group of fifty Christians in Lyon were sacrificed to wild beasts. In Asia, Polycarp, the bishop of Smyrna, when told to renounce his faith, replied, "I have served [Christ] for eighty-six years and he has done me no wrong. How can I blaspheme my king and my savior?" Polycarp, who had played an important role in spreading Christian teachings in Asia, was burned at the stake as "an offering ready and acceptable to God." In Africa, in 180, a small group of Christian men and women from near Carthage were put on trial and condemned to die: "having confessed that they live according to the Christian religion, since they obstinately persisted when given the opportunity of returning to Roman ways, [they] are to be executed by the sword." The Christians responded, "We give thanks to God."[24]

For many Christians, martyrdom meant achieving salvation by following the example of Jesus's sacrificial suffering and death on the cross. Indeed, Tertullian (tur-TULL-yun) (c. 160–c. 225), a Christian writer from Carthage, declared that Christian martyrs were "witnesses to the Grace of God." By imitating Jesus, the Christian martyrs established a model to be followed by other Christians. Said Tertullian, "No one would want to be killed unless possessed of the truth," making the blood of martyrs "the seed of the church."[25] Witnessing Christian martyrs die may well have encouraged others to convert to Christianity.

The Growth of Christianity   The sporadic persecution of Christians by the Romans in the first and second centuries did nothing to stop the growth of Christianity. In fact, it served to strengthen Christianity as an institution in the second and third centuries by causing it to shed the loose structure of the first century and move toward a more centralized organization of its various church communities. Crucial to this change was the emerging role of the bishops. Though still chosen by the community, bishops began to assume more control, with the bishop serving as leader and the presbyters emerging as clergy subject to the bishop's authority. By the third century, bishops were nominated by the clergy, simply approved by the congregation, and then officially ordained into office. The Christian church was creating a well-defined hierarchical structure in which the bishops and clergy were salaried officers separate from the laity or regular church members.

Christianity and Greco-Roman Culture   Many early Christians expressed considerable hostility toward the pagan culture of the Classical world. Tertullian had proclaimed: "What has Jerusalem to do with Athens, the Church with the Academy, the Christian with the heretic? ... After Jesus Christ we have no need of speculation, after the Gospel no need of research."[26] To many early Christians, the Bible contained all the knowledge anyone needed.

Others, however, thought it was not possible to separate Christian theological thought from Classical traditions and education and encouraged Christians to absorb the Classical heritage. As it spread in the eastern Roman world, Christianity adopted Greek as its language. The New Testament was written in Greek. Christians also turned to Greek thought for help in expressing complicated theological concepts. An especially important influence was Neoplatonism, a revival of Platonic thought that reached its high point in the third century C.E. Neoplatonists believed that one could use reason to perceive the link between the invisible spiritual world and the visible material world. Christian theologians used Neoplatonic concepts to explain doctrines on Jesus, especially the distinction between his human and divine natures. In many ways, then, Christianity served to preserve Greco-Roman culture.

The Appeal of Christianity   Christianity grew slowly in the first century, took root in the second, and had spread widely by the third. Why was Christianity able to attract so many followers? Historians are not really sure but have offered several answers. Certainly, the Christian message had much to offer the Roman world. The promise of salvation, made possible by Jesus's death and resurrection, had immense appeal in a world full of suffering and injustice. Christianity seemed to imbue life with a meaning and purpose beyond the simple material things of everyday reality. Second, Christianity was not entirely unfamiliar. It could be viewed as simply another eastern mystery religion, offering immortality as the result of the sacrificial death of a savior-god. At the same time, it offered advantages that the other mystery religions lacked. Jesus had been a human figure, not a mythological one, such as Isis or Mithra. Moreover, Christianity had universal appeal. Unlike Mithraism, it was not restricted to men. Furthermore, it did not require a difficult or expensive initiation rite as other mystery religions did. Initiation was accomplished simply by baptism—a purification by water—by which one entered into direct communion with Jesus. In addition, Christianity gave new meaning to life and offered what the Roman state religions could not—a personal relationship with God and a link to higher worlds.

Finally, Christianity fulfilled the human need to belong. Christians formed communities bound to one another in which people could express their love by helping each other and offering assistance to the poor, sick, widows, and orphans. Christianity satisfied the need to belong in a way that the huge, impersonal, and remote Roman Empire could never do.

Christianity proved attractive to all classes. The promise of eternal life was for all—rich, poor, aristocrats, slaves, men, and women. As Paul stated in his Epistle to the Colossians: "And [you] have put on the new self, which is being renewed in knowledge in the image of its Creator. Here there is no Greek nor Jew, circumcised or uncircumcised, barbarian, Scythian, slave or free, but Christ is all, and is in all."[27] Although it did not call for revolution or social upheaval, Christianity emphasized a sense of spiritual equality for all people.

Women and Early Christianity   As we have seen, first-century C.E. Christian communities had allowed both men and women to play significant roles. By the second century, however, men had gained control of church organization and restricted women to secondary roles. Women, as Paul had argued, should be subject to men.

Nevertheless, many women found that Christianity offered them new roles and new forms of companionship with other women. Christian women fostered the new religion in their own homes and preached their convictions to other people in their towns and villages. Many also died for their faith. Perpetua (d. 203) was an aristocratic woman who converted to Christianity. Her pagan family begged her to renounce her new faith, but she refused. Arrested by the Roman authorities, she chose instead to die for her faith and was one of a group of Christians who were slaughtered by wild beasts in the arena at Carthage on March 7, 203.

Persecution   As the Christian church became more organized, two emperors in the third century responded with more systematic persecutions. The emperor Decius (DEE-she-uss) (249–251) blamed the Christians for the disasters befalling the Roman Empire in the terrible third century: their refusal to acknowledge the state gods had brought the gods' retribution against the Romans. Moreover, as the administrative organization of the church grew, Christianity appeared to Decius even more like a state within a state that was undermining the empire. Accordingly, he initiated the first systematic persecution of Christians. All citizens were required to appear before their local magistrates and offer sacrifices to the Roman gods. Christians, of course, refused to do so. But Decius's scheme failed to work. Not only did local officials fail to cooperate, but Decius's reign was not very long. The last great persecution was by Diocletian (dy-uh-KLEE-shun) at the beginning of the fourth century, but by then it was too late. Christianity had become too strong to be eradicated by force.

CHRONOLOGY

RULERS OF THE EARLY EMPIRE

Julio-Claudian Dynasty

31 B.C.–A.D. 14	Augustus
14–37	Tiberius
37–41	Caligula
41–54	Claudius
54–68	Nero

Flavian Dynasty

69–79	Vespasian
79–81	Titus
81–96	Domitian

Five Good Emperors

96–98	Nerva
98–117	Trajan
117–138	Hadrian
138–161	Antoninus Pius
161–180	Marcus Aurelius

7

LATE ANTIQUITY AND THE EMERGENCE OF THE MEDIEVAL WORLD

A fifteenth-century manuscript illustration of Clovis, his wife Clotilde, and their four sons

---

CHAPTER OUTLINE

• The Late Roman Empire • The Germanic Kingdoms • Development of the Christian Church • The Byzantine Empire • The Rise of Islam

---

THE LATE ROMAN EMPIRE

At the end of the third century and the beginning of the fourth, the Roman Empire gained a new lease on life through the efforts of two strong emperors, Diocletian and Constantine (KAHN-stun-teen), who restored order and stability. The empire was virtually transformed into a new state, the Late Roman Empire, which included a new governmental structure, a rigid economic and social system, and a new state religion—Christianity.

The Reforms of Diocletian and Constantine
At the end of the troubled third century, a new emperor—Diocletian (284–305)—began the process of restoring the strength of the Roman Empire. Diocletian had risen through the ranks to become a prominent military leader, and after the murder of the emperor Numerian by his praetorian prefect, Diocletian executed the prefect and was then hailed as emperor by his soldiers. Diocletian's own rise to power led him to see the need for a new system for ruling the Roman Empire.

Political Reforms   Diocletian created a new administrative system for a restructured empire. The number of provinces was increased to almost one hundred by creating smaller districts superintended by more officials. The provinces were in turn grouped into twelve dioceses, each headed by an official called a vicar. The twelve dioceses were grouped into four prefectures (see Map 7.1), and the entire Roman Empire was divided into two parts, east and west. Each part contained two prefectures and was ruled by an "Augustus." Diocletian ruled the east, and Maximian (mak-SIM-ee-un), a strong military commander, the west. Each Augustus was assisted by a chief lieutenant or "vice-emperor" called a "Caesar," who theoretically would eventually succeed to the position of Augustus. This new system was called the **tetrarchy** (rule by four). Diocletian had obviously come to believe that one man was not capable of ruling such an enormous empire, especially in view of the barbarian invasions of the third century. Each of the four tetrarchs—two Augusti and two Caesars—resided in a different administrative capital. Diocletian, for example, established his base at Nicomedia in Bithynia. Despite the appearance of four-man rule, however, it is important to note that Diocletian's military seniority enabled him to claim a higher status and hold the ultimate authority.

Soon after Diocletian's retirement in 305, a new struggle for power ensued. The victory of Constantine (306–337) in 312 led to his control of the entire west, although he continued to share imperial authority with Licinius (ly-SIN-ee-uss), a fellow emperor. Twelve years later, in 324, Constantine's army routed Licinius's forces, and Constantine established himself as the sole ruler.

Constantine continued and even expanded the autocratic policies of Diocletian. Under these two rulers, the Roman Empire was transformed into a system in which the emperor had far more personal power than Augustus, Trajan, or any of the other emperors had had during the *Pax Romana*. The emperor, now clothed in jewel-bedecked robes of gold and blue, was seen as a divinely sanctioned monarch whose will was law. Government officials were humble servants required to kneel before the emperor and kiss his robe. The Roman senate was stripped of any power and became merely the city council for Rome.

MAP 7.1   Divisions of the Late Roman Empire, c. 300

Diocletian imposed order and a new economic and administrative structure on the Late Empire. He divided the Roman Empire into four regions, each ruled by either an "Augustus" or a "Caesar," although Diocletian retained supreme power.

Diocletian and Constantine greatly strengthened and enlarged the administrative bureaucracies of the Roman Empire. Henceforth, civil and military bureaucracies were sharply separated. Each contained a hierarchy of officials who exercised control at the various levels. The emperor presided over both hierarchies and served as the only link between them. New titles of nobility—such as *illustres* (ee-loo-STRAYSS) ("illustrious ones") and *illustrissimi* (ee-loo-STREE-see-mee) ("most illustrious ones")—were instituted to dignify the holders of positions in the civil and military bureaucracies.

Military Reforms   Additional military reforms were also instituted. The army was enlarged to 400,000 men, including units filled with Germans. By the end of Constantine's reign, the army also had a new organization. Military forces were divided between garrison troops, which were located on the frontiers to serve as a first line of defense against invaders, and mobile units, which were based behind the frontier but could be quickly moved to support frontier troops when the borders were threatened. This system gave the empire greater flexibility in responding to invasion.

Economic and Social Trends   The political and military reforms of Diocletian and Constantine greatly enlarged two institutions—the army and the civil service—that drained most of the public funds. Although more revenues were needed to pay for the military and the bureaucracy, the population was not growing, so the tax base could not be expanded. Diocletian and Constantine devised new economic and social policies to deal with these financial burdens. Like their political policies, these economic and social policies were all based on coercion and loss of individual freedom.

To fight **inflation**, in 301 Diocletian resorted to issuing an edict that established maximum wages and prices for the entire empire. It was applied mostly in the east, but despite severe penalties, like most wage and price controls, it was largely unenforceable. The decline in the coins in circulation forced Diocletian to collect taxes and make government payments in produce. Constantine, however, managed to introduce a new gold coin, the solidus, and new silver coins that remained in circulation during his reign.

In the third century, the city councils, which had formed one of the most important administrative units of the empire, had begun to decline. Since the **curiales** (KUR-ee-all-ayss) (the city councillors) were forced to pay expenses out of their own pockets when the taxes they collected were insufficient, the wealthy no longer wanted to serve in these positions. Diocletian and Constantine responded by issuing edicts that forced the rich to continue in their posts as *curiales*, making the positions virtually hereditary. Some *curiales* realized that their fortunes would be wiped out and fled the cities to escape the clutches of the imperial bureaucracy. If caught, however, they were returned to their cities like runaway slaves and forced to resume their duties.

Coercion also came to form the underlying basis for numerous occupations in the Late Roman Empire. To maintain the tax base and keep the empire going despite the shortage of labor, the emperors issued edicts that forced people to remain in their designated vocations. Hence, basic jobs, such as bakers and shippers, became hereditary.

Free tenant farmers—the *coloni*—continued to decline and increasingly found themselves bound to the land as large landowners took advantage of the depressed agricultural conditions to enlarge their landed estates. To guarantee their supply of labor, the landlords obtained the government's cooperation in attaching the tenant farmers to the estates. One imperial edict stated: "And as for *coloni* themselves, it will be proper for such as contemplate flight to be bound with chains to a servile status, so that by virtue of such condemnation to servitude they may be compelled to fulfill the duties that befit free men."[1]

In addition to facing increased restrictions on their freedom, the lower classes were burdened with enormous taxes, since the wealthiest classes in the Late Roman Empire were either exempt from paying taxes or evaded them by bribing the tax collectors. These tax pressures undermined lower-class support for the regime. A fifth-century writer reported that the Roman peasants welcomed the Visigothic invaders of southern Gaul as liberators because the enemy was more lenient to them than the tax collectors.

In general, the economic and social policies of Diocletian and Constantine were based on an unprecedented degree of control and coercion. Though temporarily successful, in the long run such authoritarian policies stifled the very vitality the Late Empire needed to revive its sagging fortunes.

Constantine's Building Program Constantine engaged in extensive building programs despite the strain they placed on the budget. Many of them took place in the provinces, as Rome had become merely a symbolic capital. It was considered too far from the frontiers to serve as an imperial administrative center. Between 324 and 330, Constantine carried out his biggest project, the construction of a new capital city in the east, on the site of the Greek city of Byzantium (bih-ZAN-tee-um), on the shores of the Bosporus. Named the "city of Constantine," or Constantinople (modern Istanbul), it was developed for defensive reasons; it had an excellent strategic location. Calling it his "New Rome," Constantine endowed the city with a forum, large palaces, and a vast amphitheater. It was officially dedicated on May 11, 330, "by the commandment of God," and in the following years, many Christian churches were built there.

Constantine did not entirely forget Rome. Earlier he was responsible for building public baths and the triumphal Arch of Constantine, erected between 312 and 315. Constantine was also the first emperor to build churches for the Christian faith in Rome, including the first basilica dedicated to Saint Peter, built on the supposed site of Saint Peter's burial. These acts by Constantine are a reminder of the new role Christianity was beginning to play in the Late Empire.

The Empire's New Religion   In the fourth century, Christianity flourished as never before, and the emperor Constantine played an important role in its new status.

The Conversion of Constantine Constantine's support for Christianity supposedly began in 312, when his army was about to fight a crucial battle against the forces of Maxentius (mak-SEN-shuss) at the Milvian Bridge, which crossed the Tiber River just north of Rome. According to the traditional story, before the battle, Constantine saw a vision of a Christian cross with the words, "In this sign you will conquer." Having won the battle, the story goes, Constantine was convinced of the power of the Christian God. Although he was probably not baptized until the end of his life, in 313 he issued the famous Edict of Milan, which officially tolerated the existence of Christianity.

After Constantine, all of the emperors were Christian with the exception of Julian (360–363), who tried briefly to restore the traditional Greco-Roman polytheistic religion. But he died in battle, and his reign was too short to make a difference. Under Theodosius (thee-uh-DOH-shuss) I "the Great" (379–395), Christianity was made the official religion of the Roman Empire. Once in control, Christian leaders used their influence and power to outlaw pagan religious practices. Christianity had triumphed.

Organization and Religious Disputes By the fourth century, the Christian church had developed a system of government based on a territorial plan borrowed from Roman administration. The Christian community in each city was headed by a bishop, whose area of jurisdiction was known as a bishopric or diocese. The bishoprics of each Roman province were clustered together under the direction of an archbishop. The bishops of four great cities, Rome, Jerusalem, Alexandria, and Antioch, held positions of special power in church affairs because the churches in these cities all asserted that they had been founded by the original apostles sent out by Jesus.

One reason the church needed a more formal organization was the problem of **heresy**. As Christianity developed and spread, contradictory interpretations of important doctrines emerged. Heresy came to be viewed as a teaching different from the official "catholic" or universal beliefs of the church. For people deeply concerned about salvation, the question of whether Jesus's nature is divine or human took on great significance. These doctrinal differences also became political issues, creating political factions that actually warred with one another. It is unlikely that ordinary people understood the issues in these debates.

One of the major heresies of the fourth century was **Arianism** (AR-ee-uh-niz-um), which was a product of the followers of Arius (AR-ee-uss), a priest from Alexandria in Egypt. Arius postulated that Jesus had been human and thus not truly God. Arius was opposed by Athanasius (ath-uh-NAY-shuss), a bishop of Alexandria, who argued that Jesus was human but also truly God. Emperor Constantine, disturbed by the controversy, called the first ecumenical council of the church, a meeting composed of representatives from the entire Christian community. The Council of Nicaea (ny-SEE-uh), held in 325, condemned Arianism and stated that Jesus was of "the same substance" as God: "We believe in one God the Father All-sovereign, maker of all things visible and invisible; And in one Lord Jesus Christ, the Son of God, begotten of the Father, only-begotten, that is, of the substance of the Father, God of God, Light of Light, true God of true God, begotten not made, of one substance with the Father."[2]

The Council of Nicaea did not end the controversy, however; not only did Arianism persist in some parts of the Roman Empire for many years, but even more important, many of the Germanic Goths who established states in the west converted to Arian Christianity (see "The Germanic Kingdoms" later in this chapter). As a result of these fourth-century religious controversies, the Roman emperor came to play an increasingly important role in church affairs, especially by taking responsibility for calling church councils.

The End of the Western Empire   After Constantine's death, the empire began to divide into western and eastern parts as fighting erupted on a regular basis between elements of the Roman army backing the claims of rival emperors. By 395, the western and eastern parts of the empire had become virtually two independent states. In the course of the fifth century, while the empire in the east remained intact under the Roman emperor in Constantinople (see "The Byzantine Empire" later in this chapter), the administrative structure of the empire in the west collapsed and was replaced by an assortment of Germanic kingdoms. The process was a gradual one, involving the movement of Germans into the empire, military failures, struggles for power on the part of both Roman and German military leaders, and the efforts of wealthy aristocrats to support whichever side seemed to offer them greater security.

The Germans   During the first and second centuries C.E., the Romans had established the Rhine and Danube Rivers as the empire's northern boundary. The Romans called all the peoples to the north of the rivers "Germans" and regarded them as uncivilized barbarians. In fact, the Germans comprised several different groups with their own customs and identities, but these constantly

Two Views of the Huns

The first selection is a description of the Huns by Ammianus Marcellinus (am-ee-AY-nuss mar-suh-LY-nuss) (c. 330–c. 393), who has been called the "last great Roman historian." Ammianus wrote a history of Rome from 96 C.E. to his own day. Only the chapters that deal with the period from 354 to 378 have survived. Historians believe that his account of the Huns is largely based on stereotypes. The second selection is taken from an account by Priscus, an envoy from the Eastern Roman Empire to the court of Attila (uh-TILL-uh *or* AT-ih-luh), king of the Huns from 434 to 453. His description of the Huns in 448 is quite different from that of Ammianus Marcellinus.

Ammianus Marcellinus, *The Later Roman Empire*

The Huns ... are quite abnormally savage. From the moment of their birth they make deep gashes in their children's cheeks, so that when in due course hair appears its growth is checked by the wrinkled scars.... They have squat bodies, strong limbs, and thick necks, and are so prodigiously ugly and bent that they might be two-legged animals.... Still, their shape, however disagreeable, is human; but their way of life is so rough that they have no use for fire or seasoned food, but live on the roots of wild plants and the half-raw flesh of any sort of animal, which they warm a little by placing it between their thighs and the backs of their horses. They have no buildings to shelter them; ... not so much as a hut thatched with reeds is to be found among them.... They wear garments of linen or of the skins of field-mice stitched together, and there is no difference between their clothing whether they are at home or abroad. Once they have put their necks in some dingy shirt they never take it off or change it till it rots and falls to pieces from incessant wear. They have round caps of fur on their heads, and protect their hairy legs with goatskins. Their shapeless shoes ... make it hard to walk easily. In consequence they are ill-fitted to fight on foot, and remain glued to their horses, hardy but ugly beasts, on which they sometimes sit like women to perform their everyday business. Buying or selling, eating or drinking, are all done by day or night on horseback, and they even bow forward over their beasts' narrow necks to enjoy a deep and dreamy sleep....

They sometimes fight by challenging their foes to single combat, but when they join battle they advance in packs, uttering their various warcries. Being lightly equipped and very sudden in their movements they can deliberately scatter

changed as tribes broke up and came together in new configurations. At times they formed larger confederations under strong warrior leaders. The Germans lived by herding and farming and also traded with people living along the northern frontiers of the Roman Empire. Their proximity to the Romans also led to some Romanization of the tribes. They were familiar with the Roman use of coins rather than barter and also gained some knowledge of both the Latin language and Roman military matters.

Contacts between Romans and Germans were common across the boundaries established along the Rhine and Danube Rivers. In fact, for some time, the Romans and gallop about at random, inflicting tremendous slaughter; their extreme nimbleness enables them to force a rampart or pillage an enemy's camp before one catches sight of them.... None of them plows or ever touches a plow-handle. They have no fixed abode, no home or law or settled manner of life, but wander like refugees with the wagons in which they live. In these their wives weave their filthy clothing, mate with their husbands, and give birth to their children, and rear them to the age of puberty.

Priscus, *An Account of the Court of Attila the Hun*

[We were invited to a banquet with Attila.] When the hour arrived we went to Attila's palace, along with the embassy from the western Romans, and stood on the threshold of the hall in the presence of Attila. The cupbearers gave us a cup, according to the national custom, that we might pray before we sat down. Having tasted the cup, we proceeded to take our seats, all the chairs being ranged along the walls of the room on either side. Attila sat in the middle on a couch; a second couch was set behind him, and from it steps led up to his bed, which was covered with linen sheets and coverlets....

[First the king and his guests pledged one another with the wine.] When this ceremony was over the cupbearers retired and tables, large enough for three or four, or even more, to sit at, were placed next to the table of Attila, so that each could take of the food on the dishes without leaving his seat. The attendant of Attila first entered with a dish full of meat, and behind him came the other attendants with bread and other dishes, which they laid on the tables. A luxurious meal, served on silver plate, had been made ready for us and the other guests, but Attila ate nothing but meat on a wooden platter. In everything else, too, he showed himself temperate; his cup was of wood, while to the guests were given goblets of gold and silver. His dress, too, was quite simple, affecting only to be clean.

Q *What motives may have prompted Ammianus Marcellinus to describe the Huns so harshly? How does the account of Priscus differ, and do you detect any strategies of the Huns to impress and overawe foreigners? How reliable do you think these descriptions of the Huns are? Why?*

Sources: Ammianus Marcellinus, *The Later Roman Empire*. From THE LATER ROMAN EMPIRE by Ammianus Marcellinus, selected and translated by Walter Hamilton (Penguin Classics, 1986). Translation copyright © Walter Hamilton, 1986. Reproduced by permission of Penguin Books Ltd. Priscus, *An Account of the Court of Attila the Hun*. From *Fragmenta Historicorum Graecorum*, trans. J. B. Bury.

had hired Germanic tribes to fight other Germanic tribes that threatened Rome and enlisted groups of Germans to fight for Rome. Until the fourth century, the empire had proved capable of absorbing these people without harm to its political structure. As that century wore on, however, the situation began to change as the Germanic tribes came under new pressures from invaders.

German Migrations   In the late fourth century, the Huns, a fierce tribe of nomads from Asia, began moving into the Black Sea region and forced the Germanic inhabitants westward. In 376, one of the largest groups, which came to be known as the

Visigoths (VIZ-uh-gahthz), asked the Roman emperor Valens (VAY-linz) (364–378) to allow them to cross the Danube and farm in the Balkans in return for providing troops for the Roman military. But the Roman military commanders mistreated them, as one ancient German historian recounted:

> Soon famine and want came upon them…. Their leaders … begged the Roman commanders to open a market. But to what will not the "cursed lust for gold" compel men to assent? The generals, swayed by greed, sold them at a high price not only the flesh of sheep and oxen, but even the carcasses of dogs and unclean animals…. When their goods and chattels failed, the greedy traders demanded their sons in return for the necessities of life. And the parents consented even to this.[3]

Outraged at this treatment, the Visigoths revolted. In 378, Emperor Valens and an army of 40,000 soldiers confronted the Visigoths at Adrianople. The emperor was killed, and two-thirds of the Roman soldiers were left dead on the battlefield.

The loss was not fatal, although the new emperor, Theodosius I, resettled the Visigoths and incorporated many of their soldiers into the Roman army. Some of the Visigoths even became army leaders. By the second half of the fourth century, Roman policy allowed Roman army units to be composed entirely of Germanic tribes, known as **federates**, or allies of Rome.

The Threat of the Germans   The existence of such military groups proved dangerous to the Late Empire. This was especially evident after Alaric (AL-uh-rik) became the leader of the Visigoths. Between 395 and 401, Alaric and his soldiers moved through the Balkans and then into Italy, seeking food and cash payments from Roman officials. When the city of Rome refused his demands in 408, Alaric marched to the gates and besieged the city, causing the senate of Rome to agree to pay 5,000 pounds of gold and 30,000 pounds of silver for his withdrawal. Two years later, frustrated in his demand that the Visigoths be given part of northern Italy, Alaric and his forces sacked Rome for three days. Alaric died soon after, and his Visigothic followers left Italy, crossed the Alps, and moved into Spain and southern Gaul as Roman allies (see Map 7.2).

By this time, other Germanic tribes were also entering the Roman Empire and settling down. As one contemporary observer noted, "the barbarians, detesting their swords, turned to their plows and now cherish the Romans as comrades and friends."[4] In the early fifth century, the Burgundians arrived in southern Gaul, while the Franks moved into northern Gaul. Another group, the Vandals, under their leader Gaiseric (GY-zuh-rik), moved through Gaul and Spain, crossed the Strait of Gibraltar into North Africa, and seized Carthage, the capital city, in 439.

As the Germanic tribes moved into the empire and settled down, Roman forces were often withdrawn from the provinces, effectively reducing the central authority of the emperors. In 410, for example, the emperor Honorius (hoh-NOR-ee-uss) recalled the last Roman legions from Britain. As one ancient commentator remarked, "Honorius sent letters to the cities in Britain, urging them to fend for themselves."[5] With the withdrawal, the Saxons, who had arrived earlier as Roman allies, now expanded their control in Britain. Within another decade, both Spain and Gaul had also become free of imperial authority.

MAP 7.2 German Migration Routes

In the fifth century, various groups of Germans migrated throughout the Western Roman Empire. Pressure from Huns in the east forced some tribes to move west into the empire, and many tribes already in the empire experienced conflict. Some fought the empire, while others were induced to move to the empire's far regions.

Role of Masters of the Soldiers   By the middle of the fifth century, the western provinces of the Roman Empire had been taken over by Germanic peoples who were in the process of creating independent kingdoms. At the same time, a semblance of imperial authority remained in Rome, although the real power behind the throne tended to rest in the hands of important military officials known as Masters of the Soldiers.

These military commanders controlled the government and dominated the imperial court. The three most prominent in the fifth century were Stilicho (STIL-i-koh), Aetius (ay-EE-shuss), and Ricimer (RISS-uh-mur). Stilicho and Ricimer were both Germans, whereas Aetius was a Roman. Although all three propped up emperors to maintain the fiction of imperial rule, they were also willing to cooperate with the Germans to maintain their power. But even the Masters of the Soldiers were never safe in the bloody world of fifth-century Roman political life. Stilicho was executed by the guards of Emperor Honorius. Aetius was killed by Emperor Valentinian

Basilica di San Giovanni Battista, Monza, Italy/The Bridgeman Art Library

Stilicho, a German Master of the Soldiers. *Half-Vandal and half-Roman, Stilicho was the power behind the imperial throne from 395 to 408. Emperor Honorius ordered his execution in 408. These ivory panels show Stilicho at the right, in Vandal clothing, with his wife and son at the left.*

(val-en-TIN-ee-un) III, who was in turn assassinated by two of Aetius's German bodyguards, who sought to avenge their betrayed leader. Ricimer died a natural death, an unusual event in fifth-century Rome. No doubt, the constant infighting at the center of the Western Empire added to the instability of imperial rule.

By the mid-fifth century, imperial authority in the west was still operating only in Italy and small parts of Gaul. Even Rome itself was not safe. In 455, after the Romans broke a treaty that they had made with Gaiseric, leader of the Vandals, Gaiseric sent a Vandal fleet to Italy and sacked the undefended city of Rome. Twenty-one years later, in 476, Odoacer (oh-doh-AY-sur), a new Master of the Soldiers, himself of German origin, deposed the Roman emperor, the boy Romulus Augustulus (RAHM-yuh-luss ow-GOOS-chuh-luss). To many historians, the deposition of Romulus signaled the end of the Roman Empire. Of course, this is only a symbolic date, since much of direct imperial rule had already been lost in the course of the fifth century. Even then the empire remained, as Odoacer presented himself as a German king obedient in theory to the Roman emperor Zeno (ZEE-noh) in Constantinople.

By the end of the fifth century, Roman imperial authority in the west had ceased. Nevertheless, the intellectual, governmental, and cultural traditions of the Late Roman Empire continued to live on in the new Germanic kingdoms.

THE GERMANIC KINGDOMS

By 500, the Western Roman Empire was being replaced politically by a series of king-doms ruled by German kings (see Map 7.3). Although the Germans now ruled, they were greatly outnumbered by the Romans, who still controlled most of the economic

MAP 7.3 The Germanic Kingdoms of the Old Western Empire

The Germanic tribes filled the power vacuum caused by the demise of the Roman Empire, building states that blended elements of Germanic customs and laws with those of Roman culture, including large-scale conversions to Christianity. The Franks established the most durable of these Germanic states.

resources. Both were Christian, but many of the Germans were Arian Christians, considered heretics by Romans who belonged to the Christian church in Rome, which had become known as the Roman Catholic Church. Gradually, the two groups merged into a common culture, although the pattern of settlement and the fusion of the Romans and Germans took different forms in the various Germanic kingdoms.

The Ostrogothic Kingdom of Italy   Zeno, the Roman emperor in Constantinople, was not pleased with Odoacer's actions and plotted to unseat him. In his desire to act against the German leader, Zeno brought another German tribe, the Ostrogoths (AHSS-truh-gahthss), into Italy. The Ostrogoths had recovered from a defeat by the Huns in the fourth century and under their king Theodoric (thee-AHD-uh-rik) (493–526) had attacked Constantinople. To divert them, Emperor Zeno invited Theodoric to act as his deputy to defeat Odoacer and bring Italy back into the empire. Theodoric accepted the challenge, marched into Italy, killed Odoacer, and then, contrary to Zeno's wishes, established himself as ruler of Italy in 493.

Theodoric's Rule   More than any other Germanic state, the Ostrogothic kingdom of Italy managed to maintain the Roman tradition of government. The Ostrogothic king, Theodoric, had received a Roman education while a hostage in Constantinople. After taking control of Italy, he was eager to create a synthesis of Ostrogothic and Roman practices. In addition to maintaining the entire structure of Roman imperial government, he established separate systems of rule for the Ostrogoths and Romans. The Italian population lived under Roman law administered by Roman officials. The Ostrogoths were governed by their own customs and their own officials. Nevertheless, although the Roman administrative system was kept intact, it was the Ostrogoths alone who controlled the army. Despite the apparent success of this "dual approach," Theodoric's system was unable to keep friction from developing between the Italian population and their Germanic overlords.

Religion proved to be a major source of trouble between Ostrogoths and Romans. The Ostrogoths had been converted earlier to Christianity, but to Arian Christianity, and consequently were viewed by western Christians and the Italians as heretics. Theodoric's rule grew ever harsher as discontent with Ostrogothic rule deepened.

End of the Ostrogothic Kingdom   After Theodoric's death in 526, it quickly became apparent that much of his success had been due to the force of his own personality. His successors soon found themselves facing opposition from the imperial forces of the Byzantine or Eastern Roman Empire. Under Emperor Justinian (juh-STIN-ee-un) (527–565) (see "The Reign of Justinian" later in this chapter), Eastern Roman armies reconquered Italy between 535 and 552, devastating much of the peninsula in the process and destroying Rome as one of the great urban centers of the Mediterranean world. The Eastern Roman reconquest proved ephemeral, however. Another German tribe, the Lombards, invaded Italy in 568 and conquered much of northern and central Italy. Unlike the Ostrogoths, the Lombards were harsh rulers and cared little for Roman structures and traditions. The Lombards' fondness for fighting each other enabled the Eastern Romans to retain control of some parts of Italy, especially the area around Ravenna, which became the capital of imperial government in the west.

The Visigothic
Kingdom of
Spain

The Visigothic kingdom in Spain demonstrated a number of parallels to the Ostrogothic kingdom of Italy. Both favored coexistence between the Roman and German populations, both featured a warrior caste dominating a larger native population, and both continued to maintain much of the Roman structure of government while largely excluding Romans from power. There were also noticeable differences, however. Perceiving that their Arianism was a stumbling block to good relations, in the late sixth century the Visigothic rulers converted to Latin or Catholic Christianity and ended the tension caused by this heresy. Laws preventing intermarriage were dropped, and the Visigothic and Hispano-Roman peoples began to fuse together. A new body of law common to both peoples also developed.

The kingdom possessed one fatal weakness, however—the Visigoths fought constantly over the kingship. The Visigoths did not have a hereditary monarchy and lacked any established procedure for choosing new rulers. Church officials tried to help develop a sense of order, as this canon from the Fourth Council of Toledo in 633 illustrates: "No one of us shall dare to seize the kingdom; no one shall arouse sedition among the citizenry; no one shall think of killing the king." Church decrees failed to stop the feuds, however, and assassinations remained a way of life in Visigothic Spain. In 711, Muslim invaders destroyed the Visigothic kingdom itself (see "The Rise of Islam" later in this chapter).

The Frankish
Kingdom

Only one of the German states on the European continent proved long-lasting—the kingdom of the Franks. The establishment of a Frankish kingdom was the work of Clovis (c. 482–511), the leader of one group of Franks who eventually became king of them all.

The Rule of Clovis   Around 500, Clovis became a Catholic Christian. He was not the first German king to convert to Christianity, but the others had joined the Arian sect of Christianity. The Roman Catholic Church regarded the Arians as heretics, people who believed in teachings that departed from the official church doctrine. Clovis found that his conversion to Catholic Christianity gained him the support of the Roman Catholic Church, which was only too eager to obtain the friendship of a major Germanic ruler who was a Catholic Christian. The conversion of the king also paved the way for the conversion of the Frankish peoples. Finally, Clovis could pose as a defender of the orthodox Catholic faith in order to justify his expansion at the beginning of the sixth century. He defeated the Alemanni (al-uh-MAH-nee) in southwest Germany and the Visigoths in southern Gaul. By 510, Clovis had established a powerful new Frankish kingdom stretching from the Pyrenees in the west to German lands in the east (modern-day France and western Germany).

Clovis was thus responsible for establishing a Frankish kingdom under the Merovingian (meh-ruh-VIN-jee-un) dynasty, a name derived from Merovech, their semilegendary ancestor. Clovis came to rely on his Frankish followers to rule in the old Roman city-states under the title of count. Often these officials were forced to share power with the Gallo-Roman Catholic bishops, producing a gradual fusion of Latin and German cultures, with the church serving to preserve the Latin culture. Clovis spent the last years of his life ensuring the survival of his dynasty by killing off relatives who were leaders of other groups of Franks.

The Successors of Clovis   After the death of Clovis, his sons divided the newly created kingdom, as was the Frankish custom. During the sixth and seventh centuries, the once-united Frankish kingdom came to be partitioned into three major areas: Neustria (NOO-stree-uh) in northern Gaul; Austrasia (aw-STRAY-zhuh), consisting of the ancient Frankish lands on both sides of the Rhine; and the former kingdom of Burgundy. All three were ruled by members of the Merovingian dynasty. Within the three territories, members of the dynasty were assisted by powerful nobles. Frankish society possessed a ruling class that gradually intermarried with the old Gallo-Roman senatorial class to form a new nobility. These noble families took advantage of their position to expand their own lands and wealth at the expense of the monarchy. Within the royal household, the position of **major domus** (my-YOR DOH-moos), or mayor of the palace, the chief officer of the king's household, began to overshadow the king. Essentially, both nobles and mayors of the palace were expanding their power at the expense of the kings.

At the beginning of the eighth century, the most important political development in the Frankish kingdom was the rise of Charles Martel, who served as mayor of the palace of Austrasia beginning in 714. Charles Martel led troops that defeated the Muslims near Poitiers (pwah-TYAY) in 732 and by the time of his death in 741 had become virtual ruler of the three Merovingian kingdoms. Though he was not king, Charles Martel's dynamic efforts put his family on the verge of creating a new dynasty that would establish an even more powerful Frankish state (see Chapter 8).

During the sixth and seventh centuries, the Frankish kingdom witnessed a process of fusion between Gallo-Roman and Frankish cultures and peoples, a process accompanied by a significant decline in Roman standards of civilization and commercial activity. The Franks were warriors and did little to encourage either urban life or trade. Commerce declined in the interior, though seacoast towns maintained some activity. By 750, Frankish Gaul was basically an agricultural society in which the old Roman estates of the Late Empire continued unimpeded. Institutionally, however, Germanic concepts of kingship and customary law replaced the Roman governmental structure.

Anglo-Saxon England   The barbarian pressures on the Western Roman Empire had forced the emperors to withdraw the Roman armies and abandon Britain by the beginning of the fifth century. This opened the door to the Angles and Saxons, Germanic tribes from Denmark and northern Germany. Although these same peoples had made plundering raids for a century, the withdrawal of the Roman armies enabled them to make settlements instead. They met with resistance from the Celtic Britons, however, who still controlled the western regions of Cornwall, Wales, and Cumberland at the beginning of the seventh century (see Map 7.3). The German invaders eventually succeeded in carving out small kingdoms throughout the island, such as Mercia, Northumberland, and Kent. This wave of German invaders would eventually be converted to Christianity by new groups of Christian missionaries (see "The Conversion of England" later in this chapter).

The Society of the Germanic Kingdoms   As the Germans infiltrated the Roman Empire, they were influenced by the Roman society they encountered. Consequently, the Germanic peoples of the fifth, sixth, and seventh centuries were probably quite different from the Germans that the forces of Augustus encountered in the first century C.E. Moreover, there was a meaningful fusion of Roman and German upper classes in the new kingdoms. In Merovingian Frankish lands, upper-class Gallo-Romans intermarried with Frankish nobles to produce a new ruling class. Each influenced the other. Franks constructed Roman-style villas; Gallo-Romans adopted Frankish weapons.

The crucial social bond among the Germanic peoples was the family, especially the extended or patriarchal family of husbands, wives, children, brothers, sisters, cousins, and grandparents. In addition to working the land together and passing it down to succeeding generations, the extended family provided protection, which was sorely needed in the violent atmosphere of Merovingian times.

Germanic Law   The German conception of family and kinship affected the way Germanic law treated the problem of crime and punishment. In the Roman system, as in our own, a crime such as murder was considered an offense against society or the state and was handled by a court that heard evidence and arrived at a decision. Germanic law tended to be personal. An injury by one person against another could lead to a blood feud in which the family of the injured party took revenge on the kin of the wrongdoer. Feuds could result in savage acts of revenge—hands or feet might be hacked off, eyes gouged out, or ears and noses sliced off. Since this system had a tendency to get out of control and allow mayhem to multiply, an alternative system arose that made use of a fine called **wergeld** (WURR-geld). This was the amount paid by a wrongdoer to the family of the person who had been injured or killed. *Wergeld*, which means "money for a man," was the value of a person in monetary terms. That value varied considerably according to social status. The law of the Salic Franks, which was first written down under Roman influence at the beginning of the sixth century, stated: "If any one shall have killed a free Frank, or a barbarian living under the Salic law, and it have been proved on him, he shall be sentenced to 8,000 denars.... But if any one has slain a man who is in the service of the king, he shall be sentenced to 24,000 denars."[6] An offense against a noble obviously cost considerably more than one against a free person or a slave.

Under German customary law, compurgation and the ordeal were the two most commonly used procedures for determining whether an accused person was guilty and should have to pay *wergeld*. Compurgation was the swearing of an oath by the accused person, backed up by a group of "oathhelpers," numbering twelve or twenty-five, who would also swear that the accused person should be believed. The ordeal functioned in a variety of ways, all of which were based on the principle of divine intervention; divine forces (whether pagan or Christian) would not allow an innocent person to be harmed.

The Frankish Family and Marriage   For the Franks, like other Germanic peoples of the Early Middle Ages, the extended family was at the center of social organization. The Frankish family structure was quite simple. Males were dominant and made all the important decisions. A woman obeyed her father until she married and then fell under the legal domination of her husband. A widow, however, could hold property without a male guardian. In Frankish law, the *wergeld* of a wife of childbearing age—of value because she could produce children—was considerably higher than that of a man. The Salic law stated: "If any one killed a free woman after she had begun bearing children, he shall be sentenced to 24,000 denars.... After she can have no more children, he who kills her shall be sentenced to 8,000 denars."[7]

Since marriage affected the extended family group, fathers or uncles could arrange marriages for the good of the family without considering their children's wishes. Most important was the engagement ceremony in which a prospective son-in-law made a payment symbolizing the purchase of paternal authority over the bride. The essential feature of the marriage itself involved placing the married couple in bed to achieve their physical union. In first marriages, it was considered important that the wife be a virgin so as to ensure that any children would be the husband's. A virgin symbolized the ability of the bloodline to continue. For this reason, adultery was viewed as pollution of the woman and her offspring, poisoning the future. Adulterous wives were severely punished (an adulterous woman could be strangled or even burned alive); adulterous husbands were not. Divorce was relatively simple and was initiated primarily by the husband. Divorced wives simply returned to their families.

For most women in the new Germanic kingdoms, their legal status reflected the material conditions of their lives. Archaeological evidence suggests that most women had life expectancies of only thirty or forty years and that about 10 to 15 percent of women died in their childbearing years, no doubt due to complications associated with childbirth.

For most women, life consisted of domestic labor: providing food and clothing for the household, caring for the children, and assisting with numerous farming chores. This labor was crucial to the family economy. In addition to clothing and feeding their own families, women could sell or barter clothes and food for additional goods. Of all the duties of women, the most important was childbearing because it was crucial to the maintenance of the family and its properties.

DEVELOPMENT OF THE CHRISTIAN CHURCH

By the end of the fourth century, Christianity had become the predominant religion of the Roman Empire. As the official Roman state disintegrated, the Christian church played an increasingly important role in the new civilization built on the ruins of the old Roman Empire.

The Church Fathers   A number of intellectuals in the early church who wrote in Latin profoundly influenced the development of Christian thought in the west. They came to be known as the Latin Fathers of the Catholic Church. They include Augustine, Jerome, Ambrose, and Gregory the Great (the last two are discussed in "Church and State" and "Pope Gregory the Great" below).

The Work of Augustine   Saint Augustine (AW-guh-steen) (354–430) was the most prominent of the Latin Fathers. His work provides one of the best examples of how Christian theologians used pagan culture in the service of Christianity.

Born in North Africa, Augustine was reared by his mother, an ardent Christian. He eventually became a professor of rhetoric at Milan in 384. But two years later, after experiencing a profound and moving religious experience, Augustine gave up his teaching position and went back to North Africa, where he served as bishop of Hippo from 396 until his death in 430.

Augustine's two most famous works are the *Confessions* and *The City of God*. Written in 397, the *Confessions* was a self-portrait not of Augustine's worldly activities but of the "history of a heart," an account of his own personal and spiritual experiences, written to help others with their search. Augustine describes how he struggled throughout his early life to find God until in his thirty-second year he experienced a miraculous conversion.

The City of God, Augustine's other major work, was a profound expression of a Christian philosophy of government and history. In it, Augustine theorized on the ideal relations between two kinds of societies existing throughout time—the City of God and the City of the World. Those who loved God would be loyal to the City of God, whose ultimate location was the kingdom of heaven. Earthly society would always be insecure because of human beings' imperfect nature and inclination to violate God's commandments. And yet the City of the World was still necessary, for it was the duty of rulers to curb the depraved instincts of sinful humans and maintain the peace necessary for Christians to live in the world. Hence, Augustine posited that secular government and authority were necessary for the pursuit of the true Christian life on earth; in doing so, he provided a justification for secular political authority that would play an important role in medieval thought.

Augustine was also important in establishing the Christian church's views on sexual desire. Many early Christians had seen **celibacy** (SELL-uh-buh-see), or complete abstinence from sexual activity, as the surest way to holiness. Augustine, too, believed Christians should reject sex, but he maintained that many Christians were unable to do so. For them, marriage was a good alternative, but with the understanding that even in marriage, sex between a man and woman had to serve a purpose—the procreation of children. It was left to the clergy of the church to uphold the high ideal of celibacy.

Jerome and the Bible   Another Latin Father was Jerome (345–420), who pursued literary studies in Rome and became a master of Latin prose. Jerome had mixed feelings about his love for liberal studies, however, and like Augustine, he experienced a spiritual conversion, after which he tried to dedicate himself more fully to Jesus. He had a dream in which Jesus appeared as his judge:

> Asked who and what I was, I replied: "I am a Christian." But He who presided said: "You lie, you are a follower of Cicero, not of Christ. For where your treasure is, there will your heart be also." Instantly, I became dumb.... Accordingly I made oath and called upon His name, saying: "Lord, if ever again I possess worldly books [the classics], or if ever again I read such, I have denied You."

After this dream, Jerome determined to "read the books of God with a zeal greater than I had previously given to the books of men."[8]

Ultimately, Jerome found a compromise by purifying the literature of the pagan world and then using it to further the Christian faith. Jerome was the greatest scholar among the Latin Fathers, and his extensive knowledge of both Hebrew and Greek enabled him to translate the Old and New Testaments into Latin. In the process, he created the so-called Latin Vulgate, or common text, of the Scriptures that became the standard edition for the Catholic Church in the Middle Ages.

The Power of the Pope

In the early centuries of Christianity, the churches in the larger cities had great influence in the administration of the church. It was only natural, then, that the bishops of those cities would also exercise considerable power. One of the far-reaching developments in the history of the Christian church was the emergence of one bishop—that of Rome—as the recognized leader of the western Christian church.

The doctrine of **Petrine supremacy,** based on the belief that the bishops of Rome occupied a preeminent position in the church, was grounded in Scripture. According to the Gospel of Matthew, when Jesus asked his disciples, "Who do you say I am?" Simon Peter answered:

> You are the Christ, the Son of the living God. Jesus replied, Blessed are you, Simon, son of Jonah, for this was not revealed by man, but by my Father in heaven. And I tell you that you are Peter, and on this rock I will build my church, and the gates of hell will not overcome it. I will give you the keys of the kingdom of heaven; whatever you bind on earth will be bound in heaven; and whatever you loose on earth will be loosed in heaven.[9]

According to church tradition, Jesus had given the keys to the kingdom of heaven to Peter, who was considered the chief apostle and the first bishop of Rome. Subsequent bishops of Rome were considered Peter's successors and later the "vicars of Christ" on earth. Though this exalted view of the bishops of Rome was by no means accepted by all early Christians, Rome's position as the traditional capital of the Roman Empire served to buttress this claim.

By the end of the fourth century, the bishops of Rome were using the title of *papa,* "father" (which became the English *pope*). Pope Leo I (440–461) was especially energetic in systematically expounding the doctrine of Petrine supremacy. He portrayed himself as the heir of Peter, whom Jesus had chosen to be head of the Christian church. But state authorities were also claiming some power over the church.

Church and State

Once the Roman emperors became Christians, they came to play a significant role in the affairs of the church. Christian emperors viewed themselves as God's representatives on earth. They not only built churches and influenced the structure of the church's organization but also became involved in church government and doctrinal controversies.

While emperors were busying themselves in church affairs, the spiritual and political vacuum left by the disintegration of the Roman state allowed bishops to play a more active role in imperial government. Increasingly, they served as advisers to Christian Roman emperors. Moreover, as imperial authority declined, bishops often played a noticeably independent political role. Ambrose (c. 339–397) of Milan was an early example of a strong and independent bishop. Through his activities and writings, which brought him recognition as another of the four Latin

Fathers of the Catholic Church. Ambrose created an image of the ideal Christian bishop. Among other things, this ideal bishop would defend the independence of the church against the tendency of imperial officials to oversee church policy: "Exalt not yourself, but if you would reign the longer, be subject to God. It is written, God's to God and Caesar's to Caesar. The palace is the Emperor's, the Churches are the Bishop's."[10] When Emperor Theodosius I ordered the massacre of many citizens of Thessalonika for refusing to obey his commands, Ambrose denounced the massacre and refused to allow the emperor to take part in church ceremonies. Theodosius finally agreed to do public penance in the cathedral of Milan for his dastardly deed. Ambrose proved himself a formidable advocate of the position that spiritual authority should take precedence over temporal power, at least in spiritual matters.

The weakness of the political authorities on the Italian peninsula also contributed to the church's independence in that area. In the Germanic kingdoms, the kings controlled both churches and bishops. But in Italy, a different tradition prevailed, fed by semilegendary accounts of papal deeds. Pope Leo I, for example, supposedly caused Attila the Hun to turn away from Rome in 452. Although Attila's withdrawal was probably due more to plague than to papal persuasion, the pope got the credit. Popes, then, played significant political roles in Italy, which only added to their claims of power vis-à-vis the secular authorities. Pope Gelasius (juh-LAY-shuss) I (492–496) could write to the emperor at Constantinople:

> There are two powers, august Emperor, by which this world is ruled from the beginning: the consecrated authority of the bishops, and the royal power. In these matters the priests bear the heavier burden because they will render account, even for rulers of men, at the divine judgment. Besides, most gracious son, you are aware that, although you in your office are the ruler of the human race, nevertheless you devoutly bow your head before those who are leaders in things divine and look to them for the means of your salvation.[11]

According to Gelasius, though there were two ruling powers, spiritual and temporal, with different functions, the church was ultimately the higher authority because all men, including emperors, must look to the church "for the means of ... salvation."

Pope Gregory the Great   Although eventually western Christians came to accept the bishop of Rome as head of the church, there was no unanimity on the extent of the powers the pope possessed as a result of his position. Nevertheless, the emergence in the sixth century of a strong pope, Gregory I, known as Gregory the Great, the last of the Latin Fathers, set the papacy and the Roman Catholic Church on an energetic path that enabled the church in the seventh and eighth centuries to play an increasingly prominent role in civilizing the Germans and aiding the emergence of a distinctly new European civilization.

As pope, Gregory I (590–604) assumed direction of Rome and its surrounding territories, which had suffered enormously from the Ostrogothic-Byzantine struggle and the Lombard invasion of the sixth century. Gregory described the conditions in a sermon to the people of Rome:

> What Rome herself, once deemed the Mistress of the World, has now become, we see— wasted away with afflictions grievous and many, with the loss of citizens, the assaults

of enemies, the frequent fall of ruined buildings.... Where is the Senate? Where is the people? The bones are all dissolved, the flesh is consumed, all the pomp of the dignities of this world is gone.[12]

Gregory took charge and made Rome and its surrounding area into an administrative unit that eventually came to be known as the Papal States. Although historians disagree about Gregory's motives in establishing papal temporal power, no doubt Gregory was probably only doing what he felt needed to be done: provide for the defense of Rome against the Lombards, establish a government for Rome, and feed the people. Gregory remained loyal to the empire and continued to address the Byzantine emperor as the rightful ruler of Italy.

Gregory also pursued a policy of extending papal authority over the Christian church in the west, although few people in Europe at this time looked to the pope as the church's ruler. He intervened in ecclesiastical conflicts throughout Italy and corresponded with the Frankish rulers, urging them to reform the church in Gaul. He successfully initiated the efforts of missionaries to convert England to Christianity and was especially active in converting the pagan peoples of Germanic Europe. His primary instrument was the monastic movement.

The Monks and Their Missions

A **monk** (Latin *monachus*, meaning "someone who lives alone") was a man who sought to live a life divorced from the world, cut off from ordinary human society, in order to pursue an ideal of godliness or total dedication to the will of God. Christian **monasticism**, which developed first in Egypt, was initially based on the model of the solitary hermit who forsakes all civilized society to pursue spirituality. Saint Anthony (c. 250–350) was a prosperous Egyptian peasant who decided to follow Jesus's injunction in the Gospel of Mark: "Go your way, sell whatsoever you have, and give to the poor, and you shall have treasure in heaven: and come, take up the cross, and follow me."[13] Anthony gave his 300 acres of land to the poor and went into the desert to pursue his ideal of holiness. Others did likewise, often to extremes. Saint Simeon the Stylite lived for three decades in a basket atop a pillar more than 60 feet high. These spiritual gymnastics established a new ideal for Christianity. Whereas the early Christian model had been the martyr who died for the faith and achieved eternal life in the process, the new ideal was the monk who died to the world and achieved spiritual life through denial, asceticism, and mystical experience of God.

These early monks, however, soon found themselves unable to live in solitude. Their feats of holiness attracted followers on a wide scale, and as the monastic ideal spread throughout the east, a new form of monasticism, based on the practice of communal life, soon became the dominant form. Monastic communities soon came to be seen as the ideal Christian society that could provide a moral example to the wider society around them.

Benedictine Monasticism

Saint Benedict of Nursia (c. 480–c. 543), who founded a monastic house and wrote a set of rules for it sometime between 520 and 530, established the fundamental form of monastic life in the western Christian church. Benedict's rules largely rejected the ascetic ideals of eastern monasticism, which had tended to emphasize such practices as fasting and self-inflicted torments (such as living atop pillars for thirty years), in favor of an ideal of moderation. In Chapter 40 of the rules, on the amount of drink a monk should imbibe, this sense of moderation becomes apparent:

> "Every man has his proper gift from God, one after this manner, another after that." And therefore it is with some misgiving that we determine the amount of food for someone else. Still, having regard for the weakness of some brothers, we believe that a hemina [a quarter liter] of wine per day will suffice for all. Let those, however, to whom God gives the gift of abstinence, know that they shall have their proper reward. But if either the circumstances of the place, the work, or the heat of summer necessitates more, let it lie in the discretion of the abbot to grant it. But let him take care in all things lest satiety or drunkenness supervene.

At the same time, moderation did not preclude a hard and disciplined existence based on the ideals of stability (staying in the monastery for life), fidelity (accepting the routine of the monastery), and obedience (to the abbot as head of the monastery).

Benedict's rules divided each day into a series of activities with primary emphasis on prayer and manual labor. Physical work of some kind was required of all monks for several hours a day because "idleness is the enemy of the soul." At the very heart of community practice was prayer, the proper "work of God." While this included private meditation and reading, all monks gathered together seven times during the day for common prayer and chanting of psalms. A Benedictine life was a communal one; monks ate, worked, slept, and worshiped together.

Each Benedictine monastery was strictly ruled by an **abbot**, or "father" of the monastery, who had complete authority over the monks, who bent unquestioningly to the will of the abbot. Each Benedictine monastery owned lands that enabled it to be a self-sustaining community, isolated from and independent of the world surrounding it. Within the monastery, however, monks were to fulfill an ideal of poverty: "Let all things be common to all, as it is written, lest anyone should say that anything is his own or arrogate it to himself."[14] By the eighth century, Benedictine monasticism had spread throughout the west.

Women, too, sought to withdraw from the world to dedicate themselves to God. Already in the third century, groups of women abandoned the cities to form communities in the deserts of Egypt and Syria. The first monastic rules for western women were produced by Caesarius of Arles for his sister in the fifth century. They strongly emphasized a rigid cloistering of female religious, known as **nuns,** to preserve them from dangers. Later in the west, in the seventh and eighth centuries, the growth of double monasteries allowed monks and nuns to reside close by and follow a common set of rules. Not all women pursued the celibate life in the desert, however. In a number of cities in the fourth century, women organized religious communities in their own homes.

Monasticism played an indispensable role in early medieval civilization. Monks became the new heroes of Christian civilization. Their dedication to God became the highest ideal of Christian life. Moreover, the monks played an increasingly significant role in spreading Christianity to all of Europe.

Irish Monks as Missionaries
Ireland had remained a Celtic outpost beyond the reach of the Roman Empire and the Germanic invaders. The most famous of the Christian missionaries to Ireland in the fifth century was Saint Patrick (c. 390–461). Son of a

Irish Monasticism and the Penitential

Irish monasticism became well known for its ascetic practices. It emphasized careful examination of conscience to determine if one had committed a sin against God. To facilitate this examination, penitentials were developed that listed possible sins with appropriate penances. Penance usually meant fasting—taking only bread and water—for a number of days each week. Although these penitentials were eventually used throughout Christendom, they were especially important in Irish Christianity. This excerpt from the penitential of Cummean, an Irish abbot, was written about 650 and demonstrates a distinctive feature of the penitentials, an acute preoccupation with sexual sins.

The Penitential of Cummean

A bishop who commits fornication shall be degraded and shall do penance for twelve years.

A priest or a deacon who commits natural fornication, having previously taken the vow of a monk, shall do penance for seven years. He shall ask pardon every hour; he shall perform a special fast during every week except in the days between Easter and Pentecost.

He who defiles his mother shall do penance for three years, with perpetual pilgrimage.

So shall those who commit sodomy do penance every seven years.

He who merely desires in his mind to commit fornication, but is not able, shall do penance for one year, especially in the three forty-day periods.

He who is willingly polluted during sleep shall arise and sing nine psalms in order, kneeling. On the following day, he shall live on bread and water.

A cleric who commits fornication once shall do penance for one year on bread and water; if he begets a son he shall do penance for seven years as an exile; so also a virgin.

He who loves any woman, but is unaware of any evil beyond a few conversations, shall do penance for forty days.

He who is in a state of matrimony ought to be continent during the three forty-day periods and on Saturday and on Sunday, night and day, and in the two appointed week days [Wednesday and Friday], and after conception, and during the entire menstrual period.

After a birth he shall abstain, if it is a son, for thirty-three [days]; if a daughter, for sixty-six [days].

Boys talking alone and transgressing the regulations of the elders [in the monastery], shall be corrected by three special fasts.

Children who imitate acts of fornication, twenty days; if frequently, forty.

But boys of twenty years who practice masturbation together and confess [shall do penance] twenty or forty days before they take communion.

Q *What does the penitential of Cummean reveal about the nature of Irish monasticism? What do you think was the theory of human sexuality held by early Irish Christianity?*

Source: From *Medieval Handbooks of Penance*, edited by John T. McNeill and Helena M. Garner. Copyright © 1990 by Columbia University Press. Reprinted by permission of the publisher.

Romano-British Christian, Patrick was kidnapped as a young man by Irish raiders and kept as a slave in Ireland. After his escape to Gaul, he became a monk and chose to return to Ireland to convert the Irish to Christianity. Irish tradition ascribes to Patrick the title of "founder of Irish Christianity," a testament to his apparent success.

Since Ireland had not been part of the Roman world and was fairly isolated from the European continent even after its conversion, Irish Christianity tended to develop along lines somewhat different from Roman Christianity. Whereas Catholic ecclesiastical structure had followed Roman government models, the absence of these models in Ireland led to a different pattern of church organization. Rather than bishoprics, monasteries became the fundamental units of church organization, and abbots, the heads of the monasteries, exercised far more control over the Irish church than bishops did.

By the sixth century, Irish monasticism was a flourishing institution with its own striking characteristics. It was strongly ascetic. Monks performed strenuous fasts, prayed and meditated frequently under extreme privations, and confessed their sins on a regular basis to their superiors. In fact, Irish monasticism gave rise to the use of penitentials or manuals that provided a guide for examining one's life to see what offenses against the will of God had been committed.

A great love of learning also characterized Irish monasticism. The Irish eagerly absorbed both Latin and Greek culture and fostered education as a major part of their monastic life. Irish monks were preserving Classical Latin at the same time spoken Latin was being corrupted on the Continent into new dialects that eventually became the Romance languages, such as Italian, French, and Spanish. Irish monasteries produced extraordinary illuminated manuscripts illustrated with abstract geometric patterns.

The emphasis on asceticism led many Irish monks to go into voluntary exile. This "exile for the love of God" was not into isolation, however, but into missionary activity. Irish monks became fervid missionaries. Saint Columba (521–597) left Ireland in 565 as a "pilgrim for Christ" and founded a highly influential monastic community off the coast of Scotland on the island of Iona. From there Irish missionaries went to northern England to begin the process of converting the Angles and Saxons. Aidan of Iona, for example, founded the island monastery of Lindisfarne (LIN-dis-farn) in the Anglo-Saxon kingdom of Northumbria. Lindisfarne in turn became a training center for monks who spread out to different parts of Anglo-Saxon England. Meanwhile, other Irish monks traveled to the European mainland. New monasteries founded by the Irish became centers of learning wherever they were located.

The Conversion of England   At the same time the Irish monks were busy bringing their version of Christianity to the Anglo-Saxons of Britain, Pope Gregory the Great had set in motion his own effort to convert England to Roman Christianity. His most important agent was Augustine, a monk from a monastery in Rome, who arrived in England in 597. England at that time had a number of Anglo-Saxon kingdoms. Augustine went first to Kent, where he converted King Ethelbert, whereupon most of the king's subjects followed suit. Pope Gregory's conversion techniques emphasized persuasion rather than force, and as seen in this excerpt from one of his letters, he was willing to assimilate old pagan practices in order to coax the pagans into the new faith:

> We wish you [Abbot Mellitus] to inform him [Augustine] that we have been giving careful thought to the affairs of the English, and have come to the conclusion that the temples of the idols among that people should on no account be destroyed. The idols

are to be destroyed, but the temples themselves are to be sprinkled with holy water, altars set up in them, and relics deposited there. For if these temples are well-built, they must be purified from the worship of demons and dedicated to the service of the true God. In this way, we hope that the people, seeing that their temples are not destroyed, may abandon their error and, flocking more readily to their accustomed resorts, may come to know and adore the true God.[15]

Freed of their pagan past, temples became churches, as one Christian commentator noted with joy: "The dwelling place of demons has become a house of God. The saving light has come to shine, where shadows covered all. Where sacrifices once took place and idols stood, angelic choirs now dance. Where God was angered once, now God is made content."[16]

Likewise, old pagan feasts were given new names and incorporated into the Christian calendar. No doubt Gregory was aware that early Christians had done the same. The Christian feast of Christmas, for example, was held on December 25, the day of the pagan celebration of the winter solstice.

As Roman Christianity spread northward in Britain, it encountered Irish Christianity moving southward. Soon arguments arose over the differences between Irish and Roman Christianity, especially over different calendar days for the feast of Easter and matters of discipline. At the Synod of Whitby, held in the kingdom of Northumbria in 664, the king of Northumbria accepted the arguments of the representatives of Roman Christianity and decided the issue in favor of Roman practices. A gradual fusion of Irish and Roman Christianity now ensued. Despite its new-found unity and loyalty to Rome, the English church retained some Irish features. Most important was the concentration on monastic culture with special emphasis on learning and missionary work. By 700, the English clergy had become the best trained and most learned in western Europe.

Following the Irish example, English monks journeyed to the European continent to carry on the work of conversion (see Map 7.4). Most important was Boniface (c. 675–754), who undertook the conversion of pagan Germans in Frisia, Bavaria, and Saxony. By 740, Saint Boniface, the "Apostle of the Germans," had become the most famous churchman in Europe. Fourteen years later, he was killed while trying to convert the pagan Frisians. Boniface was a brilliant example of the numerous Irish and English monks whose tireless efforts made Europe the bastion of the Roman Catholic faith.

Women and Monasticism Women, too, played an important role in the monastic missionary movement and the conversion of the Germanic kingdoms. Double monasteries, where monks and nuns lived in separate houses but attended church services together, were found in both the English and Frankish kingdoms. The monks and nuns followed common rules under a common head—frequently an **abbess** rather than an abbot. Many of these abbesses belonged to royal houses, especially in Anglo-Saxon England. In the kingdom of Northumbria, for example, Saint Hilda founded the monastery of Whitby in 657. As abbess, she was responsible for giving learning an important role in the life of the monastery; five future bishops were educated under her tutelage. For female intellectuals, monasteries offered opportunities for learning not found elsewhere in the society of their day.

MAP 7.4 The Spread of Christianity, 400–800

The Christian church had penetrated much of the Roman Empire by the end of the fifth century. It emerged as a major base of power after the fall of the empire, and it pushed its influence into new areas through the activities of missionaries.

Nuns of the seventh and eighth centuries were not always as heavily cloistered as they once had been and were therefore able to play an important role in the spread of Christianity. The great English missionary Boniface relied on nuns in England for books and money. He also asked the abbess of Wimborne to send groups of nuns to establish convents in newly converted German lands. A nun named Leoba established the first convent in Germany at Bischofsheim.

The Path of Celibacy   The monastic movement enabled some women to pursue a new path to holiness. Cloisters for both men and women offered the ideal place to practice the new Christian ideal of celibacy. This newfound emphasis on abstaining from sexual relations, especially evident in the emphasis on virginity, created a new image of the human body in late antiquity. To many Greeks and Romans, the human body had been a source of beauty, joy, and pleasure, an attitude evident in numerous works of art. Many Christians, however, viewed the body as a hindrance to a spiritual connection with God. The refusal to have sex was a victory over the desires of the flesh and thus an avenue to holiness.

In the fourth and fifth centuries, a cult of virginity also moved beyond the walls of monasteries and convents. Throughout the Mediterranean world, groups of women met together to study the importance and benefits of celibacy. In Rome, a woman named Marcella supported a group of aristocratic women who studied the teachings about celibacy and also aided Jerome, the church father, with his work in translating the Bible into Latin.

The Growing Wealth of Monasteries   Beginning in the sixth century, monasteries and local churches became the beneficiaries of grants of land from kings, bishops, and aristocrats. These gifts reached a high point in the eighth century. In fact, one historian has estimated that by the end of the eighth century, one-third of the land of Italy and the kingdom of the Franks was owned by church establishments. Those who gave these gifts did so in large part for religious favors, such as prayers and assurances of salvation. As a result of the gifts, however, individual monasteries sometimes became as wealthy as landed aristocrats and thus also served as instruments of political power.

Christian Intellectual Life in the Germanic Kingdoms   Although the Christian church came to accept Classical culture, it was not easy to do so in the new Germanic kingdoms. Nevertheless, some Christian scholars managed to keep learning alive.

Cassiodorus   Most prominent was Cassiodorus (c. 490–585), who came from an aristocratic Roman family and served as an official of the Ostrogothic king Theodoric. The conflicts that erupted after the death of Theodoric led Cassiodorus to withdraw from public life and retire to his landed estates in southern Italy, where he wrote his final work, *Divine and Human Readings*, a compendium of the literature of both Christian and pagan antiquity. Cassiodorus accepted the advice of earlier Christian intellectuals to make use of Classical works while treasuring the Scriptures above all else.

Cassiodorus continued the tradition of late antiquity of classifying knowledge according to certain subjects. In assembling his compendium of authors, he followed the works of late ancient authors in placing all secular knowledge into the categories of the seven **liberal arts**, which were divided into two major groups: the *trivium* (TRIV-ee-um), consisting of grammar, rhetoric, and dialectic or logic, and the *quadrivium* (kwah-DRIV-ee-um), consisting of arithmetic, geometry, astronomy, and music. The seven liberal arts would remain the cornerstone of Western education for nearly twelve hundred years.

Bede   The Venerable Bede (BEED) (c. 672–735) was a scholar and product of Christian Anglo-Saxon England. He entered a monastery at Jarrow as a small boy and remained there most of the rest of his life. His *Ecclesiastical History of the English People*, completed in 731, was a product of the remarkable flowering of English ecclesiastical and monastic culture in the eighth century. His history of England begins with the coming of Christianity to Britain. Although Bede shared the credulity of his age in regard to stories of miracles, he had a remarkable sense of history. He used his sources so judiciously that they remain our chief source of information about early Anglo-Saxon England. His work was a remarkable accomplishment for a monk from a small corner of England and reflects the high degree of intellectual achievement in England in the eighth century.

THE BYZANTINE EMPIRE

As noted earlier, in the fourth century, a separation between the western and eastern parts of the Roman Empire began to occur. Even as the Germans moved into the western part of the empire and established various kingdoms over the course of the fifth century, the Roman Empire in the east, centered on Constantinople, solidified and prospered.

The Reign of Justinian (527–565) In the sixth century, the empire in the east came under the control of one of its most remarkable rulers, the emperor Justinian. As the nephew and heir of the previous emperor, Justinian had been well trained in imperial administration. He was determined to reestablish the Roman Empire in the entire Mediterranean world and began his attempt to reconquer the west in 533.

Justinian's army under Belisarius (bell-uh-SAH-ree-uss), probably the best general of the late Roman world, presented a formidable force. Belisarius sailed to North Africa and quickly destroyed the Vandals in two major battles. From North Africa, he led his forces onto the Italian peninsula after occupying Sicily in 535. But it was not until 552 that the Ostrogoths were finally defeated. The struggle devastated Italy, which suffered more from Justinian's reconquest than from all of the previous barbarian invasions.

Justinian has been criticized for overextending his resources and bankrupting the empire. Historians now think, however, that a devastating plague in 542 and long-term economic changes were far more damaging to the Eastern Roman Empire than Justinian's conquests. Before he died, Justinian appeared to have achieved his goals. He had restored the imperial Mediterranean world; his empire included Italy, part of Spain, North Africa, Asia Minor, Palestine, and Syria (see Map 7.5). But the conquest of the Western Empire proved fleeting. Only three years after Justinian's death, the Lombards entered Italy. Although the Eastern Empire maintained the fiction of Italy as a province, its forces were limited to southern and central Italy, Sicily, and coastal areas, such as the territory around Ravenna.

The Codification of Roman Law Though his conquests proved short-lived, Justinian made a lasting contribution to Western civilization through his codification of Roman law. The Eastern Empire was heir to a vast quantity of materials connected to the development of Roman law. These included laws passed by the senate and assemblies, legal commentaries of jurists, decisions of praetors, and the edicts of emperors. Justinian had been well trained in imperial government and was thoroughly acquainted with Roman law. He wished to codify and simplify this mass of materials.

To accomplish his goal, Justinian authorized the jurist Trebonian to make a systematic compilation of imperial edicts. The result was the Code of Law, the first part of the *Corpus Iuris Civilis* (KOR-pus YOOR-iss see-VIL-liss) (Body of Civil Law), completed in 529. Four years later, two other parts of the *Corpus* appeared: the *Digest*, a compendium of writings of Roman jurists, and the *Institutes*, a brief summary of the chief principles of Roman law that could be used as a textbook on Roman law. The fourth part of the *Corpus* was the *Novels*, a compilation of the most important new edicts issued during Justinian's reign.

MAP 7.5 The Byzantine Empire in the Time of Justinian

The Byzantine emperor Justinian briefly restored much of the Mediterranean portion of the old Roman Empire. His general Belisarius quickly conquered the Vandals in North Africa but wrested Italy from the Ostrogoths only after a long and devastating struggle.

The Emperor Justinian and His Court. *As the seat of Byzantine power in Italy, the town of Ravenna was adorned with many examples of Byzantine art. The Church of San Vitale at Ravenna contains some of the finest examples of sixth-century Byzantine mosaics. Small pieces of colored glass were set in mortar on the wall to form these figures and their surroundings. The emperor is seen as both head of state (he wears a jeweled crown and a purple robe) and head of the church (he carries a gold bowl symbolizing the body of Jesus.)*

Justinian's codification of Roman law became the basis of imperial law in the Byzantine Empire until its end in 1453. More important, however, since it was written in Latin (it was, in fact, the last product of eastern Roman culture to be written in Latin, which was soon replaced by Greek), it was also eventually used in the west and in fact became the basis of the legal system of all of continental Europe.

Intellectual Life Under Justinian   The intellectual life of the Eastern Roman Empire was highly influenced by the traditions of Classical civilization. Scholars actively strived to preserve the works of the ancient Greeks while basing a great deal of their own literature on Classical models. Initially, however, the most outstanding literary achievements of the Eastern Empire were historical and religious works.

The best known of the historians was Procopius (pruh-KOH-pee-uss) (c. 500–c. 562), court historian during the reign of Justinian. Procopius served as secretary to the great general Belisarius and accompanied him on his wars on behalf of Justinian. Procopius's best historical work, the *Wars*, is a firsthand account of Justinian's wars of reconquest in the western Mediterranean and his wars against the Persians in the east. Deliberately modeled after the work of his hero, the Greek historian Thucydides (see Chapter 3), Procopius's narrative features vivid descriptions of battle scenes, clear judgment, and noteworthy objectivity.

Procopius also wrote a work that many historians consider mostly scandalous gossip, his infamous *Secret History*. At the beginning of this work, Procopius informed his readers that "what I shall write now follows a different plan, supplementing the previous formal chronicle with a disclosure of what really happened throughout the Roman Empire."[17] What he revealed constituted a scathing attack on Justinian and his wife Theodora for their alleged misdeeds.

The Empress Theodora   Theodora (thee-uh-DOR-uh) was the daughter of the "keeper of bears" for the games at Constantinople, who died when she was a child. Theodora followed in her mother's footsteps by becoming an actress, which at that time was considered a lowborn activity. Often actresses also worked as prostitutes, and Theodora was no exception. At the age of twenty-five, she met Justinian, who was forty. His uncle, the Emperor Justin, had to change the law to allow an aristocratic senator to marry a woman who had been an actress. After his uncle died in 527, Justinian became emperor and Theodora empress, a remarkable achievement for a woman from the lower classes.

Justinian and Theodora were close and loving companions. She also influenced her husband in both church and state affairs. A strong-willed and intelligent woman, she proved especially valuable in 532, when the two factions of charioteer supporters in Constantinople joined forces and rioted against the emperor. The riots soon became a revolt as the rioters burned and looted the center of the city, shouting "*Nika!*" ("win"), a word normally used to cheer on their favorite chariot teams. Justinian seemed ready to flee, but Theodora strengthened his resolve by saying, "My opinion then is that the present time, above all others, is inopportune for flight, even though it bring safety.... For one who has been emperor it is unendurable to be a fugitive,... and may I not live that day on which those who meet me shall not address me as mistress."[18] On hearing her words, Justinian resolved to stay and fight. Many of the protesters were killed as the so-called Nika Revolt was suppressed.

The Emperor's Building Program   After the riots destroyed much of Constantinople, Justinian rebuilt the city and gave it the appearance it would keep for almost a thousand years (see Map 7.6). Earlier, Emperor Theodosius II (408–450) had constructed an enormous defensive wall to protect the city on its land side. The city was dominated by an immense palace complex, a huge arena known as the Hippodrome, and hundreds of churches. No residential district was particularly fashionable; palaces, tenements, and slums ranged alongside one another. Justinian added many new buildings. His public works projects included roads, bridges, walls, public baths, law courts, and colossal underground reservoirs to hold the city's water supply. He also built hospitals, schools, monasteries, and churches. Churches were his special passion, and in Constantinople alone he built or rebuilt thirty-four of them. His greatest achievement was the famous Hagia Sophia (HAG-ee-uh soh-FEE-uh), the Church of the Holy Wisdom.

Completed in 537, Hagia Sophia was designed by a Greek architect who departed radically from the simple, flat-roofed basilica of Western architecture. The center of Hagia Sophia consisted of four huge piers crowned by an enormous

MAP 7.6 Constantinople

Constantinople was the largest city in Europe, and until the twelfth century, it was the nexus of trade between east and west. Emperor Justinian oversaw a massive building program that produced important architectural monuments such as Hagia Sophia.

dome, which seemed to be floating in space. This effect was emphasized by Procopius, the court historian, who, at Justinian's request, wrote a treatise on the emperor's building projects: "From the lightness of the building, it does not appear to rest upon a solid foundation, but to cover the place beneath as though it were suspended from heaven by the fabled golden chain." In part, this impression was created by putting forty-two windows around the base of the dome, which allowed an incredible play of light within the cathedral. Light served to remind the worshipers of God; as Procopius commented:

> Whoever enters there to worship perceives at once that it is not by any human strength or skill, but by the favor of God that this work has been perfected; his mind rises sublime to commune with God, feeling that He cannot be far off, but must especially love to dwell in the place which He has chosen; and this takes place not only when a man sees it for the first time, but it always makes the same impression upon him, as though he had never beheld it before.[19]

As darkness is illumined by invisible light, so too, it was believed, the world is illumined by invisible spirit.

The royal palace complex, Hagia Sophia, and the Hippodrome were the three greatest buildings in Constantinople. This last was a huge amphitheater, constructed of brick covered by marble, holding as many as 60,000 spectators. Although gladiator fights were held there, the main events were the chariot races; twenty-four would usually be presented in one day. The citizens of Constantinople were passionate fans of chariot racing. Successful charioteers were acclaimed as heroes and honored with public statues. Crowds in the Hippodrome also took on political significance. Being a member of the two chief factions of charioteers—the Blues or the Greens—was the only real outlet for political expression. Even emperors had to be aware of their demands and attitudes: the loss of a race in the Hippodrome frequently resulted in bloody riots, which could threaten the emperor's power.

From Eastern Roman to Byzantine Empire   Justinian's accomplishments had been spectacular, but when he died, he left the Eastern Roman Empire with serious problems: too much distant territory to protect, an empty treasury, a smaller population after the plague, and renewed threats to the frontiers. In the first half of the seventh century, during the reign of Heraclius (he-ruh-KLY-uss *or* huh-RAK-lee-uss) (610–641), the empire faced attacks from the Persians to the east and the Slavs to the north.

The empire was left exhausted by these struggles. In the midst of them, it had developed a new system of defense by creating a new administrative unit, the *theme*, which combined civilian and military offices in the hands of the same person. Thus, the civil governor was also the military leader of the area. Although this innovation helped the empire survive, it also fostered an increased militarization of the empire. By the mid-seventh century, it had become apparent that a restored Mediterranean empire was simply beyond the resources of the Eastern Empire, which now increasingly turned its back on the Latin west.

The most serious challenge to the Eastern Roman Empire came from the rise of Islam, which unified the Arab tribes and created a powerful new force that swept through the east (see "The Rise of Islam" later in this chapter). The empire lost the

Interior View of Hagia Sophia. *Pictured here is the interior of the Church of the Holy Wisdom in Constantinople (modern Istanbul), constructed under Justinian by Authemius of Tralles and Isidore of Milan. Some of the stones used in the construction of the church had been plundered from the famous Classical Temple of Diana, near Ephesus, in Asia Minor. This view gives an idea of how the window around the base of the dome produced a special play of light within the cathedral. The pulpits and plaques bearing inscriptions from the Qur'an were introduced when the Turks converted this church to a mosque in the fifteenth century.*

© Robert Harding/Getty Images

provinces of Syria and Palestine after the Arabs defeated an eastern Roman army at Yarmuk (yahr-MOOK) in 636. The Arabs also moved into the old Persian Empire and conquered it. An Arab attempt to besiege Constantinople failed, in large part due to the use of Greek fire against the Arab fleets. Greek fire was a petroleum-based compound containing quicklime and sulfur. Because it would burn under water, the Byzantines created the equivalent of modern flamethrowers by using tubes to blow Greek fire onto wooden ships, with frightening effect. Arabs and eastern Roman forces now faced each other along a frontier in southern Asia Minor.

Problems also arose along the northern frontier, especially in the Balkans, where an Asiatic people known as the Bulgars had arrived earlier in the sixth century. In 679, the Bulgars defeated the eastern Roman forces and took possession of the lower Danube valley, setting up a strong Bulgarian kingdom.

By the beginning of the eighth century, the Eastern Roman Empire was greatly diminished in size, consisting only of the eastern Balkans and Asia Minor. It was now an eastern Mediterranean state. These external challenges had important internal repercussions as well. By the eighth century, the Eastern Roman Empire had been transformed into what historians call the Byzantine Empire, a civilization with its own unique character that would last until 1453 (Constantinople was built on the site of an older city named Byzantium—hence the term *Byzantine*).

The Byzantine Empire in the Eighth Century   The Byzantine Empire was both a Greek and a Christian state. Increasingly, Latin fell into disuse as Greek became both the common and the official language of the empire. The Byzantine Empire was also built on a faith in Jesus that was shared in a profound way by almost all its citizens. An enormous amount of artistic talent was poured into the construction of churches, church ceremonies, and church decoration. Spiritual principles deeply permeated Byzantine art. The importance of religion to the Byzantines explains why theological disputes took on an exaggerated form. The most famous of these disputes, the so-called iconoclastic controversy, threatened the stability of the empire in the first half of the eighth century.

Beginning in the sixth century, the use of religious images, especially in the form of icons or pictures of sacred figures, became so widespread that charges of idolatry, the worship of images, began to be heard. The use of images or icons had been justified by the argument that icons were not worshiped but were simply used to help illiterate people understand their religion. This argument failed to stop the **iconoclasts**, as the opponents of icons were called.

Iconoclasm was not unique to the Byzantine Empire. In the neighboring Islamic empire (see "The Rise of Islam" later in the chapter), religious art did not include any physical representations of Muhammad. Iconoclasm would also play a role among some of the new religious groups that emerged in the Protestant Reformation in sixteenth-century Europe (see Chapter 13).

Beginning in 730, the Byzantine emperor Leo III (717–741) outlawed the use of icons. Strong resistance ensued, especially from monks. Leo also used the iconoclastic controversy to add to the prestige of the patriarch of Constantinople, the highest church official in the east and second in dignity only to the bishop of Rome. The Roman popes were opposed to the iconoclastic edicts, and their opposition created considerable dissension between the popes and the Byzantine emperors. Late in the eighth century, the Byzantine rulers reversed their stand on the use of images, but not before considerable damage had been done to the unity of the Christian church. Although the final separation between Roman Catholicism and Greek Orthodoxy (as the Christian church in the Byzantine Empire was called) did not occur until 1054, the iconoclastic controversy was important in moving both sides in that direction.

The emperor occupied a crucial position in the Byzantine state. Portrayed as chosen by God, the Byzantine emperor was crowned in sacred ceremonies, and his subjects were expected to prostrate themselves in his presence. His power was considered absolute and was limited in practice only by deposition or assassination. Because the emperor appointed the patriarch, he also exercised control over both church and state. The Byzantines believed that God had commanded their state to preserve the true Christian faith. Emperor, clergy, and civic officials were all bound together in service to this ideal. It can be said that spiritual values truly held the Byzantine state together.

Because of their many foreign enemies, Byzantine emperors spent considerable energy on war and preparations for war. Byzantine literature included many manuals on war, instructing people in the ways of fighting. Byzantine armies, often led by the emperors, were well trained and well equipped with the latest weapons. The Byzantines, however, often preferred to use diplomacy rather than fight. Our word *byzantine*— often defined as "extremely complicated or carried on by underhand methods"—stems from the complex and crafty instructions that Byzantine rulers sent to their envoys.

By 750, it was apparent that two of Rome's heirs, the Germanic kingdoms and the Byzantine Empire, were moving in different directions. Nevertheless, Byzantine influence on the Western world was significant. The images of a Roman imperial state that continued to haunt the west lived on in Byzantium. The legal system of the west came to owe much to Justinian's codification of Roman law. In addition, the Byzantine Empire served in part as a buffer state, protecting the west for a long time from incursions from the east. Although the Byzantine Empire would continue to influence the west until its demise in 1453, it went its own unique way.

Life in Constantinople: The Importance of Trade   With a population estimated in the hundreds of thousands, Constantinople was the largest city in Europe during the Middle Ages. It viewed itself as the center of an empire and a special Christian city. The Byzantines believed that the city was under the protection of God and the Virgin Mary. One thirteenth-century Byzantine said: "About our city you shall know: until the end she will fear no nation whatsoever, for no one will entrap or capture her, not by any means, for she has been given to the Mother of God and no one will snatch her out of Her hands. Many nations will break their horns against her walls and withdraw with shame."[20]

Until the twelfth century, Constantinople was Europe's greatest commercial center. The city was the chief entrepôt for the exchange of products between west and east, and trade formed the basis for its fabulous prosperity. This trade, however, was largely carried on by foreign merchants. As one contemporary said:

> All sorts of merchants come here from the land of Babylon, from … Persia, Media, and all the sovereignty of the land of Egypt, from the lands of Canaan, and from the empire of Russia, from Hungaria, Kharzaria, and the land of Lombardy and Sepharad. It is a busy city, and merchants come to it from every country by sea or land, and there is none like it in the world except Baghdad, the great city of Islam.[21]

Highly desired in western Europe were the products of the east: silk from China, spices from Southeast Asia and India, jewelry and ivory from India (the latter used by artisans for church items), wheat and furs from southern Russia, and flax and honey from the Balkans. Many of these eastern goods were shipped from Constantinople to the Mediterranean area and northern Europe. Despite the Germanic incursions, European trade did not entirely end.

Moreover, imported raw materials were used in Constantinople for local industries. During Justinian's reign, two Christian monks smuggled silkworms from China to begin a silk industry. The state had a monopoly on the production of silk cloth, and the workshops themselves were housed in Constantinople's royal palace complex. European demand for silk cloth made it the city's most lucrative product. It is interesting to note that the upper classes, including emperors and empresses, were not discouraged from making money through trade and manufacturing. Indeed, one empress even manufactured perfumes in her bedroom.

THE RISE OF ISLAM

The Arabs were a Semitic-speaking people of southwestern Asia with a long history. In Roman times, the Arabian peninsula came to be dominated by Bedouin (BED-oo-un *or* BED-wuhn) nomads who moved constantly to find water and food for their animals. In early times, the Bedouins had supported themselves primarily by sheepherding or by raiding passing caravans, but after the domestication of the camel during the second millennium B.C.E., the Bedouins began to participate in the caravan trade themselves and became major carriers of goods between the Persian Gulf and the Mediterranean Sea.

Although these early Arabs were polytheistic, there was a supreme God named Allah (AH-lah) (Arabic for "God") who ruled over the other gods. There was no priesthood; all members of the tribe were involved in the practice of the faith. Allah was symbolized by a sacred stone, and each tribe had its own stone. All tribes, however, worshiped a massive black meteorite—the Black Stone, which had been placed in a central shrine called the *Ka'aba* (KAH-buh) in the city of Mecca.

In the fifth and sixth centuries C.E., the Arabian peninsula took on new importance. As a result of political disorder in Mesopotamia and Egypt, the usual trade routes in the region began to change. A new trade route—from the Mediterranean through Mecca to Yemen and then by ship across the Arabian Sea and the Indian Ocean—became more popular, and communities in that part of the Arabian peninsula, including Mecca, began to prosper from this caravan trade. As a result, tensions arose between the Bedouins in the desert and the increasingly wealthy merchant classes in the towns. Into this intense world came Muhammad (moh-HAM-mud *or* moo-HAM-mud).

Muhammad   Born in Mecca to a merchant family, Muhammad (c. 570–632) was orphaned at the age of five. He grew up to become a caravan manager and eventually married a rich widow who was also his employer. In his middle years, he began to experience visions that he believed were inspired by Allah. Muhammad believed that although Allah had already revealed himself in part through Moses and Jesus—and thus through the Hebrew and Christian traditions—the final revelations were now being given to him. Out of these revelations, which were eventually written down, came the Qur'an (kuh-RAN *or* kuh-RAHN) or Koran, which contained the guidelines by which followers of Allah were to live. Muhammad's teachings formed the basis for the religion known as Islam, which means "submission to the will of Allah." Allah was the all-powerful being who had created the universe and everything in it. Humans must subject themselves to Allah if they wished to achieve everlasting life. His followers were called Muslims, meaning "practitioners of Islam."

After receiving the revelations, Muhammad set out to convince the people of Mecca that the revelations were true. At first, many thought he was insane, and others feared that his attacks on the corrupt society around him would upset the established social and political order. Discouraged by the failure of the Meccans to accept his message, in 622 Muhammad and some of his closest supporters left the city and moved north to the rival city of Yathrib, later renamed Medina (muh-DEE-nuh) ("city of the Prophet"). The year of the journey to Medina, known in history as the *Hegira* (hee-JY-ruh *or* HEH-juh-ruh) ("departure"), became year 1 in the official calendar of Islam.

Muhammad, who had been invited to the town by a number of prominent residents, soon began to win support from people in Medina as well as from members of Bedouin tribes in the surrounding countryside. From these groups, he formed the first Muslim community. Muslims saw no separation between political and religious authority; submission to the will of Allah meant submission to Muhammad, his Prophet. Muhammad soon became both a religious and a political leader. His political and military skills enabled him to put together a reliable military force, with which he returned to Mecca in 630, conquering the city and converting the townspeople to the new faith. From Mecca, Muhammad's ideas spread quickly across the Arabian peninsula and within a relatively short time had resulted in both the religious and the political unification of Arab society.

The Teachings of Islam   At the heart of Islam was its sacred book, the Qur'an, with its basic message that there is no God but Allah and Muhammad is his Prophet. Essentially, the Qur'an contains Muhammad's revelations of a heavenly book written down by secretaries. Consisting of 114 chapters, the Qur'an recorded the beliefs of the Muslims and served as their code of ethics and law.

Islam was a direct and simple faith, emphasizing the need to obey the will of Allah. This meant following a basic ethical code consisting of the **Five Pillars of Islam**: belief in Allah and Muhammad as his Prophet; standard prayer five times a day and public prayer on Friday at midday to worship Allah; observance of the holy month of Ramadan (RAH-muh-dan) (the ninth month on the Muslim calendar) with fasting from dawn to sunset; making a pilgrimage—known as the *hajj* (HAJ)—to Mecca in one's lifetime, if possible; and giving alms to the poor and unfortunate. The faithful who observed the law were guaranteed a place in an eternal paradise.

Islam was not just a set of religious beliefs but a way of life as well. After the death of Muhammad, Muslim scholars drew up a law code, called the *Shari'a* (shah-REE-uh), to provide believers with a set of prescriptions to regulate their daily lives. Much of the

© Bibliothèque Nationale, Paris//The Bridgeman Art Library

Muslims Celebrate the End of Ramadan. *Ramadan is the holy month of Islam during which all Muslims must fast from dawn to sunset. Observance of this holy month is regarded as one of the Five Pillars of the faith. Muhammad instituted the fast during his stay at Medina. It was designed to replace the single Jewish Day of Atonement. This Persian miniature depicts Muslims on horseback celebrating the end of Ramadan.*

Shari'a was drawn from the Qur'an. Believers' behavior was subject to strict guidelines. In addition to the Five Pillars, Muslims were forbidden to gamble, to eat pork, to drink alcoholic beverages, and to engage in dishonest behavior. Sexual practices were also strictly regulated. Marriages were to be arranged by parents, and contacts between unmarried men and women were discouraged. In accordance with Bedouin custom, males were permitted to have more than one wife, but Muhammad attempted to limit the practice by restricting the number of wives to four.

The Spread of Islam   The death of Muhammad presented his followers with a dilemma. Although Muhammad had not claimed to be divine, Muslims saw no separation between religious and political authority. Submission to the will of Allah was the same thing as submission to his Prophet, Muhammad. He had never named a successor, and although he had several daughters, he left no sons. In a male-oriented society, who would lead the community of the faithful? Shortly after Muhammad's death, a number of his closest followers selected Abu Bakr (ah-boo BAHK-ur), a wealthy merchant who was Muhammad's father-in-law, as **caliph** (KAY-liff), or temporal leader, of the Islamic community.

Muhammad and the early caliphs who succeeded him took up the Arab tribal custom of the *razzia* or raid in the struggle against their enemies. Some have called this activity a *jihad* (ji-HAHD), which they misleadingly interpret as a holy war. *Jihad* actually means "striving in the way of the Lord" to achieve personal betterment, although it can also mean fair, defensive fighting to preserve one's life and one's faith. Arab conquests were not carried out to convert others, since conversion to Islam was purely voluntary. Those who did not convert were required only to submit to Muslim rule and pay taxes.

The Byzantines and the Persians were the first to feel the strength of the newly united Arabs. At Yarmuk in 636, the Muslims defeated the Byzantine army, and by 640, they had taken possession of the province of Syria (see Map 7.7). To the east, the Arabs went on to conquer the entire Persian Empire by 650. In the meantime, Egypt and other areas of northern Africa had been added to the new Muslim empire. Led by a series of brilliant generals, the Arabs had put together a large and highly motivated army, whose valor was enhanced by the belief that Muslim warriors were guaranteed a place in paradise if they died in battle.

Early caliphs, ruling from Medina, organized their newly conquered territories into taxpaying provinces. By the mid-seventh century, problems arose again over the succession to the Prophet until Ali, Muhammad's son-in-law, was assassinated and the general Muawiya (moo-AH-wee-yah), the governor of Syria and one of Ali's chief rivals, became caliph in 661. Muawiya was known for one outstanding virtue: he used force only when necessary. As he said, "I never use my sword when my whip will do, nor my whip when my tongue will do."[22] Muawiya moved quickly to make the caliphate hereditary in his own family, thus establishing the Umayyad (oo-MY-ad) dynasty. As one of their first actions, the Umayyads moved the capital of the Muslim empire from Medina to Damascus in Syria. This internal dissension over the caliphate created a split in Islam between the **Shi'ites** (SHEE-yts), or those who accepted only the descendants of Ali, Muhammad's son-in-law, as the true rulers, and the **Sunnites** (SOO-nyts), who claimed that the descendants of the Umayyads were the true caliphs. This seventh-century split in Islam has lasted until the present day.

MAP 7.7   The Expansion of Islam

Muhammad, the prophet of Islam, engaged in warfare against neighboring tribes. Militaristic expansion continued with great zeal under the Prophet's successors. Islamic rule spread rapidly in the decades after Muhammad's death, stopped finally by the Byzantine Empire and the Franks.

Internal dissension, however, did not stop the expansion of Islam. After sweeping across North Africa, the Muslims crossed the Strait of Gibraltar and moved into Spain around 710. The Visigothic kingdom collapsed, and by 725, most of Spain had become a Muslim state with its center at Córdoba. In 732, a Muslim army, making a foray into southern France, was defeated at the Battle of Tours near Poitiers. Muslim expansion in Europe came to a halt.

Meanwhile, in 717, another Muslim force had launched a naval attack on Constantinople with the hope of destroying the Byzantine Empire. In the spring of 718, the Byzantines destroyed the Muslim fleet and saved the Byzantine Empire and indirectly Christian Europe, since the fall of Constantinople would no doubt have opened the door to Muslim invasion of eastern Europe. The Byzantine Empire and Islam now established an uneasy frontier in southern Asia Minor.

The Arab advance had finally come to an end, but not before the southern and eastern Mediterranean portions of the old Roman Empire had been conquered. Islam had truly become heir to much of the old Roman Empire. That part of the empire had been a prosperous one, and the new Arab Empire benefited greatly from its conquest.

The Umayyad dynasty at Damascus now ruled an enormous empire. While expansion had conveyed untold wealth and new ethnic groups into the fold of Islam, it also brought contact with Byzantine and Persian civilization. As a result, the new Arab Empire would be influenced by Greek culture as well as the older civilizations of the ancient Near East. The children of the conquerors would be educated in new ways and produce a brilliant culture that would eventually influence western Europe intellectually.

CHRONOLOGIES

THE LATE ROMAN EMPIRE

284–337	Reforms of Diocletian and Constantine
378–395	Theodosius "the Great"
395	Division of the empire
410	Alaric and Visigoths sack Rome
455	Vandals sack Rome
476	Odoacer deposes Romulus Augustulus

THE GERMANIC KINGDOMS

493	Theodoric establishes an Ostrogothic kingdom in Italy
c. 500	Frankish king Clovis converts to Christianity
535–552	Reconquest of Italy by Byzantines
711	Muslims shatter Visigoths in Spain
732	Charles Martel defeats Muslims near Poitiers

THE BYZANTINE EMPIRE

529–533	Justinian codifies Roman law
535–552	Reconquest of Italy by the Byzantines
636	Arab defeat of Byzantines at Yarmuk
679	Defeat by the Bulgars; losses in the Balkans

THE RISE OF ISLAM

c. 570	Birth of Muhammad
622	Muhammad's flight from Mecca (*Hegira*)
632	Death of Muhammad
637–650	Defeat of Persians
640–642	Seizure of Byzantine provinces of Syria and Egypt
c. 710	Invasion of Spain

8

EUROPEAN CIVILIZATION IN THE EARLY MIDDLE AGES, 750–1000

A fifteenth-century French manuscript illustration of the coronation of Charlemagne by Pope Leo III

Bibliothèque de L'Arsenal, Paris//Archives Charmet/The Bridgeman Art Library

---

CHAPTER OUTLINE

• Europeans and the Environment • The World of the Carolingians
• Disintegration of the Carolingian Empire • The Emerging World of Lords and Vassals • The Zenith of Byzantine Civilization • The Slavic Peoples of Central and Eastern Europe • The Expansion of Islam

EUROPEANS AND THE ENVIRONMENT

The number of people in early medieval Europe is a matter of considerable uncertainty. In all probability, the population of the eighth century still had not recovered from the losses caused by the plagues of the sixth and seventh centuries. Historians generally believe that in the Early Middle Ages, Europe was a sparsely populated landscape dotted with villages and clusters of villages of farmers and warriors. Although rivers, such as the Loire, Seine, Rhine, Elbe, and Oder, served as major arteries of communication, villages were still separated from one another by forests, swamps, and mountain ridges. Forests, which provided building and heating materials as well as game, covered the European landscape. In fact, it has been estimated that less than 10 percent of the land was cultivated, a figure so small that some economic historians believe that Europe had difficulty feeding even its modest population. Thus, hunting and fishing were necessary to supplement the European diet.

Farming   The cultivation of new land proved especially difficult in the Early Middle Ages. Given the crude implements of the time, it was not easy to clear forests and prepare the ground for planting. Moreover, German tribes had for centuries considered trees sacred and resisted cutting them down to make room for farms. Even conversion to Christianity did not entirely change these attitudes. In addition, the heavy soils of northern Europe were not easily plowed. Agricultural methods also worked against significant crop yields. Land was allowed to lie fallow (unplanted) every other year to regain its fertility, but even so it produced low yields. Evidence indicates that Frankish estates yielded incredibly low ratios of two measures of grain to one measure of seed.

The Climate   Climatic patterns show that European weather began to improve around 700 after several centuries of wetter and colder conditions. Nevertheless, natural disasters were always a threat, especially since the low yields meant that little surplus could be saved for bad times. Drought or too much rain could mean meager harvests, famine, and dietary deficiencies that made people susceptible to a wide range of diseases. This was a period of low life expectancy. One study of Hungarian graves found that of every five skeletons, one was a child below the age of one, and two were children between one and fourteen; more than one in five was a woman below the age of twenty. Overall, then, the picture of early medieval Europe is of a relatively small population subsisting on the basis of a limited agricultural economy and leading, in most cases, a precarious existence.

THE WORLD OF THE CAROLINGIANS

By the eighth century, the Merovingian dynasty was losing its control of the Frankish lands. Charles Martel, the Carolingian mayor of the palace of Austrasia, became the virtual ruler of these territories. When Charles Martel died in 741, his son, Pepin (PEP-in *or* pay-PANH), deposed the Merovingians and assumed the kingship of the Frankish state for himself and his family. Pepin's actions, which were approved by the pope, created a new form of Frankish kingship. Pepin (751–768) was crowned king and formally anointed by a representative of the pope with holy oil in imitation of an Old Testament practice. The anointing not only symbolized that the king had been entrusted with a sacred office but also provides yet another example of how a Germanic institution fused with a Christian practice in the Early Middle Ages.

Charlemagne and the Carolingian Empire (768–814)   Pepin's death in 768 brought to the throne of the Frankish kingdom his son, a dynamic and powerful ruler known to history as Charles the Great or Charlemagne (*Carolus magnus* in Latin—hence our word *Carolingian*). Charlemagne was a determined and decisive man, intelligent and inquisitive. A fierce warrior, he was also a wise patron of learning and a resolute statesman. He greatly expanded the territory of the Carolingian Empire during his lengthy rule.

Expansion of the Carolingian Empire   In the tradition of Germanic kings, Charlemagne was a determined warrior who undertook fifty-four military campaigns. Even though the Frankish army was relatively small—only eight thousand men gathered each spring for campaigning—supplying it and transporting it to distant areas could still present serious problems. The Frankish army comprised mostly infantry, with some cavalry armed with swords and spears.

Charlemagne's campaigns took him to many areas of Europe. In 773, he led his army into Italy, crushed the Lombards, and took control of the Lombard state. Although his son was crowned king of Italy, Charlemagne was its real ruler. Four years after subduing Italy, Charlemagne and his forces advanced into northern Spain. This campaign proved disappointing; not only did the Basques harass his army as it crossed the Pyrenees on the way home, but they also ambushed and annihilated his rear guard.

Charlemagne was considerably more successful with his eastern campaigns into Germany, especially against the Saxons, who had settled between the Elbe River and the North Sea. As Einhard, Charlemagne's biographer, recounted it:

> No war ever undertaken by the Frank nation was carried on with such persistence and bitterness, or cost so much labor, because the Saxons, like almost all the tribes of Germany, were a fierce people, given to the worship of devils, and hostile to our religion, and did not consider it dishonorable to transgress and violate all law, human and divine.[1]

Charlemagne's insistence that the Saxons convert to Christianity simply fueled their resistance. Not until 804, after eighteen campaigns, was Saxony finally pacified and added to the Carolingian domain.

Charlemagne invaded the lands of the Bavarians in southeastern Germany in 787 and had incorporated them into his empire by the following year, an expansion that brought him into contact with the southern Slavs and the Avars. The latter disappeared from history after their utter devastation at the hands of Charlemagne's army. Now at its height, Charlemagne's empire covered much of western and central Europe (see Map 8.1); not until the time of Napoleon in the nineteenth century would an empire of this size be seen again in Europe.

Governing the Empire   Charlemagne continued the efforts of his father in organizing the Carolingian kingdom. Because there was no system of public taxation,

MAP 8.1 The Carolingian Empire

Charlemagne inherited the Carolingian Empire from his father, Pepin. He expanded his territories in several directions, creating an empire that would not be rivaled in size until the conquests of Napoleon in the early nineteenth century.

Charlemagne was dependent on the royal estates for the resources he needed to govern his empire. Food and goods derived from these lands provided support for the king, his household staff, and officials. To keep the nobles in his service, Charlemagne granted part of the royal lands as lifetime holdings to nobles who assisted him.

Besides the household staff, the administration of the empire depended on counts, who were the king's chief representatives in local areas, although in dangerous border districts officials known as margraves (literally, *mark graf*, count of the border district) were used. Counts were members of the nobility who had already existed under the Merovingians. They had come to control public services in their own lands and thus acted as judges, military leaders, and agents of the king. Gradually, as the rule of the Merovingian kings weakened, many counts had simply attached the royal lands and services performed on behalf of the king to their own family possessions.

In an effort to gain greater control over his kingdom, Charlemagne attempted to limit the power of the counts. They were required to serve outside their own family lands and were moved about periodically rather than being permitted to remain in a county for life. By making the offices appointive, Charlemagne tried to prevent the counts' children from automatically inheriting their offices. Moreover, as another check on the counts, Charlemagne instituted the *missi dominici* (MISS-ee doh-MIN-i-chee) ("messengers of the lord king"), two men, one lay lord and one church official, who were sent out to local districts to ensure that the counts were executing the king's wishes. They had the power to remove counts if they were abusing their power, thus making the *missi* an important instrument in bolstering royal power. The counts also had assistants, but they were members of their households, not part of a bureaucratic office.

The last point is an important reminder that we should not think of Carolingian government in the modern sense of government offices run by officials committed to an impersonal ideal of state service. The Carolingian system was glaringly inefficient. Great distances had to be covered on horseback, making it impossible for Charlemagne and his household staff to exercise much supervision over local affairs. What held the system together was personal loyalty to a single ruler who was strong enough to ensure loyalty by force when necessary.

Charlemagne also realized that the Catholic Church could provide valuable assistance in governing his kingdom. By the late seventh century, the system of ecclesiastical government within the Christian church that had been created in the Late Roman Empire had largely disintegrated. Many church offices were not filled or were held by grossly unqualified relatives of the royal family. Both Pepin and his son Charlemagne took up the cause of church reform by creating new bishoprics and archbishoprics, restoring old ones, and seeing to it that the clergy accepted the orders of their superiors and executed their duties.

Charlemagne as Emperor   As Charlemagne's power grew, so did his prestige as the most powerful Christian ruler; one monk even wrote of his empire as the "kingdom of Europe." Charlemagne acquired a new title—emperor of the Romans—in 800, but substantial controversy surrounds this event, and it can only be understood within the context of the relationship between the papacy and the Frankish monarchs.

Already during the reign of Pepin, a growing alliance had emerged between the kingdom of the Franks and the papacy. The popes welcomed this support, and in the course of the second half of the eighth century, they severed more and more of their ties with the Byzantine Empire and drew closer to the Frankish kingdom. Charlemagne encouraged this development. In 799, after a rebellion against his authority, Pope Leo III (795–816) managed to escape from Rome and flee to safety at Charlemagne's court. Charlemagne offered assistance, and when he went to Rome in November 800 to settle affairs, he was received by the pope like an emperor. On Christmas Day in 800, after Mass, Pope Leo placed a crown on Charlemagne's head and proclaimed him emperor of the Romans.

What was the Significance of Charlemagne?   The significance of this imperial coronation has been much debated by historians. We are not even sure whether the pope or Charlemagne initiated the idea when they met in the summer of 799 in Paderborn in German lands or whether Charlemagne was pleased or displeased. His biographer Einhard claimed that "at first [he] had such an aversion that he declared that he would not have set foot in the Church the day that [it was] conferred, although it was a great feast-day, if he could have foreseen the design of the Pope."[2] But Charlemagne also perceived the usefulness of the imperial title; after all, he was now on a level of equality with the Byzantine emperor. Moreover, the papacy now had a defender of great stature, although later popes in the Middle Ages would become involved in fierce struggles with emperors over who possessed the higher power.

In any case, Charlemagne's coronation as Roman emperor certainly demonstrated the strength, even after three hundred years, of the concept of an enduring Roman Empire. More important, it symbolized the fusion of Roman, Christian, and Germanic elements. Did this fusion constitute the foundations of European civilization? A Germanic king had been crowned emperor of the Romans by the spiritual leader of western Christendom. Charlemagne had created an empire that stretched from the North Sea in the north to Italy in the south, and from France in western Europe to Vienna in central Europe. This empire differed significantly from the Roman Empire, which encompassed much of the Mediterranean world. Had a new civilization emerged? And should Charlemagne be seen, as one recent biographer has argued, as the "father of Europe"?[3] Other historians disagree and argue that there was only a weak sense of community in Europe before 1000. As one has stated, "Europe was not born in the early Middle Ages.... There was no common European culture, and certainly not any Europe-wide economy."[4]

| The Carolingian Intellectual Renewal | Charlemagne had a strong desire to revive learning in his kingdom, an attitude that stemmed from his own intellectual curiosity as well as the need to provide educated clergy for the church and literate officials for the government. His |

efforts led to a revival of learning and culture that some historians have labeled the Carolingian Renaissance, or "rebirth" of learning.

For the most part, the revival of Classical studies and the efforts to preserve Latin culture took place in the monasteries, many of which had been established by the Irish and English missionaries of the seventh and eighth centuries (see Chapter 7). By the ninth century, the work required of Benedictine monks was the copying of manuscripts. Monasteries established **scriptoria** (skrip-TOR-ee-uh), or writing rooms, where monks copied not only the works of early Christianity, such as the Bible and the treatises of the church fathers, but also the works of Classical Latin authors.

Following the example of the Irish and English monks, their Carolingian counterparts developed new ways of producing books. Their texts were written on pages made of parchment or sheepskin rather than papyrus and then bound in covers decorated with jewels and precious metals. The use of parchment made books very expensive; making a Bible required an entire herd of sheep. (Papyrus was no longer available because Egypt was in Muslim hands, and the west could no longer afford to import it.) Carolingian monastic scribes also developed a new writing style called the Carolingian minuscule. This was really hand printing rather than cursive writing and was far easier to read than the Merovingian script.

The manuscripts, some of them illustrated, that were produced in Carolingian monastic scriptoria were crucial in preserving the ancient legacy. About eight thousand manuscripts survive from Carolingian times. Some 90 percent of the ancient Roman works that we have today exist because they were copied by Carolingian monks.

Charlemagne personally promoted learning by establishing a palace school and encouraging scholars from all over Europe to come to the Carolingian court. These included men of letters from Italy, Spain, Germany, and Ireland. Best known was Alcuin (AL-kwin), from the famous school at York, founded as part of the great revival of learning in the Anglo-Saxon kingdom of Northumbria. From 782 to 796, while serving at Charlemagne's court as an adviser on ecclesiastical affairs, Alcuin also provided the leadership for the palace school. He concentrated on teaching Classical Latin and adopted Cassiodorus's sevenfold division of knowledge known as the liberal arts (see Chapter 7), which became the basis for all later medieval education.

Charlemagne's official seal carried the words "renewal of the Roman Empire." For Charlemagne, who made a number of visits to Italy, this included a revival of the arts, which meant looking to Italy for inspiration. Charlemagne encouraged his own artists to look to the arts of ancient Rome and the Byzantine Empire. The chapel he built at Aachen was modeled after the Church of San Vitale in Ravenna, a church that had been built by the emperor Justinian after his reconquest of much of Italy (see Chapter 7). All in all, the Carolingian Renaissance played an important role in keeping the Classical heritage alive.

Life in the Carolingian World   In daily life as well as intellectual life, the Europe of the Carolingian era witnessed a fusion of Roman, Germanic, and Christian practices. The last in particular seem to have exercised an ever-increasing influence.

The Family and Marriage   By Carolingian times, the Catholic Church had begun to make a significant impact on Frankish family life and marital and sexual attitudes. Marriages in Frankish society were arranged by fathers or uncles to meet the needs of the extended family. Although wives were expected to be faithful to their husbands, Frankish aristocrats often kept concubines, either slave girls or free women from their estates. Even the "most Christian king" Charlemagne had a number of concubines.

To limit such sexual license, the church increasingly emphasized its role in marriage and attempted to Christianize it. Although marriage was a civil arrangement, priests tried to add their blessings and strengthen the concept of a special marriage ceremony.

To stabilize marriages, the church also began to emphasize **monogamy** and permanence. A Frankish church council in 789 stipulated that marriage was "indissoluble" and condemned concubinage and easy divorce. During the reign of Emperor Louis the Pious (814–840), the church formally prohibited divorce. Now a husband was expected to remain with his wife "even though she were sterile, deformed, old, dirty, drunken, a frequenter of bad company, lascivious, vain, greedy, unfaithful, quarrelsome, abusive … for when that man was free, he freely engaged himself."[5] This change was not easily accepted, however, and it was not until the thirteenth century that divorce was largely stamped out among both the common people and the nobility.

Advice from a Carolingian Mother

In addition to her other responsibilities, the wife of a Carolingian aristocrat was expected to bear large numbers of children and to supervise their upbringing. This selection by Dhuoda (doo-OH-duh), wife of Bernard, marquis of Septimania (in southern France), is taken from a manual she wrote to instruct her son on his duties to his new lord, King Charles the Bald (840–877).

Dhuoda, *Handbook for William*

Direction on your comportment toward your lord.

You have Charles as your lord; you have him as lord because, as I believe, God and your father, Bernard, have chosen him for you to serve at the beginning of your career, in the flower of your youth. Remember that he comes from a great and noble lineage on both sides of his family. Serve him not only so that you please him in obvious ways, but also as one clearheaded in matters of both body and soul. Be steadfastly and completely loyal to him in all things....

This is why, my son, I urge you to keep this loyalty as long as you live, in your body and in your mind. For the advancement that it brings you will be of great value both to you and to those who in turn serve you. May the madness of treachery never, not once, make you offer an angry insult. May it never give rise in your heart to the idea of being disloyal to your lord. There is harsh and shameful talk about men who act in this fashion. I do not think that such will befall you or those who fight alongside you because such an attitude has never shown itself among your ancestors. It has not been seen among them, it is not seen now, and it will not be seen in the future.

Be truthful to your lord, my son William, child of their lineage. Be vigilant, energetic, and offer him ready assistance as I have said here. In every matter of importance to royal power take care to show yourself a man of good judgment—in your own thoughts and in public—to the extent that God gives you strength. Read the sayings and the lives of the holy Fathers who have gone before us. You will there discover how you may serve your lord and be faithful to him in all things. When you understand this, devote yourself to the faithful execution of your lord's commands. Look around as well and observe those who fight for him loyally and constantly. Learn from them how you may serve him. Then, informed by their example, with the help and support of God, you will easily reach the celestial goal I have mentioned above. And may your heavenly Lord God be generous and benevolent toward you. May he keep you safe, be your kind leader and your protector. May he deign to assist you in all your actions and be your constant defender.

Q *What advice does Dhuoda of Septimania give her son? What does this selection tell us about aristocratic women in the Early Middle Ages and their relationship with power?*

Source: Reproduced from *Handbook for William: A Carolingian Woman's Counsel for Her Son*, by Dhuoda, translated by Carol Neel, by permission of the University of Nebraska Press. Copyright © 1991 by the University of Nebraska Press.

The acceptance and spread of the Catholic Church's views on the indissolubil-
ity of marriage encouraged the development of the **nuclear family** at the expense of
the extended family. Although kinship was still an influential social and political
force, the conjugal unit came to be seen as the basic unit of society. The new practice of young couples establishing their own households had a significant impact on
women. In the extended family, the oldest woman controlled all the other female
members; in the nuclear family, the wife was still dominated by her husband, but
at least she now had control of her own household and children. In aristocratic
families, women had even more opportunity to play independent roles. The wives
of Carolingian aristocrats were often entrusted with the management of the household and even the administration of extensive landed estates while their husbands
were absent in the royal service or on a military campaign.

Christianity and Sexuality   The early church fathers had stressed that celibacy
and complete abstinence from sexual activity constituted an ideal state superior to
marriage. Subsequently, the early church gradually developed a case for clerical celibacy, although it proved impossible to enforce in the Early Middle Ages.

The early fathers had also emphasized, however, that not all people had the
self-discipline to remain celibate. It was thus permissible to marry, as Paul had indicated in his first epistle to the Corinthians: "It is good for a man not to touch a
woman. Nevertheless, to avoid fornication, let every man have his own wife, and
let every woman have her own husband.... I say therefore to the unmarried and
widows, it is good for them if they abide even as I. But if they cannot contain, let
them marry: for it is better to marry than to burn [with passion]."[6] The church thus
viewed marriage as the lesser of two evils; it was a concession to human weakness
and fulfilled the need for companionship, sex, and children. Although marriage was
the subject of much debate in the early medieval church, it was generally agreed
that marriage gave the right to indulge in sexual intercourse. Sex, then, was permissible within marriage, but only so long as it was used for the purpose of procreation, or the begetting of children, not for pleasure.

Because the church developed the tradition that sexual relations between man
and wife were legitimate only if engaged in for procreation, it condemned all
forms of contraception. The church accepted only one way to limit children:
abstinence from intercourse, either periodic or total. The church also strongly condemned abortion, although its prohibition failed to stop the practice. Various
herbal potions, whose formulas appear in writings from Roman and Byzantine
doctors, were available to prevent conception or cause abortion.

The church's condemnation of sexual activity outside marriage also included
homosexuality. Neither Roman religion nor Roman law had recognized any real
difference between homosexual and heterosexual eroticism, and the Roman Empire
had taken no legal measures against the practice of homosexuality between adults.
Later, however, in 538 the Byzantine emperor Justinian condemned homosexuality,
claiming that it brought down the wrath of God ("we have provoked Him to
anger") and endangered the welfare of the state: "For because of such crimes,
there are famines, earthquakes, and pestilences; wherefore we admonish men to
abstain from the aforesaid unlawful acts, that they may not lose their souls."[7]
Justinian recommended that the guilty parties be punished by castration. Although

the early medieval church similarly condemned homosexuality, it also pursued a flexible policy in its treatment of homosexuals. In the Early Middle Ages, homosexuals were treated less harshly than married couples who practiced contraception.

New Attitudes Toward Children   The Catholic Church also had an impact on another aspect of family life—children. The ancient Romans had limited their family size through infanticide, primarily the exposure of unwanted children, which was accepted in Classical society. The Romans then paid much attention to the children chosen to survive, as is especially evident in the education of upper-class children. In the emerging early medieval world, German practices of child rearing became influential. As we saw in Chapter 7, the Germanic law codes listed *wergelds*, whose size represented a crude evaluation of a person's importance. According to a Visigothic code of the mid-seventh century, for example, male children were valued at 60 solidi. At the age of twenty, when they had become warriors, the *wergeld* increased fivefold to 300 solidi, where it remained until the adult male reached fifty, after which it again declined. The value of females was only half that of males, although it also jumped tremendously (to 250 solidi) for women between the ages of fifteen and forty because of their importance as bearers of children.

Although the Christian church condemned infanticide, it was not able to eliminate the practice, especially among the poor and among victims of seduction who did not want to keep their illegitimate offspring. Nevertheless, priests tried to discourage such practices by urging people to abandon unwanted children in churches. Often such children were taken in by monasteries and convents and raised to be monks and nuns. Following the example of Jesus's love for children, monks and nuns tended to respect and preserve the virtues of childhood. As children grew older, however, it was thought necessary to use strict discipline to control what was considered the natural inclination of children to sin, especially by disobeying their elders.

Travel and Hospitality   Monasteries served another important function in the early medieval world as providers of hospitality. Both monasteries and aristocratic households were expected to provide a place to stay for weary travelers, who were ever at risk from thieves or violence of many kinds. Indeed, Burgundian law stipulated that "anyone who refused to offer a visitor shelter and warmth shall pay a fine of three solidi."[8] Hospitality, then, was a sacred duty, and monasteries were especially active in providing it. It was customary for monasteries to have two guest houses, one for the rich and another for the poor. The plan for the monastery of Saint Gall, for example, provided pilgrims and paupers with a house containing benches, two dormitories, and outbuildings. For travelers of high rank, there was a separate guest house with two heated rooms, servants' bedrooms, and stables for horses. One could not always be sure of hospitality in the Early Middle Ages, however. The famous English missionary to Germany, Saint Boniface, reported that female pilgrims to Rome had been forced to become prostitutes in every town along their route in order to obtain their sustenance and reach their goal. The church responded by forbidding females to go on such pilgrimages.

Diet   For both rich and poor, the main staple of the Carolingian diet was bread. The aristocratic classes, as well as the monks, consumed it in large quantities. Ovens at the monastery of Saint Gall were able to bake a thousand loaves of bread. Sometimes a gruel made of barley and oats was substituted for bread in the peasant diet.

The upper classes in Carolingian society enjoyed a much more varied diet than the peasants. Pork was the primary meat. Domestic pigs, allowed to run wild in the forests to find their own food, were collected and slaughtered in the fall, then smoked and salted to be eaten during the winter months. Because Carolingian aristocrats were especially fond of roasted meat, hunting wild game became one of their favorite activities. They ate little beef or mutton, however, because cattle were kept as dairy cows and oxen to draw plows, and sheep were raised for wool.

Dairy products were also important in the Carolingian diet. Milk, which spoiled rapidly, was made into cheese and butter. Chickens were raised for their eggs. Vegetables also formed a crucial part of the diet of both rich and poor. These included legumes, such as beans, peas, and lentils, and roots, such as garlic, onions, and carrots.

The Carolingian diet, especially of the upper classes, was also heavily dependent on honey and spices. Honey was used as a sweetener, both for foods and for many drinks, including wine and ale. Spices and herbs included domestic varieties that were grown in home gardens, such as thyme, sage, and chives, and more exotic—and outrageously expensive—varieties imported from the East, such as pepper, cumin, cloves, and cinnamon. Aristocrats enjoyed spicy dishes, not just for their taste but as a sign of prestige and wealth; spices were also believed to aid the digestion.

Gluttony and drunkenness were vices shared by many people in Carolingian society. Monastic rations were greatly enlarged in the eighth century to include a daily allotment of 3.7 pounds of bread (nuns were permitted 3 pounds), 11.2 quarts of wine or ale, 2 or 3 ounces of cheese, and 8 ounces of vegetables (4 ounces for nuns). These rations provided 6,000 calories a day, and since only heavy, fatty foods—bread, milk, and cheese—were considered nourishing, we begin to understand why some Carolingians were known for their potbellies. Malnutrition, however, remained a widespread problem for common people.

Everyone in Carolingian society, including abbots and monks, drank heavily and often to excess. Taverns became a regular feature of life and were found everywhere: in marketplaces, at pilgrimage centers, and on royal, episcopal, and monastic estates. Drinking contests were not unusual; one penitential stated: "Does drunken bravado encourage you to attempt to outdrink your friends? If so, thirty days' fast."

The aristocrats and monks favored wine above all other beverages, and much care was lavished on its production, especially by monasteries. Although ale was considered inferior in some quarters, it was especially popular in the northern and eastern parts of the Carolingian world. Water was also drunk as a beverage, but much care had to be taken to obtain pure sources from wells or clear streams.

Water was also used for bathing. Although standards of personal hygiene were not high, medieval people did not ignore cleanliness. A royal palace, such as Charlemagne's, possessed both hot and cold baths. Carolingian aristocrats changed clothes and bathed at least once a week, on Saturdays. The Saturday bath was also a regular practice in many Carolingian monasteries. To monks, bathing more than once a week seemed an unnecessary luxury; to aristocrats, it often seemed desirable.

Health　Medical practice in Carolingian times stressed the use of medicinal herbs and bleeding. Although the latter was practiced regularly, moderation was frequently recommended. Some advised carefulness as well: "Who dares to undertake a bleeding should see to it that his hand does not tremble."

Physicians were also available when people faced serious illnesses. Many were clerics, and monasteries trained their own. Monastic libraries kept medical manuscripts copied from ancient works and grew herbs to provide stocks of medicinal plants. Carolingian medical manuscripts contained scientific descriptions of illnesses, recipes for medical potions, and even gynecological advice, although monks in particular expended little effort on female medical needs. Some manuals even included instructions for operations, especially for soldiers injured in battle. Some sources clearly demonstrate that there were accurate techniques for amputating gangrenous limbs:

> If you must cut off an unhealthy limb from a healthy body, then do not cut to the limit of the healthy flesh, but cut further into the whole and quick flesh, so that a better and quicker cure may be obtained. When you set fire on the man [i.e., cauterize], take leaves of tender leek and grated salt, overlay the places so that the heat of the fire be more quickly drawn away.[9]

Bloodletting in Early Medieval Medicine.
Bleeding was a regular part of medieval medical practice. It involved the withdrawing of blood from a person in the belief that doing so would bring balance to the body and thus heal a diseased condition. This fourteenth-century manuscript illustration shows a physician bleeding his patient with a cut in the arm. As the physician squeezes the arm, the blood spurts into a bowl; the patient seems to be quite anxious about the procedure.

© British Library, London, UK/HIP/Art Resource, NY

Although scholars are not sure whether anesthesia was used for such operations, medieval manuals recommended poppy, mandrake, and henbane for their narcotic properties.

Physicians of the Early Middle Ages supplemented their medicines and natural practices with appeals for otherworldly help. Magical rites and influences were carried over from pagan times; the Germanic tribes had used magical medicine for centuries. Physicians recommended that patients wear amulets and charms around their bodies to ward off diseases:

> Procure a little bit of the dung of a wolf, preferably some which contains small bits of bone, and pack it in a tube which the patient may easily wear as an amulet.
>
> For epilepsy take a nail of a wrecked ship, make it into a bracelet and set therein the bone of a stag's heart taken from its body whilst alive; put it on the left arm; you will be astonished at the result.[10]

But as pagans were converted to Christianity, miraculous healing through the intervention of God, Jesus, or the saints soon replaced pagan practices. Medieval chronicles abound with accounts of people healed by touching a saint's body. The use of Christian prayers, written down and used as amulets, however, reminds us that for centuries Christian and pagan medical practices survived side by side.

DISINTEGRATION OF THE CAROLINGIAN EMPIRE

The Carolingian Empire began to disintegrate soon after Charlemagne's death. Charlemagne was succeeded by his son Louis the Pious. Though a decent man, Louis was not a strong ruler and was unable to control either the Frankish aristocracy or his own four sons, who fought continually. In 843, after their father's death, the three surviving brothers signed the Treaty of Verdun, which divided the Carolingian Empire among them into three major sections: Charles the Bald (843–877) obtained the western Frankish lands, which formed the core of the eventual kingdom of France; Louis the German (843–876) took the eastern lands, which became Germany; and Lothar (840–855) received the title of emperor and a "Middle Kingdom" extending from the North Sea to the Mediterranean, including the Netherlands, the Rhineland, and northern Italy. The territories of the Middle Kingdom became a source of incessant struggle between the other two Frankish rulers and their heirs. Indeed, France and Germany would fight over the territories of this Middle Kingdom for centuries.

Although this division of the Carolingian Empire was made for political reasons (dividing a kingdom among the male heirs was a traditional Frankish custom), two different cultures began to emerge. By the ninth century, inhabitants of the western Frankish area were speaking a Romance language derived from Latin that became French. Eastern Franks spoke a Germanic dialect. The later kingdoms of France and Germany did not yet exist, however. In the ninth century, the frequent struggles among the numerous heirs of the sons of Louis the Pious led to further disintegration of the Carolingian Empire. In the meantime, while powerful aristocrats acquired even more power in their own local territories at the expense of the squabbling Carolingian rulers, external attacks on different parts of the old Carolingian world added to the process of disintegration.

Invasions of the Ninth and Tenth Centuries　In the ninth and tenth centuries, western Europe was beset by a wave of invasions by several non-Christian peoples—one old enemy, the Muslims, and two new ones, the Magyars (MAG-yarz) and the Vikings (see Map 8.2). The Muslims began a new series of attacks in the Mediterranean in the ninth century. They raided the southern coasts of Europe, especially Italy, and even threatened Rome in 843. Their invasion of Sicily in 827 eventually led to a successful occupation of the island. Muslim forces also destroyed the Carolingian defenses in northern Spain and conducted forays into southern France.

The Magyars were a people from western Asia who moved into eastern and central Europe by the end of the ninth century. They established themselves on the plains of Hungary and from there made raids into western Europe. The Magyars were finally crushed at the Battle of Lechfeld (LEK-feld) in Germany in 955. At the end of the tenth century, they were converted to Christianity and settled down to establish the kingdom of Hungary.

© Cengage Learning 2012

MAP 8.2　Invasions of the Ninth and Tenth Centuries

Attacks by invading Vikings, Magyars, and Muslims terrorized much of Europe in the ninth and tenth centuries, disrupting economic activity and spurring the development of fief-holding. The Vikings were the biggest problem, but they eventually formed settlements, converted to Christianity, and were assimilated.

The Vikings Invade England

Near the end of the ninth century, a number of monks in England began to compile a series of chronicles, or yearly records of events. Although there are several chronicles, they have come to be known as the *Anglo-Saxon Chronicle*. Although much of the chronicle focuses on politics, there are also numerous accounts of events of immediate concern to the monks, such as the death of a bishop or inclement weather conditions. This selection from the *Anglo-Saxon Chronicle* focuses on the Danish Viking invasions of England. These selections, taken from the accounts for the years 994, 997, 998, 999, and 1003, show how regular and devastating the Viking invasions were.

Anglo-Saxon Chronicle

994. Olaf and Swein came to London, on the Nativity of St. Mary, with ninety-four ships, fighting constantly the city, and they meant, moreover, to set it on fire. But they there suffered more harm and evil than they ever believed any town-dwellers could have done them. In this God's holy mother showed her mercy to the town-dwellers and delivered them from their enemies; then they went from there, and wrought the most evil that any force had ever done, in burning, ravaging and killing, both along the seacoast, in Essex, and in Kent, Sussex and Hampshire; finally they seized horses for themselves, and rode as widely as they would, working unspeakable evil.

997. The Danes went around Devonshire into the mouth of the Severn, and there ravaged in Cornwall, Wales and Devon. Then they put in at Watchet and did much evil by burning and slaughtering. After that, they went around Land's End again on the south side, and went into the mouth of the Tamar, continuing up until they came to Lydford, burning or killing each thing they met—they burnt down Ordulf's monastery at Tavistock, and brought with them to their ships indescribable plunder.

The Vikings By far the most devastating and far-reaching attacks came from the Northmen or Norsemen of Scandinavia, also known to us as the Vikings. The Vikings were a Germanic people based in Scandinavia and constitute, in a sense, the final wave of Germanic migration. Why they began to move is not very clear to historians. One common explanation focuses on overpopulation, although recent research indicates that this may have been true only in western Norway. Other reasons have included the Vikings' great love of adventure and their search for wealth and new avenues of trade.

Two features of Viking society help explain what the Vikings accomplished. First of all, they were warriors. Second, they were superb shipbuilders and sailors. Their ships were the best of the period. Long and narrow with beautifully carved arched prows, the Viking dragon ships carried about fifty men. They had banks of oars as well as a single great sail. Their shallow draft enabled them to sail up European rivers and attack places at some distance inland. Although Viking raids in the eighth century tended to be small-scale and sporadic, they became more regular and more devastating in the ninth. Vikings sacked villages and towns, destroyed churches, and easily defeated small local armies. Viking attacks frightened people

998. The force went eastward again into the mouth of the Frome, and went inland as widely as they pleased into Dorset. Troops were often gathered against them, but as soon as they should have come together, always, in some way, flight was ordered, and they always had the victory in the end. Another time they settled themselves on the Isle of Wight, and fed themselves from Hampshire and Sussex.

999. The force came again into the Thames, and went up along Medway to Rochester; there the Kentish troops came against them, and they came together resolutely. But alas, they moved too quickly, and fled because they had not the help they should have had—then the Danes had the power of the battlefield, seized horses, and rode as widely as they pleased. They ravaged and destroyed nearly all West Kent.

1003. Exeter was ruined, because of the Frankish peasant Hugh, whom the lady had set up as her reeve [local official]; the Danish force destroyed the town completely, and took much booty.

A very great army was gathered from Wiltshire and Hampshire, and went very resolutely against the force. The ealdorman [town official] Aelfric should have led the army, but he displayed his old wiles. As soon as they were close enough to look on one another, he feigned sickness, and began retching to vomit, and said that he was taken ill; so he betrayed the people he should have led, as it is said: "When the war-leader weakens, all the army is greatly hindered." When Swein saw that they were not resolute, and all scattering, he led his force into Wilton, ravaged and burnt the borough, went to Salisbury, and from there went back to the sea, where he knew his wave-coursers were.

Q *What do you think were the tactics of the Viking invaders? How would you know from these accounts that the Chronicle was written by monks?*

Source: From THE ANGLO-SAXON CHRONICLES (New York: St. Martin's, 1982), translated by Anne Savage, pp. 994, 997, 998, 999, 1003. Reprinted by permission of the translator.

and led many a clergyman to exhort his parishioners to change their behavior to appease God's anger, as in this sermon by an English archbishop in 1014:

Things have not gone well now for a long time at home or abroad, but there has been devastation and persecution in every district again and again, and the English have been for a long time now completely defeated and too greatly disheartened through God's anger; and the pirates [Vikings] so strong with God's consent that often in battle one puts to flight ten, and sometimes less, sometimes more, all because of our sins.... We pay them continually and they humiliate us daily; they ravage and they burn, plunder, and rob and carry on board; and lo, what else is there in all these events except God's anger clear and visible over this people?[11]

Because there were different groups of Scandinavians, Viking expansion varied a great deal. Norwegian Vikings moved into Ireland and western England; Danes attacked eastern England, Frisia, and the Rhineland and navigated rivers to enter western Frankish lands. Swedish Vikings dominated the Baltic Sea and progressed into the Slavic areas to the east. Moving into northwestern Russia, they went down the rivers of Russia to Novgorod and Kiev and established fortified ports throughout these territories. There they made contact with the Byzantine Empire,

The Vikings Attack England. *An illustration from an eleventh-century English manuscript depicts a group of armed Vikings invading England. Two ships have already reached the shore, and a few Vikings are shown walking down a long gangplank onto English soil.*

either as traders or as invaders. They also made contact with Arab traders on the Volga River and the Sea of Azov.

Early Viking raids had been carried out largely in the summer; by the mid-ninth century, however, the Norsemen had begun to establish winter settlements in Europe from which they could make expeditions to conquer and settle new lands. By 850, groups of Norsemen had settled in Ireland, and the Danes occupied an area known as the Danelaw in northeastern England by 878. Agreeing to accept Christianity, the Danes were eventually assimilated into a larger Anglo-Saxon kingdom. Beginning in 911, the ruler of the western Frankish lands gave one band of Vikings land at the mouth of the Seine River, forming a section of France that ultimately came to be known as Normandy. This policy of settling the Vikings and converting them to Christianity was a deliberate one, since the new inhabitants served as protectors against additional Norseman attacks.

The Vikings were also daring explorers. After 860, they sailed westward in their long ships across the North Atlantic Ocean, reaching Iceland in 874. Erik the Red, a Viking exiled from Iceland, traveled even farther west and discovered Greenland in 985. A Viking site has also been found in Newfoundland in North America.

By the tenth century, Viking expansion was drawing to a close. Greater control by the monarchs of Denmark, Norway, and Sweden over their inhabitants and the increasing Christianization of the Scandinavian kings and peoples tended to inhibit Viking expansion, but not before Viking settlements had been established in many parts of Europe. Like the Magyars, the Vikings were assimilated into European civilization. Once again, Christianity proved a decisive civilizing force. Europe and Christianity were becoming virtually synonymous.

The Viking raids and settlements also had important political repercussions. The inability of royal authorities to stem these incursions caused local populations to turn instead to local aristocrats for protection. As a result, the landed aristocrats not only increased their strength and prestige but also assumed even more of the functions of local government that had previously belonged to the kings; over time these developments led to a new political and military order.

THE EMERGING WORLD OF LORDS AND VASSALS

The renewed invasions and the disintegration of the Carolingian Empire led to the emergence of a new type of relationship between free individuals. When governments ceased to be able to defend their subjects, it became important to find some powerful lord who could offer protection in exchange for service. The contract sworn between a lord and his subordinate is the basis of a form of social organization that later generations of historians called *feudalism*. But feudalism was never a system, and many historians today prefer to avoid using the term.

Vassalage   The practice of **vassalage** was derived from Germanic society, in which warriors swore an oath of loyalty to their leader. They fought for their chief, and he in turn took care of their needs. By the eighth century, an individual who served a lord in a military capacity was known as a *vassal*.

Both the breakdown of governments, which allowed powerful nobles to take control of large areas of land, and a change in fighting techniques contributed to this process. The Frankish army had originally consisted of foot soldiers, dressed in coats of mail and armed with swords. But with the introduction of larger horses and the stirrup in the eighth century, a military change began to occur. Earlier, horsemen had been throwers of spears. Now they wore armored coats of mail (the larger horse could carry the weight) and wielded long lances that enabled them to act as battering rams (the stirrups kept the riders on their horses). For almost five hundred years, warfare in Europe would be dominated by heavily armored cavalry, or *knights*, as they came to be called.

Of course, a horse, armor, and weapons were expensive to purchase and maintain, and learning to wield these instruments skillfully from horseback took much time and practice. Consequently, lords who wanted men to fight for them had to grant each vassal a piece of land that provided for the support of the vassal and his family. In return for the land, the vassal provided his lord with one major service, his fighting skills. Each needed the other. In the society of the Early Middle Ages, where there was little trade and wealth was based primarily on land ownership, land became the most important gift a lord could give to a vassal in return for military service.

The relationship between lord and vassal was made official by a public ceremony. To become a vassal, a man performed an act of homage to his lord, as described in this passage from a medieval treatise on law:

> The man should put his hands together as a sign of humility, and place them between the two hands of his lord as a token that he vows everything to him and promises faith to him; and the lord should receive him and promise to keep faith with him. Then the man should say: "Sir, I enter your homage and faith and become your man by mouth and hands [i.e., by taking the oath and placing his hands between those of the lord], and I swear and promise to keep faith and loyalty to you against all others, and to guard your rights with all my strength.[12]

As in the earlier Germanic band, loyalty to one's lord was the chief virtue.

Fief-Holding   The land or some other type of income granted to a vassal in return for military service came to be known as a **fief** (FEEF). In time, many vassals who held such grants of land came to exercise rights of jurisdiction or political and legal authority within their fiefs. As the Carolingian world disintegrated politically under the impact of dissension within and invasions from without, an increasing number of powerful lords arose. Instead of a single government, many people were now responsible for keeping order. In some areas of France, for example, some lords—called *castellans*—constructed castles and asserted their authority to collect taxes and dispense justice to the local population. Lack of effective central control led to ever-larger numbers of castles and castellans.

Fief-holding also became increasingly complicated as **subinfeudation** developed. The vassals of a king, who were themselves great lords, might also have vassals who would owe them military service in return for a grant of land from their estates. Those vassals, in turn, might likewise have vassals, who at such a level would be simple knights with barely enough land to provide their equipment. The lord-vassal relationship, then, bound together both greater and lesser landowners. Historians used to speak of a hierarchy with the king at the top, greater lords on the next level, lesser lords on the next, and simple knights at the bottom; this was only a model, however, and rarely reflected reality. Such a hierarchy implies a king at the top. The reality in the tenth-century west Frankish kingdom was that the Capetian kings (see "New Political Configurations in the Tenth Century" later in this chapter) actually controlled only the region around Paris. They possessed little real power over the great lords who held fiefs throughout France.

The lord-vassal relationship at all levels always constituted an honorable relationship between free men and did not imply any sense of servitude. Since kings could no longer provide security in the midst of the breakdown created by the invasions of the ninth century, subinfeudation became ever more widespread. With their rights of jurisdiction, fiefs gave lords virtual possession of the rights of government.

The new practice of lordship was basically a product of the Carolingian world, but it also spread to England, Germany, and central Europe, and in modified form to Italy. Fief-holding came to be characterized by a set of practices worked out in the course of the tenth century, although they became more prominent after 1000. These practices included a series of mutual obligations of lord toward vassal and vassal toward lord, but it is crucial to remember that such obligations varied considerably from place to place and even from fief to fief. As usual, practice almost always diverged from theory.

Mutual Obligations   Because the basic objective of fief-holding was to provide military support, it is no surprise to learn that the major obligation of a vassal to his lord was to perform military service. In addition to his own personal service, a great lord was also responsible for providing a group of knights for the king's army. Moreover, vassals had to furnish suit at court; this meant that a vassal was obliged to appear at his lord's court when summoned, either to give advice to the lord or to sit in judgment in a legal case, since the important vassals of a lord were peers, and only they could judge each other. Many vassals were also obliged to provide hospitality for their lord when he stayed at a vassal's castle. This obligation was especially important to medieval kings because they tended to be itinerant. Finally, vassals were responsible for aids, or financial payments, to the lord on a number of occasions, including the knighting of the lord's eldest son, the marriage of his eldest daughter, and the ransom of the lord's person if he was held captive.

In turn, a lord had responsibilities toward his vassals. His major obligation was to protect his vassal, either by defending him militarily or by taking his side in a court of law if necessary. The lord was also responsible for the maintenance of the vassal, usually by granting him a fief.

As this system of mutual obligations between lord and vassal evolved, certain practices became common. If a lord acted improperly toward his vassal, the bond between them could be dissolved. Likewise, if a vassal failed to fulfill his vow of loyalty, he was subject to forfeiture of his fief. Upon a vassal's death, his fief theoretically reverted to the lord, since it had been granted to the vassal for use, not as a possession. In practice, however, by the tenth century fiefs tended to be hereditary. Following the principle of primogeniture (pry-muh-JEN-ih-chur), the eldest son inherited the father's fief. If a vassal died without heirs, the lord could reclaim the fief.

New Political Configurations in the Tenth Century

In the tenth century, Europe began to recover from the invasions of the century before. The disintegration of the Carolingian Empire and the emergence of great and powerful lords soon produced new political configurations.

The Eastern Franks   In the east Frankish kingdom, the last Carolingian king died in 911, whereupon local rulers, especially the powerful dukes (the title of *duke* is derived from the Latin word *dux*, meaning "leader") of the Saxons, Swabians, Bavarians, Thuringians, and Franconians, who exercised much power in their large dukedoms, elected one of their own number, Conrad of Franconia, to serve as king of Germany (as we think of it) or of the eastern Franks (as contemporaries thought of it). But Conrad did not last long, and after his death, the German dukes chose Henry the Fowler, duke of Saxony, as the new king of Germany (919–936). The first of the Saxon dynasty of German kings, Henry was not particularly successful in creating a unified eastern Frankish kingdom because he lacked the resources to impose effective rule over the entire area.

The best known of the Saxon kings of Germany was Henry's son, Otto I (936–973). He defeated the Magyars at the Battle of Lechfeld in 955 and encouraged an ongoing program of Christianization of both the Slavic and the Scandinavian peoples. Even more than his father, he relied on bishops and abbots in governing his kingdom. This practice was in part a response to the tendency of the lay lords to build up their power at the expense of the king. Since the clergy were theoretically celibate, bishops and abbots could not make their offices hereditary, thus allowing the king to maintain more control over them.

Otto also intervened in Italian politics and for his efforts was crowned emperor of the Romans by the pope in 962, reviving a title that had fallen into disuse with the disintegration of Charlemagne's empire. Once again a pope had conferred the Roman imperial title on a king of the Franks, even though he was a Saxon king of the eastern Franks. Otto's creation of a new "Roman Empire" in the hands of the eastern Franks (or Germans) added a tremendous burden to the kingship of Germany. To the difficulties of governing Germany was appended the onerous task of ruling Italy as well. It proved a formidable and ultimately impossible task.

The Western Franks   In the ninth and tenth centuries, the Carolingian kings had little success in controlling the great lords of the western Frankish kingdom. The counts, who were supposed to serve as the chief administrative officials, often paid little attention to the wishes of the Carolingian kings. In 987, when the Carolingian king died, the western Frankish nobles and chief prelates of the church chose Hugh Capet (YOO ka-PAY), count of Orléans and Paris, as the new king (987–996).

The nobles who elected Hugh Capet did not intend to establish a new royal dynasty. After all, although Hugh was officially king of the western Franks and overlord of the great nobles of the kingdom, his own family controlled only the Île-de-France (eel-duh-FRAHNS), the region around Paris. Other French nobles possessed lands equal to or greater than those of the Capetians and assumed that the king would be content to live off the revenues of his personal lands and not impose any burdensome demands on the nobility. Hugh Capet did succeed in making his position hereditary, however. He asked the nobles, and they agreed, to choose his eldest son, Robert, as his anointed associate in case Hugh died on a campaign to Spain in 987. And although Hugh Capet could not know it then, the Capetian (kuh-PEE-shun) dynasty would rule the western Frankish kingdom, or France, as it eventually came to be known, for centuries. In the late tenth century, however, the territory that would become France was not a unified kingdom but a loose alliance of powerful lords who treated the king as an equal. They assisted him only when it was in their own interests to do so.

Anglo-Saxon England   England's development in the ninth and tenth centuries took a course somewhat different from that of the Frankish kingdoms. The long struggle of the Anglo-Saxon kingdoms against the Viking invasions ultimately produced a unified kingdom. Alfred the Great, king of Wessex (871–899), played a crucial role. He defeated a Danish army in 879, according to an account by Asser, his adviser, who wrote a biography of the king:

> [Alfred] gained the victory through God's will. He destroyed the Vikings with great slaughter, and pursued those who fled as far as the stronghold, hacking them down; he seized everything which he found outside the stronghold—men (whom he killed immediately), horses and cattle—and boldly made camp in front of the gate of the Viking

stronghold with all his army. When he had been there for fourteen days the Vikings, thoroughly terrified by hunger, cold and fear, and in the end by despair, sought peace.[13]

Alfred eventually made peace with the Danes in 886 after strengthening his army and creating a navy.

Alfred also believed in the power of education. He invited scholars to his court and encouraged the translation of the works of such church fathers as Augustine and Gregory the Great from Latin into Anglo-Saxon (Old English), the vernacular, or the language spoken by the people. Old English was also soon used for official correspondence as well. Alfred's successors reconquered the remaining areas occupied by the Danes and established a unified Anglo-Saxon monarchy. By the time of King Edgar (959–975), Anglo-Saxon England had a well-developed and strong monarchical government. Although the kingship was elective, only descendants of Alfred were chosen for the position. In the counties or *shires*, the administrative units into which England was divided, the king was assisted by an agent appointed and controlled by him, the shire-reeve or sheriff. An efficient chancery or writing office was responsible for issuing writs (or royal letters) conveying the king's orders to the sheriffs.

The Manorial System   The landholding class of nobles and knights comprised a military elite whose ability to function as warriors depended on having the leisure time to pursue the arts of war. Landed estates worked by a dependent peasant class provided the economic sustenance that made this way of life possible. A **manor** (see Map 8.3) was simply an agricultural

MAP 8.3 A Typical Manor

The manorial system created small, tightly knit communities in which peasants were economically and physically bound to their lord. Crops were rotated, with roughly one-third of the fields lying fallow at any one time, which helped replenish soil nutrients (see Chapter 9).

estate operated by a lord and worked by peasants. Lords provided protection; peasants gave up their freedom, became tied to the lord's land, and provided labor services for him.

Manorialism grew out of the unsettled circumstances of the Early Middle Ages, when small farmers often needed protection or food in a time of bad harvests. Free peasants gave up their freedom to the lords of large landed estates in return for protection and use of the lord's land. Although a large class of free peasants continued to exist, increasing numbers of them became bound to the land as serfs. Unlike slaves, **serfs** could not be bought and sold, but they were subservient to their lords in a variety of ways. Serfs were required to provide labor services, pay rents, and be subject to the lord's jurisdiction. By the ninth century, probably 60 percent of the population of western Europe had become serfs.

A serf's labor services consisted of working the lord's **demesne** (duh-MAYN *or* duh-MEEN), the land retained by the lord, which might encompass one-third to one-half of the cultivated lands scattered throughout the manor (the rest would have been allotted to the serfs for their maintenance), as well as building barns and digging ditches. Although labor requirements varied from manor to manor and person to person, a common work obligation was three days a week.

The serfs paid rent by giving their lord a share of every product they raised. Serfs also paid the lord for the use of the manor's common pasturelands, streams, ponds, and surrounding woodlands. For example, if tenants fished in the pond or stream on a manor, they turned over part of the catch to their lord. For grazing a cow in the common pasture, a serf paid a rent in cheese produced from the cow's milk. Serfs were also obliged to pay a **tithe** (a tenth of their produce) to their local village church.

Lords also possessed a variety of legal rights over their serfs. Serfs were legally bound to the lord's land; they could not leave without his permission. Although free to marry, serfs could not marry anyone outside their manor without the lord's approval. Moreover, lords sometimes exercised public rights or political authority on their lands. This gave the lord the right to try serfs in his own court, although only for lesser crimes (called "low justice"). In fact, the lord's manorial court provided the only law that most serfs knew. Finally, the lord's political authority enabled him to establish monopolies on certain services that provided additional revenues. Serfs could be required to bring their grain to the lord's mill and pay a fee to have it ground into flour. Thus, the rights a lord possessed on his manor gave him virtual control over both the lives and the property of his serfs.

The administration of manors varied considerably. If the lord of a manor was a simple knight, he would probably live on the estate and supervise it in person. Great lords possessed many manors and relied on a steward or bailiff to run each estate. Note that manors were controlled not only by lay lords but also by monasteries and cathedral churches. Monasteries tended to be far more conscientious about keeping accurate records of their manorial estates than lay lords, and their surveys provide some of the best sources of information on medieval village life. The relationship between manors and villages was highly variable. A single village might constitute a manor, or a large manor might encompass several villages.

In the Early Middle Ages, the vast majority of men and women, free or unfree—possibly as many as 90 percent—worked the land. This period had witnessed a precipitous decline in trade. Coins and jewelry were often hoarded, and at the local level, goods were frequently bartered because so few coins were in circulation. But trade never entirely disappeared. Even in an agrarian society, surplus products could be exchanged at local markets. More significant, however, was that both aristocrats and wealthy clerics desired merchandise not produced locally, such as spices, silk cloth, wine, and gold and silver jewelry, and it took trade to obtain these items.

Much of the trade in luxury goods, especially beginning in the ninth century, was conducted with the Byzantine Empire, particularly the city of Constantinople, and the Islamic caliphs of Baghdad. Products from the west included iron, timber, furs, and slaves (many from eastern Europe, including captured Slavs, from whom the modern word *slave* is derived). Traders, often Jews, carried goods by boat on European rivers or on caravans with horses or mules. An Arab geographer of the ninth century left this account of Jewish traders from southern France:

> [They] speak Arabic, Persian, Greek, Frankish, Spanish, and Slavonic. They travel from west to east and from east to west, by land and by sea. From the west they bring eunuchs, slavegirls, boys, brocade, marten and other furs, and swords. They take ship from Frankland in the western Mediterranean sea and land at Farama, whence they take their merchandise on camel-back to Qulzum.... Then they sail on the eastern [Red] sea from Qulzum, and onward to India and China. From China they bring back musk, aloes, camphor, cinnamon, and other products of those parts, and return to Qulzum. Then they transport them to Farama and sail again on the western sea. Some sail with their goods to Constantinople and sell them to the Greeks, and some take them to the king of the Franks and sell them there.[14]

By 900, Italian merchants, especially the Venetians, were entering the trade picture. Overall, however, compared with the Byzantine Empire or Muslim caliphates, western Europe in the Early Middle Ages was an underdeveloped, predominantly agrarian society and could not begin to match the splendor of either of the other heirs of the Roman Empire.

THE ZENITH OF BYZANTINE CIVILIZATION

In the seventh and eighth centuries, the Byzantine Empire had lost much of its territory to Slavs, Bulgars, and Muslims. By 750, the empire consisted only of Asia Minor, some lands in the Balkans, and the southern coast of Italy. Although Byzantium was beset with internal dissension and invasions in the ninth century, it was able to deal with them and not only endured but even expanded, reaching its high point in the tenth century, which some historians have called the golden age of Byzantine civilization.

During the reign of Michael III (842–867), the Byzantine Empire began to experience a revival. Iconoclasm was finally abolished in 843, and reforms were made in education, church life, the military, and the peasant economy. There was a noticeable intellectual renewal. But the Byzantine Empire under Michael was still plagued by persistent problems. The Bulgars mounted new attacks, and the Arabs continued to harass the empire. Moreover, a new church problem with political repercussions erupted over differences between the pope as leader of the western Christian church and the patriarch of Constantinople as leader of the eastern (or Orthodox) Christian church. Patriarch Photius (FOH-shuss) condemned the pope as a heretic for accepting a revised form of the Nicene Creed stating that the Holy Spirit proceeded from the Father and the Son instead of "the Holy Spirit, who proceeds from the Father." A council of eastern bishops followed Photius's wishes and excommunicated the pope, creating the so-called Photian schism. Although the differences were later papered over, this controversy served to further the division between the eastern and western Christian churches.

The Macedonian Dynasty
The problems that arose during Michael's reign were effectively dealt with by a new dynasty of Byzantine emperors known as the Macedonians (867–1056). This dynastic line managed to hold off the external enemies, go over to the offensive, and reestablish domestic order. Supported by the church, the emperors thought of the Byzantine Empire as a continuation of the Christian Roman Empire of late antiquity. Although for diplomatic reasons they occasionally recognized the imperial title of western emperors, such as Charlemagne, they still regarded them as little more than barbarian parvenus.

The Macedonian emperors could boast of a remarkable number of achievements in the late ninth and tenth centuries. They worked to strengthen the position of the free farmers, who felt threatened by the attempts of landed aristocrats to expand their estates at the expense of the farmers. The emperors were well aware that the free farmers made up the rank and file of the Byzantine cavalry and provided the military strength of the empire. The Macedonian emperors also fostered a burst of economic prosperity by expanding trade relations with western Europe, especially by selling silks and metalwork. Thanks to this prosperity, the city of Constantinople flourished. Foreign visitors continued to be astounded by its size, wealth, and physical surroundings. To western Europeans, it was the stuff of legends and fables.

In the midst of this prosperity, Byzantine cultural influence expanded due to the active missionary efforts of eastern Byzantine Christians. Eastern Orthodox Christianity was spread to eastern European peoples, such as the Bulgars and Serbs. Perhaps the greatest missionary success occurred when the prince of Kiev in Russia converted to Christianity in 987.

Under the Macedonian rulers, Byzantium enjoyed a strong civil service, talented emperors, and military advances. The Byzantine civil service was staffed by well-educated, competent aristocrats from Constantinople who oversaw the collection of taxes, domestic administration, and foreign policy. At the same time, the Macedonian dynasty produced some truly outstanding emperors skilled in administration and law, including Leo VI (886–912) and Basil II (976–1025). In the tenth century, competent emperors combined with a number of talented generals to mobilize the empire's military resources and take the offensive. The Bulgars were defeated, and both the eastern and western parts of Bulgaria were annexed to the empire. The Byzantines went on to add the islands of Crete and Cyprus to the empire and defeat the Muslim forces in Syria, expanding the empire to the upper Euphrates. By the end of the reign of Basil II in 1025, the Byzantine Empire was the largest it had been since the beginning of the seventh century.

Women in Byzantium   In Byzantium, as in western Europe, women were regarded as inferior to men, and at times, even considered to be the instrument of the devil. In general, women were expected to remain at home. They could leave to shop, visit parents, and take part in civic celebrations, but they were supposed to wear veils on these occasions.

Women were generally expected to fulfill three major functions: to marry and bear children, to maintain the household, and to weave clothes for their families. Thus, a good wife was seen as a special gift to her husband. Contrary to these ideal female roles, some women in the Byzantine world worked outside the home as artisans and sellers, especially of foodstuffs, in the markets of Constantinople. Others served as midwives, bakers, cooks, or dancers, although some dancers also worked as prostitutes.

Upper-class women had greater opportunities to play important roles in the empire. Some aristocratic wives funded the establishment of monasteries, occupied important positions at court, and patronized the arts. Imperial wives could exercise considerable political power as regents for their sons; some even became empresses in their own right. Irene, for example, served as regent for her son until 797 when she blinded and deposed him; she then ruled in her own right until her death in 802.

THE SLAVIC PEOPLES OF CENTRAL AND EASTERN EUROPE

North of Byzantium and east of the Carolingian Empire lay a spacious plain through which a number of Asiatic nomads, including the Huns, Bulgars, Avars, and Magyars, had pushed their way westward, terrorizing and plundering the settled peasant communities. Eastern Europe was ravaged by these successive waves of invaders, who found it relatively easy to create large empires that were in turn overthrown by the next invaders. Over a period of time, the invaders themselves were largely assimilated by the native Slavic peoples of the area.

The Slavic peoples were originally a single people in central and eastern Europe who through mass migrations and nomadic invasions were gradually divided into three major groups: the western, southern, and eastern Slavs (see Map 8.4).

Western Slavs   In the region east of the eastern Frankish or Germanic kingdom emerged the Polish and Bohemian kingdoms of the western Slavs. The Germans assumed responsibility for the conversion of these Slavic peoples because German emperors considered it their duty to spread Christianity to the "barbarians." Of course, it also gave them the opportunity to extend their political authority. German missionaries had converted the Czechs in Bohemia by the end of the ninth century, and a bishopric eventually occupied by a Czech bishop was established at Prague in the tenth century. The Slavs in Poland were not converted until the reign of Prince Mieszko (MYESH-koh) (c. 960–992). In 1000, an independent Polish archbishopric was set up at Gniezno by the pope. The non-Slavic kingdom of Hungary, which emerged after the Magyars settled down after their defeat at Lechfeld in 955, was also converted to Christianity by German missionaries. Saint Stephen, king of Hungary from 997 to 1038, facilitated the acceptance of Christianity by his people. The Poles, Czechs, and Hungarians all accepted Catholic or western Christianity and became closely tied to the Roman Catholic Church and its Latin culture.

MAP 8.4 The Migrations of the Slavs

Originally from east-central Europe, the Slavic people broke into three groups. The western Slavs converted to Catholic Christianity, while the eastern Slavs and southern Slavs, under the influence of the Byzantine Empire, embraced the Eastern Orthodox faith.

Southern Slavs   The southern and eastern Slavic populations largely took a different path because of their proximity to the Byzantine Empire. The southern Slavic peoples were converted to the Eastern Orthodox Christianity of the Byzantine Empire by two Byzantine missionary brothers, Cyril and Methodius, who began their activities in 863. They created a Slavonic (Cyrillic) alphabet, translated the Bible into Slavonic, and developed Slavonic church services. Although the southern Slavic peoples accepted Christianity, a split eventually developed between the Croats, who accepted the Roman church, and the Serbs, who remained loyal to eastern Christianity.

Although the Bulgars were originally an Asiatic people who conquered much of the Balkan peninsula, they were eventually absorbed by the larger native southern Slavic population. Together, by the ninth century, they formed a largely Slavic Bulgarian kingdom. Although the conversion to Christianity of this state was complicated by the rivalry between the Roman Catholic and Eastern Orthodox

Churches, the Bulgarians eventually accepted the latter. By the end of the ninth century, they embraced the Slavonic church services earlier developed by Cyril and Methodius. The acceptance of Eastern Orthodoxy by the southern Slavic peoples, the Serbs and Bulgarians, meant that their cultural life was also linked to the Byzantine state.

Eastern Slavs   The eastern Slavic peoples, from whom the modern Russians, White Russians (Byelorussians), and Ukrainians are descended, had settled in the territory of present-day Ukraine and European Russia. There, beginning in the late eighth century, they began to contend with Viking invaders. Swedish Vikings, known to the eastern Slavs as Varangians, moved down the extensive network of rivers into the lands of the eastern Slavs in search of booty and new trade routes. After establishing trading links with the Byzantine state, the Varangians built trading settlements, became involved in the civil wars among the Slavic peoples, and eventually came to dominate the native peoples, just as their fellow Vikings were doing in parts of western Europe. According to the traditional version of the story, the semilegendary Rurik (ROO-rik) secured his ruling dynasty in the Slavic settlement of Novgorod (NAHV-guh-rahd) in 862. Rurik and his fellow Vikings were called the Rus (ROOSS *or* ROOSH), from which the name that eventually became attached to the state they founded, Russia, is derived. Although much about Rurik is unclear, it is certain that his follower Oleg (c. 873–913) took up residence in Kiev (KEE-yev) and created the Rus state, a union of eastern Slavic territories known as the principality of Kiev. Oleg's successors extended their control over the eastern Slavs and expanded the territory of Kiev until it encompassed the lands between the Baltic and Black Seas and the Danube and Volga Rivers. By marrying Slavic wives, the Viking ruling class was gradually assimilated into the Slavic population, a process confirmed by their assumption of Slavic names.

The growth of the principality of Kiev attracted religious missionaries, especially from the Byzantine Empire. One Rus ruler, Vladimir (c. 980–1015), married the Byzantine emperor's sister and officially accepted Christianity for himself and his people in 987. His primary motive was probably not spiritual. By all accounts, Vladimir was a cruel and vicious man who believed an established church would be helpful in developing an organized state. From the end of the tenth century on, Byzantine Christianity became the model for Russian religious life, just as Byzantine imperial ideals came to influence the outward forms of Russian political life.

Women in the Slavic World   As in western Europe, women in central and eastern Europe were subordinated to men and expected to focus their lives on their families, nurturing their children, providing food and clothing, and helping their husbands and fathers. Female labor thus made up a significant part of the early medieval economy in the Slavic world. In the centuries after 1000, more opportunities for women became available, especially for aristocratic women. Beginning in the eleventh century, for example, noble women in Russia could administer the household and the family's property.

A Muslim's Description of the Rus

Despite the difficulties that travel presented, early medieval civilization did witness some contact among the various cultures. This might occur through trade, diplomacy, or the conquest and migration of peoples. This document is a description of the Swedish Rus who eventually merged with the native Slavic peoples to form the principality of Kiev, commonly regarded as the first Russian state. This account was written by Ibn Fadlan, a Muslim diplomat sent from Baghdad in 921 to a settlement on the Volga River. His comments on the filthiness of the Rus reflect the Muslim emphasis on cleanliness.

Ibn Fadlan, *Description of the Rus*

I saw the Rus folk when they arrived on their trading-mission and settled at the river Atul (Volga). Never had I seen people of more perfect physique. They are tall as date-palms, and reddish in color. They wear neither coat nor kaftan, but each man carried a cape which covers one half of his body, leaving one hand free. No one is ever parted from his ax, sword, and knife. Their swords are Frankish in design, broad, flat, and fluted. Each man has a number of trees, figures, and the like from the fingernails to the neck. Each woman carried on her bosom a container made of iron, silver, copper or gold—its size and substance depending on her man's wealth....

They [the Rus] are the filthiest of God's creatures. They do not wash after discharging their natural functions, neither do they wash their hands after meals. They are as lousy as donkeys.

They arrive from their distant river, and there they build big houses on its shores. Ten or twenty of them may live together in one house, and each of them has a couch of his own where he sits and diverts himself with the pretty slave girls whom he had brought along for sale. He will make love with one of them while a comrade looks on; sometimes they indulge in a communal orgy, and, if a customer should turn up to buy a girl, the Rus man will not let her go till he has finished with her.

They wash their hands and faces every day in incredibly filthy water. Every morning the girl brings her master a large bowl of water in which he washes his hands and face and hair, then blows his nose into it and spits into it. When he has finished the girl takes the bowl to his neighbor—who repeats the performance. Thus, the bowl goes the rounds of the entire household....

If one of the Rus folk falls sick they put him in a tent by himself and leave bread and water for him. They do not visit him, however, or speak to him, especially if he is a serf. Should he recover he rejoins the others; if he dies they burn him. But if he happens to be a serf they leave him for the dogs and vultures to devour. If they catch a robber they hang him to a tree until he is torn to shreds by wind and weather.

Q *What was Ibn Fadlan's impression of the Rus? Why do you think he was so critical of their behavior?*

Source: From THE VIKINGS by Johannes Brøndsted, translated by Kalle Skov (Penguin Books, 1965) copyright © Johannes Brøndsted, 1960, 1965. Reproduced by permission of Penguin Books Ltd.

THE EXPANSION OF ISLAM

The Umayyad dynasty of caliphs had established Damascus as the center of an Islamic empire created by Arab expansion in the seventh and eighth centuries. But Umayyad rule aroused resentment, and the Umayyads' corrupt behavior also helped bring about their end. One caliph, for example, supposedly swam in a pool of wine and drank enough of it to lower the wine level considerably. Finally, in 750, Abu al-Abbas (uh-BOO al-uh-BUSS), a descendant of the uncle of Muhammad, brought an end to the Umayyad dynasty and established the Abbasid (uh-BAH-sid *or* AB-uh-sid) dynasty, which lasted until 1258.

The Abbasid Dynasty   The Abbasid rulers brought much change to the world of Islam. They tried to break down the distinctions between Arab and non-Arab Muslims. All Muslims, regardless of their ethnic background, could now hold both civil and military offices. This helped open Islamic life to the influences of the civilizations the Arabs had conquered. Many Arabs now began to intermarry with the peoples they had conquered.

In 762, the Abbasids built a new capital city, Baghdad, on the Tigris River far to the east of Damascus. The new capital was well placed. It took advantage of river traffic to the Persian Gulf and at the same time was located on the caravan route from the Mediterranean to Central Asia. The move eastward allowed Persian influence to come to the fore, encouraging a new cultural orientation. Under the Abbasids, judges, merchants, and government officials, rather than warriors, were viewed as the ideal citizens.

The new Abbasid dynasty experienced a period of splendid rule well into the ninth century. Best known of the caliphs of the time was Harun al-Rashid (huh-ROON al-rah-SHEED) (786–809), whose reign is often described as the golden age of the Abbasid caliphate. His son al-Ma'mun (al-muh-MOON) (813–833) was a great patron of learning. He founded an astronomical observatory and created a foundation for translating Classical Greek works. This was also a period of growing economic prosperity. The Arabs had conquered many of the richest provinces of the old Roman Empire, and they now controlled the trade routes to the east. Baghdad became the center of an enormous trade empire that extended into Europe, Asia, and Africa, greatly adding to the wealth of the Islamic world.

Despite the prosperity, all was not quite well in the empire of the Abbasids. There was much fighting over the succession to the caliphate. When Harun al-Rashid died, his two sons fought to succeed him in a struggle that almost destroyed the city of Baghdad. As the tenth-century Muslim historian al-Mas'udi wrote: "Mansions were destroyed, most remarkable monuments obliterated; prices soared.... Brother turned his sword against brother, son against father, as some fought for Amin, others for Ma'mun. Houses and palaces fueled the flames; property was put to the sack."[15]

Vast wealth also gave rise to financial corruption. By awarding important positions to court favorites, the Abbasid caliphs began to undermine the foundations of their own power and soon became figureheads. Rulers of the provinces of the empire broke away from the control of the caliphs and established their own independent dynasties. In the eighth century, Spain had already established its own caliphate when Abd al-Rahman (AHB-d al-rahkh-MAHN) of the Umayyad dynasty had fled there. In 756, he seized control of southern Spain and then expanded his power into the center of the peninsula. He took the title of *emir*, or commander, and set up the emirate of al-Andalus (the Arabic name for Spain) with its center at Córdoba (KOR-duh-buh). In 929, Abd al-Rahman III (912–961) proclaimed himself caliph. The rulers of al-Andalus developed a unique society in which all religions were tolerated. The court also supported writers and artists, creating a brilliant and flourishing culture.

The fragmentation of the Islamic empire accelerated in the tenth century. The Fatimid (FAT-i-mid) family established a caliphate in Egypt in 973, and an independent dynasty also operated in North Africa. Despite the political disunity of the Islamic world, however, there was an underlying Islamic civilization based on two common bonds, the Qur'an and the Arabic language.

Islamic Civilization   From the beginning of their empire, Muslim Arabs had demonstrated a willingness to absorb the culture of their conquered territories. The Arabs were truly heirs to the remaining Greco-Roman culture of the Roman Empire. Just as readily, they assimilated Byzantine and Persian culture. In the eighth and ninth centuries, numerous Greek, Syrian, and Persian scientific and philosophical works were translated into Arabic. As the chief language in the southern Mediterranean and the Near East and the required language of Muslims, Arabic became a truly international tongue.

The Muslims created a brilliant urban culture at a time when western Europe was predominantly a rural world of farming villages. This can be seen in such new cities as Baghdad and Cairo, but also in Córdoba, the capital of the Umayyad caliphate in Spain. With a population of possibly 100,000, Córdoba was Europe's largest city after Constantinople. It had seventy public libraries, and the number of manuscripts in the caliph's private library reached 400,000. One caliph, al-Hakem (961–976), collected books from different parts of the world and then had them translated into Arabic and Latin. These included works on geography that later proved valuable to Western sailors and merchants. Schools were also established, and the Great Mosque of Córdoba became a center for scholars from all over the Islamic world. Large numbers of women served as teachers and librarians in Córdoba.

Islamic cities had a distinctive physical appearance due to their common use of certain architectural features, such as the pointed arch and traceried windows, and specific kinds of buildings. The latter included palaces and public buildings with fountains and secluded courtyards, mosques for worship, public baths, and bazaars or marketplaces. Muslims embellished their buildings with a unique decorative art that avoided representation of living things because their religion prohibited the making of graven images.

Although the Qur'an instructed men to treat women with respect, the male was dominant in Muslim society. Women were to be good mothers and wives by raising their children and caring for their husbands. Nevertheless, women did have the right to own and inherit property.

Islamic custom required that women be secluded in their homes and kept from social contacts with males outside their own families. One jurist wrote that "a woman should leave her house on three occasions only: when she is conducted to the house of her bridegroom, on the deaths of her parents, and when she goes to her own grave."[16] The custom of requiring women to cover virtually all parts of their bodies when appearing in public was common in the cities and is still practiced today in many Islamic societies. It should be noted, however, that these customs owed more to traditional Arab practice than to the Qur'an.

The Culture of Islam During the first few centuries of the Arab Empire, it was the Islamic world that saved and spread the scientific and philosophical works of ancient civilizations. At a time when the ancient Greek philosophers were largely unknown in Europe, key works by Plato and Aristotle were translated into Arabic. They were put in a library called the House of Wisdom in Baghdad, where they were read and studied by Muslim scholars. Texts on mathematics were brought from India. The preservation of ancient texts was aided by the use of paper.

Topkapi Palace Museum, Istanbul/The Bridgeman Art Library

Preserving Greek Literature. *After the collapse of the Western Roman Empire, the philosophical works of ancient Greece were virtually forgotten in Europe. It was thanks to Muslim scholars, who stored copies and translations in libraries in the Arab world, that many Classical Greek writings survived. Here young Muslim scholars are being trained in the Greek language so that they can translate Classical Greek literature into Arabic. Later the works were translated back into Latin and served as a catalyst for an intellectual revival in medieval and Renaissance Europe.*

The making of paper was introduced from China in the eighth century, and by the end of that century, paper factories had been established in Baghdad. Booksellers and libraries soon followed. European universities later benefited from this scholarship when these works were translated from Arabic into Latin.

Although Islamic scholars are rightly praised for preserving much of Classical knowledge for the West, they also made considerable advances of their own. Nowhere is this more evident than in their contributions to mathematics and the natural sciences. The list of achievements in mathematics and astronomy alone is impressive. The Muslims adopted and passed on the numerical system of India, including the use of the zero. In Europe, it became known as the Arabic system. Al-Khwarizmi (al-KHWAR-iz-mee), a ninth-century Persian mathematician, developed the discipline of algebra. In astronomy, the Muslims were aware that the earth was round, and they set up an observatory at Baghdad to study the stars, many of which they named. They also perfected the astrolabe, an instrument used by sailors to determine their location by observing the positions of heavenly bodies. It was the astrolabe that made it possible for Europeans to sail to the Americas.

Muslim scholars also made discoveries in chemistry and developed medicine as a field of scientific study. Especially renowned was Ibn Sina (ib-un SEE-nuh) (980–1037), known as Avicenna (av-i-SENN-uh) in the West, who wrote a medical encyclopedia that, among other things, stressed the contagious nature of certain diseases and showed how they could be spread by contaminated water supplies. After its translation into Latin, Avicenna's work became a basic medical textbook for medieval European university students. Avicenna was but one of many Muslim scholars whose work was translated into Latin and contributed to the development of intellectual life in Europe in the twelfth and thirteenth centuries.

CHRONOLOGIES

THE CAROLINGIAN EMPIRE

751	Pepin crowned king of the Franks
768–814	Reign of Charlemagne
814–840	Reign of Louis the Pious
843	Treaty of Verdun divides Carolingian Empire

NEW POLITICAL CONFIGURATIONS OF THE TENTH CENTURY

Eastern Franks	
962	Coronation of Otto I as emperor
Western Franks	
987	Election of Hugh Capet as king
Anglo-Saxon England	
871–899	Alfred the Great, king of Wessex

BYZANTIUM, THE SLAVS, AND THE ISLAMIC WORLD

Byzantine Empire

842–867	Michael III
867–1081	Macedonian dynasty

Slavic Peoples of Central and Eastern Europe

863	Cyril and Methodius begin to convert Moravian Slavs
c. 873–913	Oleg creates principality of Kiev
987	Vladimir's conversion to Christianity

World of Islam

750	Overthrow of Umayyad dynasty by Abbasids
786–809	Harun al-Rashid
813–833	al-Ma'mun
973	Establishment of Fatimid caliphate in Egypt

9

THE RECOVERY AND GROWTH OF EUROPEAN SOCIETY IN THE HIGH MIDDLE AGES

A town street scene in thirteenth-century England

© Mary Evans Picture Library/The Image Works

CHAPTER OUTLINE

• Land and People in the High Middle Ages • The New World of Trade and Cities • The Intellectual and Artistic World of the High Middle Ages

---

LAND AND PEOPLE IN THE HIGH MIDDLE AGES

The period from 1000 to 1300 witnessed an improvement in climate as a small but nevertheless significant rise in temperature made for longer and better growing seasons. At the same time, the European population experienced a dramatic increase, virtually doubling between 1000 and 1300, from 38 million to 74 million people. As Table 9.1 indicates, the rate of growth tended to vary from region to region. This rise in population was physically evident in the growth of agricultural villages, towns, and cities and the increase in arable land.

What accounted for this dramatic increase in population? Obviously, fertility rates increased sufficiently to gradually outstrip the relatively high mortality rates of medieval society, which were especially acute in infancy and the childhood years. Traditionally, historians have cited two factors to explain the population increase: increased security stemming from more settled and peaceful conditions after the invasions of the Early Middle Ages had stopped and a dramatic increase in agricultural production capable of sustaining a larger population.

The New Agriculture   During the High Middle Ages, significant changes occurred in the way Europeans farmed. Although the warmer climate played an underlying role by improving growing conditions, another factor contributing to the increased production of food was the expansion

TABLE 9.1 | POPULATION ESTIMATES (IN MILLIONS), 1000 AND 1340

Area	1000	1340
Mediterranean		
Greece and Balkans	5	6
Italy	5	10
Iberia	7	9
Total	17	25
Western and Central Europe		
France and Low Countries	6	19
British Isles	2	5
Germany and Scandinavia	4	11.5
Total	12	35.5
Eastern Europe		
Russia	6	8
Poland	2	3
Hungary	1.5	2
Total	9.5	13
Grand Total	38.5	73.5

Source: J. C. Russell, *The Control of Late Ancient and Medieval Population* (Philadelphia: American Philosophical Society, 1985), p. 36. Demographic specialists caution that these are merely estimates. Some figures, especially those for eastern Europe, could be radically revised by new research.

of arable land, achieved chiefly by clearing forested areas for cultivation. Eager for land, peasants cut down trees, drained swamps, and in the Netherlands even began to reclaim land from the sea. By the thirteenth century, the total acreage available for farming in Europe was greater than at any time before or since.

Technological Changes   Technological changes also furthered the expansion of agriculture. Many of these depended on the use of iron, which was mined in various areas of Europe and traded to places where it was not found. Iron was in demand to make swords and armor as well as scythes, axheads, new types of farming implements such as hoes, and saws, hammers, and nails for building purposes. It was crucial for making the heavy, wheeled plow, the carruca (kuh-ROO-kuh), which made an enormous impact on medieval agriculture north of the Alps.

The plow of the Mediterranean and Near Eastern worlds had been the *aratrum* (uh-RAH-trum), a nonwheeled, light scratch plow made mostly of wood that was sufficient to break the top layer of the light soils of those areas. It could be pulled by a single donkey, ox, or horse. But such a light plow was totally ineffective in the heavy clay soils north of the Alps. The carruca, a heavy, wheeled plow with an iron plowshare, came into widespread use by the tenth century. It could turn over heavy soils and allow them to drain. Because the carruca was so heavy, six or eight oxen were needed to pull it, but oxen were slow. Two new inventions for the horse made made it possible to plow faster. In the tenth century, a new horse collar appeared that distributed the weight around the shoulders and chest rather than the throat and could be used to hitch up a series of horses, enabling them to pull the new heavy plow faster and cultivate more land. The use of horseshoes, iron shoes nailed to a horse's hooves, produced greater traction and better protection against the rocky and heavy clay soils of northern Europe.

The use of the heavy, wheeled plow also led to cooperative agricultural villages. Because iron was expensive, the plow had to be purchased by the entire community. Similarly, an individual family could not afford a team of animals, so villagers shared their beasts. Moreover, the plow's size and weight made it hard to maneuver, so land was cultivated in long strips to minimize the amount of turning that would have to be done.

People in the High Middle Ages also learned to harness the power of water and wind to do jobs formerly done by humans or animals. Although the watermill had been invented as early as the second century B.C.E., it did not come into widespread use until the High Middle Ages. Mills, located along streams and powered by the rushing water, were used to grind grain and produce flour. Often dams were built to increase the force of the water. The development of the cam enabled millwrights to mechanize entire industries; waterpower was used in certain phases of cloth production and to run trip-hammers for the working of metals. The Chinese had made use of the cam in operating trip-hammers for hulling rice by the third century C.E. but had apparently not extended its use to other industries.

Europeans also developed windmills to capture the power of the wind. Historians are uncertain whether windmills were imported into Europe (they were invented in Persia) or designed independently by Europeans. In either case, by the end of the twelfth century, they were beginning to dot the European landscape. The watermill and windmill were the most important devices for harnessing power before the invention of the steam engine in the eighteenth century.

The Three-Field System   The shift from a two-field to a three-field system of crop rotation also contributed to the increase in agricultural production. In the Early Middle Ages, farmers commonly planted one field while allowing another of equal size to lie fallow to regain its fertility. Now estates were divided into three parts. One field was planted in the fall with grains such as rye and wheat, while spring-sown grains, such as oats and barley, and legumes, such as peas, beans, or lentils, were planted in the second field. The third was allowed to lie fallow. By rotating their use, only one-third, rather than one-half, of the land lay fallow at any time. The rotation of crops also prevented the soil from being exhausted so quickly, especially since legumes improve soil fertility because their roots fix nitrogen in the soil. Grain yields increased as well.

By the thirteenth century, the growing demand for agricultural produce in the towns and cities led to higher food prices. This encouraged lords to try to grow more food for profit. One way to do so was to lease their demesne land to their serfs and to transform labor services into money payments or fixed rents, thereby converting many serfs into free peasants. Although many peasants still remained economically dependent on their lords, they were no longer legally tied to the land. Lords, in turn, became collectors of rents rather than operators of manors with political and legal privileges. The political and legal powers formerly exercised by lords were increasingly reclaimed by the monarchical states.

The Life of the Peasantry   Peasant activities were largely determined by the seasons of the year. Each season brought a new round of tasks appropriate for the time, although some periods, especially summer and fall, were considerably more hectic than others. The basic staple of the peasant diet was bread, so an adequate harvest of grains was crucial to survival in the winter months. A new cycle began in October when peasants prepared the ground for the planting of winter crops. In November came the slaughter of excess livestock because there was usually insufficient fodder to keep animals all winter. The meat would be salted to preserve it for winter use. In February and March, the land was plowed for spring crops—oats, barley, peas, beans, and lentils. Early summer was a comparatively relaxed time, although weeding and sheepshearing still had to be done. In every season, the serfs worked not only their own land but also the lord's demesne. They also tended the gardens adjacent to their dwellings where they grew the vegetables and fruits that made up part of their diet.

Holidays and the Village Church   But peasants did not face a life of constant labor thanks to the feast days or holidays of the Catholic Church, which commemorated the great events of the Christian faith or the lives of Christian saints or holy persons. The three great feasts of the Catholic Church were Christmas (celebrating the birth of Jesus), Easter (celebrating the resurrection of Jesus), and Pentecost (celebrating the descent of the Holy Spirit on Jesus's disciples fifty days after his resurrection). Numerous other feasts dedicated to saints or the Virgin Mary, the mother of Jesus, were also celebrated, making a total of more than fifty holidays.

Religious feast days, Sunday Mass, baptisms, marriages, and funerals all brought peasants into contact with the village church, a crucial part of manorial life. In the village church, the peasant was baptized as an infant, confirmed in the

Peasant Activities.

The seasons of the year largely determined the life of the European peasant. The kind of work that peasants did was dictated by the month and the season. This French calendar from 1460 shows a number of medieval farming activities, including sowing seeds, harvesting crops, pruning plants, shearing sheep, threshing, pressing grapes, and taking care of animals.

Musée Condé, Chantilly//© Réunion des Musées Nationaux/Art Resource, NY

faith, sometimes married, and given the sacrament of Holy Communion; before death, the peasant would receive the last rites of the church. The village priest instructed the peasants in the basic elements of Christianity so that they might attain the Christian's ultimate goal—salvation. But village priests were often barely literate peasants themselves, and it is hard to know how much church doctrine the peasants actually understood. Very likely, they regarded God as an all-powerful force who needed to be appeased by prayer to bring good harvests.

The Peasant Household Peasant dwellings were very simple. The cottages were built with wood frames with walls made of laths or sticks; the spaces between the laths were stuffed with straw and rubble and then plastered over with clay. Roofs were often thatched with reeds or straw. In timber-poor areas, peasants built their houses out of stone. The houses of poorer peasants consisted of a single room, but others had at least two rooms—a main room for cooking, eating, and other activities and another room for sleeping. There was little privacy in a medieval household. A hearth in the main room was used for heating and cooking; the smoke from fires in the hearth went out a hole in the roof or gable.

Family and the Role of Women Surveys of monastic manors reveal that the typical peasant household consisted of a husband and wife with two or three children. Infant mortality rates were high. Peasant women occupied both an important and a difficult position in manorial society. They were expected to carry and bear children, as well as provide for their socialization and religious training. Peasant women also did the spinning and weaving that provided the household's clothes, tended the family's vegetable garden and chickens, and cooked the meals. A woman's ability to manage the household might determine whether her family would starve or survive in difficult times. In addition to managing the household, peasant women often worked with men in the fields, especially at harvest time.

Indeed, as one historian has noted, peasant marriage was an "economic partnership" in which both husbands and wives contributed their own distinctive labor.

The Peasant Diet Though simple, a peasant's daily diet was potentially nutritious when food was available. The basic staple of the peasant diet, and the medieval diet in general, was bread. Women made the dough for the bread, but the loaves were usually baked in community ovens, which were a monopoly of the lord of the manor. Peasant bread was made of the cheaper grains (rye, barley, millet, and oats), rather than expensive wheat. It was dark and had a very heavy, hard texture. Bread was supplemented by legumes (peas and beans) from the household gardens, bacon from the family pig, cheese from cow's or goat's milk, and where available, wild game and fish from hunting and fishing. Manorial lords tended to regulate fishing, however, and were especially reluctant to allow peasants to hunt for fear that insufficient game would remain for the nobility. Woodlands also provided nuts, berries, and a foraging area for pigs. Fruits, such as apples, pears, and cherries, were also available. Chickens provided eggs and occasionally meat. Peasants usually ate fresh meat only on the great feast days, such as Christmas, Easter, and Pentecost.

Grains were important not only for bread but also for making ale. In many northern European countries, ale was the most common drink of the poor. If records are accurate, enormous quantities of ale were consumed. A monastery in the twelfth century recorded a daily allotment of three gallons a day to each monk, far above the weekend consumption of many present-day college students. Peasants in the field undoubtedly consumed even more. This high consumption of alcohol might explain the large number of fights and accidents recorded in medieval court records.

The Aristocracy of the High Middle Ages In the High Middle Ages, European society was dominated by a group of men whose primary preoccupation was warfare. King Alfred of England had said that a "well-peopled land" must have "men of prayer, men of war, and men of work," and medieval ideals held to a tripartite division of society into these three basic groups. The "men of war" were the **aristocracy** who came to form a distinct social group, albeit one with considerable variation in wealth among its members. Nevertheless, they, along with their wives and children, shared a common ethos and a distinctive lifestyle.

The Significance of the Aristocracy King Alfred's "men of war" were the lords and vassals of medieval society. The lords were the kings, dukes, counts, barons, and viscounts (and even bishops and archbishops) who held extensive lands and considerable political power. They formed an aristocracy or nobility that consisted of people who held real political, economic, and social power. Nobles relied for military help on knights, mounted warriors who fought for them in return for weapons and daily sustenance. Knights initially were by no means the social equals of nobles; many knights in fact possessed little more than peasants. But in the course of the twelfth and thirteenth centuries, knights improved their social status and joined the ranks of the nobility. In the process, *noble* and *knight* came to mean much the same thing, and warfare likewise tended to become a distinguishing characteristic of the nobleman. The great lords and knights came to form a common caste. Although social divisions based on extremes of wealth and landholdings persisted, they were all warriors united by the institution of knighthood.

The Men of War   Medieval theory maintained that the warlike qualities of the nobility were justified by their role as defenders of society. Knights, however, were also notorious for fighting each other. The Catholic Church intervened, and though it could not stop the incessant bloodletting, it did at least try to limit it by instituting the "Peace of God." Beginning in the eleventh century, the church encouraged knights to take an oath to respect churches and pilgrimage centers and to refrain from attacking noncombatants, such as clergy, poor people, merchants, and women. It was, of course, permissible to continue killing each other. At the same time, the church initiated the "Truce of God," which forbade fighting on Sundays and the primary feast days.

In addition to trying to diminish fighting, the church also worked to redirect the nobility's warlike energy into different channels, such as the Crusades against the Muslims (see Chapter 10), and was quite willing to justify violence when used against peace-breakers and especially against non-Christians. Hence, being a warrior on behalf of God easily vindicated the nobles' love of war and in fact justified their high social status as the defenders of Christian society. The church furthered this process by steeping knighthood in Christian symbols. A knight formally received his arms in a religious ceremony, and a priest blessed his weapons for Christian service. Throughout the Middle Ages, a constant tension existed between the ideals of a religion founded on the ideal of peace and the ethos of a nobility based on the love of war.

Castles   The growth of the European nobility in the High Middle Ages was made visible by an increasing number of castles scattered across the landscape. Although castle architecture varied considerably, castles did possess two common features: they were permanent residences for the noble family, its retainers, and servants, and they were defensible fortifications. For defensive purposes, castles were surrounded by open areas and large stone walls. At the heart of the castle was the keep, a large, multistoried building that housed kitchens, stables, and storerooms; numerous rooms for sleeping and living; and a great hall for visitors, dining, and administrative business. The growing wealth of the High Middle Ages made it possible for the European nobility to build more secure castles with thicker walls and more elaborately decorated interiors. With their sturdier construction, castles were easier to defend and harder to seize by force.

Aristocratic Women   Although women could legally hold and inherit property, most women remained under the control of men—their fathers until they married and their husbands after they married. Nevertheless, aristocratic women had numerous opportunities to play important roles. Because the lord was often away at war, on a Crusade, or at court, the lady of the castle had to manage the estate, a considerable responsibility in view of the fact that households, even of lesser aristocrats, could include large numbers of officials and servants. Supervising financial accounts, both for the household and for the landed estate, alone required considerable financial knowledge. The lady of the castle was also often responsible for overseeing the food supply and maintaining all other supplies for the smooth operation of the household.

Childhood ended early for the daughters of aristocrats. Since aristocratic girls were married in their teens (usually at the age of fifteen or sixteen) and were expected by their husbands to assume their responsibilities immediately, the training of girls in a large body of practical knowledge could never start too early. Sent at a young age to the castles of other nobles to be brought up, girls were trained as ladies-in-waiting. The lady of the castle taught them how to sew and weave and instructed them in all the skills needed for running an estate. They also learned how to read and write, dance, sing, and play musical instruments.

Although women were expected to be subservient to their husbands, there were many strong women who advised and sometimes even dominated their husbands. Perhaps the most famous was Eleanor of Aquitaine (c. 1122–1204), heiress to the duchy of Aquitaine in southwestern France. Married first to King Louis VII of France (1137–1180), Eleanor even accompanied her husband on a Crusade, but her failure to bear sons led Louis to have their marriage annulled. Eleanor then married Henry, count of Anjou (AHN-zhoo), who became King Henry II of England (1154–1189) and duke of Normandy. She bore him both sons and daughters and took an active role in politics, even assisting her sons in rebelling against Henry in 1173–1174. Imprisoned by her husband for her activities, after Henry's death she again assumed an active political life, providing both military and political support for her sons.

Blanche of Castile (1188–1252) was another powerful medieval queen. She became regent while her son Louis IX was a boy and ruled France with a powerful hand during much of the 1220s and 1230s. She repelled the attempt of some rebellious French nobles to seize her son, the young king, and defeated Henry III of England when he tried to incite an uprising in France in order to reconquer Normandy. Blanche's political sense was so astute that even when Louis IX came of age, he continued to rely on her as his chief adviser. One medieval chronicler gave her the highest compliment he could think of: "she ruled as a man."

The Way of the Warrior   At the age of seven or eight, aristocratic boys were sent either to a clerical school to pursue a religious career or to another nobleman's castle, where they prepared for the life of a noble. The chief lessons for those learning to be nobles were military; they learned how to joust, hunt, ride, and handle weapons properly. Occasionally, aristocrats' sons might also learn the basic fundamentals of reading and writing. After his apprenticeship in knighthood, at about the age of twenty-one, a young man formally entered the adult world in the ceremony of "knighting." A sponsor girded a sword on the young candidate and struck him on the cheek or neck with an open hand (or later touched him three times on the shoulder with the blade of a sword), possibly signifying the passing of the sponsor's military valor to the new knight.

In the eleventh and twelfth centuries, under the influence of the church, an ideal of civilized behavior called **chivalry** gradually evolved among the nobility. Chivalry represented a code of ethics that knights were supposed to uphold. In addition to

Women in Medieval Thought

Whether a nun or the wife of an aristo-crat, townsman, or peasant, a woman in the Middle Ages was considered inferior to a man and subject to a man's authority. Although there are a number of examples of strong women who ignored such atti-tudes, church teachings also reinforced these notions. The first selection from Gratian (GRAY-shee-un *or* GRAY-shun), the twelfth-century jurist who wrote the first systematic work on canon law (church law), supports this view. The sec-ond selection was written in the 1390s by a wealthy fifty-year-old Parisian who wanted to instruct his fifteen-year-old bride on how to be a good wife.

Gratian, *Decretum*

Women should be subject to their men. The natural order for mankind is that women should serve men and children their parents, for it is just that the lesser serve the greater.

The image of God is in man and it is one. Women were drawn from man, who has God's jurisdiction as if he were God's vicar, because he has the image of one God. Therefore woman is not made in God's image.

Woman's authority is nil; let her in all things be subject to the rule of man.... And neither can she teach, nor be a witness, nor give a guarantee, nor sit in judgment.

Adam was beguiled by Eve, not she by him. It is right that he whom woman led into wrongdoing should have her under his direction, so that he may not fail a second time through female levity.

A Merchant of Paris, *On Marriage*

I entreat you to keep his linen clean, for this is up to you. Because the care of out-side affairs is men's work, a husband must look after these things, and go and come, run here and there in rain, wind, snow, and hail—sometimes wet, sometimes dry, sometimes sweating, other times shiver-ing, badly fed, badly housed, badly shod, badly bedded—and nothing harms him because he is cheered by the anticipation of the care his wife will take of him on his return—of the pleasures, joys, and com-forts she will provide, or have provided for him in her presence: to have his shoes off before a good fire, to have his feet washed, to have clean shoes and hose, to be well fed, provided with good drink, well served, well honored, well bedded in white sheets and white nightcaps, well covered with good furs, and comforted with other joys and amusements, intima-cies, affections, and secrets about which I am silent. And on the next day fresh linen and garments....

Also keep peace with him. Remember the country proverb that says there are three things that drive a good man from his home: a house with a bad roof, a smoking chimney, and a quarrelsome woman. I beg you, in order to preserve your husband's love and good will, be loving, amiable, and sweet with him.... Thus protect and shield your husband from all troubles, give him all the com-fort you can think of, wait on him, and have him waited on in your home.... If you do what is said here, he will always have his affection and his heart turned toward you and your service, and he will forsake all other homes, all other women, all other help, and all other households.

Q *What do these two documents reveal about male attitudes toward women in the Middle Ages? How do the authors justify these attitudes?*

Source: From *Not in God's Image: Women in History from the Greeks to Victorians* by Julia O'Faolain and Lauro Martines. Copyright © 1973 by Julia O'Faolain and Lauro Martines. Reprinted by permission of the authors.

defending the church and the defenseless, knights were expected to treat captives as honored guests instead of throwing them in dungeons. Chivalry also implied that knights should fight only for glory, but this account of a group of English knights by a medieval writer reveals another motive for battle: "The whole city was plundered to the last farthing, and then they proceeded to rob all the churches throughout the city,... and seizing gold and silver, cloth of all colors, women's ornaments, gold rings, goblets, and precious stones.... They all returned to their own lords rich men."[1] Apparently, not all chivalric ideals were taken seriously.

After his formal initiation into the world of warriors, a young man returned home to find himself once again subject to his parents' authority. Young men were discouraged from marrying until their fathers died, at which time they could marry and become lords of the castle. Trained to be warriors but with no adult responsibilities, young knights naturally gravitated toward military activities and often furthered the private warfare endemic to the noble class.

The Role of Tournaments   In the twelfth century, tournaments began to appear as an alternative to the socially destructive fighting that the church was trying to curb. Initially, tournaments consisted of the "melee," in which warriors on horseback fought with blunted weapons in free-for-all combat. The goal was to take prisoners who would then be ransomed, making success in tournaments a path to considerable wealth. Within an eight-month span, the English knight William Marshall made a tour of the tournament circuit, defeated 203 knights, and made so much money that he had to hire two clerks to take care of it.

By the late twelfth century, the melee was preceded by the joust, or individual combat between two knights. Gradually, jousts became the main part of the tournament. No matter how much the church condemned tournaments, knights themselves continued to see them as an excellent way to train for war. As one knight explained: "A knight cannot distinguish himself in that [war] if he has not trained for it in tourneys. He must have seen his blood flow, heard his teeth crack under fist blows, felt his opponent's weight bear down upon him as he lay on the ground and, after being twenty times unhorsed, have risen twenty times to fight."[2]

Marriage Patterns of the Aristocracy   Aristocratic marriages were expected to establish alliances with other families, bring new wealth, and provide heirs to carry on the family line. Parents therefore supervised the choice of spouses for their children. One of the most noticeable features of aristocratic marriages was the usually wide discrepancy in the ages of the marital partners. Daughters of the nobles married at fifteen or sixteen, but their husbands might be in their thirties or even forties, since men did not marry until they came into their inheritances.

By the twelfth century, the efforts of the church since Carolingian times to end divorce (see Chapter 8) had borne much fruit. As a sacrament, marriage was intended to last for a lifetime and could not be dissolved. In certain cases, however, the church allowed married persons to separate by granting them an annulment or official recognition that their marriage had not been valid in the first place. If it could be established that the couple had not consented to the marriage, that one or the other suffered from a sexual incapacity that prevented the consummation of the marriage, or that the couple were related by blood (more closely than sixth or,

after 1215, third cousins), the church would approve an annulment of their marriage, and the partners would be free to marry again.

THE NEW WORLD OF TRADE AND CITIES

Medieval Europe was an overwhelmingly agrarian society with most people living
in small villages. In the eleventh and twelfth centuries, however, new elements were
introduced that began to transform the economic foundation of Western civilization: a revival of trade, considerable expansion in the circulation of money, the
emergence of specialized craftspeople and artisans, and the growth and development of towns. These changes were made possible by the new agricultural practices
and subsequent increase in food production, which freed some European families
from the need to produce their own food. Merchants and craftspeople could now
buy their necessities.

The Revival of   The revival of commercial activity was a gradual process.
Trade   During the chaotic conditions of the Early Middle Ages,
                       large-scale trade had declined in western Europe except for
Byzantine contacts with Italy and the Jewish traders who moved back and forth
between the Muslim and Christian worlds. By the end of the tenth century, however, people with both the skills and the products for commercial activity were
emerging in Europe.

Cities in Italy assumed a leading role in the revival of trade (see Map 9.1). By
the end of the eighth century, Venice, on the northeastern coast, had emerged as a
town with close trading ties to the Byzantine Empire. Venice developed a trading
fleet and by the end of the tenth century had become the chief western trading center for Byzantine and Islamic commerce. Venice sent wine, grain, and timber to
Constantinople in exchange for silk cloth, which was then peddled to other communities. Other coastal communities in western Italy, such as Genoa and Pisa, also
opened new trade routes. By 1100, Italian merchants began to benefit from the
Crusades and were able to establish new trading centers in eastern ports. There
the merchants obtained silks, sugar, and spices, which they subsequently carried
back to Italy and the West.

In the High Middle Ages, Italian merchants became even more daring in their
trade activities. They established trading posts in Cairo, Damascus, and a number
of Black Sea ports, where they acquired goods brought by Muslim merchants from
India, China, and Southeast Asia. A few Italian merchants even journeyed to India
and China in search of trade.

While the northern Italian cities were busy trading in the Mediterranean, the
towns of Flanders were doing likewise in northern Europe. Flanders, the area
along the coast of present-day Belgium and northern France, was known for the
production of a much desired high-quality woolen cloth. Flanders's location made
it a logical entrepôt for the traders of northern Europe. Merchants from England,
Scandinavia, France, and Germany converged there to trade their wares for woolen
cloth. Flanders prospered in the eleventh and twelfth centuries, and Flemish towns
such as Bruges (BROOZH) and Ghent became centers for the trade and manufac-
ture of woolen cloth.

MAP 9.1 Medieval Trade Routes

Italian cities and Flanders were the centers of gradually expanding trade in Europe. They fostered the exchange of goods from the Byzantine Empire and the Far East with those of various regions of Europe. The decline in the level of violence over time greatly helped trade.

By the twelfth century, it was almost inevitable that a regular exchange of goods would develop between Flanders and Italy. To encourage this trade, the counts of Champagne in northern France devised a series of six fairs held annually in the chief towns of their territory. The fairs of Champagne became the largest commercial marketplace in western Europe where the goods of northern Europe could be exchanged for the goods of southern Europe and the East. Northern merchants brought the furs, woolen cloth, tin, hemp, and honey of northern Europe and exchanged them for the cloth and swords of northern Italy and the silks, sugar, and spices of the East. The prosperity of the Champagne fairs caused lords everywhere to follow their example and establish trading fairs.

As trade increased, both gold and silver came to be in demand at fairs and trading markets of all kinds. Slowly, a money economy began to emerge. New trading companies and banking firms were set up to manage the exchange and sale of goods. New techniques, including double-entry bookkeeping, commercial contracts,

Two Views of Trade and Merchants

The revival of trade in Europe was a gradual process, but by the High Middle Ages, it had begun to expand dramatically. During the medieval period, trade already flourished in other parts of the world, especially in the Islamic world and in China. Nevertheless, many people in these societies, including rulers, nobles, and religious leaders, had some reservations about the success of merchants. The first selection is taken from the life of Godric, a twelfth-century European merchant who became a saint. The second selection is from the *Prolegomena* (proh-lih-GAHM-uh-nuh), the first part of a universal history written by Ibn Khaldun (ib-un kahl-DOON), a Muslim historian who traveled widely in the Muslim world in the fourteenth century.

Life of Saint Godric

At first, he lived as a peddler for four years in Lincolnshire, going on foot and carrying the smallest wares; then he traveled abroad, first to St. Andrews in Scotland and then for the first time to Rome. On his return, having formed a familiar friendship with certain other young men who were eager

for merchandise, he began to launch upon bolder courses, and to coast frequently by sea to the foreign lands that lay around him. Thus, sailing often to and fro between Scotland and Britain, he traded in many divers wares and, amid these occupations, learned much worldly wisdom....

Thus aspiring ever higher and higher, and yearning upward with his whole heart, at length his great labors and cares bore much fruit of worldly gain. For he labored not only as a merchant but also as a shipman ... to Denmark and to Flanders and Scotland; in all which lands he found certain rare, and therefore more precious, wares, which he carried to other parts wherein he knew them to be least familiar, and coveted by the inhabitants beyond the price of gold itself; wherefore he exchanged these wares for others coveted by men of other lands; and thus he chaffered [traded] most freely and assiduously. Hence he made great profit in all his bargains, and gathered much wealth in the sweat of his brow; for he sold dear in one place the wares which he had bought elsewhere at a small price.

And now he had lived sixteen years as a merchant, and began to think of

---

and insurance, also appeared to facilitate the expansion of businesses. All of these new practices were part of a commercial revolution based on the growth of **capitalism**, an economic system in which commerce and industry are controlled by private owners who invest in trade and goods in order to make profits.

The Growth of Cities

The revival of trade led to a revival of cities. Merchants needed places where they could live and build warehouses to store their goods. Towns had greatly declined in the Early Middle Ages, especially in Europe north of the Alps. Old Roman cities continued to exist but had dwindled in size and population. With the revival of trade, merchants began to settle in these old cities, followed by craftworkers or artisans, people who had developed skills on manors or elsewhere and now perceived the spending on charity, to God's honor and service, the goods which he had so laboriously acquired. He therefore took the cross as a pilgrim to Jerusalem.... [When he had returned to England] Godric, that he might follow Christ the more freely, sold all his possessions and distributed them among the poor [and began to live the life of a hermit].

Ibn Khaldun, *Prolegomena*

As for Trade, although it be a natural means of livelihood, yet most of the methods it employs are tricks aimed at making a profit by securing the difference between the buying and selling prices, and by appropriating the surplus. This is why [religious] Law allows the use of such methods, which, although they come under the heading of gambling, yet do not constitute the taking without return of other people's goods....

Should their [traders'] standard of living, however, rise, so that they begin to enjoy more than the bare necessities, the effect will be to breed in them a desire for repose and tranquillity. They will therefore cooperate to secure superfluities; their food and clothing will increase in quantity and refinement; they will enlarge their houses and plan their towns for defense. A further

improvement in their conditions will lead to habits of luxury, resulting in extreme refinement in cooking and the preparation of food; in choosing rich clothing of the finest silk; in raising lofty mansions and castles and furnishing them luxuriously, and so on. At this stage the crafts develop and reach their height. Lofty castles and mansions are built and decorated sumptuously, water is drawn to them and a great diversity takes place in the way of dress, furniture, vessels, and household equipment. Such are the townsmen, who earn their living in industry or trade.

Q *What did the biographer of Godric and Ibn Khaldun see as valuable in mercantile activity? What reservations did they have about trade? How are the two perspectives alike? How are they different, and how do you explain the differences? What generalizations can you make about Christian and Muslim attitudes toward trade?*

Sources: Life of Saint Godric. From Reginald of Durham, "Life of St. Godric," in G. G. Coulton, ed., Social Life in Britain from the Conquest to the Reformation, (Cambridge: Cambridge University Press, 1918), pp. 415–20. Ibn Khaldun, Prolegomena. From An Arab Philosophy of History. Ed. and trans. by Charles Issawi. New York: Darwin Press, 1987. Reprinted by permission of the Darwin Press.

opportunity to ply their trade producing objects that could be sold by the merchants. In the course of the eleventh and twelfth centuries, the old Roman cities came alive with new residents. By 1100, the old areas of these cities had been repopulated; soon the population outgrew the walls, necessitating the construction of new city walls outside the old.

In the Mediterranean world, cities had survived in a more visible fashion. Spain's Islamic cities had a flourishing urban life, and southern Italy still possessed such thriving cities as Bari, Salerno, Naples, and Amalfi. Although greatly reduced in size, Rome, the old capital of the Roman world, had survived as the center of papal administration. In northern Italy, Venice had already emerged as a town by the end of the eighth century because of its commercial connections to the Byzantine Empire.

Tuul/Getty Images

Fortified Town of Carcassonne. *The expansion of commerce and industry led to an ongoing growth of towns and cities in the High Middle Ages. As seen in this picture of the French town of Carcassonne, medieval towns were surrounded by walls strengthened by defensive towers and punctuated by gates. As is evident here, medieval urban skylines were dominated by towers of all kinds.*

Founding of New Cities and Towns   Beginning in the late tenth century, many new cities or towns were founded, particularly in northern Europe. Usually, a group of artisans and merchants established a settlement near some fortified stronghold, such as a castle or monastery. Castles were particularly favored because they were usually located along major routes of transportation or at the intersection of two trade routes; the lord of the castle also offered protection. If the settlement prospered and expanded, walls were built to protect it. The original meaning of the English *borough* or *burgh* and the German *Burg* as a fortress or walled enclosure is still evident in the names of many cities, such as Edinburgh and Hamburg. The merchants and artisans of these boroughs and burghs came to be called burghers or **bourgeoisie**.

Most towns were closely tied to their surrounding territories because they were dependent on the countryside for their food supplies. In addition, they were often part of the territory belonging to a lord and were subject to his jurisdiction. Although lords wanted to treat towns and townspeople as they would their vassals and serfs, cities had totally different needs and a different perspective. Townspeople needed mobility to trade. Consequently, the merchants and artisans of the towns constituted a revolutionary group who needed their own unique laws to meet their requirements. Since the townspeople were profiting from the growth of trade and sales of their products, they were willing to pay for the right to make their own laws and govern themselves. In many instances, lords and kings saw the potential for vast new sources of revenues and were willing to grant (or more accurately, sell) to the townspeople the liberties they were beginning to demand.

The Rights of Townspeople   By 1100, townspeople were obtaining charters of liberties from their territorial lords that granted them the privileges they wanted,

including the right to bequeath goods and sell property, freedom from military obligation to the lord, written urban law that guaranteed their freedom, and the right for
serfs to become free after residing a year and a day in the town. The last provision
made it possible for a runaway serf who could avoid capture to become a free person
in a city. Almost all new urban communities gained these elementary liberties, but
only some towns obtained the right to govern themselves by choosing their own officials and administering their own courts of law. Where townspeople experienced difficulty in obtaining privileges, they often swore an oath, forming an association called
a **commune**, and resorted to force against their lay or ecclesiastical lords.

Communes appeared first in Italy, where urban communities existed even in the
Early Middle Ages. In northern Italy, in the regions called Tuscany and Lombardy,
towns were governed by their bishops, but the nobles whose lands surrounded the
towns took an active interest in them. Bishops were usually supported by the
emperors, who used them as their chief administrators. In the eleventh century,
city residents rebelled against the rule of the bishops, swore communal associations
with the bishops' noble vassals, and overthrew the authority of the bishops by
force. The alliance between town residents and rural nobles was overwhelming,
and in the course of the eleventh and twelfth centuries, bishops were shorn of
their authority. Communes took over the rights of government and created new
offices, such as consuls and city councils, for self-rule. Pisa, Milan, Arezzo, and
Genoa all attained self-government by the end of the eleventh century.

Although communes were also sworn in northern Europe, especially in France
and Flanders, townspeople did not have the support of rural nobles. Revolts against
lay lords were usually brutally suppressed; those against bishops, as in Laon
(LAHn) at the beginning of the twelfth century, were more frequently successful.
When they succeeded, communes received the right to choose their own officials,
hold their own courts, and run their own cities. Unlike the towns in Italy, however,
where the decline of the emperor's authority ensured that the northern Italian cities
could function as self-governing republics, towns in France and England did not
become independent city-states but remained ultimately subject to royal authority.

Medieval cities, then, possessed varying degrees of self-government, depending
on the amount of control retained over them by the lord or king in whose territory
they were located. Nevertheless, all towns, regardless of the degree of outside control, evolved institutions of government for running the affairs of the community.

City Governments   Medieval cities defined citizenship narrowly and accorded it
only to males who had been born in the city or who had lived there for some
time. In many cities, citizens elected members of a city council that bore primary
responsibility for running the affairs of the city. City councillors (known as *consuls*
in Italy and southern France) not only enacted legislation but also served as judges
and city magistrates. The electoral process was carefully engineered to ensure that
only members of the wealthiest and most powerful families, who came to be called
the *patricians*, were elected. They kept the reins of government in their hands
despite periodic protests from lesser merchants and artisans. In the twelfth and thirteenth centuries, cities added some kind of sole executive leader, even if he was
only a figurehead. Although the title varied from town to town, this executive officer was frequently called a *mayor*.

City governments kept close watch over the activities of their community. To care for the welfare and safety of the community, a government might regulate air and water pollution; provide water barrels and delegate responsibility to people in every section of the town to fight fires, which were an ever-present danger; construct warehouses to stockpile grain in the event of food emergencies; and establish and supervise the standards of weights and measures used in the various local trades and industries.

Crime was not a major problem in the towns of the High Middle Ages because the relatively small size of communities made it difficult for criminals to operate openly. Nevertheless, medieval urban governments did organize town guards to patrol the streets by night and the city walls by day. People caught committing criminal acts were quickly tried for their offenses. Serious offenses, such as murder, were punished by execution, usually by hanging. Lesser crimes were punished by fines, flogging, branding, public exposure (as in the pillory), or expulsion.

Medieval cities remained relatively small in comparison with either ancient or modern cities. A large trading city would number about 5,000 inhabitants. By 1300, London was the largest city in England, with 80,000 people or more. Otherwise, north of the Alps, only a few great commercial urban centers, such as Bruges and Ghent, had a population close to 40,000. Italian cities tended to be larger, with Venice, Florence, Genoa, Milan, and Naples numbering almost 100,000. Even the largest European city, however, seemed insignificant alongside the Byzantine capital of Constantinople or the Arab cities of Damascus, Baghdad, and Cairo. For a long time to come, Europe remained predominantly rural, but in the long run, the rise of towns and the growth of trade laid the foundation for the eventual transformation of Europe from a rural agricultural society to an urban industrial one.

Life in the Medieval City   Medieval towns were surrounded by stone walls that were expensive to build, so the space within was precious and tightly filled. This gave medieval cities their characteristic appearance of narrow, winding streets with houses crowded against each other. Until the thirteenth century, streets were generally left unpaved, and buildings fronted directly on them. To gain more space, inhabitants frequently added balconies or built the second and third stories of their dwellings out over the streets. Since dwellings were crowded so closely together and candles and wood fires were used for light and heat, the danger of fire was great.

A medieval urban skyline was dominated by the towers of castles and town halls, but especially of churches, whose number could be staggering. At the beginning of the thirteenth century, London had 120 monastic and parish churches. If a city was the center of a bishop's see, a large cathedral would dominate the other buildings and be visible for miles outside the city.

Most of the people who lived in the cities were merchants involved in trade and artisans engaged in manufacturing of some kind. Sometimes merchants and artisans had their own sections in a city. The merchant area included warehouses, inns, and taverns. Artisan sections were usually divided along craft lines, and each craft might have its own street where its activity was pursued.

The physical environment of medieval cities was not pleasant. They were often dirty and rife with smells from animal and human waste deposited in backyard privies or on the streets. In some places, city governments required citizens to periodically collect garbage and waste and cart it outside the town. Atmospheric pollution was also a fact of life, not only from the ubiquitous wood fires but also from the use of coal, a cheap fuel that was used industrially by lime-burners, brewers, and dyers. Burning coal emitted foul-smelling, noxious fumes and was sometimes prohibited under pain of fine.

Cities were also unable to stop water pollution, especially from the animal-slaughtering and tanning industries. Butchers dumped blood and other waste products from their butchered animals into the river, while tanners unloaded tannic acids, dried blood, fat, hair, and the other waste products of their operations. Forcing both industries to locate downstream to avoid polluting the water used by the city upstream was only partly effective. Tanneries and slaughterhouses existed in every medieval town, so the river could rapidly become polluted from other towns' wastes.

Because of the pollution, cities were not inclined to use the rivers for drinking water but relied instead on wells. Occasionally, communities repaired the system of aqueducts or conduits left over from Roman times and sometimes even constructed new ones. Private and public baths also existed in medieval towns. Paris, for example, had thirty-two public baths for men and women. City laws did not allow lepers and people with "bad reputations" to use them, but such measures did not prevent the public baths from being known for permissiveness due to public nudity. One contemporary commented on what occurred in public bathhouses: "Shameful things. Men make a point of staying all night in the public baths and women at the break of day come in and through 'ignorance' find themselves in the men's rooms."[3] Authorities came under increasing pressure to close the baths down, and the great plague of the fourteenth century sealed their fate. The standards of medieval hygiene broke down, and late medieval and early modern European society would prove to be remarkably dirty.

Because of the limited space in medieval towns, houses were narrow, built next to one another, and usually multistoried. In many houses, the shops or workrooms of merchants and craftspeople occupied the ground floor. Inhabitants, who might include husband and wife, children, servants, and apprentices, would live upstairs.

Women in Medieval Cities For most ordinary merchants and artisans, then, home life and work life were closely intertwined. Merchants and artisans taught their trades to their children and their wives and apprentices, or their children might be apprenticed to another merchant or artisan. Married women, in addition to supervising the household, purchasing food and preparing meals, washing clothes, managing the family finances, and bearing and taking care of children, were also often expected to help their husbands in their trades. While men produced goods at home, their wives often peddled them at markets or fairs.

Single women and widows had little alternative but to become involved in activities to generate income in order to provide for themselves financially. Some women earned money by practicing a trade, such as brewing ale, manufacturing glass, or making hats and cloth. Other women became midwives, innkeepers, or prostitutes. A widow often carried on her husband's trade. Some women in medieval towns were thus able to lead lives of considerable independence and made important contributions to the market economy. Nevertheless, women often earned less than men and faced obstacles that kept them from more rewarding opportunities. For example, women in textile production usually were given the most menial jobs. Many were forced to become domestic servants and received room and board in return for cooking, cleaning, and other domestic services.

Industry in Medieval Cities   The revival of trade enabled cities and towns to become important centers for manufacturing a wide range of goods, such as cloth, metalwork, shoes, and leather goods. A host of crafts were carried on in houses along the narrow streets of the medieval cities. From the twelfth century on, merchants and artisans began to organize themselves into **guilds**, which came to play a leading role in the economic life of the cities.

By the thirteenth century, virtually every group of craftspeople, such as tanners, carpenters, and bakers, had their own guild, and specialized groups of merchants, such as dealers in silk, spices, wool, or banking, had their separate guilds as well. Florence alone had fifty different guilds. Some communities were so comprehensive in covering all trades that they even had guilds for prostitutes.

Craft guilds directed almost every aspect of the production process. They set standards for the articles produced, specified the methods of production to be used, and even fixed the price at which the finished goods could be sold. Guilds also determined the number of individuals who could enter a specific trade and the procedure they must follow to do so.

A person who wanted to learn a trade first became an apprentice to a master craftsman, usually at around the age of ten. Apprentices were not paid but did receive room and board from their masters. After five to seven years of service, during which they learned their craft, apprentices became journeymen (or journeywomen, although most were male) who then worked for wages for other masters. Journeymen aspired to become masters as well. To do so, a journeyman had to produce a "masterpiece," a finished piece in his craft that allowed the master craftsmen of the guild to judge whether the journeyman was qualified to become a master and join the guild.

Craft guilds continued to dominate manufacturing in industries where raw materials could be acquired locally and the products sold locally. But in industries that required raw materials from outside the local area to produce high-quality products for growing markets abroad, a new form of industry dependent on large concentrations of capital and unskilled labor began to emerge. It was particularly evident in the "putting-out" or domestic system used in the production of woolen cloth in both Flanders and northern Italy. An entrepreneur, whose initial capital outlay probably came from commercial activities, bought raw wool and distributed it to workers who carried out the various stages of carding, spinning, weaving, dyeing, and fulling to produce a finished piece of woolen cloth. These laborers worked in their own homes and were paid wages. As wage earners, they were dependent on their employers and the fluctuations in prices that occurred periodically in the international market for the finished goods. The entrepreneur collected the final products and sold the finished cloth, earning a profit that could then be invested in more production. Woolen industries operated by capitalist entrepreneurs in seventeen principal centers in northern Europe, mostly in Flanders, produced most of the woolen cloth used in northern Europe. An Italian chronicler at the beginning of the fourteenth century estimated that the woolen industry in Florence produced 80,000 pieces of cloth a year and employed 30,000 men, women, and children, usually at pitiful wages.

THE INTELLECTUAL AND ARTISTIC WORLD OF THE HIGH MIDDLE AGES

The High Middle Ages was a time of tremendous intellectual and artistic vitality. The period witnessed the growth of educational institutions, a rebirth of interest in ancient culture, a quickening of theological thought, a revival of law, the development of a vernacular literature, and a burst of activity in art and architecture. Although monks continued to play an important role in intellectual activity, increasingly the secular clergy, cities, and courts, whether of kings, princes, or high church officials, began to exert a newfound influence. Especially significant were the new cultural expressions that emerged in towns and cities.

The Rise of Universities   The university as we know it with faculty, students, and degrees was a product of the High Middle Ages. The word *university* is derived from the Latin word *universitas* (yoo-nee-VAYR-see-tahss), meaning a corporation or guild, and referred to either a guild of teachers or a guild of students. Medieval universities were educational guilds or corporations that produced educated and trained individuals.

The Origins of Universities   Education in the Early Middle Ages rested primarily with the clergy, especially the monks. Although monastic schools were the centers of learning from the ninth century, they were surpassed in the course of the eleventh century by the cathedral schools organized by the secular (nonmonastic) clergy. Cathedral schools, like the cities in which they were located, expanded rapidly in the eleventh century. There were twenty of them in 900, but by 1100 the number had grown to at least two hundred since every cathedral city felt compelled to establish one. The most famous were Chartres, Reims, Paris, Laon, and Soissons, all in France, which was the intellectual center of Europe by the twelfth century (see Map 9.2). Although the primary purpose of cathedral schools was to educate priests to be more literate men of God, they also attracted other individuals who desired some education but did not want to become priests. Many university administrators today carry titles, such as chancellor, provost, and dean, that were originally used for the officials of cathedral chapters.

The first European university was founded in Bologna, Italy, and coincided with the revival of interest in Roman law, especially the rediscovery of Justinian's *Corpus Iuris Civilis* (see "The Revival of Roman Law" later in this chapter). In the twelfth century, Irnerius (1088–1125), a great teacher of Roman law in Bologna (buh-LOHN-yuh) attracted students from all over Europe. Most of them were laymen, usually older individuals who served as administrators to kings and princes and were eager to learn more about law so that they could apply it in their jobs. To protect themselves, students at Bologna formed a guild or *universitas*, which was recognized by Emperor Frederick Barbarossa and given a charter in 1158. Although the faculty also organized itself as a group, the *universitas* of students at

MAP 9.2 Intellectual Centers of Medieval Europe

Products of the High Middle Ages, universities provided students with a basic liberal arts education and the opportunity to pursue further studies in law, medicine, or theology. Courses were taught in Latin, primarily by professors reading from books. There were no exams in individual courses, but students had to pass a comprehensive oral exam to gain a degree.

Bologna was far more influential. It obtained a promise of freedom for students from local authorities, regulated the price of lodging, and determined the curriculum, fees, and standards for their masters. Teachers were fined if they missed a class or began their lectures late. The University of Bologna remained the greatest law school in Europe throughout the Middle Ages.

In northern Europe, the University of Paris became the first recognized university. A number of teachers or masters who had received licenses to teach from the cathedral school of Notre-Dame in Paris began to take on extra students for a fee. By the end of the twelfth century, these masters teaching at Paris had formed a *universitas* or guild of masters. By 1200, the king of France, Philip Augustus, officially acknowledged the existence of the University of Paris.

The University of Oxford in England, organized on the Paris model, first appeared in 1208. A migration of scholars from Oxford in 1209 led to the establishment of Cambridge University. In the Late Middle Ages, kings, popes, and princes vied to found new universities. By the end of the Middle Ages, there were eighty universities in Europe, most of them located in France, Italy, Germany, and England.

Teaching in the Medieval University   A student's initial studies at a medieval university centered around the traditional liberal arts curriculum. The *trivium* consisted of grammar, rhetoric, and logic, and the *quadrivium* comprised arithmetic, geometry, astronomy, and music. All classes were conducted in Latin, which provided a common means of communication for students, regardless of their country of origin. Basically, medieval university instruction used the lecture method. The word *lecture* is derived from Latin and means "to read." Before the development of the printing press in the fifteenth century, books were expensive, and few students could afford them, so masters read from a text (such as a collection of laws when the subject was law) and then added commentaries, which came to be known as glosses. No exams were given after a series of lectures, but when a student applied for a degree, he (women did not attend universities in the Middle Ages) was given a comprehensive oral examination by a committee of teachers. These exams were taken after a four- or six-year period of study. The first degree a student could earn was an A.B., the *artium baccalaureus* (ar-TEE-um bak-uh-LAR-ee-uss), or bachelor of arts; later he might receive an A.M., *artium magister* (ar-TEE-um muh-GISS-ter), master of arts. All degrees were technically licenses to teach, although most students receiving them did not become teachers.

After completing the liberal arts curriculum, a student could go on to study law, medicine, or theology, which was the most highly regarded subject of the medieval curriculum. The study of law, medicine, or theology was a long process that could take a decade or more. A student who passed his final oral examinations was granted a doctor's degree, which officially enabled him to teach his subject. Most students who pursued advanced degrees received their master's degrees first and taught the arts curriculum while continuing to pursue their advanced degrees. Students who received degrees from medieval universities could pursue other careers besides teaching that were much more lucrative. A law degree was deemed essential for those who wished to serve as advisers to kings and princes. The growing administrative bureaucracies of popes and kings also demanded a supply of clerks with a university education who could keep records and draw up official documents.

Students in the Medieval University   Students at medieval universities stemmed predominantly from the middle groups of medieval society, the families of lesser knights, merchants, and artisans. All were male; many were poor but ambitious and upwardly mobile. Many students started when they were fourteen to eighteen years old and received their bachelor's or master's degrees by their early twenties. Study for a doctorate in one of the specialized schools of law, medicine, or theology entailed at least another ten years. It was not unusual for men to receive their doctorates in their late thirties or early forties.

There are obvious similarities between medieval and modern students. Then as now, many students took their studies seriously and worked hard. Then as now, alcohol, sex, and appeals for spending money were all too common. In medieval universities, handbooks provided form letters that students could use in requesting money from their fathers, guardians, or patrons. This is an example from Oxford:

> B. to his venerable master A., greeting. This is to inform you that I am studying at Oxford with the greatest of diligence, but the matter of money stands greatly in the way of my promotion, as it is now two months since I have spent the last of what you sent me. The city is expensive and makes many demands; I have to rent lodgings, buy necessaries, and provide for many other things which I cannot now specify. Wherefore I respectfully beg your paternity that by the promptings of divine pity you may assist me, so that I may be able to complete what I have well begun.[4]

Lack of studiousness is not just a modern phenomenon, as this letter from a medieval father to his son illustrates:

> To his son G. residing at Orleans, P. of Besançon sends greetings with paternal zeal. It is written, "He also that is slothful in his work is brother to him that is a great waster." I have recently discovered that you live dissolutely and slothfully, preferring license to restraint and play to work and strumming a guitar while the others are at their studies, whence it happens that you have read but one volume of law while your more industrious companions have read several. Wherefore I have decided to exhort you herewith to repent utterly of your dissolute and careless ways, that you may no longer be called a waster and your shame may be turned to good repute.[5]

We have no idea whether the letter convinced the student to change his ways.

Medieval universities shared in the violent atmosphere of the age. Records from courts of law reveal numerous disturbances at European universities. One German professor was finally dismissed for stabbing one too many of his colleagues in faculty meetings. A student in Bologna was attacked in the classroom by another student armed with a sword. Oxford regulations attempted to dampen the violence by forbidding students to bring weapons to class. Not uncommonly, town and gown struggles (*gown* refers to the academic robe worn by teachers and students) escalated into bloody riots between townspeople and students.

Despite the violence, universities proved important to medieval civilization, not only for the growth of learning, which, after all, is the main task of the university, but also by providing a mechanism for training the personnel who served as teachers, administrators, lawyers, and doctors in an increasingly specialized society.

A Revival of Classical Antiquity   Another aspect of the intellectual revival of the High Middle Ages was a resurgence of interest in the works of Classical antiquity—the works of the Greeks and Romans. In the twelfth century, western Europe was introduced to a large number of Greek scientific and philosophical works, including those of Galen and Hippocrates on medicine, Ptolemy on geography and astronomy, and Euclid on mathematics. Above all, the West now had available the complete works of Aristotle. During the second half of the twelfth century, all of Aristotle's scientific works were translated into Latin, which served as an international language for both speaking and writing in the West. This great influx of Aristotle's works had an overwhelming impact on the West. He came to be viewed as the "master of those who know," the man who seemed to have understood every field of knowledge.

The recovery of Greek scientific and philosophical works was not a simple process, however. Little knowledge of Greek had survived in Europe. Thus, it was through the Muslim world that the West recovered Aristotle and other Greek works. The translation of Greek works into Arabic had formed but one aspect of a brilliant Muslim civilization. In the twelfth century, these writings were now translated from Arabic into Latin, making them available to the West. Wherever Muslim and Christian cultures met—in the Norman kingdom of Sicily, southern Italy, and above all Spain—the work of translation was carried on by both Arabic and Jewish scholars.

The Islamic world had more to contribute intellectually to the West than translations, however. Scientific work in the ninth and tenth centuries had enabled it to forge far ahead of the Western world, and in the twelfth and thirteenth centuries, Arabic works on physics, mathematics, medicine, and optics became available to the West in Latin translations. Adelard of Bath (1090–1150) was one source of these works. Having traveled throughout the Mediterranean region, he later translated an Arabic version of Euclid's Chapter 4) into Latin, as well as the mathematical works of al-Khwarizmi (see Chapter 8). Adelard also introduced to Europeans the astrolabe, an Arabic astronomical instrument that proved valuable to sailors.

When Aristotle's works arrived in the West in the second half of the twelfth century, they were accompanied by commentaries written by outstanding Arabic and Jewish philosophers. One example was Ibn-Rushd (ib-un-RUSHT *or* ib-un-RUSH-ed), or Averroës (uh-VERR-oh-eez) (1126–1198), who lived in Córdoba and composed a systematic commentary on virtually all of Aristotle's surviving works. The works of Arabic philosophers proved highly influential to Western intellectuals.

The West was also receptive to the works of Jewish scholars living in the Islamic world. Perhaps the best known is Moses ben Maimon, or Maimonides (my-MAH-nuh-deez) (1135–1204), who also lived in Córdoba. He was conversant with Greek and Arabic traditions and interested in the problem of reconciling faith and reason. In his *Guide for the Perplexed*, written in Arabic, Maimonides attempted to harmonize the rational and natural philosophy of Aristotle with the basic truths of Judaism. Although it was attacked by some Orthodox Jews, Western scholars in the thirteenth century paid close attention to it after its translation into Latin.

The Development of Scholasticism   Christianity's importance in medieval society probably made it inevitable that theology would play a central role in the European intellectual world. Whether in monastic or cathedral schools or the new universities, theology, the formal study of religion, reigned as "queen of the sciences."

Beginning in the eleventh century, the effort to apply reason or logical analysis to the church's basic theological doctrines had a significant impact on the study of theology. The philosophical and theological system of the medieval schools is known as **scholasticism**. A primary preoccupation of scholasticism was the attempt to reconcile faith and reason, to demonstrate that what was accepted on faith was in harmony with what could be learned by reason. The scholastic method came to be the basic instructional mode of the universities. In essence, this method consisted of posing a question, presenting contradictory authorities on that question, and then arriving at conclusions. It was a system that demanded rigorous analytical thought. Although scholasticism reached its high point in the thirteenth century, it had its beginnings in the theological world of the eleventh and twelfth centuries, especially in the work of Abelard.

Abelard   Peter Abelard (1079–1142) studied in northern France but scorned his teachers as insignificant and took up the teaching of theology in Paris. Possessed of a colorful personality, Abelard was a very popular teacher who attracted many students. A man with a strong ego, he became known for the zest with which he entered into arguments with fellow students as well as for his affair with his student Heloise. Heloise bore a child by Abelard and secretly married him. But her uncle, who had hired Abelard as a tutor for his niece, sought revenge, as Abelard related in an account of his life titled *History of My Misfortunes*: "One night they took from me a most cruel and shameful vengeance, as I was resting and sleeping in the inner room of my lodging.... For they cut off those parts of my body, by which I had committed the deed which sorrowed them."[6]

Above all others, Abelard was responsible for furthering the new scholastic approach to theology. In his most famous work, *Sic et Non (Yes and No)*, he listed passages from Scripture and the church fathers that stood in direct contradiction to one another and stressed the need to use logic or dialectical reasoning to reconcile the apparent differences systematically. He summed up his method thus: "By doubting we come to inquiry, through inquiry to the truth."

The Problem of Universals   Beginning in the twelfth century, a major controversy—the problem of universals—began to occupy many theologians. The basic issue involved the nature of reality itself: What constitutes what is real? Theologians were divided into two major schools of thought reflecting the earlier traditions of Greek thought, especially the divergent schools of Plato and Aristotle.

Following Plato, the scholastic **realists** took the position that the individual objects that we perceive with our senses, such as trees, are not real but merely manifestations of universal ideas ("treeness") that exist in the mind of God. All knowledge, then, is based on the ideas implanted in human reason by the creator. To the realists, truth can be discovered only by contemplating universals. The **nominalists** were adherents of Aristotle's ideas and believed that only individual objects are real. In their view, universal ideas and concepts were simply names (Latin *nomina*, hence *nominalism*). Truth could be discovered only by examining individual objects.

By the thirteenth century, the scholastics were confronting a new challenge—how to harmonize Christian revelation with the work of Aristotle. The great influx of Aristotle's works into the West in the High Middle Ages threw many theologians into consternation. Aristotle was so highly regarded that he was called "the philosopher," yet he had arrived at his conclusions by rational thought, not revelation, and some of his doctrines, such as the mortality of the individual soul, contradicted the teachings of the church. The most famous attempt to reconcile Aristotle and the doctrines of Christianity was that of Saint Thomas Aquinas (uh-KWY-nuss).

Aquinas Thomas Aquinas (1225–1274) studied theology at Cologne and Paris and taught at both Naples and Paris, and it was at the latter that he worked on his famous *Summa Theologica* (SOO-muh tay-oh-LOG-jee-kuh) (*A Summa of Theology*—a summa was a compendium of knowledge that attempted to bring together all the received learning of the preceding centuries on a given subject into a single whole). Aquinas's masterpiece was organized according to the dialectical method of the scholastics. Aquinas first posed a question, then cited sources that offered opposing opinions on the question, and finally resolved the issue by arriving at his own conclusions. In this fashion, Aquinas raised and discussed some six hundred articles or issues.

Aquinas's reputation derives from his masterful attempt to reconcile faith and reason. He took it for granted that there were truths derived by reason and truths derived by faith. He was certain, however, that the two truths could not be in conflict with each other:

> The light of faith that is freely infused into us does not destroy the light of natural knowledge [reason] implanted in us naturally. For although the natural light of the human mind is insufficient to show us these things made manifest by faith, it is nevertheless impossible that these things which the divine principle gives us by faith are contrary to these implanted in us by nature [reason]. Indeed, were that the case, one or the other would have to be false, and since both are given to us by God, God would have to be the author of untruth, which is impossible.
>
> … It is impossible that those things which are of philosophy can be contrary to those things which are of faith.[7]

The natural mind, unaided by faith, could arrive at truths concerning the physical universe. Without God's help, however, unaided reason alone could not grasp spiritual truths, such as the Trinity (the belief that God, Jesus, and the Holy Spirit are three manifestations of the same unique deity) or the Incarnation (the belief that Jesus in his lifetime was God in human form).

The Revival of Roman Law A systematic approach to knowledge was also expressed in the area of law. Of special importance was the rediscovery of the great legal work of Justinian, the *Corpus Iuris Civilis*, known to the medieval West before 1100 only at second hand. Initially, teachers of law, such as Irnerius of Bologna, were content merely to explain the meaning of Roman legal terms to their students. Gradually, they became more sophisticated so that by the mid-twelfth century, "doctors of law" had developed commentaries and systematic treatises on the legal texts. Italian cities, above all Pavia and Bologna, became prominent centers for the study of Roman law. By the thirteenth century, Italian jurists were systematizing the various professional commentaries on Roman law into a single commentary known as the ordinary gloss. Study of Roman law at the universities came to consist of learning the text of the law along with this gloss.

This revival of Roman law occurred in a world dominated by a body of law quite different from that of the Romans. European law comprised a hodgepodge of Germanic law codes, feudal customs, and urban regulations. The desire to know a more orderly world, already evident in the study of theology, perhaps made it inevitable that Europeans would enthusiastically welcome the more systematic approach of Roman law.

The training of students in Roman law at medieval universities led to further application of its principles as these students became judges, lawyers, scribes, and councillors for the towns and monarchies of western Europe. By the beginning of the thirteenth century, the old system of the ordeal was being replaced by a rational, decision-making process based on the systematic collection and analysis of evidence, a clear indication of the impact of Roman law on the European legal system.

Literature in the High Middle Ages   Latin was the universal language of medieval civilization. Used in the church and schools, it enabled learned people to communicate anywhere in Europe. The intellectual revival of the High Middle Ages included an outpouring of Latin literature. Much of medieval Latin poetry was religious verse, but there was also a large body of Latin verse dedicated to themes of love and nature. Many of these poems constitute the so-called Goliardic (gohl-YAR-dik) poetry.

While Latin continued to be used for literary purposes, by the twelfth century much creative literature was being written in the **vernacular** (the local language, such as Spanish, French, English, or German). Throughout the Middle Ages, there had been a popular vernacular literature, especially manifest in the Germanic, Celtic, Old Icelandic, and Slavonic sagas. But a new market for vernacular literature appeared in the twelfth century when educated laypeople at courts and in the new urban society sought fresh avenues of entertainment.

Troubadour Poetry   Perhaps the most popular vernacular literature of the twelfth century was *troubadour poetry*, chiefly the product of nobles and knights. This poetry focused on themes of courtly love, the love of a knight for a lady, generally a married noble lady, who inspires him to become a braver knight and a better poet. A good example is found in the laments of Jaufré Rudel (zhoh-FRAY roo-DEL), a crusading noble who cherished a dream lady from afar whom he said he would always love but feared he would never meet:

> *Most sad, most joyous shall I go away,*
> *Let me have seen her for a single day,*
> *   My love afar,*
> *I shall not see her, for her land and mine*
> *Are sundered, and the ways are hard to find,*
> *So many ways, and I shall lose my way,*
> *   So wills it God.*
> *Yet shall I know no other love but hers,*
> *And if not hers, no other love at all.*
> *   She has surpassed all.*
> *So fair she is, so noble, I would be*
> *   A captive with the hosts of paynimrie [the*
> *   Muslims]*
> *In a far land, if so be upon me*
> *   Her eyes might fall.*[8]

Although it originated in southern France, troubadour poetry also spread to northern France, Italy, and Germany.

Goliardic Poetry: The Archpoet

The Goliards (GOHL-yurds *or* GOHL-yards) were a group of Latin writers who wrote poems satirizing the hypocrisy of the church while celebrating the joys of wine, women, and song. Although it was once thought that the Goliards were "wandering scholars"—vagabond students and teachers—many historians today believe that they were established poets living at courts or in monasteries. One of these poets was a German known only as the Archpoet, who was probably from the knightly order and was in service at the court of the archbishop of Cologne. This selection is from his most famous work, *The Confession of Golias*.

The Archpoet, *The Confession of Golias*

Dull and dour sobriety
  Never takes my money,
Give me loose society
  Where the jokes are funny;
Love will bring variety,
  Toil that's sweet as honey.
Pillars of propriety,
  Have you hearts as sunny?
Down the primrose path I post
  Straight to Satan's grotto,
Shunning virtue, doing most
  Things that I ought not to;
Little hope of heaven I boast,
  Charmed by pleasure's otto
  [fragrance]:

Since the soul is bound to roast
  Save the skin's my motto....
Much too hard it is, I find,
  So to change my essence
As to keep a virgin mind
  In a virgin's presence.
Rigid laws can never bind
  Youth to acquiescence;
Light o' loves must seek their kind,
  Bodies take their pleasance....
Next, I'm called in terms precise
  Monstrous fond of gaming;
Losing all my clothes at dice
  Gains me this worth naming:
While outside I'm cool as ice,
  Inwardly I'm flaming,
Then with daintiest device
  Poems and songs I'm framing....
My intention is to die
  In the tavern drinking;
Wine must be at hand, for I
  Want it when I'm sinking.
Angels when they come shall cry,
  At my frailties winking:
"Spare this drunkard, God, he's high,
  Absolutely stinking!"

Q What groups of people in medieval society would be attracted to Goliardic poetry? Why?

Source: From George Whicher, *The Goliard Poets: Medieval Songs and Satires in New Verse Translations* (New Directions, 1949), pp. 107–111.

The Heroic Epic   Another type of vernacular literature was the **chanson de geste** (shahn-SAWNH duh ZHEST), or heroic epic. The earliest and finest example is the *Chanson de Roland (The Song of Roland)*, which appeared around 1100 and was written in a dialect of French, a Romance language derived from Latin. The *chansons de geste* were written for a male-dominated society. The chief events described in these poems, as in *The Song of Roland*, are battles and political contests. Their world is one of combat in which knights fight courageously for their kings and lords. Women play little or no role in this literary genre.

The Courtly Romance   Although *chansons de geste* were still written in the twelfth century, a different kind of long poem, the *courtly romance*, also became popular. It was composed in rhymed couplets and dwelt on romantic subjects: brave knights, virtuous ladies, evil magicians, bewitched palaces, fairies, talking animals, and strange forests. The story of King Arthur, the legendary king of the fifth-century Britons, became a popular subject for the courtly romance. The best versions of the Arthurian legends survive in the works of Chrétien de Troyes (kray-TYEN duh TRWAH), a French writer in the second half of the twelfth century, whose courtly romances were viewed by contemporaries as the works of a master storyteller.

Romanesque Architecture: "A White Mantle of Churches"   The eleventh and twelfth centuries witnessed an explosion of building, both private and public. The construction of castles and churches absorbed most of the surplus resources of medieval society and at the same time reflected its basic pre-occupations, warfare and God. The churches were by far the most conspicuous of the public buildings. As a chronicler of the eleventh century commented:

> [After the] year of the millennium, which is now about three years past, people all over the world, but especially in Italy and France, began to rebuild their churches. Although most of them were well built and in little need of alterations, Christian nations were rivaling each other to have the most beautiful edifices. One might say the world was shaking herself, throwing off her old garments, and robing herself with a white mantle of churches. Then nearly all the cathedrals, the monasteries dedicated to different saints, and even the small village chapels were reconstructed more beautifully by the faithful.[9]

Hundreds of new cathedrals and abbey and pilgrimage churches, as well as thousands of parish churches in rural villages, were built in the eleventh and twelfth centuries. This building spree reflected both the revived religious culture and the increased wealth of the period produced by agriculture, trade, and the growth of cities.

The cathedrals of the eleventh and twelfth centuries were built in a truly international style, the **Romanesque** (roh-man-ESK). The construction of churches required the services of professional master builders, whose employment throughout Europe guaranteed an international unity in basic features. Prominent examples of Romanesque churches can be found in Germany, France, and Spain.

Romanesque churches were normally built in the rectangular basilica shape used in the construction of churches in the Late Roman Empire. Romanesque builders made a significant innovation by replacing the earlier flat wooden ceiling with a long, round stone vault called a barrel vault or a cross vault where two barrel vaults intersected (a vault is simply a curved roof made of masonry). The latter was used when a transept was added to create a church plan in the shape of a cross. Although barrel and cross vaults were technically difficult to construct, they were considered aesthetically pleasing and technically proficient and had fine acoustics.

Because stone vaults were extremely heavy, Romanesque churches required massive pillars and walls to hold them up. This left little space for windows, making Romanesque churches notoriously dark on the inside. Their massive walls and pillars gave the churches a sense of solidity and almost the impression of a fortress. Indeed, massive walls and slit windows were also characteristic of the castle architecture of the period.

The Gothic Cathedral   Begun in the twelfth century and brought to perfection in the thirteenth, the **Gothic** cathedral remains one of the greatest artistic triumphs of the High Middle Ages. Soaring skyward, almost as if to reach heaven, it was a fitting symbol for medieval people's preoccupation with God.

Two fundamental innovations of the twelfth century made Gothic cathedrals possible. The combination of ribbed vaults and pointed arches replaced the barrel vault of Romanesque churches and enabled builders to make Gothic churches higher than their Romanesque counterparts. The use of pointed arches and ribbed vaults created an impression of upward movement, a sense of weightless upward thrust that implied the energy of God. Another technical innovation, the flying buttress, a heavy arched pier of stone built onto the outside of the walls, made it possible to distribute the weight of the church's vaulted ceilings outward and downward and thereby eliminate the heavy walls used in Romanesque churches to hold the weight of the massive barrel vaults. Thus, Gothic cathedrals could be built with thin walls that were filled with magnificent stained-glass windows, which created a play of light inside that varied with the sun at different times of the day.

Medieval craftspeople of the twelfth and thirteenth centuries perfected the art of stained glass. Small pieces of glass were stained in glowing colors like jewels. The colored light that filled Gothic cathedrals was not accidental but was achieved by people inspired by the belief that natural light was a symbol of the divine light of God. Light is invisible but enables people to see; so too is God invisible, but the existence of God allows the world of matter to be. Those impressed by the mystical significance of light were also impressed by the mystical significance of number. The proportions of Gothic cathedrals were based on mathematical ratios that their

The Gothic Cathedral. *The Gothic cathedral was one of the great artistic triumphs of the High Middle Ages. Shown here is the cathedral of Notre-Dame in Paris. Begun in 1163, it was not completed until the beginning of the fourteenth century.*

builders believed were derived from the ancient Greek school of Pythagoras and expressed the intrinsic harmony of the world as established by its creator.

The first fully Gothic church was the abbey church of Saint-Denis near Paris, which was built between 1140 and 1150 at the inspiration of Suger, the famous abbot of the monastery from 1122 to 1151. Although the Gothic style was the product of northern France, by the mid-thirteenth century French Gothic architecture had spread to England, Spain, Germany—indeed, to virtually all of Europe. This French Gothic style was seen most brilliantly in cathedrals in Paris (Notre-Dame), Reims, Amiens, and Chartres.

A Gothic cathedral was the work of an entire community. All classes contributed to its construction. Money was raised from wealthy townspeople who had profited from the new trade and industries as well as from kings and nobles. Master masons who were both architects and engineers designed the cathedrals. They drew up the plans and supervised the work of construction. Stonemasons and other craftspeople were paid a daily wage and provided the skilled labor to build the cathedrals. Indeed, these buildings were the first monumental structures of consequence built by free, salaried labor.

The building of cathedrals often became highly competitive as communities vied with one another to build the highest tower, a rivalry that sometimes ended in disaster. The cathedral of Beauvais in northern France collapsed in 1284 after reaching the height of 157 feet. Gothic cathedrals also depended on a community's faith. After all, it often took two or more generations to complete a cathedral, and the first generation of builders must have begun with the knowledge that they would not live to see the completed project. Most important, a Gothic cathedral symbolized the chief preoccupation of a medieval Christian community, its dedication to a spiritual ideal. As we have observed before, the largest buildings of an era reflect the values of its society. The Gothic cathedral, with its towers soaring toward heaven, gave witness to an age when a spiritual impulse still underlay most of existence.

CHRONOLOGY

EUROPEAN SOCIETY IN THE HIGH MIDDLE AGES

c. 950–1050	Emergence of new towns
c. 1000–1100	Romanesque cathedrals
c. 1100	The Song of Roland
c. 1100	Beginning of fairs in Champagne
c. 1140–1300	Age of Gothic cathedrals
c. 1150–1210	The rise of universities
c. 1150–1250	Growth of guilds
c. 1250–1280	Work of Thomas Aquinas

10

THE RISE OF KINGDOMS AND THE GROWTH OF CHURCH POWER

A medieval abbot and his monks

A. Dagli Orti/De Agostini/Getty Images

CHAPTER OUTLINE

- The Emergence and Growth of European Kingdoms, 1000–1300
- The Recovery and Reform of the Catholic Church • Christianity and Medieval Civilization • The Crusades

---

The Emergence and Growth of European Kingdoms, 1000–1300

The domination of society by the nobility reached its apex in the High Middle Ages. During this time, however, kings began the process of extending their power in more effective ways. Out of this growth in the monarchies would eventually come the European states that dominated much of later European history.

In theory, kings were regarded as the heads of their kingdoms and were expected to lead their vassals and subjects into battle. The king's power, however, was strictly limited. As we saw in Chapter 8, he had to honor the rights and privileges of his vassals, and if he failed to observe his vassals' rights, they could and did rebel. Weak kings were overthrown or, like the later Carolingians, replaced by another ruling dynasty.

Nevertheless, kings did possess some sources of power that other lords did not. Kings were anointed by holy oil in ceremonies reminiscent of Old Testament precedents; thus, their positions seemed sanctioned by divine favor. War and marriage alliances enabled them to increase their power, and their conquests enabled them to reward their followers with grants of land and bind powerful nobles to them. In the High Middle Ages, kings found ways to strengthen governmental institutions and consequently to extend their powers. The revival of commerce, the growth of cities, and the emergence of a money economy eventually enabled monarchs to hire soldiers and officials and to rely less on their vassals.

England in the High Middle Ages   At the beginning of the eleventh century, Anglo-Saxon England had fallen subject to Scandinavian control after a successful invasion by the Danes in 1016. King Canute (kuh-NOOT) (1016–1035) continued English institutions and laws and even supported the Catholic Church. His dynastic line proved unable to maintain itself, however, and in 1042, the Anglo-Saxon line of kings was restored in the person of Edward the Confessor (1042–1066). After his death, the kingship was taken by Harold Godwinson, who belonged to one of England's greatest noble families.

A cousin of Edward the Confessor, William of Normandy, however, laid claim to the throne of England. William crossed the English Channel with his forces in late September. The Anglo-Saxon forces of Harold Godwinson were in northern England, where they had defeated an invading Viking army, and had to return quickly to the south to face the new invaders. The Anglo-Saxon and Norman forces met on October 14, 1066, at Hastings, in one of the most famous battles in English history. Both forces numbered about 7,000 men. The Anglo-Saxon army, consisting mostly of foot soldiers armed with shields, swords, and battle-axes, created a shield wall at the top of a hill. Opposing them were the Norman forces of archers and the heavily armed knights that were a product of the fief-holding order that we examined in Chapter 8. Exhausted from their march from the north, the Anglo-Saxon forces fought bravely but were gradually worn down by the charges of the Norman knights. The battle lasted almost the entire day, but after the death of Harold Godwinson on the battlefield, the Anglo-Saxon forces fled. William then began his advance to London, where he was crowned king of England at Christmastime.

William of Normandy   After his conquest, William (1066–1087) treated all of England as a royal possession. Based on the Domesday (DOOMZ-day) Book, which William commissioned in 1086 by sending out royal officials to ascertain who owned or held land in tenancy, modern historians have estimated that the Norman royal family took possession of about one-fifth of the land in England as the royal demesne (domain). The remaining English land was held by nobles or the church as fiefs from the king; each of these vassals was in turn responsible for supplying a quota of knights for the royal army. The great landed nobles were allowed to divide their lands among their subvassals as they wished. In 1086, however, by the Oath of Salisbury Plain, William required all subvassals to swear loyalty to him as their king and liege lord. Henceforth, all subvassals owed their primary loyalty to the king rather than to their immediate lords.

Thus, the Norman conquest of England had brought a dramatic change. In Anglo-Saxon England, the king had only limited lands while great families controlled large stretches of territory and acted rather independently of the king. In contrast, the Normans established a hierarchy of nobles holding land as fiefs from the king. William of Normandy had created a strong, centralized monarchy. Gradually, a process of fusion between the victorious Normans and the defeated Anglo-Saxons created a new England. Although the Norman ruling class spoke French, Anglo-Saxon and French gradually merged into a new English language as the Norman-French intermarried with the Anglo-Saxon nobility.

William maintained the Anglo-Saxon administrative system in which counties (shires) were divided into hundreds (groups of villages). Within each shire, the sheriff was the chief royal officer responsible for leading the military forces of the county, collecting royal tolls, and presiding over the county court. William retained the office but replaced the Anglo-Saxon sheriffs with Normans. William also more fully developed the system of taxation and royal courts begun by the Anglo-Saxon and Danish kings of the tenth and eleventh centuries.

The Norman conquest of England had repercussions in France as well. Because the new king of England was still the duke of Normandy, he was both a king (of England) and at the same time a vassal to a king (of France), but a vassal who was now far more powerful than his lord. This connection with France kept England heavily involved in Continental affairs throughout the High Middle Ages.

A New Dynasty In the twelfth century, the power of the English monarchy increased substantially during the reign of Henry II (1154–1189), the founder of the new Plantagenet (plan-TAJ-uh-net) dynasty . Henry was particularly successful in developing administrative and legal institutions that strengthened the royal government. He continued the development of the **exchequer** (EKS-chek-ur), or permanent royal treasury. Royal officials, known as "barons of the exchequer," received taxes collected by the sheriffs while seated around a table covered by a checkered cloth that served as a counting device. (*Exchequer* is derived from the French word for chessboard.) The barons gave receipts to the sheriffs, while clerks recorded the accounts on sheets of parchment that were then rolled up. These so-called pipe rolls have been an important source of economic and social information for historians.

Perhaps even more significant than Henry's financial reforms were his efforts to strengthen the royal courts. Henry expanded the number of criminal cases tried in the king's courts and also devised ways of taking property cases from local courts to the royal courts. Henry's goals were clear: expanding the jurisdiction of the royal

Magna Carta

After the dismal defeat of King John at the hands of the French king, some of the English barons rebelled against their king. At Runnymede in 1215, King John agreed to seal Magna Carta, the "great charter" of liberties regulating the relationship between the king and his vassals. Magna Carta was, above all, a feudal document but was used in later years to strengthen the concept of limited monarchy.

Magna Carta

John, by the Grace of God, king of England, lord of Ireland, duke of Normandy and Aquitaine, count of Anjou, to the archbishops, bishops, abbots, earls, barons, justiciars, foresters, sheriffs, reeves, servants, and all bailiffs and his faithful people greeting.

1. In the first place we have granted to God, and by this our present charter confirmed, for us and our heirs forever, that the English church shall be free, and shall hold its rights entire and its liberties uninjured.... We have granted moreover to all free men of our kingdom for us and our heirs forever all the liberties written below, to be had and holden by themselves and their heirs from us and our heirs.

2. If any of our earls or barons, or others holding from us in chief by military service shall have died, and when he had died his heir shall be of full age and owe relief, he shall have his inheritance by the ancient relief; that is to say, the heir or heirs of an earl for the whole barony of an earl a hundred pounds; the heir or heirs of a baron for a whole barony a hundred pounds; the heir or heirs of a knight, for a whole knight's fee, a hundred shillings at most; and who owes less let him give less according to the ancient custom of fiefs.

3. If moreover the heir of any one of such shall be under age, and shall be in wardship, when he comes of age he shall have his inheritance without relief and without a fine....

12. No scutage or aid shall be imposed in our kingdom except by the common

courts extended the king's power and, of course, brought revenues into his coffers. Moreover, because the royal courts were now found throughout England, a body of **common law** (law that was common to the whole kingdom) began to replace the local law codes, which varied from place to place.

Henry was less successful at imposing royal control over the church. The king claimed the right to punish clergymen in the royal courts, but Thomas à Becket, archbishop of Canterbury and thus the highest-ranking English cleric, claimed that only church courts could try clerics. Attempts at compromise failed, and in 1170 the angry king publicly expressed the desire to be rid of Becket: "Who will free me of this priest?" he screamed. Four knights took the challenge, went to Canterbury, and murdered the archbishop in the cathedral. Faced with public outrage, Henry was forced to allow the right of appeal from English church courts to the papal court.

King John and Magna Carta   Many English nobles came to resent the ongoing growth of royal power and rose in rebellion during the reign of Henry's son, King John (1199–1216). Following in his father's footsteps, John continued council of our kingdom, except for the ransoming of our body, for the making of our oldest son a knight, and for once marrying our oldest daughter, and for these purposes it shall be only a reasonable aid....

13. And the city of London shall have all its ancient liberties and free customs, as well by land as by water. Moreover, we will and grant that all other cities and boroughs and villages and ports shall have all their liberties and free customs.

14. And for holding a common council of the kingdom concerning the assessment of an aid otherwise than in the three cases mentioned above, or concerning the assessment of a scutage we shall cause to be summoned the archbishops, bishops, abbots, earls, and greater barons by our letters under seal; and besides we shall cause to be summoned generally, by our sheriffs and bailiffs, all those who hold from us in chief, for a certain day, that is at the end of forty days at least, and for a certain place; and in all the letters of that summons, we will express the cause of the summons, and when the summons has

thus been given, the business shall proceed on the appointed day, on the advice of those who shall be present, even if not all of those who were summoned have come....

39. No free man shall be taken or imprisoned or dispossessed, or outlawed, or banished, or in any way destroyed, nor will we go upon him, nor send upon him, except by the legal judgment of his peers or by the law of the land....

60. Moreover, all those customs and franchises mentioned above in which we have conceded in our kingdom, and which are to be fulfilled, as far as pertains to us, in respect to our men; all men of our kingdom, as well as clergy as laymen, shall observe as far as pertains to them, in respect to their men.

Q *What are the major principles of Magna Carta as seen in this excerpt? Why has Magna Carta been considered such an important historical document?*

Source: From University of Pennsylvania Translation and Reprints, translated by E. P. Cheyney (Philadelphia, PA: University of Pennsylvania Press), 1897, Volume I, No. 6, pp. 6–16.

the effort to strengthen royal power and proved particularly ingenious at finding novel ways to levy taxes. The barons of England came to resent him deeply. By 1205, John had lost the duchy of Normandy, Maine, Anjou, and Touraine to the French king, Philip Augustus; when John's attempt to reconquer the duchy ended in a devastating defeat, many of the English barons rose in rebellion. At Runnymede (RUHN-ee-meed) in 1215, John was forced to assent to Magna Carta, the "great charter" of feudal liberties. Much of Magna Carta was aimed at limiting government practices that affected the relations between the king and his vassals on the one hand and between the king and the church on the other.

Despite later interpretations and efforts to broaden its principles, Magna Carta remains, above all, a feudal document. Feudal custom had always recognized that the relationship between king and vassals was based on mutual rights and obligations. Magna Carta gave written recognition to that fact and was used in subsequent years to underscore the concept that the monarch should be limited rather than absolute.

Edward I and the Emergence of Parliament   In the late thirteenth century, a very talented and powerful monarch ascended the throne in the person of Edward I (1272–1307). He began the process of uniting all of the British Isles into a single kingdom. Although Wales was eventually conquered and pacified, his attempt to subdue Scotland failed. Edward managed merely to begin a lengthy conflict between England and Scotland that lasted for centuries.

Edward was successful in reestablishing monarchical rights after a period of baronial control. During his reign, the role of the English Parliament, an institution of great importance in the development of representative government, began to be defined.

Originally, the word *parliament* was applied to meetings of the king's Great Council in which the greater barons and chief prelates of the church met with the king's judges and principal advisers to deal with judicial affairs. But in need of money in 1295, Edward I invited two knights from every county and two residents (known as burgesses) from each city and town to meet with the Great Council to consent to new taxes. This was the first Parliament.

The English Parliament, then, came to be composed of two knights from every county and two burgesses from every town or city, as well as the barons and ecclesiastical lords. Eventually, the barons and church lords formed the House of Lords; the knights and burgesses, the House of Commons. The Parliaments of Edward I granted taxes, discussed politics, passed laws, and handled judicial business. Although not yet the important body it would eventually become, the English Parliament had clearly emerged as an institution by the end of the thirteenth century. The law of the realm was beginning to be determined not by the king alone but by the king in consultation with representatives of various groups that constituted the community. By the beginning of the fourteenth century, England had begun to develop a unique system of national monarchy.

The Growth of the French Kingdom   The Capetian dynasty of French kings had emerged at the end of the tenth century. Although they bore the title of king, the Capetians had little real power. They controlled as the royal domain (the lands of the king) only the lands around Paris known as the Île-de-France (eel-duh-FRAHNS). As kings of France, the Capetians were formally the overlords of the great lords of France, such as the dukes of Normandy, Brittany, Burgundy, and Aquitaine. In reality, however, many of the dukes were considerably more powerful than the Capetian kings. It would take the Capetian dynasty hundreds of years to create a truly centralized monarchical authority in France.

The Conquests of Philip II   The reign of King Philip II Augustus (1180–1223) was an important turning point. He perceived that the power of the French monarch would never be extended until the Plantagenets' power was defeated. After all, Henry II and his sons were not only kings of England but also rulers of the French territories of Normandy, Maine, Anjou, and Aquitaine. Accordingly, Philip II waged war against King John of England and was successful in wresting control of Normandy, Maine, Anjou, and Touraine from the English king (see Map 10.1). Through these conquests, Philip II quadrupled the income of the French monarchy and greatly enlarged its power. To administer justice and collect royal revenues in his new territories, Philip appointed new royal officials, thus inaugurating a French royal bureaucracy.

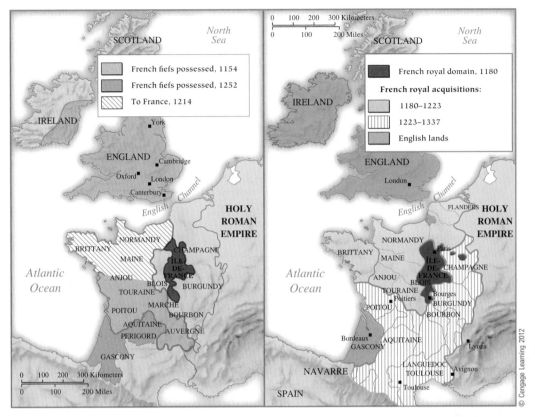

MAP 10.1   England and France (1154–1337): *(left)* **England and Its French Holdings;** *(right)* **Growth of the French State**

King Philip II Augustus of France greatly expanded the power of the Capetian royal family through his victories over the Plantagenet monarchy of England, which enabled Philip to gain control over much of north-central France.

The Saintly Louis IX   Capetian rulers after Philip II continued to add lands to the royal domain. Although Philip had used military force, other kings used both purchase and marriage to achieve the same end. Much of the thirteenth century was dominated by Louis IX (1226–1270), one of the most celebrated of the medieval French kings. A deeply religious man, he was later canonized as a saint by the church, an unusual action regardless of the century. Louis was known for his attempts to bring justice to his people and ensure their rights. He sent out royal agents to check on the activities of royal officials after hearing complaints that they were abusing their power. Sharing in the religious sentiments of his age, Louis played a major role in two of the later Crusades (see "The Crusades" later in this chapter). Both were failures, and he met his death during an invasion of North Africa.

Philip IV and the Estates-General   One of Louis's successors, Philip IV the Fair (1285–1314), was particularly effective in strengthening the French monarchy. The machinery of government became even more specialized. French kings going back to the early Capetians had possessed a household staff for running their affairs. In effect, the division and enlargement of this household staff produced the three major branches of royal administration: a council for advice; a chamber of accounts for finances; and the *Parlement* (par-luh-MAHNH), or royal court (the French *Parlement* was not the same as the English Parliament). By the beginning of the fourteenth century, the Capetians had established an efficient royal bureaucracy.

Philip IV also brought a French parliament into being by summoning representatives of the three estates, or classes—the clergy (First Estate), the nobles (Second Estate), and the townspeople (Third Estate)—to meet with him. They did so in 1302, inaugurating the Estates-General, the first French parliament. The Estates-General came to function as an instrument to bolster the king's power because he could ask representatives of the major French social classes to change the laws or grant new taxes. By the end of the thirteenth century, France was the largest, wealthiest, and best-governed monarchical state in Europe.

Christian Reconquest: The Spanish Kingdoms   Much of Spain had been part of the Islamic world since the eighth century. Muslim Spain had flourished in the Early Middle Ages. Córdoba became a major urban center with a population exceeding 300,000 people. Agriculture prospered, and Spain became known for excellent leather, wool, silk, and paper. Beginning in the tenth century, however, the most noticeable feature of Spanish history was the weakening of Muslim power and the beginning of a Christian reconquest that lasted until the final expulsion of the Muslims at the end of the fifteenth century. The **Reconquista** (ray-con-KEES-tuh), as the Spaniards called it, became over a period of time a sacred mission to many of the Christian rulers and inhabitants of the peninsula.

The Reconquest   By the eleventh century, a number of small Christian kingdoms in northern Spain—Leon, Castile (ka-STEEL), Navarre, Aragon, and Catalonia—were ready to take the offensive against the Muslims. Rodrigo Diaz de Vivar, known as El Cid ("The Master"), was the most famous military adventurer of the time. Unlike the Christian warriors of France, El Cid (ell SID *or* ell THEED) fought under either Christian or Muslim rulers. He carved out his own kingdom of Valencia in 1094 but failed to create a dynasty when it was reconquered by the Muslims after his death.

By the end of the twelfth century, the Christian reconquest of Spain had slowed considerably. The northern half had been consolidated into the Christian kingdoms of Castile, Navarre, Aragon, and Portugal, which had emerged by 1179 as a separate kingdom (see Map 10.2). The southern half of Spain remained under the control of the Muslims.

In the thirteenth century, Christian rulers again took the offensive against the Muslims. Aragon and Castile had become the two strongest Spanish kingdoms, and Portugal had reached its modern boundaries. All three states made significant conquests of Muslim territory. Castile subdued most of Andalusia in the south, down to the Atlantic and the Mediterranean; at the same time, Aragon conquered Valencia. The crucial battle occurred in 1212 at Las Navas de Tolosa (lahss

MAP 10.2 Christian Reconquests in the Western Mediterranean

Muslims seized most of Spain in the eighth century, near the end of the period of rapid Islamic expansion. In the eleventh century, small Christian kingdoms in the north began the Reconquista, finally conquering the last Moors near the end of the fifteenth century.

nah-vahss day toh-LOH-suh). Alfonso VIII of Castile (1155–1214) had amassed an army of 60,000 men and crushed the Muslim forces, leading to Christian victories over the next forty years. By the mid-thirteenth century, the Muslims held only the kingdom of Granada, along the southeastern edge of the Iberian peninsula.

As the Christian armies moved down the peninsula, the rulers followed a policy known as *repartimiento* (ray-par-tuh-my-EN-toh). They distributed houses, land, and property in the countryside to individuals who had made the conquests and new Christian colonists. The former—consisting of nobles, important churchmen, high-ranking soldiers, and royal officials—often received the best lands. The colonists, some of them ordinary foot soldiers, also received land. Muslims who were not expelled or killed and chose to stay under Christian rule were known as *mudejares* (moo-theh-KHAH-rayss); most of them continued to work in small industrial enterprises or as farmers.

To encourage other settlers to move into the newly conquered regions, Spanish kings issued written privileges that guaranteed rule in accordance with the law for most of the communities in their kingdoms. These privileges, or *fueros* (FWYA-rohss), stipulated the punishments for crimes committed within community boundaries and the means for resolving civil disputes. They also established a procedure for acquiring citizenship in the community, rules for service in the local militia, and laws protecting the rights of women and children living in the towns. By the thirteenth century, kings were increasingly required to swear that they would respect these community customs before they were confirmed in office by assemblies of their leading citizens.

The Spanish kingdoms followed no consistent policy in the treatment of the conquered Muslim population. Muslim farmers continued to work the land but were forced to pay very high rents in Aragon. In Castile, King Alfonso X (1252–1284), who called himself the "King of Three Religions," encouraged the continued development of a cosmopolitan culture shared by Christians, Jews, and Muslims.

The Lands of the Holy Roman Empire: Germany and Italy   The Saxon kings of the tenth century had strengthened their hold over the German kingdom and revived the empire of Charlemagne. A new dynasty, known as the Salian kings, began in 1024 with the election of Conrad II (1024–1039) of Franconia (see Map 10.3). Both Conrad and his successors, Henry III (1039–1056) and Henry IV (1056–1106), managed to create a strong German monarchy and a powerful empire by leading armies into Italy. The great lords of Germany took advantage of the early death of Henry III and the minority of Henry IV to extend their own power at the expense of the latter. The elective nature of the German monarchy posed a problem for the German kings. Although some dynasties were strong enough for their members to be elected regularly, the great lords who were the electors did at times deliberately choose otherwise. It was to their advantage to select a weak king.

To compensate for their weaknesses, German kings came to rely on their ability to control the church and select bishops and abbots whom they could then use as royal administrators. But the struggle between church and state during the reign of Henry IV weakened the king's ability to use church officials in this way (see "The Investiture Controversy" later in this chapter).

Involvement in Italy   The German kings also tried to bolster their power by using their position as emperors to exploit the resources of Italy. Italy seemed a likely area for intervention because it had no central political authority. While important nobles struggled to dominate northern Italy, central Italy remained under the control of the Papal States. In southern Italy, the Lombard dukes, Muslims, and Byzantines seemed to be in constant conflict.

In the latter half of the eleventh century, a group of Norman adventurers led by Robert Guiscard (gees-KAR) ("the cunning") conquered much of southern Italy. Robert's brother Roger subdued Muslim Sicily in 1091 after a thirty-year struggle. In 1130, Roger II, the son of Roger of Sicily, was crowned king of Sicily. By the end of the twelfth century, the Norman kingdom was one of the most powerful in Europe as well as one of the most fascinating. A melting pot of Christian, Jewish, and Muslim culture, the state issued its official documents in Latin, Greek, and Arabic.

The Norman kingdom in southern Italy was beyond any claims of the German kings, but the wealthy cities of northern Italy, which by the twelfth century had become virtually independent after overthrowing the rule of their bishops, were a

MAP 10.3 The Lands of the Holy Roman Empire in the Twelfth Century

The Hohenstaufen rulers Frederick I and Frederick II sought to expand the Holy Roman Empire to include all of Italy. Frederick II had only fleeting success: after his death, several independent city-states arose in northern Italy, while at home, German nobles had virtually free rein within their domains.

tempting prize to the German kings, who never entirely gave up their dreams of a restored empire. No German dynasty proved more susceptible to the allure of this dream than the Hohenstaufens (hoh-en-SHTOW-fenz).

Frederick I   Both Frederick I (1152–1190) and Frederick II (1212–1250) tried to create a foundation for a new kind of empire. Frederick I, known as Barbarossa (bar-buh-ROH-suh) (Redbeard) to the Italians, was a powerful lord from the house of Hohenstaufen when he was elected king. Previous German kings had focused on building a strong German kingdom, to which Italy might be added as an appendage. Frederick I, however, planned to get his chief revenues from Italy as the center of a "holy empire," as he called it—the Holy Roman Empire. But his attempt to conquer northern Italy ran into severe difficulties. The pope opposed him, fearful that the emperor wanted to incorporate Rome and the Papal States into his empire. The cities of northern Italy, which had become used to their freedom, were also not willing to be Frederick's subjects. An alliance of these northern Italian cities, with the support of the papacy, defeated the forces of the Emperor Frederick at Legnano (leh-NYAH-noh) in 1176.

Later Frederick returned to Italy and arranged a settlement with the northern Italian cities by which they retained their independence in return for an annual payment to the emperor. Frederick now had the financial base he had sought. Moreover, by marrying his son (who became Henry VI, 1190–1197) to the heiress of the Norman kingdom of southern Italy, Frederick seemed to be creating the foundation for making the Holy Roman Empire a reality and for realizing the pope's nightmare: the encirclement of Rome and the Papal States. After Frederick's death, Henry VI's control of Germany and both northern and southern Italy made him the strongest European ruler since Charlemagne. Henry's empire soon collapsed, however, for he died prematurely, leaving as his heir a son only two years old.

Frederick II   The son, Frederick II, grew up to become the most brilliant of the Hohenstaufen rulers. King of Sicily in 1198, king of Germany in 1212, and crowned emperor in 1220, Frederick II was a truly remarkable man who awed his contemporaries. Frederick was raised in Sicily, with its diverse peoples, languages, and religions. His court there brought together a brilliant array of lawyers, poets, artists, and scientists, and he himself took a deep interest in their work.

Until he was crowned emperor, Frederick spent much time in Germany; once he left in 1220, though, he rarely returned. He gave the German princes full control of their territories, voluntarily surrendering any real power over Germany in exchange for revenues while he pursued his main goal, the establishment of a strong centralized state in Italy dominated by his kingdom in Sicily. Frederick's major task was to gain control of northern Italy. In reaching to extend his power in Italy, he became involved in a deadly struggle with the popes, who realized that a single ruler of northern and southern Italy meant the end of papal secular power in central Italy. The northern Italian cities were also unwilling to give up their freedom. Frederick waged a bitter struggle in northern Italy, winning many battles but ultimately losing the war.

Frederick's preoccupation with the creation of an empire in Italy left Germany in confusion and chaos until 1273, when the major German princes, serving as electors, chose an insignificant German noble, Rudolf of Habsburg (HAPS-burg), as the new German king. In choosing a weak king, the princes were ensuring that the German monarchy would remain impotent and incapable of reestablishing a centralized monarchical state. The failure of the Hohenstaufens had led to a situation in which his exalted majesty, the German king and Holy Roman Emperor, had no real power over either Germany or Italy. Unlike France and England, neither Germany nor Italy created a unified national monarchy in the Middle Ages. Both became geographic designations for loose confederations of hundreds of petty independent states under the vague direction of king or emperor. In fact, neither Germany nor Italy would become united until the nineteenth century.

Following the death of Frederick II, Italy fell into political confusion. While the papacy remained in control of much of central Italy, the defeat of imperial power left the cities and towns of northern Italy independent of any other authority. Gradually, the larger ones began to emerge as strong city-states. Florence assumed the leadership of Tuscany, while Milan, under the guidance of the Visconti family, took control of the Lombard region. With its great commercial wealth, the republic of Venice dominated the northeastern part of the peninsula.

New Kingdoms in Northern and Eastern Europe   The Scandinavian countries of northern Europe had little political organization before 1000, and it was not until the second half of the tenth century and the first half of the eleventh that the three Scandinavian kingdoms—Denmark, Norway, and Sweden (see Map 10.4)—emerged with a noticeable political structure. At the same time, the three kingdoms were converted to Christianity by kings who believed that an organized church was a necessary accompaniment to an organized state. The adoption of Christianity, however, did not eliminate the warlike tendencies of the Scandinavians. Not only did the three kingdoms fight each other in the eleventh and twelfth centuries, but rival families were in regular conflict over the throne in each state. This period also witnessed the growth of a powerful noble landowning class.

To the south, in eastern Europe, Hungary, which had been a Christian state since 1000, remained relatively stable throughout the High Middle Ages, but the history of Poland and Russia was more turbulent. In the thirteenth century, eastern Europe was beset by two groups of invaders, the Teutonic Knights from the west and the Mongols from the east.

In the eleventh century, a Polish kingdom existed as a separate state but with no natural frontiers. Consequently, German settlers encroached on its territory on a regular basis, leading to considerable intermarriage between Slavs and Germans. During the thirteenth century, relations between the Germans and the Slavs of eastern Europe worsened due to the aggression of the Teutonic Knights. The Teutonic Knights had been founded near the end of the twelfth century to protect the Christian Holy Land. In the early thirteenth century, however, these Christian knights found greater opportunity to the east of Germany, where they attacked the pagan Slavs. East Prussia was given to the military order in 1226, and five years later, the knights moved into the lands beyond the Vistula River, where they waged war against the Slavs for another thirty years. By the end of the thirteenth century, Prussia had become German and Christian as the pagan Slavs were forced to convert.

Central and eastern Europe had periodically been subject to invasions from fierce Asiatic nomads, such as the Huns, Avars, Bulgars, and Magyars. In the thirteenth century, the Mongols exploded onto the scene, causing far more disruption than earlier invaders.

MAP 10.4 Northern and Eastern Europe c. 1150

Acceptance of Christianity gave many northern and eastern European kingdoms greater control over their subjects. Warfare was common in the region: dynastic struggles occurred in Scandinavia, and the Teutonic Knights, based in East Prussia, attacked pagan Slavs.

Impact of the Mongol Empire

The Mongols rose to power in Asia with stunning speed. A pastoral people in the region of modern-day Mongolia, they were loosely organized into clans and tribes that were often warring with each other. This changed when one leader, Temuchin (TEM-yuh-jin), unified the Mongol tribes and gained the title of Genghis Khan (c. 1162–1227), which means "universal ruler." From that time on, Genghis Khan (GENG-uss *or* JING-uss KAHN) created a powerful military force and devoted himself to fighting. "Man's highest joy," Genghis Khan remarked, "is in victory: to conquer one's enemies, to pursue them, to deprive them of their possessions, to make their beloved weep, to ride on their horses, and to embrace their wives and daughters."[1] Genghis Khan was succeeded by equally competent sons and grandsons.

The Mongols burst onto the scene in the thirteenth century. They advanced eastward, eventually conquering China and Korea. One of Genghis Khan's grandsons, Khubilai Khan (KOO-bluh KAHN), completed the conquest of China and established a new Chinese dynasty of rulers known as the Yuan (YOO-enn *or* YWAHN). In 1279, Khubilai Khan moved the capital of China northward to Khanbaliq (kahn-bah-LEEK) ("city of the khan"), which would later be known by the Chinese name Beijing (bay-ZHING).

The Mongols also moved westward against the Islamic empire. Persia fell by 1233, and by 1258, they had conquered Baghdad and destroyed the Abbasid caliphate. Beginning in the 1230s, the Mongols moved into Europe. They conquered Russia, advanced into Poland and Hungary, and destroyed a force of Poles and Teutonic Knights in Silesia in 1241 (see Map 10.5). Europe then seemingly got lucky when the Mongol hordes turned back because of internal fighting; western and southern Europe thus escaped the wrath of the Mongols. Overall, the Mongols had little impact in Europe, although their occupation of Russia had some residual effects.

The Development of Russia   The Kievan Rus state, which had formally become Christian in 987, prospered considerably afterward, reaching its high point in the first half of the eleventh century. Kievan society

MAP 10.5   The Mongol Empire in the Thirteenth Century

Beginning with the exploits of Genghis Khan, the Mongols used unorthodox but effective military tactics to establish an empire that stretched from Russia to China and included India and South Asia. The empire was divided into khanates. The Golden Horde, the khanate in Russia, was eventually overwhelmed by princes of Moscow who went on to establish the Russian state.

was dominated by a noble class of landowners known as the **boyars** (boh-YARS). Kievan merchants maintained regular trade with Scandinavia to the northwest and the Islamic and Byzantine worlds to the south. But destructive civil wars and new invasions by Asiatic nomads caused the principality of Kiev to disintegrate into a number of constituent parts, and the sack of Kiev by north Russian princes in 1169 brought an inglorious end to the first Russian state.

The fundamental civilizing and unifying force of early Russia was the Christian church. The Russian church imitated the liturgy and organization of the Byzantine Empire, whose Eastern Orthodox priests had converted the Kievan Rus to Christianity at the end of the tenth century. The Russian church became known for its rigid religious orthodoxy. Although Christianity provided a common bond between Russian and European civilization, Russia's religious development guaranteed an even closer affinity between Russian and Byzantine civilization.

In the thirteenth century, the Mongols conquered Russia and cut it off even more from western Europe. The Mongols were not numerous enough to settle the vast Russian lands but were content to rule directly an area along the lower Volga and north of the Caspian and Black Seas to Kiev and rule indirectly elsewhere. In the latter territories, Russian princes were required to pay tribute to the Mongol overlords.

One Russian prince soon emerged as more visible and powerful than the others. Alexander Nevsky (NYEF-skee) (c. 1220–1263), prince of Novgorod, defeated a German invading army at Lake Peipus in northwestern Russia in 1242. His cooperation with the Mongols, which included denouncing his own brother and crushing native tax revolts, won him their favor. The khan, the acknowledged leader of the western part of the Mongol Empire, rewarded Alexander Nevsky with the title of grand-prince, enabling his descendants to become the princes of Moscow and eventually leaders of all Russia.

THE RECOVERY AND REFORM OF THE CATHOLIC CHURCH

In the Early Middle Ages, the Catholic Church had played a leading role in converting and civilizing first the Germanic invaders and later the Vikings and Magyars. Although highly successful, this had not been accomplished without challenges that undermined the spiritual life of the church itself.

The Problems of Decline   Since the eighth century, the popes had reigned supreme over the affairs of the Catholic Church. They had also come to exercise control over the territories in central Italy known as the Papal States; this kept the popes involved in political matters, often at the expense of their spiritual obligations. At the same time, the church became increasingly entangled in the evolving lord-vassal relationships. High officials of the church, such as bishops and abbots, came to hold their offices as fiefs from nobles. As vassals, they were obliged to carry out the usual duties, including military service. Of course, lords assumed the right to choose their vassals, even when those vassals included bishops and abbots. Because lords often selected their vassals from other noble families for political reasons, these bishops and abbots were often worldly figures who cared little about their spiritual responsibilities.

The monastic ideal had also suffered during the Early Middle Ages. Benedictine monasteries had sometimes been exemplary centers of Christian living and learning, but the invasions of Vikings, Magyars, and Muslims wreaked havoc with many monastic establishments. Discipline declined, and with it the monastic reputation for learning and holiness. At the same time, a growing number of monasteries fell under the control of local lords, as did much of the church. A number of people believed that the time for reform had come.

The Cluniac Reform Movement   Reform of the Catholic Church began in Burgundy in eastern France in 910 when Duke William of Aquitaine founded the abbey of Cluny (KLOO-nee). The monastery began with a renewed dedication to the highest spiritual ideals of the Benedictine rule and was fortunate in having a series of abbots in the tenth century who maintained these ideals. Cluny was deliberately kept independent from secular control. As Duke William stipulated in his original charter, "It has pleased us also to insert in this document that, from this day, those same monks there congregated shall be subject neither to our yoke, nor to that of our relatives, nor to the sway of the royal might, nor to that of any earthly power."[2] The new monastery at Cluny tried to eliminate some of the abuses that had crept into religious communities by stressing the need for work, replacing manual labor with the copying of manuscripts, and demanding more community worship and less private prayer.

The Cluniac reform movement sparked an enthusiastic response, first in France and eventually in all of western and central Europe. Hundreds of new monasteries were founded on Cluniac ideals, and existing monasteries rededicated themselves by adopting the Cluniac program. The movement also began to reach beyond monasticism and into the papacy itself, which was in dire need of help.

Reform of the Papacy   By the eleventh century, a movement for change, led by a series of reforming popes, was sweeping through the Catholic Church. One of the reformers' primary goals was to free the church from the interference of lords in the election of church officials. This issue was dramatically taken up by the greatest of the reform popes of the eleventh century, Gregory VII (1073–1085).

Pope Gregory VII and Reform   Elected pope in 1073, Gregory was absolutely certain that he had been chosen by God to reform the church. In pursuit of those aims, Gregory claimed that he—the pope—was God's "vicar on Earth" and that the pope's authority extended over all of Christendom and included the right to depose emperors if they disobeyed his wishes. Gregory sought nothing less than the elimination of **lay investiture** (both interference by nonmembers of the clergy in elections and their participation in the installation of prelates). Only then could the church regain its freedom, by which Gregory meant the right of the church to appoint its own clergy and run its own affairs. If rulers did not accept these "divine" commands, they could be deposed by the pope in his capacity as the vicar of Christ. Gregory VII soon found himself in conflict with the king of Germany over these claims. (The king of Germany was also the emperor-designate since it had been accepted by this time that only kings of Germany could be emperors, but they did not officially use the title "emperor" until they were crowned by the pope.)

King Henry IV of Germany was just as determined as the pope. For many years, German kings had appointed high-ranking clerics, especially bishops, as their vassals in order to use them as administrators. Without them, the king could not hope to maintain his own power vis-à-vis the powerful German nobles. In 1075, Pope Gregory issued a decree forbidding important clerics from receiving investiture from lay leaders: "We decree that no one of the clergy shall receive the investiture with a bishopric or abbey or church from the hand of an emperor or king or of any lay person."[3] Henry had no intention of obeying a decree that challenged the very heart of his administration.

The Investiture Controversy   The immediate cause of the so-called Investiture Controversy was a disputed election to the bishopric of Milan in northern Italy, an important position because the bishop was also the ruler of the city. Control of the bishopric was crucial if the king wished to reestablish German power in northern Italy. Since Milan was considered second only to Rome in importance as a bishopric, papal interest in the office was also keen. Pope Gregory VII and King Henry IV backed competing candidates for the position.

To gain acceptance of his candidate, the pope threatened the king with **excommunication**. Excommunication is a censure by which a person is deprived of receiving the sacraments of the church. To counter this threat, the king called a synod or assembly of German bishops, all of whom he had appointed, and had them depose the pope.

Pope Gregory VII responded by excommunicating the king and freeing his subjects from their allegiance to him. The latter was a clever move. The German nobles were only too eager to diminish the power of a centralized monarchy because of the threat it posed to their own power, and they welcomed this opportunity to rebel against the king. Both the nobles and the bishops of Germany agreed to hold a meeting in Germany with the pope to solve the problem, possibly by choosing a new king. Gregory set out for Germany. Henry, realizing the threat to his power, forestalled the pope by traveling to northern Italy, where he met the pope at Canossa, a castle belonging to Countess Matilda of Tuscany, an avid supporter of the papal reform program. There, in January 1077, the king admitted his transgressions and begged for forgiveness and absolution. Although he made the king wait three days, the pope was constrained by his priestly responsibility to grant absolution to a penitent sinner and lifted the ban of excommunication. This did not end the problem, however. Within three years, pope and king were again locked in combat.

The struggle continued until 1122, when a new German king and a new pope achieved a compromise called the Concordat of Worms (WURMZ *or* VORMPS). Under this agreement, a bishop in Germany was first elected by church officials.

After election, the nominee paid homage to the king as his secular lord, who in turn invested him with the symbols of temporal office. A representative of the pope then invested the new bishop with the symbols of his spiritual office.

This struggle between church and state was an important element in the history of Europe in the High Middle Ages. In the Early Middle Ages, popes had been dependent on emperors and had allowed them to exercise considerable authority over church affairs. But a set of new ideals championed by activist reformers in the eleventh century now supported the "freedom of the church," which meant not only the freedom of the church to control its own affairs but also extreme claims of papal authority. Not only was the pope superior to all other bishops, but popes now claimed the right to depose kings under certain circumstances. Such papal claims ensured further church-state confrontations.

CHRISTIANITY AND MEDIEVAL CIVILIZATION

Christianity was an integral part of the fabric of medieval European society and the consciousness of Europe. Papal directives affected the actions of kings and princes alike, while Christian teaching and practices touched the economic, social, intellectual, cultural, and daily lives of all Europeans.

Growth of the Papal Monarchy   The popes of the twelfth century did not abandon the reform ideals of Gregory VII, but they were less dogmatic and more inclined to consolidate their power and build a strong administrative system. By the twelfth century, the Catholic Church possessed a clearly organized, hierarchical structure. The pope and **papal curia** (KYUR-ee-uh) were at the apex of the administrative structure. The curia was staffed by high church officials known as cardinals, who served as major advisers and administrators to the popes; at the pope's death, the college of cardinals, as they were collectively called, elected the new pope. Below the pope and cardinals were the archbishops, each of whom controlled a large region called an archdiocese. Each archdiocese was divided into smaller units called dioceses, each headed by a bishop. Each diocese was divided into parishes, each headed by a priest. Theoretically, the bishop chose all priests in his diocese, administered his diocese, and was responsible only to the pope.

The Pontificate of Innocent III   In the thirteenth century, the Catholic Church reached the height of its political, intellectual, and secular power. The papal monarchy extended its sway over both ecclesiastical and temporal affairs, as was especially evident during the papacy of Pope Innocent III (1198–1216). At the beginning of his pontificate, in a letter to a priest, Innocent made a clear statement of his views on papal supremacy:

> As God, the creator of the universe, set two great lights in the firmament of heaven, the greater light to rule the day, and the lesser light to rule the night, so He set two great dignities in the firmament of the universal church,... the greater to rule the day, that is, souls, and the lesser to rule the night, that is, bodies. These dignities are the papal authority and the royal power. And just as the moon gets her light from the sun, and is inferior to the sun ... so the royal power gets the splendor of its dignity from the papal authority.[4]

Sacro Speco, Subiaco//© Scala/Art Resource, NY

Pope Innocent III. *Innocent III was an active and powerful pope during the High Middle Ages. He approved the creation of the Franciscan and Dominican religious orders and inaugurated the Fourth Crusade. He is shown here with the papal bull he issued to establish the monastery of Sacro Speco in Subiaco, Italy.*

Innocent's actions were those of a man who believed that he, the pope, was the supreme judge of European affairs. He forced King Philip II Augustus of France to take back his wife and queen after Philip had tried to have the marriage annulled. The pope intervened in German affairs and installed his candidate as emperor. He compelled King John of England to accept the papal choice for the position of archbishop of Canterbury. To achieve his political ends, Innocent did not hesitate to use the spiritual weapons at his command, especially the **interdict**, which forbade priests to dispense the **sacraments** of the church in the hope that the people, deprived of the comforts of religion, would exert pressure against their ruler. Pope Innocent's interdict was so effective that it caused King Philip Augustus to restore his wife to her rightful place as queen of France.

New Religious Orders and Spiritual Ideals In the second half of the eleventh century and the first half of the twelfth, a wave of religious enthusiasm seized Europe, leading to a spectacular growth in the number of monasteries and the emergence of new monastic orders. Most important was the Cistercian (sis-TUR-shun) order, founded in 1098 by a group of monks dissatisfied with the lack of strict discipline at their Benedictine monastery.

Cistercian monasticism spread rapidly from southern France into the rest of Europe.

The Cistercians were strict. They ate a simple diet and possessed only a single robe apiece. All decorations were eliminated from their churches and monastic buildings. More time for prayer and manual labor was provided by shortening the number of hours spent at religious services. The Cistercians played a major role in developing a new activist spiritual model for twelfth-century Europe. A Benedictine monk often spent hours in prayer to honor God. The Cistercian ideal had a different emphasis: "Arise, soldier of Christ, arise! Get up off the ground and return to the battle from which you have fled! Fight more boldly after your flight, and triumph in glory!"[5] These were the words of Saint Bernard of Clairvaux (klair-VOH) (1090–1153), who more than any other person embodied the new spiritual ideal of Cistercian monasticism.

Women in Religious Orders   Women were also active participants in the spiritual movements of the age. The number of women joining religious houses increased perceptibly with the spread of the new orders of the twelfth century. In the High Middle Ages, most nuns were from the ranks of the landed aristocracy. Convents were convenient for families unable or unwilling to find husbands for their daughters and for aristocratic women who did not wish to marry. Female intellectuals found them a haven for their activities. Most of the learned women of the Middle Ages, especially in Germany, were nuns. One of the most distinguished was Hildegard of Bingen (HIL-duh-gard of BING-un) (1098–1179), who became abbess of a convent at Disibodenberg in western Germany.

Hildegard shared in the religious enthusiasm of the twelfth century. Soon after becoming abbess, she began to write an account of the mystical visions she had experienced for years. "A great flash of light from heaven pierced my brain and ... in that instant my mind was imbued with the meaning of the sacred books," she wrote in a description typical of the world's mystical literature. Eventually, she produced three books based on her visions. Hildegard gained considerable renown as a mystic and prophet, and popes, emperors, kings, dukes, and bishops eagerly sought her advice.

Hildegard of Bingen was also one of the first important female composers and a major contributor to the body of music known as Gregorian chant or plainsong. Gregorian chant was basically monophonic—a single line of unaccompanied vocal music—set to Latin texts and chanted by a group of monks or nuns during church services. Hildegard's work is especially remarkable because she succeeded at a time when music in general, and sacred music in particular, was almost exclusively the domain of men.

Living the Gospel Life   In the early thirteenth century, two religious leaders, Saint Francis and Saint Dominic, founded two new religious orders whose members did not remain in the cloister like the monks of the contemplative orders, such as the Benedictines and Cistercians, but rather went out into the secular arena of the towns to preach the word of God. By their example, the new orders strove to provide a more personal religious experience for ordinary people. The new orders were known as mendicant ("begging") orders because their members adopted lives of deliberate poverty. In this, they were reacting against the growing wealth of the High Middle Ages, especially evident in the cities, which they considered harmful to a Christian's soul. After all, Jesus had stated in the New Testament: "How hard it is for a rich man to enter the kingdom of God! Indeed, it is easier for a camel to go through the eye of a needle than for a rich man to enter the kingdom of God."[6]

Saint Francis of Assisi (1182–1226) was born to a wealthy Italian merchant family, but as a young man he abandoned all worldly goods and began to live and preach in poverty after a series of dramatic spiritual experiences. His simplicity, joyful nature, and love for others soon attracted a band of followers, all of whom took vows of absolute poverty, agreeing to reject all property and live by working and begging for their food. Francis drew up a simple rule for his followers that focused on the need to preach and the importance of poverty. He sought approval for his new rule from Pope Innocent III, who confirmed the new order as the Order of Friars Minor, more commonly known as the Franciscans. The Franciscans struck a responsive chord among many Europeans and became very popular. The Franciscans lived among the people, preaching repentance and aiding the poor. Their calls for a return to the simplicity and poverty of the early church, reinforced by their own example, were especially effective. The Franciscans had a female branch as well, known as the Poor Clares, which was founded by Saint Clare, an aristocratic lady of Assisi who was a great admirer of Francis.

The second new religious order of the early thirteenth century arose out of the desire to defend orthodox church teachings from heresy (see "Voices of Protest and Intolerance" later in this chapter). The Order of Preachers, popularly known as the Dominicans, was created through the efforts of a Spanish priest, Dominic de Guzmán (DAH-muh-nik duh gooz-MAHN) (1170–1221). Unlike Francis, Dominic was an intellectual who was particularly appalled by the recent growth of heretical movements. He came to believe that a new religious order of men who lived lives of poverty but were learned and capable of preaching effectively would best be able to attack heresy. With the approval of Pope Innocent III, the Dominicans became an order of mendicant friars in 1215.

In addition to the friars, the thirteenth century witnessed the development of yet another kind of religious order. Known as Beguines (bay-GEENZ), these were communities of women dwelling together in poverty. Devout and dedicated to prayer, they begged for their daily support or worked as laundresses in hospitals or at other menial tasks. They did not take religious vows and were free to leave the community at will. Although the Beguines originated in the Low Countries, they eventually became quite strong in the Rhineland area of Germany as well.

Monasticism and Social Services   Monastic life in all of its different forms was the most important component of religious life in the Middle Ages. Monks and nuns performed a remarkable variety of tasks, including praying for themselves and others, copying manuscripts, maintaining libraries and schools, acting as missionaries to the heathen, preaching to the poor, and fighting heresy. But in an age unlike our own, when governments provide basic social services, monks and nuns also worked for society by providing a number of social welfare services.

Monasteries often provided both food and clothing for the poor. Otto of Freising, a German writer of history in the twelfth century, declared, "There is always a pious, Godfearing friar sitting [at the gate] receiving all arriving guests, pilgrims, and poor people, as friendly and kind-hearted as Christ himself." Due to a shortage of inns, monasteries also provided hospitality for pilgrims and other travelers. As the Rule of St. Benedict noted, "All who arrive as guests are to be welcomed like Christ." Monks and nuns also took care of the sick. They planted herb gardens so that they could prepare the herbal remedies that were commonly used in medieval medicine. In addition, monks and nuns ran hospitals, especially for poor people who could not receive care elsewhere. Unlike modern-day hospitals, medieval hospitals were primarily residences for the elderly, the terminally ill, or the blind. Separate quarters were provided for lepers. There were about two thousand leper houses in France in the thirteenth century, a good indication of the widespread nature of the disease.

Popular Religion in the High Middle Ages   We have witnessed the actions of popes, bishops, monks, and nuns. But what of ordinary clergy and laypeople? What were their religious hopes and fears? What were their spiritual aspirations?

The sacraments of the Catholic Church ensured that the church was an integral part of people's lives, from birth to death. There were (and still are) seven sacraments—the Eucharist (the Lord's Supper), baptism, marriage, penance, extreme unction, holy orders, and confirmation—administered only by the clergy. The sacraments were viewed as outward symbols of an inward grace (grace was God's freely given gift that enabled humans to be saved) and were considered imperative for a Christian's salvation. Therefore, the clergy were seen to have a key role in the attainment of salvation.

The Importance of Saints   Other church practices were also important to ordinary people. Saints, it was believed, were men and women who, through their holiness, had achieved a special position in heaven, enabling them to act as intercessors before God. The saints' ability to protect poor souls enabled them to take on great importance at the popular level. Jesus's apostles were recognized throughout Europe as saints, but there were also numerous local saints that were of special significance to the area. New cults rapidly developed, particularly in the intense religious atmosphere of the eleventh and twelfth centuries. The English introduced Saint Nicholas, the patron saint of children, who remains instantly recognizable today through his identification with Santa Claus.

Of all the saints, the Virgin Mary, the mother of Jesus, occupied the foremost position in the High Middle Ages. Mary was viewed as the most important mediator with her son Jesus, the judge of all sinners. Moreover, from the eleventh century on, a fascination with Mary as Jesus's human mother became more evident. A sign of Mary's growing importance was the number of churches all over Europe that were dedicated to "Our Lady" in the twelfth and thirteenth centuries, including the cathedral of Notre-Dame in Paris.

The Use of Relics   Emphasis on the role of the saints was closely tied to the use of **relics**, which also increased noticeably in the High Middle Ages. Relics were usually the bones of saints or objects intimately connected to saints that were considered worthy of veneration by the faithful. A twelfth-century English monk began his description of the abbey's relics by saying, "There is kept there a thing more precious than gold,... the right arm of St. Oswald.... This we have seen with our own eyes and have kissed, and have handled with our own hands.... There are kept here also part of his ribs and of the soil on which he fell."[7] The monk went on to list additional purported relics possessed by the abbey, including two pieces of Jesus's swaddling clothes, pieces of Jesus's manger, and parts of the five loaves of bread with which Jesus miraculously fed five thousand people. Because the holiness of the saint was considered to be inherent in his relics, these objects were believed to be capable of healing people or producing other miracles.

In the High Middle Ages, it became a regular practice of the church to attach **indulgences** to these relics. Indulgences brought a remission of time spent in **purgatory**. Purgatory was believed to be a place of punishment in which the soul of the departed could be purified before ascending to heaven. The living could ease that suffering through Masses and prayers offered on behalf of the deceased or through indulgences. Indulgences were granted for good works such as charitable contributions and viewing the relics of saints. The church specified the number of years and days of each indulgence, enabling the soul to spend less time in purgatory.

The Pilgrimage   Medieval Christians believed that a pilgrimage to a holy shrine was of particular spiritual benefit. The greatest shrine but the most difficult to reach was the Holy City of Jerusalem (see Map 10.6). On the European continent, two pilgrim centers were especially popular in the High Middle Ages: Rome, which contained the relics of Saints Peter and Paul, and the town of Santiago de Compostela, supposedly the site of the tomb of the Apostle James. Local attractions, such as shrines dedicated to the Virgin Mary, also became pilgrimage centers.

Voices of Protest and Intolerance   The desire for more personal and deeper religious experience, which characterized the spiritual revival of the High Middle Ages, also led people into directions hostile to the institutional church. From the twelfth century on, heresy, the holding of religious doctrines different from the orthodox teachings of the church as determined by church authorities, became a serious problem for the Catholic Church.

The best-known heresy of the twelfth and thirteenth centuries was Catharism (KA-thuh-riz-um). The Cathars (the word *Cathar* means "pure") were often called Albigensians (al-buh-JEN-see-unz) after the city of Albi, one of their strongholds in southern France. They believed in a dualist system in which good and evil were separate and distinct. Things of the spirit were good because they were created by God, the source of light; things of the world were evil because they were created by Satan, the prince of darkness. Humans, too, were enmeshed in **dualism**. Their souls, which were good, were trapped in material bodies, which were evil. According to the

North Sea

Lübeck

Walsingham

Magdeburg

Canterbury

Cologne

Trier

Worms

Amiens

Paris

Mont-Saint-Michel

Clairvaux

Atlantic
Ocean

Chartres

Tours

Vézelay

Cluny

Turin

Milan

Moissac

Assisi

Santiago de
Compostela

Avignon

Toulouse

Rome

Black Sea

Bari

Constantinople

Miletus

Mediterranean Sea

Jerusalem

0   300   600   900 Kilometers
0   300   600 Miles

~ Major pilgrimage routes, 1100–1500

☩ Pilgrimage shrine

© Cengage Learning 2012

MAP 10.6 Pilgrimage Routes in the Middle Ages

Some Christians sought spiritual solace by traveling to pilgrimage sites. Many went to local shrines honoring the Virgin Mary, but Jerusalem, Rome, and Santiago de Compostela were the most desired locations.

Cathars, the Catholic Church, itself a materialistic institution, had nothing to do with God and was essentially evil. There was no need to follow its teachings or recognize its authority. The Cathar movement gained valuable support from important nobles in southern France and northern Italy.

The spread of heresy in southern France alarmed the church authorities. Pope Innocent III appealed to the nobles of northern France for a **Crusade** (a military campaign in defense of Christendom) against the heretics. The Crusade against the Albigensians, which began in the summer of 1209 and lasted for almost two decades, was a bloody one. Thousands of heretics (and the innocent) were slaughtered, including entire populations of some towns. In Beziers, for example, seven thousand men, women, and children were massacred when they took refuge in the local church.

Southern France was devastated, but Catharism persisted, which caused the Catholic Church to devise a regular method for discovering and dealing with heretics. This led to the emergence of the Holy Office, as the papal Inquisition was called, a formal court whose job it was to ferret out and try heretics.

Gradually, the Holy Office developed its inquisitorial procedure. Anyone could be accused of heresy since the identity of the accuser was not revealed to the indicted heretic. If the accused heretic confessed, he or she was forced to perform public penance and was subjected to punishment, such as flogging; the heretic's property was then confiscated and divided between the secular authorities and the church. Beginning in 1252, those not confessing voluntarily were subjected to

Expulsion of Albigensian Heretics. *In 1209, Pope Innocent III authorized a Crusade against the heretical Albigensians. In this medieval illustration, French knights are shown expelling Albigensian heretics from the town of Carcassonne near Albi, an Albigensian stronghold in southern France.*

© British Library Board/The Bridgeman Art Library

torture. Relapsed heretics—those who confessed, did penance, and then reverted to heresy—were turned over to the secular authorities for execution.

To the Christians of the thirteenth century, who believed that there was only one path to salvation, heresy was a crime against God and against humanity, and force was justified to save souls from damnation. The fanaticism and fear unleashed in the struggle against heretics were also used against others, especially the best-known outgroup of Western society, the Jews.

Persecution of the Jews   The Jews were the only religious minority in Christian Europe that was allowed to practice a non-Christian religion. In the Early Middle Ages, Jews were actively involved in trade and crafts. Later, after being excluded from practicing most trades by the guild system, some Jews turned to money-lending as a way to survive.

There is little certainty about the number of Jews in Europe. England had relatively few Jews, probably 2,500 to 3,000, or one of every thousand inhabitants. Larger numbers lived in southern Italy, Spain, France, and Germany. In southern Europe, Jews served an important function as cultural and intellectual intermediaries between the Muslim and Christian worlds.

The religious enthusiasm of the High Middle Ages produced an outburst of intolerance against the supposed enemies of Christianity. Although this was evident in the Crusades against the Muslims (see "The Crusades" later in this chapter), Christians also took up the search for enemies at home, persecuting Jews in France and the Rhineland at the time of the first Crusades. Jews in Speyer, Worms, Mainz, and Cologne were all set upon by bands of Christian crusaders. A contemporary chronicler described how a band of English crusaders who stopped at Lisbon, Portugal, en route to the Holy Land "drove away the pagans and Jews, servants of the king, who dwelt in the city and plundered their property and possessions, and burned their houses; and they then stripped their vineyards, not leaving them so much as a grape or a cluster."[8] Even people who tried to protect the Jews were in danger. When the archbishop of Mainz provided shelter for the Jews, a mob stormed his palace and forced him to flee. Popes also came to the Jews' defense by issuing decrees ordering that Jews were not to be persecuted.

Nevertheless, in the thirteenth century, in the supercharged religious atmosphere created by the struggle with heretics, Jews were persecuted more and more. Friars urged action against these "murderers of Christ," referring to the traditional Christian view of the Jews as being responsible for the death of Jesus, and organized public burnings of Jewish books. The Fourth Lateran Council in 1215 decreed that Jews must wear special clothing so that they could be distinguished from Christians. The same council encouraged the development of Jewish ghettos, or walled enclosures, not to protect the Jews but to isolate them from Christians. The persecutions and the new image of the hated Jew stimulated a tradition of anti-Semitism that proved to be one of Christian Europe's most insidious contributions to the Western heritage.

By the end of the thirteenth century, European kings, who had earlier portrayed themselves as protectors of the Jews, had fleeced the Jewish communities of their money and then renounced their protection. Edward I expelled all Jews from England in 1290. The French king followed suit in 1306 but readmitted the Jews in 1315. They then left on their own accord in 1322. As the policy of expulsion spread into central Europe, most northern European Jews were forced to move into Poland as a last refuge.

Intolerance and Homosexuality   The climate of intolerance that characterized thirteenth-century attitudes toward Muslims, heretics, and Jews was also evident toward homosexuals. Although the church had condemned homosexuality in the Early Middle Ages, it had not been overly concerned with homosexual behavior, an attitude also prevalent in the secular world. By the thirteenth century, however, these tolerant attitudes had altered drastically. Some historians connect this change to the century's climate of fear and intolerance against any group that deviated from the standards of the majority. A favorite approach of the critics was to identify homosexuals with other detested groups. Homosexuality was portrayed as a regular practice of Muslims and such notorious heretics as the Albigensians. Between 1250 and 1300, what had been tolerated in most of Europe became a criminal act deserving of death.

The legislation against homosexuality commonly referred to it as a "sin against nature." This is precisely the argument developed by Thomas Aquinas (see Chapter 9), who formed Catholic opinion on the subject for centuries to come. In his *Summa Theologica*, Aquinas argued that because the purpose of sex was procreation, it could legitimately take place only in ways that did not exclude this possibility. Hence, homosexuality was "contrary to nature" and a deviation from the natural order established by God. This argument and laws prohibiting homosexual activity on pain of severe punishment remained the norm in Europe and elsewhere in the Christian world until the twentieth century.

THE CRUSADES

Another manifestation of the wave of religious enthusiasm that seized Europe in the High Middle Ages was the series of Crusades mounted against the Muslims. The Crusades gave the revived papacy of the High Middle Ages yet another opportunity to demonstrate its influence over European society. The Crusades were a curious mix of God and warfare, two of the chief concerns of the Middle Ages.

Background to the Crusades   Although European civilization developed in relative isolation, it had never entirely lost contact with the lands and empires of the east. At the end of the eleventh century, that contact increased, in part because developments in the Islamic and Byzantine worlds prompted the first major attempt of the new European civilization to expand beyond Europe proper.

Islam and the Seljuk Turks   By the mid-tenth century, the Islamic empire led by the Abbasid caliphate in Baghdad was disintegrating. An attempt was made in the tenth century to unify the Islamic world under the direction of a Shi'ite dynasty known as the Fatimids. Their origins lay in North Africa, but they managed to conquer Egypt and establish the new city of Cairo as their capital. In establishing a Shi'ite caliphate, they became rivals to the Sunni caliphate of Baghdad and divided the Islamic world.

Nevertheless, the Fatimid dynasty prospered and surpassed the Abbasid caliphate as the dynamic center of Islam. Benefiting from their position in the heart of the Nile delta, the Fatimids played a major role in the regional trade passing from the Mediterranean to the Red Sea and beyond. They were tolerant in matters of religion and created a strong army by using nonnative peoples as mercenaries. One of these peoples, the Seljuk (SEL-jook) Turks, soon posed a threat to the Fatimids themselves.

The Seljuk Turks were a nomadic people from Central Asia who had been converted to Islam and flourished as military mercenaries for the Abbasid caliphate. Moving gradually into Persia and Armenia, their numbers grew until by the eleventh century they were able to take over the eastern provinces of the Abbasid empire. In 1055, a Turkish leader captured Baghdad and assumed command of the Abbasid empire with the title of **sultan** ("holder of power"). While the Abbasid caliph remained the chief representative of Sunni religious authority, the real military and political power of the state was in the hands of the Seljuk Turks. In Europe and within the Muslim world itself, the Turks were initially regarded as a disaster. They were viewed as barbarians who destroyed civilizations and oppressed populations. In many respects, however, Turkish rule in the Middle East was probably beneficial by bringing an end to the squabbles between Sunni and Shi'ite Muslims while supporting the Sunnis. The Turks also put their energies into revitalizing Islamic law and institutions.

By the latter part of the eleventh century, the Seljuk Turks were exerting military pressure on Egypt and the Byzantine Empire. When the Byzantine emperor foolishly challenged the Turks, the latter routed the Byzantine army at Manzikert in 1071. In dire straits, the Byzantines looked west for help, setting in motion the papal pleas that led to the Crusades. To understand the complexities of the situation, however, we need to look first at the Byzantine Empire.

The Byzantine Empire   The Macedonian dynasty of the tenth and eleventh centuries had restored much of the power of the Byzantine Empire; its incompetent successors, however, reversed most of the gains. After the Macedonian dynasty was extinguished in 1056, the empire was beset by internal struggles for power between ambitious military leaders and aristocratic families who attempted to buy the support of the great landowners of Anatolia by allowing them greater control over their peasants. This policy was self-destructive, however, because the peasant-warrior was the traditional backbone of the Byzantine state.

The growing division between the Catholic Church of the West and the Eastern Orthodox Church of the Byzantine Empire also weakened the Byzantine state. The Eastern Orthodox Church was unwilling to accept the pope's claim that he was the sole head of the church. This dispute reached a climax in 1054 when Pope Leo IX and Patriarch Michael Cerularius (seer-oo-LAR-ee-uss), head of the Byzantine church, formally excommunicated each other, initiating a schism between the two great branches of Christianity that has not been healed to this day.

The Byzantine Empire faced external threats to its security as well. The greatest challenge came from the Seljuk Turks who had moved into Asia Minor—the heartland of the empire and its main source of food and manpower. After defeating the Byzantine forces at Manzikert in 1071, the Turks advanced into Anatolia, where many peasants, already disgusted by their exploitation at the hands of Byzantine landowners, readily accepted Turkish control.

A new dynasty, however, soon breathed new life into the Byzantine Empire. The Comneni, under Alexius I Comnenus (kahm-NEE-nuss) (1081–1118), were victorious on the Greek Adriatic coast against the Normans, defeated the Pechenegs in the Balkans, and stopped the Turks in Anatolia. Lacking the resources to undertake additional campaigns against the Turks, Emperor Alexius I turned to the West for military assistance. The positive response to the emperor's request led to the Crusades. The Byzantine Empire lived to regret it.

The Early Crusades   The Crusades were based on the idea of a holy war against the infidels or unbelievers. The wrath of Christians was directed against the Muslims and had already found some expression in the attempt to reconquer Spain from the Muslims and the success of the Normans in reclaiming Sicily. At the end of the eleventh century, Christian Europe found itself with a glorious opportunity to attack the Muslims.

The immediate impetus for the Crusades came when the Byzantine emperor, Alexius I, asked Pope Urban II (1088–1099) for help against the Seljuk Turks. The pope saw a golden opportunity to provide papal leadership for a great cause: to rally the warriors of Europe for the liberation of Jerusalem and the Holy Land from the infidel. As we have seen, the Holy City of Jerusalem had long been the object of Christian pilgrimages. At the Council of Clermont in southern France near the end of 1095, Urban challenged Christians to take up their weapons against the infidel and join in a holy war to recover the Holy Land. The pope promised

The Bridgeman Art Library/Getty Images

The First Crusade: The Capture of Jerusalem. *Recruited from the noble class of western Europe, the first crusading army had taken Antioch by 1098. Working down the coast of Palestine, the crusaders captured Jerusalem in 1099. Shown here in a fifteenth-century manuscript illustration is a fanciful re-creation of the looting of Jerusalem after its capture by the Christian crusaders.*

remission of sins: "All who die by the way, whether by land or by sea, or in battle against the pagans, shall have immediate remission of sins. This I grant them through the power of God with which I am invested."[9]

The initial response to Urban's speech reveals how appealing many people found this combined call to military arms and religious fervor. The First Crusade was preceded by an exercise in religious fanaticism and futility. A self-appointed leader, Peter the Hermit, who preached of his visions of the Holy City of Jerusalem, convinced a large mob, most of them poor and many of them peasants, to undertake a Crusade to the east. One person who encountered Peter described him in in these words: "Outdoors he wore a woolen tunic, which revealed his ankles, and above it a hood; he wore a cloak to cover his upper body, a bit of his arms, but his feet were bare. He drank wine and ate fish, but scarcely ever ate bread. This man, partly because of his reputation, partly because of his preaching, [assembled] a very large army."[10]

This "Peasants' Crusade," or "Crusade of the Poor," comprised a ragtag rabble that moved through the Balkans, terrorizing the natives and looting food and supplies. Their misplaced religious enthusiasm led to another tragic by-product as well, the persecution of the Jews, long depicted by the church as the murderers of Christ. As a contemporary chronicler put it, "they persecuted the hated race of the Jews wherever they were found." Two bands of peasant crusaders, led by Peter the Hermit, managed to reach Constantinople. Emperor Alexius wisely shipped them over to Asia Minor where the Turks massacred the undisciplined and poorly armed rabble.

The First Crusade Pope Urban II did not share the wishful thinking of the peasant crusaders but was more inclined to trust knights who had been well trained in the art of war. The warriors of western Europe, particularly France, formed the first crusading armies. The knights who made up this first serious crusading host were motivated by religious fervor, but there were other attractions as well. Some sought adventure and welcomed a legitimate opportunity to pursue their favorite pastime—fighting. Others saw an opportunity to gain territory, riches, status, possibly a title, and even salvation—had the pope not offered a full remission of sins for those who participated in these "armed pilgrimages"? From the perspective of the pope and European monarchs, the Crusades offered a way to rid Europe of contentious young nobles who disturbed the peace and wasted lives and energy fighting each other. The Catholic Church had tried earlier with the "Peace of God" and "Truce of God" to limit the ongoing bloodletting, but without a great deal of success (see Chapter 9). And merchants in many Italian cities relished the prospect of new trading opportunities in Muslim lands.

In the First Crusade, begun in 1096, three organized bands of noble warriors, most of them French, made their way to the east (see Map 10.7). The crusading

MAP 10.7 The Early Crusades

Pope Urban II launched the Crusades to recapture the Holy Land from the "enemies of God," a call met with great enthusiasm in Europe. The fighters of the First Crusade massacred the inhabitants of Jerusalem and established the crusader states.

army probably numbered several thousand cavalry and as many as 10,000 foot soldiers. After the capture of Antioch in 1098, much of the crusading host proceeded down the coast of Palestine, evading the garrisoned coastal cities, and reached Jerusalem in June 1099. After a five-week siege, the Holy City was taken amid a horrible massacre of the inhabitants, men, women, and children.

After further conquest of Palestinian lands, the crusaders ignored the wishes of the Byzantine emperor (who foolishly believed the crusaders were working on his behalf) and organized four crusader states (Edessa, Antioch, Tripoli, and Jerusalem). Because the crusader states were surrounded by Muslim enemies, they grew increasingly dependent on the Italian commercial cities for supplies from Europe. Some Italian cities, such as Genoa, Pisa, and especially Venice, became rich and powerful in the process.

The Second Crusade   At first, Muslim rulers in the Middle East were taken aback by the invading crusaders, whose armored cavalry presented a new challenge to local warriors, and their response was ineffectual. The Seljuk Turks by that time were preoccupied with events taking place farther to the east and took no action themselves. But the crusader states soon foundered, and by the 1120s, the Muslims were striking back. In 1144, Edessa became the first of the four Latin states to be recaptured. Its fall led to renewed calls for another Crusade, especially from the monastic firebrand Saint Bernard of Clairvaux, who exclaimed, "Now, on account of our sins, the sacrilegious enemies of the cross have begun to show their faces.... What are you doing, you servants of the cross? Will you throw to the dogs that which is most holy? Will you cast pearls before swine?"[11] Bernard aimed his message at knights and even managed to enlist two powerful rulers, King Louis VII of France and Emperor Conrad III of Germany. Their Second Crusade, however, proved to be a total failure.

The Third Crusade   In 1169, Sunni Muslims under the leadership of Saladin (SAL-uh-din) brought an end to the Fatimid dynasty in Egypt. Proclaiming himself sultan, Saladin succeeded in establishing his control over both Egypt and Syria and began to confront the Christian states in the area with united Muslim power on two fronts. In 1187, Saladin's army invaded the kingdom of Jerusalem and destroyed the Christian forces there. Further operations reduced Christian occupation in the area to a handful of fortresses along the northern coast. Unlike the Christians of the First Crusade, who had slaughtered much of the population of Jerusalem when they captured the city, Saladin did not permit a massacre of the civilian population and even tolerated Christian religious services in conquered territories. For a time, Christian occupation forces even carried on a lively trade with Muslim communities in the region.

The fall of the Holy City of Jerusalem, however, set all of Christendom ablaze with calls for a new Crusade. Three major monarchs agreed to lead the Third Crusade in person: Emperor Frederick Barbarossa of Germany, King Richard I the Lionhearted of England (1189–1199), and Philip II Augustus, king of France. Some of the crusaders finally arrived in the Middle East by 1189 only to encounter problems. Frederick Barbarossa drowned while swimming in a local river, and his army quickly fell apart. The English and French arrived by sea and met with success against the coastal cities, where they had the support of their fleets, but when they moved inland, they failed miserably. Eventually, after Philip went home, Richard negotiated a settlement whereby Saladin agreed to allow Christian pilgrims free access to Jerusalem.

The Crusades of the Thirteenth Century

After the death of Saladin in 1193, Pope Innocent III initiated the Fourth Crusade. On its way to the Holy Land, the crusading army became involved in a dispute over the succession to the Byzantine throne. The Venetian leaders of the Fourth Crusade saw an opportunity to neutralize their greatest commercial competitor, the Byzantine Empire. Diverted to Constantinople, the crusaders sacked the great capital city in 1204 and created a new Latin Empire of Constantinople. Not until 1261 did a Byzantine army recapture Constantinople. The Byzantine Empire had been saved, but it was no longer a great Mediterranean power. The restored empire now comprised only the city of Constantinople and its surrounding territory as well as some lands in Asia Minor. Though reduced in size, the empire limped along for another 190 years until its weakened condition finally enabled the Ottoman Turks to conquer it in 1453.

Despite the failures, the crusading ideal was not yet completely lost. In Germany in 1212, a youth known as Nicholas of Cologne announced that God had inspired him to lead a Children's Crusade to the Holy Land. Thousands of young people joined Nicholas and made their way down the Rhine and across the Alps to Italy, where the pope told them to go home. Most tried to do so. The next Crusade of adult warriors was hardly more successful. The Fifth Crusade (1219–1221) attempted to recover the Holy Land by way of the powerful Muslim state of Egypt. The Crusade achieved some early successes, but its ultimate failure marked an end to papal leadership of the western crusaders.

The Sixth Crusade, which was led by the German emperor Frederick II, took place without papal support because the emperor had been excommunicated by the pope for starting late. In 1228, Frederick marched into Jerusalem and accepted the crown as king of Jerusalem after he had made an agreement with the sultan of Egypt. The Holy City had been taken without a fight and without papal support. Once Frederick left, however, the city fell once again, this time to a group of Turks allied with the sultan of Egypt. The last two major Crusades, poorly organized by the pious king of France, Louis IX, were complete failures. Soon the remaining Christian possessions in the Middle East were retaken. Acre, the last foothold of the crusaders, surrendered in 1291. All in all, the Crusades had failed to accomplish their primary goal of holding the Holy Land for the Christian West.

What Were the Effects of the Crusades?

Whether the Crusades had much effect on European civilization is debatable. The crusaders made little long-term impact on the Middle East, where the only visible remnants of their conquests were their castles. There may have been some broadening of perspective that comes from the exchange between two cultures, but

The Siege of Jerusalem: Christian and Muslim Perspectives

During the First Crusade, Christian knights laid siege to Jerusalem in June 1099. The first excerpt is taken from an account by Fulcher of Chartres, who accompanied the crusaders to the Holy Land. The second selection is by a Muslim writer, Ibn al-Athir, whose account of the First Crusade can be found in his history of the Muslim world.

Fulcher of Chartres, *Chronicle of the First Crusade*

Then the Franks entered the city magnificently at the noonday hour on Friday, the day of the week when Christ redeemed the whole world on the cross. With trumpets sounding and with everything in an uproar, exclaiming: "Help, God!" they vigorously pushed into the city, and straightway raised the banner on the top of the wall. All the heathen, completely terrified, changed their boldness to swift flight through the narrow streets of the quarters. The more quickly they fled, the more quickly they put to flight.

Count Raymond and his men, who were bravely assailing the city in another section, did not perceive this until they saw the Saracens [Muslims] jumping from the top of the wall. Seeing this, they joyfully ran to the city as quickly as they could, and helped the others pursue and kill the wicked enemy.

Then some, both Arabs and Ethiopians, fled into the Tower of David; others shut themselves in the Temple of the Lord and of Solomon, where in the halls a very great attack was made on them. Nowhere was there a place where the Saracens could escape swordsmen.

On the top of Solomon's Temple, to which they had climbed in fleeing, many were shot to death with arrows and cast down headlong from the roof. Within this Temple, about ten thousand were beheaded. If you had been there, your feet would have been stained up to the ankles with the blood of the slain. What more shall I tell? Not one of them was

the interaction of Christian Europe with the Muslim world was actually both more intense and more meaningful in Spain and Sicily than in the Holy Land.

Did the Crusades help stabilize European society by removing large numbers of young warriors who would have fought each other in Europe? Some historians think so and believe that Western monarchs established their control more easily as a result. There is no doubt that the Crusades did contribute to the economic growth of the Italian port cities, especially Genoa, Pisa, and Venice. But it is important to remember that the growing wealth and population of twelfth-century Europe had made the Crusades possible in the first place. The Crusades may have enhanced the revival of trade, but they certainly did not cause it. Even without the Crusades, Italian merchants would have pursued new trade contacts with the eastern world.

allowed to live. They did not spare the women and children.

Account of Ibn al-Athir

In fact Jerusalem was taken from the north on the morning of Friday 22 Sha'ban 492/15 July 1099. The population was put to the sword by the Franks, who pillaged the area for a week. A band of Muslims barricaded themselves into the Oratory of David and fought on for several days. They were granted their lives in return for surrendering. The Franks honored their word, and the group left by night for Ascalon. In the Masjid al-Aqsa the Franks slaughtered more than 70,000 people, among them a large number of Imams and Muslim scholars, devout and ascetic men who had left their homelands to live lives of pious seclusion in the Holy Place. The Franks stripped the Dome of the Rock of more than forty silver candelabra, each of them weighing 3,600 drams, and a great silver lamp weighing forty-four Syrian pounds, as well as a hundred and fifty smaller candelabra and more than twenty gold ones, and a great deal more booty. Refugees from Syria reached Baghdad in Ramadan, among them the qadi Abu sa'd al-Harawi. They told the Caliph's ministers a story that wrung their hearts and brought tears to their eyes. On Friday they went to the Cathedral Mosque and begged for help, weeping so that their hearers wept with them as they described the sufferings of the Muslims in that Holy City: the men killed, the women and children taken prisoner, the homes pillaged. Because of the terrible hardships they had suffered, they were allowed to break the fast.

Q *What happened to the inhabitants of Jerusalem when the Christian knights captured the city? How do you explain the extreme intolerance and brutality of the Christian knights? How do these two accounts differ, and how are they similar?*

Sources: Fulcher of Chartres, *Chronicle of the First Crusade.* From *The First Crusade: The Chronicle of Fulcher of Chartres and Other Source Materials*, 2nd ed., ed. Edward Peters (University of Pennsylvania Press, 1998), pp. 90–91. Account of Ibn al-Athir. From *Arab Historians of the Crusades*, ed. and trans. E. J. Costello. Berkeley: University of California Press, 1969.

Did the Crusades have side effects that would haunt European society for generations? Some historians have argued that the Crusades might be considered a "Christian holy war," whose memories still trouble the relationship between the Muslim world and the West today. Other historians argue that the early crusaders were motivated as much by economic and political reasons as religious ones.

Another possible side effect is more apparent. The first widespread attacks on the Jews began with the Crusades. As some Christians argued, to undertake holy wars against infidel Muslims while the "murderers of Christ" ran free at home was unthinkable. With the crusades, the massacre of Jews became a regular feature of medieval European life.

CHRONOLOGIES

GROWTH OF THE EUROPEAN KINGDOMS

England

1066–1087	William the Conqueror
1154–1189	Henry II, first of the Plantagenet dynasty
1215	Magna Carta

France

1180–1223	Philip II Augustus
1226–1270	Louis IX
1285–1314	Philip IV

Germany, the Holy Roman Empire, and Italy

1056–1106	Henry IV
1152–1190	Frederick I Barbarossa
1212–1250	Frederick II
1273	Election of Rudolf of Habsburg as king of Germany

Eastern Europe

1230s	Mongol conquest of Russia
c. 1220–1263	Alexander Nevsky, prince of Novgorod

THE CRUSADES

1096–1099	First Crusade
1147–1149	Second Crusade
1189–1192	Third Crusade
1204	Fourth Crusade—sack of Constantinople
1219–1221	Fifth Crusade
1291	Surrender of Acre and end of Christian presence in the Holy Land

11

THE LATER MIDDLE AGES: CRISIS AND DISINTEGRATION IN THE FOURTEENTH CENTURY

A medieval illustration of Death as a mounted hunter and reaper during the Black Death

---

CHAPTER OUTLINE

• A Time of Troubles: Black Death and Social Crisis • War and Political Instability • The Decline of the Church • The Cultural World of the Fourteenth Century • Society in an Age of Adversity

A TIME OF TROUBLES: BLACK DEATH AND SOCIAL CRISIS

Well into the thirteenth century, Europe had experienced good harvests and an expanding population. By the end of the century, however, a period of disastrous changes had begun.

Famine and Population   For one thing, there were noticeable changes in weather patterns as Europe entered a "little ice age." Shortened growing seasons and disastrous weather conditions, including severe storms and constant rain, led to widespread famine and hunger. The great famine of 1315–1317 in northern Europe destroyed harvests and caused serious food shortages, resulting in extreme hunger and starvation. The great famine expanded to other parts of Europe in an all-too-familiar pattern, as is evident in this scene described by a contemporary chronicler:

> We saw a large number of both sexes, not only from nearby places but from as much as five leagues away, barefooted and maybe even, except for women, in a completely nude state, together with their priests coming in procession at the Church of the Holy Martyrs, their bones bulging out, devoutly carrying bodies of saints and other relics to be adorned hoping to get relief.[1]

Some historians estimate that famine killed 10 percent of the European population in the first half of the fourteenth century.

Europe had experienced a great increase in population in the High Middle Ages. By 1300, however, indications are that Europe had reached the upper limit in the number of people who could be supported by existing agricultural production and technology. Virtually all productive land was being farmed, including many marginal lands that needed intensive cultivation and proved easily susceptible to changing weather patterns.

There was also a movement from overpopulated rural areas to urban locations. Eighteen percent of the people in the village of Broughton in England, for example, migrated between 1288 and 1340. There is no certainty that these migrants found better economic opportunities in urban areas. We might in fact conclude the opposite, based on the reports of increasing numbers of poor people in the cities. In 1330, for example, one chronicler estimated that of the 100,000 inhabitants of Florence, 17,000 were paupers. Moreover, evidence suggests that because of the growing population, by 1300 individual peasant holdings were shrinking in size to an acreage that could no longer support a peasant family. Europe seemed to have reached an upper limit to population growth, and the number of poor appeared to have increased noticeably.

Some historians have pointed out that famine may have led to chronic malnutrition, which in turn contributed to increased infant mortality, lower birthrates, and higher susceptibility to disease because malnourished people are less able to resist infection. This, they argue, helps explain the high mortality of the great plague known as the Black Death.

The Black Death: From Asia to Europe   In the mid-fourteenth century, the disaster known as the **Black Death** struck Asia, North Africa, and Europe. Although there were several types of plague, the most common and most important form in the diffusion of the Black

Death was bubonic plague, which was spread by black rats infested with fleas who were host to the deadly bacterium *Yersinia pestis*.

Role of the Mongols   This great plague originated in Asia. After disappearing from Europe and the Middle East in the Middle Ages, bubonic plague continued to haunt areas of southwestern China. In the early 1300s, rats accompanying Mongol troops spread the plague into central China and by 1331 to northeastern China. In one province near Beijing, it was reported that 90 percent of the population died. Overall, China's population may have declined from 120 million in the mid-fourteenth century to 80 million by 1400.

In the thirteenth century, the Mongols had brought much of the Eurasian land-mass under a single rule, which in turn facilitated long-distance trade, particularly along the Silk Road (see Chapter 6), now dominated by Muslim merchants from Central Asia. The movement of people and goods throughout this Eurasian land-mass also facilitated the spread of the plague.

In the 1330s, there were outbreaks of plague in Central Asia; by 1339, it had reached Samarkand, a caravan stop on the Silk Road. From Central Asia, trading caravans carried the plague westward, to Caffa, on the Black Sea, in 1346, and Constantinople by 1347. Its arrival in the Byzantine Empire was noted by Emperor John VI, who lost a son: "Upon arrival in Constantinople she [the empress] found Andronikos, the youngest born, dead from the invading plague, which ... attacked almost all the seacoasts of the world and killed most of their people."[2] By 1348, the plague had spread to Egypt, Mecca, and Damascus as well as to other parts of the Middle East.

The Black Death in Europe   The Black Death of the mid-fourteenth century was the most devastating natural disaster in European history, ravaging Europe's population and causing economic, social, political, and cultural upheaval. Contemporary chroniclers lamented that parents attempted to flee, abandoning their children; one related the words of a child left behind: "Oh father, why have you abandoned me? ... Mother where have you gone?"[3] People were horrified by an evil force they could not understand and by the subsequent breakdown of all normal human relations.

Symptoms of bubonic plague included high fever, aching joints, swelling of the lymph nodes, and dark blotches caused by bleeding beneath the skin. Bubonic plague was actually the least toxic form of plague but nevertheless killed 50 to 60 percent of its victims. In pneumonic plague, the bacterial inflection spread to the lungs, resulting in severe coughing, bloody sputum, and the relatively easy spread of the bacillus from human to human by coughing.

The plague reached Europe in October 1347 when Genoese merchants brought it from Caffa to the island of Sicily off the coast of Italy. One contemporary wrote: "As it happened, among those who escaped from Caffa by boat, there were a few sailors who had been infected with the poisonous disease. Some boats were bound for Genoa, others went to Venice and other Christian areas. When the sailors reached these places and mixed with the people there, it was as if they had brought evil spirits with them."[4] The plague spread quickly, reaching southern Italy and southern France and Spain by the end of 1347 (see Map 11.1). Usually, the

MAP 11.1 Spread of the Black Death

The plague entered Europe by way of Sicily in 1347 and within three years had killed between one-quarter and one-half of the population. Outbreaks continued into the early eighteenth century, and the European population took two hundred years to return to the level it had reached before the Black Death.

diffusion of the Black Death followed commercial trade routes. In 1348, the plague spread through France and the Low Countries and into Germany. By the end of that year, it had moved to England, ravaging it in 1349. By the end of 1349, the plague had expanded to northern Europe and Scandinavia. Eastern Europe and Russia were affected by 1351, although mortality rates were never as high in eastern Europe as they were in western and central Europe.

Mortality figures for the Black Death were incredibly high. Italy was hit especially hard. As the commercial center of the Mediterranean, Italy possessed scores of ports where the plague could be introduced. Italy's crowded cities, whether large, such as Florence, Genoa, and Venice, with populations near 100,000, or small, such as Orvieto and Pistoia, suffered losses of 50 to 60 percent. France and England were also particularly devastated. In northern France, farming villages suffered mortality rates of 30 percent, while cities such as Rouen were more severely affected and experienced losses as high as 40 percent. In England and Germany, entire villages simply disappeared. In Germany, of approximately 170,000 inhabited locations, only 130,000 were left by the end of the fourteenth century.

It has been estimated that the European population declined by 25 to 50 percent between 1347 and 1351. If we accept the recent scholarly assessment of a European population of 75 million in the early fourteenth century, this means a death toll of 19 to 38 million people in four years. And the plague did not end in 1351. There were major outbreaks again in 1361–1362 and 1369 and then recurrences every five or six to ten or twelve years, depending on climatic and ecological conditions, until the end of the fifteenth century. The European population thus did not begin to recover until around 1500 and took several generations after that to reattain thirteenth-century levels.

Life and Death: Reactions to the Plague   Natural disasters of the magnitude of the great plague produce extreme psychological reactions. Knowing they could be dead in a matter of days, people began to live for the moment; some threw themselves with abandon into sexual and alcoholic orgies. The fourteenth-century Italian writer Giovanni Boccaccio (joe-VAH-nee boh-KAH-choh) gave a classic description of this kind of reaction to the plague in Florence in the preface to his famous *Decameron*:

> [Some people] held that plenty of drinking and enjoyment, singing and free living and the gratification of the appetite in every possible way, letting the devil take the hindmost, was the best preventative ... ; and as far as they could, they suited the action to the word. Day and night they went from one tavern to another drinking and carousing unrestrainedly. At the least inkling of something that suited them, they ran wild in other people's houses, and there was no one to prevent them, for everyone had abandoned all responsibility for his belongings as well as for himself, considering his days numbered.[5]

Wealthy and powerful people fled to their country estates, as Boccaccio recounted: "Still others ... maintained that no remedy against plagues was better than to leave them miles behind. Men and women without number ..., caring for nobody but themselves, abandoned the city, their houses and estates, their own flesh and blood even, and their effects, in search of a country place."[6]

The attempt to explain the Black Death and mitigate its harshness led to extreme sorts of behavior. To many people, the plague had either been sent by God as a punishment for humans' sins or been caused by the devil. Some resorted to extreme asceticism to cleanse themselves of sin and gain God's forgiveness. Such were the flagellants (FLAJ-uh-lunts), whose movement became popular in 1348, especially in Germany. Groups of flagellants, both men and women, wandered from town to town, flogging themselves with whips to win the forgiveness of God, whom they believed had sent the plague to punish humans for their sinful ways. One contemporary chronicler described a flagellant procession:

> The penitents went about, coming first out of Germany. They were men who did public penance and scourged themselves with whips of hard knotted leather with little iron spikes. Some made themselves bleed very badly between the shoulder blades and some foolish women had cloths ready to catch the blood and smear it on their eyes, saying it was miraculous blood. While they were doing penance, they sang very mournful songs about the nativity and the passion of Our Lord. The object of this penance was to put a stop to the mortality, for in that time ... at least a third of all the people in the world died.[7]

The flagellants attracted attention and created mass hysteria wherever they went. The Catholic Church, however, became alarmed when flagellant groups began to

Bavarian State Library, Munich//© Interfoto/Alamy

The Flagellants. *Reactions to the plague were extreme at times. Believing that asceticism could atone for humanity's sins and win God's forgiveness, flagellants wandered from town to town flogging themselves and each other with whips as in this illustration from a fifteenth-century German manuscript.*

kill Jews and attack clergy who opposed them. Some groups also developed a millenarian aspect, anticipating the imminent end of the world, the return of Jesus, and the establishment of a thousand-year kingdom under his governance. Pope Clement VI condemned the flagellants in October 1349 and urged the public authorities to crush them. By the end of 1350, most of the flagellant movement had been destroyed.

An outbreak of virulent anti-Semitism also accompanied the Black Death. Jews were accused of causing the plague by poisoning town wells. Although Jews were persecuted in Spain, the worst organized massacres, or **pogroms** (POH-grums), against this helpless minority were carried out in Germany; more than sixty major Jewish communities in Germany had been exterminated by 1351. Many Jews fled eastward to Russia and especially to Poland, where the king offered them protection. Eastern Europe became home to large Jewish communities.

The prevalence of death because of the plague and its recurrences affected people in profound ways. Some survivors apparently came to treat life as something cheap and transient. Violence and violent death appeared to be more common after the plague than before. Postplague Europe also demonstrated a morbid preoccupation with death. In their sermons, priests reminded parishioners that each night's sleep might be their last. Tombstones were decorated with macabre scenes of naked corpses in various stages of decomposition with snakes entwined in their bones and their innards filled with worms.

The Cremation of the Strasbourg Jews

In their attempt to explain the widespread horrors of the Black Death, medieval Christian communities looked for scapegoats. As at the time of the Crusades, the Jews were blamed for poisoning wells and thereby spreading the plague. This selection by a contemporary chronicler, written in 1349, gives an account of how Christians in the town of Strasbourg in the Holy Roman Empire dealt with their Jewish community. It is apparent that financial gain was also an important motive in killing the Jews.

Jacob von Konigshofen, "The Cremation of the Strasbourg Jews"

In the year 1349 there occurred the greatest epidemic that ever happened. Death went from one end of the earth to the other.... And from what this epidemic came, all wise teachers and physicians could only say that it was God's will.... This epidemic also came to Strasbourg in the summer of the above-mentioned year, and it is estimated that about sixteen thousand people died.

In the matter of this plague the Jews throughout the world were reviled and accused in all lands of having caused it through the poison which they are said to have put into the water and the wells—that is what they were accused of—and for this reason the Jews were burnt all the way from the Mediterranean into Germany....

[The account then goes on to discuss the situation of the Jews in the city of Strasbourg.]

On Saturday ... they burnt the Jews on a wooden platform in their cemetery. There were about two thousand people of them.

Those who wanted to baptize themselves were spared. [About one thousand accepted baptism.] Many small children were taken out of the fire and baptized against the will of their fathers and mothers. And everything that was owed to the Jews was canceled, and the Jews had to surrender all pledges and notes that they had taken for debts. The council, however, took the cash that the Jews possessed and divided it among the working-men proportionately. The money was indeed the thing that killed the Jews. If they had been poor and if the lords had not been in debt to them, they would not have been burnt....

Thus were the Jews burnt at Strasbourg, and in the same year in all the cities of the Rhine, whether Free Cities or Imperial Cities or cities belonging to the lords. In some towns they burnt the Jews after a trial, in others, without a trial. In some cities the Jews themselves set fire to their houses and cremated themselves.

It was decided in Strasbourg that no Jew should enter the city for 100 years, but before 20 years had passed, the council and magistrates agreed that they ought to admit the Jews again into the city for 20 years. And so the Jews came back again to Strasbourg in the year 1368 after the birth of our Lord.

Q *What charges were made against the Jews in regard to the Black Death? Can it be said that these charges were economically motivated? Why or why not?*

Source: From *The Jew in the Medieval World* by Jacob R. Marcus. Copyright 1972 by Atheneum. Reprinted with permission of The Hebrew Union College Press.

Art and the Black Death The Black Death made a visible impact on art. For one thing, it wiped out entire guilds of artists. At the same time, survivors, including the newly rich who patronized artists, were no longer so optimistic. Some were more guilty about enjoying life and more concerned about gaining salvation. Postplague art began to concentrate on pain and death. A fairly large number of artistic works came to be based on the *ars moriendi* (AHRS moh-ree-EN-dee), the art of dying. A morbid concern with death is especially evident in the fresco *The Triumph of Death* by Francesco Traini (frahn-CHES-koh TRAY-nee) in Pisa. On the left side of the fresco, several young nobles encounter three coffins containing decomposing bodies, while on the right young aristocrats engage in pleasant pursuits but are threatened by a grim figure of Death in the form of a witch flying through the air swinging a large scythe. Beneath her lie piles of dead citizens and clergy cut down in the prime of life.

Economic Dislocation and Social Upheaval   The population collapse of the fourteenth century had dire economic and social consequences. Economic dislocation was accompanied by social upheaval. Between 1000 and 1300, Europe had been relatively stable. The division of society into the three estates of clergy (those who pray), nobility (those who fight), and laborers (those who work) had already begun to disintegrate in the thirteenth century, however. In the fourteenth century, a series of urban and rural revolts rocked European society.

Noble Landlords and Peasants   Both peasants and noble landlords were affected by the demographic crisis of the fourteenth century. Most noticeably, Europe experienced a serious labor shortage that caused a dramatic rise in the price of labor. At Cuxham manor in England, for example, a farm laborer who had received two shillings a week in 1347 was paid seven in 1349 and almost eleven by 1350. At the same time, the decline in population depressed or held stable the demand for agricultural produce, resulting in stable or falling prices for output (although in England prices remained high until the 1380s). The chronicler Henry Knighton observed: "And the price of everything was cheap.... A man could buy a horse for half a mark [six shillings], which before was worth forty shillings."[8] Because landlords were having to pay more for labor at the same time that their rents or incomes were declining, they began to experience considerable adversity and lower standards of living. In England, aristocratic incomes dropped more than 20 percent between 1347 and 1353.

Landed aristocrats responded by seeking to lower the wage rate. The English Parliament passed the Statute of Laborers (1351), which attempted to limit wages to preplague levels and forbid the mobility of peasants as well. Although such laws proved largely unworkable, they did keep wages from rising as high as they might have in a free market. Overall, the position of landlords continued to deteriorate during the late fourteenth and early fifteenth centuries. At the same time, conditions for peasants improved, though not uniformly throughout Europe.

The decline in the number of peasants after the Black Death accelerated the process of converting labor services to rents, freeing peasants from the obligations of servile tenure and weakening the system of manorialism. But there were limits to how much the peasants could advance. Not only did they face the same economic hurdles as the lords, but the latter attempted to impose wage restrictions and reinstate old forms of labor service. New governmental taxes also hurt. Peasant complaints became widespread and soon gave rise to rural revolts.

Peasant Revolt in France   In 1358, a peasant revolt, known as the *Jacquerie* (zhahk-REE), broke out in northern France. The destruction of normal order by the Black Death and the subsequent economic dislocation were important factors in causing the revolt, but the ravages created by the Hundred Years' War also affected the French peasantry (see "War and Political Instability" later in this chapter). Both the French and English forces followed a deliberate policy of laying waste to peasants' fields while bands of mercenaries lived off the land by taking peasants' produce as well.

Growing class tensions also exacerbated peasant anger. Landed nobles were eager to hold on to their politically privileged position and felt increasingly threatened in the new postplague world of higher wages and lower prices. Many aristocrats looked on peasants with utter contempt. A French tale told to upper-class audiences contained this remarkable passage:

> Tell me, Lord, if you please, by what right or title does a villein [peasant] eat beef? ... Should they eat fish? Rather let them eat thistles and briars, thorns and straw and hay on Sunday and peapods on weekdays. They should keep watch without sleep and have trouble always; that is how villeins should live. Yet each day they are full and drunk on the best wines, and in fine clothes. The great expenditures of villeins come as a high cost, for it is this that destroys and ruins the world. It is they who spoil the common welfare. From the villein comes all unhappiness. Should they eat meat? Rather should they chew grass on the heath with the horned cattle and go naked on all fours.[9]

The peasants reciprocated this contempt for their so-called social superiors.

The outburst of peasant anger led to savage confrontations. Castles were burned and nobles murdered. Such atrocities did not go unanswered, however. The *Jacquerie* soon failed as the privileged classes closed ranks, savagely massacred the rebels, and ended the revolt.

An English Peasant Revolt   The English Peasants' Revolt of 1381 was the most prominent of all. It was a product not of desperation but of rising expectations. After the Black Death, the condition of the English peasants had improved as they enjoyed greater freedom and higher wages or lower rents. Aristocratic landlords had fought back with legislation to depress wages and attempted to reimpose old feudal dues. The most immediate cause of the revolt, however, was the monarchy's attempt to raise revenues by imposing a poll tax or a flat charge on each adult member of the population. Peasants in eastern England, the wealthiest part of the country, refused to pay the tax and expelled the collectors forcibly from their villages.

This action sparked a widespread rebellion of both peasants and townspeople led by a well-to-do peasant called Wat Tyler and a preacher named John Ball. The latter preached an effective message against the noble class, as recounted by the French chronicler Jean Froissart (ZHAHNH frwah-SAR):

> Good people, things cannot go right in England and never will, until goods are held in common and there are no more villeins and gentlefolk, but we are all one and the same. In what way are those whom we call lords greater masters than ourselves? How have they deserved it? Why do they hold us in bondage? If we all spring from a single father and mother, Adam and Eve, how can they claim or prove that they are lords more than us, except by making us produce and grow the wealth which they spend?[10]

A Revolt of French Peasants

In 1358, French peasants rose up in a revolt known as the *Jacquerie*. The relationship between aristocrats and peasants had degenerated as a result of the social upheavals and privations caused by the Black Death and the Hundred Years' War. This excerpt from the chronicle of an aristocrat paints a horrifying picture of the barbarities that occurred during the revolt.

Jean Froissart, *Chronicles*

There were very strange and terrible happenings in several parts of the kingdom of France.... They began when some of the men from the country towns came together in the Beauvais region. They had no leaders and at first they numbered scarcely 100. One of them got up and said that the nobility of France, knights and squires, were disgracing and betraying the realm, and that it would be a good thing if they were all destroyed. At this they all shouted: "He's right! He's right! Shame on any man who saves the nobility from being wiped out!"

They banded together and went off, without further deliberation and unarmed except for pikes and knives, to the house of a knight who lived nearby. They broke in and killed the knight, with his lady and his children, big and small, and set fire to the house. Next they went to another castle and did much worse; for, having seized the knight and bound him securely to a post, several of them violated his wife and daughter before his eyes. Then they killed the wife, who was pregnant, and the daughter and all the other children, and finally put the knight to death with great cruelty and burned and razed the castle.

They did similar things in a number of castles and big houses, and their ranks swelled until there were a good 6,000 of them. Wherever they went their numbers grew, for all the men of the same sort joined them. The knights and squires fled before them with their families. They took their wives and daughters many miles away to put them in safety, leaving their houses open with their possessions inside. And those evil men, who had come together without leaders or arms, pillaged and burned everything and violated and killed all the ladies and girls without mercy, like mad dogs. Their barbarous acts were worse than anything that ever took place between Christians and Saracens [Muslims]. Never did men commit such vile deeds. They were such that no living creature ought to see, or even imagine or think of, and the men who committed the most were admired and had the highest places among them. I could never bring myself to write down the horrible and shameful things which they did to the ladies. But, among other brutal excesses, they killed a knight, put him on a spit, and turned him at the fire and roasted him before the lady and her children. After about a dozen of them had violated the lady, they tried to force her and the children to eat the knight's flesh before putting them cruelly to death.

Q *Why did the peasants react so strongly against their aristocratic lords? Do you think this is an unbiased account? Why or why not?*

Source: From CHRONICLES by Froissart, translated by Geoffrey Brereton (Penguin Classics, 1968, Revised 1978). Translation copyright © Geoffrey Brereton, 1968. Reproduced by permission of Penguin Books, Ltd.

The revolt was initially successful as the rebels burned down the manor houses of aristocrats, lawyers, and government officials and murdered several important officials, including the archbishop of Canterbury. After the peasants marched on London, the young King Richard II, age fifteen, promised to accept the rebels' demands if they returned to their homes. They accepted the king's word and dispersed, but the king reneged and with the assistance of the aristocrats arrested hundreds of the rebels. The poll tax was eliminated, however, and in the end most of the rebels were pardoned.

Revolts in the Cities   Revolts also erupted in the cities. Commercial and industrial activity suffered almost immediately from the Black Death. An oversupply of goods and an immediate drop in demand led to a decline in trade after 1350. Some industries suffered greatly. Florence's woolen industry, one of the giants, produced 70,000 to 80,000 pieces of cloth in 1338; in 1378, it was yielding only 24,000 pieces. Bourgeois merchants and manufacturers responded to the decline in trade and production by attempting to restrict competition and resist the demands of the lower classes.

In urban areas, where capitalist industrialists paid low wages and managed to prevent workers from forming organizations to help themselves, industrial revolts broke out throughout Europe. Ghent experienced one in 1381, Rouen in 1382. Most famous, however, was the revolt of the *ciompi* (CHAHM-pee) in Florence in 1378. The *ciompi* were wool workers in Florence's most prominent industry. In the 1370s, not only was the woolen industry depressed, but the wool workers saw their real wages decline when the coinage in which they were paid was debased. Their revolt won them some concessions from the municipal government, including the right to form guilds and be represented in the government. But their newly won rights were short-lived; authorities ended *ciompi* participation in the government by 1382.

Although the peasant and urban revolts sometimes resulted in short-term gains for the participants, the uprisings were quickly crushed and their gains lost. Accustomed to ruling, the established classes easily formed a united front and quashed dissent. Nevertheless, the rural and urban revolts of the fourteenth century ushered in an age of social conflict that characterized much of later European history.

WAR AND POLITICAL INSTABILITY

Famine, plague, economic turmoil, social upheaval, and violence were not the only problems of the fourteenth century. War and political instability must also be added to the list. Of all the struggles that ensued in the fourteenth century, the Hundred Years' War was the most famous and the most violent.

Causes of the Hundred Years' War   In 1259, the English king, Henry III, had relinquished his claims to all the French territories previously held by the English monarchy except for one relatively small possession known as the duchy of Gascony. As duke of Gascony, the English king pledged loyalty as a vassal to the French king. But this territory gave rise to numerous disputes between the kings of England and France. By the thirteenth century, the Capetian monarchs had greatly increased their power over

Philip III
King of France (1270–1285)

Philip IV
(1285–1314)

Charles of Valois
(*d.* 1325)

Louis X
(1314–1316)

Philip V
(1316–1322)

Charles IV
(1322–1328)

Isabella = Edward II
King of England
(1307–1327)

Philip VI
King of France
(1328–1350)

John I
(1316)

(daughters)

(daughters)

Edward III
King of England
(1327–1377)

John II
King of France
(1350–1364)

CHART 11.1   Background to the Hundred Years' War: Kings of France and England

their more important vassals, the great lords of France. Royal officials interfered regularly in the affairs of the vassals' fiefs, especially in matters of justice. Although this policy irritated all the vassals, it especially annoyed the king of England, who considered himself the peer of the French king.

A dispute over the right of succession to the French throne also complicated relations between the French and the English. In the fourteenth century, the Capetian dynasty failed to produce a male heir for the first time in almost four hundred years. In 1328, the last son of King Philip IV died without a male heir. The closest male relative in line to the throne was King Edward III of England (1327–1377), whose mother was Isabella, the daughter of Philip IV (see Chart 11.1). Known for her strong personality (she was nicknamed the "she-wolf of France"), Isabella, with the assistance of her lover, led a revolt against her husband, King Edward II, overthrew him, and ruled England until her teenage son, Edward III, took sole control of the throne in 1330. As the son of the daughter of King Philip IV, King Edward III of England had a claim to the French throne, but the French nobles argued that the inheritance of the monarchy could not pass through the female line and chose a cousin of the Capetians, Philip, duke of Valois (val-WAH), as King Philip VI (1328–1350).

The immediate cause of the war between France and England was yet another quarrel over Gascony. In 1337, when Edward III, the king of England and duke of Gascony, refused to do homage to Philip VI for Gascony, the French king seized the duchy. Edward responded by declaring war on Philip, the "so-called king of France." There is no doubt that the personalities of the two monarchs also had much to do with the outbreak of the Hundred Years' War. Both Edward and Philip loved luxury and shared a desire for the glory and prestige that came from military engagements. Both were only too willing to use their respective nation's resources to satisfy their own desires. Moreover, for many nobles, the promise of plunder and territorial gain was an incentive to follow the disruptive path of their rulers.

Conduct and Course of the War

The Hundred Years' War began in a burst of knightly enthusiasm. Trained to be warriors, knights viewed the clash of battle as the ultimate opportunity to demonstrate their fighting abilities. But this struggle would change the nature of warfare, for as it dragged on, it was not knights but peasant foot soldiers who increasingly determined the outcomes of battles. The French army of 1337, with its heavily armed noble cavalry, resembled its twelfth- and thirteenth-century forebears. The noble cavalrymen considered themselves the fighting elite and looked with contempt on the foot soldiers and crossbowmen, their social inferiors.

The English army, however, had evolved differently and had included peasants as paid foot soldiers since at least Anglo-Saxon times. Armed with pikes, many of these foot soldiers had also adopted the longbow, invented by the Welsh. The longbow had a more rapid speed of fire than the more powerful crossbow. Although the English made use of heavily armed cavalry, they relied even more on large numbers of foot soldiers.

Early Phases of the War   Edward III's early campaigns in France achieved little. When Edward renewed his efforts in 1346 with an invasion of Normandy, Philip responded by raising a large force to crush the English army and met Edward's forces at Crécy (kray-SEE), just south of Flanders. The larger French army followed no battle plan but simply attacked the English lines in a disorderly fashion. The arrows of the English archers devastated the French cavalry. As Jean Froissart described it, "The English continued to shoot [their longbows] into the thickest part of the crowd, wasting none of their arrows. They impaled or wounded horses and riders, who fell to the ground in great distress, unable to get up again [because of their heavy armor] without the help of several men."[11] It was a stunning victory for the English. Edward followed up by capturing the French port of Calais (ka-LAY) to serve as a staging ground for future invasions.

The Battle of Crécy was not decisive, however. The English simply did not possess the resources to subjugate all of France. Truces, small-scale hostilities, and some major operations were combined in an orgy of seemingly incessant struggle. The English campaigns were waged by Edward III and his son Edward, the prince of Wales, known as the Black Prince. The Black Prince's campaigns in France were devastating. Avoiding pitched battles, his forces deliberately ravaged the land, burning crops and entire unfortified villages and towns and stealing anything of value. For the English, such campaigns were profitable; for the French people, they meant hunger, deprivation, and death. When the army of the Black Prince was finally forced to do battle, the French, under their king, John II (1350–1364), were once again defeated. This time even the king was captured. This Battle of Poitiers (pwah-TYAY) (1356) ended the first phase of the Hundred Years' War. Under the Peace of Brétigny (bray-tee-NYEE) (1359), the French agreed to pay a large ransom for King John, the English territories in Gascony were enlarged, and Edward renounced his claims to the throne of France in return for John's promise to give up control over English lands in France. This first phase of the war made it clear that despite their victories, the English were not really strong enough to subdue all of France and make Edward III's claim to the French monarchy a reality.

Monarchs, however, could be slow learners. The Treaty of Brétigny was never really enforced. In the next phase of the war, in the capable hands of John's son Charles V (1364–1380), the French recovered what they had previously lost. The English returned to plundering the French countryside and avoiding pitched battles. That pleased Charles, who did not want to engage in set battles, preferring to use armed bands to reduce the English fortresses systematically.

By 1374, the French had recovered their lost lands, although France itself continued to be plagued by "free companies" of mercenaries who, no longer paid by the English, simply lived off the land by plunder and ransom. Nevertheless, for the time being, the war seemed over, especially when a twenty-year truce was negotiated in 1396.

Renewal of the War In 1415, however, the English king, Henry V (1413–1422), renewed the war at a time when the French were enduring civil war as the dukes of Burgundy and Orléans (or-lay-AHN) competed to control the weak French king, Charles VI (1380–1422). In the summer of 1413, Paris exploded with bloody encounters. Taking advantage of the chaos, Henry V invaded France in 1415. At the Battle of Agincourt (AH-zhen-koor) (1415), the French suffered a disastrous defeat, and 1,500 French nobles died when the heavy, armor-plated French knights attempted to attack across a field turned to mud by heavy rain. Altogether, French losses were 6,000 dead; the English lost only three hundred men.

Henry went on to reconquer Normandy and forge an alliance with the duke of Burgundy, which led Charles VI to agree to the Treaty of Troyes (TRWAH) in 1420. By this treaty, Henry V was married to Catherine, daughter of Charles VI, and recognized as the heir to the French throne. By 1420, the English were masters of northern France (see Map 11.2).

The seemingly hopeless French cause fell into the hands of Charles the dauphin (DAH-fin *or* doh-FAN) (heir to the throne), the son of Charles VI, who, despite being disinherited by the Treaty of Troyes, still considered himself the real heir to the French throne. The dauphin governed the southern two-thirds of French lands from Bourges. Charles was weak and timid and was unable to rally the French against the English, who in 1428 had turned south and were besieging the city of Orléans to gain access to the valley of the Loire. The French monarch was saved, quite unexpectedly, by a French peasant woman.

Joan of Arc Joan of Arc was born in 1412 to well-to-do peasants from the village of Domrémy in Champagne. Deeply religious, Joan experienced visions and came to believe that her favorite saints had commanded her to free France and have the dauphin crowned as king. In February 1429, Joan made her way to the dauphin's court, where her sincerity and simplicity persuaded Charles to allow her to accompany a French army to Orléans. Apparently inspired by the faith of the peasant girl, the French armies found new confidence in themselves and liberated Orléans, changing the course of the war. Within a few weeks, the entire Loire valley had been freed of the English. In July 1429, fulfilling Joan's other task, the

France in the Mid-Fourteenth Century

— Boundary of kingdom of France, 1360

······· Lands held by Edward III of England on accession, 1327

→ Route taken by Edward III, 1346–1347

→ Route taken by Edward, Black Prince, 1355–1357

⚔ Site and date of important battle

▨ Lands ceded to Edward III of England

▢ Domain of king of France, 1360

▢ Lands held by relatives of the king of France

▢ Other territories held by the king of France

France in the Early Fifteenth Century

— Boundary of kingdom of France, 1429

······· Boundary of lands left to England, 1377

→ Route taken by Henry V, 1415–1416

→ Route taken by Joan of Arc, 1429–1431

⚔ Site and date of important battle

▨ Lands held by Henry VI of England, 1429

▢ Lands held by Charles VII of France

▢ Lands held by the duke of Burgundy

▢ Burgundian lands recognizing Henry VI

© Cengage Learning 2012

MAP 11.2 The Hundred Years' War

This long, exhausting struggle began in 1337 and dragged on until 1453. The English initially gained substantial French territory, but in the later phases of the war, France turned the tide, eventually expelling the English from all Continental lands except the port of Calais.

dauphin was crowned king of France and became Charles VII (1422–1461). In accomplishing the two commands of her angelic voices, Joan had brought the war to a decisive turning point.

Joan did not live to see the war concluded, however. She was captured by the Burgundian allies of the English in 1430. Wishing to eliminate the "Maid of Orléans" for obvious political reasons, the English turned Joan over to the Inquisition on charges of witchcraft. In the fifteenth century, spiritual visions were thought to be inspired by either God or the devil. Because Joan dressed in men's clothing, it was easy for her enemies to believe that she was in league with the "prince of darkness." She was condemned to death as a heretic and burned at the stake in

Joan of Arc. *Pictured here in a fifteenth-century design for a window for the cathedral of Orléans, Joan of Arc is seen in a suit of armor entering the city. There are no known portraits of Joan made from life.*

DEA/G. Dagli Orti//Getty Images

1431, at the age of nineteen. To the end, as the flames rose up around her, she declared that her voices came from God and had not deceived her. Twenty-five years later, a church court exonerated her of these charges. To a contemporary French writer, Christine de Pizan (kris-TEEN duh pee-ZAHN), Joan was a feminist heroine. In 1920, she was made a saint of the Roman Catholic Church.

End of the War   Joan of Arc's accomplishments proved decisive. Although the war dragged on for another two decades, defeats of English armies in Normandy and Aquitaine ultimately led to French victory. Important to the French success was the use of the cannon, a new weapon made possible by the invention of gunpowder. The Chinese had invented gunpowder in the eleventh century and devised a simple cannon by the thirteenth century. The Mongols greatly improved this technology, developing more accurate cannons and cannonballs; both spread to the Middle East by the thirteenth century and to Europe by the fourteenth.

The deaths of England's best commanders and the instability of the English government under King Henry VI (1422–1471) also contributed to England's defeat. By 1453, the only part of France that was left in English hands was the coastal town of Calais, which remained English for another century.

**Political
Instability**

The fourteenth century was a period of adversity for the internal political stability of European governments. Although government bureaucracies grew ever larger, at the same time the question of who should control the bureaucracies led to internal conflict and instability. Like the lord-serf relationship, the lord-vassal relationship based on land and military service was being replaced by a contract based on money. Especially after the Black Death, money payments called **scutage** (SKYOO-tij) were increasingly substituted for military service. Monarchs welcomed this development because they could now hire professional soldiers, who tended to be more reliable anyway. As lord-vassal relationships became less personal and less important, new relationships based on political advantage began to be formed, creating new avenues for political influence—and for corruption as well. Especially noticeable as the landed aristocrats suffered declining rents and social uncertainties with the new relationships was the formation of factions of nobles who looked for opportunities to advance their power and wealth at the expense of other noble factions and of their monarchs as well. Other nobles went to the royal courts, offering to serve the kings.

The kings had their own problems, however. By the mid-fifteenth century, reigning monarchs in many European countries were not the direct descendants of the rulers of 1300. The founders of these new dynasties had to struggle for position as factions of nobles vied to gain material advantages for themselves. As the fifteenth century began, there were two claimants to the throne of France, two aristocratic factions fighting for control of England, and three German princes struggling to be recognized as Holy Roman Emperor.

Fourteenth-century monarchs of old dynasties and new ones faced financial problems as well. The shift to using mercenary soldiers left monarchs perennially short of cash. Traditional revenues, especially rents from property, increasingly proved insufficient to meet their needs. Monarchs attempted to generate new sources of revenues, especially through taxes, which often meant going through parliaments. This opened the door for parliamentary bodies to gain more power by asking for favors first. Although unsuccessful in most cases, the parliaments simply added another element of uncertainty and confusion to fourteenth-century politics. Turning now to a survey of western and central European states (eastern Europe will be examined in Chapter 12), we can see how these disruptive factors worked.

**The Growth
of England's
Political
Institutions**

The fifty-year reign of Edward III (1327–1377) was important for the evolution of English political institutions in the fourteenth century. Parliament increased in prominence and developed its basic structure and functions during Edward's reign. Due to his constant need for money to fight the Hundred Years' War, Edward came to rely on Parliament to levy new taxes. In return for regular grants, Edward made several concessions, including a commitment to levy no direct tax without Parliament's consent and to allow Parliament to examine the government accounts to ensure that the money was being spent properly. By the end of Edward's reign, Parliament had become an important component of the English governmental system.

During this same period, Parliament began to assume the organizational structure it has retained to this day. The Great Council of barons became the House of Lords and evolved into a body composed of the chief bishops and abbots of the realm and aristocratic peers whose position in Parliament was hereditary. The representatives of the shires and boroughs, who were considered less important than the lay and ecclesiastical lords, held collective meetings and soon came to be regarded as the House of Commons. Together, the House of Lords and House of Commons constituted Parliament. Although the House of Commons did little beyond approving measures proposed by the Lords, during Edward's reign the Commons did begin the practice of drawing up petitions, which, if accepted by the king, became law.

After Edward III's death, England began to experience the internal instability of aristocratic factionalism that was racking other European countries. The early years of the reign of Edward's grandson, Richard II (1377–1399), began inauspiciously with the peasant revolt that ended only when the king made concessions. Richard's reign was troubled by competing groups of nobles who sought to pursue their own interests. One faction, led by Henry of Lancaster, defeated the king's forces and then deposed and killed him. Henry of Lancaster became King Henry IV (1399–1413). In the fifteenth century, factional conflict would lead to a devastating series of civil wars.

The Problems of the French Kings   At the beginning of the fourteenth century, France was the most prosperous monarchy in Europe. By the end of the century, much of its wealth had been dissipated, and rival factions of aristocrats had made effective monarchical rule virtually impossible.

The French monarchical state had always had an underlying inherent weakness that proved its undoing in difficult times. Although the Capetian monarchs had found ways to enlarge their royal domain and extend their control by developing a large and effective bureaucracy, the various territories that made up France still maintained their own princes, customs, and laws. The parliamentary institutions of France provide a good example of France's basic lack of unity. The French parliament, known as the Estates-General and composed of representatives of the clergy, the nobility, and the **Third Estate** (everyone else), usually represented only the north of France, not the entire kingdom. The southern provinces had their own estates, and local estates existed in other parts of France. Unlike the English Parliament, which was evolving into a crucial part of the English government, the French Estates-General was simply one of many such institutions.

When Philip VI (1328–1350) became involved in the Hundred Years' War with England, he found it necessary to devise new sources of revenue, including a tax on salt known as the *gabelle* (gah-BELL) and a hearth tax eventually called the *taille* (TY). These taxes weighed heavily on the French peasantry and middle class. Consequently, when additional taxes were needed to pay for the ransom of King John II after his capture at the Battle of Poitiers, the middle-class inhabitants of the towns tried to use the Estates-General to reform the French government and tax structure.

At the meeting of the Estates-General in 1357, under the leadership of the Parisian provost Étienne Marcel (ay-TYEN mahr-SEL), representatives of the

Third Estate granted taxes in exchange for a promise from King John's son, the dauphin Charles, not to tax without the Estates-General's permission and to allow the Estates-General to meet on a regular basis and participate in important political decisions. After Marcel's movement was crushed in 1358, this attempt to make the Estates-General a functioning part of the French government collapsed. The dauphin became King Charles V (1364–1380) and went on to recover much of the land lost to the English. His military successes underscored his efforts to reestablish strong monarchical powers. He undermined the role of the Estates-General by getting it to grant him taxes with no fixed time limit. Charles's death in 1380 soon led to a new time of troubles for the French monarchy, however.

The insanity of Charles VI (1380–1422), which first became apparent in 1392, opened the door to rival factions of French nobles aspiring to power and wealth. The dukes of Burgundy and Orléans competed to control Charles and the French monarchy. Their struggles created chaos for the French government and the French people. Many nobles supported the Orléanist faction, while Paris and other towns favored the Burgundians. By the beginning of the fifteenth century, France seemed hopelessly mired in a civil war. When the English renewed the Hundred Years' War in 1415, the Burgundians supported the English cause and the English monarch's claim to the throne of France.

The German Monarchy　　England and France had developed strong national monarchies in the High Middle Ages. Nevertheless, by the end of the fourteenth century, they seemed in danger of disintegrating due to dynastic problems and the pressures generated by the Hundred Years' War. In contrast, the Holy Roman Empire, whose core consisted of the lands of Germany, had already begun to fall apart in the High Middle Ages. Northern Italy, which the German emperors had tried to include in their medieval empire, had been free from any real imperial control since the end of the Hohenstaufen dynasty in the thirteenth century. In Germany itself, the failure of the Hohenstaufens ended any chance of centralized monarchical authority, and Germany became a land of hundreds of states that varied in size and power. These included princely states, such as the duchies of Bavaria and Saxony; free imperial city-states (self-governing cities directly under the control of the Holy Roman Emperor rather than a German territorial prince), such as Nuremberg; modest territories of petty imperial knights; and ecclesiastical states, such as the archbishopric of Cologne, in which an ecclesiastical official, such as a bishop, archbishop, or abbot, served in a dual capacity as an administrative official of the Catholic Church and as secular lord over the territories of the state. Although all of the rulers of these different states had some obligations to the German king and Holy Roman Emperor, more and more they acted independently.

Electoral Nature of the German Monarchy　　Because of its unique pattern of development in the High Middle Ages, the German monarchy had become established on an elective rather than a hereditary basis. This principle of election was standardized in 1356 by the Golden Bull issued by Emperor Charles IV (1346–1378). This document stated that four lay princes (the count palatine of the Rhine, the duke of Saxony, the margrave of Brandenburg, and the king of Bohemia) and three ecclesiastical rulers (the archbishops of Mainz, Trier, and Cologne) would serve as electors with the legal power to elect the "king of the Romans and future emperor, to be ruler of the world and of the Christian people."[12] "King of the Romans" was the official title of the German king; after his imperial coronation, he would also have the title of emperor.

In the fourteenth century, the electoral principle further ensured that kings of Germany were generally weak. Their ability to exercise effective power depended on the extent of their own family possessions. At the beginning of the fifteenth century, three emperors claimed the throne. Although the dispute was quickly settled, Germany entered the fifteenth century in a condition that verged on anarchy. Princes fought princes and leagues of cities. The emperors were virtually powerless to control any of them.

The States of Italy   Italy, too, had failed to develop a centralized monarchical state by the fourteenth century. Papal opposition to the rule of the Hohenstaufen emperors in northern Italy had virtually guaranteed that. Moreover, southern Italy was divided into the kingdom of Naples, ruled by the French house of Anjou, and Sicily, whose kings came from the Spanish house of Aragon. The center of the peninsula remained under the rather shaky control of the papacy. Lack of centralized authority had enabled numerous city-states in northern Italy to remain independent of any political authority.

In fourteenth-century Italy, two general tendencies can be discerned: the replacement of republican governments by tyrants and the expansion of the larger city-states at the expense of the less powerful ones. Nearly all the cities of northern Italy began their existence as free communes with republican governments. But in the fourteenth century, intense internal strife led city-states to resort to temporary expedients, allowing rule by one man with dictatorial powers. Limited rule, however, soon became long-term despotism as tyrants proved willing to use force to maintain themselves in power. Eventually, such tyrants tried to legitimize their power by purchasing titles from the emperor (still nominally the ruler of northern Italy as Holy Roman Emperor). In this fashion, the Visconti became the dukes of Milan and the d'Este, the dukes of Ferrara.

The other change of great significance was the development of larger, regional states as the larger states conquered the smaller ones. To fight their battles, city-states came to rely on mercenary soldiers, whose leaders, called **condottieri** (kahn-duh-TYAY-ree), sold the services of their bands to the highest bidder. These mercenaries wreaked havoc on the countryside, living by blackmail and looting when they were not actively engaged in battles. Many were foreigners who flocked to Italy during the periods of truce in the Hundred Years' War. By the end of the fourteenth century, three major states came to dominate northern Italy: the despotic state of Milan and the republican states of Florence and Venice.

Duchy of Milan   Located in the fertile Po valley, at the intersection of the chief trade routes from Italian coastal cities to the Alpine passes, Milan was one of the richest city-states in Italy. Politically, it was also one of the most agitated until the Visconti family established themselves as the hereditary despots of Milan in 1322. Giangaleazzo Visconti (jahn-gah-lay-AH-tsoh vees-KOHN-tee), who ruled from 1385 to 1402, transformed this despotism into a hereditary duchy by purchasing the title of duke from the emperor in 1395. Under Giangaleazzo's direction, the duchy of Milan extended its power over all of Lombardy and even threatened to conquer much of northern Italy until the duke's untimely death before the gates of Florence in 1402.

Republic of Florence   Florence, like the other Italian towns, was initially a free commune dominated by a patrician class of nobles known as the *grandi* (GRAHN-dee). But the rapid expansion of Florence's economy made possible the development of a wealthy merchant-industrialist class known as the *popolo grasso* (PAWP-oo-loh GRAH-soh)—literally the "fat people." In 1293, the *popolo grasso* assumed a dominant role in government by establishing a new constitution known as the Ordinances of Justice. It provided for a republican government controlled by the seven major guilds of the city, which represented the interests of the wealthier classes. Executive power was vested in the hands of a council of elected priors. Around the mid-fourteenth century, revolutionary activity by the *popolo minuto*, the small shopkeepers and artisans, won them a share in the government. Even greater expansion occurred briefly when the *ciompi*, or industrial wool workers, were allowed to be represented in the government after their revolt in 1378. Only four years later, however, a counterrevolution brought the "fat people" back into virtual control of the government. After 1382, the Florentine government was controlled by a small merchant oligarchy that manipulated the supposedly republican government. By that time, Florence had also been successful in a series of wars against its neighbors. It had conquered most of Tuscany and established itself as a major territorial state in northern Italy.

Republic of Venice   The other major northern Italian state was the republic of Venice, which had grown rich from commercial activity throughout the eastern Mediterranean and into northern Europe. A large number of merchant families became extremely wealthy. In the constitution of 1297, these patricians took control of the republic. In this year, the Great Council, the source of all political power, was closed to all but the members of about two hundred families. Since all other magistrates of the city were chosen either from or by this council, these families now formed a hereditary patriciate that completely dominated the city. Although the doge (DOHJ) (or duke) had been the executive head of the republic since the Early Middle Ages, by 1300 he had become largely a figurehead. Actual power was vested in the hands of the Great Council and the legislative body known as the Senate, while an extraordinary body known as the Council of Ten, first formed in 1310, came to be the real executive power of the state. The Venetian government was respected by contemporaries for its stability. A sixteenth-century Italian historian noted that Venice had "the best government of any city not only in our own times but also in the classical world."[13]

In the fourteenth century, Venice also embarked on a policy of expansion. By the end of the century, it had created a commercial empire by establishing colonies and trading posts in the eastern Mediterranean and Black Sea as well as continuing its commercial monopolies in the Byzantine Empire. At the same time, Venice began to conquer the territory adjoining it in northern Italy.

THE DECLINE OF THE CHURCH

The papacy of the Roman Catholic Church reached the height of its power in the thirteenth century. Theories of papal supremacy included a doctrine of "fullness of
power" as the spiritual head of Christendom and claims to universal temporal authority over all secular rulers. But papal claims of temporal supremacy were increasingly
out of step with the growing secular monarchies of Europe and ultimately brought the
papacy into a conflict with the territorial states that it was unable to win.

Boniface VIII
and the Conflict
with the State

The struggle between the papacy and the monarchies began
during the pontificate of Pope Boniface VIII (1294–1303). One
major issue appeared to be at stake between the pope and King
Philip IV (1285–1314) of France. In his desire to acquire new
revenues, Philip claimed the right to tax the French clergy. Boniface VIII responded
that the clergy of any state could not pay taxes to their secular ruler without the
pope's consent. Underlying this issue, however, was a basic conflict between the claims
of the papacy to universal authority over both church and state, which necessitated
complete control over the clergy, and the claims of the king that all subjects, including
the clergy, were under the jurisdiction of the crown and subject to the king's authority
on matters of taxation and justice. In short, the fundamental issue was the universal
sovereignty of the papacy versus the royal sovereignty of the monarch.

Boniface VIII asserted his position in a series of papal bulls or letters, the most
important of which was *Unam Sanctam* (OO-nam SAHNK-tahm), issued in 1302.
It was the strongest statement ever made by a pope on the supremacy of the spiritual authority over the temporal authority. When it became apparent that the pope
had decided to act on his principles by excommunicating Philip IV, the latter sent a
small contingent of French forces to capture Boniface and bring him back to France
for trial. The pope was captured in Anagni, although Italian nobles from the surrounding countryside soon rescued him. The shock of this experience, however,
soon led to the pope's death. Philip's strong-arm tactics had produced a clear victory for the national monarchy over the papacy, and no later pope has dared
renew the extravagant claims of Boniface VIII.

To ensure his position and avoid any future papal threat, Philip IV brought
enough pressure to bear on the college of cardinals to achieve the election of a
Frenchman as pope in 1305. Using the excuse of turbulence in the city of Rome,
the new pope, Clement V (1305–1314), took up residence in Avignon (ah-
veen-YOHN) on the east bank of the Rhône River. Although Avignon was located
in the Holy Roman Empire and was not a French possession, it lay just across the
river from the territory of King Philip IV. Clement may have intended to return to
Rome, but he and his successors remained in Avignon for the next seventy-two
years, thereby creating yet another crisis for the church.

The Papacy
at Avignon
(1305–1377)

The residency of the popes in Avignon for most of the fourteenth century led to a decline in papal prestige and growing
antipapal sentiment. The city of Rome was the traditional
capital of the universal church. The pope was the bishop of
Rome, and his position was based on being the successor to the Apostle Peter,

traditionally considered the first bishop of Rome. It was unseemly that the head of the Catholic Church should reside elsewhere. In the 1330s, the popes began to construct a stately palace in Avignon, a clear indication that they intended to stay for some time.

Other factors also contributed to the decline in papal prestige during the Avignonese residency. It was widely believed that the popes at Avignon were captives of the French monarchy. Although questionable, since Avignon did not belong to the French monarchy, it was easy to believe in view of Avignon's proximity to French lands. Moreover, during the seventy-two years of the Avignonese papacy, of the 134 new cardinals created by the popes, 113 were French. The papal residency at Avignon was also an important turning point in the church's attempt to adapt to the changing economic and political conditions of Europe. Like the growing monarchical states, the popes centralized their administration by developing a specialized bureaucracy. In fact, the papal bureaucracy in the fourteenth century under the leadership of the pope and college of cardinals became the most sophisticated administrative system in the medieval world.

At the same time, the popes attempted to find new sources of revenue to compensate for their loss of income from the Papal States and began to impose new taxes on the clergy. Furthermore, the splendor in which the pope and cardinals were living in Avignon led to highly vocal criticism of both clergy and papacy in the fourteenth century. Avignon had become a powerful symbol of abuses within the church, and many people began to call for the pope's return to Rome.

One of the most prominent calls came from Catherine of Siena (c. 1347–1380), whose saintly demeanor and claims of visions from God led the city of Florence to send her on a mission to Pope Gregory XI (1370–1378) in Avignon. She told the pope, "Because God has given you authority and because you have accepted it, you ought to use your virtue and power; if you do not wish to use it, it might be better for you to resign what you have accepted; it would give more honor to God and health to your soul."[14]

The Great Schism   Catherine of Siena's admonition seemed to be heeded in 1377, when at long last Pope Gregory XI, perceiving the disastrous decline in papal prestige, returned to Rome. He died soon afterward, however, in the spring of 1378. When the college of cardinals met in conclave to elect a new pope, the citizens of Rome, fearful that the French majority would choose another Frenchman who would return the papacy to Avignon, threatened that the cardinals would not leave Rome alive unless they elected a Roman or at least an Italian as pope. Indeed, the guards of the conclave warned the cardinals that they "ran the risk of being torn in pieces" if they did not choose an Italian. Wisely, the terrified cardinals duly elected the Italian archbishop of Bari, who was subsequently crowned as Pope Urban VI (1378–1389) on Easter Sunday. Following his election, Urban VI made clear his plans to reform the papal curia and even to swamp the college of cardinals with enough new Italian cardinals to eliminate the French majority. After many of the cardinals (the French ones) withdrew from Rome in late summer and were finally free of the Roman mob, they issued a manifesto, saying that they had been coerced by the mob and that Urban's election was therefore null and void. The dissenting cardinals thereupon chose one of their number, a Frenchman, who took the title of Clement VII and promptly returned to Avignon. Since Urban remained in Rome, there were now two popes, initiating what has been called the **Great Schism** of the church.

Europe's loyalties soon became divided: France, Spain, Scotland, and southern Italy supported Clement, while England, Germany, Scandinavia, and most of Italy supported Urban. These divisions generally followed political lines and reflected the bitter division between the English and the French in the Hundred Years' War. Because the French supported the Avignonese pope, so did their allies; their enemies, particularly England and its allies, supported the Roman pope. The need for political support caused both popes to subordinate their policies to the policies of these states.

The Great Schism lasted for nearly forty years and had a baleful effect on the Catholic Church and Christendom in general. The schism greatly aggravated the financial abuses that had developed within the church during the Avignonese papacy. Two papal administrative systems (with only half the accustomed revenues) worked to increase taxation. At the same time, the schism badly damaged the faith of Christian believers. The pope was widely believed to be the leader of Christendom and, as Boniface VIII had pointed out, held the keys to the kingdom of heaven. Since each line of popes denounced the other as the Antichrist, such a spectacle could not help but undermine the institution that had become the very foundation of the church.

New Thoughts on Church and State and the Rise of Conciliarism   As dissatisfaction with the papacy grew, so did the calls for a revolutionary approach to solving the church's institutional problems. One of the most systematic was provided by Marsiglio of Padua (mar-SIL-yoh of PAD-juh-wuh) (c. 1270–1342), rector of the University of Paris and author of a remarkable book, *Defender of the Peace*. Marsiglio denied that the temporal authority was subject to the spiritual authority, as many popes had maintained. Instead, he argued that the church was only one element of society and must confine itself solely to spiritual functions. Furthermore, Marsiglio argued, the church is a community of the faithful in which all authority is ultimately derived from the entire community. The clergy hold no special authority from God but serve only to administer the affairs of the church on behalf of all Christians. Thus, final authority in spiritual matters must reside not with the pope but with a general church council representing all members.

The Conciliar Movement   The Great Schism led large numbers of churchmen to take up this theory, known as **conciliarism**, in the belief that only a general council of the church could end the schism and bring reform to the church in its "head and members." The only serious issue left to be decided was who should call the council. Church law held that only a pope could convene a council. Professors of theology argued, however, that since the competing popes would not do so, either members of the church hierarchy or even secular princes, especially the Holy Roman Emperor, could convene a council to settle all relevant issues.

In desperation, a group of cardinals from both camps finally convened a general council on their own. This Council of Pisa, which met in 1409, deposed the two popes and elected a new one, Alexander V. The council's action proved disastrous, however, when the two deposed popes refused to step down. There were now three popes, and the church seemed more hopelessly divided than ever.

Leadership in convening a new council now passed to the Holy Roman Emperor, Sigismund. As a result of his efforts, a new ecumenical church council met at Constance from 1414 to 1418. Ending the schism proved a surprisingly easy task: after the three competing popes either resigned or were deposed, a new conclave elected Cardinal Oddone Colonna, a member of a prominent Roman family, as Pope Martin V (1417–1431). The Great Schism had finally been ended.

Popular Religion in an Age of Adversity   The seeming preoccupation of the popes and leading clerics with finances and power during the struggles of Boniface VIII, the Avignonese papacy, and the Great Schism could not help but lead to a decline in prestige and respect for the institutional church, especially the papacy. At the same time, in the fourteenth century, the Black Death and its recurrences made an important impact on the religious life of ordinary Christians by heightening their preoccupation with death and salvation. The church often failed to provide sufficient spiritual comfort as many parish priests fled from the plague.

Christians responded in different ways to the adversities of the fourteenth century. First of all, there was a tendency to stress the performance of good works, including acts of charity, as a means of ensuring salvation. Bequests to hospitals and other charitable foundations increased. Family chapels were established, served by priests whose primary responsibility was to say Mass for the good of the souls of deceased family members. These chapels became even more significant as the importance of purgatory rose. Purgatory was defined by the church as the place where souls went after death to be purged of punishment for sins committed in life. In effect, the soul was purified in purgatory before it ascended into heaven. It was believed that like indulgences, prayers and private Masses for the dead could shorten the amount of time souls spent in purgatory.

All of these developments were part of a larger trend—a new emphasis in late medieval Christianity on a mechanical path to salvation. Chalking up good deeds to ensure salvation was done in numerous ways but was nowhere more evident than in the growing emphasis on indulgences. We should also note that pilgrimages, which became increasingly popular, and charitable contributions were good works that could be accomplished without the involvement of clerics, a reflection of the loss of faith in the institutional church and its clergy and another noticeable feature of popular religious life. At the same time, interest in Christianity itself did not decline. Indeed, people sought to play a more active role in their own salvation. This is particularly evident in the popularity of mysticism and lay piety in the fourteenth century.

Mysticism and Lay Piety   The mysticism of the fourteenth century was certainly not new, for Christians throughout the Middle Ages had claimed to have had mystical experiences. Simply defined, **mysticism** is the immediate experience of oneness with God. It is this experience that characterized the teaching of Meister Eckhart (MY-stur EK-hart) (1260–1327), who sparked a mystical movement in western

Germany. Eckhart was a well-educated Dominican theologian who wrote learned Latin works on theology, but he was also a popular preacher whose message on the union of the soul with God was typical of mysticism. According to Eckhart, such a union was attainable by all who pursued it wholeheartedly.

Eckhart's movement spread from Germany into the Low Countries, where it took on a new form, called the **Modern Devotion**, founded by Gerard Groote (GROH-tuh) (1340–1384). After a religious conversion, Groote entered a monastery for several years of contemplation before reentering the world. His messages were typical of a practical mysticism. To achieve true spiritual communion with God, people must imitate Jesus and lead lives dedicated to serving the needs of their fellow human beings. Groote emphasized a simple inner piety and morality based on Scripture and an avoidance of the complexities of theology.

Eventually, Groote attracted a group of followers who came to be known as the Brothers of the Common Life. From this small beginning, a movement developed that spread through the Netherlands and back into Germany. Houses of the Brothers, as well as separate houses for women (Sisters of the Common Life), were founded in one city after another. The Sisters and Brothers of the Common Life did not constitute regular religious orders. They were laypeople who took no formal monastic vows but were nevertheless regulated by rules that they imposed on their own communities. They also established schools throughout Germany and the Netherlands in which they stressed their message of imitating the life of Jesus by serving others. The Brothers and Sisters of the Common Life attest to the vitality of spiritual life among lay Christians in the fourteenth century.

Unique Female Mystical Experiences   A number of female mystics had their own unique spiritual experiences. For them, fasting and receiving the Eucharist (the communion wafer that, according to Roman Catholic doctrine, contains the body of Jesus) became the mainstay of their religious practices. Catherine of Siena, for example, gave up eating any solid food at the age of twenty-three and thereafter lived only on cold water and herbs that she sucked and then spat out. Her primary nourishment, however, came from the Eucharist. She wrote: "The immaculate lamb [Christ] is food, table, and servant.... And we who eat at that table become like the food [that is, Christ], acting not for our own utility but for the honor of God and the salvation of neighbor."[15] For Catherine and a number of other female mystics, reception of the Eucharist was their primary instrument in achieving a mystical union with God.

Changes in Theology   The fourteenth century presented challenges not only to the institutional church but also to its theological framework, especially evident in the questioning of the grand synthesis attempted by Thomas Aquinas. In the thirteenth century, Aquinas's grand synthesis of faith and reason was not widely accepted outside his own Dominican order. At the same time, differences with Aquinas were kept within a framework of commonly accepted scholastic thought. In the fourteenth century, however, the philosopher William of Occam (1285–1329) posed a severe challenge to the scholastic achievements of the High Middle Ages.

Occam posited a radical interpretation of nominalism. He asserted that all universals or general concepts were simply names and that only individual objects perceived by the senses were real. Although the mind was capable of analyzing individual objects, it could not establish any truths about the nature of external, higher reality. Reason could not be used to substantiate spiritual truths. It could not, for example, prove the statement "God exists." For William of Occam as a Christian believer, this did not mean that God did not exist, however. It simply indicated that the truths of religion could only be known by an act of faith and were not demonstrable by reason. The acceptance of Occam's nominalist philosophy at the University of Paris brought an element of uncertainty to late medieval theology by seriously weakening the synthesis of faith and reason that had characterized the theological thought of the High Middle Ages. Nevertheless, Occam's emphasis on using reason to analyze the observable phenomena of the world had an important impact on the development of physical science by creating support for rational and scientific analysis. Some late medieval theologians came to accept the compatibility of rational analysis of the material world with mystical acceptance of spiritual truths.

THE CULTURAL WORLD OF THE FOURTEENTH CENTURY

The cultural life of the fourteenth century was also characterized by ferment. In literature, several writers used their vernacular languages to produce notable works. In art, in addition to the morbid themes inspired by the Black Death and other problems of the century, the period also produced Giotto, whose paintings expressed a new realism that would be developed further by the artists of the next century.

The Development of Vernacular Literature   Although Latin remained the language of the church liturgy and the official documents of both church and state throughout Europe, the fourteenth century witnessed the rapid growth of vernacular literature, especially in Italy. The development of an Italian vernacular literature was mostly the result of the efforts of three writers in the fourteenth century: Dante, Petrarch (PEE-trark *or* PET-trark), and Boccaccio. Their use of the Tuscan dialect common in Florence and its surrounding countryside ensured that it would prevail as the basis of the modern Italian language.

Dante   Dante Alighieri (DAHN-tay al-lih-GAIR-ee) (1265–1321) came from an old Florentine noble family that had fallen on hard times. Although he had held high political office in republican Florence, factional conflict led to his exile from the city in 1302. Until the end of his life, Dante hoped to return to his beloved Florence, but his wish remained unfulfilled.

Dante's masterpiece in the Italian vernacular was the *Divine Comedy*, written between 1313 and 1321. Cast in a typical medieval framework, the *Divine Comedy* is basically the story of the soul's progression to salvation, a fundamental medieval preoccupation. The lengthy poem was divided into three major sections corresponding to the realms of the afterworld: hell, purgatory, and heaven or paradise. In the "Inferno," Dante is led by his guide, the Classical author Virgil, who is a symbol of human reason. But Virgil (or reason) can lead the poet only so far on his journey.

At the end of "Purgatory," Beatrice (the true love of Dante's life), who represents revelation—which alone can explain the mysteries of heaven—becomes his guide into "Paradise." Here Beatrice presents Dante to Saint Bernard, a symbol of mystical contemplation. The saint turns Dante over to the Virgin Mary, since grace is necessary to achieve the final step of entering the presence of God, where one beholds "the love that moves the sun and the other stars."[16]

Petrarch   Like Dante, Francesco Petrarca, known as Petrarch (1304–1374), was a Florentine who spent much of his life outside his native city. Petrarch's role in the revival of the classics made him a seminal figure in the literary Italian Renaissance (see Chapter 12). His primary contribution to the development of the Italian vernacular was made in his sonnets. He is considered one of the greatest European lyric poets. His sonnets were inspired by his love for a married lady named Laura, whom he had met in 1327. Though honoring an idealized female figure was a long-standing medieval tradition, Laura was very human and not just an ideal. She was a real woman with whom Petrarch was involved for a long time. He poured forth his lamentations in sonnet after sonnet:

> *I am as tired of thinking as my thought*
> *Is never tired to find itself in you,*
> *And of not yet leaving this life that brought*
> *Me the too heavy weight of signs and rue;*
>
> *And because to describe your hair and face*
> *And the fair eyes of which I always speak,*
> *Language and sound have not become too weak*
> *And day and night your name they still embrace.*
>
> *And tired because my feet do not yet fail*
> *After following you in every part,*
> *Wasting so many steps without avail,*
>
> *From whence derive the paper and the ink*
> *That I have filled with you; if I should sink,*
> *It is the fault of Love, not of my art.*[17]

In analyzing every aspect of the unrequited lover's feelings, Petrarch appeared less concerned to sing his lady's praise than to immortalize his own thoughts. This interest in his own personality reveals a sense of individuality stronger than in any previous medieval literature.

Boccaccio   Although he too wrote poetry, Giovanni Boccaccio (1313–1375) is known primarily for his prose. Another Florentine, he also used the Tuscan dialect. While working for the Bardi banking house in Naples, he fell in love with a noble lady, and under her inspiration, he began to write prose romances. His best-known work, the *Decameron*, however, was not written until after he had returned to Florence. The *Decameron* is set at the time of the Black Death. Ten young people flee to a villa outside Florence to escape the plague and decide to while away the time by telling stories. Although the stories are not new and still reflect the acceptance of basic Christian values, Boccaccio does present the society of his time from a secular point of view. It is the seducer of women, not the knight or philosopher or pious monk, who is the real hero. Perhaps, as some historians have argued, the *Decameron* reflects the immediate easygoing, cynical postplague values. Boccaccio's later work certainly became gloomier and more pessimistic; as he grew older, he even rejected his earlier work as irrelevant. He commented in a 1373 letter, "I am certainly not pleased that you have allowed the illustrious women in your house to read my trifles.... You know how much in them is less than decent and opposed to modesty, how much stimulation to wanton lust, how many things that drive to lust even those most fortified against it."[18]

Chaucer   Another leading vernacular author was Geoffrey Chaucer (c. 1340–1400), who brought a new level of sophistication to the English vernacular language in his famous *Canterbury Tales*. His beauty of expression and clear, forceful language were important in transforming his East Midland dialect into the chief ancestor of the modern English language. *The Canterbury Tales* is a collection of stories told by a group of twenty-nine pilgrims journeying from the London suburb of Southwark to the tomb of Saint Thomas à Becket at Canterbury. This format gave Chaucer the chance to portray an entire range of English society, both high- and low-born. Among others, he presented the Knight, the Yeoman, the Prioress, the Monk, the Merchant, the Student, the Lawyer, the Carpenter, the Cook, the Doctor, the Plowman, and, "A Good Wife was there from beside the city of Bath—a little deaf, which was a pity." The stories these pilgrims told to while away the time on the journey were just as varied as the storytellers themselves: knightly romances, fairy tales, saints' lives, sophisticated satires, and crude anecdotes.

Chaucer also used some of his characters to criticize the corruption of the church in the late medieval period. His portrayal of the Friar leaves no doubt of Chaucer's disdain for the corrupt practices of clerics. Of the Friar, he says:

> *He knew the taverns well in every town.*
> *The barmaids and innkeepers pleased his mind*
> *Better than beggars and lepers and their kind.*[19]

And yet Chaucer was still a pious Christian, never doubting basic Christian doctrines and remaining optimistic that the church could be reformed.

Christine de Pizan   One of the extraordinary vernacular writers of the age was Christine de Pizan (c. 1364–1430). Because of her father's position at the court of Charles V of France, she received a good education. Her husband died when she was only twenty-five (they had been married for ten years), leaving her with little income and three small children and her mother to support. Christine took the unusual step of becoming a writer in order to earn her living. Her poems were soon in demand, and by 1400 she had achieved financial security.

Christine de Pizan is best known, however, for her French prose works written in defense of women. In *The Book of the City of Ladies*, written in 1404, she denounced the many male writers who had argued that women needed to be controlled by men because women by their very nature were prone to evil, unable to learn, and easily swayed. With the help of Reason, Righteousness, and Justice, who appear to her in a vision, Christine refutes these antifeminist attacks. Women, she

Scrovegni Chapel, Padua//© Scala/Art Resource, NY

Giotto, *Lamentation*. *The work of Giotto marked the first clear innovation in fourteenth-century painting, making him a forerunner of the early Renaissance. This fresco was part of a series done on the walls of the Arena Chapel in Padua begun in 1305. Giotto painted thirty-eight scenes on three levels: the lives of Mary, the mother of Jesus, and her parents (top panel); the life and work of Jesus (middle panel); and his passion, crucifixion, and resurrection (bottom panel). Shown here from the bottom panel is the* Lamentation. *A group of Jesus's followers, including his mother and Mary Magdalene, mourn over the body of Jesus before it is placed in its tomb. The solidity of Giotto's human figures gives them a three-dimensional sense. He also captured the grief and despair felt by the mourners.*

argues, are not evil by nature, and they could learn as well as men if they were permitted to attend the same schools: "Should I also tell you whether a woman's nature is clever and quick enough to learn speculative sciences as well as to discover them, and likewise the manual arts. I assure you that women are equally well-suited and skilled to carry them out and to put them to sophisticated use once they have learned them."[20] Much of the book includes a detailed discussion of women from the past and present who have distinguished themselves as leaders, warriors, wives, mothers, and martyrs for their religious faith. She ends by encouraging women to defend themselves against the attacks of men, who are incapable of understanding them.

A New Art:
Giotto

The fourteenth century produced an artistic outburst in new directions as well as a large body of morbid work influenced by the Black Death and the recurrences of the plague. The city of Florence witnessed the first dramatic break with medieval tradition in the work of Giotto (JOH-toh) (1266–1337), often considered a forerunner of Italian

Renaissance painting. Born into a peasant family, Giotto acquired his painting skills in a workshop in Florence. Although he worked throughout Italy, his most famous works were done in Padua and Florence.

Coming out of the formal Byzantine school, Giotto transcended it with a new kind of realism, a desire to imitate nature that Renaissance artists later identified as the basic component of Classical art. Giotto's figures were solid and rounded; placed realistically in relationship to each other and their background, they conveyed three-dimensional depth. The expressive faces and physically realistic bodies gave his sacred figures human qualities with which spectators could identify. Although Giotto had no direct successors, Florentine painting in the early fifteenth century pursued even more dramatically the new direction his work represents.

SOCIETY IN AN AGE OF ADVERSITY

In the midst of disaster, the fourteenth century proved creative in its own way. New inventions made an impact on daily life at the same time that the effects of the plague were felt in many areas of medieval urban life.

Changes in Urban Life   One immediate by-product of the Black Death was greater regulation of urban activities by town governments. Authorities tried to keep cities cleaner by enacting new ordinances against waste products in the streets. Viewed as unhealthy places, bathhouses were closed down, leading to a noticeable decline in personal cleanliness. Efforts at regulation also affected the practice of female prostitution.

Medieval society had tolerated prostitution as a lesser evil: it was better for males to frequent prostitutes than to seduce virgins or married women. Since many males in medieval towns married late, the demand for prostitutes was high and was met by a regular supply, derived no doubt from the need of many poor girls and women to survive. The recession of the fourteenth century probably increased the supply of prostitutes, while the new hedonism prevalent after the Black Death also increased demand. As a result, cities intensified their regulation of prostitution.

By organizing brothels, city authorities could supervise as well as tax prostitutes. Officials granted charters to citizens who were allowed to set up brothels, provided they were located only in certain areas of town. Prostitutes were also expected to wear special items of clothing—such as red hats—to distinguish them from other women. It was assumed that the regulation of prostitution made it easier to supervise and hence maintained public order.

Family Life and Gender Roles in Late Medieval Cities   The basic unit of the late medieval town was the nuclear family of husband, wife, and children. Especially in wealthier families, there might also be servants, apprentices, and other relatives, including widowed mothers and the husband's illegitimate children.

Before the Black Death, late marriages were common for urban couples. It was not unusual for husbands to be in their late thirties or forties and wives in their early twenties. The expense of setting up a household probably necessitated the delay in marriage. But the situation changed dramatically after the plague, reflecting new economic opportunities for the survivors and a new reluctance to postpone living in the presence of so much death.

The economic difficulties of the fourteenth century also tended to strengthen the development of gender roles. Based on the authority of Aristotle, Thomas Aquinas and other scholastic theologians had advanced the belief that according to the natural order, men were active and domineering while women were passive and submissive. As more and more lawyers, doctors, and priests, who had been trained in universities where these notions were taught, entered society, these ideas about the different natures of men and women became widely accepted. This was evident in legal systems, many of which limited the legal capacity of women. Increasingly, women were expected to give up any active functions in society and remain subject to direction from males. A fourteenth-century Parisian provost commented that among glass cutters, "no master's widow who keeps working at his craft after her husband's death may take on apprentices, for the men of the craft do not believe that a woman can master it well enough to teach a child to master it, for the craft is a very delicate one."[21] Although this statement suggests that some women were, in fact, running businesses, it also reveals that they were viewed as incapable of undertaking all of men's activities. Europeans in the fourteenth century imposed a division of labor roles between men and women that persisted until the Industrial Revolution.

In practice, however, some women in the fourteenth century benefited from the effects of the Black Death. The deaths of many male workers in cities opened up new jobs for women, such as metalworkers and stevedores. In cloth making, women were allowed to assume better-paying jobs as weavers. Brewing became an all-female profession by 1450. Widows also occasionally carried on their husbands' shops or businesses.

Medieval Children   Parents in the High and Later Middle Ages invested considerable resources and affection in rearing their children (see Images of Everyday Life. The dramatic increase in specialized roles that accompanied the spread of commerce and the growth of cities demanded a commitment to educating children in the marketable skills needed for the new occupations. Philip of Navarre noted in the twelfth century that boys ought to be taught a trade "as soon as possible. Those who early become and long remain apprentices ought to be the best masters."[22] Some cities provided schools to educate the young. A chronicler in Florence related that between 8,000 and 10,000 boys and girls between the ages of six and twelve attended the city's grammar schools, a figure that probably represented half of all school-aged children. Although grammar school completed education for girls, some 1,100 boys went on to six secondary schools that prepared them for business careers, while another 600 studied Latin and logic in four other schools that readied them for university training and a career in medicine, law, or the church. In the High Middle Ages, then, urban communities demonstrated a commitment to training the young.

As a result of the devastating effects of the plague and its recurrences, these same communities became concerned about investing in the survival and health of children. A number of hospitals existed in both Florence and Rome in the fourteenth century, and in the 1420s and 1430s, hospitals were established that catered

Entertainment in the Middle Ages

Medieval people engaged in a variety of activities for entertainment. City dwellers enjoyed feast days and holidays, when minstrels and jugglers amused people with their arts and tricks. Castle life had its courtly feasts, featuring tournaments accompanied by banquets, music, and dancing. Games were popular at all levels of society; castle dwellers played backgammon, checkers, and chess. The illustration at the left, from a fifteenth-century fresco, shows a group of ladies and gentlemen playing cards.

Like children in all ages, medieval children joined with other children in playing a variety of games. A number of writers on children saw play as a basic symbol of childhood itself. In these illustrations from medieval manuscripts, we see children engaged in riding hobby-horses (undoubtedly popular in a society dependent on horses) and playing a game of blind man's bluff.

The Art Archive/Bodleian Library (Douce 276 folio 124v), Oxford, UK

The Art Archive/Bibliothèque Universitaire de Médecine, Montpellier/Gianni Dagli Orti

only to the needs of foundlings, supporting them until boys could be taught a trade and girls could marry.

New Directions in Medicine   The medical community comprised a number of functionaries. At the top of the medical hierarchy were the physicians, usually clergymen, who received their education in the universities, where they studied ancient authorities, such as Hippocrates and Galen. As a result, physicians were highly trained in theory but had little or no clinical practice. By the fourteenth century, they were educated in six chief medical schools—Salerno, Montpellier, Bologna, Oxford, Padua, and Paris. Paris was regarded as the most prestigious.

The preplague medicine of university-trained physicians was theoretically grounded in the Classical Greek theory of the "four humors," each connected to a particular organ: blood (from the heart), phlegm (from the brain), yellow bile (from the liver), and black bile (from the spleen). Because the four humors corresponded in turn to the four elemental qualities of the universe—air (blood), water (phlegm), fire (yellow bile), and earth (black bile)—a human being was considered a microcosm of the cosmos. Good health resulted from a perfect balance of the four humors; sickness meant that the humors were out of balance. The task of the medieval physician was to restore proper order through a number of remedies, such as rest, diet, herbal medicines, or bloodletting.

Beneath the physicians in the hierarchy of the medical profession stood the surgeons, whose activities included performing operations, setting broken bones, and bleeding patients. Their knowledge was based largely on practical experience. Below surgeons were midwives, who delivered babies, and barber-surgeons, who were less trained than surgeons and performed menial tasks such as bloodletting and setting simple bone fractures. Barber-surgeons supplemented their income by shaving and cutting hair and pulling teeth. Apothecaries also constituted part of the medical establishment. They filled herbal prescriptions recommended by physicians and also prescribed drugs on their own authority.

All of these medical practitioners proved unable to deal with the plague. When King Philip VI of France requested the opinion of the medical faculty of the University of Paris on the plague, their advice proved worthless. This failure to understand the Black Death, however, produced a crisis in medieval medicine that resulted in some new approaches to health care.

One result was the rise of surgeons to greater prominence because of their practical knowledge. Surgeons were now recruited by universities, which placed them on an equal level with physicians and introduced a greater emphasis on practical anatomy into the university curriculum. Connected to this was a burgeoning of medical textbooks, often written in the vernacular and stressing practical, how-to approaches to medical and surgical problems.

Finally, as a result of the plague, cities, especially in Italy, gave increased attention to public health and sanitation. Public health laws were instituted, and municipal boards of health came into being. The primary concern of the latter was to prevent plague, but gradually they came to control almost every aspect of health and sanitation. Boards of public health, consisting of medical practitioners and public officials, were empowered to enforce sanitary conditions, report on and attempt to isolate epidemics by quarantine (rarely successful), and regulate the activities of doctors.

Inventions and New Patterns   Despite its problems, the fourteenth century witnessed a continuation of the technological innovations that had characterized the High Middle Ages.

The Clock   The most extraordinary of these inventions, and one that made a visible impact on European cities, was the clock. The mechanical clock was invented at the end of the thirteenth century but not perfected until the fourteenth. The time-telling clock was actually a by-product of a larger astronomical clock. The best-designed one was constructed by Giovanni di Dondi in the mid-fourteenth century. Dondi's clock contained the signs of the zodiac but also struck on the hour. Since clocks were expensive, they were usually installed only in the towers of churches or municipal buildings. The first clock striking equal hours was in a church in Milan; in 1335, a chronicler described it as "a wonderful clock, with a very large clapper which strikes a bell twenty-four times according to the twenty-four hours of the day and night and thus at the first hour of the night gives one sound, at the second two strikes ... and so distinguishes one hour from another, which is of greatest use to men of every degree."[23]

Clocks revolutionized how people thought about and used time. Throughout most of the Middle Ages, time was determined by natural rhythms (daybreak and nightfall) or church bells that were rung at more or less regular three-hour intervals, corresponding to the ecclesiastical offices of the church. Clocks made it possible for people to plan their day and organize activities around the regular striking of bells. This brought a new regularity into the lives of workers and merchants, defining urban existence and enabling merchants and bankers to see the value of time in a new way.

Eyeglasses and Paper   Like clocks, eyeglasses were introduced in the thirteenth century but not refined until the fourteenth. Even then they were not particularly effective by modern standards and were still extremely expensive. The high cost of parchment forced people to write in extremely small script; eyeglasses made it more readable. At the same time, a significant change in writing materials occurred in the fourteenth century when parchment was supplemented by much cheaper paper made from cotton rags. Although it was more subject to insect and water damage than parchment, medieval paper was actually superior to modern papers made of high-acid wood pulp.

Gunpowder and Cannons   Invented earlier by the Chinese, gunpowder also made its appearance in the West in the fourteenth century. The use of gunpowder eventually brought drastic changes to European warfare. Its primary use was in cannons, although early cannons were prone to blow up, making them as dangerous to the people firing them as to the enemy. Even as late as 1460, an attack on a castle using an enormous Flemish cannon called the "Lion" proved disastrous for the Scottish king James II when the "Lion" blew up, killing the king and a number of his retainers. Continued improvement in the construction of cannons, however, soon made them extremely valuable in reducing both castles and city walls. Gunpowder made castles, city walls, and armored knights obsolete.

CHRONOLOGIES

The Hundred Years' War

1337	Outbreak of hostilities
1396	Twenty-year truce declared
1415	Henry V (1413–1422) renews the war
1429–1431	French recovery under Joan of Arc
1453	End of the war

The States of Western and Central Europe

England

1327–1377	Edward III
1377–1399	Richard II

France

1328–1350	Philip VI
1364–1380	Charles V
1380–1422	Charles VI

German Monarchy

1356	Golden Bull

Italy

1293	Ordinances of Justice (Florence)
1297	Closing of Great Council (Venice)
1322	Visconti establish themselves as rulers of Milan

The Decline of the Church

1294–1303	Pope Boniface VIII
1305–1377	Papacy at Avignon
1378	Great Schism begins
1414–1418	Council of Constance

12

RECOVERY AND REBIRTH: THE AGE OF THE RENAISSANCE

Michelangelo's Creation of Adam *on the Sistine Chapel ceiling*

Sistine Chapel, Vatican Palace//© Erich Lessing/Art Resource, NY

CHAPTER OUTLINE

- Meaning and Characteristics of the Italian Renaissance • The Making of Renaissance Society • The Italian States in the Renaissance • The Intellectual Renaissance in Italy • The Artistic Renaissance • The European State in the Renaissance • The Church in the Renaissance

MEANING AND CHARACTERISTICS
OF THE ITALIAN RENAISSANCE

Renaissance means "rebirth." Many people who lived in Italy between 1350 and 1550 believed that they had witnessed a rebirth of antiquity or Greco-Roman civilization, marking a new age. To them, the thousand or so years between the end of the Roman Empire and their own era constituted a middle period (the "Middle Ages"), characterized by darkness because of its lack of Classical culture. Historians of the nineteenth century later used similar terminology to describe this period in Italy. The Swiss historian and art critic Jacob Burckhardt (YAK-ub BOORK-hart) created the modern concept of the **Renaissance** in his celebrated book *The Civilization of the Renaissance in Italy*, published in 1860. He portrayed Italy in the fourteenth and fifteenth centuries as the birthplace of the modern world (the Italians were "the firstborn among the sons of modern Europe") and saw the revival of antiquity, the "perfecting of the individual," and secularism ("worldliness of the Italians") as its distinguishing features. Burckhardt exaggerated the individuality and secularism of the Renaissance and failed to recognize the depths of its religious sentiment; nevertheless, he established the framework for all modern interpretations of the period. Although contemporary scholars do not believe that the Renaissance represents a sudden or dramatic cultural break with the Middle Ages, as Burckhardt argued—there was, after all, much continuity in economic, political, and social life—the Renaissance can still be viewed as a distinct period of European history that manifested itself first in Italy and then spread to the rest of Europe.

Renaissance Italy was largely an urban society. As a result of its commercial preeminence and political evolution, northern Italy by the mid-fourteenth century was mostly a land of independent cities that dominated the country districts around them. These city-states became the centers of Italian political, economic, social, and cultural life. Within this new urban society, a secular spirit emerged as increasing wealth created new possibilities for the enjoyment of worldly things.

Above all, the Renaissance was an age of recovery from the calamitous fourteenth century, a time for the slow process of recuperating from the effects of the Black Death, political disorder, and economic recession. This recovery was accompanied by a rediscovery of the culture of Classical antiquity. Increasingly aware of their own historical past, Italian intellectuals became intensely interested in the Greek and Roman culture of the ancient Mediterranean world. This revival of Classical antiquity (the Middle Ages had in fact preserved much of ancient Latin culture) affected activities as diverse as politics and art and led to new attempts to reconcile the pagan philosophy of the Greco-Roman world with Christian thought, as well as new ways of viewing human beings.

A revived emphasis on individual ability became a characteristic of the Italian Renaissance. As the fifteenth-century Florentine architect Leon Battista Alberti (LAY-un buh-TEESS-tuh al-BAYR-tee) expressed it, "Men can do all things if they will."[1] A high regard for human dignity and worth and a realization of individual potentiality created a new social ideal of the well-rounded personality or universal person—*l'uomo universale* (LWOH-moh OO-nee-ver-SAH-lay)—who was capable of achievements in many areas of life.

These general features of the Italian Renaissance were not characteristic of all Italians but were primarily the preserve of the wealthy upper classes, who constituted a small percentage of the total population. The achievements of the Italian Renaissance were the product of an elite, rather than a mass, movement. Nevertheless, indirectly it did have some impact on ordinary people, especially in the cities, where so many of the intellectual and artistic accomplishments of the period were most visible.

THE MAKING OF RENAISSANCE SOCIETY

After the severe economic reversals and social upheavals of the fourteenth century, the European economy gradually recovered as the volume of manufacturing and trade increased.

Economic Recovery   By the fourteenth century, Italian merchants were carrying on a flourishing commerce throughout the Mediterranean and had also expanded their lines of trade north along the Atlantic seaboard. The great galleys of the Venetian Flanders Fleet maintained a direct sea route from Venice to England and the Netherlands, where Italian merchants came into contact with the increasingly powerful Hanseatic League of merchants. Hard hit by the plague, the Italians lost their commercial preeminence while the Hanseatic League continued to prosper.

Expansion of Trade   As early as the thirteenth century, a number of North German coastal towns had formed a commercial and military association known as the Hansa, or Hanseatic League. By 1500, more than eighty cities belonged to the League, which had established settlements and commercial bases in many cities in England and northern Europe, including the chief towns of Denmark, Norway, and Sweden. For almost two hundred years, the Hansa had a monopoly on northern European trade in timber, fish, grain, metals, honey, and wines. Its southern outlet in Flanders, the port city of Bruges, became the economic crossroads of Europe in the fourteenth century, serving as the meeting place between Hanseatic merchants and the Flanders Fleet of Venice. In the fifteenth century, however, silting of the port caused Bruges to enter a slow decline. So did the Hanseatic League, which was increasingly unable to compete with the developing larger territorial states.

Overall, trade recovered dramatically from the economic contraction of the fourteenth century. The Italians and especially the Venetians, despite new restrictive pressures on their eastern Mediterranean trade from the Ottoman Turks (see "The Ottoman Turks and the End of the Byzantine Empire" later in this chapter), continued to maintain a wealthy commercial empire. Not until the sixteenth century, when transatlantic discoveries gave new importance to the states along the ocean, did the petty Italian city-states begin to suffer from the competitive advantages of the ever-growing and more powerful national territorial states.

Industries Old and New   The economic depression of the fourteenth century also affected patterns of manufacturing. The woolen industries of Flanders and the northern Italian cities had been particularly devastated. By the beginning of the fifteenth century, however, the Florentine woolen industry had begun to recover. At the same time, the Italian cities began to develop and expand luxury industries, especially silk, glassware, and handworked items in metal and precious stones.

Other new industries, especially printing, mining, and metallurgy, began to rival the textile industry in importance in the fifteenth century. New machinery and techniques for digging deeper mines and for separating metals from ore and purifying them were devised, and entrepreneurs quickly developed large mining operations to produce copper, iron, and silver. Especially valuable were the rich mineral deposits in central Europe. Expanding iron production and new skills in metalworking in turn contributed to the development of firearms that were more effective than the crude weapons of the fourteenth century.

Banking and the Medici   The city of Florence regained its preeminence in banking in the fifteenth century, due primarily to the Medici (MED-ih-chee) family. The Medici had expanded from cloth production into commerce, real estate, and banking. In its best days (in the fifteenth century), the House of Medici was the greatest bank in Europe, with branches in Venice, Milan, Rome, Avignon, Bruges, London, and Lyons. Moreover, the family had controlling interests in industrial enterprises for wool, silk, and the mining of alum, used in the dyeing of textiles. Except for a brief period, the Medici were also the principal bankers for the papacy, a position that produced big profits and influence at the papal court. Despite its great success in the early and middle part of the fifteenth century, the Medici bank suffered a rather sudden decline at the end of the century due to poor leadership and a series of bad loans, especially uncollectible loans to rulers. In 1494, when the French expelled the Medici from Florence and confiscated their property, the Medici financial edifice collapsed.

Social Changes in the Renaissance   The Renaissance inherited its social structure from the Middle Ages. Society remained fundamentally divided into three **estates**: the First Estate, the clergy, whose preeminence was grounded in the belief that people should be guided to spiritual ends; the Second Estate, the nobility, whose privileges were based on the principle that the nobles provided security and justice for society; and the Third Estate, which consisted of the peasants and inhabitants of the towns and cities. This social order experienced certain adaptations in the Renaissance, which we can see by examining the Second and Third Estates (the clergy will be examined in Chapter 13).

The Nobility   Throughout much of Europe, the landholding nobles faced declining real incomes during the greater part of the fourteenth and fifteenth centuries. Nevertheless, many members of the old nobility survived, and new blood infused their ranks. A reconstruction of the aristocracy was well under way by 1500. As a result of this reconstruction, the nobles, old and new, who constituted between 2 and 3 percent of the population in most countries, managed to dominate society as they had done in the Middle Ages, serving as military officers and holding important political posts as well as advising the king. In the sixteenth century, members of the aristocracy increasingly pursued education as the means to maintain their role in government.

By 1500, certain ideals came to be expected of the noble or aristocrat. These ideals were best expressed in *The Book of the Courtier* by the Italian Baldassare Castiglione (bal-duh-SAH-ray ka-steel-YOH-nay) (1478–1529). First published in 1528, Castiglione's work soon became popular throughout Europe and remained a fundamental handbook for European aristocrats for centuries.

In his book, Castiglione described the three basic attributes of the perfect courtier. First, nobles should possess fundamental native endowments, such as impeccable character, grace, talents, and noble birth. The perfect courtier must also cultivate certain achievements. Primarily, he should participate in military and bodily exercises, because the principal profession of a courtier was bearing arms. But unlike the medieval knight, who had been required only to have military skill, the Renaissance courtier was also expected to have a Classical education and to adorn his life with the arts by playing a musical instrument, drawing, and painting. In Castiglione's hands, the Renaissance ideal of the well-developed personality became a social ideal of the aristocracy. Finally, the aristocrat was expected to follow a certain standard of conduct. Nobles were to make a good impression; while remaining modest, they should not hide their accomplishments but show them with grace.

What was the purpose of these courtly standards? Castiglione wrote:

> I think that the aim of the perfect Courtier, which we have not spoken of up to now, is so to win for himself, by means of the accomplishments ascribed to him by these gentlemen, the favor and mind of the prince whom he serves that he may be able to tell him, and always will tell him, the truth about everything he needs to know, without fear or risk of displeasing him; and that when he sees the mind of his prince inclined to a wrong action, he may dare to oppose him ... so as to dissuade him of every evil intent and bring him to the path of virtue.[2]

The aim of the perfect noble, then, was to serve his prince in an effective and honest way. Nobles would adhere to these principles for hundreds of years while they continued to dominate European life socially and politically.

Peasants and Townspeople   Peasants made up the overwhelming mass of the Third Estate and continued to constitute 85 to 90 percent of the European population, except in the highly urbanized areas of northern Italy and Flanders. The most noticeable trend produced by the economic crisis of the fourteenth century was the decline of the manorial system and the continuing elimination of serfdom. This process had already begun in the twelfth century when the introduction of a money economy made possible the conversion of servile labor dues into rents paid in money, although they also continued to be paid in kind or labor. The contraction of the peasantry after the Black Death simply accelerated this process, since lords found it convenient to deal with the peasants by granting freedom and accepting rents. The lords' lands were then tilled by hired workers or rented out. By the end of the fifteenth century, serfdom was declining in western Europe, and more and more peasants were becoming legally free.

The remainder of the Third Estate centered around the inhabitants of towns and cities, originally the merchants and artisans who formed the bourgeoisie. The Renaissance town or city of the fifteenth century actually was home to a multitude of townspeople widely separated socially and economically.

At the top of urban society were the patricians, whose wealth from capitalistic enterprises in trade, industry, and banking enabled them to dominate their urban communities economically, socially, and politically. Below them were the petty burghers—the shopkeepers, artisans, guildmasters, and guild members, who were largely concerned with providing goods and services for local consumption. Below these two groups were the propertyless workers earning pitiful wages and the unemployed, living squalid and miserable lives; these people constituted 30 to 40 percent of the population living in cities. In many places in Europe in the late fourteenth and fifteenth centuries, urban poverty increased dramatically. One rich merchant of Florence wrote:

> Those that are lazy and indolent in a way that does harm to the city, and who can offer no just reason for their condition, should either be forced to work or expelled from the Commune. The city would thus rid itself of that most harmful part of the poorest class.... If the lowest order of society earn enough food to keep them going from day to day, then they have enough.[3]

But even this large group was not at the bottom of the social scale; beneath them were the slaves, especially in the Italian cities.

Slavery in the Renaissance   Agricultural slavery existed in the Early Middle Ages but had declined for economic reasons and been replaced by serfdom by the ninth century. Although some domestic slaves remained, slavery in European society had largely disappeared by the eleventh century. It reappeared first in Spain, where both Christians and Muslims used captured prisoners as slaves during the lengthy *Reconquista*. In the second half of the fourteenth century, the shortage of workers after the Black Death led Italians to introduce slavery on a fairly large scale.

In the Italian cities, slaves were used as skilled workers, making handcrafted goods for their masters, or as household workers. Girls served as nursemaids and boys as playmates. Fiammetta Adimari wrote to her husband in 1469: "I must remind you that when Alfonso is weaned we ought to get a little slave-girl to look after him, or else one of the black boys to keep him company."[4] Most slaves, though, were females, many of them young girls. In Florence, wealthy merchants might own two or three slaves. Often men of the household took slaves as concubines, which sometimes led to the birth of illegitimate children. In 1392, the wealthy merchant Francesco Datini fathered an illegitimate daughter by Lucia, his twenty-year-old slave. His wife, Margherita, who was unable to bear any children, reluctantly agreed to raise the girl as their own daughter. Many illegitimate children were not as fortunate.

Slaves for the Italian market were obtained primarily from the eastern Mediterranean and the Black Sea region and included Tartars, Russians, Albanians, and Dalmatians. There were also slaves from Africa, either Moors or Ethiopians, and Muslims from Spain. Because of the lucrative nature of the slave trade, Italian merchants became involved in the transportation of slaves. Between 1414 and 1423, ten thousand slaves were sold on the Venetian market.

By the end of the fifteenth century, slavery had declined dramatically in the Italian cities. Many slaves had been freed by their owners for humanitarian reasons, and the major source of slaves dried up as the Black Sea slave markets were closed to Italian traders after the Turks conquered the Byzantine Empire. Moreover, a general feeling had arisen that slaves—the "domestic enemy," as they were called—were dangerous and not worth the effort. By the sixteenth century, slaves were in evidence only at princely courts, where they were kept as curiosities; this was especially true of black slaves.

In the fifteenth century, the Portuguese had imported increasing numbers of African slaves for southern European markets. It has been estimated that between 1444 and 1505, some 140,000 slaves were shipped from Africa. The presence of blacks in European society was not entirely new. Saint Maurice, a Christian martyr of the fourth century, was portrayed by medieval artists as a black knight and became the center of a popular cult in the twelfth and thirteenth centuries. The number of blacks in Europe was small, however, until their importation as slaves.

The Family in Renaissance Italy   The family played an important role in Renaissance Italy (see Images of Everyday Life. Family meant, first of all, the extended household of parents, children, and servants (if the family was wealthy) and could also include grandparents, widowed mothers, and even unmarried sisters. Families that were related and bore the same surname often lived near each other and might dominate an entire urban district. Old family names—Strozzi (STRAWT-see), Rucellai (roo-CHELL-eye), Medici—conferred great status and prestige. The family bond was a source of great security in a dangerous and violent world, and its importance helps explain the vendetta in the Italian Renaissance. A crime committed by one family member fell on the entire family, ensuring that retaliation by the offended family would be a bloody affair involving large numbers of people.

Marriage   To maintain the family, parents gave careful attention to arranging marriages, often to strengthen business or family ties. Details were worked out well in advance, sometimes when children were only two or three years old, and reinforced by a legally binding marriage contract. The important aspect of the contract was the amount of the dowry, money presented by the wife's family to the husband upon marriage. The dowry could involve large sums and was expected of all families. The size of the dowry was an indication of whether the bride was moving upward or downward in society. With a large dowry, a daughter could marry a man of higher social status, thereby enabling her family to move up in society; if the daughter married a man of lower social status, however, her dowry would be smaller because the reputation of her family would raise the status of her husband's family.

The father-husband was the center of the Italian family. He gave it his name, was responsible for it in all legal matters, managed all finances (his wife had no share in his wealth), and made the crucial decisions that determined his children's lives. A father's authority over his children was absolute until he died or formally freed his children. In Renaissance Italy, children did not become adults on reaching a certain age; adulthood came only when the father went before a judge and formally emancipated them. The age of emancipation varied from early teens to late twenties.

Children   The wife managed the household, a position that gave women a certain degree of autonomy in their daily lives. Women of the upper and middle classes,

Family and Marriage in Renaissance Italy

The family was an important unit in Renaissance Italy. For the upper classes, family meant an extended household of parents, children, and servants, as in evident in the portrait of the Gonzaga family by Andrea Mantegna (ahn-DRAY-uh mahn-TEN-yah) below. Ludovico Gonzaga, marquis of Mantua, is shown at the left listening to a messenger. To his right are his wife Barbara, two sons, and two daughters, as well as servants. In the lower right corner is a dwarf. Dwarfs were common at Italian Renaissance courts, where they were kept as a source of entertainment.

In the upper classes, parents arranged marriages to reinforce business or family connections. The marriage ceremony involved an exchange of vows and the placing of a ring by the bridegroom on the bride's hand. The ring was a sign of affection and a symbol of the union of the

Camera degli Sposi, Palazzo Ducale, Mantua//Scala/Art Resource, NY

however, were expected to remain at home, under the supervision of their father or husband. Moreover, most wives knew that their primary function was to bear children. Upper-class wives were frequently pregnant; Alessandra Strozzi of Florence, for example, who had been married at the age of sixteen, bore eight children in ten years. Poor women did not conceive at the same rate because they nursed their own babies. Wealthy women gave their infants out to wet nurses, which enabled them to become pregnant more quickly after the birth of a child.

For women in the Renaissance, childbirth was a fearful occasion. Not only was it painful, but it could be deadly; as many as 10 percent of mothers died in childbirth. In his memoirs, the Florentine merchant Gregorio Dati recalled that three of his four wives had died in childbirth. His third wife, after bearing eleven children in fifteen years, "died in childbirth after lengthy suffering, which she bore with remarkable strength and patience."[5] Nor did the tragedies end with childbirth. Surviving mothers two families. The church encouraged the presence of a priest, but it was not necessary. The wedding was then recorded in a marriage contract that was considered a crucial part of the marital arrangements. So was a wedding feast, as seen in the painting by Sandro Botticelli below. It shows the wedding banquet that celebrated the marriage of Nastagio degli Onesti and the daughter of Paulo Traversaro in Florence. After the feast, the couple retired to a bedroom, usually in the house of the bride, where they physically consummated their marriage. Later, the husband introduced his bride to his household, usually on Sunday, in order to make it public knowledge that the marriage had been consummated.

often faced the death of their children. In Florence in the fifteenth century, for example, almost 50 percent of the children born to merchant families died before the age of twenty. Given these mortality rates, many upper-class families sought to have as many children as possible to ensure that there would be a surviving male heir to the family fortune. This concern is evident in the Florentine humanist Leon Battista Alberti's treatise *On the Family*, where one of the characters remarks, "How many families do we see today in decadence and ruin! ... Of all these families not only the magnificence and greatness but the very men, not only the men but the very names are shrunk away and gone. Their memory ... is wiped out and obliterated."[6]

Sexual Norms   Considering that marriages were arranged, marital relationships ran the gamut from deep emotional attachments to purely formal ties. The lack of emotional attachment in arranged marriages did encourage extramarital relationships, especially among groups whose lifestyle offered special temptations. Although sexual license for males was the norm for princes and their courts, women were supposed to follow different guidelines. The first wife of Duke Filippo Maria Visconti of Milan had an affair with the court musician and was executed for it.

The great age difference between husbands and wives in Italian Renaissance marriage patterns also encouraged the tendency to seek sexual outlets outside marriage. In Florence in 1427–1428, the average difference was thirteen years. Though females married between the ages of sixteen and eighteen, factors of environment, wealth, and demographic trends favored relatively late ages for the first marriages of males, who were usually in their thirties or even early forties. The existence of large numbers of young, unmarried males encouraged extramarital sex as well as prostitution. Prostitution was viewed as a necessary vice; since it could not be eliminated, it should be regulated. In Florence in 1415, the city fathers established communal brothels:

> Desiring to eliminate a worse evil by means of a lesser one, the lord priors … have decreed that the priors … may authorize the establishment of two public brothels in the city of Florence, in addition to the one which already exists…. [They are to be located] in suitable places or in places where the exercise of such scandalous activity can best be concealed, for the honor of the city and of those who live in the neighborhood in which these prostitutes must stay to hire their bodies for lucre.[7]

A prostitute in Florence was required to wear a traditional garb of "gloves on her hands and a bell on her head."

THE ITALIAN STATES IN THE RENAISSANCE

By the fifteenth century, five major powers dominated the Italian peninsula: Milan, Venice, Florence, the Papal States, and Naples (see Map 12.1).

The Five Major States   Northern Italy was divided between the duchy of Milan and the republic of Venice. After the death of the last Visconti ruler of Milan in 1447, Francesco Sforza (frahn-CHESS-koh SFORT-sah), one of the leading *condottieri* of the time (see Chapter 11), turned on his Milanese employers, conquered the city, and became its new duke. Both the Visconti and the Sforza rulers worked to create a highly centralized territorial state. They were especially successful in devising systems of taxation that generated enormous revenues for the government. The maritime republic of Venice remained an extremely stable political entity governed by a small oligarchy of merchant-aristocrats. Its commercial empire brought in enormous revenues and gave it the status of an international power. At the end of the fourteenth century, Venice embarked on the conquest of a territorial state in northern Italy to protect its food supply and its overland trade routes. Although expansion on the mainland made sense to the Venetians, it frightened Milan and Florence, which worked to curb what they perceived as the expansionary designs of the Venetians.

Republic of Florence   The republic of Florence dominated the region of Tuscany. By the beginning of the fifteenth century, Florence was governed by a small merchant oligarchy that manipulated the apparently republican government. In 1434,

MAP 12.1 Renaissance Italy

Italy in the late fourteenth century was a land of five major states and numerous independent city-states. Increased prosperity and a supportive intellectual climate helped create the atmosphere for the middle and upper classes to "rediscover" Greco-Roman culture. Modern diplomacy was also a product of Renaissance Italy.

Cosimo de' Medici took control of this oligarchy. Although the wealthy Medici family maintained republican forms of government for appearances' sake, it ran the government from behind the scenes. Through lavish patronage and careful courting of political allies, Cosimo (1434–1464) and later his grandson, Lorenzo the Magnificent (1469–1492), were successful in dominating the city at a time when Florence was the center of the cultural Renaissance.

Papal States   The Papal States lay in central Italy. Although these lands were nominally under the political control of the popes, papal residence in Avignon and the Great Schism had enabled individual cities and territories, such as Urbino (ur-BEE-noh), Bologna (buh-LOHN-yuh), and Ferrara, to become independent of papal authority. The Renaissance popes of the fifteenth century directed much of their energy toward reestablishing their control over the Papal States (see "The Renaissance Papacy" later in this chapter).

Kingdom of Naples   The kingdom of Naples, which encompassed most of southern Italy and usually the island of Sicily, was fought over by the French and the Aragonese until the latter established their domination in the mid-fifteenth century. Throughout the Renaissance, the kingdom of Naples remained a backward monarchy with a population consisting largely of poverty-stricken peasants dominated by unruly nobles. It shared little in the cultural glories of the Renaissance.

Independent City-States   Besides the five major states, there were a number of independent city-states under the control of powerful ruling families that became brilliant centers of Renaissance culture in the fifteenth century. These included Mantua (MAN-choo-uh), under the enlightened rule of the Gonzaga (gun-DZAH-gah) lords; Ferrara, governed by the flamboyant d'Este (DESS-tay) family; and perhaps the most famous, Urbino, ruled by the Montefeltro dynasty.

Urbino   Federigo da Montefeltro (fay-day-REE-goh dah mahn-tuh-FELL-troh), who ruled Urbino from 1444 to 1482, received a Classical education typical of the famous humanist school in Mantua run by Vittorino da Feltre (vee-tor-EE-noh dah FELL-tray) (1378–1446) (see "Education in the Renaissance" below). He also learned the skills of fighting, since the Montefeltro family compensated for the poverty of Urbino by hiring themselves out as *condottieri*. Federigo was not only a good ruler but also a rather unusual *condottiere* by fifteenth-century standards. Although not a brilliant general, he was reliable and honest. He did not break his promises, even when urged to do so by a papal legate. At the same time, Duke Federigo was one of the greatest patrons of Renaissance culture. Under his direction, Urbino became a well-known cultural and intellectual center. Though a despot, Federigo was also benevolent. It was said of him that he could walk safely through the streets of Urbino unaccompanied by a bodyguard, a feat few Renaissance rulers dared to emulate.

The Role of Women   A noticeable feature of these smaller Renaissance courts was the important role played by women. Battista Sforza (buh-TEESS-tuh SFORT-sah), niece of the ruler of Milan, was the wife of Federigo da Montefeltro. The duke called his wife "the delight of both my public and my private hours." An intelligent woman, she was well versed in both Greek and Latin and did much to foster art and letters in Urbino. As a prominent *condottiere*, Federigo was frequently absent, and like the wives of medieval lords, Battista Sforza was respected for governing the state "with firmness and good sense."

Perhaps the most famous of the Renaissance ruling women was Isabella d'Este (1474–1539), daughter of the duke of Ferrara, who married Francesco Gonzaga, marquis of Mantua. Their court was another important center of art and learning in the Renaissance. Educated at the brilliant court of Ferrara, Isabella was known for her intelligence and political wisdom. Called the "first lady of the world," she attracted artists and intellectuals to the Mantuan court and was responsible for amassing one of the finest libraries in all of Italy. Her numerous letters to friends, family, princes, and artists all over Europe reveal her political acumen as well as her good sense of humor. Both before and after the death of her husband, she effectively ruled Mantua and won a reputation as a clever negotiator.

Warfare in Italy   The fragmented world of the Italian territorial states gave rise to a political practice that was later used on a larger scale by competing European states. This was the concept of a balance of power, designed to prevent the aggrandizement of any one state at the expense of the others. This system was especially evident after 1454 when the Italian states signed the Peace of Lodi (LAH-dee), which ended almost a half-century of war and inaugurated a relatively peaceful forty-year era in Italy. An alliance system (Milan, Florence, and Naples versus Venice and the papacy) was created that led to a workable balance of power within Italy. It failed, however, to establish lasting cooperation among the major powers.

The growth of powerful monarchical states (see "The European State in the Renaissance" later in this chapter) led to trouble for the Italians. Italy soon became a battlefield for the great power struggle between the French and Spanish monarchies. Italian wealth and splendor would probably have been inviting to its northern neighbors under any circumstances, but it was actually the breakdown of the Italian balance of power that encouraged the invasions and began the Italian wars. Feeling isolated, Ludovico Sforza, the duke of Milan, foolishly invited the French to intervene in Italian politics. The French king Charles VIII (1483–1498) was eager to do so, and in 1494, with an army of 30,000 men, he advanced through Italy and occupied the kingdom of Naples. Other Italian states turned to the Spanish for help, and Ferdinand of Aragon indicated his willingness to intervene. For the next fifteen years, the French and Spanish competed to dominate Italy. After 1510, the war was continued by a new generation of rulers, Francis I of France and Charles I of Spain (see Chapter 13). This war was part of a long struggle for power throughout Europe between the Valois and Habsburg dynasties. Italy was only a pawn for the two great powers, a convenient arena for fighting battles. The terrible sack of Rome in 1527 by the armies of the Spanish king Charles I brought a temporary end to the Italian wars. Thereafter, the Spaniards dominated Italy.

Although some Italians had differentiated between Italians and "barbarians" (all foreigners), few Italians conceived of creating an alliance or confederation of states that could repel foreign invaders. Italians remained fiercely loyal to their own petty states, making invasion a fact of life in Italian history for all too long. Italy would not achieve unification and nationhood until 1870.

The Birth of Modern Diplomacy   The modern diplomatic system was a product of the Italian Renaissance. There were ambassadors in the Middle Ages, but they were used only on a temporary basis. Moreover, an ambassador, regardless of whose subject he was, regarded himself as the servant of all Christendom, not just of his particular employer. As a treatise on diplomacy stated, "An ambassador is sacred because he acts for the general welfare." Since he was the servant of all Christendom, "the business of an ambassador is peace."[8]

This concept of an ambassador changed during the Italian Renaissance because of the political situation in Italy. A large number of states existed, many so small that their security was easily threatened by their neighbors. To survive, the Italian states began to send resident diplomatic agents to each other to ferret out useful information. During the Italian wars, the practice of resident diplomats spread to the rest of Europe, and in the course of the sixteenth and seventeenth centuries, Europeans developed the diplomatic machinery still in use today, such as the rights of ambassadors in host countries and the proper procedures for conducting diplomatic business.

With the use of permanent resident agents or ambassadors, the conception of the purpose of an ambassador also changed. A Venetian diplomat attempted to define an ambassador's function in a treatise written at the end of the fifteenth century. He wrote, "The first duty of an ambassador is exactly the same as that of any other servant of a government, that is, to do, say, advise, and think whatever may best serve the preservation and aggrandizement of his own state."[9] An ambassador was now an agent only of the territorial state that sent him, not the larger body of Christendom. He could use any methods that were beneficial to the political interests of his own state. We are at the beginning of modern politics when the interests of the state supersede all other considerations.

Machiavelli and the New Statecraft   No one gave better expression to the Renaissance preoccupation with political power than Niccolò Machiavelli (nee-koh-LOH mahk-ee-uh-VEL-ee) (1469–1527). He entered the service of the Florentine republic in 1498, four years after the Medici family had been expelled from the city. As a secretary to the Florentine Council of Ten, he made numerous diplomatic missions, including trips to France and Germany, and saw the workings of statecraft at first hand. Machiavelli's political activity occurred during the period of tribulation and devastation for Italy that followed the French invasion in 1494. In 1512, French defeat and Spanish victory led to the reestablishment of Medici power in Florence. Staunch republicans, including Machiavelli, were sent into exile. Forced to give up politics, the great love of his life, Machiavelli now reflected on political power and wrote books, including *The Prince* (1513), one of the most famous treatises on political power in the Western world.

The Prince   Machiavelli's ideas on politics stemmed from two major sources, his knowledge of ancient Rome and his preoccupation with Italy's political problems. As a result of his experiences, Machiavelli fully realized that the small Italian states were no match for the larger monarchical states outside Italy's borders and that Italy itself had become merely a battleground for the armies of foreign states. His major concerns in *The Prince* were the acquisition and expansion of political power as the means to restore and maintain order in his time. In the Middle Ages, many political theorists stressed the ethical side of a prince's activity—how a ruler ought to behave based on Christian moral principles. Machiavelli bluntly contradicted this approach:

> My hope is to write a book that will be useful, at least to those who read it intelligently, and so I thought it sensible to go straight to a discussion of how things are in real life and not waste time with a discussion of an imaginary world.... For the gap

between how people actually behave and how they ought to behave is so great that anyone who ignores everyday reality in order to live up to an ideal will soon discover he has been taught how to destroy himself, not how to preserve himself.[10]

Machiavelli considered his approach far more realistic than that of his medieval forebears.

In Machiavelli's view, a prince's attitude toward power must be based on an understanding of human nature, which he perceived as basically self-centered: "For of men one can, in general, say this: They are ungrateful, fickle, deceptive and deceiving, avoiders of danger, eager to gain." Political activity, therefore, could not be restricted by moral considerations. The prince acts on behalf of the state and for the sake of the state must be willing to let his conscience sleep. As Machiavelli put it:

> You need to understand this: A ruler, and particularly a ruler who is new to power, cannot conform to all those rules that men who are thought good are expected to respect, for he is often obliged, in order to hold on to power, to break his word, to be uncharitable, inhumane, and irreligious. So he must be mentally prepared to act as circumstances and changes in fortune require. As I have said, he should do what is right if he can; but he must be prepared to do wrong if necessary.[11]

Machiavelli found a good example of the new Italian ruler in Cesare Borgia (CHAY-zah-ray BOR-juh), the son of Pope Alexander VI, who used ruthless measures to achieve his goal of carving out a new state in central Italy. As Machiavelli said: "So anyone who decides that the policy to follow when one has newly acquired power is to destroy one's enemies, to secure some allies, to win wars, whether by force or by fraud, to make oneself both loved and feared by one's subjects, ... cannot hope to find, in the recent past, a better model to imitate than Cesare Borgia."[12] Machiavelli was among the first to abandon morality as the basis for the analysis of political activity.

THE INTELLECTUAL RENAISSANCE IN ITALY

Individualism and **secularism**—two characteristics of the Italian Renaissance—were most noticeable in the intellectual and artistic realms. Italian culture had matured by the fourteenth century. For the next two centuries, Italy was the cultural leader of Europe. This new Italian culture was primarily the product of a relatively wealthy, urban lay society. The most important literary movement associated with the Renaissance was **humanism**.

Italian Renaissance Humanism   Renaissance humanism was an intellectual movement based on the study of the Classical literary works of Greece and Rome. Humanists examined the *studia humanitatis* ("the studies of humanity")—grammar, rhetoric, poetry, moral philosophy or ethics, and history—all based on the writings of ancient Greek and Roman authors. These are the subjects we call the humanities.

The central importance of literary preoccupations in Renaissance humanism is evident in the professional status or occupations of the humanists. Some of them were teachers of the humanities in secondary schools and universities, where they

OPPOSING VIEWPOINTS

The Renaissance Prince: The Views of Machiavelli and Erasmus

At the beginning of the sixteenth century, two writers produced very different views of political power and how a ruler should conduct affairs of state. In 1513, Niccolò Machiavelli wrote a short treatise on political power that, justly or unjustly, has given him a reputation as a political opportunist. In this selection from Chapter 17 of *The Prince*, Machiavelli analyzes whether it is better for a ruler to be loved than to be feared. Three years later the Dutch intellectual Erasmus, leader of the Christian humanists (see Chapter 13), also wrote a treatise on political power, entitled *Education of a Christian Prince*. As is evident in this excerpt from his treatise, Erasmus followed in the footsteps of medieval theorists on power by insisting that a true prince should think only of his moral obligations to the people he rules.

Machiavelli, *The Prince* (1513)

This leads us to a question that is in dispute: Is it better to be loved than feared, or vice versa? My reply is one ought to be both loved and feared; but, since it is difficult to accomplish both at the same time, I maintain it is much safer to be feared than loved, if you have to do without one of the two. For of men one can, in general, say this: They are ungrateful, fickle, deceptive and deceiving, avoiders of danger, eager to gain. As long as you serve their interests, they are devoted to you. They promise you their blood, their possessions, their lives, and their children, as I said before, so long as you seem to have no need of them. But as soon as you need help, they turn against you. Any ruler who relies simply on their promises and makes no other preparations, will be destroyed. For you will find that those whose support you buy, who do not rally to you because they admire your strength of character and nobility of soul, these are people you pay for, but they are never yours, and in the end you cannot get the benefit of your investment. Men are less nervous of offending someone who makes himself lovable, than someone who makes himself frightening. For love attaches men by ties of obligation, which, since men are wicked, they break whenever their interests are at stake. But fear restrains men because they are afraid of punishment, and this fear never leaves them. Still, a ruler should make himself feared in such a way that, if he does not inspire love, at least he does not provoke hatred. For it is perfectly possible to be feared and not hated. You will only be hated if you seize the property or the women of your subjects and citizens. Whenever you have to kill someone, make sure that you have a suitable excuse and an obvious reason; but, above all else, keep your hands off other people's property; for men are quicker to forget the death of their father than the loss of their inheritance. Moreover, there are always reasons why you might want to

either gave occasional lectures or held permanent positions, often as professors of rhetoric. Others served as secretaries in the chancelleries of Italian city-states or at the courts of princes or popes. All of these occupations were largely secular, and most humanists were laymen rather than members of the clergy.

seize people's property; and he who begins to live by plundering others will always find an excuse for seizing other people's possessions; but there are fewer reasons for killing people, and one killing need not lead to another.

When a ruler is at the head of his army and has a vast number of soldiers under his command, then it is absolutely essential to be prepared to be thought cruel; for it is impossible to keep an army united and ready for action without acquiring a reputation for cruelty.

Erasmus, *Education of a Christian Prince* (1516)

Follow the right, do violence to no one, plunder no one, sell no public office, be corrupted by no bribes.... As you would rather stand for an injury than avenge it at great loss to the state, perchance you will lose a little something of your empire. Bear that; consider that you have gained a great deal because you have brought hurt to fewer than you would otherwise have done.... If you cannot defend your realm without violating justice, without wanton loss of human life, without great loss to religion, give up and yield to the importunities of the age!...

A good prince ... is a living likeness of God, who is at once good and powerful. His goodness makes him want to help all; his power makes him able to do so. On the other hand, an evil prince, who is like a plague to his country, is the incarnation of the devil, who has great power joined with his wickedness. All his resources to the very last, he uses for the undoing of the human race....

[A good prince is one] who holds the life of each individual dearer than his own; who works and strives night and day for just one end—to be the best he can for everyone; with whom rewards are ready for all good men ... for so much does he want to be of real help to his people, without thought of recompense, that if necessary he would not hesitate to look out for their welfare at great risk to himself; who considers his wealth to lie in the advantage of his country; who is ever on the watch so that everyone else may sleep deeply; who grants no leisure to himself so that he may spend his life in the peace of his country; who worries himself with continual cares so that his subjects may have peace and quiet.... He does everything and allows everything that will bring everlasting peace to his country, for he realizes that war is the source of all misfortunes to the state.

Q *What does Machiavelli have to say about being loved rather than feared? How does this view contrast with that of Erasmus on the characteristics of a good ruler? Which viewpoint do you consider more modern? Why? Which viewpoint do you think is correct? Why?*

Sources: Machiavelli, *The Prince* (1513). From The Prince by Machiavelli, translated by David Wootton, pp. 51–52. Copyright © 1995 by Hackett Publishing Company, Inc. Reprinted by permission of Hackett Publishing Company, Inc. All rights reserved. Erasmus, *Education of a Christian Prince* (1516). From *The Education of a Christian Prince*, by Erasmus, translated by L. K. Born. Copyright © 1936 by Columbia University Press. Reprinted with permission of the publisher.

The Emergence of Humanism   Petrarch (1304–1374) has often been called the father of Italian Renaissance humanism (see Chapter 11 on his use of the Italian vernacular). Petrarch rejected his father's desire that he become a lawyer and took up a literary career instead. Although he lived in Avignon for a time, most of his last decades were spent in Italy as the guest of various princes and city govern-ments. With his usual lack of modesty, Petrarch once exclaimed, "Some of the greatest kings of our time have loved me and cultivated my friendship.... When I was their guest it was more as if they were mine."[13]

Petrarch did more than any other individual in the fourteenth century to foster the development of Renaissance humanism. He was the first intellectual to charac-terize the Middle Ages as a period of darkness, promoting the mistaken belief that medieval culture was ignorant of Classical antiquity. Petrarch's interest in the clas-sics led him on a quest for forgotten Latin manuscripts and set in motion a ransack-ing of monastic libraries throughout Europe. In his preoccupation with the classics and their secular content, Petrarch worried at times that he might not be sufficiently attentive to spiritual ideals. His qualms, however, did not prevent him from inaugu-rating the humanist emphasis on the use of pure Classical Latin, making it fashion-able for humanists to use Cicero as a model for prose and Virgil for poetry. As Petrarch said, "Christ is my God; Cicero is the prince of the language."

Humanism in Fifteenth-Century Italy   In Florence, the humanist movement took a new direction at the beginning of the fifteenth century when it became closely tied to Florentine civic spirit and pride, giving rise to what one modern scholar has labeled **civic humanism**. Fourteenth-century humanists such as Petrarch had described the intellectual life as one of solitude. They rejected family and a life of action in the community. In the busy civic world of Florence, however, intellectuals began to take a new view of their role as intellectuals. The Classical Roman statesman and intellectual Cicero became their model. Leonardo Bruni (leh-ah-NAHR-doh BROO-nee) (1370–1444), a humanist, Florentine patriot, and chancellor of the city, wrote a biography of Cicero titled *The New Cicero*, in which he waxed enthusiastic about the fusion of political action and literary creation in Cicero's life. From Bruni's time on, Cicero served as the inspiration for the Renaissance ideal that intellectuals had a duty to live an active life for their state. An individual only "grows to maturity—both intellectually and morally—through participation" in the life of the state. Civic humanism reflected the values of the urban society of the Italian Renaissance. Humanists came to believe that their study of the humanities should be put to the service of the state. It is no accident that humanists served the state as chancellors, councillors, and advisers.

Also evident in the humanism of the first half of the fifteenth century was a grow-ing interest in Classical Greek civilization. Bruni was one of the first Italian humanists to gain a thorough knowledge of Greek. He became an enthusiastic pupil of the Byzantine scholar Manuel Chrysoloras (man-WEL kris-uh-LAHR-uss), who taught in Florence from 1396 to 1400. Humanists eagerly perused the works of Plato as well as those of Greek poets, dramatists, historians, and orators, such as Euripides, Sophocles, and Thucydides, all of whom had been ignored by the scholastics of the High Middle Ages as irrelevant to the theological questions they were examining.

By the fifteenth century, a consciousness of being humanists had emerged. This was especially evident in the career of Lorenzo Valla (1407–1457). Valla was brought up in Rome and educated in both Latin and Greek. Eventually, he achieved his chief ambition of becoming a papal secretary. Valla's major work, *The Elegances of the Latin Language*, was an effort to purify medieval Latin and restore Latin to its proper position over the vernacular. The treatise examined the proper use of Classical Latin and created a new literary standard. Early humanists had tended to take as Classical models any author (including Christians) who had written before the seventh century C.E. Valla identified different stages in the development of the Latin language and accepted only the Latin of the last century of the Roman Republic and the first century of the empire.

Humanism and Philosophy   In the second half of the fifteenth century, a dramatic upsurge of interest in the works of Plato occurred, especially evident among the members of an informal discussion group known as the Florentine Platonic Academy. Cosimo de' Medici, the de facto ruler of Florence, encouraged this development by commissioning a translation of Plato's dialogues by Marsilio Ficino (mar-SIL-yoh fee-CHEE-noh) (1433–1499), one of the academy's leaders. Ficino dedicated his life to the translation of Plato and the exposition of the Platonic philosophy known as **Neoplatonism.**

In two major works, Ficino undertook the synthesis of Christianity and Platonism into a single system. His Neoplatonism was based on two primary ideas, the Neoplatonic hierarchy of substances and a theory of spiritual love. The former postulated the idea of a hierarchy of substances, or great chain of being, from the lowest form of physical matter (plants) to the purest spirit (God), in which humans occupied a central or middle position. They were the link between the material world (through the body) and the spiritual world (through the soul), and their highest duty was to ascend toward that union with God that was the true end of human existence. Ficino's theory of spiritual or Platonic love maintained that just as all people are bound together in their common humanity by love, so too are all parts of the universe held together by bonds of sympathetic love.

Renaissance Hermeticism   **Hermeticism** was another product of the Florentine intellectual environment of the late fifteenth century. At the request of Cosimo de' Medici, Ficino translated into Latin a Greek work titled *Corpus Hermeticum* (KOR-pus hur-MET-i-koom). The Hermetic manuscripts contained two kinds of writings. One type stressed the occult sciences, with an emphasis on astrology, alchemy, and magic; the other focused on theological and philosophical beliefs and speculations. Some Hermetic writings espoused **pantheism**, seeing divinity embodied in all aspects of nature and in the heavenly bodies as well as in earthly objects. As Giordano Bruno (jor-DAHN-oh BROO-noh), one of the most prominent sixteenth-century Hermeticists, stated, "God as a whole is in all things."[14]

For Renaissance intellectuals, the Hermetic revival offered a new view of humankind. They believed that human beings had been created as divine beings endowed with divine creative power but had freely chosen to enter the material world (nature). Humans could recover their divinity, however, through a regenerative experience or purification of the soul. Thus regenerated, they became true sages or magi, as the Renaissance called them, who had knowledge of God and of truth. In regaining their original divinity, they reacquired an intimate knowledge of nature and the ability to employ the powers of nature for beneficial purposes.

In Italy, the most prominent magi in the late fifteenth century were Ficino and his friend and pupil, Giovanni Pico della Mirandola (PEE-koh DELL-uh mee-RAN-doh-lah) (1463–1494). Pico produced one of the most famous pieces of writing of the Renaissance, the *Oration on the Dignity of Man*. Pico combed diligently through the works of many philosophers of different backgrounds for the common "nuggets of universal truth" that he believed were all part of God's revelation to humanity. In the *Oration*, Pico offered a ringing statement of unlimited human potential: "To him it is granted to have whatever he chooses, to be whatever he wills."[15] Like Ficino, Pico took an avid interest in Hermetic philosophy, accepting it as the "science of the Divine," which "embraces the deepest contemplation of the most secret things, and at last the knowledge of all nature."[16]

Education in the Renaissance   The humanist movement had a profound effect on education. Renaissance humanists believed that human beings could be dramatically changed by education. They wrote books on education and developed secondary schools based on their ideas. Most famous was the school founded in 1423 by Vittorino da Feltre at Mantua, where the ruler of that small Italian state, Gian Francesco I Gonzaga, wished to provide a humanist education for his children. Vittorino based much of his educational system on the ideas of Classical authors, particularly Cicero and Quintilian.

At the core of humanist schools were the "liberal studies." A treatise on education called *Concerning Character* by Pietro Paolo Vergerio (PYAY-troh PAH-oh-loh vur-JEER-ee-oh) (1370–1444) especially influenced the Renaissance view of the value of the liberal arts. This work stressed the importance of liberal studies as the key to true freedom, enabling individuals to reach their full potential. According to Vergerio, "We call those studies liberal which are worthy of a free man; those studies by which we attain and practice virtue and wisdom; that education which calls forth, trains, and develops those highest gifts of body and mind which ennoble men."[17] The liberal studies included history, moral philosophy, eloquence (rhetoric), letters (grammar and logic), poetry, mathematics, astronomy, and music. The purpose of a liberal education was thus to produce individuals who followed a path of virtue and wisdom and possessed the rhetorical skills with which to persuade others to do the same. Following the Greek precept of a sound mind in a sound body, Vittorino's school at Mantua also stressed physical education. Pupils were taught the skills of javelin throwing, archery, and dancing and encouraged to run, wrestle, hunt, and swim.

Humanist education was thought to be a practical preparation for life. Its aim was not to create great scholars but rather to produce complete citizens who could participate in the civic life of their communities. As Vittorino said, "Not everyone is obliged to excel in philosophy, medicine, or the law, nor are all equally favored by nature; but all are destined to live in society and to practice virtue."[18] Humanist schools, combining the classics and Christianity, provided the model for the basic education of the European ruling classes until the twentieth century.

Although a small number of children from the lower classes received free educations, humanist schools such as Vittorino's were primarily geared for the education of an elite, the ruling classes of their communities. Also largely absent from such schools were females. Vittorino's only female pupils were the two daughters of the Gonzaga ruler of Mantua. Though these few female students studied the classics and were encouraged to know some history and to ride, dance, sing, play the

A Woman's Defense of Learning

As a young woman, Laura Cereta was proud of her learning but was condemned by a male world that found it unseemly for women to be scholars. One monk said to her father, "She gives herself to things unworthy of her—namely, the classics." Before being silenced, Laura Cereta wrote a series of letters, including one to a male critic who had argued that her work was so good it could not have been written by a woman.

Laura Cereta, *Defense of the Liberal Instruction of Women*

My ears are wearied by your carping. You brashly and publicly not merely wonder but indeed lament that I am said to possess as fine a mind as nature ever bestowed upon the most learned man. You seem to think that so learned a woman has scarcely before been seen in the world. You are wrong on both counts....

I would have been silent.... But I cannot tolerate your having attacked my entire sex. For this reason my thirsty soul seeks revenge, my sleeping pen is aroused to literary struggle, raging anger stirs mental passions long chained by silence. With just cause I am moved to demonstrate how great a reputation for learning and virtue women have won by their inborn excellence, manifested in every age as knowledge....

Only the question of the rarity of outstanding women remains to be addressed. The explanation is clear: women have been able by nature to be exceptional, but have chosen lesser goals. For some women are concerned with parting their hair correctly, adorning themselves with lovely dresses, or decorating their fingers with pearls and other gems. Others delight in mouthing carefully composed phrases, indulging in dancing, or managing spoiled puppies. Still others wish to gaze at lavish banquet tables, to rest in sleep, or, standing at mirrors, to smear their lovely faces. But those in whom a deeper integrity yearns for virtue, restrain from the start their youthful souls, reflect on higher things, harden the body with sobriety and trials, and curb their tongues, open their ears, compose their thoughts in wakeful hours, their minds in contemplation, to letters bonded to righteousness. For knowledge is not given as a gift, but [is gained] with diligence. The free mind, not shirking effort, always soars zealously toward the good, and the desire to know grows ever more wide and deep. It is because of no special holiness, therefore, that we [women] are rewarded by God the Giver with the gift of exceptional talent. Nature has generously lavished its gifts upon all people, opening to all the doors of choice through which reason sends envoys to the will, from which they learn and convey its desires. The will must choose to exercise the gift of reason....

I have been praised too much; showing your contempt for women, you pretend that I alone am admirable because of the good fortune of my intellect.... Do you suppose, O most contemptible man on earth, that I think myself sprung [like Athena] from the head of Jove? I am a school girl, possessed of the sleeping embers of an ordinary mind. Indeed I am too hurt, and my mind, offended, too swayed by passions, sighs, tormenting itself, conscious of the obligation to defend my sex. For absolutely everything—that which is within us and that which is without—is made weak by association with my sex.

Q *How did Cereta explain her intellectual interests and accomplishments? Why were Renaissance women rarely taken seriously when they sought educational opportunities and recognition for their intellectual talents? Were any of those factors unique to the Renaissance era?*

Source: Laura Cereta, "Defense of the Liberal Instruction of Women," from *Her Immaculate Hand: Selected Works by and about the Women Humanists of Quattrocentro Italy*, ed. by Margaret King and Albert Rabil (Pegasus Press, Asheville, NC, 2000). Reprinted by permission.

lute, and appreciate poetry, they were discouraged from learning mathematics and rhetoric. In the educational treatises of the time, religion and morals were thought to "hold the first place in the education of a Christian lady."

Was there a Renaissance for Women?   Historians have disagreed over the benefits of the Renaissance for women. Some maintain that during the Middle Ages upper-class women in particular had greater freedom to satisfy their emotional needs and that upper-class women in the Renaissance experienced a contraction of both social and personal options as they became even more subject to male authority and patterns. Other historians have argued that although conditions remained bleak for most women, some women, especially those in courtly, religious, and intellectual environments, found ways to develop a new sense of themselves as women. This may be especially true of women who were educated in the humanist fashion and went on to establish their own literary careers.

Isotta Nogarola (ee-ZAHT-uh NOH-guh-roll-uh), born to a noble family in Verona, mastered Latin and wrote numerous letters and treatises that brought her praise from male Italian intellectuals. Cassandra Fedele (FAY-duh-lee) of Venice, who learned both Latin and Greek from humanist tutors hired by her family, became well known in Venice for her public recitations of orations. Laura Cereta (say-REE-tuh) was educated in Latin by her father, a physician from Brescia. Laura defended the ability of women to pursue scholarly pursuits.

Humanism and History   Humanism had a strong impact on the writing of history. Influenced by Roman and Greek historians, the humanists approached the writing of history differently from the chroniclers of the Middle Ages. The humanists' belief that Classical civilization had been followed by an age of barbarism (the Middle Ages), which had in turn been succeeded by their own age, with its rebirth of the study of the classics, enabled them to think in terms of the passage of time, of the past as past. Their division of the past into ancient world, dark ages, and their own age provided a new sense of chronology or periodization in history.

The humanists were also responsible for secularizing the writing of history. Humanist historians reduced or eliminated the role of miracles in historical interpretation, not because they were anti-Christian but because they took a new approach to sources. They wanted to use documents and exercised their newly developed critical skills in examining them. Greater attention was paid to the political events and forces that affected their city-states or larger territorial units. Thus, Leonardo Bruni wrote the *History of the Florentine People*. The new emphasis on secularization was also evident in the humanists' conception of causation in history. Medieval historical literature often portrayed historical events as being caused by God's active involvement in human affairs. Humanists de-emphasized divine intervention in favor of human motives, stressing political forces or the role of individuals in history.

Guicciardini   The high point of Renaissance historiography was achieved at the beginning of the sixteenth century in the works of Francesco Guicciardini (frahn-CHESS-koh gwee-char-DEE-nee) (1483–1540). To many historians, his *History of*

Italy and *History of Florence* represent the beginning of "modern analytical historiography." To Guicciardini, the purpose of writing history was to teach lessons, but he was so impressed by the complexity of historical events that he felt those lessons were not always obvious. From his extensive background in government and diplomatic affairs, he developed the skills that enabled him to analyze political situations precisely and critically. Emphasizing political and military history, his works relied heavily on personal examples and documentary sources.

The Impact of Printing   The Renaissance witnessed the invention of printing, one of the most important technological innovations of Western civilization. The art of printing made an immediate impact on European intellectual life and thought. Printing from hand-carved wooden blocks had been done in the West since the twelfth century and in China even before that. What was new to Europe in the fifteenth century was multiple printing with movable metal type. The development of printing from movable type was a gradual process that culminated between 1445 and 1450; Johannes Gutenberg (yoh-HAH-nuss GOO-ten-bayrk) of Mainz played an important role in bringing the process to completion. Gutenberg's Bible, completed in 1455 or 1456, was the first true book in the West produced from movable type.

The new printing spread rapidly throughout Europe in the second half of the fifteenth century. Printing presses were established throughout the Holy Roman Empire in the 1460s and within ten years had spread to both western and eastern Europe. Especially well known as a printing center was Venice, home by 1500 to almost one hundred printers who had produced almost 2 million volumes.

By 1500, there were more than a thousand printers in Europe who had published almost 40,000 titles (between 8 million and 10 million copies). Probably 50 percent of these books were religious—Bibles and biblical commentaries, books of devotion, and sermons. Next in importance were the Latin and Greek classics, medieval grammars, legal handbooks, works on philosophy, and an ever-growing number of popular romances.

Printing became one of the largest industries in Europe, and its effects were soon felt in many areas of European life. The printing of books encouraged the development of scholarly research and the desire to attain knowledge. Moreover, printing facilitated cooperation among scholars and helped produce standardized and definitive texts. Printing also stimulated the development of an ever-expanding lay reading public, a development that had an enormous impact on European society. Indeed, without the printing press, the new religious ideas of the Reformation would never have spread as rapidly as they did in the sixteenth century.

THE ARTISTIC RENAISSANCE

Leonardo da Vinci (dah VEEN-chee), one of the great Italian Renaissance artists, once explained: "Hence the painter will produce pictures of small merit if he takes for his standard the pictures of others, but if he will study from natural objects he will bear good fruit.... Those who take for their standard any one but nature ... weary themselves in vain."[19] Renaissance artists considered the imitation of nature their primary goal. Their search for naturalism became an end in itself: to persuade

Galleria degli Uffizi, Florence//Scala/Art Resource, NY

Botticelli, *Primavera*. *This work reflects Botticelli's strong interest in Classical antiquity. At the center of the painting is Venus, the goddess of love. At the right stands Flora, a Roman goddess of flowers and fertility, while the Three Graces dance playfully at the left. Cupid, the son of Venus, aims his arrow at the Three Graces. At the far left of the picture is Mercury, the messenger of the gods. Later in life, Botticelli experienced a profound religious crisis, leading him to reject his earlier preoccupation with pagan gods and goddesses. He burned many of his early paintings and thereafter produced only religious works.*

onlookers of the reality of the object or event they were portraying. At the same time, the new artistic standards reflected a new attitude of mind as well, one in which human beings became the focus of attention, the "center and measure of all things," as one artist proclaimed.

Art in the Early Renaissance   Leonardo and other Italians maintained that it was Giotto in the fourteenth century (see Chapter 11) who began the imitation of nature. But what Giotto had begun was not taken up again until the work of Masaccio (muh-ZAH-choh) (1401–1428) in Florence. Masaccio's cycle of frescoes in the Brancacci Chapel has long been regarded as the first masterpiece of Early Renaissance art. With his use of monumental figures, a more realistic relationship between figures and landscape, and visual representation of the laws of perspective, a new realistic style of painting was born. Onlookers become aware of a world of reality that appears to be a continuation of their own world. Masaccio's massive, three-dimensional human figures provided a model for later generations of Florentine artists.

During the fifteenth century, other Florentine painters absorbed and modified this new Renaissance style. Especially important was the development of an experimental trend that took two directions. One emphasized the mathematical side of painting, the working out of the laws of perspective and the organization of outdoor space and light by geometry and perspective. In the work of Paolo Uccello (PAH-oh-loh oo-CHELL-oh) (1397–1475), figures became mere stage props to show off his mastery of the laws of perspective. The other aspect of the experimental trend involved the investigation of movement and anatomical structure. *The Martyrdom of Saint Sebastian* by Antonio Pollaiuolo (pohl-ly-WOH-loh) (c. 1432–1498) revels in Classical motifs and attempts to portray the human body under stress. Indeed, the realistic portrayal of the human nude became one of the foremost preoccupations of Italian Renaissance art. The fifteenth century, then, was a period of experimentation and technical mastery.

During the last decades of the fifteenth century, a new sense of invention emerged in Florence, especially in the circle of artists and scholars who formed part of the court of the city's leading citizen, Lorenzo the Magnificent. One of this group's prominent members was Sandro Botticelli (SAHN-droh bot-i-CHELL-ee) (1445–1510), whose interest in Greek and Roman mythology was well reflected in one of his most famous works, *Primavera* (Spring). The painting is set in the garden of Venus, a garden of eternal spring. Though Botticelli's figures are well defined, they also possess an otherworldly quality that is far removed from the realism that characterized the painting of the Early Renaissance.

The revolutionary achievements of Florentine painters in the fifteenth century were matched by equally stunning advances in sculpture and architecture. Donato di Donatello (doh-NAH-toh dee doh-nuh-TELL-oh) (1386–1466) spent time in Rome studying and copying the statues of antiquity. His subsequent work in Florence reveals how well he had mastered the essence of what he saw. Among his numerous works was a statue of David, which is the first known life-size, freestanding bronze nude in European art since antiquity. With the severed head of the giant Goliath beneath David's feet, Donatello's statue may have celebrated Florentine heroism in the triumph of Florence over the Milanese in 1428. Like Donatello's other statues, *David* also radiated a simplicity and strength that reflected the dignity of humanity.

Filippo Brunelleschi (fee-LEE-poh BROO-nuh-LESS-kee) (1377–1446), a friend of Donatello's, accompanied the latter to Rome. Brunelleschi drew much inspiration from the architectural monuments of Roman antiquity, and when he returned to Florence, he poured his new insights into the creation of a new architecture. His first project involved the challenge of building a dome for the unfinished cathedral of Florence (the Duomo). The cathedral had been started in 1296, but it was Brunelleschi who devised new building techniques and machinery to create a dome, built between 1420 and 1436, that spanned a 140-foot opening.

An even better example of Brunelleschi's new Renaissance architectural style is evident in the Church of San Lorenzo. When the Medici commissioned him to design the church, Brunelleschi, inspired by Roman models, created a church interior very different from that of the great medieval cathedrals. San Lorenzo's Classical columns, rounded arches, and coffered ceiling created an environment that did not overwhelm the worshiper materially and psychologically, as Gothic cathedrals did, but comforted as a space created to fit human, not divine, measurements. Like painters and sculptors, Renaissance architects sought to reflect a human-centered world.

Filippo Brunelleschi, Dome of the Duomo. Brunelleschi was first commissioned to design the dome for the unfinished cathedral of Florence in 1417, but work did not begin until 1420. Although Brunelleschi would have preferred the Roman hemispheric dome, for practical reasons he was forced to elevate the center of the dome and then lessen the weight of the structure by building a thin double shell around a structure of twenty-four ribs. The most important ribs were placed on the outside of the dome (four of them are visible in this illustration).

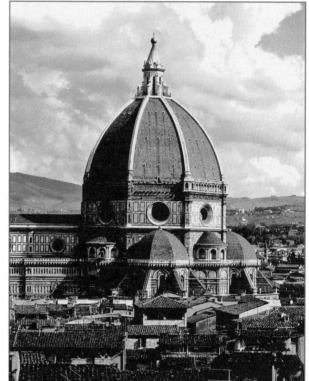

© Scala/Art Resource, NY

The new assertion of human individuality, evident in Early Renaissance art, was also reflected in the new emphasis on portraiture. Patrons appeared in the corners of sacred pictures, and monumental tombs and portrait statues honored many of Florence's prominent citizens. By the mid-fifteenth century, artists were giving an accurate rendering of their subjects' facial features while revealing the inner qualities of their personalities. The portraits of the duke and duchess of Urbino by Piero della Francesca (c. 1410–1492) provide accurate representations as well as a sense of both the power and the wealth of the rulers of Urbino (see p. 388).

The Artistic High Renaissance

By the end of the fifteenth century, Italian painters, sculptors, and architects had created a new artistic environment. Many artists had mastered the new techniques for a scientific observation of the world around them and were now ready to move into individualistic forms of creative expression. This final stage of Renaissance art, which flourished between 1480 and 1520, is called the High Renaissance. The shift to the High Renaissance was marked by the increasing importance of Rome as a new cultural center of the Italian Renaissance.

The High Renaissance was dominated by the work of three artistic giants: Leonardo da Vinci (1452–1519), Raphael (1483–1520), and Michelangelo (1475–1564). Leonardo represents a transitional figure in the shift to High Renaissance principles. He carried on the fifteenth-century experimental tradition by studying everything and even dissecting human bodies to see more clearly how nature worked. But Leonardo stressed the need to advance beyond such realism and initiated the High Renaissance's preoccupation with the idealization of nature, or the attempt to generalize from realistic portrayal to an ideal form. Leonardo's *Last Supper*, painted in Milan, is a brilliant summary of fifteenth-century trends in its organization of space and use of perspective to depict subjects three-dimensionally in a two-dimensional medium. But it is also more. The figure of Philip is idealized, and the work embodies profound psychological dimensions. The words of Jesus that "one of you shall betray me" are experienced directly as each of the apostles reveals his personality and his relationship to Jesus. Through gestures and movement, Leonardo hoped to reveal a person's inner life.

Raphael (RAFF-ee-ul) blossomed as a painter at an early age; at twenty-five, he was already regarded as one of Italy's best painters. Raphael was acclaimed for his numerous madonnas, in which he attempted to achieve an ideal of beauty far surpassing human standards. He is well known for his frescoes in the Vatican Palace; his *School of Athens* reveals a world of balance, harmony, and order—the underlying principles of the art of the Classical world of Greece and Rome.

Michelangelo (my-kuh-LAN-juh-loh), an accomplished painter, sculptor, and architect, was another giant of the High Renaissance. Fiercely driven by his desire to create, he worked with great passion and energy on a remarkable number of projects. Michelangelo was influenced by Neoplatonism, especially evident in his figures on the ceiling of the Sistine Chapel in Rome. In 1508, Pope Julius II had called Michelangelo to Rome and commissioned him to decorate the chapel ceiling. This colossal project was not completed until 1512. Michelangelo attempted to tell the story of the Fall of Man by depicting nine scenes from the biblical book of Genesis. In his *Creation of Adam* (reproduced at the start of this chapter), the well-proportioned figure of Adam awaits the divine spark. Adam, like the other muscular figures on the ceiling, reveals an ideal type of human being with perfect proportions. In good Neoplatonic fashion, the beauty of these figures is meant to be a reflection of divine beauty; the more beautiful the body, the more God-like the figure.

Another manifestation of Michelangelo's search for ideal beauty was his *David*, a colossal marble statue commissioned by the Florentine government in 1501 and completed in 1504. Michelangelo maintained that the form of a statue already resided in the uncarved piece of stone: "I only take away the surplus, the statue is already there."[20] Out of a piece of marble that had remained unused for fifty years, Michelangelo created a 14-foot-high figure, the largest sculpture in Italy since the time of Rome. An awe-inspiring hero, Michelangelo's *David* proudly proclaims the beauty of the human body and the glory of human beings.

The High Renaissance was also evident in architecture, especially in the work of Donato Bramante (doh-NAH-toh brah-MAHN-tay) (1444–1514). He came from Urbino but took up residence in Rome, where he designed a small temple on the supposed site of Saint Peter's martyrdom. The Tempietto, or little temple, with its Doric columns surrounding a sanctuary enclosed by a dome, summarized the architectural ideals of the High Renaissance. Columns, dome, and sanctuary form a monumental and harmonious whole. Inspired by antiquity, Bramante had recaptured the grandeur of ancient Rome.

The Artist and
Social Status

Early Renaissance artists began their careers as apprentices to masters in craft guilds. Apprentices with unusual talent might eventually become masters and run their own workshops. As in the Middle Ages, artists were still largely viewed as artisans. Since guilds depended on commissions for their projects, patrons played an important role in the art of the Early Renaissance. The wealthy upper classes determined both the content and the purpose of the paintings and pieces of sculpture they commissioned.

By the end of the fifteenth century, a transformation in the position of the artist had occurred. Especially talented individuals, such as Leonardo, Raphael, and Michelangelo, were no longer regarded as artisans but as artistic geniuses with creative energies akin to the divine. Artists were heroes, individuals who were praised more for their creativity than for their competence as craftspeople. Michelangelo, for example, was frequently addressed as "Il Divino"—the Divine One. As society excused their eccentricities and valued their creative genius, the artists of the High Renaissance became the first to embody the modern concept of the artist.

As respect for artists grew, so did their ability to profit economically from their work and to rise on the social scale. Now welcomed as equals into the circles of the upper classes, they mingled with the political and intellectual elite of their society and became more aware of new intellectual theories, which they then embodied in their art. The Platonic Academy and Renaissance Neoplatonism had an especially important impact on Florentine painters.

The Northern
Artistic
Renaissance

In trying to provide an exact portrayal of their world, the artists of the north (especially the Low Countries) and Italy took different approaches. In Italy, the human form became the primary vehicle of expression as Italian artists sought to master the technical skills that allowed them to portray humans in realistic settings. The large wall spaces of Italian churches had given rise to the art of fresco painting, but in the north, the prevalence of Gothic cathedrals with their stained-glass windows resulted in more emphasis on illuminated manuscripts and wooden panel painting for altarpieces. The space available in these works was limited, and great care was required to depict each object, leading northern painters to become masters at rendering details.

The most influential northern school of art in the fifteenth century was centered in Flanders. Jan van Eyck (YAHN vahn YK *or* van AYK) (c. 1390–1441) was among the first to use oil paint, a medium that enabled the artist to use a varied range of colors and create fine details. In the famous *Giovanni Arnolfini and His Bride*, van Eyck's attention to detail is staggering: precise portraits, a glittering chandelier, and a mirror reflecting the objects in the room. Although each detail was rendered as observed, it is evident that van Eyck's comprehension of perspective was still uncertain. His work is truly indicative of northern Renaissance painters, who, in their effort to imitate nature, did so not by mastery of the laws of perspective and proportion but by empirical observation of visual reality and the accurate portrayal of details. Moreover, northern painters placed great emphasis on the emotional intensity of religious feeling and created great works of devotional art, especially in their altarpieces. Michelangelo summarized the difference between northern and Italian Renaissance painting in these words:

> In Flanders, they paint, before all things, to render exactly and deceptively the outward appearance of things. The painters choose, by preference, subjects provoking transports of piety, like the figures of saints or of prophets. But most of the time they paint what are called landscapes with plenty of figures. Though the eye is agreeably impressed, these pictures have neither choice of values nor grandeur. In short, this art is without power and without distinction; it aims at rendering minutely many things at the same time, of which a single one would have sufficed to call forth a man's whole application.[21]

By the end of the fifteenth century, however, artists from the north began to study in Italy and were visually influenced by what artists were doing there.

One northern artist of this later period who was greatly affected by the Italians was Albrecht Dürer (AHL-brekht DOO-rur) (1471–1528) from Nuremberg. Dürer made two trips to Italy and absorbed most of what the Italians could teach, as is evident in his mastery of the laws of perspective and Renaissance theories of

Galleria degli Uffizi, Florence//© Erich Lessing/Art Resource, NY

Dürer, *Adoration of the Magi.* *By the end of the fifteenth century, northern artists had begun to study in Italy and to adopt many of the techniques used by Italian painters. As is evident in this painting, which was the central panel for an altarpiece done for Frederick the Wise in 1504, Albrecht Dürer masterfully incorporated the laws of perspective and the ideals of proportion into his works. At the same time, he did not abandon the preoccupation with detail typical of northern artists. Dürer portrayed himself in the center as the wise man with long hair.*

proportion. He wrote detailed treatises on both subjects. At the same time, as in his famous *Adoration of the Magi*, Dürer did not reject the use of minute details characteristic of northern artists. He did try, however, to integrate those details more harmoniously into his works and, like the Italian artists of the High Renaissance, to achieve a standard of ideal beauty by a careful examination of the human form.

Music in the Renaissance   For much of the fifteenth century, an extraordinary cultural environment was fostered in the domains of the dukes of Burgundy in northern Europe. The court of the dukes attracted some of the best artists and musicians of the time. Among them was Guillaume Dufay (gee-YOHM doo-FAY) (c. 1400–1474), perhaps the most important composer of his era. Born in northern France, Dufay lived for a few years in Italy and was thus well suited to combine the late medieval style of France with the early Renaissance style of Italy. One of Dufay's greatest contributions was a change in the composition of the Mass. He was the first to use secular tunes to replace Gregorian chants as the fixed melody that served as the basis for the Mass. Dufay also composed a number of secular songs, an important reminder that during the Renaissance, music ceased to be used chiefly in the service of God and moved into the secular world of courts and cities. In Italy and France, the chief form of secular music was the madrigal.

The Renaissance madrigal was a poem set to music, and it originated in the fourteenth-century Italian courts. The texts were usually twelve-line poems written in the vernacular, and their theme was emotional or erotic love. By the mid-sixteenth century, most madrigals were written for five or six voices and employed a technique called text painting, in which the music tried to portray the literal meaning of the text. Thus, the melody would rise for the word *heaven* or use a wavelike motion to represent the word *water*. By the mid-sixteenth century, the madrigal had also spread to England, where the most popular form was characterized by the *fa-la-la* refrain like that found in the English carol "Deck the Halls."

THE EUROPEAN STATE IN THE RENAISSANCE

In the first half of the fifteenth century, European states continued the disintegrative patterns of the previous century. In the second half of the century, however, recovery set in, and attempts were made to reestablish the centralized power of monarchical governments. To characterize the results, some historians have used the label "Renaissance states"; others have spoken of the "**new monarchies**," especially those of France, England, and Spain at the end of the fifteenth century (see Map 12.2). Although monarchs in western Europe succeeded to varying degrees at extending their political authority, rulers in central and eastern Europe were often weak and unable to impose their authority.

The Growth of the French Monarchy   The Hundred Years' War had left France prostrate. Depopulation, desolate farmlands, ruined commerce, and independent and unruly nobles had made it difficult for the kings to assert their authority. But the war had also developed a strong degree of French national feeling toward a common enemy that the kings

MAP 12.2   Europe in the Second Half of the Fifteenth Century

By the second half of the fifteenth century, states in western Europe, particularly France, Spain, and England, had begun the process of modern state building. With varying success, they reined in the power of the church and nobles, increased the ability to levy taxes, and established effective government bureaucracies.

could use to reestablish monarchical power. The need to prosecute the war provided an excuse to strengthen the authority of the king, already evident in the policies of Charles VII (1422–1461) after he was crowned king at Reims. With the consent of the Estates-General, Charles established a royal army composed of cavalry and archers. The Estates-General also granted him the right to levy the *taille*, an annual direct tax usually on land or property, without any need for further approval from the Estates-General. Losing control of the purse meant less power for this parliamentary body.

The process of developing a French territorial state was greatly advanced by King Louis XI (1461–1483), known as the Spider because of his wily and devious ways. By retaining the *taille* as a permanent tax imposed by royal authority, Louis secured a sound, regular source of income. Louis was not, however, completely successful in repressing the French nobility, whose independence posed a threat to his own state building. A major problem was his supposed vassal, Charles the Bold, duke of Burgundy (1467–1477). Charles attempted to create a middle kingdom between France and Germany, stretching from the Low Countries to Switzerland. Louis opposed his efforts, and when Charles was killed in 1477 fighting the Swiss, Louis added part of Charles's possessions, the duchy of Burgundy, to his own lands. Three years later, the provinces of Anjou, Maine, Bar, and Provence were brought under royal control. Many historians believe that Louis created a base for the later development of a strong French monarchy.

England: Civil War and a New Monarchy   The Hundred Years' War had also strongly affected the other protagonist in that conflict. The cost of the war in its final years and the losses in manpower strained the English economy. Moreover, even greater domestic turmoil came to England when a period of civil wars broke out in the 1450s. These wars pitted the ducal house of Lancaster against the ducal house of York. (The wars are popularly known as the "Wars of the Roses" because Shakespeare a hundred years later created the fiction that a white rose symbolized the Yorkists and a red rose, the Lancasters.) Many aristocratic families of England were drawn into the conflict. Finally, in 1485, Henry Tudor, duke of Richmond, defeated the last Yorkist king, Richard III (1483–1485), at Bosworth Field and established the new Tudor dynasty.

As the first Tudor king, Henry VII (1485–1509) worked to reduce internal dissension and establish a strong monarchical government. Henry ended the private wars of the nobility by abolishing "livery and maintenance," the practice by which wealthy aristocrats maintained private armies of followers dedicated to the service of their lord. Since England, unlike France and Spain, did not possess a standing army, the king relied on special commissions to trusted nobles to raise troops for a specific campaign, after which the troops were disbanded. Henry also controlled the irresponsible activity of the nobles by establishing the Court of Star Chamber, which did not use juries and allowed torture to be used to extract confessions.

Henry VII was particularly successful in extracting income from the traditional financial resources of the English monarch, such as the crown lands, judicial fees and fines, and customs duties. By using diplomacy to avoid wars, which are always expensive, the king avoided having to call Parliament on any regular basis to grant him funds. By not overburdening the landed gentry and middle class with taxes, Henry won their favor, and they provided much support for his monarchy. Henry's policies enabled him to leave England with a stable and prosperous government and an enhanced status for the monarchy itself.

The Unification of Spain   During the Middle Ages, several independent Christian kingdoms had emerged in the course of the long reconquest of the Iberian peninsula from the Muslims. Aragon and Castile were the strongest Spanish kingdoms; in the west was the independent monarchy of Portugal; in the north, the small kingdom of Navarre, oriented toward France; and in the south, the Muslim kingdom of Granada (see Map 12.3). Few people at the beginning of the fifteenth century could have predicted the unification of the Iberian kingdoms.

A major step in that direction was taken with the marriage of Isabella of Castile (1474–1504) and Ferdinand of Aragon (1479–1516) in 1469. This was a dynastic

MAP 12.3 The Iberian Peninsula

The marriage of Isabella of Castile to Ferdinand of Aragon laid the foundation for the unification of Spain and its rise as a major European power. The two monarchs instituted military and bureaucratic reforms and forced Jews and Muslims to flee the country.

union of two rulers, not a political union. Both kingdoms maintained their own parliaments (Cortes), courts, laws, coinage, speech, customs, and political organs. Nevertheless, the two rulers worked to strengthen royal control of government, especially in Castile. The royal council, which was supposed to supervise local administration and oversee the implementation of government policies, was stripped of aristocrats and filled primarily with middle-class lawyers. Trained in the principles of Roman law, these officials operated on the belief that the monarchy embodied the power of the state.

Seeking to replace the undisciplined feudal levies they had inherited with a more professional royal army, Ferdinand and Isabella reorganized the military forces of Spain. The development of a strong infantry force as the heart of the new Spanish army made it the best in Europe by the sixteenth century.

Because of its vast power and wealth, Ferdinand and Isabella recognized the importance of controlling the Catholic Church. They secured from the pope the right to select the most important church officials in Spain, virtually guaranteeing the creation of a Spanish Catholic Church in which the clergy became an instrument for the extension of royal power. The monarchs also used their authority over the church to institute reform. Isabella's chief minister, the able and astute Cardinal Ximenes (khee-MAY-ness), restored discipline and eliminated immorality among the monks and secular clergy.

The religious zeal exhibited in Cardinal Ximenes's reform program was also evident in the policy of strict religious uniformity pursued by Ferdinand and Isabella. Of course, it served a political purpose as well: to create unity and further bolster royal power. Spain possessed two large religious minorities, the Jews and Muslims, both of which had generally been tolerated in medieval Spain. Although anti-Semitism had become a fact of life in medieval Europe, Spain had largely remained tolerant. In some areas of Spain, Jews exercised much influence in economic and intellectual affairs. During the fourteenth century, however, increased persecution led the majority of Spanish Jews to convert to Christianity. Although many of these converted Jews came to play important roles in Spanish society, complaints that they were secretly reverting to Judaism prompted Ferdinand and Isabella to ask the pope to introduce the Inquisition into Spain in 1478. Under royal control, the Inquisition worked with cruel efficiency to guarantee the orthodoxy of the converts but had no authority over practicing Jews. Consequently, in 1492, flush with the success of their conquest of Muslim Granada, Ferdinand and Isabella took the drastic step of expelling all professed Jews from Spain. It is estimated that 150,000 out of possibly 200,000 Jews fled.

Ferdinand and Isabella also pursued a policy of battling the Muslims by attacking the kingdom of Granada. The war against this remaining Muslim kingdom lasted eleven years until the final bastion of the city of Granada fell in 1492. Muslims were now "encouraged" to convert to Christianity, and in 1502 Isabella issued a decree expelling all professed Muslims from her kingdom. To a very large degree, the "Most Catholic" monarchs had achieved their goal of absolute religious orthodoxy as a basic ingredient of the Spanish state. To be Spanish was to be Catholic, a policy of uniformity enforced by the Inquisition. It was no accident that Spain became a staunch pillar of the Catholic Church during the era of the Reformation in the sixteenth century (see Chapter 13).

The Holy Roman Empire: The Success of the Habsburgs   Unlike France, England, and Spain, the Holy Roman Empire failed to develop a strong monarchical authority. After 1438, the position of Holy Roman Emperor remained in the hands of the Habsburg dynasty. Having gradually acquired a number of possessions along the Danube, known collectively as Austria, the house of Habsburg had become one of the wealthiest landholders in the empire and by the mid-fifteenth century began to play an important role in European affairs.

Much of the Habsburg success in the fifteenth century was due not to military success but to a well-executed policy of dynastic marriages. As the old Habsburg motto said, "Leave the waging of wars to others! But you, happy Austria, marry; for the realms which Mars [god of war] awards to others, Venus [goddess of love] transfers to you." By marrying his son Maximilian to Mary, the daughter of Duke Charles the Bold of Burgundy, Emperor Frederick III (1440–1493) gained Franche-Comté in east-central France, Luxembourg, and a large part of the Low Countries. The addition of these territories made the Habsburg dynasty an international power and brought it the undying opposition of the French monarchy because the rulers of France feared they would be surrounded by the Habsburgs.

Much was expected of the flamboyant Maximilian I (1493–1519) when he became emperor. Through the Reichstag, the imperial diet or parliament, Maximilian attempted to centralize the administration by creating new institutions common to the entire empire. Opposition from the German princes doomed these efforts, however. Maximilian's only real success lay in his marriage alliances. Philip of Burgundy, the son of Maximilian's marriage to Mary, was married to Joanna, the daughter of Ferdinand and Isabella. Philip and Joanna produced a son, Charles, who, through a series of unexpected deaths, became heir to all three lines, the Habsburg, Burgundian, and Spanish, making him the leading monarch of his age (see Chapter 13).

The Struggle for Strong Monarchy in Eastern Europe   In eastern Europe, rulers struggled to achieve the centralization of their territorial states but faced serious obstacles. Although the population was mostly Slavic, there were islands of other ethnic groups that caused untold difficulties. Religious differences also troubled the area, as Roman Catholics, Greek Orthodox Christians, and pagans confronted each other.

Much of Polish history revolved around a bitter struggle between the crown and the landed nobility until the end of the fifteenth century, when the preoccupation of Poland's rulers with problems in Bohemia and Hungary, as well as war with the Russians and Turks, enabled the aristocrats to reestablish their power. Through their control of the Sejm (SAYM) or national diet, the magnates reduced the peasantry to serfdom by 1511 and established the right to elect their kings. The Polish kings proved unable to establish a strong royal authority.

Bohemia, Poland's neighbor, was part of the Holy Roman Empire, but distrust of the Germans and close ethnic ties to the Poles and Slovaks encouraged the Czechs of Bohemia to associate with their northeastern Slavic neighbors. The Hussite wars (see "The Problems of Heresy and Reform" later in this chapter) led to further dissension and civil war. Because of a weak monarchy, the Bohemian nobles increased their authority and wealth at the expense of both crown and church.

The history of Hungary had been closely tied to that of central and western Europe by its conversion to Roman Catholicism by German missionaries. The church became a large and prosperous institution. Wealthy bishops, along with the great territorial lords, became powerful, independent political figures. For a brief while, Hungary developed into an important European state, the dominant power in eastern Europe. King Matthias Corvinus (muh-THY-uss kor-VY-nuss) (1458–1490) broke the power of the wealthy lords and created a well-organized bureaucracy. Like a typical Renaissance prince, he patronized the new humanist culture, brought Italian scholars and artists to his capital at Buda, and made his court one of the most brilliant outside Italy. After his death, however, Hungary returned to weak rule, and the work of Corvinus was largely undone.

Since the thirteenth century, Russia had been under the domination of the Mongols. Gradually, the princes of Moscow rose to prominence by using their close relationship to the Mongol khans to increase their wealth and expand their possessions. In the reign of the great prince Ivan III (1462–1505), a new Russian state—the principality of Moscow—was born. Ivan III annexed other Russian principalities and took advantage of dissension among the Mongols to throw off their yoke by 1480.

MAP 12.4   The Ottoman Empire and Southeastern Europe

Long a buffer between Christian Europe and the Muslim Middle East, the Byzantine Empire quickly waned in power and territory after Constantinople was sacked by crusaders in 1204. The Ottoman Turks slowly gained Byzantine territory and ended the thousand-year reign with the fall of Constantinople in 1453.

The Ottoman Turks and the End of the Byzantine Empire

Eastern Europe was increasingly threatened by the steadily advancing Ottoman Turks (see Map 12.4). The Byzantine Empire had, of course, served as a buffer between the Muslim Middle East and the Latin West for centuries, but it had been severely weakened by the sack of Constantinople in 1204 and its occupation by the West. Although the Palaeologus dynasty (1260–1453) had tried to reestablish Byzantine power in the Balkans after the overthrow of the Latin empire, the threat from the Turks finally doomed the long-lasting empire.

Beginning in northeastern Asia Minor in the thirteenth century, the Ottoman Turks spread rapidly, seizing the lands of the Seljuk Turks and the Byzantine Empire. In 1345, they bypassed Constantinople and moved into the Balkans. Under Sultan Murad (moo-RAHD), Ottoman forces moved through Bulgaria and into the lands of the Serbs, who provided a strong center of opposition under King Lazar (lah-ZAR). But in 1389, at the Battle of Kosovo (KAWSS-suh-voh), Ottoman forces defeated the Serbs; both King Lazar and Sultan Murad perished in the battle. Kosovo became a battlefield long revered and remembered by the Serbs. Not until 1480 were Bosnia, Albania, and the rest of Serbia added to the Ottoman Empire in the Balkans.

In the meantime, in 1453, the Ottomans completed the demise of the Byzantine Empire. With 80,000 troops ranged against only 7,000 defenders, Sultan Mehmet II (meh-MET) laid siege to Constantinople. In their attack on the city, the Turks made use of massive cannons with 26-foot barrels that could launch stone balls weighing up to 1,200 pounds each. Finally, the walls were breached; the Byzantine emperor died in the final battle. Mehmet II, standing before the palace of the emperor, paused to reflect on the passing nature of human glory.

After their conquest of Constantinople, the Ottoman Turks tried to complete their conquest of the Balkans, where they had been established since the fourteenth century. Although they were successful in taking the Romanian territory of Wallachia (wah-LAY-kee-uh) in 1476, the resistance of the Hungarians initially kept the Turks from advancing up the Danube valley. Until the end of the fifteenth century, internal problems and the need to consolidate their eastern frontiers kept the Turks from any further attacks on Europe. But at the beginning of the sixteenth century, the Ottomans would renew their offensive against the West, challenging Hungary, Austria, Bohemia, and Poland and threatening to turn the Mediterranean into a Turkish lake.

THE CHURCH IN THE RENAISSANCE

As a result of the efforts of the Council of Constance, the Great Schism had finally been brought to an end in 1417 (see Chapter 11). The ending of the schism proved to be the council's easiest task; it was much less successful in dealing with the problems of heresy and reform.

The Problems of Heresy and Reform Heresy was not a new problem, and in the thirteenth century, the church had developed inquisitorial machinery to deal with it. But two widespread movements in the fourteenth and early fifteenth centuries—Lollardy and Hussitism—posed new threats to the church.

Wyclif and Lollardy   English Lollardy was a product of the Oxford theologian John Wyclif (WIK-lif) (c. 1328–1384), whose disgust with clerical corruption led him to make a far-ranging attack on papal authority and medieval Christian beliefs and practices. Wyclif alleged that there was no basis in Scripture for papal claims of temporal authority and advocated that the popes be stripped of their authority and their property. Believing that the Bible should be a Christian's sole authority, Wyclif urged that it be made available in the vernacular languages so that every Christian could read it. Rejecting all practices not mentioned in Scripture, Wyclif condemned pilgrimages, the veneration of saints, and a whole series of rituals and rites that had developed in the medieval church. Wyclif attracted a number of followers who came to be known as Lollards.

Hus and the Hussites   A marriage between the royal families of England and Bohemia enabled Lollard ideas to spread to Bohemia, where they reinforced the ideas of a group of Czech reformers led by the chancellor of the university at Prague, John Hus (1374–1415). In his call for reform, Hus urged the elimination of the worldliness and corruption of the clergy and attacked the excessive power of the papacy within the Catholic Church. Hus's objections fell on receptive ears, for the Catholic Church, as one of the largest landowners in Bohemia, was already widely criticized. Moreover, many clergymen were German, and the native Czechs' strong resentment of the Germans who dominated Bohemia also contributed to Hus's movement.

The Council of Constance attempted to deal with the growing problem of heresy by summoning John Hus to the council. Granted safe conduct by Emperor Sigismund, Hus went in the hope of a free hearing of his ideas. Instead he was arrested, condemned as a heretic (by a narrow vote), and burned at the stake in 1415. This action turned the unrest in Bohemia into revolutionary upheaval, and the resulting Hussite wars racked the Holy Roman Empire until a truce was arranged in 1436.

Reform of the Church   The efforts of the Council of Constance to reform the church were even less successful than its attempt to eradicate heresy. The council passed two reform decrees. *Sacrosancta* (sak-roh-SANK-tuh) stated that a general council of the church received its authority from God; hence, every Christian, including the pope, was subject to its authority. The decree *Frequens* (FREE-kwens) provided for the regular holding of general councils to ensure that church reform would continue. Taken together, *Sacrosancta* and *Frequens* provided for a legislative system within the church superior to the popes.

Decrees alone, however, proved insufficient to reform the church. Councils could issue decrees, but popes had to execute them, and popes would not cooperate with councils that diminished their authority. Beginning as early as Martin V in 1417, successive popes worked steadfastly for thirty years to defeat the conciliar movement. The final blow came in 1460, when Pope Pius II issued the papal bull *Execrabilis* (ek-suh-KRAB-uh-liss), condemning appeals to a council over the head of a pope as heretical.

By the mid-fifteenth century, the popes had reasserted their supremacy over the Catholic Church. No longer, however, did they have any possibility of asserting supremacy over temporal governments as the medieval papacy had. Although the papal monarchy had been maintained, it had lost much moral prestige. In the fifteenth century, the Renaissance papacy contributed to an even further decline in the moral leadership of the popes.

The Renaissance Papacy   The Renaissance papacy encompasses the line of popes from the end of the Great Schism (1417) to the beginnings of the Reformation in the early sixteenth century. The primary concern of the papacy is governing the Catholic Church as its spiritual leader. But as heads of the church, popes had temporal preoccupations as well, and the story of the Renaissance papacy is really an account of how the latter came to overshadow the popes' spiritual functions.

The manner in which Renaissance popes pursued their interests in the Papal States and Italian politics, especially their use of intrigue and even bloodshed, seemed shocking. Of all the Renaissance popes, Julius II (1503–1513) was most involved in war and politics. The fiery "warrior-pope" personally led armies against his enemies, much to the disgust of pious Christians, who viewed the pope as a spiritual leader. As one intellectual wrote, "How, O bishop standing in the room of the Apostles, dare you teach the people the things that pertain to war?"

To further their territorial aims in the Papal States, the popes needed loyal servants. Because they were not hereditary monarchs, popes could not build dynasties over several generations and came to rely on the practice of **nepotism** to promote their families' interests. Pope Sixtus IV (1471–1484), for example, made five of his nephews cardinals and gave them an abundance of church offices to build up their finances (the word *nepotism* is in fact derived from the Latin *nepos*, meaning "nephew"). Alexander VI (1492–1503), a member of the Borgia family who was known for his debauchery and sensuality, raised one son, one nephew, and the brother of one mistress to the cardinalate. A Venetian envoy stated that Alexander, "joyous by nature, thought of nothing but the aggrandizement of his children." Alexander scandalized the church by encouraging his son Cesare to carve out a state for himself from the territories of the Papal States in central Italy.

The Renaissance popes were great patrons of Renaissance culture, and their efforts made Rome a cultural leader at the beginning of the sixteenth century. For the warrior-pope Julius II, the patronage of Renaissance culture was mostly a matter of policy as he endeavored to add to the splendor of his pontificate by tearing down the Basilica of Saint Peter, which had been built by the emperor Constantine, and beginning construction of the greatest building in Christendom, the present Saint Peter's Basilica.

Julius's successor, Leo X (1513–1521), was also a patron of Renaissance culture, not as a matter of policy but as a deeply involved participant. Such might be expected of the son of Lorenzo de' Medici. Made an archbishop at the age of eight and a cardinal at thirteen, he acquired a refined taste in art, manners, and social life among the Florentine Renaissance elite. He became pope at the age of thirty-seven, reportedly remarking to the Venetian ambassador, "Let us enjoy the papacy, since God has given it to us." Raphael was commissioned to do paintings, and the construction of Saint Peter's was accelerated as Rome became the literary and artistic center of the Renaissance.

CHRONOLOGIES

THE ITALIAN STATES IN THE RENAISSANCE

1311–1447	The Viscontis (Duchy of Milan)
1450–1494	The Sforzas (Duchy of Milan)
1434–1464	Cosimo de' Medici (Florence)
1469–1492	Lorenzo de' Medici (Florence)
1494	Beginning of Italian wars—French invasion of Italy
1527	Sack of Rome

EUROPE IN THE RENAISSANCE

France
1461–1483	Louis XI the Spider

England
1450s–1485	War of the Roses
1485–1509	Henry VII

Spain
1469	Marriage of Ferdinand and Isabella

Holy Roman Empire
1440–1493	Frederick III
1493–1519	Maximilian I

Eastern Europe
1462–1505	Russia: Ivan III
1453	Fall of Constantinople and Byzantine Empire

THE CHURCH IN THE RENAISSANCE

1492–1503	Pope Alexander VI
1503–1513	Pope Julius II
1513–1521	Pope Leo X

13

REFORMATION AND RELIGIOUS WARFARE IN THE SIXTEENTH CENTURY

A nineteenth-century engraving showing Luther before the Diet of Worms

CHAPTER OUTLINE

• Prelude to Reformation • Martin Luther and the Reformation in Germany • The Spread of the Protestant Reformation • The Social Impact of the Protestant Reformation • The Catholic Reformation • Politics and the Wars of Religion in the Sixteenth Century

PRELUDE TO REFORMATION

Martin Luther's reform movement was by no means the first. During the second half of the fifteenth century, the new Classical learning that was part of Italian Renaissance humanism spread to northern Europe and spawned a movement called **Christian** or **northern Renaissance humanism** whose major goal was the reform of Christianity.

Christian or Northern Renaissance Humanism   Like their Italian counterparts, northern humanists cultivated a knowledge of the classics, the bond that united all humanists into a kind of international fellowship. In returning to the writings of antiquity, northern humanists (also called Christian humanists because of their profound preoccupation with religion) focused on the sources of early Christianity, the Holy Scriptures and the writings of such church fathers as Augustine, Ambrose, and Jerome. In these early Christian writings, they discovered a simple religion that they came to feel had been distorted by the complicated theological arguments of the Middle Ages.

The most important characteristic of northern humanism was its reform program. Convinced of the ability of human beings to reason and improve themselves, the northern humanists felt that through education in the sources of Classical, and especially Christian, antiquity, they could instill a true inner piety or an inward religious feeling that would bring about a reform of the church and society. For this reason, Christian humanists supported schools, brought out new editions of the classics, and prepared new editions of the Bible and writings of the church fathers. In the preface to his edition of the Greek New Testament, the famous humanist Erasmus wrote:

> I disagree very much with those who are unwilling that Holy Scripture, translated into the vulgar tongue, be read by the uneducated, as if Christ taught such intricate doctrines that they could scarcely be understood by very few theologians, or as if the strength of the Christian religion consisted in men's ignorance of it.... I would that even the lowliest women read the Gospels and the Pauline Epistles. And I would that they were translated into all languages so that they could be read and understood not only by Scots and Irish but also by Turks and Saracens.... Would that, as a result, the farmer sing some portion of them at the plow, the weaver hum some parts of them to the movement of his shuttle, the traveler lighten the weariness of the journey with stories of this kind![1]

This belief in the power of education would remain an important characteristic of European civilization. Like later intellectuals, Christian humanists believed that to change society, they must first change the human beings who compose it. Although some critics have called the Christian humanists naive, they were in fact merely optimistic. The turmoil of the Reformation, however, shattered much of this intellectual optimism, as the lives and careers of two of the most prominent Christian humanists, Desiderius Erasmus and Thomas More, illustrate.

Erasmus   The most influential of all the Christian humanists was Desiderius Erasmus (dez-ih-DEER-ee-uss ih-RAZZ-mus) (1466–1536), who formulated and popularized the reform program of Christian humanism. Born in Holland, Erasmus was educated at one of the schools of the Brothers of the Common Life (see Chapter 11). He wandered to France, England, Italy, Germany, and Switzerland, conversing everywhere in the Classical Latin that might be called his mother tongue. The *Handbook of the Christian Knight*, printed in 1503, reflected his preoccupation with religion. He called his conception of religion "the philosophy of Christ," by which he meant that Christianity should be a guiding philosophy for the direction of daily life rather than the system of dogmatic beliefs and practices that the medieval church seemed to stress. In other words, he emphasized inner piety and de-emphasized the external forms of religion (such as the sacraments, pilgrimages, fasts, veneration of saints, and relics). To return to the simplicity of the early church, people needed to understand the original meaning of the Scriptures and the writings of the early church fathers. Because Erasmus thought that the standard Latin edition of the Bible, known as the Vulgate, contained errors, he edited the Greek text of the New Testament from the earliest available manuscripts and published it, along with a new Latin translation, in 1516. Erasmus also wrote *Annotations*, a detailed commentary on the Vulgate Bible itself. In his day, Erasmus's work on the New Testament was considered his most outstanding achievement, and Martin Luther himself would use Erasmus's work as the basis for his German translation of the New Testament.

To Erasmus, the reform of the church meant spreading an understanding of the philosophy of Jesus, providing enlightened education in the sources of early Christianity, and making common-sense criticisms of the abuses in the church. This last is especially evident in *The Praise of Folly*, written in 1509, in which Erasmus engaged in humorous yet effective criticism of the most corrupt practices of his own society. He was especially harsh on the abuses within the ranks of the clergy.

Erasmus's program did not achieve the reform of the church that he so desired. His moderation and his emphasis on education were quickly overwhelmed by the passions of the Reformation. Undoubtedly, though, his work helped prepare the way for the Reformation; as contemporaries proclaimed, "Erasmus laid the egg that Luther hatched." Yet Erasmus eventually disapproved of Luther and the Protestant reformers. He had no intention of destroying the unity of the medieval Christian church; rather, his whole program was based on reform within the church.

Thomas More   The son of a London lawyer, Thomas More (1478–1535) received the benefits of a good education. Although trained in the law, he took an avid interest in the new Classical learning and became proficient in both Latin and Greek. Like the Italian humanists, who believed in putting their learning at the service of the state, More embarked on a public career that ultimately took him to the highest reaches of power as lord chancellor of England.

His career in government service, however, did not keep More from the intellectual and spiritual interests that were so dear to him. He was well acquainted with other English humanists and became an intimate friend of Erasmus. He made translations from Greek authors and wrote both prose and poetry in Latin. A devout man, he spent many hours in prayer and private devotions. Contemporaries praised his household as a shining model of Christian family life.

More's most famous work, and one of the most controversial of his age, was *Utopia*, written in 1516. This literary masterpiece is an account of the idealistic life and institutions of the community of Utopia (Greek for "nowhere"), an imaginary island in the vicinity of the recently discovered New World. It reflects More's own concerns with the economic, social, and political problems of his day. He presented a new social system in which cooperation and reason replaced power and fame as the proper motivating agents for human society. Utopian society, therefore, was based on communal ownership rather than private property. All residents of Utopia worked nine hours a day, regardless of occupation, and were rewarded according to their needs. Possessing abundant leisure time and relieved of competition and greed, Utopians were free to lead wholesome and enriching lives.

In serving King Henry VIII, More came face to face with the abuses and corruption he had criticized in *Utopia*. But he did not allow idealism to outweigh his own ultimate realism, and in *Utopia* itself he justified his service to the king:

> If you can't completely eradicate wrong ideas, or deal with inveterate vices as effectively as you could wish, that's no reason for turning your back on public life altogether.... On the other hand, it's no use attempting to put across entirely new ideas, which will obviously carry no weight with people who are prejudiced against them. You must go to work indirectly. You must handle everything as tactfully as you can, and what you can't put right you must try to make as little wrong as possible. For things will never be perfect, until human beings are perfect—which I don't expect them to be for quite a number of years.[2]

More's religious devotion and belief in the universal Catholic Church ultimately proved even more important than his service to the king, however. While in office, More's intolerance of heresy led him to advocate persecution of those who would fundamentally change the Catholic Church. Moreover, always the man of conscience, More willingly gave up his life opposing England's break with the Roman Catholic Church over the divorce of King Henry VIII.

Church and Religion on the Eve of the Reformation   Corruption in the Catholic Church was another factor that spurred people to want reform. No doubt the failure of the Renaissance popes to provide spiritual leadership had affected the spiritual life of all Christendom. The papal court's preoccupation with finances had an especially strong impact on the clergy. So did the economic changes of the fourteenth and fifteenth centuries. Increasingly, nobles or wealthy members of the bourgeoisie held the highest positions among the clergy. Moreover, to increase their revenues, high church officials (bishops, archbishops, and cardinals) took over more than one church office. This so-called **pluralism** led in turn to absenteeism: church officeholders ignored their duties and hired underlings who sometimes lacked the proper qualifications. Complaints about the ignorance and ineptness of parish priests became widespread in the fifteenth century.

The Search for Salvation   While many of the leaders of the church were failing to meet their responsibilities, ordinary people were clamoring for meaningful religious expression and certainty of salvation. As a result, for some the salvation process became almost mechanical. As more and more people sought certainty of salvation through veneration of relics, collections of such objects grew. Frederick the Wise, elector of Saxony and Martin Luther's prince, had amassed more than 19,000 relics to which were attached indulgences that could reduce one's time in purgatory by nearly 2 million years. (An indulgence, you will recall, is a remission, after death, of all or part of the punishment for sin.) Other people sought certainty of salvation in the popular mystical movement known as the Modern Devotion, which downplayed religious dogma and stressed the need to follow the teachings of Jesus. Thomas à Kempis, author of *The Imitation of Christ*, wrote that "truly, at the day of judgment we shall not be examined by what we have read, but what we have done; not how well we have spoken, but how religiously we have lived."

What is striking about the revival of religious piety in the fifteenth century— whether expressed through such external forces as the veneration of relics and the buying of indulgences or the mystical path—was its adherence to the orthodox beliefs and practices of the Catholic Church. The agitation for certainty of salvation and spiritual peace occurred within the framework of the "holy mother Church." But disillusionment grew as the devout experienced the clergy's inability to live up to their expectations. The deepening of religious life, especially in the second half of the fifteenth century, found little echo among the worldly-wise clergy, and this environment helps explain the tremendous and immediate impact of Luther's ideas.

Calls for Reform   At the same time, several sources of reform were already at work within the Catholic Church at the end of the fifteenth and the beginning of the sixteenth century. Especially noticeable were the calls for reform from the religious orders of the Franciscans, Dominicans, and Augustinians. Members of these groups put particular emphasis on preaching to laypeople. One of the popular preachers was Johannes Geiler of Kaisersberg (KY-zerz-bayrk), who denounced the corruption of the clergy.

The Oratory of Divine Love, first organized in Italy in 1497, was not a religious order but an informal group of clergy and laymen who worked to foster reform by emphasizing personal spiritual development and outward acts of charity. The "philosophy of Christ," advocated by the Christian humanist Erasmus, was especially appealing to many of them. The Oratory's members included a number of cardinals who favored church reform. A Spanish archbishop, Cardinal Ximenes, was especially active in using Christian humanism to reform the church. To foster spirituality among the people, he had a number of religious writings, including Thomas à Kempis's *The Imitation of Christ*, translated into Spanish.

MARTIN LUTHER AND THE REFORMATION IN GERMANY

The Protestant Reformation began with a typical medieval question: What must I do to be saved? Martin Luther, a deeply religious man, found an answer that did not fit within the traditional teachings of the late medieval church. Ultimately, he split with that church, destroying the religious unity of western Christendom. That other people were concerned with the same question is evident in the rapid spread of the Reformation. But religion was so entangled in the social, economic, and political forces of the period that the Protestant reformers' hope of transforming the church quickly proved illusory.

The Early Luther   Martin Luther was born in Germany on November 10, 1483. His father wanted him to become a lawyer, so Luther enrolled at the University of Erfurt, where he received his bachelor's degree in 1502. Three years later, after becoming a master in the liberal arts, the young man began to study law. But Luther was not content, not in small part due to his long-standing religious inclinations. That summer, while returning to Erfurt after a brief visit home, he was caught in a ferocious thunderstorm and vowed that if he survived unscathed, he would become a monk. He then entered the monastic order of the Augustinian Hermits in Erfurt, much to his father's disgust. In the monastery, Luther focused on his major concern, the assurance of salvation. The traditional beliefs and practices of the church seemed unable to relieve his obsession with this question, especially evident in his struggle with the sacrament of penance or **confession**. The sacraments were a Catholic's chief means of receiving God's grace; confession offered the opportunity to have one's sins forgiven. Luther spent hours confessing his sins, but he was always doubtful. Had he remembered all of his sins? Even more, how could a hopeless sinner be acceptable to a totally just and all-powerful God? Luther threw himself into his monastic routine with a vengeance:

> I was indeed a good monk and kept my order so strictly that I could say that if ever a monk could get to heaven through monastic discipline, I was that monk.... And yet my conscience would not give me certainty, but I always doubted and said, "You didn't do that right. You weren't contrite enough. You left that out of your confession." The more I tried to remedy an uncertain, weak and troubled conscience with human traditions, the more I daily found it more uncertain, weaker and more troubled.[3]

Despite his strenuous efforts, Luther achieved no certainty.

To help overcome his difficulties, his superiors recommended that the monk study theology. He received his doctorate in 1512 and then became a professor in the theological faculty at the University of Wittenberg (VIT-ten-bayrk), lecturing on the Bible. Sometime between 1513 and 1516, through his study of the Bible, he arrived at an answer to his problem.

Catholic doctrine had emphasized that both faith and good works were required for a Christian to achieve personal salvation. In Luther's eyes, human beings, weak and powerless in the sight of an almighty God, could never do enough good works to merit salvation. Through his study of the Bible, especially his work on Paul's Epistle to the Romans, Luther rediscovered another way of viewing this problem. To Luther, humans are saved not through their good works but through faith in the promises of God, made possible by the sacrifice of Jesus on the cross. The doctrine of salvation or justification by grace through faith alone became the primary doctrine of the Protestant Reformation (**justification** is the act by which a person is made deserving of salvation). Because Luther had arrived at this doctrine from his study of the Bible, the Bible became for Luther, as for all other Protestants, the chief guide to religious truth. Justification by faith and the Bible as the sole authority in religious affairs were the twin pillars of the Protestant Reformation.

The Indulgence Controversy   Luther did not see himself as either an innovator or a heretic, but his involvement in the indulgence controversy propelled him into an open confrontation with church officials and forced him to see the theological implications of justification by faith alone. In 1517, Pope Leo X had issued a special jubilee indulgence to finance the ongoing construction of Saint Peter's Basilica in Rome. Johann Tetzel, a rambunctious Dominican, hawked the indulgences in Germany with the slogan "As soon as the coin in the coffer rings, the soul from purgatory springs."

Luther was greatly distressed by the sale of indulgences, certain that people who relied on these pieces of paper to assure themselves of salvation were guaranteeing their eternal damnation instead. Angered, he issued his Ninety-Five Theses, although scholars are unsure whether he nailed them to a church door in Wittenberg, as is traditionally alleged, or mailed them to his ecclesiastical superior. In either case, his theses were a stunning indictment of the abuses in the sale of indulgences. It is doubtful that Luther intended any break with the church over the issue of indulgences. If the pope had clarified the use of indulgences, as Luther wished, he would probably have been satisfied, and the controversy would have ended. But Pope Leo X did not take the issue seriously and is even reported to have said that Luther was simply "some drunken German who will amend his ways when he sobers up." Thousands of copies of a German translation of the Ninety-Five Theses were quickly printed and were received sympathetically in a Germany that had a long tradition of dissatisfaction with papal policies and power.

Of course, Luther was not the first theologian to criticize the powers of the papacy. As we saw in Chapter 12, John Wyclif at the end of the fourteenth century and John Hus at the beginning of the fifteenth century had attacked the excessive power of the papacy. Luther was certainly well aware of John Hus's fate at the Council of Constance, where he was burned at the stake on charges of heresy.

The Quickening Rebellion   The controversy reached an important turning point with the Leipzig Debate in July 1519. In Leipzig, Luther's opponent, the capable Catholic theologian Johann Eck, forced Luther to move beyond indulgences and deny the authority of popes and councils. During the debate, Eck also identified Luther's ideas with those of John Hus, the condemned heretic. Luther was now compelled to see the consequences of his new theology. At the beginning of 1520, he proclaimed: "Farewell, unhappy, hopeless, blasphemous Rome! The Wrath of God has come upon you, as you deserve. We have cared for Babylon, and she is not healed: let us then, leave her, that she may be the habitation of dragons, spectres, and witches."[4] At the same time, Luther was convinced that he was doing God's work and had to proceed regardless of the consequences.

In three pamphlets published in 1520, Luther moved toward a more definite break with the Catholic Church. The *Address to the Nobility of the German*

Nation was a political tract written in German in which Luther called on the German princes to overthrow the papacy in Germany and establish a reformed German church. The *Babylonian Captivity of the Church*, written in Latin for theologians, attacked the sacramental system as the means by which the pope and church had held the real meaning of the Gospel captive for a thousand years. Luther called for the reform of monasticism and for the clergy to marry. Though virginity is good, he argued, marriage is better, and freedom of choice is best. *On the Freedom of a Christian Man* was a short treatise on the doctrine of salvation. It is faith alone, not good works, that justifies, frees, and brings salvation through Jesus. Being saved and freed by his faith in Jesus, however, does not free the Christian from doing good works. Rather, he performs good works out of gratitude to God. "Good works do not make a good man, but a good man does good works."[5]

Unable to accept Luther's forcefully worded dissent from traditional Catholic teachings, the church excommunicated him in January 1521. He was also summoned to appear before the Reichstag (RYKHSS-tahk), the imperial diet of the Holy Roman Empire, in Worms (WURMZ *or* VORMPS), convened by the recently elected Emperor Charles V (1519–1556). Expected to recant the heretical doctrines he had espoused, Luther refused and made the famous reply that became the battle cry of the Reformation:

> Since then Your Majesty and your lordships desire a simple reply, I will answer without horns and without teeth. Unless I am convicted by Scripture and plain reason— I do not accept the authority of popes and councils, for they have contradicted each other—my conscience is captive to the Word of God. I cannot and I will not recant anything, for to go against conscience is neither right nor safe. Here I stand, I cannot do otherwise. God help me. Amen.[6]

Emperor Charles was outraged at Luther's audacity and gave his opinion that "a single friar who goes counter to all Christianity for a thousand years must be wrong." By the Edict of Worms, Martin Luther was made an outlaw within the empire. His works were to be burned, and Luther himself was to be captured and delivered to the emperor. Instead, Luther's prince, the Elector of Saxony, sent him into hiding at the Wartburg (VART-bayrk) Castle, where he remained for nearly a year.

The Rise of Lutheranism   At the beginning of 1522, Luther returned to Wittenberg in Electoral Saxony and began to organize a reformed church. While at the Wartburg Castle, Luther's foremost achievement was his translation of the New Testament into German. Within twelve years, his German New Testament had sold almost 200,000 copies. Lutheranism had wide appeal and spread rapidly, but not primarily through the written word since only 4 to 5 percent of people in Germany were literate. And most of these were in urban areas.

Instead, the primary means of disseminating Luther's ideas was the sermon. The preaching of evangelical sermons, based on a return to the original message of the Bible, found favor throughout Germany. In city after city, the arrival of preachers presenting Luther's teachings was soon followed by a public debate in which the churches in Germany (and later in Scandinavia) quickly became territorial or state churches in which the state supervised and disciplined church members.

As part of the development of these state-dominated churches, Luther also instituted new religious services to replace the Mass. These featured a worship service consisting of a vernacular liturgy that focused on Bible reading, preaching the word of God, and song. Following his own denunciation of clerical celibacy, Luther married a former nun, Katherina von Bora (kat-uh-REE-nuh fun BOH-rah), in 1525. His union provided a model of married and family life for the new Protestant minister.

Germany and the Reformation: Religion and Politics From its very beginning, the fate of Luther's movement was closely tied to political affairs. In 1519, Charles I, king of Spain and grandson of Emperor Maximilian (see Chart 13.1), was elected Holy Roman Emperor as Charles V. Charles ruled over an immense empire, consisting of Spain and its overseas possessions, the traditional Austrian Habsburg lands, Bohemia, Hungary, the Low Countries, and the kingdom of Naples in southern Italy (see Map 13.1). The extent of his possessions was reflected in the languages he used: "I speak Spanish to God, Italian to women, French to men, and German to my horse." Politically, Charles wanted to maintain his dynasty's control over his enormous empire; religiously, he hoped to preserve the unity of the Catholic faith throughout his empire. Despite Charles's strengths, his empire was overextended, and he spent a lifetime in futile pursuit of his goals. Four major problems—the French, the papacy, the Turks, and Germany's internal situation—cost him both his dream and his health. At the same time, the emperor's problems gave Luther's movement time to grow and organize before facing the concerted onslaught of the Catholic forces.

CHART 13.1 The Habsburgs as Holy Roman Emperors and Kings of Spain

MAP 13.1 The Empire of Charles V

Charles V spent much of his reign fighting wars in Italy, against France and the Ottoman Empire, and within the borders of the Holy Roman Empire. He failed in his main goal to secure Europe for Catholicism: the 1555 Peace of Augsburg recognized the equality of Catholicism and Lutheranism and let each German prince choose his realm's religion.

The French and the Papacy   Charles V's chief political concern was his rivalry with the Valois king of France, Francis I (1515–1547). Encircled by the possessions of the Habsburg empire, Francis became embroiled in a series of conflicts with Charles over disputed territories in southern France, the Netherlands, the Rhineland, northern Spain, and Italy. These conflicts, known as the Habsburg-Valois Wars, were fought intermittently for twenty-four years (1521–1544), preventing Charles from concentrating on the Lutheran problem in Germany.

Meanwhile, Charles faced two other enemies. The Habsburg emperor expected papal cooperation in dealing with the Lutheran heresy. Papal policy, however, was guided by political considerations, not religious ones, a clear indication that, like the Catholic king of France, a pope could act against his religious interests because of the political situation. Fearful of Charles's power in Italy, Pope Clement VII (1523–1534) joined the side of Francis I in the second

Habsburg-Valois War (1527–1529), with catastrophic results. In April 1527, the Spanish-imperial army of Charles V went berserk while attacking Rome and gave the capital of Catholicism a fearful and bloody sacking. Sobered by the experience, Clement came to terms with the emperor, and by 1530, Charles V stood supreme over much of Italy.

The Ottoman Empire   In the meantime, Charles V also faced problems in the eastern part of his empire. In the fifteenth century, the Ottoman Turks had overrun Constantinople and established control over much of the Balkans in southeastern Europe (see Chapter 12). Now, in the first decades of the sixteenth century, the Ottomans posed a new threat to Europe. Ottoman armies had taken control of much of the North African coast and captured the Christian island of Rhodes. Under their new leader, Suleiman (SOO-lay-mahn) the Magnificent (1520–1566), Ottoman forces had defeated and killed King Louis of Hungary, Charles's brother-in-law, at the Battle of Mohács (MOH-hach) in 1526. Subsequently, the Ottomans overran most of Hungary, moved into Austria, and advanced as far as Vienna, where they were finally repulsed in 1529. The emperor and much of Christian Europe breathed a sigh of relief but still remained fearful of another Ottoman attack.

Politics in Germany   By the end of 1529, Charles was ready to deal with Germany. The second Habsburg-Valois War had ended, the Turks had been defeated temporarily, and the pope had been subdued. The internal political situation in the Holy Roman Empire was not in his favor, however. Germany was a land of several hundred territorial states: princely states, ecclesiastical principalities, and free imperial cities. Though all owed loyalty to the emperor, Germany's medieval development had enabled these states to become quite independent of imperial authority. They had no desire to have a strong emperor.

Charles's attempt to settle the Lutheran problem at the Diet of Augsburg in 1530 proved completely inadequate, and the emperor wound up demanding that the Lutherans return to the Catholic Church by April 15, 1531. In February 1531, fearful of Charles's intentions, eight princes and eleven imperial cities—all Lutheran—formed a defensive alliance known as the Schmalkaldic League. These Protestant German states vowed to assist each other "whenever any one of us is attacked on account of the Word of God and the doctrine of the Gospel." Religion was dividing the empire into two armed camps.

The renewed threat of the Turks against Vienna forced Charles once again to seek compromise instead of war with the Protestant authorities. From 1532 to 1535, Charles was forced to fight off an Ottoman, Arab, and Barbary attack on the Mediterranean coasts of Italy and Spain. Two additional Habsburg-Valois Wars (1535–1538 and 1542–1544) soon followed and kept Charles preoccupied with military campaigns in southern France and the Low Countries. Finally, Charles made peace with Francis in 1544 and the Turks in 1545. Fifteen years after the Diet of Augsburg, Charles was finally free to resolve his problem in Germany.

By the time of Luther's death in February 1546, all hopes of a peaceful compromise had faded. Charles brought a sizable imperial army of German, Dutch, Italian, and Spanish troops to do battle with the Protestants. In the first phase of the Schmalkaldic Wars (1546–1547), the emperor's forces decisively defeated the Lutherans at the Battle of Mühlberg (MOOL-bayrk). Charles V was at the zenith of his power, and the Protestant cause seemed doomed.

Appearances proved misleading, however. The Schmalkaldic League was soon reestablished, and the German Protestant princes allied themselves with the new French king, Henry II (1547–1559)—a Catholic—to revive the war in 1552. This time Charles was less fortunate and had to negotiate a truce. Exhausted by his efforts to maintain religious orthodoxy and the unity of his empire, Charles abandoned German affairs to his brother Ferdinand, abdicated all of his titles in 1556, and retired to his country estate in Spain to spend the remaining two years of his life in solitude.

An end to religious warfare in Germany came in 1555 with the Peace of Augsburg, which marked an important turning point in the history of the Reformation. The agreement formally acknowledged the division of Christianity, with Lutheranism granted equal legal standing with Catholicism. Moreover, the peace settlement accepted the right of each German ruler to determine the religion of his subjects (but not the right of the subjects to choose their religion). Charles's hope for a united empire had been completely dashed, and the ideal of medieval Christian unity was irretrievably lost. The rapid proliferation of new Protestant groups served to underscore that new reality.

THE SPREAD OF THE PROTESTANT REFORMATION

For both Catholics and Protestant reformers, Luther's heresy raised the question of what constituted the correct interpretation of the Bible. The inability to agree on this issue led not only to theological confrontations but also to bloody warfare as each Christian group was unwilling to admit that it could be wrong.

Lutheranism in Scandinavia   In 1397, the Union of Kalmar had brought about the unification of Denmark, Norway, and Sweden under the rule of one monarch, the king of Denmark. This union, however, failed to achieve any real social or political unification of the three states, particularly since the independent-minded landed nobles worked to frustrate any increase in monarchical centralization. By the beginning of the sixteenth century, the union was on the brink of disintegration. In 1520, Christian II (1513–1523) of Denmark, ruler of the three Scandinavian kingdoms, was overthrown by Swedish barons led by Gustavus Vasa. Three years later, Vasa became king of an independent Sweden (1523–1560) and took the lead in establishing a Lutheran Reformation in his country. By the 1530s, the Swedish Lutheran National Church had been created.

Meanwhile, Christian II had also been deposed as the king of Denmark by the Danish nobility; he was succeeded by his uncle, who became Frederick I (1523–1533). Frederick encouraged Lutheran preachers to spread their evangelical doctrines and to introduce a Lutheran liturgy into the Danish church service. In the 1530s, under Frederick's successor, Christian III (1534–1559), a Lutheran state church was installed with the king as the supreme authority in all ecclesiastical affairs. Christian was also instrumental in spreading Lutheranism to Norway. By the 1540s, Scandinavia had become a Lutheran stronghold. Like the German princes, the Scandinavian monarchs had been the dominant force in establishing state-run churches.

The Zwinglian Reformation   In the sixteenth century, the Swiss Confederation was a loose association of thirteen self-governing states called cantons. Theoretically part of the Holy Roman Empire, they had become virtually independent in 1499. The six forest cantons were democratic republics; the seven urban cantons, which included Zürich, Bern, and Basel, were for the most part governed by city councils controlled by narrow oligarchies of wealthy citizens.

Ulrich Zwingli (OOL-rikh TSFING-lee) (1484–1531) was a product of the Swiss forest cantons. The precocious son of a relatively prosperous peasant, the young Zwingli eventually obtained both bachelor of arts and master of arts degrees. During his university education at Vienna and Basel, Zwingli was strongly influenced by Christian humanism. Ordained a priest in 1506, he accepted a parish post in rural Switzerland until his appointment as a cathedral priest in the Great Minster of Zürich in 1518. Through his preaching there, Zwingli began the Reformation in Switzerland.

Zwingli's preaching of the Gospel caused such unrest that in 1523 the city council held a public disputation or debate in the town hall. The disputation became a standard method of spreading the Reformation to many cities. It gave an advantage to reformers, since they had the power of new ideas and Catholics were not used to defending their teachings. The victory went to Zwingli's party, and the council declared that "Mayor, Council and Great Council of Zürich, in order to do away with disturbance and discord, have upon due deliberation and consultation decided and resolved that Master Zwingli should continue as heretofore to proclaim the Gospel and the pure sacred Scripture."[7]

Reforms in Zürich   Over the next two years, a city council strongly influenced by Zwingli promulgated evangelical reforms in Zürich. Zwingli looked to the state to supervise the church. "A church without the magistrate is mutilated and incomplete," he declared. The city council abolished relics and images, removed all paintings and decorations from the churches, and replaced them with whitewashed walls. As Zwingli remarked, "The images are not to be endured; for all that God has forbidden, there can be no compromise."[8] A new liturgy consisting of Scripture reading, prayer, and sermons replaced the Mass, and music was eliminated from the service as a distraction from the pure word of God. Monasticism, pilgrimages, the veneration of saints, clerical celibacy, and the pope's authority were all abolished as remnants of papal Christianity. Zwingli's movement soon spread to other cities in Switzerland, including Bern in 1528 and Basel in 1529.

A Futile Search for Unity   By 1528, Zwingli's reform movement faced a serious political problem as the forest cantons remained staunchly Catholic. Zürich feared that they would ally with the Habsburgs. To counteract this danger, Zwingli attempted to build a league of evangelical cities by seeking an agreement with Luther and the German reformers. An alliance between them seemed possible, since the Reformation had spread to the southern German cities, especially Strasbourg, where a moderate reform movement containing characteristics of both Luther's and Zwingli's movements had been instituted by Martin Bucer (1491–1551). Both the German and the Swiss reformers realized the need for unity to defend against imperial and conservative opposition.

Protestant political leaders, especially Landgrave Philip of Hesse, fearful that Charles V would take advantage of the division between the reformers, attempted to promote an alliance of the Swiss and German reformed churches by persuading the leaders of both groups to attend a colloquy (conference) at Marburg to resolve their differences. Able to agree on virtually everything else, the gathering splintered over the interpretation of the Lord's Supper. Zwingli believed that the scriptural words "This is my body" and "This is my blood" should be taken symbolically, not literally. To Zwingli, the Lord's Supper was only a meal of remembrance, and he refused to accept Luther's insistence on the real presence of the body and blood of Jesus "in, with, and under the bread and wine." The Marburg Colloquy of 1529 produced no agreement and no evangelical alliance. It was a foretaste of the issues that would divide one reform group from another and lead to the creation of different Protestant groups.

In October 1531, war erupted between the Swiss Protestant and Catholic cantons. Zürich's army was routed, and Zwingli was found wounded on the battlefield. His enemies killed him, cut up his body, burned the pieces, and scattered the ashes. This Swiss civil war of 1531 provided an early indication of what religious passions would lead to in the sixteenth century. Unable to find peaceful ways to agree on the meaning of the Gospel, the disciples of Christianity resorted to violence and decision by force. When he heard of Zwingli's death, Martin Luther, who had not forgotten the confrontation at Marburg, is supposed to have remarked that Zwingli "got what he deserved."

The Radical Reformation: The Anabaptists   Although many reformers were ready to allow the state to play an important, if not dominant, role in church affairs, some people rejected this kind of magisterial reformation and favored a far more radical reform movement. Collectively called the Anabaptists, these radicals were actually members of a large variety of groups who shared some common characteristics. Anabaptism was especially attractive to the peasants, weavers, miners, and artisans who had been adversely affected by the economic changes of the age.

The Ideas of the Anabaptists   Anabaptists everywhere held certain ideas in common. All felt that the true Christian church was a voluntary association of believers who had undergone spiritual rebirth and had then been baptized into the church. Anabaptists advocated adult rather than infant baptism. No one, they believed, should be forced to accept the truth of the Bible. They also tried to return literally to the practices and spirit of early Christianity. Adhering to the accounts of early Christian communities in the New Testament, they followed a strict sort of democracy in which all believers were considered equal. Each church chose its own minister, who might be any member of the community, since all Christians were considered priests (though women were often excluded). Those chosen as ministers had the duty to lead services, which were very simple and contained nothing not found in the early church. Like early Christians, Anabaptists, who called themselves "Christians" or "Saints," accepted that they would have to suffer for their faith. Anabaptists rejected theological speculation in favor of simple Christian living according to what they believed was the pure word of God. The Lord's Supper was interpreted as a remembrance, a meal of fellowship celebrated in the evening in private houses according to Jesus's example.

Unlike the Catholics and other Protestants, most Anabaptists believed in the complete separation of church and state. Not only was government to be excluded from the realm of religion, but it was not even supposed to exercise political jurisdiction over real Christians. Human law had no power over those whom God had saved. Anabaptists refused to hold political office or bear arms because many took the commandment "Thou shall not kill" literally, although some Anabaptist groups did become quite violent. Their political beliefs as much as their religious beliefs caused the Anabaptists to be regarded as dangerous radicals who threatened the very fabric of sixteenth-century society. Indeed, the chief thing Protestants and Catholics could agree on was the need to stamp out the Anabaptists.

Varieties of Anabaptists   One early group of Anabaptists known as the Swiss Brethren arose in Zürich. Their ideas, especially adult baptism, frightened Zwingli, and they were expelled from the city in 1523. Because the first members of the Swiss Brethren who were baptized as adults had already been baptized as children (in the Catholic Church), their opponents labeled them Anabaptists or Rebaptists. Under Roman law, such people were subject to the death penalty.

As the teachings of the Swiss Brethren spread through southern Germany, the Austrian Habsburg lands, and Switzerland, Anabaptists suffered ruthless persecution, especially after the Peasants' War of 1524–1525, when the upper classes resorted to repression. Virtually eradicated in Germany, Anabaptist survivors emerged in Moravia and Poland, and in the Netherlands, Anabaptism took on a strange form.

In the 1530s, the city of Münster, in Westphalia in northwestern Germany near the Dutch border, was the site of an Anabaptist uprising that determined the fate of Dutch Anabaptism. Seat of a powerful Catholic prince-bishop, Münster had experienced severe economic disasters, including crop failure and plague. Although converted to Lutheranism in 1532, Münster experienced a more radical mass religious hysteria that led to legal recognition for the Anabaptists. Soon Münster became a haven for Anabaptists from the surrounding neighborhood, especially the more wild-eyed variety known as Melchiorites, who adhered to a vivid **millenarianism**. They believed that the end of the world was at hand and that they would usher in the kingdom of God with Münster as the New Jerusalem. By the end of February 1534, these

A Reformation Debate: Conflict at Marburg

Debates played a crucial role in the Reformation period. They were a primary instrument in introducing the Reformation into innumerable cities as well as a means of resolving differences among like-minded Protestant groups. This selection contains an excerpt from the vivacious and often brutal debate between Luther and Zwingli over the sacrament of the Lord's Supper at Marburg in 1529. The two protagonists failed to reach agreement.

The Marburg Colloquy, 1529

THE HESSIAN CHANCELLOR FEIGE: My gracious prince and lord [Landgrave Philip of Hesse] has summoned you for the express and urgent purpose of settling the dispute over the sacrament of the Lord's Supper.... Let everyone on both sides present his arguments in a spirit of moderation, as becomes such matters.... Now then, Doctor Luther, you may proceed.

LUTHER: Noble prince, gracious lord! Undoubtedly the colloquy is well intentioned.... Although I have no intention of changing my mind, which is firmly made up, I will nevertheless present the grounds of my belief and show where the others are in error.... Your basic contentions are these: In the last analysis you wish to prove that a body cannot be in two places at once, and you produce arguments about the unlimited body which are based on natural reason. I do not question how Christ can be God and man and how the two natures can be joined. For God is more powerful than all our ideas, and we must submit to his word.

Prove that Christ's body is not there where the Scripture says, "This is my body!" Rational proofs I will not listen to.... God is beyond all mathematics and the words of God are to be revered and carried out in awe. It is God who commands, "Take, eat, this is my body." I request, therefore, valid scriptural proof to the contrary. *Luther writes on the table in chalk, "This is my body," and covers the words with a velvet cloth.*

OECOLAMPADIUS [leader of the reform movement in Basel and a Zwinglian partisan]: The sixth chapter of John clarifies the other scriptural passages. Christ is not speaking there about a local presence. "The flesh is of no avail," he says. It is not my intention to employ rational, or geometrical, arguments—neither am I denying the power of God—but as long as I have the complete faith I will speak from that. For Christ is risen; he sits at the

millenarian Anabaptists had taken control of the city, driven out everyone they considered godless or unbelievers, burned all books except the Bible, and proclaimed communal ownership of all property. Eventually, the leadership of this New Jerusalem fell into the hands of one man, John of Leiden, who proclaimed himself king of the New Jerusalem. As king, he would lead the elect from Münster out to cover the entire world and purify it of evil by the sword in preparation for Jesus's Second Coming and the creation of a New Age. In this new kingdom, John of Leiden believed, all goods would be held in common and the saints would live without suffering.

right hand of God; and so he cannot be present in the bread. Our view is neither new nor sacrilegious, but is based on faith and Scripture....

ZWINGLI: I insist that the words of the Lord's Supper must be figurative. This is ever apparent, and even required by the article of faith: "taken up into heaven, seated at the right hand of the Father." Otherwise, it would be absurd to look for him in the Lord's Supper at the same time that Christ is telling us that he is in heaven. One and the same body cannot possibly be in different places....

LUTHER: I call upon you as before: your basic contentions are shaky. Give way, and give glory to God!

ZWINGLI: And we call upon you to give glory to God and to quit begging the question! The issue at stake is this: Where is the proof of your position? I am willing to consider your words carefully—no harm meant! You're trying to outwit me. I stand by this passage in the sixth chapter of John, verse 63, and shall not be shaken from it. You'll have to sing another tune.

LUTHER: You're being obnoxious.

ZWINGLI: (excitedly) Don't you believe that Christ was attempting in John 6 to help those who did not understand?

LUTHER: You're trying to dominate things! You insist on passing judgment! Leave that to someone else! ... It is your point that must be proved, not mine. But let us stop this sort of thing. It serves no purpose.

ZWINGLI: It certainly does! It is for you to prove that the passage in John 6 speaks of a physical repast.

LUTHER: You express yourself poorly and make about as much progress as a cane standing in a corner. You're going nowhere.

ZWINGLI: No, no, no! This is the passage that will break your neck!

LUTHER: Don't be so sure of yourself. Necks don't break this way. You're in Hesse, not Switzerland.

Q *How did the positions of Zwingli and Luther on the sacrament of the Lord's Supper differ? What was the purpose of this debate? Based on this example, why do you think Reformation debates led to further hostility rather than compromise and unity between religious and sectarian opponents? What implications did this have for the future of the Protestant Reformation?*

Source: "The Marburg Colloquy," from GREAT DEBATES OF THE REFORMATION, edited by Donald Ziegler, copyright © 1969 by Donald Ziegler. Used by permission of Modern Library, a division of Random House, Inc.

But it was not to be. As the Catholic prince-bishop of Münster gathered a large force and laid siege to the city, the new king repeatedly had to postpone the ushering forth from Münster. Finally, after many inhabitants had starved, a joint army of Catholics and Lutherans recaptured the city in June 1535 and executed the radical Anabaptist leaders in gruesome fashion. The New Jerusalem had ceased to exist.

Purged of its fantasies and its more extreme elements, Dutch Anabaptism reverted to its pacifist tendencies, especially evident in the work of Menno Simons

(1496–1561), the man most responsible for rejuvenating Dutch Anabaptism. A popular leader, Menno dedicated his life to the spread of a peaceful, evangelical Anabaptism that stressed separation from the world in order to truly emulate the life of Jesus. Simons imposed strict discipline on his followers and banned those who refused to conform to the rules. The Mennonites, as his followers were called, spread from the Netherlands into northwestern Germany and eventually into Poland and Lithuania as well as the New World. Both the Mennonites and the Amish, who are also descended from the Anabaptists, maintain communities in the United States and Canada today.

The Reformation in England   The English Reformation was initiated by King Henry VIII (1509–1547), who wanted to divorce his first wife, Catherine of Aragon, because she had failed to produce a male heir. Furthermore, Henry had fallen in love with Anne Boleyn (BUH-lin *or* buh-LIN), a lady-in-waiting to Queen Catherine. Anne's unwillingness to be only the king's mistress and the king's desire to have a legitimate male heir made their marriage imperative, but the king's first marriage stood in the way.

Henry relied on Cardinal Wolsey, the highest-ranking English church official and lord chancellor to the king, to obtain from Pope Clement VII an annulment of the king's marriage. Normally, the pope might have been willing to oblige, but the sack of Rome in 1527 had made the pope dependent on the Holy Roman Emperor Charles V, who happened to be the nephew of Queen Catherine. Discretion dictated delay in granting the English king's request. Impatient with the process, Henry dismissed Wolsey in 1529.

Two new advisers now became the king's agents in fulfilling his wishes. These were Thomas Cranmer (1489–1556), who became archbishop of Canterbury in 1532, and Thomas Cromwell (1485–1540), the king's principal secretary after the fall of Wolsey. They advised the king to obtain an annulment of his marriage in England's own ecclesiastical courts. The most important step toward this goal was an act of Parliament cutting off all appeals from English church courts to Rome, a piece of legislation that essentially abolished papal authority in England. Henry no longer needed the pope to obtain his annulment. He was now in a hurry because Anne Boleyn had become pregnant and he had secretly married her in January 1533 to legitimize the expected heir. In May, as archbishop of Canterbury and head of the highest ecclesiastical court in England, Thomas Cranmer ruled that the king's marriage to Catherine was "null and absolutely void" and then validated Henry's marriage to Anne. At the beginning of June, Anne was crowned queen. Three months later, a child was born. Much to the king's disappointment, the baby was a girl, whom they named Elizabeth.

In 1534, Parliament completed the break of the Church of England with Rome by passing the Act of Supremacy, which declared that the king was "taken, accepted, and reputed the only supreme head on earth of the Church of England." This meant that the English monarch now controlled the church in all matters of doctrine, clerical appointments, and discipline. In addition, Parliament passed the Treason Act, making it punishable by death to deny that the king was the supreme head of the church.

One who challenged the new order was Thomas More, the humanist and for-mer lord chancellor, who saw clearly to the heart of the issue: loyalty to the pope in Rome was now treason in England. More refused to support the new laws and was duly tried for treason. At his trial, he asked, rhetorically, what the effect of the actions of the king and Parliament would be: "Therefore am I not bound ... to con-form my conscience to the Council of one realm [England] against the general Council of Christendom?"[9] Because his conscience could not accept the victory of the national state over the church, nor would he, as a Christian, bow his head to a secular ruler in matters of faith, More was beheaded in London on July 6, 1535.

Recent research that emphasizes the strength of Catholicism in England sug-gests that Thomas More was not alone in his view of the new order. In fact, one historian has argued that Catholicism was vibrant in England in both the fifteenth and sixteenth centuries; in his view, the English Reformation was alien to many English people.

The New Order Thomas Cromwell worked out the details of the Tudor govern-ment's new role in church affairs based on the centralized power exercised by the king and Parliament. Cromwell also came to his extravagant king's financial rescue with a daring plan for the dissolution of the monasteries. About four hundred reli-gious houses were closed in 1536, and the king confiscated their lands and posses-sions. Many were sold to nobles, gentry, and some merchants. The king added enormously to his treasury and also to his ranks of supporters, who now had a stake in the new Tudor order.

Although Henry VIII had broken with the papacy, little change occurred in matters of doctrine, theology, and ceremony. Some of his supporters, such as Archbishop Thomas Cranmer, wished to have a religious reformation as well as an administrative one, but Henry was unyielding. Nevertheless, some clergymen ignored Henry on the matter of priestly celibacy and secretly married.

The final decade of Henry's reign was preoccupied with foreign affairs, fac-tional intrigue, and a continued effort to find the perfect wife. Henry soon tired of Anne Boleyn and had her beheaded in 1536 on a charge of adultery. His third wife, Jane Seymour, produced the long-awaited male heir but died twelve days later. His fourth marriage, to Anne of Cleves, a German princess, was arranged for political reasons. Henry relied on a painted portrait of Anne when he made the arrangements, but he was disappointed at her physical appearance when he saw her in person and soon divorced her. His fifth wife, Catherine Howard, was more attractive but less moral. When she committed adultery, Henry had her beheaded. His last wife was Catherine Parr, who married the king in 1543 and outlived him. Henry was succeeded by the underage and sickly Edward VI (1547–1553), the son of his third wife.

Since the new king was only nine years old at the time of his accession to the throne, real control of England passed to a council of regency. During Edward's reign, Archbishop Cranmer and others inclined toward Protestant doctrines were able to move the Church of England in a more Protestant direction. New acts of Parliament instituted the right of the clergy to marry, eliminated images, and autho-rized a revised Protestant liturgy that was elaborated in a new prayer book and liturgical guide known as the Book of Common Prayer. These rapid changes in doctrine and liturgy aroused much opposition and prepared the way for the reaction that occurred when Mary, Henry's first daughter by Catherine of Aragon, came to the throne.

Reaction Under Mary   Mary (1553–1558) was a Catholic who fully intended to restore England to the Roman Catholic fold. But her restoration of Catholicism, achieved by joint action of the monarch and Parliament, aroused opposition. There was widespread antipathy to Mary's unfortunate marriage to Philip II, son of Charles V and the future king of Spain. Philip was strongly disliked in England, and Mary's foreign policy of alliance with Spain aroused further hostility, especially when her forces lost Calais, the last English possession in France after the Hundred Years' War. The burning of more than three hundred Protestant heretics aroused further ire against "bloody Mary." As a result of her policies, Mary managed to achieve the opposite of what she had intended: England was more Protestant by the end of her reign than it had been at the beginning. When she came to power, Protestantism had become identified with church destruction and religious anarchy. Now people identified it with English

Hampton Court Palace, London//Eurasia/Getty Images

Henry VIII and His Successor. *Henry VIII finally achieved his goal of a male heir in 1537 when his third wife, Jane Seymour, gave birth to a son. Edward VI, who succeeded his father in 1547 at the age of nine, ruled for only six years before dying, probably of tuberculosis. Edward, his father, and his mother are seen here in a sixteenth-century portrait in the Great Hall of Hampton Court Palace.*

resistance to Spanish interference. Mary's death in 1558 ended the restoration of Catholicism in England.

John Calvin and Calvinism   Of the second generation of Protestant reformers, one stands out as the systematic theologian and organizer of the Protestant movement—John Calvin (1509–1564). Calvin received a remarkably diverse education in humanistic studies and law in his native France. He was also influenced by Luther's writings, which were being circulated and read by French intellectuals as early as 1523. In 1533, Calvin experienced a religious crisis that determined the rest of his life's work. He described it in these words:

> God, by a sudden conversion, subdued and brought my mind to a teachable frame, which was more hardened in such matters than might have been expected from one at my early period of life. Having thus received some taste and knowledge of true godliness, I was immediately inflamed with so intense a desire to make progress therein, although I did not leave off other studies, I yet pursued them with less ardor.[10]

Calvin's conversion was solemn and straightforward. He was so convinced of the inner guidance of God that he became the most determined of all the Protestant reformers.

After his conversion and newfound conviction, Calvin was no longer safe in Paris, since King Francis I periodically persecuted Protestants. Eventually, Calvin made his way to Basel, where in 1536 he published the first edition of the *Institutes of the Christian Religion*, a masterful synthesis of Protestant thought that immediately secured his reputation as one of the new leaders of Protestantism.

Calvin's Ideas   On most important doctrines, Calvin stood very close to Luther. He adhered to the doctrine of justification by faith alone to explain how humans achieved salvation. Calvin also placed much emphasis on the absolute sovereignty of God or the "power, grace, and glory of God." Thus, "God asserts his possession of omnipotence, and claims our acknowledgment of this attribute; not such as is imagined by sophists, vain, idle, and almost asleep, but vigilant, efficacious, operative and engaged in continual action."[11]

One of the ideas derived from his emphasis on the absolute sovereignty of God—**predestination**—gave a unique cast to Calvin's teachings, although Luther also believed in this principle. This "eternal decree," as Calvin called it, meant that God had predestined some people to be saved (the elect) and others to be damned (the reprobate). According to Calvin, "He has once for all determined, both whom he would admit to salvation, and whom he would condemn to destruction."[12] Calvin identified three tests that might indicate possible salvation: an open profession of faith, a "decent and godly life," and participation in the sacraments of baptism and communion. In no instance did Calvin ever suggest that worldly success or material wealth was a sign of election. Significantly for the future of Calvinism, although Calvin himself stressed that there could be no absolute certainty of salvation, some of his followers did not always make this distinction. The practical psychological effect of predestination was to give some later Calvinists an unshakable conviction that they were doing God's work on earth. It is no accident that Calvinism became the activist international form of Protestantism.

To Calvin, the church was a divine institution responsible for preaching the word of God and administering the sacraments. Calvin kept the same two sacraments as other Protestant reformers, baptism and the Lord's Supper. Baptism was a sign of the remission of sins. Calvin believed in the real presence of Jesus in the sacrament of the Lord's Supper, but only in a spiritual sense. Jesus's body is at the right hand of God and thus cannot be in the sacrament, but to the believer, Jesus is spiritually present in the Lord's Supper.

Calvin's Geneva   Before 1536, John Calvin had essentially been a scholar. But in that year, he took up a ministry in Geneva that lasted, except for a brief exile (1538–1541), until his death in 1564. Calvin achieved a major success in 1541 when the city council accepted his new church constitution, known as the Ecclesiastical Ordinances.

This document created a church government that used both clergy and laymen in the service of the church. The Consistory, a special body for enforcing moral discipline, was set up as a court to oversee the moral life and doctrinal purity of Genevans. As its power increased, the Consistory went from "fraternal corrections" to the use of public penance and excommunication. More serious cases could be turned over to the city council for punishments greater than excommunication. During Calvin's last years, stricter laws against blasphemy were enacted and enforced with banishment and public whippings.

Calvin's success in Geneva enabled the city to become a vibrant center of Protestantism. John Knox, the Calvinist reformer of Scotland, called it "the most perfect school of Christ on earth." Following Calvin's lead, missionaries trained in Geneva were sent to all parts of Europe. Calvinism became established in France, the Netherlands, Scotland, and central and eastern Europe. By the mid-sixteenth century, Calvinism had replaced Lutheranism as the international form of Protestantism, and Calvin's Geneva stood as the fortress of the Reformation.

THE SOCIAL IMPACT OF THE PROTESTANT REFORMATION

Because Christianity was such an integral part of European life, it was inevitable that the Reformation would have an impact on the family, education, and popular religious practices.

The Family   For centuries, Catholicism had praised the family and sanctified its existence by making marriage a sacrament. But the Catholic Church's high regard for abstinence from sex as the surest way to holiness made the celibate state of the clergy preferable to marriage. Nevertheless, because not all men could remain chaste, marriage offered the best means to control sexual intercourse and give it a purpose, the procreation of children. To some extent, this attitude persisted among the Protestant reformers; Luther, for example, argued that sex in marriage allowed one to "make use of this sex in order to avoid sin," and Calvin advised that every man should "abstain from marriage only so long as he is fit to observe celibacy." If "his power to tame lust fails him," then he must marry.

But the Reformation did bring some change to the conception of the family. Both Catholic and Protestant clergy preached sermons advocating a more positive approach to family relationships. The Protestants were especially important in developing this new view of the family. Because Protestantism had eliminated any idea of special holiness for celibacy, abolishing both monasticism and a celibate clergy, the family could be placed at the center of human life, and a new stress on "mutual love between man and wife" could be extolled. But were doctrine and reality the same? For more radical religious groups, at times they were. One Anabaptist wrote to his wife before his execution, "My faithful helper, my loyal friend. I praise God that he gave you to me, you who have sustained me in all my trial."[13] But more often reality reflected the traditional roles of husband as the ruler and wife as the obedient servant whose chief duty was to please her husband. Luther stated it clearly:

> The rule remains with the husband, and the wife is compelled to obey him by God's command. He rules the home and the state, wages war, defends his possessions, tills the soil, builds, plants, etc. The woman on the other hand is like a nail driven into the wall ... so the wife should stay at home and look after the affairs of the household, as one who has been deprived of the ability of administering those affairs that are outside and that concern the state. She does not go beyond her most personal duties.[14]

Obedience to her husband was not a wife's only role; her other important duty was to bear children. To Calvin and Luther, this function of women was part of the divine plan. God punishes women for the sins of Eve by the burdens of procreation and feeding and nurturing their children, but, said Luther, "it is a gladsome punishment if you consider the hope of eternal life and the honor of motherhood which had been left to her."[15] Although the Protestant reformers sanctified this role of woman as mother and wife, viewing it as a holy vocation, Protestantism also left few alternatives for women. Because monasticism had been destroyed, that career avenue was no longer available; for most Protestant women, family life was their only destiny. At the same time, by emphasizing the father as "ruler" and hence the center of household religion, Protestantism even removed the woman from her traditional role as controller of religion in the home.

Protestant reformers called on men and women to read the Bible and participate in religious services together. In this way, the reformers did provide a stimulus for the education of girls so that they could read the Bible and other religious literature. The city council of Zwickau, for example, established a girls' school in 1525. But these schools were designed to encourage proper moral values rather than intellectual development and really did little to improve the position of women in society. Likewise, when women attempted to take more active roles in religious life, reformers—Lutheran and Calvinist alike—shrank back in horror. To them, the equality of the Gospel did not mean overthrowing the inequality of social classes or the sexes. Overall, the

Protestant Reformation did not noticeably transform women's subordinate place in society.

Education in the Reformation The Reformation had an important effect on the development of education in Europe. Renaissance humanism had significantly altered the content of education, and Protestant educators were very successful in implementing and using humanist methods in Protestant secondary schools and universities. Unlike the humanist schools, however, which had been mostly for an elite, the sons and a few daughters of the nobility and wealthier bourgeoisie, Protestant schools were aimed at a much wider audience. Protestantism created an increased need for at least a semiliterate body of believers who could read the Bible for themselves.

While adopting the Classical emphasis of humanist schools, Protestant reformers broadened the base of the people being educated. Convinced of the need to provide the church with good Christians and good pastors as well as the state with good administrators and citizens, Martin Luther advocated that all children should have the opportunity of an education provided by the state. To that end, he urged the cities and villages of Saxony to establish schools paid for by the public. Luther's ideas were shared by his Wittenberg coworker Philip Melanchthon, whose educational efforts earned him the title of *Praecepter Germaniae* (PREE-sep-tur gayr-MAHN-ee-ee), the Teacher of Germany. In his scheme for education in Saxony, Melanchthon divided students into three classes or divisions based on their age or capabilities.

Following Melanchthon's example, the Protestants in Germany were responsible for introducing the gymnasium, or secondary school, where the humanist emphasis on the liberal arts based on instruction in Greek and Latin was combined with religious instruction. Most famous was the school in Strasbourg founded by Johannes Sturm in 1538, which served as a model for other Protestant

A Sixteenth-Century Classroom. *Protestants in Germany developed secondary schools that combined instruction in the liberal arts with religious education. This scene from a painting by Ambrosius Holbein shows a schoolmaster instructing a pupil in the alphabet while his wife helps a little girl.*

© Roger-Viollet, Paris/The Bridgeman Art Library

schools. John Calvin's Genevan Academy, founded in 1559, was organized in two distinct parts. The "private school" or gymnasium was divided into seven classes for young people who were taught Latin and Greek grammar and literature as well as logic. In the "public school," students were taught philosophy, Hebrew, Greek, and theology. The Genevan Academy, which eventually became a university, came to concentrate on preparing ministers to spread the Calvinist view of the Gospel.

Religious Practices and Popular Culture   The Protestant reformers' attacks on the Catholic Church led to radical changes in religious practices. The Protestant Reformation abolished or severely curtailed such customary practices as indulgences, the veneration of relics and saints, pilgrimages, monasticism, and clerical celibacy. The elimination of saints put an end to the numerous celebrations of religious holy days and changed a community's sense of time. Thus, in Protestant communities, religious ceremonies and imagery, such as processions and statues, tended to be replaced with individual private prayer, family worship, and collective prayer and worship at the same time each week on Sunday.

In addition to abolishing saints' days and religious carnivals, some Protestant reformers even tried to eliminate customary forms of entertainment. The Puritans (as English Calvinists were called), for example, attempted to ban drinking in taverns, dramatic performances, and dancing. Dutch Calvinists denounced the tradition of giving small presents to children on the feast of Saint Nicholas, in early December. Many of these Protestant attacks on popular culture were unsuccessful, however. The importance of taverns in English social life made it impossible to eradicate them, and celebrating at Christmastime persisted in the Dutch Netherlands.

THE CATHOLIC REFORMATION

By the mid-sixteenth century, Lutheranism had become established in parts of Germany and Scandinavia, and Calvinism in parts of Switzerland, France, the Netherlands, and eastern Europe (see Map 13.2). In England, the split from Rome had resulted in the creation of a national church. The situation in Europe did not look particularly favorable for the Roman Catholic Church. Yet constructive, positive forces were already at work within the Catholic Church.

Catholic Reformation or Counter-Reformation?   There is no doubt that the Catholic Church underwent a revitalization in the sixteenth century. But was this reformation a **Catholic Reformation** or a Counter-Reformation? Some historians prefer to call it a "Counter-Reformation" to focus on the aspects that were a direct reaction against the Protestant movement. Historians who prefer to use "Catholic Reformation" point out that elements of reform were already present in the Catholic Church at the end of the fifteenth century and the beginning of the sixteenth, and that by the mid-sixteenth century, they came to be directed by a revived and reformed papacy, giving the church new strength.

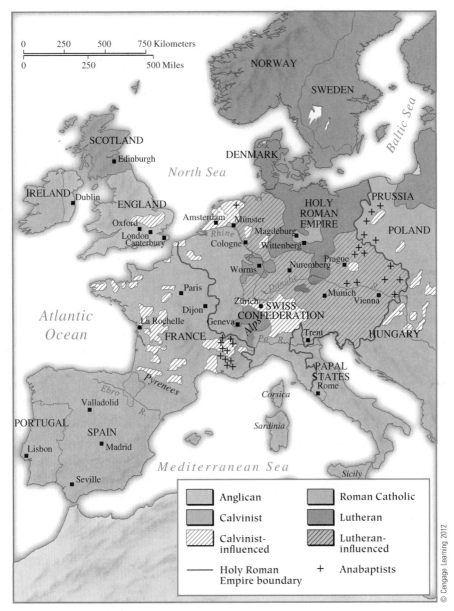

MAP 13.2 Catholics and Protestants in Europe by 1560

The Reformation continued to evolve beyond the basic split of the Lutherans from the Catholics. Several Protestant sects broke away from the teachings of Martin Luther, each with a separate creed and different ways of worship. In England, Henry VIII broke with the Catholic Church for political and dynastic reasons.

No doubt, both positions on the nature of the reformation of the Catholic Church contain elements of truth. The Catholic Reformation revived the best features of medieval Catholicism and then adjusted them to meet new conditions, as is most apparent in the revival of mysticism and monasticism. The emergence of a new mysticism, closely tied to the traditions of Catholic piety, was especially evident in the life of the Spanish mystic Saint Teresa of Avila (1515–1582). A nun of the Carmelite order, Teresa experienced mystical visions that she claimed resulted in the ecstatic union of her soul with God. But Teresa also believed that mystical experience should lead to an active life of service on behalf of her Catholic faith. Consequently, she founded a new order of barefoot Carmelite nuns and worked to foster their mystical experiences.

The regeneration of religious orders also proved valuable to the reform of Catholicism. Old orders, such as the Benedictines and Dominicans, were reformed and renewed. The Capuchins emerged when a group of Franciscans decided to return to the simplicity and poverty of Saint Francis of Assisi, the medieval founder of the Franciscan order. In addition to caring for the sick and the poor, the Capuchins focused on preaching the Gospel directly to the people and emerged as an effective force against Protestantism. New religious orders and brotherhoods were also created. The Theatines, founded in 1524, placed their emphasis on reforming the secular clergy and encouraging those clerics to fulfill their duties among the laity. The Theatines also founded orphanages and hospitals to care for the victims of war and plague. The Ursulines, a new order of nuns founded in Italy in 1535, focused their attention on establishing schools for the education of girls.

The Society of Jesus   Of all the new religious orders, the most important was the Society of Jesus, known as the Jesuits, who became the chief instrument of the Catholic Reformation. The Society of Jesus was founded by a Spanish nobleman, Ignatius of Loyola (ig-NAY-shuss of loi-OH-luh) (1491–1556), whose injuries in battle cut short his military career. Loyola experienced a spiritual torment similar to Luther's but, unlike Luther, resolved his problems not by a new doctrine but by a decision to submit his will to the will of the church. Unable to be a real soldier, he vowed to be a soldier of God. Over a period of twelve years, Loyola prepared for his lifework by prayer, pilgrimages, going to school, and working out a spiritual program in his brief but powerful book, *The Spiritual Exercises*. This was a training manual for spiritual development emphasizing exercises by which the human will could be strengthened and made to follow the will of God as manifested through his instrument, the Catholic Church.

Loyola gathered together a small group of individuals who were eventually recognized as a religious order, the Society of Jesus, by a papal bull in 1540. The new order was grounded on the principles of absolute obedience to the papacy, a strict hierarchical order for the society, the use of education to achieve its goals, and a dedication to engage in "conflict for God." The Jesuits' organization came to resemble the structure of a military command. A two-year novitiate weeded out all but the most dedicated adherents. Executive leadership was put in the hands of a general, who nominated all important positions in the order and was to be revered as the absolute head of the order. Loyola served as the first general of the order until his death in 1556. A special vow of absolute obedience to the pope made the Jesuits an important instrument for papal policy.

Activities of the Jesuits   The Jesuits pursued three major activities. They established highly disciplined schools, borrowing freely from humanist schools

Ignatius of Loyola.
The Jesuits became the most important new religious order of the Catholic Reformation. Shown here in a sixteenth-century painting by an unknown artist is Ignatius of Loyola, founder of the Society of Jesus. Loyola is seen kneeling before Pope Paul III, who officially recognized the Jesuits in 1540.

Il Gesu, Rome//© Scala/Art Resource, NY

for their educational methods. To the Jesuits, the thorough education of young people was crucial to combating the advance of Protestantism. In the course of the sixteenth century, the Jesuits took over the premier academic posts in Catholic universities, and by 1600, they were the most famous educators in Europe.

Another prominent Jesuit activity was the propagation of the Catholic faith among non-Christians. Francis Xavier (ZAY-vee-ur) (1506–1552), one of the original members of the Society of Jesus, carried the message of Catholic Christianity to the East. After converting tens of thousands in India, he traveled to Malacca and the Moluccas before reaching Japan in 1549. He spoke highly of the Japanese: "They are a people of excellent morals—good in general and not malicious."[16] Thousands of Japanese, especially in the southernmost islands, became Christians. In 1552, Xavier set out for China but died of a fever before he reached the mainland.

Although conversion efforts in Japan proved short-lived, Jesuit activity in China, especially that of the Italian Matteo Ricci (ma-TAY-oh REE-chee) (1552–1610), was more long-lasting. Recognizing the Chinese pride in their own culture, the Jesuits attempted to draw parallels between Christian and Confucian concepts and to show the similarities between Christian morality and Confucian ethics. For their part, the missionaries were impressed with many aspects of Chinese civilization, and reports of their experiences heightened European curiosity about this great society on the other side of the world.

The Jesuits were also determined to carry the Catholic banner and fight Protestantism. Jesuit missionaries succeeded in restoring Catholicism to parts of Germany and eastern Europe. Poland was largely won back for the Catholic Church through Jesuit efforts.

A Revived Papacy
The involvement of the Renaissance papacy in dubious finances and Italian political and military affairs had given rise to numerous sources of corruption. The meager steps taken to control corruption left the papacy still in need of serious reform, and it took the jolt of the Protestant Reformation to bring it about.

The pontificate of Pope Paul III (1534–1549) proved to be a turning point in the reform of the papacy. Raised in the lap of Renaissance luxury, Paul III continued Renaissance papal practices by appointing his nephews as cardinals, involving himself in politics, and patronizing arts and letters on a lavish scale. Nevertheless, he perceived the need for change and expressed it decisively. He made advocates of reform, such as Gasparo Contarini (GAHS-puh-roh kahn-tuh-REE-nee) and Gian Pietro Caraffa (JAHN PYAY-troh kuh-RAH-fuh), cardinals. In 1535, Paul took the audacious step of appointing a reform commission to study the condition of the church. The commission's report in 1537 blamed the church's problems on the corrupt policies of popes and cardinals. Paul III also formally recognized the Jesuits and summoned the Council of Trent (see the next section).

A decisive turning point in the direction of the Catholic Reformation and the nature of papal reform came in the 1540s. In 1541, a colloquy had been held at Regensburg in a final attempt to settle the religious division peacefully. Here Catholic moderates, such as Cardinal Contarini, who favored concessions to Protestants in the hope of restoring Christian unity, reached a compromise with Protestant moderates on a number of doctrinal issues. When Contarini returned to Rome with these proposals, Cardinal Caraffa and other hard-liners, who regarded all compromise with Protestant innovations as heresy, accused him of selling out to the heretics. It soon became apparent that the conservative reformers were in the ascendancy when Caraffa was able to persuade Paul III to establish the Roman Inquisition or Holy Office in 1542 to ferret out doctrinal errors. There was to be no compromise with Protestantism.

When Cardinal Caraffa was chosen pope as Paul IV (1555–1559), he so increased the power of the Inquisition that even liberal cardinals were silenced. This "first true pope of the Catholic Counter-Reformation," as he has been called, also created the Index of Forbidden Books, a list of books that Catholics were not allowed to read. It included all the works of Protestant theologians as well as authors considered "unwholesome," a category general enough to include the works of Erasmus. Rome, the capital of Catholic Christianity, was rapidly becoming Fortress Rome; any hope of restoring Christian unity by compromise was fast fading. The activities of the Council of Trent made compromise virtually impossible.

**The Council
of Trent**
In 1542, Pope Paul III took the decisive step of calling for a general council of Christendom to resolve the religious differences created by the Protestant revolt. It was not until March 1545, however, that a group of cardinals, archbishops, bishops, abbots, and theologians met in the city of Trent on the border between Germany and Italy and initiated the Council of Trent. But a variety of problems, including an outbreak of plague, war between France and Spain, and the changing of popes, prevented the council from holding regular annual meetings. Nevertheless, the council met intermittently in three major sessions between 1545 and 1563. Moderate Catholic reformers hoped that the council would make compromises in formulating doctrinal definitions that would encourage Protestants to return to the church. Conservatives, however, favored an uncompromising restatement of Catholic doctrines in strict opposition to Protestant positions. After a struggle, the latter group won.

The final doctrinal decrees of the Council of Trent reaffirmed traditional Catholic teachings in opposition to Protestant beliefs. The council affirmed Scripture and tradition as equal authorities in religious matters; only the church could interpret Scripture. Other decrees declared both faith and good works to be necessary for salvation and upheld the seven sacraments, the Catholic doctrine of transubstantiation, and clerical celibacy. The council also affirmed the belief in purgatory and in the efficacy of indulgences, although it prohibited the hawking of indulgences. Of the reform decrees that were passed, the most important established theological seminaries in every diocese for the training of priests.

After the Council of Trent, the Roman Catholic Church possessed a clear body of doctrine and a unified church under the acknowledged supremacy of the popes, who had triumphed over bishops and councils. The Roman Catholic Church had become one Christian denomination among many with an organizational framework and doctrinal pattern that would not be significantly altered for four hundred years. With renewed confidence, the Catholic Church entered a new phase of its history.

POLITICS AND THE WARS OF RELIGION IN THE SIXTEENTH CENTURY

By the middle of the sixteenth century, Calvinism and Catholicism had become activist religions dedicated to spreading the word of God as they interpreted it. Although this struggle for the minds and hearts of Europeans is at the heart of the religious wars of the sixteenth century, economic, social, and political forces also played an important role in these conflicts. Of the sixteenth-century religious wars, none were more momentous or shattering than the French civil wars known as the French Wars of Religion.

**The French
Wars of Religion
(1562–1598)**
Religion was the engine that drove the French civil wars of the sixteenth century. Concerned by the growth of Calvinism, the French kings tried to stop its spread by persecuting Calvinists but had little success. **Huguenots** (HYOO-guh-nots),

as the French Calvinists were called, came from all levels of society: artisans and shopkeepers hurt by rising prices and a rigid guild system, merchants and lawyers in provincial towns whose local privileges were tenuous, and members of the nobility. Possibly 40 to 50 percent of the French nobility became Huguenots, including the house of Bourbon (boor-BOHN), which stood next to the Valois (val-WAH) in the royal line of succession and ruled the southern French kingdom of Navarre (nuh-VAHR). The conversion of so many nobles made the Huguenots a potentially dangerous political threat to monarchical power. Though the Calvinists constituted only about 10 percent of the population, they were a strong-willed and well-organized minority.

The Catholic majority greatly outnumbered the Calvinist minority. The Valois monarchy was staunchly Catholic, and its control of the Catholic Church gave it little incentive to look on Protestantism favorably. When King Henry II was killed accidentally in a tournament in 1559, he was succeeded by a series of weak and neurotic sons, two of whom were dominated by their mother, Catherine de' Medici (1519–1589). As regent for her sons, the moderate Catholic Catherine looked to religious compromise as a way to defuse the political tensions but found to her consternation that both sides possessed their share of religious fanatics unwilling to make concessions. The extreme Catholic party—known as the ultra-Catholics—favored strict opposition to the Huguenots and was led by the Guise (GEEZ) family. Possessing the loyalty of Paris and large sections of northern and northwestern France through their client-patronage system, the Guises could recruit and pay for large armies and received support abroad from the papacy and Jesuits who favored the family's uncompromising Catholic position.

But religion was not the only factor contributing to the French civil wars. Resentful of the growing power of monarchical centralization, towns and provinces were only too willing to join a revolt against the monarchy. This was also true of the nobility, and because so many of them were Calvinists, they formed an important base of opposition to the crown. The French Wars of Religion, then, presented a major constitutional crisis for France and temporarily halted the development of the French centralized territorial state. The claim of the state's ruling dynasty to a person's loyalties was temporarily superseded by loyalty to one's religious belief. For some people, the unity of France was less important than religious truth. But there also emerged in France a group of public figures who placed politics before religion and believed that no religious truth was worth the ravages of civil war. These **politiques** (puh-lee-TEEKS) ultimately prevailed, but not until both sides were exhausted by bloodshed.

Course of the Struggle   The wars erupted in 1562 when the powerful duke of Guise massacred a peaceful congregation of Huguenots at Vassy. In the decade of the 1560s, the Huguenots held their own. Though too small a group to conquer France, their armies were so good at defensive campaigns that they could not be defeated either, despite the infamous Saint Bartholomew's Day massacre.

This massacre of Huguenots occurred in August 1572 at a time when the Catholic and Calvinist parties had apparently been reconciled through the marriage of the sister of the reigning Valois king, Charles IX (1560–1574), and Henry of Navarre, the Bourbon ruler of Navarre. Henry was the son of Jeanne d'Albret (ZHAHN dahl-BRAY), queen of Navarre, who had been responsible for introducing Calvinist ideas into her kingdom. Henry was also the acknowledged political leader of the Huguenots, and many Huguenots traveled to Paris for the wedding.

But the Guise family persuaded the king and his mother, Catherine de' Medici, that this gathering of Huguenots posed a threat to them. Charles and his advisers decided to eliminate the Huguenot leaders with one swift blow. According to one French military leader, Charles and his advisers believed that civil war would soon break out anyway and that "it was better to win a battle in Paris, where all the leaders were, than to risk it in the field and fall into a dangerous and uncertain war."[17]

The massacre began early in the day on August 24 when the king's guards sought out and killed some prominent Huguenot leaders. These murders soon unleashed a wave of violence that gripped the city of Paris. For three days, frenzied Catholic mobs roamed the streets of Paris, killing Huguenots in an often cruel and bloodthirsty manner. According to one eyewitness account: "Then they took

The Saint Bartholomew's Day Massacre. *Although the outbreak of religious war seemed unlikely in France, the collapse of the strong monarchy with the death of Henry II unleashed forces that led to a series of civil wars. Pictured here is the Saint Bartholomew's Day massacre of 1572. This contemporary painting by the Huguenot artist François Dubois vividly depicts a number of the incidents of that day when approximately three thousand Huguenots were murdered in Paris.*

© Musée Cantonal des Beaux-Arts de Lausanne/Photo © Held Collection/The Bridgeman Art Library her [Françoise Lussault] and dragged her by the hair a long way through the streets, and spying the gold bracelets on her arms, without having the patience to unfasten them, cut off her wrists."[18] Three days of killing left three thousand Huguenots dead, although not Henry of Navarre, who saved his life by promising to turn Catholic. Thousands more were killed in provincial towns. The massacre boomeranged, however, because it discredited the Valois dynasty without ending the conflict.

The fighting continued. The Huguenots rebuilt their strength, and in 1576, the ultra-Catholics formed a "Holy League," vowing to exterminate heresy and seat a true Catholic champion—Henry, duke of Guise—on the French throne in place of the ruling king, Henry III (1574–1589), who had succeeded his brother Charles IX. The turning point in the conflict came in the War of the Three Henries in 1588–1589. Henry, duke of Guise, in the pay of Philip II of Spain, seized Paris and forced King Henry III to make him chief minister. To rid himself of Guise influence, Henry III assassinated the duke of Guise and then joined with Henry of Navarre (who meanwhile had returned to Calvinism), who was next in line to the throne, to crush the Catholic Holy League and retake the city of Paris. Although successful, Henry III was assassinated in 1589 by a monk who was repelled by the spectacle of a Catholic king cooperating with a Protestant. Henry of Navarre now claimed the throne. Realizing, however, that he would never be accepted by Catholic France, Henry took the logical way out and converted once again to Catholicism. With his coronation in 1594, the French Wars of Religion finally came to an end.

Nevertheless, the religious problem persisted until the Edict of Nantes (NAHNT) was issued in 1598. The edict acknowledged Catholicism as the official religion of France but guaranteed the Huguenots the right to worship in selected places in every district and allowed them to retain a number of fortified towns for their protection. In addition, Huguenots were allowed to enjoy all political privileges, including the holding of public offices. Although the Edict of Nantes recognized the rights of the Protestant minority and ostensibly the principle of religious toleration, it did so only out of political necessity, not out of conviction.

Philip II and Militant Catholicism   The greatest advocate of activist Catholicism in the second half of the sixteenth century was King Philip II of Spain (1556–1598), the son and heir of Charles V. Philip's reign ushered in an age of Spanish greatness, both politically and culturally.

The first major goal of Philip II was to consolidate and secure the lands he had inherited from his father. These included Spain, the Netherlands, and possessions in Italy (see Map 13.3) and the New World. For Philip, this meant strict conformity to Catholicism, enforced by aggressive use of the Spanish Inquisition, and the establishment of strong, monarchical authority. The latter was not an easy task because Philip had inherited a governmental structure in which each of the various states and territories of his empire stood in an individual relationship to the king. Philip did manage, however, to expand royal

MAP 13.3 The Height of Spanish Power Under Philip II

Like his father, Charles V, Philip II, the "Most Catholic King," was a champion of the Catholic cause against Protestantism. He sought to maintain Habsburg control in the Netherlands by combating a Protestant revolt, a rebellion eventually supported by Queen Elizabeth of England. Spain's attempt to invade England in 1588 ended in disaster.

power in Spain by making the monarchy less dependent on the traditional landed aristocracy. Philip tried to be the center of the whole government and supervised the work of all departments, even down to the smallest details. Unwilling to delegate authority, he failed to distinguish between important and trivial matters and fell weeks behind on state correspondence, where he was inclined to make marginal notes and even correct spelling. One Spanish official said, "If God used the Escorial [the royal palace where Philip worked] to deliver my death sentence, I would be immortal."

One of Philip's aims was to make Spain a dominant power in Europe. To a great extent, Spain's preeminence depended on a prosperous economy fueled by its importation of gold and silver from its New World possessions, its agriculture, its commerce, and its industry, especially in textiles, silk, and leather goods. The importation of silver also had detrimental effects, however, as it helped set off a spiraling inflation that disrupted the Spanish economy, eventually hurting both textile production and agriculture. Moreover, the expenses of war, especially after 1580, proved devastating to the Spanish economy. American gold and silver never constituted more than 20 percent of the royal revenue, leading the government to impose a crushing burden of direct and indirect taxes. Even then the government was forced to borrow. Philip repudiated his debts seven times; still, two-thirds of state income went to pay interest on the debt by the end of his reign. The attempt to make Spain a great power led to its decline after Philip's reign.

Crucial to an understanding of Philip II is the importance of Catholicism to the Spanish people and their ruler. Driven by a heritage of crusading fervor, the Spanish had little difficulty seeing themselves as a nation of people divinely chosen to save Catholic Christianity from the Protestant heretics. Philip II, the "Most Catholic King," became the champion of Catholicism throughout Europe, a role that led to spectacular victories and equally spectacular defeats for the Spanish king. Spain's leadership of a holy league against Turkish encroachments in the Mediterranean, especially the Muslim attack on the island of Cyprus, resulted in a stunning victory over the Turkish fleet at the Battle of Lepanto (LEH-pahn-toh *or* LIH-pan-toh) in 1571. Philip's greatest misfortunes came from his attempt to crush the revolt in the Netherlands and his tortured relations with Queen Elizabeth of England.

Revolt of the Netherlands   As one of the richest parts of Philip's empire, the Spanish Netherlands was of great importance to the Most Catholic King. The Netherlands consisted of seventeen provinces (the modern Netherlands, Belgium, and Luxembourg). The seven northern provinces were largely Germanic in culture and Dutch speaking, while the French- and Flemish-speaking southern provinces were closely tied to France. Situated at the commercial crossroads of northwestern Europe, the Netherlands had become prosperous through commerce and a flourishing textile industry. Because of its location, the Netherlands was open to the religious influences of the age. Though some inhabitants had adopted Lutheranism or Anabaptism, by the time of Philip II, Calvinism was also making inroads. These provinces had no real political bond holding them together except their common ruler, and that ruler was Philip II, a foreigner who was out of touch with the local situation.

Philip II hoped to strengthen his control in the Netherlands, regardless of the traditional privileges of the separate provinces. This was strongly opposed by the nobles, towns, and provincial states, which stood to lose politically if their jealously guarded privileges and freedoms were weakened. Resentment against Philip increased when the residents of the Netherlands realized that the taxes they paid were being used for Spanish interests. Finally, religion became a major catalyst for rebellion when Philip attempted to crush Calvinism. Violence erupted in 1566 when Calvinists—especially nobles—began to destroy statues and stained-glass windows in Catholic churches. Philip responded by sending the duke of Alva with 10,000 veteran Spanish and Italian troops to crush the rebellion.

The repressive policies of the duke proved counterproductive. The levying of a permanent sales tax alienated many merchants and commoners, who now joined the nobles and Calvinists in the struggle against Spanish rule. A special tribunal, known as the Council of Troubles (nicknamed the Council of Blood by the Dutch), inaugurated a reign of terror in which even powerful aristocrats were executed. As a result, the revolt now became organized, especially in the northern provinces, where William of Nassau, the prince of Orange, also known as William the Silent, and Dutch pirates known as the "Sea Beggars" mounted growing resistance. In 1573, Philip removed the duke of Alva and shifted to a more conciliatory policy to bring an end to the costly revolt.

William of Orange wished to unify all seventeen provinces, a goal seemingly realized in 1576 with the Pacification of Ghent. This agreement stipulated that all the provinces would stand together under William's leadership, respect religious differences, and demand that the Spanish troops be withdrawn. But religious differences proved too strong for any lasting union. When the duke of Parma, the next Spanish leader, arrived in the Netherlands, he astutely played on the religious differences of the provinces and split their united front. The southern provinces formed a Catholic union—the Union of Arras—in 1579 and accepted Spanish control. To counter this, William of Orange organized the seven northern, Dutch-speaking states into a Protestant union—the Union of Utrecht—determined to oppose Spanish rule. The Netherlands was now divided along religious, geographic, and political lines into two hostile camps. The struggle dragged on until 1609, when a twelve-year truce ended the war, virtually recognizing the independence of the northern provinces. These "United Provinces" soon emerged as the Dutch Republic, although the Spanish did not formally recognize them as independent until 1648. The ten southern provinces remained a Spanish possession (see Map 13.3).

The England of Elizabeth   After the death of Queen Mary in 1558, her half-sister Elizabeth (1558–1603) ascended the throne of England. During Elizabeth's reign, England rose to prominence as the relatively small island kingdom became the leader of the Protestant nations of Europe, laid the foundations for a world empire, and experienced a cultural renaissance.

The daughter of King Henry VIII and Anne Boleyn, Elizabeth had had a difficult early life. During Mary's reign, she had even been imprisoned for a while and had learned early to hide her true feelings from both private and public sight. Intelligent, cautious, and self-confident, she moved quickly to solve the difficult religious problem she had inherited from Mary, who had become extremely unpopular when she tried to return England to the Catholic fold.

Religious Policy Elizabeth's religious policy was based on moderation and compromise. As a ruler, she wished to prevent England from being torn apart over matters of religion. Parliament cooperated with the queen in initiating the Elizabethan religious settlement in 1559. The Catholic legislation of Mary's reign was repealed, and the new Act of Supremacy designated Elizabeth as "the only supreme governor of this realm, as well in all spiritual or ecclesiastical things or causes, as temporal." She used this title rather than "supreme head of the church," which had been used by both Henry VIII and Edward VI, because she did not want to upset the Catholics, who considered the pope the supreme head, or radical Protestants, who thought that Christ alone was head of the church. The Act of Uniformity restored the church service of the Book of Common Prayer from the reign of Edward VI with some revisions to make it more acceptable to Catholics. The Thirty-Nine Articles, a new confession of faith, defined theological issues midway between Lutheranism and Calvinism. Elizabeth's religious settlement was basically Protestant, but it was a moderate Protestantism that avoided overly subtle distinctions and extremes.

The new religious settlement worked, at least to the extent that it smothered religious differences in England in the second half of the sixteenth century. Two groups, however, the Catholics and the Puritans, continued to oppose it. One of Elizabeth's greatest challenges came from her Catholic cousin, Mary, queen of Scots, who was next in line to the English throne. Mary was ousted from Scotland by rebellious Calvinist nobles in 1568 and fled for her life to England. There Elizabeth placed her under house arrest and for fourteen years tolerated her involvement in a number of ill-planned Catholic plots designed to kill Elizabeth and replace her on the throne with the Catholic Mary. Finally, in 1587, after Mary became embroiled in a far more serious plot, Elizabeth had her cousin beheaded to end the threats to her regime.

Potentially more dangerous to Anglicanism in the long run were the **Puritans**. The word *Puritan* first appeared in 1564 when it was used to refer to Protestants within the Anglican Church who, inspired by Calvinist theology, wanted to remove any trace of Catholicism from the Church of England. Elizabeth managed to keep the Puritans in check during her reign.

Elizabeth proved as adept in government and foreign policy as in religious affairs. She was well served administratively by the principal secretary of state. The talents of Sir William Cecil and Sir Francis Walsingham, who together held the office for thirty-two years, ensured much of Elizabeth's success in foreign and domestic affairs. Elizabeth also handled Parliament with much skill; it met only thirteen times during her entire reign.

Foreign Policy   Caution, moderation, and expediency also dictated Elizabeth's foreign policy. Fearful of other countries' motives, Elizabeth realized that war could be disastrous for her island kingdom and her own rule. Unofficially, however, she encouraged English seamen to raid Spanish ships and colonies. Francis Drake was especially adept at plundering Spanish fleets loaded with gold and silver from Spain's New World empire. While encouraging English piracy and providing clandestine aid to French Huguenots and Dutch Calvinists to weaken France and Spain, Elizabeth pretended complete aloofness and avoided alliances that would force her into war with any major power. Gradually, however, Elizabeth was drawn into more active involvement in the Netherlands. This move accelerated the already mounting friction between Spain and England. After years of resisting the idea of invading England as impractical, Philip II of

Queen Elizabeth I: "I Have the Heart of a King"

Queen Elizabeth I ruled England from 1558 to 1603 with a consummate skill that contemporaries considered unusual in a woman. Though shrewd and paternalistic, Elizabeth, like other sixteenth-century monarchs, depended for her power on the favor of her people. When England faced the threat of an invasion by the Spanish armada of Philip II in 1588, Elizabeth sought to rally her troops with a speech at Tilbury, a town on the Thames River. This selection is taken from her speech.

Queen Elizabeth I, Speech at Tilbury

My loving people, we have been persuaded by some, that are careful of our safety, to take heed how we commit ourselves to armed multitudes, for fear of treachery; but I assure you, I do not desire to live to distrust my faithful and loving people. Let tyrants fear; I have always so behaved myself that, under God, I have placed my chiefest strength and safeguard in the loyal hearts and good will of my subjects. And therefore I am come amongst you at this time, not as for my recreation or sport, but being resolved, in the midst and heat of the battle, to live or die amongst you all; to lay down, for my God, and for my kingdom, and for my people, my honor and my blood, even in the dust. I know I have but the body of a weak and feeble woman; but I have the heart of a king, and of a king of England, too; and think foul scorn that Parma or Spain, or any prince of Europe, should dare to invade the borders of my realm: to which, rather than any dishonor should grow by me, I myself will take up arms; I myself will be your general, judge, and rewarder of every one of your virtues in the field. I know already, by your forwardness, that you have deserved rewards and crowns; and we do assure you, on the word of a prince, they shall be duly paid you. In the mean my lieutenant general shall be in my stead, than whom never prince commanded a more noble and worthy subject; not doubting by your obedience to my general, by your concord in the camp and by your valor in the field, we shall shortly have a famous victory over the enemies of my God, of my kingdom, and of my people.

Q *What qualities evident in Elizabeth's speech would have endeared her to her listeners? How was her popularity connected to the events of the late sixteenth century?*

Source: From Elizabeth I's Speech at Tilbury in 1588 to the troops.

Spain was finally persuaded to do so by advisers who assured him that the people of England would rise against their queen when the Spaniards arrived. Moreover, Philip was easily convinced that the revolt in the Netherlands would never be crushed as long as England provided support for it. In any case, a successful invasion of England would mean the overthrow of heresy and the return of England to Catholicism, surely an act in accordance with the will of God. Accordingly, Philip ordered preparations for a fleet of warships that would rendezvous with the army of the duke of Parma in Flanders and escort his troops across the English Channel for the invasion.

The Spanish Armada   The armada proved to be a disaster. The Spanish fleet that finally set sail had neither the ships nor the troops that Philip had planned to send. A conversation between a papal emissary and an officer of the Spanish fleet before the armada departed reveals the fundamental flaw:

> "And if you meet the English armada in the Channel, do you expect to win the battle?" "Of course," replied the Spaniard.
>
> "How can you be sure?" [asked the emissary].
>
> "It's very simple. It is well known that we fight in God's cause. So, when we meet the English, God will surely arrange matters so that we can grapple and board them, either by sending some strange freak of weather or, more likely, just by depriving the English of their wits. If we can come to close quarters, Spanish valor and Spanish steel (and the great masses of soldiers we shall have on board) will make our victory certain. But unless God helps us by a miracle the English, who have faster and handier ships than ours, and many more long-range guns, and who know their advantage just as well as we do, will never close with us at all, but stand aloof and knock us to pieces with their culverins [cannons], without our being able to do them any serious hurt. So," concluded the captain, and one fancies a grim smile, "we are sailing against England in the confident hope of a miracle."[19]

The hoped-for miracle never materialized. The Spanish fleet, battered by a number of encounters with the English, sailed back to Spain by a northward route around Scotland and Ireland, where it was further battered by storms. Although the English and Spanish would continue their war for another sixteen years, the defeat of the Spanish armada guaranteed for the time being that England would remain a Protestant country. Although Spain made up for its losses within a year and a half, the defeat was a psychological blow to the Spaniards.

CHRONOLOGY

REFORMATION AND RELIGIOUS WARFARE

1517–1521	Luther and the Indulgence controversy
1518	Zwingli made cathedral priest at Zurich
1521–1544	Hapsburg-Valois Wars
1524–1525	Peasants' War
1534–1535	Anabaptists at Munster
1534–1547	Henry VIII's Reformation in England
1536–1564	Calvin's church at Geneva
1542	Establishment of Roman Inquisition (Holy Office)
1545–1563	Council of Trent
1546–1555	Schmalkaldic Wars

1555	Peace of Augsburg
1556–1598	Philip II's Militant Catholicism in Spain
1562–1598	The French Wars of Religion
1566–1609	Revolt of the Netherlands
1588	Spanish armada
1598	Edict of Nantes

14

EUROPE AND THE WORLD:
NEW ENCOUNTERS, 1500–1800

© Everett Collection

A 1536 Mercator projection map showing the route of Ferdinand Magellan's first circumnavigation of the world

---

CHAPTER OUTLINE

• On the Brink of a New World • New Horizons: The Portuguese and Spanish Empires • New Rivals on the World Stage • The Impact of European Expansion • Toward a World Economy

---

ON THE BRINK OF A NEW WORLD

Nowhere has the dynamic and even ruthless energy of Western civilization been more apparent than in its expansion into the rest of the world. By the late sixteenth century, the Atlantic seaboard had become the center of a commercial activity that raised Portugal and Spain and later the Dutch Republic, England, and France to prominence. The age of expansion was a crucial factor in the European transition from the agrarian economy of the Middle Ages to a commercial and industrial capitalistic system. Expansion also brought Europeans into new and lasting contacts with non-European peoples that inaugurated a new age of world history in the sixteenth century.

The Motives for Expansion   For almost a millennium, Catholic Europe had been confined to one geographic area. Its one major attempt to expand beyond those frontiers, the Crusades, had largely failed. Of course, Europe had never completely lost touch with the outside world: the goods of Asia and Africa made their way into medieval castles, the works of Muslim philosophers were read in medieval universities, and in the ninth and tenth centuries, the Vikings had even made their way to the eastern fringes of North America. But in all cases, contacts with non-European civilizations remained limited until the end of the fifteenth century, when Europeans embarked on a remarkable series of overseas journeys. What caused Europeans to undertake such dangerous voyages to the ends of the earth?

Fantastic Lands   Europeans had long felt the lure of lands outside Europe as a result of a large body of fantasy literature about "other worlds" that blossomed in the Middle Ages. In the fourteenth century, the author of *The Travels of John Mandeville* spoke of realms (which he had never seen) filled with precious stones and gold. Other lands were more frightening and considerably less appealing. In one country, "the folk be great giants of twenty-eight foot long, or thirty foot long.... And they eat more gladly man's flesh than any other flesh." Farther north was a land inhabited by "full cruel and evil women. And they have precious stones in their eyes. And they be of that kind that if they behold any man with wrath they slay him at once with the beholding."[1] Other writers, however, enticed Europeans with descriptions of mysterious Christian kingdoms: the magical kingdom of Prester John in Africa and a Christian community in southern India that was supposedly founded by Thomas, an apostle of Jesus.

Economic Motives   Although Muslim control of Central Asia cut Europe off from the countries farther east, the Mongol conquests in the thirteenth century had reopened the doors. The most famous medieval travelers to the East were the Polos of Venice. Niccolò and Maffeo, merchants from Venice, accompanied by Niccolò's son Marco, undertook the lengthy journey to the court of the great Mongol ruler Khubilai Khan (1259–1294) in 1271. An account of Marco's experiences, the *Travels*, was the most informative of all the descriptions of Asia by medieval European travelers. Others followed the Polos, but in the fourteenth century, the conquests of the Ottoman Turks and then the breakup of the Mongol

Empire reduced Western traffic to the East. With the closing of the overland routes, a number of people in Europe became interested in the possibility of reaching Asia by sea to gain access to the spices and other precious items of the region. Christopher Columbus had a copy of Marco Polo's *Travels* in his possession when he began to envision his epoch-making voyage across the Atlantic Ocean.

An economic motive thus loomed large in European expansion in the Renaissance. Merchants, adventurers, and government officials had high hopes of finding new areas of trade, especially more direct access to the spices of the East. These continued to come to Europe via Arab intermediaries but were outrageously expensive. In addition to the potential profits to be made from the spice trade, many European explorers and conquerors did not hesitate to express their desire for material gain in the form of gold and other precious metals. One Spanish conquistador (kahn-KEESS-tuh-dor) explained that the purpose of their mission to the New World was to "serve God and His Majesty, to give light to those who were in darkness, and to grow rich, as all men desire to do."[2]

Religious Zeal   The conquistador's statement expressed another major reason for the overseas voyages—religious zeal. A crusading mentality was particularly strong in Portugal and Spain, where the Muslims had largely been driven out in the Middle Ages. Contemporaries of Prince Henry the Navigator of Portugal (see "The Development of a Portuguese Maritime Empire" later in this chapter) said that he was motivated by "his great desire to make increase in the faith of our Lord Jesus Christ and to bring him all the souls that should be saved." Although most scholars believe that the religious motive was secondary to economic considerations, it would be foolish to overlook the genuine desire of explorers and conquistadors, let alone missionaries, to convert the heathen to Christianity. Hernán Cortés (hayr-NAHN kor-TAYSS *or* kor-TEZ), the conqueror of Mexico, asked his Spanish rulers if it was not their duty to ensure that the native Mexicans "are introduced into and instructed in the holy Catholic faith" and predicted that if "the devotion, trust and hope which they now have in their idols turned so as to repose with the divine power of the true God … they would work many miracles."[3] Spiritual and secular affairs were closely intertwined in the sixteenth century. No doubt, the desire for grandeur and glory as well as plain intellectual curiosity and a spirit of adventure also played some role in European expansion.

The Means for Expansion   If "God, glory, and gold" were the primary motives, what made the voyages possible? First of all, the expansion of Europe was connected to the growth of centralized monarchies during the Renaissance. Although historians still debate the degree of that centralization, the reality is that Renaissance expansion was a state enterprise. By the second half of the fifteenth century, European monarchies had increased both their authority and their resources and were in a position to turn their energies beyond their borders. For France, that meant the invasion of Italy, but for Portugal, a state not strong enough to pursue power in Europe, it meant going abroad. The Spanish monarchy was strong enough by the sixteenth century to pursue power both in Europe and beyond.

Maps   At the same time, Europeans had achieved a level of wealth and technology that enabled them to make a regular series of voyages beyond Europe. Although the highly schematic and symbolic medieval maps were of little help to sailors, the **portolani** (pohr-tuh-LAH-nee), or charts made by medieval navigators and mathematicians in the thirteenth and fourteenth centuries, were more useful. With details on coastal contours, distances between ports, and compass readings, these charts proved of great value for voyages in European waters. But because the *portolani* were drawn on a flat scale and took no account of the curvature of the earth, they were of little use for longer overseas voyages. Only when seafarers began to venture beyond the coast of Europe did they begin to accumulate information about the actual shape of the earth. By the end of the fifteenth century, cartography had developed to the point that Europeans possessed fairly accurate maps of the known world.

One of the most important world maps available to Europeans at the end of the fifteenth century was that of Ptolemy (TAHL-uh-mee), an astronomer of the second century C.E. Ptolemy's work, the *Geography*, had been known to Arab geographers as early as the eighth century, but it was not until the fifteenth century that a Latin translation was made of the work. Printed editions of Ptolemy's *Geography*, which contained his world map, became available from 1477 on. Ptolemy's map (see the illustration below) showed the world as spherical with three major landmasses—Europe, Asia, and Africa—and only two oceans. In addition to showing the oceans as considerably smaller than the landmasses, Ptolemy had also drastically underestimated the circumference of the earth, which led Columbus and other adventurers to believe that it would be feasible to sail west from Europe to reach Asia.

Ships and Sailing   Europeans had also developed remarkably seaworthy ships as well as new navigational techniques. European shipmakers had mastered the use of the axial rudder (an import from China) and had learned to combine the use of lateen sails with a square rig. With these innovations, they could construct ships mobile enough to sail against the wind and engage in naval warfare and also large enough to mount heavy cannons and carry a substantial amount of goods over long distances. Previously, sailors had used a quadrant and their knowledge of the position of the Pole Star to ascertain their latitude. Below the equator, however, this technique was useless. Only with the assistance of new navigational aids such as the compass and the astrolabe were they able to explore the high seas with confidence.

A final spur to exploration was the growing knowledge of the wind patterns in the Atlantic Ocean. The first European fleets sailing southward along the coast of West Africa had found their efforts to return hindered by the strong winds that blew steadily from the north along the coast. By the late fifteenth century, however, sailors had learned to tack out into the ocean, where they were able to catch westerly winds in the vicinity of the Azores that brought them back to the coast of western Europe. Christopher Columbus used this technique in his voyages to the Americas, and others relied on their new knowledge of the winds to round the continent of Africa in search of the Spice Islands.

NEW HORIZONS: THE PORTUGUESE
AND SPANISH EMPIRES

Portugal took the lead in the European age of expansion when it began to explore the coast of Africa under the sponsorship of Prince Henry the Navigator (1394–1460). His motives were a blend of seeking a Christian kingdom as an ally against the Muslims, acquiring trade opportunities for Portugal, and spreading Christianity.

**The
Development
of a Portuguese
Maritime
Empire**
In 1419, Prince Henry founded a school for navigators on the southwestern coast of Portugal. Shortly thereafter, Portuguese fleets began probing southward along the western coast of Africa in search of gold, which had been carried northward from south of the Atlas Mountains in central Morocco for centuries. In 1441, Portuguese ships reached the Senegal River, just north of Cape Verde, and brought home a cargo of black Africans, most of whom were then sold as slaves to wealthy buyers elsewhere in Europe. Within a few years, an estimated one thousand slaves were shipped annually from the area back to Lisbon.

Through regular expeditions, the Portuguese gradually crept down the African coast, and in 1471, they discovered a new source of gold along the southern coast of the hump of West Africa (an area that would henceforth be known to Europeans as the Gold Coast). A few years later, they established contact with the state of Bakongo, near the mouth of the Zaire (Congo) River in Central Africa. To facilitate trade in gold, ivory, and slaves (some slaves were brought back to Lisbon, while others were bartered to local merchants for gold), the Portuguese leased land from local rulers and built stone forts along the coast.

The Portuguese in India   Hearing reports of a route to India around the southern tip of Africa, Portuguese sea captains continued their probing. In 1488, Bartholomeu Dias (bar-toh-loh-MAY-oo DEE-ush) (c. 1450–1500) took advantage of westerly winds in the South Atlantic to round the Cape of Good Hope, but he feared a mutiny from his crew and returned (see Map 14.1). Ten years later, a fleet under the command of Vasco da Gama (VAHSH-koh dah GAHM-uh) (c. 1460–1524) rounded the cape and stopped at several ports controlled by Muslim merchants along the coast of East Africa. Da Gama's fleet then crossed the Arabian Sea and reached the port of Calicut, on the southwestern coast of India, on May 18, 1498. On arriving in Calicut, da Gama announced to his surprised hosts that he had come in search of "Christians and spices." He found no Christians, but he did find the spices he sought. Although he lost two ships en route, da Gama's remaining vessels returned to Europe with their holds filled with ginger and cinnamon, a cargo that earned the investors a profit of several thousand percent.

Portuguese fleets returned annually to the area, seeking to destroy Arab shipping and establish a monopoly in the spice trade. In 1509, a Portuguese armada defeated a combined fleet of Turkish and Indian ships off the coast of India and began to impose a blockade on the entrance to the Red Sea to cut off the flow of

Principal Voyages of Discovery

A Portuguese expeditions, 1430s–1480s
B Dias, 1487–1488
C Da Gama, 1497–1499
D Portuguese voyages to the East, 1509–1514
E Columbus's first voyage, 1492
F Columbus's three successive voyages, 1493–1502
G Voyages attended by Vespucci, 1499–1502
H Magellan–Del Cano, 1519–1522
I Cabot, 1497

Areas under Spanish control
Areas under Portuguese control
—— Line of Demarcation, Treaty of Tordesillas, 1494

■ Spanish trading cities
▫ Portuguese trading cities
▫ Independent trading cities

⟶ Spanish routes
⟶ Portuguese routes
- - -▶ Other routes

© Cengage Learning 2012

MAP 14.1 Discoveries and Possessions in the Fifteenth and Sixteenth Centuries

Desire for wealth was the main motivation of the early explorers, though spreading Christianity was also an important factor. Portugal under Prince Henry the Navigator initiated the first voyages in the early fifteenth century; Spain's explorations began at the century's end.

spices to Muslim rulers in Egypt and the Ottoman Empire. The following year, seeing the need for a land base in the area, Admiral Afonso de Albuquerque (ah-FAHN-soh day AL-buh-kur-kee) (c. 1462–1515) set up port facilities at Goa (GOH-uh), on the western coast of India south of present-day Mumbai (Bombay). Goa henceforth became the headquarters for Portuguese operations throughout the entire region.

In Search of Spices   In the early sixteenth century, the Portuguese expanded their search for spices. In 1511, Albuquerque sailed into the harbor of Malacca (muh-LAK-uh) on the Malay peninsula. Malacca had been transformed by its Muslim rulers into a thriving port and a major stopping point in the spice trade. After a short but bloody battle, the Portuguese seized the city and massacred the local Arab population. This slaughter initiated a fierce and brutal struggle between the Portuguese and the Arabs. According to one account, "To enhance the terror of his name he [Albuquerque] always separated Arabs from the other inhabitants of a captured city, and cut off the right hand of the men, and the noses and ears of the women."[4] By seizing Malacca, the Portuguese had not only weakened Arab control of the spice trade but obtained a major port en route to the Moluccas (muh-LUHK-uhz), then known as the Spice Islands.

From Malacca, the Portuguese launched expeditions farther east, to China and the Spice Islands. There they signed a treaty with a local ruler for the purchase and export of cloves to the European market. The new trading empire was now complete. Within a few years, the Portuguese had managed to seize control of the spice trade from Muslim traders and had garnered substantial profits for the Portuguese monarchy. Nevertheless, the Portuguese Empire remained limited, consisting only of trading posts on the coasts of India and China. The Portuguese lacked the power, the population, and the desire to colonize the Asian regions.

Why were the Portuguese so successful? Basically, their success was a matter of guns and seamanship. The first Portuguese fleet to arrive in Indian waters was relatively modest in size, consisting of three ships and twenty guns, a force sufficient for self-defense and intimidation but not for serious military operations. Later Portuguese fleets, which began to arrive with regularity early in the sixteenth century, were more heavily armed and were able not only to intimidate but also to inflict severe defeats if necessary on local naval and land forces. The Portuguese by no means possessed a monopoly on the use of firearms and explosives, but their effective use of naval technology, their heavy guns that could be mounted in the hulls of their sturdy vessels, and their tactics gave them military superiority over lightly armed rivals that they were able to exploit until the arrival of other European forces several decades later.

Voyages to the New World   While the Portuguese were seeking access to the spice trade of the Indies by sailing eastward through the Indian Ocean, the Spanish were attempting to reach the same destination by sailing westward across the Atlantic. Although the Spanish came to overseas discovery and exploration after the initial efforts of Henry the Navigator, their greater resources enabled them to establish a far grander overseas empire than that of the Portuguese—and one that was quite different.

The Voyages of Columbus   An important figure in the history of Spanish exploration was an Italian known as Christopher Columbus (1451–1506). Knowledgeable Europeans were aware that the world was round but had little understanding of its circumference or the extent of the continent of Asia. Convinced that the circumference of the earth was less than contemporaries believed and that Asia was larger than people thought, Columbus felt that Asia could be reached by sailing west instead of around Africa. After being rejected by the Portuguese, he persuaded Queen Isabella of Spain to finance his exploratory expedition.

With three ships, the *Santa María*, the *Niña*, and the *Pinta*, and a crew of ninety men, Columbus set sail on August 3, 1492. On October 12, he reached the Bahamas and then went on to explore the coastline of Cuba and the northern shores of Hispaniola (present-day Haiti and the Dominican Republic). Columbus believed that he had reached Asia, and in his reports to Queen Isabella and King

Christopher Columbus. *Columbus was an Italian explorer who worked for the queen of Spain. He has become a symbol for two entirely different perspectives. To some, he was a great and heroic explorer who discovered the New World; to others, especially in Latin America, he was responsible for beginning a process of invasion that led to the destruction of an entire way of life. Because Columbus was never painted during his lifetime, the numerous portraits of him are more fanciful than accurate. The portrait shown here was probably done by the Italian painter Ridolfo Ghirlandaio.*

© Museo Navale, Genova-Pegli/SuperStock

Ferdinand upon his return to Spain, he assured them not only that he would eventually find gold but also that they had a golden opportunity to convert the natives —whom Columbus persisted in calling "Indians"—to Christianity. In three subsequent voyages (1493, 1498, 1502), Columbus sought in vain to find a route to the Asian mainland. In his four voyages, Columbus landed on all the major islands of the Caribbean and the mainland of Central America, still convinced that he had reached the Indies in Asia.

New Voyages   Although Columbus clung to his belief until his death, other explorers soon realized that he had discovered a new frontier altogether. State-sponsored explorers joined the race to the New World. A Venetian seaman, John Cabot, explored the New England coastline of the Americas under a license from King Henry VII of England. The continent of South America was discovered accidentally by the Portuguese sea captain Pedro Cabral (kuh-BRAL) in 1500. Amerigo Vespucci (ahm-ay-REE-goh vess-POO-chee), a Florentine, accompanied several voyages and wrote a series of letters describing the geography of the New World. The publication of these letters led to the use of the name "America" (after Amerigo) for the new lands.

The first two decades of the sixteenth century witnessed numerous overseas voyages that explored the eastern coasts of both North and South America. Vasco Nuñez de Balboa (VAHS-koh NOON-yez day bal-BOH-uh) (1475–1519), a

Spanish explorer, led an expedition across the Isthmus of Panama and reached the Pacific Ocean in 1513. Perhaps the most dramatic of all these expeditions was the journey of Ferdinand Magellan (1480–1521) in 1519. After passing through the strait named after him at the southern tip of South America, he sailed across the Pacific Ocean and reached the Philippines, where he was killed by the natives. Although only one of his fleet of five ships completed the return voyage to Spain, Magellan's name is still associated with the first known circumnavigation of the earth.

The Europeans referred to the newly discovered territories as the New World, even though they held flourishing civilizations populated by millions of people. But the Americas were indeed new to the Europeans, who quickly saw opportunities for conquest and exploitation. The Spanish, in particular, were interested because the 1494 Treaty of Tordesillas (tor-day-SEE-yass) had divided up the newly discovered world into separate Portuguese and Spanish spheres of influence, and it turned out that most of South America (except for the eastern hump) fell within the Spanish sphere (see Map 14.1). Hereafter the route east around the Cape of Good Hope was to be reserved for the Portuguese while the route across the Atlantic was assigned to Spain.

The Spanish Empire in the New World   The Spanish conquerors known as **conquistadors** were hardy individuals motivated by a typical sixteenth-century blend of glory, greed, and religious crusading zeal. Although authorized by the Castilian crown, these groups were financed and outfitted privately, not by the government. Their superior weapons, organizational skills, and determination brought the conquistadors incredible success. They also benefited from rivalries among the native peoples and the decimation of the native peoples by European diseases (see "Disease in the New World" later in this chapter).

Early Civilizations in Mesoamerica   Before the Spaniards arrived in the New World, Mesoamerica (modern Mexico and Central America) had already hosted a number of flourishing civilizations. Beginning around 300 C.E., on the Yucatán peninsula a people known as the Maya (MY-uh) had built one of the most sophisticated civilizations in the Americas. The Maya built splendid temples and pyramids, were accomplished artists, and developed a sophisticated calendar, as accurate as any in existence in the world at that time. The Maya were an agrarian people who cleared the dense rain forests, developed farming, and built a patchwork of city-states. Mayan civilization came to include much of Central America and southern Mexico. For unknown reasons, Mayan civilization began to decline around 800 and had collapsed less than a hundred years later.

Sometime during the early twelfth century C.E., a people known as the Aztecs began a long migration that brought them to the Valley of Mexico. They established their capital at Tenochtitlán (tay-nawch-teet-LAHN), on an island in the middle of Lake Texcoco (now the location of Mexico City). For the next hundred years, the Aztecs built their city, constructing temples, other public buildings, houses, and causeways of stone across Lake Texcoco to the north, south, and west, linking the many islands to the mainland. At the beginning of the fifteenth century, they built an aqueduct to bring fresh water from a spring 4 miles away.

The Aztecs were outstanding warriors, and while they were building their capital city, they also set out to bring the entire area around the city under their control. By the early fifteenth century, they had become the leading city-state in the lake region. For the remainder of the fifteenth century, the Aztecs consolidated their rule over much of what is modern Mexico, from the Atlantic to the Pacific Ocean and as far south as the Guatemalan border. The new kingdom was not a centralized state but a collection of semi-independent territories governed by local lords. These rulers were confirmed in their authority by the Aztec ruler in return for the payment of tribute. This loose political organization would later contribute to the downfall of the Aztec Empire.

Spanish Conquest of the Aztec Empire   In 1519, a Spanish expedition under the command of Hernán Cortés (1485–1547) landed at Veracruz, on the Gulf of Mexico. He marched to the city of Tenochtitlán at the head of a small contingent of troops (550 soldiers and 16 horses); as he went, he made alliances with city-states that had tired of the oppressive rule of the Aztecs.

Biblioteca Laurenziana, Florence//NYPL/Science Source/Getty Images

Aztec Victims of Smallpox. *The indigenous populations of the New World had no immunities to the diseases of the Old World, such as smallpox. By 1520, smallpox had spread throughout the Caribbean and Mesoamerica. This sixteenth-century drawing by a Franciscan friar portrays Native Americans afflicted with smallpox. The pustules that often covered the body are clearly depicted. The figure at the lower right twists in agony, reflecting the immense pain experienced by those who contracted the disease.*

Especially important was Tlaxcala (tuh-lah-SKAH-lah), a state that the Aztecs had not been able to conquer. In November, Cortés arrived at Tenochtitlán, where he received a friendly welcome from the Aztec monarch Moctezuma (mahk-tuh-ZOO-muh) (often called Montezuma). At first, Moctezuma believed that his visitor was a representative of Quetzalcoatl (KWET-sul-koh-AHT-ul), the god who had departed from his homeland centuries before and had promised that he would return. Riddled with fears, Moctezuma offered gifts of gold to the foreigners and gave them a palace to use while they were in the city.

But the Spaniards quickly wore out their welcome. They took Moctezuma hostage and proceeded to pillage the city. In the fall of 1520, one year after Cortés had arrived, the local population revolted and drove the invaders from the city. Many of the Spaniards were killed, but the Aztecs soon experienced new disasters. As one Aztec related, "At about the time that the Spaniards had fled from Mexico, there came a great sickness, a pestilence, the smallpox." With no natural immunity to the diseases of the Europeans, many Aztecs fell sick and died (see "Disease in the New World" later in this chapter). Meanwhile, Cortés received fresh soldiers from his new allies; the state of Tlaxcala alone provided 50,000 warriors. After four months, the city capitulated.

The Spaniards then embarked on a new wave of destruction. The pyramids, temples, and palaces were leveled, and the stones were used to build Spanish government buildings and churches. The rivers and canals were filled in. The mighty Aztec Empire on mainland Mexico was no more. Between 1531 and 1550, the Spanish gained control of northern Mexico.

The Inca   In the late fourteenth century, the Inca were a small community in the area of Cuzco (KOOS-koh), a city located at an altitude of 10,000 feet in the mountains of southern Peru. In the 1440s, however, under the leadership of their powerful ruler Pachakuti (pah-chah-KOO-tee), the Inca launched a campaign of conquest that eventually brought the entire region under their control. Pachakuti created a highly centralized state. Cuzco, the capital, was transformed from a city of mud and thatch into an imposing city of stone. Under Pachakuti and his immediate successors, Topa Inca and Huayna Inca (the word *Inca* means "ruler"), the boundaries of the Inca Empire were extended as far as Ecuador, central Chile, and the edge of the Amazon basin. The empire included perhaps 12 million people.

Pachakuti divided his realm into four quarters, each ruled by a governor. The quarters were in turn divided into provinces, each also ruled by a governor. The governors were usually chosen from relatives of the royal family. Each province was supposed to contain about 10,000 residents. At the top of the entire system was the emperor, who was believed to be descended from the sun god.

The Inca were great builders. One major project was a system of 24,800 miles of roads that extended from the border of modern-day Colombia to a point south of modern-day Santiago, Chile. Two major roadways extended in a north-south direction, one through the Andes Mountains and the other along the coast, with connecting routes between them. Rest houses, located a day's walk apart, and

The Spanish Conquistador: Cortés and the Conquest of Mexico

Hernán Cortés was a minor Spanish nobleman who came to the New World in 1504 to seek his fortune. Contrary to his superior's orders, Cortés waged an independent campaign of conquest and overthrew the Aztec Empire in Mexico (1519–1522). Cortés wrote a series of five reports to Emperor Charles V to justify his action. The second report includes a description of Tenochtitlán, the capital of the Aztec Empire. The Spanish conquistador and his men were obviously impressed by this city, awesome in its architecture yet built by people who lacked European technology, such as wheeled vehicles and tools of hard metal.

Cortés's Description of Tenochtitlán

The great city Tenochtitlán is built in the midst of this salt lake, and it is two leagues from the heart of the city to any point on the mainland. Four causeways lead to it, all made by hand and some twelve feet wide. The city itself is as large as Seville or Córdoba. The principal streets are very broad and straight, the majority of them being of beaten earth, but a few and at least half of the smaller thoroughfares are waterways along which they pass in their canoes. Moreover, even the principal streets have openings at regular distances so that the water can freely pass from one to another, and these openings which are very broad are spanned by great bridges of huge beams, very stoutly put together, so firm indeed that over many of them ten horsemen can ride at once. Seeing that if the natives intended any treachery against us they would have every opportunity from the way in which the city is built, for by removing the bridges from the entrances and exits they could leave us to die of hunger with no possibility of getting to the mainland, I immediately set to work as soon as we entered the city on the building of four brigs, and in a short space of time had them finished so that we could ship 300 men and the horses to the mainland whenever we so desired.

The city has many open squares in which markets are continuously held and storage depots were placed along the roads. The Inca also built various types of bridges, including some of the finest examples of suspension bridges in premodern times, over the ravines and waterways.

Spanish Conquest of the Inca Empire   The Inca Empire was still flourishing when the first Spanish expeditions arrived in the area. In December 1530, Francisco Pizarro (frahn-CHESS-koh puh-ZAHR-oh) (c. 1475–1541) landed on the Pacific coast of South America with a band of about 180 men, but like Cortés, he had steel weapons, gunpowder, and horses, none of which were familiar to his hosts. Pizarro was also lucky because the Inca Empire had already succumbed to an epidemic of smallpox. Like the Aztecs, the Inca had no immunities to European diseases, and all too soon, smallpox was devastating entire villages. In another stroke of good fortune for Pizarro, even the Inca emperor was a victim. Upon the emperor's death, two sons claimed the throne, setting off a civil war. Pizarro took the general business of buying and selling proceeds. One square in particular is twice as big as that of Salamanca and completely surrounded by arcades where there are daily more than 60,000 folk buying and selling. Every kind of merchandise such as may be met with in every land is for sale there, whether of food and victuals, or ornaments of gold and silver, or lead, brass, copper, tin, precious stones, bones, shells, snails and feathers; limestone for building is likewise sold there, stone both rough and polished, bricks burnt and unburnt, wood of all kinds and in all stages of preparation.... There is a street of herb-sellers where there are all manner of roots and medicinal plants that are found in the land. There are houses as it were of apothecaries where they sell medicines made from these herbs, both for drinking and for use as ointments and salves. There are barbers' shops where you may have your hair washed and cut. There are other shops where you may obtain food and drink....

Finally, to avoid being wordy in telling all the wonders of this city, I will simply say that the manner of living among the people is very similar to that in Spain, and considering that this is a barbarous nation shut off from a knowledge of the true God or communication with enlightened nations, one may well marvel at the orderliness and good government which is everywhere maintained.

The actual service of Montezuma and those things which call for admiration by their greatness and state would take so long to describe that I assure your Majesty I do not know where to begin with any hope of ending. For as I have already said, what could there be more astonishing than that a barbarous monarch such as he should have reproductions made in gold, silver, precious stones, and feathers of all things to be found in his land, and so perfectly reproduced that there is no goldsmith or silversmith in the world who could better them, nor can one understand what instrument could have been used for fashioning the jewels; as for the featherwork its like is not to be seen in either wax or embroidery; it is so marvelously delicate.

Q *What did Cortés focus on in his description of this Aztec city? Why do you think he felt justified in overthrowing the Aztec Empire?*

Source: From *The European Reconnaissance: Selected Documents* by John H. Parry. Copyright © 1968 by John H. Parry. Reprinted by permission Walker & Co.

advantage of the situation by seizing Atahualpa (ah-tuh-WAHL-puh), whose forces had just defeated his brother's. Armed only with stones, arrows, and light spears, Incan soldiers were no match for the charging horses of the Spanish, let alone their guns and cannons. After executing Atahualpa, Pizarro and his soldiers, aided by their Incan allies, marched on Cuzco and captured the Incan capital. By 1535, Pizarro had established a capital at Lima for a new colony of the Spanish Empire.

Administration of the Spanish Empire   Spanish policy toward the Indians of the New World was a combination of confusion, misguided paternalism, and cruel exploitation. Whereas the conquistadors made decisions based on expediency and their own interests, Queen Isabella declared the native peoples to be subjects of Castile and instituted the Spanish *encomienda* (en-koh-MYEN-dah), an economic and social system that permitted the conquering Spaniards to collect tribute from the Indians and use them as laborers. In return, the holders of an *encomienda* were supposed to protect the Indians, pay them wages, and supervise their spiritual needs. In practice, this meant that the settlers were free to implement the paternalistic system of the government as they pleased. Three thousand miles from Spain, Spanish settlers largely ignored their government and brutally used the Indians to pursue their own economic interests. Indians were put to work on plantations and in the lucrative gold and silver mines. In Peru, the Spanish made use of the *mita*, a system that allowed authorities to draft native labor to work in the silver mines.

Forced labor, starvation, and especially disease took a fearful toll of Indian lives. Voices were raised to protest the harsh treatment of the Indians, especially by Dominican friars. In a 1510 sermon, Antón Montecino startled churchgoers in Santo Domingo by saying:

> And you are heading for damnation ... for you are destroying an innocent people. For they are God's people, these innocents, whom you destroyed. By what right do you make them die? Mining gold for you in your mines or working for you in your fields, by what right do you unleash enslaving wars upon them? They lived in peace in this land before you came, in peace in their own homes. They did nothing to harm you to cause you to slaughter them wholesale.[5]

In 1542, largely in response to the publications of Bartolomé de Las Casas (bahr-toh-loh-MAY day lahs KAH-sahs), a Dominican friar who championed the Indians, the government abolished the *encomienda* system and provided more protection for the natives.

In the New World, the Spanish developed an administrative system based on viceroys. Spanish possessions were initially divided into two major administrative units: New Spain (Mexico, Central America, and the Caribbean islands), with its center in Mexico City, and Peru (western South America), governed by a **viceroy** in Lima. According to legislation of 1542, "the kingdoms of New Spain and Peru are to be ruled and governed by viceroys, who shall represent our royal person, hold the superior government, do and administer justice equally to all our subjects and vassals, and concern themselves with everything that will promote the calm, peace, ennoblement and pacification of those provinces."[6] Each viceroy served as the king's chief civil and military officer and was aided by advisory groups called **audiencias** (ow-dee-en-SEE-uss), which also functioned as supreme judicial bodies.

By papal agreement, the Catholic monarchs of Spain were given extensive rights over ecclesiastical affairs in the New World. They could appoint all bishops and clergy, build churches, collect fees, and supervise the various religious orders that sought to convert the heathen. Catholic missionaries converted and baptized hundreds of thousands of Indians in the early years of the conquest.

The mass conversion of the Indians brought the organizational and institutional structures of Catholicism to the New World. Dioceses, parishes, cathedrals, schools, and hospitals—all the trappings of civilized European society—soon appeared in the Spanish Empire. So, too, did the Spanish Inquisition, established first in Peru in 1570 and in Mexico the following year.

Disease in   When Columbus reached the Caribbean island of Hispaniola
the New World   in 1492, he brought more than gunpowder, horses, attack
                        dogs, and soldiers to the shores of the New World. With no
natural resistance to European diseases, the Indians of America were ravaged by
smallpox, influenza, measles, and pneumonic plague, and later by typhus, yellow
fever, and cholera.

Smallpox, a highly contagious disease, was spread through droplets in the air
or direct contact with contaminated objects, such as clothing. In 1518, a smallpox
epidemic erupted and quickly spread along trade routes from the Caribbean to
Mesoamerica, killing a third of the Indian population. The disease ultimately
reached Tenochtitlán and helped make possible its conquest by Hernán Cortés.
When the Spaniards reentered the city in 1521, they found an appalling scene, as
reported by Bernal Díaz (ber-NAHL DEE-ass), who accompanied Cortés:

> We could not walk without treading on the bodies and heads of dead Indians.
> I have read about the destruction of Jerusalem, but I do not think the mortality
> was greater there than here in Mexico, where most of the warriors who had
> crowded in from all the provinces and subject towns had died. As I have said, the
> dry land and the stockades were piled with corpses. Indeed, the stench was so
> bad that no one could endure it.... Even Cortés was ill from the odors which
> assailed his nostrils.[7]

Smallpox ravaged the Aztecs. The Inca suffered a similar fate from smallpox
and measles as well.

Throughout the sixteenth century, outbreaks of Old World diseases continued
to spark epidemics that killed off large proportions of the local populations. By
1630, smallpox had reached New England. The ferocity of the epidemics left few
survivors to tend the crops, leading to widespread starvation and higher mortality
rates. Although scholarly estimates vary drastically, a reasonable guess is that 30 to
40 percent of the local populations died. On Hispaniola alone, out of an initial
population of 100,000 Indians when Columbus arrived in 1492, only 300 survived
by 1570. The population of central Mexico, estimated at roughly 11 million in
1519, had declined to 6.5 million by 1540 and 2.5 million by the end of the sixteenth century.

The high mortality rates among the native populations resulted in a shortage of
workers for the Europeans, which led them to turn to Africa for the labor needed
for the silver mines and sugar plantations (see "Africa: The Slave Trade" later in
this chapter). Despite the Europeans' technological advantages, the biological weapons that they brought with them from the Old World proved to have an even
greater impact on the Americas.

NEW RIVALS ON THE WORLD STAGE

Portugal and Spain had been the first Atlantic nations to take advantage of the age
of exploration, starting in the late fifteenth century, and both had become great
colonial powers. In the seventeenth century, however, their European neighbors to
the north—first the Dutch and then the French and English—moved to replace the
Portuguese and Spanish and create their own colonial empires. The new rivals and

their rivalry soon had an impact on much of the rest of the world—in Africa, Asia, and the Americas.

Africa: The Slave Trade   Although the primary objective of the Portuguese in sailing around Africa was to find a sea route to the Spice Islands, they soon discovered that profits could be made in Africa itself. So did other Europeans.

The Portuguese built forts on both the western and eastern coasts of Africa and tried, above all, to dominate the trade in gold. During the mid-seventeenth century, however, the Dutch seized a number of Portuguese forts along the West African coast and at the same time took control of much of the Portuguese trade across the Indian Ocean.

The Dutch East India Company, a trading company established in 1602 under government sponsorship, also set up a settlement in southern Africa, at the Cape of Good Hope, to serve as a base to supply food and other provisions to Dutch ships en route to the Spice Islands. Eventually, however, it developed into a permanent colony. Dutch farmers, known as Boers, began to settle in areas outside the city of Cape Town. The area's moderate climate and freedom from tropical diseases made it attractive for Europeans to settle there.

The European exploration of the African coastline did not affect most Africans living in the interior of the continent, but for peoples living on or near the coast, the impact was great indeed. As the trade in slaves increased during the sixteenth through the eighteenth centuries, thousands and then millions of Africans were removed from their homes and forcibly shipped to plantations in the New World.

Origins of the Slave Trade   Traffic in slaves was not new. As in other areas of the world, slavery had been practiced in Africa since ancient times. In the fifteenth century, it continued at a fairly steady level. The primary market for African slaves was the Middle East, where most were used as domestic servants. Slavery also existed in many European countries, where some slaves from Africa or war captives from the regions north of the Black Sea were used as household help or agricultural workers.

At first, the Portuguese simply replaced European slaves with African ones. During the second half of the fifteenth century, about a thousand slaves were taken to Portugal each year. Most ended up serving as domestic servants for affluent families in Europe. But the discovery of the Americas in the 1490s and the planting of sugarcane in South America and the islands of the Caribbean changed the situation drastically.

Cane sugar had first been introduced to Europeans from the Middle East during the Crusades. At the end of the fifteenth century, the Portuguese set up sugar plantations worked by African laborers on an island off the central coast of Africa. During the sixteenth century, sugarcane plantations were set up along the eastern coast of Brazil and on several islands in the Caribbean. Because the growing of cane sugar demands both skill and large quantities of labor, the new plantations required more workers than could be provided by the small American Indian population in the New World, decimated by diseases imported from the Old World.

Since the climate and soil of much of West Africa were not conducive to the cultivation of sugar, African slaves began to be shipped to Brazil and the Caribbean to work on the plantations. The first were sent from Portugal, but in 1518, a Spanish ship carried the first boatload of African slaves directly from Africa to the New World.

Growth of the Slave Trade   During the next two centuries, the trade in slaves grew dramatically and became part of the **triangular trade** connecting Europe, Africa, and the American continents that characterized the new Atlantic economy (see Map 14.2). European merchant ships (primarily those of England, France, Spain, Portugal, and the Dutch Republic) carried European manufactured goods,

MAP 14.2 Triangular Trade Route in the Atlantic Economy

As the trade in slaves grew, it became a part of the triangular trade route that characterized the Atlantic economy, involving the exchange of goods and slaves between the western coast of Europe, the slave depots on the African coast, and the ports of North and South America.

The Atlantic Slave Trade

One of the most odious practices of early modern Western society was the Atlantic slave trade, which reached its height in the eighteenth century. Blacks were transported in densely packed cargo ships from the western coast of Africa to the Americas to work as slaves in the plantation economy. Not until late in the eighteenth century did a rising chorus of voices raise serious objections to this trade in human beings. This excerpt presents a criticism of the slave trade from an anonymous French writer.

Diary of a Citizen

As soon as the ships have lowered their anchors off the coast of Guinea, the price at which the captains have decided to buy the captives is announced to the Negroes who buy prisoners from various princes and sell them to Europeans. Presents are sent to the sovereign who rules over that particular part of the coast, and permission to trade is given. Immediately

the slaves are brought by inhuman brokers like so many victims dragged to a sacrifice. White men who covet that portion of the human race receive them in a little house they have erected on the shore, where they have entrenched themselves with two pieces of cannon and twenty guards. As soon as the bargain is concluded, the Negro is put in chains and led aboard the vessel, where he meets his fellow sufferers. Here sinister reflections come to his mind; everything shocks and frightens him and his uncertain destiny gives rise to the greatest anxiety....

The vessel sets sail for the Antilles, and the Negroes are chained in a hold of the ship, a kind of lugubrious prison where the light of day does not penetrate, but into which the air is introduced by means of a pump. Twice a day some disgusting food is distributed to them. Their consuming sorrow and the sad state to which they are reduced would make them commit suicide if they were not deprived of all the means for an attempt

such as guns, gin, and cloth, to Africa, where they were traded for a cargo of slaves. The slaves were then shipped to the Americas and sold. European merchants then bought tobacco, molasses, sugar, rum, coffee, and raw cotton and shipped them back to Europe to be sold in European markets.

An estimated 275,000 enslaved Africans were exported to other countries during the sixteenth century, with 2,000 going annually to the Americas alone. The total climbed to over a million in the seventeenth century and jumped to 6 million in the eighteenth century, when the trade spread from West and Central Africa to East Africa. Even during the nineteenth century, when Great Britain and other European countries tried to end the slave trade, nearly 2 million were exported. Altogether as many as 10 million African slaves were transported to the Americas between the sixteenth and nineteenth centuries. About half were transported in British ships, with the rest divided among French, Dutch, Portuguese, Danish, and later, American ships.

One reason for the astonishing numbers of slaves, of course, was the high death rate. The journey of slaves from Africa to the Americas became known as the **Middle Passage**, the middle leg of the triangular trade route. African slaves were upon their lives. Without any kind of clothing it would be difficult to conceal from the watchful eyes of the sailors in charge any instrument apt to alleviate their despair. The fear of a revolt, such as sometimes happens on the voyage from Guinea, is the basis of a common concern and produces as many guards as there are men in the crew. The slightest noise or a secret conversation among two Negroes is punished with utmost severity. All in all, the voyage is made in a continuous state of alarm on the part of the white men, who fear a revolt, and in a cruel state of uncertainty on the part of the Negroes, who do not know the fate awaiting them.

When the vessel arrives at a port in the Antilles, they are taken to a warehouse where they are displayed, like any merchandise, to the eyes of buyers. The plantation owner pays according to the age, strength, and health of the Negro he is buying. He has him taken to his plantation, and there he is delivered to an overseer who then and there becomes his tormentor. In order to domesticate him, the Negro is granted a few days of rest in his new place, but soon he is given a hoe and a sickle and made to join a work gang. Then he ceases to wonder about his fate; he understands that only labor is demanded of him. But he does not know yet how excessive this labor will be. As a matter of fact, his work begins at dawn and does not end before nightfall; it is interrupted for only two hours at dinnertime. The food a full-grown Negro is given each week consists of two pounds of salt beef or cod and two pots of tapioca meal.... A Negro of twelve or thirteen years or under is given only one pot of meal and one pound of beef or cod. In place of food some planters give their Negroes the liberty of working for themselves every Saturday; others are even less generous and grant them this liberty only on Sundays and holidays.

Q *What does this account reveal about the nature of the slave trade and white attitudes toward blacks in the eighteenth century?*

Source: From *European Society in the Eighteenth Century*, ed. Robert and Elborg Forster. New York: Walker & Co., 1969. Reprinted by permission of Walker & Co.

closely packed into cargo ships, 300 to 450 per ship, and chained in holds without sanitary facilities or room to stand up; there they remained during the voyage to America, which took at least 100 days. Mortality rates averaged 10 percent; longer journeys due to storms or adverse winds resulted in even higher death rates. The Africans who survived the journey were subject to high death rates from diseases to which they had little or no immunity. Death rates were lower for slaves born and raised in the New World: the new generation developed immunity to many of the more fatal diseases. Owners, however, rarely encouraged their slaves to have children. Many slave owners, especially in the West Indies, believed that buying a new slave was less expensive than raising a child from birth to working age at adolescence.

Conduct of the Slave Trade   Before the coming of Europeans in the fifteenth century, most slaves in Africa were prisoners of war. Many served as domestic servants or as wageless workers for the local ruler. When Europeans first began to take part in the slave trade, they bought slaves from local African merchants at slave markets in return for gold, guns, or other European goods such as textiles or copper or iron utensils.

At first, local slave traders obtained their supply from regions nearby, but as demand increased, they had to move farther inland to find their victims. In a few cases, local rulers became concerned about the impact of the slave trade on the well-being of their societies. In a letter to the king of Portugal in 1526, King Affonso of Congo (Bakongo) complained:

> And we cannot reckon how great the damage is, since the mentioned merchants are taking every day our natives, sons of the land and the sons of our noblemen and vassals and our relatives, ... and so great, Sir, is the corruption and licentiousness that our country is being completely depopulated, and Your Highness should not agree with this nor accept it as in your service.[8]

But protests from Africans were generally ignored by Europeans as well as by other Africans. As a general rule, local rulers viewed the slave trade as a source of income, and many sent raiders into defenseless villages in search of unsuspecting victims.

Historians once thought that Europeans controlled the terms of the slave trade and were able to obtain victims at bargain prices. It is now clear, however, that African middlemen—merchants, local elites, or rulers—were active in the process and were often able to dictate the price and number of slaves to European purchasers. Payment to the slave merchant was often made in goods, such as textiles, furniture, and guns.

Effects of the Slave Trade   The effects of the slave trade varied from area to area. Of course, it had tragic effects on the lives of the slaves and their families. There was also an economic price as the importation of cheap manufactured goods from Europe undermined local cottage industries and forced countless families into poverty. The slave trade also led to the depopulation of some areas and deprived many African communities of their youngest and strongest men and women.

The political effects of the slave trade were also devastating. The need to maintain a constant supply of slaves led to increased warfare and violence as African chiefs and their followers, armed with guns acquired from the trade in slaves, increased their raids and wars on neighboring peoples. A few Europeans lamented what they were doing to traditional African societies. One Dutch slave trader remarked, "From us they have learned strife, quarrelling, drunkenness, trickery, theft, unbridled desire for what is not one's own, misdeeds unknown to them before, and the accursed lust for gold."[9] Nevertheless, the slave trade continued, with devastating effects for some African states.

Despite a rising chorus of humanitarian sentiments from European intellectuals, the use of black slaves remained largely acceptable to Western society. Europeans continued to view blacks as inferior beings fit primarily for slave labor. Not until the Society of Friends, known as the Quakers, began to criticize slavery in the 1770s and exclude from their church any member adhering to slave trafficking did European sentiment for the abolition of slavery begin to build. Even then, it was not until the radical stage of the French Revolution in the 1790s that the French abolished slavery. The British followed suit in 1807. Despite the elimination of the African source, slavery continued in the newly formed United States until the Civil War of the 1860s.

The West in
Southeast Asia

Portugal's efforts to dominate the trade of Southeast Asia were never totally successful. The Portuguese lacked both the numbers and the wealth to overcome local resistance and colonize the Asian regions. Portugal's empire was simply too large and Portugal too small to maintain it. One Portuguese chronicler lamented, "My country, oh my country. Too heavy is the task that has been laid on your shoulders. Day after day I watch the ships leaving your shores filled always with your best and bravest men. And too many do not return.... Who then is left to till the fields, to harvest the grapes, to keep the enemy on our frontiers at bay?"[10] By the end of the sixteenth century, new European rivals had entered the fray.

One of them was Spain. The Spanish had established themselves in the region when Magellan landed in the Philippines. Although he was killed there, the Spanish were able to gain control over the Philippines, which eventually became a major Spanish base in the trade across the Pacific. Spanish ships carried silk and other luxury goods to Mexico in return for silver from the mines of Mexico.

The primary threat to the Portuguese Empire in Southeast Asia, however, came with the arrival of the Dutch and the English, who were better financed than the Portuguese. The shift in power began in the early seventeenth century when the Dutch seized a Portuguese fort in the Moluccas and then gradually pushed the Portuguese out of the spice trade. During the next fifty years, the Dutch occupied most of the Portuguese coastal forts along the trade routes throughout the Indian Ocean, including the island of Ceylon (today's Sri Lanka), and seized Malacca in 1641. The aggressive Dutch drove the English traders out of the spice market as well, eventually restricting the English to a single port on the southern coast of Sumatra.

The Dutch also began to consolidate their political and military control over the entire area. On the island of Java, where they had established a fort at Batavia (buh-TAY-vee-uh) (modern Jakarta) in 1619, the Dutch found that it was necessary to bring the inland regions under their control to protect their position. On Java and the neighboring island of Sumatra, the Dutch East India Company established pepper plantations, which soon became the source of massive profits for Dutch merchants in Amsterdam. By the end of the eighteenth century, the Dutch had succeeded in bringing almost the entire Indonesian archipelago under their control.

The arrival of the Europeans had less impact on mainland Southeast Asia, where strong monarchies in Burma—now Myanmar (MYAN-mahr)—Thailand, and Vietnam resisted foreign encroachment. In the sixteenth century, the Portuguese established limited trade relations with several mainland states, including Thailand, Burma, Vietnam, and the remnants of the old Angkor kingdom in Cambodia. By the early seventeenth century, other nations had followed and had begun to compete actively for trade and missionary privileges. To obtain economic advantages, the Europeans soon became involved in local factional disputes. In general, however, these states were able to unite and drive the Europeans out.

In Vietnam, the arrival of Western merchants and missionaries coincided with a period of internal conflict among ruling groups in the country. Expansion had led to a civil war that temporarily divided the country into two separate states, one in the south and one in the north. After their arrival in the mid-seventeenth century, the European powers began to take sides in local politics, with the

© The Art Archive

Europe in Asia. *As Europeans began to move into parts of Asia, they reproduced many of the physical surroundings of their homeland in the port cities they built there. For example, shown here is a seventeenth-century view of Batavia, which the Dutch built as their headquarters on the northern coast of Java in 1619, and which strongly resembled Amsterdam, the financial and commercial capital of Europe at the time.*

Portuguese and the Dutch supporting rival factions. The Europeans also set up trading posts for their merchants, but by the end of the seventeenth century, when it became clear that economic opportunities were limited, most of them were abandoned. French missionaries attempted to remain, but their efforts were blocked by the authorities, who viewed converts to Catholicism as a threat to the prestige of the Vietnamese emperor.

Why were the mainland states better able to resist the European challenge than the states in the Malay world? One factor, no doubt, was the cohesive nature of these states. The mainland states in Burma, Thailand, and Vietnam had begun to define themselves as distinct political entities. The Malay states had less cohesion. Moreover, the Malay states were victims of their own resources. The spice trade was enormously profitable. European merchants and rulers were determined to gain control of the sources of the spices, and that determination led them to take direct control of the Indonesian archipelago.

The French and British in India   When a Portuguese fleet arrived at the port of Calicut in the spring of 1498, the Indian subcontinent was divided into a number of Hindu and Muslim kingdoms. But it was on the verge of a new era of unity that would be brought about by a foreign dynasty called the Mughals (MOO-guls).

The Mughal Empire   The founders of the Mughal Empire were not natives of India but came from the mountainous region north of the Ganges River valley. The founder of the dynasty, Babur (BAH-burr) (1483–1530), had an illustrious background. His father was descended from the great Asian conqueror Tamerlane; his mother, from the Mongol conqueror Genghis Khan. It was Akbar (AK-bar)

(1556–1605), Babur's grandson, however, who brought Mughal rule to most of India, creating the greatest Indian empire since the Mauryan dynasty nearly two thousand years earlier.

The Impact of the Western Powers   As we have seen, the first Europeans to arrive in India were the Portuguese. At first, Portugal dominated regional trade in the Indian Ocean, but at the end of the sixteenth century, the English and the Dutch arrived on the scene. Soon both powers were competing with Portugal, and with each other, for trading privileges in the region.

During the first half of the seventeenth century, the English presence in India steadily increased. By 1650, English trading posts had been established at Surat (a thriving port along the northwestern coast of India), Fort William (now the great city of Calcutta) near the Bay of Bengal, and Madras (now Chennai) on the southeastern coast. From Madras, English ships carried Indian-made cotton goods to the East Indies, where they were bartered for spices, which were shipped back to England.

English success in India attracted rivals, including the Dutch and the French. The Dutch abandoned their interests to concentrate on the spice trade in the middle of the seventeenth century, but the French were more persistent and established their own forts on the east coast. For a brief period, the French competed successfully with the British, even capturing the British fort at Madras.

But the British were saved by the military genius of Sir Robert Clive (CLYV), an aggressive British empire-builder who eventually became the chief representative of the East India Company in India. (The East India Company had been founded as a joint-stock company in 1600—see "The Growth of Commercial Capitalism" later in this chapter.) The British were aided as well by the refusal of the French government to provide financial support for French efforts in far-off India. Eventually, the French were restricted to the fort at Pondicherry and a handful of small territories on the southeastern coast.

In the meantime, Clive began to consolidate British control in Bengal, where the local ruler had attacked Fort William and imprisoned the local British population in the "Black Hole of Calcutta" (an underground prison for holding the prisoners, many of whom died in captivity). In 1757, a small British force numbering about three thousand defeated a Mughal-led army more than ten times its size in the Battle of Plassey (PLASS-ee). As part of the spoils of victory, the British East India Company received from the now-decrepit Mughal court the authority to collect taxes from lands in the area surrounding Calcutta. During the Seven Years' War (1756–1763), the British forced the French to withdraw completely from India (see Chapter 18).

To officials of the East India Company, the expansion of their authority into the interior of the subcontinent probably seemed like a simple economic decision. It made sense to seek regular revenues that would pay for increasingly expensive military operations in India. To historians, it marks a major step in the gradual transfer of all of the Indian subcontinent to the British East India Company and later, in 1858, to the British crown as a colony (see Chapter 24).

China   In 1514, a Portuguese fleet dropped anchor off the coast of China. It was the first direct contact between the Chinese

West Meets East: An Exchange of Royal Letters

Economic gain was not the only motivation of Western rulers who wished to establish a European presence in the East. In 1681, King Louis XIV of France wrote a letter to the king of Tonkin (the Trinh family head, then acting as viceroy to the Vietnamese emperor) asking permission for Christian missionaries to proselytize in Vietnam. The king of Tonkin politely declined the request.

A Letter to the King of Tonkin from Louis XIV

Most high, most excellent, most mighty and most magnanimous Prince, our very dear and good friend, may it please God to increase your greatness with a happy end!

We hear from our subjects who were in your Realm what protection you accorded them. We appreciate this all the more since we have for you all the esteem that one can have for a prince as illustrious through his military valor as he is commendable for the justice which he exercises in his Realm. We have even been informed that you have not been satisfied to extend this general protection to our subjects but, in particular, that you gave effective proofs of it to Messrs. Deydier and de Bourges. We would have

wished that they might have been able to recognize all the favors they received from you by having presents worthy of you offered you; but since the war which we have had for several years, in which all of Europe had banded together against us, prevented our vessels from going to the Indies, at the present time, when we are at peace after having gained many victories and expanded our Realm through the conquest of several important places, we have immediately given orders to the Royal Company to establish itself in your kingdom as soon as possible, and have commanded Messrs. Deydier and de Bourges to remain with you in order to maintain a good relationship between our subjects and yours, also to warn us on occasions that might present themselves when we might be able to give you proofs of our esteem and of our wish to concur with your satisfaction as well as with your best interests.

By way of initial proof, we have given orders to have brought to you some presents which we believe might be agreeable to you. But the one thing in the world which we desire most, both for you and for your Realm, would be to obtain for your subjects who have already embraced the law of the only true God of heaven and earth, the freedom to profess it, since this law is the

Empire and Europe since the journeys of Marco Polo two hundred years earlier. At the time, the Chinese thought little of the event. China appeared to be at the height of its power as the most magnificent civilization on earth. Its empire stretched from the steppes of Central Asia to the China Sea, from the Gobi Desert to the tropical rain forests of Southeast Asia. From the lofty perspective of the imperial throne in Beijing, the Europeans could only be seen as an unusual form of barbarian. To the Chinese ruler, the rulers of all other countries were simply "younger brothers" of the Chinese emperor, who was regarded as the Son of Heaven.

highest, the noblest, the most sacred and especially the most suitable to have kings reign absolutely over the people.

We are even quite convinced that, if you knew the truths and the maxims which it teaches, you would give first of all to your subjects the glorious example of embracing it. We wish you this incomparable blessing together with a long and happy reign, and we pray God that it may please Him to augment your greatness with the happiest of endings.

Written at Saint-Germain-en-Laye, the 10th day of January, 1681,

Your very dear and good friend,

Louis

Answer from the King of Tonkin to Louis XIV

The King of Tonkin sends to the King of France a letter to express to him his best sentiments, saying that he was happy to learn that fidelity is a durable good of man and that justice is the most important of things. Consequently practicing of fidelity and justice cannot but yield good results. Indeed, though France and our Kingdom differ as to mountains, rivers, and boundaries, if fidelity and justice reign among our villages, our conduct will express all of our good feelings and contain precious gifts. Your communication, which comes from a country which is a thousand leagues away, and which proceeds from the heart as a testimony of your sincerity, merits repeated consideration and infinite praise. Politeness toward strangers is nothing unusual in our country. There is not a stranger who is not well received by us. How then could we refuse a man from France, which is the most celebrated among the kingdoms of the world and which for love of us wishes to frequent us and bring us merchandise? These feelings of fidelity and justice are truly worthy to be applauded. As regards your wish that we should cooperate in propagating your religion, we do not dare to permit it, for there is an ancient custom, introduced by edicts, which formally forbids it. Now, edicts are promulgated only to be carried out faithfully; without fidelity nothing is stable. How could we disdain a well-established custom to satisfy a private friendship? ...

We beg you to understand well that this is our communication concerning our mutual acquaintance. This then is my letter. We send you herewith a modest gift, which we offer you with a glad heart.

This letter was written at the beginning of winter and on a beautiful day.

Q *What are the underlying beliefs and approaches of these two rulers? How are they alike? How are they different? What is the significance of the way the two rulers date their letters?*

Source: From *The World of Southeast Asia: Selected Historical Readings*, Harry J. Benda and John A. Larkin, eds. Copyright © 1967 by Harper & Row Publishers. Used with permission of John A. Larkin.

The Ming and Qing Dynasties   By the time the Portuguese fleet arrived off the coast of China, the Ming dynasty, which ruled from 1369 to 1644, had already begun a new era of greatness in Chinese history. Under a series of strong rulers, China extended its rule into Mongolia and Central Asia. The Ming even briefly reconquered Vietnam. Along the northern frontier, they strengthened the Great Wall and made peace with the nomadic tribesmen who had troubled China for centuries.

But the days of the Ming dynasty were numbered. In the 1630s, a major epidemic devastated the population in many areas. The suffering caused by the epidemic helped spark a peasant revolt led by Li Zicheng (lee zee-CHENG). In 1644, Li and his forces occupied the capital of Beijing. The last Ming emperor committed suicide by hanging himself from a tree in the palace gardens.

The overthrow of the Ming dynasty created an opportunity for the Manchus, a farming and hunting people who lived northeast of China in the area known today as Manchuria. The Manchus conquered Beijing, and Li Zicheng's army fell. The victorious Manchus then declared the creation of a new dynasty with the reign title of the Qing ("Pure").

The Qing (CHING) were blessed with a series of strong early rulers who pacified the country, corrected the most serious social and economic ills, and restored peace and prosperity. Two Qing monarchs, Kangxi (KAHNG-shee) and Qian-long (CHAN-loong), ruled China for well over a century, from the middle of the seventeenth century to the end of the eighteenth. They were responsible for much of the greatness of Manchu China.

Western Inroads   Although China was at the height of its power and glory in the mid-eighteenth century, the first signs of internal decay in the Manchu dynasty were beginning to appear. Qing military campaigns along the frontier were expensive and placed heavy demands on the treasury. At the same time, increasing pressure on the land because of population growth led to economic hardship for many peasants and even rebellion.

Unfortunately for China, the decline of the Qing dynasty occurred just as Europe was increasing pressure for more trade. The first conflict had come from the north, where Russian traders sought skins and furs. Formal diplomatic relations between China and Russia were established in 1689 and provided for regular trade between the two countries.

Dealing with the foreigners who arrived by sea was more difficult. By the end of the seventeenth century, the English had replaced the Portuguese as the dominant force in European trade. Operating through the East India Company, which served as both a trading unit and the administrator of English territories in Asia, the English established their first trading post at Canton in 1699.

Over the next several decades, trade with China, notably the export of tea and silk to England, increased rapidly. To limit contacts between Europeans and Chinese, the Qing government confined all European traders to a small island just outside the city walls of Canton and permitted them to reside there only from October through March.

For a while, the British accepted this system, which brought considerable profit to the East India Company. But by the end of the eighteenth century, some British traders had begun to demand access to other cities along the Chinese coast and insist that the country be opened to British manufactured goods. In 1793, a British mission under Lord Macartney visited Beijing to press for liberalization of trade restrictions. But Emperor Qianlong expressed no interest in British products. An exasperated Macartney compared the Chinese Empire to "an old, crazy, first-rate man-of-war" that had once awed its neighbors "merely by her bulk and appearance" but was now destined under incompetent leadership to be "dashed to pieces on the shore." The Chinese would later pay for their rejection of the British request (see Chapter 24).

Japan

At the end of the fifteenth century, Japan was at a point of near anarchy, but in the course of the sixteenth century, a number of powerful individuals achieved the unification of Japan. One of them, Tokugawa Ieyasu (toh-koo-GAH-wah ee-yeh-YAH-soo) (1543–1616), took the title of shogun ("general") in 1603, an act that initiated the most powerful and longest lasting of all the Japanese shogunates. The Tokugawa rulers completed the restoration of central authority and remained in power until 1868.

Opening to the West   Portuguese traders had landed on the islands of Japan in 1543, and in a few years, Portuguese ships began stopping at Japanese ports on a regular basis to take part in the regional trade between Japan, China, and Southeast Asia. The first Jesuit missionary, Francis Xavier, arrived in 1549 and had some success in converting the local population to Christianity.

Initially, the visitors were welcomed. The curious Japanese were fascinated by tobacco, clocks, eyeglasses, and other European goods, and local nobles were interested in purchasing all types of European weapons and armaments. Japanese rulers found the new firearms especially helpful in defeating their enemies and unifying the islands. The effect on Japanese military architecture was especially striking, as local lords began to erect castles in stone on the European model.

The success of the Catholic missionaries, however, provoked a strong reaction against the presence of Westerners. When the missionaries interfered in local politics, Tokugawa Ieyasu, newly come to power, expelled all missionaries. Japanese Christians were now persecuted. When a group of Christian peasants on the island of Kyushu revolted in 1637, they were bloodily suppressed.

The European merchants were the next to go. The government closed the two major foreign trading posts on the island of Hirado and at Nagasaki (nah-gah-SAH-kee). Only a small Dutch community in Nagasaki was allowed to remain in Japan. The Dutch, unlike the Spanish and Portuguese, had not allowed missionary activities to interfere with their trade interests. But the conditions for staying were strict. Dutch ships were allowed to dock at Nagasaki harbor just once a year and could remain for only two or three months.

The Americas

In the sixteenth century, Spain and Portugal had established large colonial empires in the Americas. Portugal continued to profit from its empire in Brazil. The Spanish also maintained an enormous South American empire, but Spain's importance as a commercial power declined rapidly in the seventeenth century because of a drop in the output of the silver mines and the poverty of the Spanish monarchy. By the beginning of the seventeenth century, both Portugal and Spain found themselves with new challenges to their American empires from the Dutch, English, and French, who increasingly sought to create their own colonial empires in the New World.

West Indies   Both the French and English colonial empires in the New World included large parts of the West Indies. The English held Barbados, Jamaica, and Bermuda, and the French possessed Saint-Domingue, Martinique, and Guadeloupe. On these tropical islands, both the English and the French developed plantation economies, worked by African slaves, which produced tobacco, cotton, coffee, and sugar, all products increasingly in demand in Europe.

The "sugar factories," as the sugar plantations in the Caribbean were called, played an especially prominent role. By the early eighteenth century, sugar was Britain's main export from its American colonies. By the last two decades of the century, the British colony of Jamaica, one of Britain's most important, was producing 50,000 tons of sugar annually with the slave labor of 200,000 blacks. The French colony of Saint-Domingue (later Haiti) had 500,000 slaves working on three thousand plantations. This colony produced 100,000 tons of sugar a year, but at the expense of a high death rate from the brutal treatment of the slaves. It is not surprising that Saint-Domingue was the site of the first successful slave uprising in 1793 (see Chapter 19).

British North America   Although Spain claimed all of North America as part of its American overseas empire, other nations largely ignored its claim. The British argued that "prescription without possession availeth nothing." The Dutch were among the first to establish settlements on the North American continent. Their activities began after 1609 when Henry Hudson, an English explorer hired by the Dutch, discovered the river that bears his name. Within a few years, the Dutch had established the mainland colony of New Netherland, which stretched from the mouth of the Hudson River as far north as Albany, New York. Present-day names such as Staten Island and Harlem remind us that it was the Dutch who initially settled the Hudson River valley. In the second half of the seventeenth century, competition from the English and French and years of warfare with those rivals led to the decline of the Dutch commercial empire. In 1664, the English seized the colony of New Netherland and renamed it New York; soon afterward, the Dutch West India Company went bankrupt.

In the meantime, the English had begun to establish their own colonies in North America. The first permanent English settlement in America was Jamestown, founded in 1607 in modern Virginia. It barely survived, making it evident that the colonizing of American lands was not necessarily conducive to quick profits. But the desire to practice one's own religion, combined with economic interests, could lead to successful colonization, as the Massachusetts Bay Company demonstrated. The Massachusetts colony had 4,000 settlers in its early years but by 1660 had swelled to 40,000. By the end of the seventeenth century, the English had established control over most of the eastern seaboard of the present United States.

British North America came to consist of thirteen colonies. They were thickly populated, containing about 1.5 million people by 1750, and were also prosperous. Supposedly run by the British Board of Trade, the Royal Council, and Parliament, these thirteen colonies had legislatures that tended to act independently. Merchants in such port cities as Boston, Philadelphia, New York, and Charleston resented and resisted regulation from the British government.

The British colonies in both North America and the West Indies were assigned roles in keeping with mercantilist theory (see "Mercantilism" later in this chapter). They provided raw materials, such as cotton, sugar and tobacco, for the mother country while buying the latter's manufactured goods. Navigation acts regulated what could be taken from and sold to the colonies. Theoretically, the system was supposed to provide a balance of trade favorable to the mother country.

French North America   The French also established a colonial empire in North America. Already in 1534, the French explorer Jacques Cartier (ZHAK kar-TYAY) had discovered the Saint Lawrence River and laid claim to Canada as a French possession. It was not until 1608, however, when Samuel de Champlain (shahm-PLAN *or* SHAM-playn) established a settlement at Quebec that the French began to take a more serious interest in Canada as a colony. In 1663, Canada was made the property of the French crown and administered by a French governor like a French province.

French North America was run autocratically as a vast trading area, where valuable furs, leather, fish, and timber were acquired. The inability of the French state to get its people to emigrate to its Canadian possessions, however, left the territory thinly populated. By the mid-eighteenth century, there were only about 15,000 French Canadians, most of whom were hunters, trappers, missionaries, or explorers. The French failed to provide adequate men or money, allowing their European wars to take precedence over the conquest of the North American continent. Already in 1713, by the Treaty of Utrecht, the French began to cede some of their American possessions to their British rival. As a result of the Seven Years' War, they would surrender the rest of their Canadian lands in 1763 (see Chapter 18).

British and French rivalry was also evident in the Spanish and Portuguese colonial empires in Latin America. The decline of Spain and Portugal had led these two states to depend even more on resources from their colonies, and they imposed strict mercantilist rules to keep others out. Spain, for example, tried to limit all trade with its colonies to Spanish ships. But the British and French were too powerful to be excluded. The British cajoled the Portuguese into allowing them into the lucrative Brazilian trade. The French, however, were the first to break into the Spanish Latin American market when the French Bourbons became kings of Spain at the beginning of the eighteenth century. Britain's first entry into Spanish American markets came in 1713, when the British were granted the privilege, known as the *asiento* (ah-SYEN-toh), of transporting 4,500 slaves a year to Spanish Latin America.

THE IMPACT OF EUROPEAN EXPANSION

Between 1500 and 1800, the Atlantic nations of Europe moved into all parts of the world. The first had been Spain and Portugal, the two great colonial powers of the sixteenth century, followed by the Dutch, who built their colonial empire in the seventeenth century as Portugal and Spain declined. The Dutch were soon challenged by the British and French, who outstripped the others in the eighteenth century while becoming involved in a bitter rivalry. By the end of the eighteenth century, it appeared that Great Britain would become the great European imperial power. European expansion made a great impact on both the conquered and the conquerors.

The Conquered   Different regions experienced different effects from the European expansion. The native American civilizations, which had their own unique qualities and a degree of sophistication not much appreciated by Europeans, were virtually destroyed. In addition to devastating losses of population from European diseases, ancient social and political structures were ripped up and replaced by European institutions, religion, language, and culture. In Africa, the real demographic impact of the slave trade is uncertain due to a lack of records; however, estimates of the population in West Africa suggest that the slave trade negated any population growth, rather than causing a decline. Politically and socially, the slave trade encouraged the growth of territories in West Africa, such as Dahomey and Benin, where the leaders waged internal wars to secure more slaves to trade for guns and gunpowder. Without the slave trade, these territories became susceptible to European control in the nineteenth century. The Portuguese trading posts in the East had little direct impact on native Asian civilizations, although Dutch control of the Indonesian archipelago was more pervasive. China and Japan were still little affected by Westerners, although India was subject to ever-growing British encroachment.

In Central and South America, a new civilization arose that we have come to call Latin America. It was a multiracial society. Spanish and Portuguese settlers who arrived in the Western Hemisphere were few in number relative to the native Indians; many of the newcomers were males who not only used female natives for their sexual pleasure but married them as well. Already by 1501, Spanish rulers had authorized intermarriage between Europeans and native American Indians, whose offspring became known as mestizos (mess-TEE-zohz). Another group of people brought to Latin America were the Africans. Over a period of three centuries, possibly as many as 8 million slaves were brought to Spanish and Portuguese America to work the plantations. Africans also contributed to Latin America's multiracial character. Mulattoes (muh-LAH-tohz)—the offspring of Africans and whites—joined mestizos and descendants of whites, Africans, and native Indians to produce a unique society in Latin America. Unlike Europe, and unlike British North America, which remained a largely white offshoot of Europe, Latin America developed a multiracial society with less rigid attitudes about race.

The ecology of the conquered areas was also affected by the European presence. Europeans brought horses and cattle to the Americas, which revolutionized the life of the Indians. Cattle farming supplanted the Indian agricultural practice of growing maize (Indian corn), eventually leading to the development of large estates for raising cattle. South America would later become a great exporter of beef. Europeans also brought new crops, such as wheat and cane sugar, to be cultivated on large plantations by native or imported slave labor. In their trips to other parts of the world, Europeans also carried New World plants with them. Thus, Europeans introduced sweet potatoes and maize to Africa in the sixteenth century.

Catholic Missionaries   Although there were some Protestant missionaries in the world outside Europe, Catholic missionaries were far more active in spreading Christianity. From the beginning of their conquest of the New World, Spanish and Portuguese rulers were determined to Christianize the native peoples. This policy gave the Catholic Church an important role to play in the New World, one that added considerably to church power. Catholic missionaries—especially the Dominicans, Franciscans, and Jesuits—fanned out to different parts of the Spanish Empire.

To facilitate their efforts, missionaries brought Indians together into villages, where they could be converted, taught trades, and encouraged to grow crops. These missions enabled the missionaries to control the lives of the Indians and helped ensure that they would remain docile members of the empire. Missions generally benefited the missionaries more than the Indians. In frontier districts such as California and Texas, missions also served as military barriers to foreign encroachment.

The Catholic Church constructed hospitals, orphanages, and schools. Monastic schools instructed Indian students in the rudiments of reading, writing, and arithmetic. The Catholic Church also provided outlets for women other than marriage. Nunneries were places of prayer and quiet contemplation, but women in religious orders, many of them of aristocratic background, often lived well and worked outside their establishments by running schools and hospitals. Indeed, one of these nuns, Sor Juana Inés de la Cruz (SAWR HWAH-nuh ee-NAYSS day lah KROOZ) (1651–1695), was one of seventeenth-century Latin America's best-known literary figures. She wrote poetry and prose and promoted the education of women.

Christian missionaries also made the long voyage to China on European merchant ships. The Jesuits were among the most active and the most effective. Many of the early Jesuit missionaries to China were highly educated men who were familiar with European philosophical and scientific developments. They brought along clocks and various other instruments that impressed Chinese officials and made them more open to Western ideas.

The Jesuits used this openness to promote Christianity. To make it easier for the Chinese to accept Christianity, the Jesuits pointed to similarities between Christian morality and Confucian ethics. The Italian priest Matteo Ricci described the Jesuit approach:

> In order that the appearance of a new religion might not arouse suspicion among the Chinese people, the Jesuit Fathers did not speak openly about religious matters when they began to appear in public.... They did, however, try to teach this pagan people in a more direct way, namely, by virtue of their example and by the sanctity of their lives. In this way they attempted to win the good will of the people and little by little to dispose their minds to receive what they could not be persuaded to accept by word of mouth.... From the time of their entrance they wore the ordinary Chinese outer

garment, which was somewhat similar to their own religious habits; a long robe reaching down to the heels and with very ample sleeves, which are much in favor with the Chinese.[11]

The efforts of the Christian missionaries reached their height in the early eighteenth century. Several hundred Chinese officials became Catholics, as did an estimated 300,000 ordinary Chinese. But ultimately squabbling among the religious orders themselves undermined the Christian effort. To make it easier for the Chinese to convert, the Jesuits had allowed the new Catholics to continue the practice of ancestor worship. Jealous Dominicans and Franciscans complained to the pope, who condemned the practice. Soon Chinese authorities began to suppress Christian activities throughout China.

The Jesuits also had some success in Japan, where they converted a number of local nobles. By the end of the sixteenth century, thousands of Japanese on the southernmost islands of Kyushu and Shikoku had become Christians. But the Jesuit practice of destroying local idols and shrines and turning some temples into Christian schools or churches caused a severe reaction. When a new group of Spanish Franciscans continued the same policies, the government ordered the execution of nine missionaries and a number of their Japanese converts. When missionaries continued to interfere in local politics, Tokugawa Ieyasu expelled all missionaries. Japanese Christians were now persecuted.

The Conquerors   For some Europeans, expansion abroad brought the possibility of obtaining land, riches, and social advancement. One Spaniard commented in 1572 that many "poor young men" had left Spain for Mexico, where they hoped to acquire landed estates and call themselves "gentlemen." Although some wives accompanied their husbands abroad, many ordinary European women found new opportunities for marriage in the New World because of the lack of white women. Indeed, as one commentator bluntly put it, even "a whore, if handsome, [can] make a wife for some rich planter."[12] In the violence-prone world of early Spanish America, a number of women also found themselves rich after their husbands were killed unexpectedly. In one area of Central America, women owned about 25 percent of the landed estates by 1700.

European expansion also had other economic effects on the conquerors. Wherever they went in the New World, Europeans looked for sources of gold and silver. One Aztec commented that the Spanish conquerors "longed and lusted for gold. Their bodies swelled with greed, and their hunger was ravenous; they hungered like pigs for that gold."[13] Rich silver deposits were found and exploited in Mexico and southern Peru (modern Bolivia). When the mines at Potosí in Peru opened in 1545, the value of precious metals imported into Europe quadrupled. Between 1503 and 1650, an estimated 16 million kilograms (more than 35 million pounds) of silver and 185,000 kilograms (407,000 pounds) of gold entered the port of Seville and set off a price revolution that affected the Spanish economy.

But gold and silver were only two of the products that became part of the exchange between the New World and the Old. Historians refer to the reciprocal importation and exportation of plants and animals between Europe and the

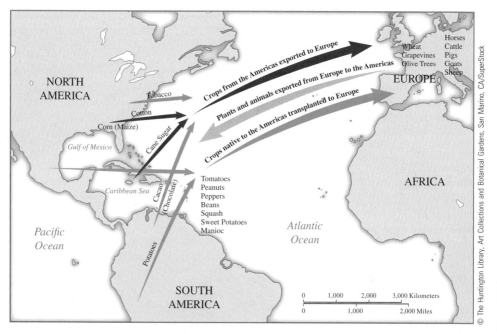

The Huntington Library, Art Collections and Botanical Gardens, San Marino, CA/SuperStock

MAP 14.3 The Columbian Exchange

In addition to their diseases, which killed vast numbers of indigenous inhabitants of the Americas, Europeans transplanted many of their crops and domestic animals to the New World. Europeans also imported plants from the New World that increased food production and nutrition in Europe.

Americas as the **Columbian Exchange** (see Map 14.3). While Europeans were bringing horses, cattle, and wheat to the New World, they were taking new agricultural products such as potatoes, chocolate, corn, tomatoes, and tobacco back to Europe. Potatoes became especially popular as a dietary staple in some areas of Europe. High in carbohydrates and rich in vitamins A and C, potatoes could be easily stored for winter use and enabled more people to survive on smaller plots of land. This improvement in nutrition was soon reflected in a rapid increase in population. Other products, such as cochineal, a red dye discovered in Mexico, gave European artists and artisans a "perfect red" for their paintings and cloth.

The European lifestyle was greatly affected by new products from abroad. In addition to new foods, new drinks also appeared in Europe. Chocolate, which had been brought to Spain from Aztec Mexico, became a common drink by 1700. The first coffee and tea houses opened in London in the 1650s and spread rapidly to other parts of Europe. In the eighteenth century, a craze for Chinese furniture and porcelain spread among the upper classes. Chinese ideas would also have an impact on intellectual attitudes (see Chapter 17).

European expansion, which was in part a product of European rivalries, also deepened that competition and increased the tensions among European states.

A Seventeenth-Century World Map. *This beautiful world map was prepared in 1630 by Henricus Hondius. The four portraits are of Caesar, the Roman statesman; Ptolemy, the second-century astronomer; Mercator, the Flemish cartographer whose map projection Hondius followed; and Hondius himself. By comparing this map with the map created by Ptolemy at the beginning of the chapter, one can see how much Europeans had learned about the shape of the world by the seventeenth century.*

Bitter conflicts arose over the cargoes coming from the New World and Asia. The Anglo-Dutch trade wars and the British-French rivalry over India and North America became part of a new pattern of worldwide warfare in the eighteenth century (see Chapter 18). Bitter rivalries also led to state-sponsored piracy as governments authorized private captains to attack enemy shipping and keep part of the proceeds for themselves.

In the course of their expansion, Europeans also came to have a new view of the world. When the travels began in the fifteenth century, Europeans were dependent on maps that were often fanciful and inaccurate. Their explorations helped them create new maps that gave a more realistic portrayal of the world, as well as new techniques called map projections that allowed them to represent the round surface of a sphere on a flat piece of paper. The most famous of these is the Mercator projection, the work of a Flemish cartographer, Gerardus Mercator (juh-RAHR-dus mur-KAY-tur) (1512–1594). A Mercator projection is what mapmakers call a conformal projection. It tries to show the true shape of landmasses, but only in a limited area. On the Mercator projection, the shapes of lands near the equator are quite accurate, but the farther away from the equator they lie, the more exaggerated their size becomes. For example, the island of Greenland on a Mercator projection appears to be larger than the continent of South America. In fact, Greenland is about one-ninth the size of South America. Nevertheless, the Mercator projection was valuable to ship captains. Every straight line on a Mercator projection is a line of true direction, whether north, south, east, or west. For four centuries, ship captains were very grateful to Mercator.

The psychological impact of colonization on the colonizers is awkward to evaluate but hard to deny. Europeans were initially startled by the discovery of new peoples in the Americas. Some deemed them inhuman and thus fit to be exploited for labor. Others, however, found them to be refreshingly natural and as yet untouched by European corruption. But even the latter group still believed that the Indians should be converted—if not forcefully, at least peacefully—to Christianity. Overall, the relatively easy European success in dominating native peoples (be they Africans or Indians) reinforced Christian Europe's belief in the inherent superiority of European civilization and religion. The Scientific Revolution of the seventeenth century (see Chapter 16), the Enlightenment of the eighteenth (see Chapter 17), and the imperialism of the nineteenth (see Chapter 24) would all bolster this Eurocentric perspective, which has pervaded Western civilization's relations with the rest of the world.

Toward a World Economy

During the High Middle Ages, Europeans had engaged in a commercial revolution that created new opportunities for townspeople in a basically agrarian economy. Although this commercial thrust was slowed by the devastating crises of the fourteenth century, Europe's discovery of the world outside in the fifteenth century led to an even greater burst of commercial activity and the inception of a world market.

Economic Conditions in the Sixteenth Century   Inflation became a major economic problem in the sixteenth and early seventeenth centuries. This so-called **price revolution** was a Europe-wide phenomenon, although it affected different areas at different times. Though the inflation rate was probably a relatively low 2 to 3 percent a year, it was noticeable in a Europe accustomed to stable prices. Foodstuffs were most subject to price increases, especially evident in the price of wheat. An upward surge in wheat prices was first noticed in the Mediterranean area—in Spain, southern France, and Italy—and reached its peak there in the 1590s.

Although precise data are lacking, economic historians believe that as a result of the price revolution, wages failed to keep up with price increases. Wage earners, especially agricultural laborers and salaried workers in urban areas, saw their standard of living drop. At the same time, landed aristocrats, who could raise rents, managed to prosper. Commercial and industrial entrepreneurs also benefited from the price revolution because of rising prices, expanding markets, and relatively cheaper labor costs. Some historians regard this profit inflation as a valuable stimulus to investment and the growth of capitalism, helping to explain the economic expansion and prosperity of the sixteenth century. Governments were likewise affected by inflation. They borrowed heavily from bankers and imposed new tax burdens on their subjects, often stirring additional discontent.

The causes of the price revolution are a subject of much historical debate. Already in the 1560s, European intellectuals associated the rise in prices with the great influx of precious metals from the New World. Although this view was accepted for a long time, many economic historians now believe that the increase in population in the sixteenth century played an important role in creating inflationary pressures. A growing population increased the demand for land and food and drove up prices for both.

The Growth of Commercial Capitalism   The flourishing European trade of the sixteenth century revolved around three major areas: the Mediterranean in the south, the Low Countries and the Baltic region in the north, and central Europe, whose inland trade depended on the Rhine and Danube Rivers. As overseas trade expanded, however, the Atlantic seaboard began to play a more important role, linking the Mediterranean, Baltic, and central European trading areas together and making the whole of Europe into a more integrated market that was all the more vulnerable to price shifts. With their cheaper and faster ships, the Dutch came to monopolize both European and world trade, although they were increasingly challenged by the English and French in the seventeenth century.

The commercial expansion of the sixteenth and seventeenth centuries was made easier by new forms of commercial organization, especially the **joint-stock company**. Individuals bought shares in a company and received dividends on their investment while a board of directors ran the company and made the important business decisions. The return on investments could be spectacular. During its first ten years, investors received 30 percent on their money from the Dutch East India Company, which opened the Spice Islands and Southeast Asia to Dutch activity. The joint-stock company made it easier to raise large amounts of capital for world trading ventures.

Enormous profits were also being made in shipbuilding and in mining and metallurgy, where technological innovations, such as the use of pumps and new methods of extracting metals from ores, proved highly successful. The mining industry was closely tied to sixteenth-century family banking firms. In exchange for arranging large loans to Charles V, Jacob Fugger (YAH-gawp FOO-gurr) was given a monopoly over silver, copper, and mercury mines in the Habsburg possessions of central Europe that produced profits in excess of 50 percent per year. Though these close relationships between governments and entrepreneurs could lead to stunning successes, they could also be precarious. The House of Fugger went bankrupt at the end of the sixteenth century when the Habsburgs defaulted on their loans.

By the seventeenth century, the traditional family banking firms were no longer able to supply the numerous services needed for the expanding commercial capitalism. New institutions arose to take their place. The city of Amsterdam created the Bank of Amsterdam in 1609 as both a deposit and a transfer institution and the Amsterdam Bourse, or Exchange, where the trading of stocks replaced the exchange of goods. By the first half of the seventeenth century, the Amsterdam Exchange had emerged as the hub of the European business world, just as Amsterdam itself had replaced Antwerp as the greatest commercial and banking center of Europe.

Despite the growth of commercial capitalism, most of the European economy still depended on an agricultural system that had experienced few changes since the thirteenth century. At least 80 percent of Europeans still worked on the land. Almost all of the peasants of western Europe were free of serfdom, although many still owed a variety of feudal dues to the nobility. Despite the expanding markets and rising prices, European peasants saw little or no improvement in their lot as they faced increased rents and fees and higher taxes imposed by the state. In eastern Europe, the peasants' position even worsened as they were increasingly tied to the land in a new serfdom enforced by powerful landowners (see Chapter 15).

Mercantilism   In the seventeenth century, a set of economic tendencies that historians call **mercantilism** came to dominate economic practices. Fundamental to mercantilism was the belief that the total volume of trade was unchangeable. Therefore, states protected their economies by following certain practices: hoarding precious metals, implementing protectionist trade policies, promoting colonial development, increasing shipbuilding, supporting trading companies, and encouraging the manufacturing of products to be used in trade.

According to the mercantilists, the prosperity of a nation depended on a plentiful supply of bullion (gold and silver). For this reason, it was desirable to achieve a favorable balance of trade in which goods exported were of greater value than those imported, promoting an influx of gold and silver payments that would increase the quantity of bullion. Furthermore, to encourage exports, governments should stimulate and protect export industries and trade by granting trade monopolies, encouraging investment in new industries through subsidies, importing foreign artisans, and improving transportation systems by building roads, bridges, and canals. By imposing high tariffs on foreign goods, they could be kept out of the country and prevented from competing with domestic industries. Colonies were also deemed valuable as sources of raw materials and markets for finished goods.

The mercantilists also focused on the role of the state, believing that state intervention in some aspects of the economy was desirable for the sake of the national good. Government regulations to ensure the superiority of export goods, the construction of roads and canals, and the granting of subsidies to create trade companies were all predicated on government involvement in economic affairs.

Overseas Trade and Colonies: Movement Toward Globalization   Mercantilist theory on the role of colonies was matched in practice by Europe's overseas expansion. With the development of colonies and trading posts in the Americas and the East, Europeans embarked on an adventure in international commerce in the seventeenth century. Although some historians speak of a nascent world economy, we should remember that local, regional, and intra-European trade still predominated. At the end of the seventeenth century, for example, English imports totaled 360,000 tons, but only 5,000 tons came from the East Indies. About one-tenth of English and Dutch exports were shipped across the Atlantic; slightly more went to the East. What made the transoceanic trade rewarding, however, was not the volume but the value of its goods. Dutch, English, and French merchants were bringing back products that were still consumed largely by the wealthy but were beginning to make their way into the lives of artisans and merchants. Pepper and spices from the Indies, West Indian and Brazilian sugar, and Asian coffee and tea were becoming more readily available to European consumers.

Trade within Europe remained strong throughout the eighteenth century as wheat, timber, and naval stores from the Baltic, wines from France, wool and fruit from Spain, and silk from Italy were exchanged along with a host of other products. But this trade increased only slightly while overseas trade boomed. From 1716 to 1789, total French exports quadrupled; intra-European trade, which constituted 75 percent of these exports in 1716, accounted for only 50 percent of the total in 1789. This increase in overseas trade has led some historians to proclaim the emergence of a truly global economy in the eighteenth century. Trade patterns now interlocked Europe, Africa, the East, and the Americas.

CHRONOLOGIES

THE PORTUGUESE AND SPANISH EMPIRES IN THE SIXTEENTH CENTURY

1488	Bartholomeu Dias sails around the tip of Africa
1492–1502	The voyages of Columbus
1494	Treaty of Tordesillas
1498	Vasco da Gama lands at Calicut in India
1511	Portuguese seize Malacca
1514	Landing of Portuguese ships in southern China
1519–1522	Magellan's voyage around the world
1519–1522	Spanish conquest of Mexico
1530–1535	Pizarro's conquest of the Inca

NEW RIVALS ON THE WORLD STAGE

1543	Portuguese traders land in Japan
1600	British East India Company formed
1602	Dutch East India Company formed
1607	English settlement at Jamestown
1608	Champlain establishes settlement at Quebec
1619	Dutch fort established at Batavia
1641	Dutch seize Malacca from the Portuguese

1664	English seize New Netherlands
1699	English establish trading post at Canton
1757	Battle of Plassey
1763	French cede Canada to British
1793	British mission to China

15

STATE BUILDING AND THE SEARCH FOR ORDER IN THE SEVENTEENTH CENTURY

Nicolas-René Jollain the Elder's portrait of Louis XIV captures the king's sense of royal grandeur

Chateaux de Versailles et de Trianon, Versailles//© Réunion des Musées Nationaux/Art Resource, NY

CHAPTER OUTLINE

• Social Crises, War, and Rebellions • The Practice of Absolutism: Western Europe • Absolutism in Central, Eastern, and Northern Europe • Limited Monarchy and Republics • The Flourishing of European Culture

SOCIAL CRISES, WAR, AND REBELLIONS

The inflation-fueled prosperity of the sixteenth century showed signs of slackening by the beginning of the seventeenth. Economic contraction was evident in some parts of Europe in the 1620s. In the 1630s and 1640s, as imports of silver from the Americas declined, economic recession intensified, especially in the Mediterranean area. Once the industrial and financial center of Europe in the Renaissance, Italy was now becoming an economic backwater. Spain's economy was also seriously failing by the 1640s.

Population trends of the sixteenth and seventeenth centuries also reveal Europe's worsening conditions. The sixteenth century was a period of expanding population, possibly related to a warmer climate and increased food supplies. It has been estimated that the population of Europe increased from 60 million in 1500 to 85 million by 1600, the first major recovery of the European population since the devastation of the Black Death in the mid-fourteenth century. Records also indicate a leveling off of the population by 1620, however, and even a decline by 1650, especially in central and southern Europe. Only the Dutch, English, and French grew in number in the first half of the seventeenth century. Europe's longtime adversaries—war, famine, and plague—continued to affect population levels. After the middle of the sixteenth century, another "little ice age," when average temperatures fell, affected harvests and caused famines. These problems created social tensions that came to a boil in the witchcraft craze.

The Witchcraft Craze   Hysteria over witchcraft affected the lives of many Europeans in the sixteenth and seventeenth centuries. Witchcraft trials were held in England, Scotland, Switzerland, Germany, some parts of France, and the Low Countries, and even in New England in America.

Witchcraft was not a new phenomenon. Its practice had been part of traditional village culture for centuries, but it came to be viewed as both sinister and dangerous when the medieval church began to connect witches to the activities of the devil, thereby transforming witchcraft into a heresy that had to be wiped out. After the establishment of the Inquisition in the thirteenth century, some people were accused of a variety of witchcraft practices and, following the biblical injunction "Thou shalt not suffer a witch to live," were turned over to secular authorities for burning at the stake or, in England, hanging.

The Spread of Witchcraft   What distinguished witchcraft in the sixteenth and seventeenth centuries from these previous developments was the increased number of trials and executions of presumed witches. Perhaps more than 100,000 people throughout Europe were prosecuted on charges of witchcraft. Although larger cities were affected first, the trials spread to smaller towns and rural areas as the hysteria persisted well into the seventeenth century.

The accused witches usually confessed to a number of practices, most often after intense torture. Many said that they had sworn allegiance to the devil and attended sabbats or nocturnal gatherings where they feasted, danced, and even copulated with the devil in sexual orgies. More common, however, were admissions of using evil incantations and special ointments and powders to wreak havoc on neighbors by killing their livestock, injuring their children, or raising storms to destroy their crops.

A number of contributing factors have been suggested to explain why the witchcraft frenzy became so widespread in the sixteenth and seventeenth centuries. Religious uncertainties clearly played some part. Many witchcraft trials occurred in areas where Protestantism had recently been victorious or in regions, such as southwestern Germany, where Protestant-Catholic controversies still raged. As religious passions became inflamed, accusations of being in league with the devil became common on both sides.

Recently, however, historians have emphasized the importance of social conditions, especially the problems of a society in turmoil, in explaining the witchcraft hysteria. At a time when the old communal values that stressed working together for the good of the community were disintegrating before the onslaught of a new economic ethic that emphasized looking out for oneself, property owners became more fearful of the growing numbers of poor in their midst and transformed them psychologically into agents of the devil. Old women were particularly susceptible to suspicion. Many of them, no longer the recipients of the local charity available in traditional society, may even have tried to survive by selling herbs, potions, or secret remedies for healing. When problems arose—and there were many in this crisis-laden period—these people were handy scapegoats.

That women should be the chief victims of witchcraft trials was hardly accidental. Nicholas Rémy, a witchcraft judge in France in the 1590s, found it "not unreasonable that this scum of humanity [witches] should be drawn chiefly from the feminine sex." To another judge, it came as no surprise that witches would confess to sexual experiences with Satan: "The Devil uses them so, because he knows that women love carnal pleasures, and he means to bind them to his allegiance by such agreeable provocations."[1] Of course, witch hunters were not the only ones who held women in such low esteem. Most theologians, lawyers, and philosophers in early modern Europe believed in the natural inferiority of women and thus would have found it plausible that women would be more susceptible to witchcraft.

Decline   By the mid-seventeenth century, the witchcraft hysteria began to subside. The destruction caused by the religious wars had forced people to accept at least a grudging toleration, tempering religious passions. Moreover, as governments began to stabilize after the period of crisis, fewer magistrates were willing to accept the unsettling and divisive conditions generated by the trials of witches. Finally, by the turn of the eighteenth century, more and more educated people were questioning traditional attitudes toward religion and finding it contrary to reason to believe in the old view of a world haunted by evil spirits.

The Thirty Years' War   Although many Europeans responded to the upheavals of the second half of the sixteenth century with a desire for peace and order, the first fifty years of the seventeenth century continued to be plagued by crises. A devastating war that affected much of Europe and rebellions seemingly everywhere protracted the atmosphere of disorder and violence.

Background to the War Religion, especially the struggle between Catholicism and Calvinism, played an important role in the outbreak of the Thirty Years' War (1618–1648), often called the "last of the religious wars." As the war progressed, however, it became increasingly clear that secular, dynastic-nationalist considerations were far more important. Although much of the fighting during the Thirty Years' War took place in the Germanic lands of the Holy Roman Empire, it became a Europe-wide struggle (see Map 15.1). In fact, some historians view it as part of a larger conflict for European leadership between the Bourbon dynasty of France and the Habsburg dynasties of Spain and the Holy Roman Empire and date it from 1609 to 1659.

© Cengage Learning 2012

MAP 15.1 The Thirty Years' War

The conflict began in the German states as Europe's major powers backed either the northern Protestant Union or the southern Catholic League. As the war progressed, religion receded in importance, replaced by a dynastic struggle between the French Bourbons and the Spanish and Austrian Habsburgs.

The Peace of Augsburg in 1555 had brought an end to religious warfare between German Catholics and Lutherans. Religion, however, continued to play a divisive role in German life as Lutherans and Catholics persisted in vying for control of various principalities. In addition, although the treaty had not recognized the rights of Calvinists, a number of German states had adopted Calvinism as their state church. At the beginning of the seventeenth century, the Calvinist ruler of the Palatinate (puh-LAT-uh-nuht *or* puh-LAT-uh-nayt), the Elector Palatine (PAL-uh-tyn) Frederick IV, assumed the leadership in forming a league of German Protestant states called the Protestant Union. To counteract it, Duke Maximilian of the south German state of Bavaria organized the Catholic League of German states. By 1609, then, Germany was dividing into two armed camps in anticipation of religious war.

The religious division was exacerbated by a constitutional issue. The desire of the Habsburg emperors to consolidate their authority in the Holy Roman Empire was resisted by the princes, who fought for their "German liberties," their constitutional rights and prerogatives as individual rulers. To pursue their policies, the Habsburg emperors looked to Spain (ruled by another branch of the family) for assistance while the princes turned to the enemies of Spain, especially France, for help against the emperors. The divisions in the Holy Roman Empire and Europe made it almost inevitable that if war did erupt, it would be widespread and difficult to stop.

The Bohemian Phase   Historians have traditionally divided the Thirty Years' War into four major phases. The Bohemian phase (1618–1625) began in one of the Habsburgs' own territories. In 1617, the Bohemian Estates (primarily the nobles) accepted the Habsburg Archduke Ferdinand as their king but soon found themselves unhappy with their choice. Though many of the nobles were Calvinists, Ferdinand was a devout Catholic who began a process of re-Catholicizing Bohemia and strengthening royal power. The Protestant nobles rebelled against Ferdinand in May 1618 and proclaimed their resistance by throwing two of the Habsburg governors and a secretary out of a window in the royal castle in Prague, the seat of Bohemian government. The Catholic side claimed that their seemingly miraculous escape from death in the 70-foot fall from the castle was due to the intercession of the Virgin Mary, while Protestants pointed out that they fell into a manure pile. The Bohemian rebels now seized control of Bohemia, deposed Ferdinand, and elected as his replacement the Protestant ruler of the Palatinate, Elector Frederick V, who was also the head of the Protestant Union.

Ferdinand, who in the meantime had been elected Holy Roman Emperor, refused to accept his deposition. Realizing that the election of Frederick V, if allowed to stand, could upset the balance of religious and political power in central Europe and give the Protestant forces greater control of the Holy Roman Empire, Ferdinand sought the aid of the imposing forces of Duke Maximilian of Bavaria and the Catholic League. With their help, the imperial forces defeated Frederick and the Bohemian nobles at the Battle of White Mountain outside Prague on November 8, 1620. Spanish troops took advantage of Frederick's predicament by invading the Palatinate and conquering it by the end of 1622. The unfortunate

Frederick fled into exile in the United Provinces. The Spanish took control of the western part of the Palatinate (to gain the access route from Italy to the Netherlands that they had wanted), and Maximilian of Bavaria took the rest of the territory. Reestablished as king of Bohemia, Emperor Ferdinand declared Bohemia a hereditary Habsburg possession, confiscated the land of the Protestant nobles, and established Catholicism as the sole religion. The Spanish renewed their attack on the Dutch, and the forces of Catholicism seemed on the road to victory. But the war was far from over.

The Danish Phase   The second phase of the war, the Danish phase (1625–1629), began when King Christian IV of Denmark (1588–1648), a Lutheran, intervened on behalf of the Protestant cause by leading an army into northern Germany. Christian had made an anti-Habsburg and anti-Catholic alliance with the United Provinces and England. He also wanted, however, to gain possession of some Catholic territories in northern Germany to benefit his family.

In the meantime, Ferdinand had gained a new commander for the imperial forces in Albrecht von Wallenstein (AWL-brekht fun VAHL-en-shtyn). A brilliant and enigmatic commander, Wallenstein was a Bohemian nobleman who had taken advantage of Ferdinand's victory to become the country's wealthiest landowner. Wallenstein's forces defeated a Protestant army at Dessau and then continued to operate in northern Germany. The forces of Christian IV, despite substantial aid from their allies, were defeated in 1626 by an army of the Catholic League under Count Tilly and then suffered an even more devastating loss to Wallenstein's forces the following year. Wallenstein now occupied parts of northern Germany, including the Baltic ports of Hamburg, Lübeck, and Bremen. Christian IV's defeat meant the end of Danish supremacy in the Baltic.

After the success of the imperial armies, Emperor Ferdinand II was at the height of his power and took this opportunity to issue the Edict of Restitution in March 1629. His proclamation prohibited Calvinist worship and restored all property taken by Protestant princes or cities during the past seventy-five years to the Catholic Church. But this sudden growth in the power of the Habsburg emperor frightened many German princes, who feared for their independent status and reacted by forcing the emperor to dismiss Wallenstein.

The Swedish Phase   The Swedish phase (1630–1635) marked the entry of Gustavus Adolphus (goo-STAY-vus uh-DAHL-fuss), king of Sweden (1611–1632), into the war. Gustavus Adolphus was responsible for reviving Sweden and transforming it into a great Baltic power. A military genius, he brought a disciplined and well-equipped Swedish army to northern Germany. He was also a devout Lutheran who felt compelled to aid his coreligionists in Germany.

Gustavus's army swept the imperial forces out of the north and moved into the heart of Germany. In desperation, the imperial side recalled Wallenstein, who was given command of the imperial army that met Gustavus's troops near Leipzig. At the Battle of Lützen (LOOT-sun) in 1632, the Swedish forces prevailed but paid a high price for the victory when the Swedish king was killed in the battle. Although the Swedish forces remained in Germany, they proved much less effective. Despite the loss of Wallenstein, who was assassinated in 1634 on the orders of Emperor Ferdinand, the imperial army decisively defeated the Swedes at the Battle of Nördlingen at the end of 1634 and drove them out of southern Germany. This imperial victory guaranteed that southern Germany would remain Catholic. The emperor used this opportunity to make peace with the German princes by agreeing to annul the Edict of Restitution of 1629. But peace failed to come to war-weary Germany. The Swedes wished to continue, while the French, under the direction of Cardinal Richelieu (REESH-uh-lyoo), the chief minister of King Louis XIII, entered the war directly, beginning the fourth and final phase of the war, the Franco-Swedish phase (1635–1648).

The Franco-Swedish Phase   By this time, religious issues were losing their significance. The Catholic French were now supporting the Protestant Swedes against the Catholic Habsburgs of Germany and Spain. The Battle of Rocroi (roh-KRWAH) in 1643 proved decisive as the French beat the Spanish and brought an end to Spanish military greatness. The French then moved on to victories over the imperialist-Bavarian armies in southern Germany. By this time, all parties were ready for peace, and after five years of protracted negotiations, the war in Germany was officially ended by the Peace of Westphalia in 1648. The war between France and Spain, however, continued until the Peace of the Pyrenees in 1659. By that time, Spain had become a second-class power, and France had emerged as the dominant nation in Europe.

Outcomes of the War   What were the results of what one historian has called a "basically meaningless conflict"? The Peace of Westphalia ensured that all German states, including the Calvinist ones, were free to determine their own religion. Territorially, France gained parts of western Germany, part of Alsace, and the three cities of Metz, Toul, and Verdun, giving the French control of the Franco-German border area. While Sweden and the German states of Brandenburg and Bavaria gained some territory in Germany, the Austrian Habsburgs did not really lose any but did see their authority as rulers of Germany further diminished. The more than three hundred states that made up the Holy Roman Empire were recognized as virtually independent, since each received the power to conduct its own foreign policy. The Habsburg emperor had been reduced to a figurehead in the Holy Roman Empire. The Peace of Westphalia also made it clear that religion and politics were now separate. The pope was completely ignored in all decisions at Westphalia, and political motives became the guiding forces in public affairs as religion moved closer to becoming primarily a matter of personal conviction and individual choice. Some historians also argue that the Peace of Westphalia marks the beginning of a modern international order in which sovereign states began to operate as equals within a secular framework.

The economic and social effects of the Thirty Years' War on Germany are still debated. Some areas of Germany were completely devastated, but others remained relatively untouched and even experienced economic growth. The most recent work pictures a damaged economy and a population decline of 15 to 20 percent in the Holy Roman Empire. Although historians may debate the degree of devastation, many people in Germany would have understood this description by a traveler journeying along the Main River in 1636:

> [We] came to a wretched little village called Neukirchen, which we found quite uninhabited yet with one house on fire. Here, since it was now late, we were obliged to stay all night, for the nearest town was four miles away; but we spent that night walking up and down with guns in our hands, and listening fearfully to the sound of shots in the woods around us.... Early next morning, His Excellency went to inspect the church and found it had been plundered and that the pictures and the altar had been desecrated. In the churchyard we saw a dead body, scraped out of the grave, while outside the churchyard we found another dead body.[2]

The Thirty Years' War was undoubtedly the most destructive conflict Europeans had yet experienced.

Was There a Military Revolution?   By the seventeenth century, war played an increasingly important role in European affairs. Military power was considered essential to a ruler's reputation and power; thus, the pressure to build an effective military machine was intense. Some historians believe that the changes that occurred in the science of warfare between 1560 and 1660 warrant the title of military revolution.

Medieval warfare, with its mounted knights and supplementary archers, had been transformed in the Renaissance by the employment of infantry armed with pikes and halberds (long-handled weapons combining an axe with a spike) and arranged in massed rectangles known as squadrons or battalions. The use of firearms required adjustments to the size and shape of the massed infantry and made the cavalry less effective.

It was Gustavus Adolphus, the king of Sweden, who developed the first standing army of conscripts, notable for the flexibility of its tactics. The infantry brigades of Gustavus's army were composed of equal numbers of musketeers and pikemen, standing six men deep. They employed the salvo, in which all rows of the infantry fired at once instead of row by row. These salvos of fire, which cut up the massed ranks of the opposing infantry squadrons, were followed by a pike charge, giving the infantry a primarily offensive deployment. Gustavus also used his cavalry in a more mobile fashion. After shooting a pistol volley, they charged the enemy with their swords. Additional flexibility was obtained by using lighter artillery pieces that were more easily moved during battle. All of these changes required coordination, careful training, and better discipline, forcing rulers to move away from undisciplined mercenary forces. Naturally, the success of Gustavus Adolphus led to imitation.

Some historians have questioned the use of the phrase "military revolution" to describe the military changes from 1560 to 1660, arguing instead that military developments were gradual. In any case, for the rest of the seventeenth century, warfare continued to change. Standing armies, based partly on conscription, grew ever larger and more expensive. Standing armies necessitated better-disciplined and better-trained soldiers and led to the education of officers in military schools. Armies also introduced the use of linear rather than square formations to provide greater flexibility and mobility in tactics. There was also an increased use of firearms as the musket with attached bayonet increasingly replaced the pike in the ranks of the infantry. A naval arms race in the seventeenth century led to more and bigger warships or capital ships known as "ships of the line." By the end of the seventeenth century, most of these had two or three decks and were capable of carrying between fifty and one hundred heavy cannon.

Larger armies and navies could be maintained only by levying heavier taxes, making war a greater economic burden and an ever more important part of the early modern European state. The creation of large bureaucracies to supervise the military resources of the state led to growth in the power of state governments.

Rebellions   Before, during, and after the Thirty Years' War, a series of rebellions and civil wars stemming from the discontent of both nobles and commoners rocked the domestic stability of many European governments. To increase their power, monarchs attempted to extend their authority at the expense of traditional powerful elements who resisted the rulers' efforts. At the same time, to fight their battles, governments increased taxes and created such hardships that common people also rose in opposition.

Between 1590 and 1640, peasant and lower-class revolts erupted in central and southern France, Austria, and Hungary. In the decades of the 1640s and 1650s, even greater unrest occurred. Portugal and Catalonia rebelled against the Spanish government in 1640. The common people in Naples and Sicily revolted against both the government and the landed nobility in 1647. Russia, too, was rocked by urban uprisings in 1641, 1645, and 1648. Nobles rebelled in France from 1648 to 1652 in an effort to halt the growth of royal power. The northern states of Sweden, Denmark, and the United Provinces were not immune from upheavals involving clergy, nobles, and mercantile groups. The most famous and widest-ranging struggle, however, was the civil war and rebellion in England, commonly known as the English Revolution (discussed later in this chapter).

THE PRACTICE OF ABSOLUTISM: WESTERN EUROPE

Absolute monarchy or **absolutism** meant that the sovereign power or ultimate authority in the state rested in the hands of a king who claimed to rule by divine right. But what did sovereignty mean? The late-sixteenth-century political theorist Jean Bodin (ZHAHN boh-DAN) believed that sovereign power consisted of the authority to make laws, tax, administer justice, control the state's administrative system, and determine foreign policy. These powers made a ruler sovereign.

One of the chief theorists of **divine-right monarchy** in the seventeenth century was the French theologian and court preacher Bishop Jacques Bossuet (ZHAHK baw-SWAY) (1627–1704), who expressed his ideas in a book titled *Politics Drawn from the Very Words of Holy Scripture*. Bossuet argued first that government was divinely ordained so that humans could live in an organized society. God established kings and through them reigned over all the peoples of the world. Since kings received their power from God, their authority was absolute. They were responsible to no one (including parliaments) except God. For Bossuet, though, his last point was especially important. Because God would hold a king accountable for his actions, Bossuet believed that kings faced serious responsibilities as well as real limits on their power. There was also a large gulf between the theory of absolutism as expressed by Bossuet and the practice of absolutism. A monarch's absolute power was often limited greatly by practical realities.

Absolute Monarchy in France   France during the reign of Louis XIV (1643–1715) has traditionally been regarded as the best example of the practice of absolute monarchy in the seventeenth century. French culture, language, and manners influenced all levels of European society. French diplomacy and wars shaped the political affairs of western and central Europe. The court of Louis XIV seemed to be imitated everywhere in Europe. Of course, the stability of Louis's reign was magnified by the instability that had preceded it.

Foundations of French Absolutism: Cardinal Richelieu   In the half century before Louis XIV came to power, royal and ministerial governments struggled to avoid the breakdown of the French state. The line between order and anarchy was often a narrow one. The situation was complicated by the fact that both Louis XIII (1610–1643) and Louis XIV were only boys when they succeeded to the throne in 1610 and 1643, respectively, leaving the government dependent on royal ministers. Two especially competent ministers played crucial roles in maintaining monarchical authority.

Cardinal Richelieu, Louis XIII's chief minister from 1624 to 1642, initiated policies that eventually strengthened the power of the monarchy. By eliminating the political and military rights of the Huguenots while preserving their religious privileges, Richelieu transformed the Huguenots into more reliable subjects. Richelieu acted more cautiously in "humbling the pride of the great men," the important French nobility. He understood the influential role played by the nobles in the French state. The dangerous ones were those who asserted their territorial independence when they were excluded from participating in the central government. Proceeding slowly but determinedly, Richelieu developed an efficient network of spies to uncover noble plots and then crushed the conspiracies and executed the conspirators, thereby eliminating a major threat to royal authority.

To reform and strengthen the central administration, initially for financial reasons, Richelieu sent out royal officials called ***intendants*** (anh-tahnh-DAHNHZ *or* in-TEN-dunts) to the provinces to execute the orders of the central government. As the functions of the *intendants* grew, they came into conflict with provincial governors. Since the *intendants* were victorious in most of these disputes, they further strengthened the power of the crown. Richelieu proved less capable in financial matters, however. Not only was the basic system of state finances corrupt, but so many people benefited from the

Cardinal Richelieu.
A key figure in the emergence of a strong monarchy in France was Cardinal Richelieu, pictured here in a portrait by Philippe de Champagne. Chief minister to Louis XIII, Richelieu strengthened royal authority by eliminating the private armies and fortified cities of the Huguenots and by crushing aristocratic conspiracies.

© National Gallery, London/The Bridgeman Art Library

system's inefficiency and injustice that the government faced strong resistance when it tried to institute reforms. The *taille* (TY) (an annual direct tax usually levied on land or property) was increased—in 1643 it was two and a half times what it had been in 1610. Richelieu's foreign policy goal of confronting the growing power of the Habsburgs in the Thirty Years' War, however, led to ever-increasing expenditures, which soon outstripped the additional revenues. French debt continued its upward spiral under Richelieu.

Cardinal Mazarin   Richelieu died in 1642, followed five months later by King Louis XIII, who was succeeded by his son Louis XIV, then but four years old. This necessitated a regency under Anne of Austria, the mother of Louis XIV. But she allowed Cardinal Mazarin (maz-uh-RANH), Richelieu's trained successor, to dominate the government. An Italian who had come to France as a papal legate and then become naturalized, Mazarin attempted to carry on Richelieu's policies until his death in 1661.

The most important event during Mazarin's rule was a revolt of the nobles known as the Fronde (FROHND). As a foreigner, Mazarin was greatly disliked by all elements of the French population. The nobles, who particularly resented the centralized administrative power being built up at the expense of the provincial nobility, temporarily allied with the members of the Parlement (par-luh-MAHNH) of Paris, who opposed the new taxes levied by the government to pay the costs of the Thirty Years' War (Mazarin continued Richelieu's anti-Habsburg policy), and with the people of Paris, who were also angry at the additional taxes. The Parlement of Paris was the most important court in France, with jurisdiction over half of the kingdom, and its members formed the nobles of the robe, the service nobility of lawyers and administrators. These nobles of the robe led the first Fronde (1648–1649), which broke out in Paris and was ended by compromise. The second Fronde, begun in 1650, was led by the nobles of the sword, who were descended from the medieval nobility. They were interested in overthrowing Mazarin for their own purposes: to secure their positions and increase their own power. The second Fronde was crushed by 1652, a task made easier when the nobles began fighting each other instead of Mazarin. With the end of the Fronde, the vast majority of the French concluded that the best hope for stability in France lay in the crown. When Mazarin died in 1661, the greatest of the seventeenth-century monarchs, Louis XIV, took over supreme power.

The Reign of Louis XIV (1643–1715)	The day after Cardinal Mazarin's death, Louis XIV, age twenty-three, expressed his determination to be a real king and the sole ruler of France:

> Up to this moment I have been pleased to entrust the government of my affairs to the late Cardinal. It is now time that I govern them myself. You [secretaries and ministers of state] will assist me with your counsels when I ask for them. I request and order you to seal no orders except by my command.... I order you not to sign anything, not even a passport ... without my command; to render account to me personally each day and to favor no one.[3]

His mother, who was well aware of Louis's proclivity for fun and games and getting into the beds of the maids in the royal palace, laughed aloud at these words. But Louis was quite serious.

Louis proved willing to pay the price of being a strong ruler. He established a conscientious routine from which he seldom deviated. Eager for glory (in the French sense of achieving what was expected of one in an important position), Louis created a grand and majestic spectacle at the court of Versailles (vayr-SY). Consequently, Louis and his court came to set the standard for monarchies and aristocracies all over Europe. Just a few decades after the king's death, the great French writer Voltaire dubbed the period from 1661 to 1715 the "Age of Louis XIV," and historians have tended to call it that ever since.

Although Louis may have believed in the theory of absolute monarchy and consciously fostered the myth of himself as the Sun King, the source of light for all of his people, historians are quick to point out that the realities fell far short of the aspirations. Despite the centralizing efforts of Cardinals Richelieu and Mazarin, seventeenth-century France still possessed a bewildering system of overlapping authorities. Provinces had their own regional courts, their own local Estates (parliaments), their own sets of laws. Members of the high nobility, with their huge estates and clients among the lesser nobility, still exercised much authority. Both towns and provinces possessed privileges and powers seemingly from time immemorial that they would not easily relinquish.

Administration of the Government   One of the keys to Louis's power was that he was able to restructure the central policy-making machinery of government because it was part of his own court and household. The royal court located outside the city of Paris at Versailles was an elaborate structure that served different purposes: it was the personal household of the king, the location of central governmental machinery, and the place where powerful subjects came to find favors and offices for themselves and their clients as well as the main arena where rival aristocratic factions jostled for power. The greatest danger to Louis's personal rule came from the very high nobles and princes of the blood (the royal princes), who considered it their natural function to assert the policy-making role of royal ministers. Louis eliminated this threat by removing them from the royal council, the chief administrative body of the king and overseer of the central machinery of government, and enticing them to his court, where he could keep them preoccupied with court life and out of politics. Instead of using the high nobility and royal princes, Louis relied on other nobles for his ministers. His ministers were expected to be subservient; said Louis, "I had no intention of sharing my authority with them."

Louis's domination of his ministers and secretaries gave him control of the central policy-making machinery of government and thus authority over the traditional areas of monarchical power: the formulation of foreign policy, the making of war and peace, the assertion of the secular power of the crown against any religious authority, and the ability to levy taxes to fulfill these functions. Louis had considerably less success with the internal administration of the kingdom, however. The traditional groups and institutions of French society—the nobles, officials, town councils, guilds, and representative Estates in some provinces—were simply too powerful for the king to have direct control over the lives of his subjects. Consequently, control of the provinces and the people was achieved largely by bribing the individuals responsible for executing the king's policies. Nevertheless, local officials could still obstruct the execution of policies they disliked, indicating clearly that a so-called absolute monarch was not always absolute. A recent study of Louis's relationship with the **parlements**, however, asserts that he was able to exercise both political and economic control over these provincial law courts, which were responsible for registering new laws sent to them by the king.

Religious Policy   The maintenance of religious harmony had long been considered an area of monarchical power. The desire to keep it brought Louis into conflict with the French Huguenots. Louis XIV did not want to allow Protestants to practice their faith in largely Catholic France. Perhaps he was motivated by religion, but it is more likely that Louis, who believed in the motto "One king, one law, one faith," felt that the existence of this minority undermined his own political authority. In October 1685, Louis issued the Edict of Fontainebleau (fawnh-ten-BLOH). In addition to revoking the Edict of

Nantes, the new edict provided for the destruction of Huguenot churches and the closing of Protestant schools. It is estimated that 200,000 Huguenots defied the prohibition against their leaving France and sought asylum in England, the United Provinces, and the German states. Although it was once believed that this exodus weakened the French economy, others maintain that an influx of English and Irish political and religious refugees into France offset the loss. Support for the expulsion of the Protestants came from Catholic laypeople, who rejected Protestant legal rights, banned them from government meetings, and destroyed Protestant churches in an effort to regain Catholic control of heavily populated Protestant regions.

Financial Issues   The cost of building Versailles and other palaces, maintaining his court, and pursuing his wars made finances a crucial issue for Louis XIV. He was most fortunate in having the services of Jean-Baptiste Colbert (ZHAHNH-bah-TEEST kohl-BAYR) (1619–1683) as controller general of finances. Colbert sought to increase the wealth and power of France through general adherence to mercantilism, which stressed government regulation of economic activities to benefit the state. To decrease the need for imports and increase exports, Colbert founded new luxury industries, such as the royal tapestry works at Beauvais; invited Venetian glassmakers and Flemish clothmakers to France; drew up instructions regulating the quality of goods produced; oversaw the training of workers; and granted special privileges, including tax exemptions, loans, and subsidies, to individuals who established new industries. To improve communications and the transportation of goods internally, he built roads and canals. To decrease imports directly, Colbert raised tariffs on foreign manufactured goods and created a merchant marine to carry French goods.

Although Colbert's policies are given much credit for fostering the development of manufacturing in France, some historians are dubious about the usefulness of many of his mercantilistic policies and question whether Colbert stuck to rigid mercantilistic convictions. Regulations were often evaded, and the imposition of high tariffs brought foreign retaliation. French trading companies entered the scene too late to be really competitive with the English and the Dutch. And above all, Colbert's economic policies, which were geared to making his king more powerful, were ultimately self-defeating. The more revenue Colbert collected to enable the king to make war, the faster Louis depleted the treasury. At the same time, the burden of taxes fell increasingly on the peasants, who still constituted the overwhelming majority of the French population. Nevertheless, some historians argue that although Louis bankrupted the treasury in order to pay for his wars, the economic practices implemented under Colbert, including investment in the shipping and textile industries and improvements in transportation facilities, allowed for greater economic growth in the eighteenth century.

Daily Life at the Court of Versailles   The court of Louis XIV at Versailles set a standard that was soon followed by other European rulers. In 1660, Louis decided to convert a hunting lodge at Versailles, not far from the capital city of Paris, into a chateau. Not until 1688, after untold sums of money had been

spent and tens of thousands of workers had labored incessantly, was construction completed on the enormous palace.

Versailles served many purposes. It was the residence of the king, a reception hall for state affairs, an office building for the members of the king's
government, and the home of thousands of royal officials and aristocratic courtiers. Versailles also served a practical political purpose. It became home to the
high nobility and princes of the blood. By keeping them involved in the myriad
activities that made up daily life at the court of Versailles, Louis excluded them
from real power while allowing them to share in the mystique of power as companions of the king. Versailles became a symbol for the French absolutist state
and the power of the Sun King, Louis XIV. As a visible manifestation of
France's superiority and wealth, this lavish court was intended to overawe subjects and impress foreign powers.

Life at Versailles became a court ceremony with Louis XIV at the center of
it all. The king had little privacy; only when he visited his wife or mother or

Chateaux de Versailles et de Trianon, Versailles//© Réunion des Musées Nationaux/Art Resource, NY

Interior of Versailles: The Hall of Mirrors. *Pictured here is the exquisite Hall of
Mirrors at Versailles. Located on the second floor, the hall overlooks the park below.
Three hundred and fifty-seven mirrors were placed on the wall opposite the windows in
order to create an illusion of even greater width. Careful planning went into every detail
of the interior decoration. Even the doorknobs were specially designed to reflect the
magnificence of Versailles. This photo shows the Hall of Mirrors after the restoration
work that was completed in June 2007, a project that took three years, cost 12 million
euros (more than $16 million), and included the restoration of the Bohemian crystal
chandeliers.*

mistress or met with ministers was he free of the noble courtiers who swarmed about the palace. Most daily ceremonies were carefully staged, such as those attending Louis's rising from bed, dining, praying, attending Mass, and going to bed. A mob of nobles aspired to assist the king in carrying out these solemn activities. It was considered a great honor for a noble to be chosen to hand the king his shirt while dressing. But why did nobles participate in so many ceremonies, some of which were so obviously demeaning? Active involvement in the activities at Versailles was the king's prerequisite for obtaining the offices, titles, and pensions that only he could grant. This policy reduced great nobles and ecclesiastics, the "people of quality," to a plane of equality, allowing Louis to exercise control over them and prevent them from interfering in the real lines of power. To maintain their social prestige, the "people of quality" were expected to adhere to rigid standards of court etiquette appropriate to their rank.

Indeed, court etiquette became a complex matter. Nobles and royal princes were arranged in an elaborate order of seniority and expected to follow certain rules of precedence. Who could sit down and on what kind of chair was a subject of much debate. When Philip of Orléans, the king's brother, and his wife Charlotte sought to visit their daughter, the duchess of Lorraine, they encountered problems with Louis. Charlotte explained why in one of her letters:

> The difficulty is that the Duke of Lorraine claims that he is entitled to sit in an armchair in the presence of Philip and myself because the Emperor gives him an armchair. To this the King [Louis] replied that the Emperor's ceremonial is one thing and the King's another, and that, for example, the Emperor gives the cardinals armchairs, whereas here they may never sit at all in the King's presence.[4]

Louis refused to compromise; the duke of Lorraine was only entitled to a stool. The duke balked, and Philip and Charlotte canceled their visit.

Daily life at Versailles also included numerous forms of entertainment. Walks through the gardens, boating trips, performances of tragedies and comedies, ballets, and concerts all provided sources of pleasure. Three evenings a week, from seven to ten, Louis also held an *appartement* (uh-par-tuh-MAHNH) where he was "at home" to his court. The *appartement* was characterized by a formal informality. Relaxed rules of etiquette even allowed people to sit down in the presence of their superiors. The evening's entertainment began with a concert, followed by games of billiards or cards, and ended with a sumptuous buffet.

The Wars of Louis XIV   Both the increase in royal power that Louis pursued and his desire for military glory led the king to wage war. Under the secretary of war, François-Michel Le Tellier (frahnh-SWAH-mee-SHEL luh tel-YAY), the marquis of Louvois (loo-VWAH), France developed a professional army numbering 100,000 men in peacetime and 400,000 in time of war. Louis made war an almost incessant activity of his reign. To achieve the prestige and military glory befitting the Sun King as well as to ensure the domination of his Bourbon dynasty over European affairs, Louis waged four wars between 1667 and 1713 (see Map 15.2).

France in 1630

Acquisitions to 1659
(minority of Louis XIV)

Acquisitions to 1679

Acquisitions to 1697
(Treaty of Ryswick)

UNITED PROVINCES

Amsterdam
Ryswick
Utrecht
Nimwegen

Rhine R.

HOLY

Brussels   Cologne
Calais
SPANISH
NETHERLANDS

ROMAN

Lille

ARTOIS

Mosel R.

Mainz

EMPIRE

Seine R.

Reims   Verdun
Metz

Battle of
Blenheim

Paris

Rastatt
LORRAINE   Strasbourg

ALSACE

FRANCE

FRANCHE-
COMTÉ

SWISS
CANTONS

0   50   100   150 Kilometers   CHAROLAIS

0   50   100 Miles

Saône R.

Lake
Geneva

© Cengage Learning 2012

MAP 15.2 The Wars of Louis XIV

The Sun King instigated several wars in his efforts to expand the power of France
and the Bourbon dynasty. Each military thrust was met by a coalition of European
states that kept French gains minimal compared to the amount of blood spilled and
capital spent.

In 1667, Louis began his first war by invading the Spanish Netherlands to
his north and Franche-Comté to the east. But the Triple Alliance of the Dutch,
English, and Swedes forced Louis to sue for peace in 1668 and accept a few
towns in the Spanish Netherlands for his efforts. He never forgave the Dutch
for arranging the Triple Alliance, and in 1672, after isolating the Dutch, France
invaded the United Provinces with some initial success. But the French victories
led Brandenburg, Spain, and the Holy Roman Empire to form a new coalition
that forced Louis to end the Dutch War by making peace at Nimwegen (NIM-
vay-gun) in 1678. While Dutch territory remained intact, France received

Franche-Comté from Spain, which served merely to stimulate Louis's appetite for even more land.

This time, Louis moved eastward against the Holy Roman Empire, which he perceived from his previous war as feeble and unable to resist. The gradual annexation of the provinces of Alsace and Lorraine was followed by the occupation of the city of Strasbourg, a move that led to widespread protest and the formation of a new coalition. The creation of this League of Augsburg, consisting of Spain, the Holy Roman Empire, the United Provinces, Sweden, and England, led to Louis's third war, the War of the League of Augsburg (1689–1697). This bitterly contested eight-year struggle brought economic depression and famine to France. The Treaty of Ryswick (RYZ-wik) ending the war forced Louis to give up most of his conquests in the empire, although he was allowed to keep Strasbourg and part of Alsace. The gains were hardly worth the bloodshed and the misery he had caused the French people.

Louis's fourth war, the War of the Spanish Succession (1702–1713), was over bigger stakes, the succession to the Spanish throne. Charles II, the sickly and childless Habsburg ruler, left the throne of Spain in his will to a grandson of Louis XIV. When the latter became King Philip V of Spain after Charles's death, the suspicion that Spain and France would eventually be united in the same dynastic family caused the formation of a new coalition, determined to prevent a Bourbon hegemony that would mean the certain destruction of the European balance of power. This coalition of England, the United Provinces, Habsburg Austria, and German states opposed France and Spain in a war that dragged on in Europe and the colonial empires in North America for eleven years. In a number of battles, including the memorable defeat of the French forces at Blenheim (BLEN-im) in 1704 by allied troops led by the English commander, John Churchill, duke of Marlborough, the coalition wore down Louis's forces. An end to the war finally came with the Peace of Utrecht in 1713 and of Rastatt in 1714. Although these peace treaties confirmed Philip V as the Spanish ruler, initiating a Spanish Bourbon dynasty that would last into the twentieth century, they also affirmed that the thrones of Spain and France were to remain separated. The Spanish Netherlands, Milan, and Naples were given to Austria, and the emerging state of Brandenburg-Prussia gained additional territories. The real winner at Utrecht, however, was England, which received Gibraltar as well as the French possessions of Newfoundland, Hudson Bay Territory, and Nova Scotia in America. Though France, by its sheer size and position, remained a great power, England had emerged as a formidable naval force.

Only two years after the treaty, the Sun King was dead, leaving France in debt and surrounded by enemies. On his deathbed, the seventy-six-year-old monarch seemed remorseful when he told his successor:

> Soon you will be King of a great kingdom. I urge you not to forget your duty to God; remember that you owe everything to Him. Try to remain at peace with your neighbors. I loved war too much. Do not follow me in that or in overspending. Take advice in everything; try to find the best course and follow it. Lighten your people's burden as soon as possible, and do what I have had the misfortune not to do myself.[5]

Did Louis mean it? Did Louis ever realize how tarnished the glory he had sought had become? Ten years before the end of his reign one of his subjects wrote: "Even the people ... who have so much loved you, and have placed such trust in you, begin to lose their love, their trust, and even their respect.... They believe you have no pity for their sorrows, that you are devoted only to your power and your glory."[6] In any event, the advice to his successor was probably not remembered; his great-grandson was only five years old.

The Decline of Spain   At the beginning of the seventeenth century, Spain possessed the most populous empire in the world, controlling almost all of South America and a number of settlements in Asia and Africa. To most Europeans, Spain still seemed the greatest power of the age, but the reality was quite different. The treasury was empty; Philip II went bankrupt in 1596 from excessive expenditures on war, and his successor, Philip III, did the same in 1607 by spending a fortune on his court. The armed forces were out-of-date, the government was inefficient, and the commercial class was weak in the midst of a suppressed peasantry, a luxury-loving class of nobles, and an oversupply of priests and monks. Spain continued to play the role of a great power, but appearances were deceiving.

During the reign of Philip III (1598–1621), many of Spain's weaknesses became apparent. Interested only in court luxury or miracle-working relics, Philip III allowed his first minister, the greedy duke of Lerma, to run the country. The aristocratic Lerma's primary interest was accumulating power and wealth for himself and his family. As important offices were filled with his relatives, crucial problems went unsolved.

The Reign of Philip IV   The reign of Philip IV (1621–1665) seemed to offer hope for a revival of Spain's energies, especially in the capable hands of his chief minister, Gaspar de Guzman (gahs-PAR day goos-MAHN), the count of Olivares (oh-lee-BAH-rayss). This clever, hardworking, and power-hungry statesman dominated the king's every move and worked to revive the interests of the monarchy. A flurry of domestic reform decrees, aimed at curtailing the power of the Catholic Church and the landed aristocracy, was soon followed by a political reform program whose purpose was to further centralize the government of all Spain and its possessions in monarchical hands. All of these efforts met with little real success, however, because both the number (estimated at one-fifth of the population) and the power of the Spanish aristocrats made them too strong to curtail in any significant fashion.

At the same time, most of the efforts of Olivares and Philip were undermined by their desire to pursue Spain's imperial glory and by a series of internal revolts. Spain's involvement in the Thirty Years' War led to a series of frightfully expensive military campaigns that incited internal revolts and years of civil war. Unfortunately for Spain, the campaigns also failed to produce victory. As Olivares wrote to King Philip IV, "God wants us to make peace; for He is depriving us visibly and absolutely of all the means of war."[7] At the Battle of Rocroi in 1643, much of the Spanish army was destroyed.

The defeats in Europe and the internal revolts of the 1640s ended any illusions about Spain's greatness. The actual extent of Spain's economic difficulties is still debated, but there is no question about its foreign losses. Dutch independence was formally recognized by the Peace of Westphalia in 1648, and the Peace of the Pyrenees with France in 1659 meant the surrender of Artois and the outlying defenses of the Spanish Netherlands as well as certain border regions that went to France.

ABSOLUTISM IN CENTRAL, EASTERN, AND NORTHERN EUROPE

During the seventeenth century, a development of great importance for the modern Western world took place in central and eastern Europe, as three new powers made their appearance: Prussia, Austria, and Russia.

The German States   The Peace of Westphalia, which officially ended the Thirty Years' War in 1648, left each of the states in the Holy Roman Empire virtually autonomous and sovereign. Properly speaking, there was no longer a German state but rather more than three hundred little Germanies. Of these, two emerged as great European powers in the seventeenth and eighteenth centuries.

The Rise of Brandenburg-Prussia   The evolution of Brandenburg into a powerful state was largely the work of the Hohenzollern (hoh-en-TSULL-urn) dynasty, which in 1415 had come to rule the insignificant principality in northeastern Germany. In 1609, the Hohenzollerns inherited some lands in the Rhine valley in western Germany; nine years later, they received the duchy of Prussia (East Prussia). By the seventeenth century, then, the dominions of the house of Hohenzollern, now called Brandenburg-Prussia, consisted of three disconnected masses in western, central, and eastern Germany; only the person of the Hohenzollern ruler connected them (see Map 15.3).

The foundation for the Prussian state was laid by Frederick William the Great Elector (1640–1688), who came to power in the midst of the Thirty Years' War. Realizing that Brandenburg-Prussia was a small, open territory with no natural frontiers for defense, Frederick William built a competent and efficient standing army. By 1678, he possessed a force of 40,000 men that absorbed more than 50 percent of the state's revenues. To sustain the army and his own power, Frederick William established the General War Commissariat to levy taxes for the army and oversee its growth and training. The Commissariat soon evolved into an agency for civil government as well. Directly responsible to the elector, the new bureaucratic machine became his chief instrument for governing the state. Many of its officials were members of the Prussian landed aristocracy, the Junkers (YOONG-kers), who also served as officers in the all-important army.

The nobles' support for Frederick William's policies derived from the tacit agreement that he made with them. In order to eliminate the power that the

MAP 15.3 The Growth of Brandenburg-Prussia

Frederick William the Great Elector laid the foundation for a powerful state when he increased the size and efficiency of the army, raised taxes and created an efficient bureaucracy to collect them, and gained the support of the landed aristocracy. Later rulers added more territory.

members of the nobility could exercise in their provincial Estates-General, Frederick William made a deal with the nobles. In return for a free hand in running the government (in other words, for depriving the provincial Estates of their power), he gave the nobles almost unlimited power over their peasants, exempted the nobles from taxation, and awarded them the highest ranks in the army and the Commissariat with the understanding that they would not challenge his political control. As for the peasants, the nobles were allowed to appropriate their land and bind them to the soil as serfs. Serfdom was not new to Brandenburg-Prussia, but Frederick William reinforced it through his concessions to the nobles.

To build Brandenburg-Prussia's economy, Frederick William followed the fashionable mercantilist policies, constructing roads and canals and using high tariffs, subsidies, and monopolies for manufacturers to stimulate domestic industry. At the same time, however, he continued to favor the interests of the nobility at the expense of the commercial and industrial middle classes in the towns.

Frederick William laid the groundwork for the Prussian state. His son Frederick III (1688–1713) made one further significant contribution: in return for aiding the Holy Roman Emperor, he was officially granted the title of king-in-Prussia. Thus was Elector Frederick III transformed into King Frederick I, ruler of an important new player on the European stage.

The Emergence of Austria   The Austrian Habsburgs had long played a significant role in European politics as Holy Roman Emperors, but by the end of the Thirty Years' War, the Habsburg hopes of creating an empire in Germany had been dashed. In the seventeenth century, the house of Austria made an important transition; the German empire was lost, but a new empire was created in eastern and southeastern Europe.

The nucleus of the new Austrian Empire remained the traditional Austrian hereditary possessions: Lower and Upper Austria, Carinthia, Carniola, Styria, and Tyrol (see Map 15.4). To these had been added the kingdom of Bohemia and parts of northwestern Hungary in the sixteenth century.

In the seventeenth century, Leopold I (1658–1705) encouraged the eastward movement of the Austrian Empire, but he was sorely challenged by the revival of Ottoman power. Having moved into Transylvania, the Ottomans eventually pushed westward and laid siege to Vienna in 1683. A European army, led by the Austrians, counterattacked and decisively defeated the Ottomans in 1687. By the Treaty of Karlowitz (KARL-oh-vits) in 1699, Austria took control of Hungary,

MAP 15.4 The Growth of the Austrian Empire

The Habsburgs had hoped to establish an empire of Germans, but the results of the Thirty Years' War crushed that dream. So Austria expanded to the east and the south, primarily at the expense of the Ottoman Empire, and also gained the Spanish Netherlands and former Spanish territories in Italy.

Transylvania, Croatia, and Slovenia, thus establishing an Austrian Empire in southeastern Europe. At the end of the War of the Spanish Succession, Austria gained the Spanish Netherlands and received formal recognition of its occupation of the Spanish possessions in Italy, namely, Milan, Mantua, Sardinia, and Naples. By the beginning of the eighteenth century, the house of Austria had acquired an empire of considerable size.

The Austrian monarchy, however, never became a highly centralized, absolutist state, primarily because it included so many different national groups. The Austrian Empire remained a collection of territories held together by a personal union. The Habsburg emperor was archduke of Austria, king of Bohemia, and king of Hungary. Each of these territories had its own laws, Estates-General, and political life. The landed aristocrats throughout the empire were connected by a common bond of service to the house of Habsburg, as military officers or government bureaucrats, but no other common sentiment tied the regions together. Nevertheless, by the beginning of the eighteenth century, Austria was a populous empire in central Europe of great potential military strength.

Italy: From Spanish to Austrian Rule

By 1530, Emperor Charles V had managed to defeat the French armies in Italy and become the arbiter of Italy (see Chapter 13). Initially, he was content to establish close ties with many native Italian rulers and allowed them to rule, provided that they recognized his dominant role. But in 1540, he gave the duchy of Milan to his son Philip II and transferred all imperial rights over Italy to the Spanish monarchy.

From the beginning of Philip II's reign in 1556 until 1713, the Spanish presence was felt everywhere in Italy. Only Florence, the Papal States, and Venice managed to maintain relatively independent policies. At the same time, the influence of the papacy became oppressive in Italy as the machinery of the Catholic Counter-Reformation—the Inquisition, the Index, and the Jesuits—was used to stifle all resistance to the Catholic orthodoxy created by the Council of Trent (see Chapter 13).

At the beginning of the eighteenth century, Italy suffered further from the struggles between France and Spain. But it was Austria, not France, that benefited the most from the War of the Spanish Succession. By gaining Milan, Mantua, Sardinia, and Naples, Austria supplanted Spain as the dominant power in Italy.

Russia: From Fledgling Principality to Major Power

A new Russian state had emerged in the fifteenth century under the leadership of the principality of Moscow and its grand dukes (see Chapter 12). In the sixteenth century, Ivan IV the Terrible (1533–1584), who was the first ruler to take the title of tsar ("Caesar"), expanded the territories of Russia eastward after finding westward expansion blocked by the powerful Swedish and Polish states. Ivan also extended the autocracy of the tsar by crushing the power of the Russian nobility, known as the **boyars** (boh-YARS). Ivan's dynasty came to an end in 1598 and was followed by a resurgence of aristocratic power in a period of anarchy known as the Time of Troubles. It did not end until the Zemsky Sobor (ZEM-skee suh-BOR), or national assembly, chose Michael Romanov (ROH-muh-nahf) (1613–1645) as the new tsar, beginning a dynasty that lasted until 1917.

In the seventeenth century, Muscovite society was highly stratified. At the top was the tsar, who claimed to be a divinely ordained autocratic ruler. Russian society was dominated by an upper class of landed aristocrats who, in the course of the seventeenth century, managed to bind their peasants to the land. An abundance of land and a shortage of peasants made serfdom desirable to the landowners. Townspeople were also controlled. Many merchants were not allowed to move from their cities without government permission or to sell their businesses to anyone outside their class. In the seventeenth century, merchant and peasant revolts as well as a schism in the Russian Orthodox Church created very unsettled conditions. In the midst of these political and religious upheavals, seventeenth-century Moscow was experiencing more frequent contacts with the West, and Western ideas were beginning to penetrate a few Russian circles. Nevertheless, Russia remained largely outside the framework of the West: the Renaissance, the Reformation, and the geographic discoveries of the sixteenth and seventeenth centuries made little impact on Russia. At the end of the seventeenth century, Peter the Great (1689–1725) noticeably accelerated the westernizing process.

The Reign of Peter the Great (1689–1725)   Peter the Great was an unusual character. A strong man, towering 6 feet 9 inches tall, Peter was coarse in his tastes and rude in his behavior. He enjoyed a low kind of humor—belching contests, crude jokes, comical funerals—and vicious punishments including floggings, impalings, roastings, and beard burnings. Peter gained a firsthand view of the West when he made a trip there in 1697–1698 and returned to Russia with a firm determination to westernize or Europeanize his realm. He admired European technology and gadgets and desired to transplant these to Russia. Only this kind of modernization could give him the army and navy he needed to make Russia a great power.

As could be expected, one of Peter's first priorities was the reorganization of the army and the creation of a navy. Employing both Russians and Europeans as officers, he conscripted peasants for twenty-five-year stints of service to build a standing army of 210,000 men. Peter has also been given credit for forming the first Russian navy.

Peter also reorganized the central government, partly along Western lines. In 1711, he created the Senate to supervise the administrative machinery of the state while he was away on military campaigns. In time, the Senate became something like a ruling council, but its ineffectiveness caused Peter to borrow the Western institution of "colleges," or boards of administrators entrusted with specific functions, such as foreign affairs, war, and justice. To impose the rule of the central government more effectively throughout the land, Peter divided Russia into eight provinces and later, in 1719, into fifty. Although he hoped to create a "police state," by which he meant a well-ordered community governed in accordance with law, few of his bureaucrats shared his concept of honest service and duty to the state. Peter hoped for a sense of civic duty, but his own forceful personality created an atmosphere of fear that prevented it. He wrote to one administrator, "According to these orders act, act, act. I won't write more, but you will pay with your head if you interpret orders again."[8]

To further his administrative aims, Peter demanded that all members of the landholding class serve in either military or civil offices. Moreover, in 1722, Peter instituted the Table of Ranks to create opportunities for nonnobles to serve the state and join the nobility. He had all civil offices ranked according to fourteen levels and created a parallel list of fourteen grades for all military offices. Every official was then required to begin at level one and work his way up the ranks. When a nonnoble reached the eighth rank, he acquired noble status. Peter's successors did not continue his attempt to create a new nobility based on merit, however.

To obtain the enormous amount of money needed for an army and navy that absorbed as much as four-fifths of the state revenue, Peter adopted Western mercantilistic policies to stimulate economic growth. He tried to increase exports and develop new industries while exploiting domestic resources like the iron mines in the Urals. But his military needs were endless, and he came to rely on the old expedient of simply raising taxes, imposing additional burdens on the hapless peasants, who were becoming ever more oppressed in Peter's Russia.

Peter also sought to establish state control over the Russian Orthodox Church. In 1721, he abolished the position of patriarch and created a body called the Holy Synod to make decisions for the church. At its head stood a **procurator**, a layman who represented the interests of the tsar and assured Peter of effective domination of the church.

Shortly after his return from the West in 1698, Peter had begun to introduce Western customs, practices, and manners into Russia. He ordered the preparation of the first Russian book of etiquette to teach Western manners. Among other things, it pointed out that it was not polite to spit on the floor or to scratch oneself at dinner. Because Europeans at that time did not wear beards or traditional long-skirted coats, Russian beards had to be shaved and coats shortened, a reform Peter personally enforced at court by shaving off his nobles' beards and cutting their coats at the knees with his own hands. Outside the court, barbers and tailors planted at town gates enforced the edicts by cutting the beards and cloaks of those who entered or left.

One group of Russians benefited greatly from Peter's cultural reforms—women. Having watched women mixing freely with men in Western courts, Peter shattered the seclusion of upper-class Russian women and demanded that they remove the traditional veils that covered their faces. Peter also decreed that social gatherings be held three times a week in the large houses of Saint Petersburg where men and women could mix for conversation, card games, and dancing, which Peter had learned in the West. The tsar also now insisted that women could marry of their own free will.

Russia as a Military Power   The object of Peter's domestic reforms was to make Russia into a great state and a military power. His primary goal was to "open a window to the West," meaning a port easily accessible to Europe. This could only be achieved on the Baltic, but at that time the Baltic coast was controlled by

Sweden, the most important power in northern Europe. Desirous of these lands, Peter, with the support of Poland and Denmark, attacked Sweden in the summer of 1700 believing that the young king of Sweden, Charles XII, could easily be defeated. Charles, however, proved to be a brilliant general. He smashed the Danes, flattened the Poles, and with a well-disciplined force of only 8,000 men, routed the Russian army of 40,000 at the Battle of Narva (1700). The Great Northern War (1701–1721) soon ensued.

But Peter fought back. He reorganized his army along Western lines and at the Battle of Poltava (pul-TAH-vuh) in 1709 defeated Charles's army decisively. Although the war dragged on for another twelve years, the Peace of Nystadt (NEE-shtaht) in 1721 gave formal recognition to what Peter had already achieved: the acquisition of Estonia, Livonia, and Karelia (see Map 15.5). Sweden had become a second-rate power, and Russia was now the great European state Peter had wanted. And he was building it a fine capital. Early in the war, in the northern marshlands along the Baltic, Peter had begun to construct a new city, Saint Petersburg, his window on the West and a symbol that Russia was looking westward to Europe. Though its construction cost the lives of thousands of peasants, Peter completed the city during his lifetime. It remained the Russian capital until 1917.

Peter modernized and westernized Russia to the extent that it became a great military power and, by his death in 1725, an important member of the European state system. But his policies were also detrimental to Russia. Westernization was a bit of a sham because Western culture reached only the upper classes, and the

MAP 15.5 Russia: From Principality to Nation-State

Russia had swelled in size since its emergence in the fifteenth century. Peter the Great, however, modernized the country, instituting bureaucratic and taxation reforms and building up the military. He won territory on the Baltic from Sweden, giving Russia a port at Saint Petersburg.

real object of the reforms, the creation of a strong military, only added more burdens to the masses of the Russian people. The forceful way in which Peter the Great imposed westernization led his people to distrust Europe and Western civilization rather than embrace them.

The Great Northern States   As the economic thoroughfare for the products of eastern Europe and the West, the Baltic Sea bestowed special importance on the lands surrounding it. In the sixteenth century, Sweden had broken its ties with Denmark and emerged as an independent state (see Chapter 13). Despite their common Lutheran religion, Denmark's and Sweden's territorial ambitions in northern Europe kept them in almost constant rivalry during the seventeenth century.

Denmark   Under Christian IV (1588–1648), Denmark seemed a likely candidate for expansion, but it met with little success. The system of electing monarchs forced the kings to share their power with the Danish nobility, who exercised strict control over the peasants who worked their lands. Danish ambitions for ruling the Baltic were severely curtailed by the losses they sustained in the Thirty Years' War and later in the so-called Northern War (1655–1660) with Sweden.

Danish military losses led to a constitutional crisis in which a meeting of Denmark's Estates brought to pass a bloodless revolution in 1660. The power of the nobility was curtailed, a hereditary monarchy was reestablished, and a new absolutist constitution was proclaimed in 1665. Under Christian V (1670–1699), a centralized administration was instituted with the nobility as the chief officeholders.

Sweden   Compared with Denmark, Sweden seemed a relatively poor country, and historians have had difficulty explaining why it played such a large role in European affairs in the seventeenth century. Sweden's economy was weak, and the monarchy was still locked in conflict with the powerful Swedish nobility. During the reign of Gustavus Adolphus (1611–1632), his wise and dedicated chief minister, Axel Oxenstierna (AHK-sul OOK-sen-shur-nah), persuaded the king to adopt a new policy in which the nobility formed a "First Estate" occupying the bureaucratic positions of an expanded central government. This created a stable monarchy and freed the king to raise a formidable army and participate in the Thirty Years' War, only to be killed in battle in 1632.

Sweden entered a period of severe political crisis after the death of Gustavus Adolphus. His daughter Christina (1633–1654) proved to be far more interested in philosophy and religion than ruling. Her tendency to favor the interests of the nobility caused the other estates of the Riksdag (reeks-TAGH), Sweden's parliament—the burghers, clergy, and peasants—to protest. In 1654, tired of ruling and wishing to become a Catholic, which was forbidden in Sweden, Christina abdicated in favor of her cousin, who became King Charles X (1654–1660). His accession to the throne defused a potentially explosive peasant revolt against the nobility.

Charles X reestablished domestic order, but it was his successor, Charles XI (1660–1697), who did the painstaking work of building the Swedish monarchy along the lines of an absolute monarchy. By retaking control of the crown lands and the revenues attached to them from the nobility, Charles managed to weaken the independent power of the nobles. He built up a bureaucracy, subdued both the Riksdag and the church, improved the army and navy, and left to his son, Charles XII (1697–1718), a well-organized Swedish state that dominated northern Europe. In 1693, he and his heirs were acclaimed as "absolute, sovereign kings, responsible for their actions to no man on earth."

Charles XII was primarily interested in military affairs. Though he was energetic and regarded as a brilliant general, his grandiose plans and strategies, which involved Sweden in conflicts with Poland, Denmark, and Russia, proved to be Sweden's undoing. By the time he died in 1718, Charles XII had lost much of Sweden's northern empire to Russia, and Sweden was no longer a first-class northern power.

The Ottoman Empire   After conquering Constantinople in 1453, the Ottoman Turks tried to complete their conquest of the Balkans, where they had been established since the fourteenth century (see Map 15.6). Although they were successful in taking the Romanian territory of Wallachia in 1476, the resistance of the Hungarians kept them from advancing up the Danube valley. From 1480 to 1520, internal problems and the need to consolidate their eastern frontiers kept the Turks from any further attacks on Europe. The reign of Sultan Suleiman (SOO-lay-mahn) I the Magnificent (1520–1566), however, brought the Turks back to Europe's attention. Advancing up the Danube, the Turks seized Belgrade in 1521 and Hungary by 1526, although their attempts to conquer Vienna in 1529 were repulsed. At the same time, the Turks extended their power into the western Mediterranean, threatening to turn it into a Turkish lake until the Spanish destroyed a large Turkish fleet at Lepanto (in modern-day Greece) in 1571. Despite the defeat, the Turks continued to hold nominal control over the southern shores of the Mediterranean.

Although Europeans frequently spoke of new Christian Crusades against the "infidel" Turks, by the beginning of the seventeenth century European rulers seeking alliances and trade concession were treating the Ottoman Empire like another European power. The Ottoman Empire possessed a highly effective governmental system, especially when it was led by strong sultans or powerful grand viziers (prime ministers). The splendid capital, Constantinople, had a population far larger than that of any European city. Nevertheless, Ottoman politics periodically degenerated into bloody intrigues as factions fought each other for influence and the throne. In one particularly gruesome practice, a ruling sultan would murder his brothers to avoid challenges to his rule. Despite the periodic bouts of civil chaos, a well-trained bureaucracy of civil servants continued to administer state affairs efficiently.

A well-organized military system also added to the strength of the Ottoman Empire. Especially outstanding were the **Janissaries** (JAN-nih-say-reez), composed of Christian boys who had been taken from their parents, converted to the Muslim

MAP 15.6 The Ottoman Empire

In the sixteenth and seventeenth centuries, the Ottoman Empire possessed an effective bureaucracy and military. During this period, it conquered much of the Balkans and made inroads into eastern Europe; by 1699, however, it had lost the farthest reaches of its European territory and would never again pose a serious threat to Europe.

faith, and subjected to rigid military discipline to form an elite core of 8,000 troops personally loyal to the sultan.

In the first half of the seventeenth century, the Ottoman Empire was a "sleeping giant." Occupied by domestic bloodletting and severely threatened by a challenge from Persia, the Ottomans were content with the status quo in eastern Europe. But under a new line of grand viziers in the second half of the seventeenth century, the Ottoman Empire again took the offensive. By 1683, the Ottomans had marched through the Hungarian plain and laid siege to Vienna. Repulsed by a mixed army of Austrians, Poles, Bavarians, and Saxons, the Turks retreated and were pushed out of Hungary by a new European coalition. Although they retained the core of their empire, the Ottoman Turks would never again be a threat to Europe.

The Limits of Absolutism
In recent decades, historical studies of local institutions have challenged the traditional picture of absolute monarchs. We now recognize that their power was far from absolute, and it is misleading to think that they actually controlled the lives of their subjects. In 1700, government for most people still meant the local institutions that affected their lives: local courts, local tax collectors, and local organizers of armed forces. Kings and ministers might determine policies and issue guidelines, but they still had to function through local agents and had no guarantee that their wishes would be carried out. A mass of urban and provincial privileges, liberties, and exemptions (including from taxation) and a whole host of corporate bodies and interest groups—provincial and national Estates, clerical officials, officeholders who had bought or inherited their positions, and provincial nobles—limited what monarchs could achieve. The most successful rulers were not those who tried to destroy the old system but rather those like Louis XIV, who knew how to use the old system to their advantage. Above all other considerations stood the landholding nobility. Everywhere in the seventeenth century, the landed aristocracy played an important role in the European monarchical system. As military officers, judges, officeholders, and landowners in control of vast, untaxed estates, their power remained immense. In some places, their strength put severe limits on how effectively even absolute monarchs could rule.

LIMITED MONARCHY AND REPUBLICS

Almost everywhere in Europe in the seventeenth century, kings and their ministers were in control of central governments that sought to impose order by strengthening their powers. But not all European states followed the pattern of absolute monarchy. In eastern Europe, the Polish aristocracy controlled a virtually powerless king. In western Europe, two great states—the Dutch Republic and England—successfully resisted the power of hereditary monarchs.

The Weakness of the Polish Monarchy
Much of Polish history revolved around the bitter struggle between the crown and the landed nobility. The dynastic union of Jagiello (yahg-YEL-oh), grand prince of Lithuania, with the Polish queen Jadwiga (yahd-VEE-guh) resulted in a large Lithuanian-Polish state in 1386, although it was not until 1569 that a formal merger occurred between the two crowns. The union of Poland and Lithuania under the Jagiello dynasty had created the largest kingdom in Christendom at the beginning of the fifteenth century. As a result, Poland-Lithuania played a major role in eastern Europe in the fifteenth century and also ruled much of Ukraine by the end of the sixteenth century. Poland-Lithuania had a rather unique governmental system in that assemblies of nobles elected the king and carefully limited royal power. The power of the nobles also enabled them to keep the Polish peasantry in a state of serfdom.

In 1572, when the Jagiello dynasty came to an end, a new practice arose of choosing outsiders as kings, with the idea that they would bring in new alliances. When the throne was awarded to the Swede Sigismund III (1587–1631), the new king dreamed of creating a vast Polish empire that would include Russia and possibly Finland and Sweden. Poland not only failed to achieve this goal but by the end of the seventeenth century had become a weak, decentralized state.

It was the elective nature of the Polish monarchy that reduced it to impotence. The Sejm (SAYM), or Polish diet, was a two-chamber assembly in which landowners completely dominated the few townspeople and lawyers who were also members. To be elected to the kingship, prospective monarchs had to agree to share power with the Sejm (in effect with the nobles) in matters of taxation, foreign and military policy, and the appointment of state officials and judges. The power of the Sejm had disastrous results for central monarchical authority, for the real aim of most of its members was to ensure that central authority would not affect their local interests. The acceptance of the liberum veto in 1652, whereby the meetings of the Sejm could be stopped by a single dissenting member, reduced government to virtual chaos.

Poland, then, was basically a confederation of semi-independent estates of landed nobles. By the late seventeenth century, it had also become a battleground for foreign powers, who found the nation easy to invade but difficult to rule.

The Golden Age of the Dutch Republic   The seventeenth century has often been called the golden age of the Dutch Republic as the United Provinces held center stage as one of Europe's great powers. Like France and England, the United Provinces was an Atlantic power, underlining the importance of the shift of political and economic power from the Mediterranean basin to the countries on the Atlantic seaboard. As a result of the sixteenth-century revolt of the Netherlands, the seven northern provinces, which began to call themselves the United Provinces of the Netherlands in 1581, became the core of the modern Dutch state. The new state was officially recognized by the Peace of Westphalia in 1648.

With independence came internal dissension. There were two chief centers of political power in the new state. Each province had an official known as a stadholder (STAD-hohl-dur) who was responsible for leading the army and maintaining order. Beginning with William of Orange and his heirs, the house of Orange occupied the stadholderate in most of the seven provinces and favored the development of a centralized government with themselves as hereditary monarchs. The States General, an assembly of representatives from every province, opposed the Orangist ambitions and advocated a decentralized or republican form of government. For much of the seventeenth century, the republican forces were in control. But in 1672, burdened with war against both France and England, the United Provinces turned to William III (1672–1702) of the house of Orange to establish a monarchical regime. But his death in 1702 without a direct heir enabled the republican forces to gain control once more, although the struggle persisted throughout the eighteenth century.

Underlying Dutch prominence in the seventeenth century was economic prosperity, fueled by the role of the Dutch as carriers of European trade. But warfare proved disastrous to the Dutch Republic. Wars with France and England placed heavy burdens on Dutch finances and manpower. English shipping began to challenge what had been Dutch commercial supremacy, and by 1715, the Dutch were experiencing a serious economic decline.

Life in Seventeenth-Century Amsterdam   By the beginning of the seventeenth century, Amsterdam had replaced Antwerp as the financial and commercial capital of Europe. In 1570, Amsterdam had 30,000 inhabitants; by 1610, that number had doubled as refugees poured in, especially from the Spanish Netherlands. In 1613, this rapid growth caused the city government to approve an "urban expansion plan" that increased the city's territory from 500 to 1,800 acres through the construction of three large concentric canals. Builders prepared plots for the tall, narrow-fronted houses that were characteristic of the city by hammering wooden columns through the mud to the firm sand underneath. The canals in turn made it possible for merchants and artisans to use the upper stories of their houses as storerooms for their goods. Wares carried by small boats were hoisted to the top windows of these dwellings by block and tackle beams fastened to the gables of the roofs. Amsterdam's physical expansion was soon matched by its population as the city grew to 200,000 by 1660.

The exuberant expansion of Amsterdam in the seventeenth century owed much to the city's role as the commercial and financial center of Europe. But what had made this possible? For one thing, Amsterdam merchants possessed vast fleets of ships, many of which were used for the lucrative North Sea herring catch. Amsterdam-based ships were also important carriers for the products of other countries. The Dutch invention of the *fluyt* (FLYT), a shallow-draft ship of large capacity, enabled them to transport enormous quantities of cereals, timber, and iron.

Amsterdam merchants unloaded their cargoes at Dam Square, and the city soon became a crossroads for the exchange of many of Europe's chief products. Amsterdam was also, of course, the chief port for the Dutch West Indian and East Indian trading companies. Moreover, city industries turned imported raw materials into finished goods, making Amsterdam an important producer of woolen cloth, refined sugar and tobacco products, glass, beer, paper, books, jewelry, and leather goods. Some of the city's great wealth came from war profits: by 1700, Amsterdam was the principal supplier of military goods in Europe; its gun foundries had customers throughout the Continent.

Another factor in Amsterdam's prosperity was its importance as a financial center. Trading profits provided large quantities of capital for investment. The city's financial role was greatly facilitated by the foundation in 1609 of the Exchange Bank of Amsterdam, long the greatest public bank in northern Europe. The city also founded the Amsterdam Stock Exchange for speculating in commodities.

At the very top of Amsterdam's society stood a select number of very prosperous manufacturers, shipyard owners, and merchants whose wealth enabled them to control the city's government. In the first half of the seventeenth century, the Calvinist background of the wealthy Amsterdam burghers led them to adopt a simple lifestyle. They wore dark clothes and lived in substantial but simply furnished houses known for their steep, narrow stairways. The oft-quoted phrase that "cleanliness is next to godliness" was literally true for these self-confident Dutch burghers.

IMAGES OF EVERYDAY LIFE

Dutch Domesticity

During the golden age of the Dutch Republic, Dutch painters delighted in painting scenes of domestic life, especially the lives of the wealthy burghers who prospered from trade, finance, and manufacturing. The Dutch painter Pieter

Museum der Bildenden Kuenste, Leipzig/© Erich Lessing/Art Resource, NY

Their houses were spotless and orderly (see Images of Everyday Life); foreigners often commented that Dutch housewives always seemed to be scrubbing. But in the second half of the seventeenth century, the wealthy burghers began to reject their Calvinist heritage, a transformation that is especially evident in their more elaborate and colorful clothes.

England and the Emergence of Constitutional Monarchy

One of the most prominent examples of resistance to absolute monarchy came in seventeenth-century England, where king and Parliament struggled to determine the role each should play in governing the nation. But the struggle over this political issue was complicated by a deep and profound de Hooch (PEE-ter duh HOHKH) specialized in painting pictures of Dutch interiors. In *Two Women Teach a Child to Walk* (on page 530), the artist shows a well-furnished and spotless interior; the polished floors reflect the sunlight streaming in through the open door. The rooms are clean and in good order. Household manuals, such as *The Experienced and Knowledgeable Hollands Householder*, provided detailed outlines of the cleaning tasks that should be performed each day of the week. In *The Linen Cupboard* (below), a Dutch mother, assisted by her daughter, is shown storing her clean sheets in an elegant cupboard in another well-polished Dutch room. The Chinese porcelain on top of the cupboard and the antique statue indicate that this is the residence of a wealthy family.

Rijksmuseum, Amsterdam//Alinari/Art Resource, NY

religious controversy. With the victory of Parliament came the foundation for constitutional monarchy by the end of the seventeenth century.

King James I and Parliament   Upon the death of Queen Elizabeth in 1603, the Tudor dynasty became extinct, and the Stuart line of rulers was inaugurated with the accession to the throne of Elizabeth's cousin, King James VI of Scotland (son of Mary, queen of Scots), who became James I (1603–1625) of England. Although used to royal power as king of Scotland, James understood little about the laws, institutions, and customs of the English. He espoused the divine right of kings, the belief that kings receive their power directly from God and are responsible to no one except God. This viewpoint alienated Parliament, which had grown accustomed under the Tudors to act on the premise that monarch and Parliament together ruled England as a "balanced polity." Parliament expressed its displeasure with James's claims by refusing his requests for additional monies needed by the king to meet the increased cost of government. Parliament's power of the purse proved to be its trump card in its relationship with the king.

Some members of Parliament were also alienated by James's religious policy. The Puritans—Protestants in the Anglican Church inspired by Calvinist theology—wanted James to eliminate the episcopal system of church organization used in the Church of England (in which the bishop or *episcopos* played the major administrative role) in favor of a Presbyterian model (used in Scotland and patterned after Calvin's church organization in Geneva, where ministers and elders—also called presbyters—played an important governing role). James refused because he realized that the Anglican Church, with its bishops appointed by the crown, was a major support of monarchical authority. But the Puritans were not easily cowed and added to the rising chorus of opposition to the king. Many of England's **gentry**, mostly well-to-do landowners below the level of the nobility, had become Puritans, and these Puritan gentry not only formed an important and substantial part of the House of Commons, the lower house of Parliament, but also held important positions locally as justices of the peace and sheriffs. It was not wise to alienate them.

Charles I and the Move Toward Revolution   The conflict that had begun during the reign of James came to a head during the reign of his son, Charles I (1625–1649). In 1628, Parliament passed the Petition of Right, which the king was supposed to accept before being granted any tax revenues. This petition prohibited taxation without Parliament's consent, arbitrary imprisonment, the quartering of soldiers in private houses, and the declaration of martial law in peacetime. Although he initially accepted it, Charles later reneged on the agreement because of its limitations on royal power. In 1629, Charles decided that since he could not work with Parliament, he would not summon it to meet. From 1629 to 1640, Charles pursued a course of personal rule, which forced him to find ways to collect taxes without the cooperation of Parliament. One expedient was a tax called ship money, a levy on seacoast towns to pay for coastal defense, which was now collected annually by the king's officials throughout England and used to finance other government operations besides defense. This use of ship money aroused opposition from middle-class merchants and landed gentry, who objected to the king's attempts to tax without Parliament's consent.

The king's religious policy also proved disastrous. His marriage to Henrietta Maria, the Catholic sister of King Louis XIII of France, aroused suspicions about the king's own religious inclinations. Even more important, however, the efforts of Charles and William Laud, the archbishop of Canterbury, to introduce more ritual into the Anglican Church struck the Puritans as a return to Catholic popery. Grievances mounted. Charles might have survived unscathed if he could have avoided calling Parliament, which alone could provide a focus for the many cries of discontent throughout the land. But when the king and Archbishop Laud attempted to impose the Anglican Book of Common Prayer on the Scottish Presbyterian Church, the Scots rose up in rebellion against the king. Financially strapped and unable to raise troops to defend against the Scots, the king was forced to call Parliament into session. Eleven years of frustration welled up to create a Parliament determined to deal the king his due.

In its first session, from November 1640 to September 1641, the so-called Long Parliament (because it lasted in one form or another from 1640 to 1660) took a series of steps that placed severe limitations on royal authority. These included the abolition of arbitrary courts; the abolition of taxes that the king had collected without Parliament's consent, such as ship money; and the passage of the revolutionary Triennial Act, which specified that Parliament must meet at least once every three years, with or without the king's consent. By the end of 1641, one group in Parliament was prepared to go no further, but a group of more radical parliamentarians pushed for more change, including the elimination of bishops in the Anglican Church. When the king tried to take advantage of the split by arresting some members of the more radical faction in Parliament, a large group in Parliament led by John Pym and his fellow Puritans decided that the king had gone too far. England slipped into civil war.

Civil War in England   Parliament proved victorious in the first phase of the English Civil War (1642–1646). Most important to Parliament's success was the creation of the New Model Army, which was composed primarily of more extreme Puritans known as the Independents, who believed they were doing battle for the Lord. It is striking to read in the military reports of Oliver Cromwell (1599–1658), one of the group's leaders, such statements as "Sir, this is none other but the hand of God; and to Him alone belongs the glory." We might also attribute some of the credit to Cromwell himself, since his crusaders were well disciplined and trained in the latest military tactics. Supported by the New Model Army, Parliament ended the first phase of the civil war with the capture of King Charles I in 1646.

A split now occurred in the parliamentary forces. A Presbyterian majority wanted to disband the army and restore Charles I with a Presbyterian state church. The army, composed mostly of the more radical Independents, who opposed an established Presbyterian church, marched on London in 1647 and began negotiations with the king. Charles took advantage of this division to flee and seek help from the Scots. Enraged by the king's treachery, Cromwell and the army engaged in a second civil war (1648) that ended with Cromwell's victory and the capture of the king. This time, Cromwell was determined to achieve a victory for the army's point of view. The Presbyterian members of Parliament were purged, leaving a Rump Parliament of fifty-three members of the House of Commons who then tried and condemned the king on a charge of treason and adjudged that "he, the said Charles Stuart, as a tyrant, traitor, murderer, and public enemy to the good people of this nation, shall be put to death by the severing of his head from his body." On January 30, 1649, Charles was beheaded, a most uncommon act in the seventeenth century. The revolution had triumphed, and the monarchy in England had been destroyed, at least for the moment.

Cromwell and New Governments   After the death of the king, the Rump Parliament abolished the monarchy and the House of Lords and proclaimed England a republic or commonwealth (1649–1653). This was not an easy period for Cromwell. As commander in chief of the army, he had to crush a Catholic uprising in Ireland, which he accomplished with a brutality that earned him the eternal enmity of the Irish people, as well as an uprising in Scotland on behalf of the son of Charles I.

Cromwell also faced opposition at home, especially from more radically minded groups who took advantage of the upheaval in England to push their agendas. The Levellers, for example, advocated such advanced ideas as freedom of speech, religious toleration, and a democratic republic, arguing for the right to vote for all male householders over the age of twenty-one. The Levellers also called for annual Parliaments, women's equality with men, and government programs to care for the poor. As one Leveller said, "The poorest he that is in England has a life to live as the greatest he." To Cromwell, a country gentleman, only people of property had the right to participate in the affairs of state, and he warned in a fit of rage: "I tell you … you have no other way to deal with these men but to break them or they will break you; and make void all that work that, with so many years' industry, toil, and pains, you have done … I tell you again, you are necessitated to break them."[9] And break them he did; Cromwell smashed the radicals by force. More than a century would pass before their ideas of democracy and equality became fashionable.

At the same time that Cromwell was dealing with the Levellers, he also found it difficult to work with the Rump Parliament and finally dispersed it by force. As the members of Parliament departed (in April 1653), he shouted after them, "It's you that have forced me to do this, for I have sought the Lord night and day that He would slay me rather than put upon me the doing of this work." With the certainty of one who is convinced he is right, Cromwell had destroyed both king and Parliament.

The army provided a new government when it drew up the Instrument of Government, England's first and only written constitution. Executive power was vested in the Lord Protector (a position held by Cromwell) and legislative power in a reconstituted Parliament. But the new system failed to work. Cromwell found it difficult to work with Parliament, especially when its members debated his authority and advocated once again the creation of a Presbyterian state church. In 1655, Cromwell dissolved Parliament and divided the country into eleven regions, each ruled by a major general who served virtually as a military governor. To meet the cost of military government, Cromwell levied a 10 percent land tax on all former Royalists. Unable to establish a constitutional basis for a working government, Cromwell had resorted to military force to maintain the rule of the Independents, ironically using even more arbitrary policies than those of Charles I.

Oliver Cromwell died in 1658. After floundering for eighteen months, the military establishment decided that arbitrary rule by the army was no longer

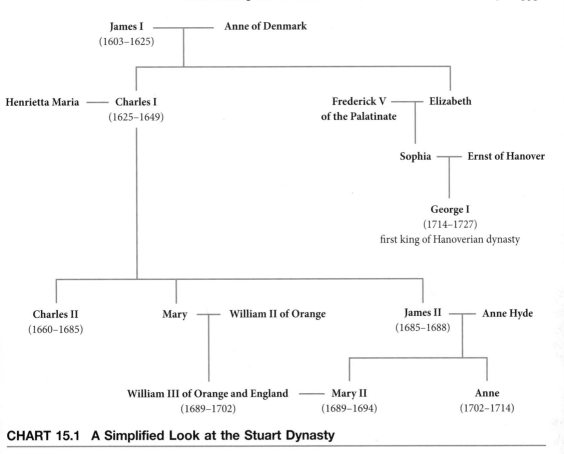

CHART 15.1 A Simplified Look at the Stuart Dynasty

feasible and reestablished the monarchy in the person of Charles II, the eldest son of Charles I (see Chart 15.1). The restoration of the Stuart monarchy ended England's time of troubles, but it was not long before yet another constitutional crisis arose.

Restoration of the Monarchy After eleven years of exile, Charles II (1660–1685) returned to England. As he entered London amid the acclaim of the people, he remarked cynically, "I never knew that I was so popular in England." The restoration of the monarchy and the House of Lords did not mean, however, that the work of the English Revolution was undone. Parliament kept much of the power it had won: its role in government was acknowledged, the necessity for its consent to taxation was accepted, and arbitrary courts were still abolished. Yet Charles continued to push his own ideas, some of which were clearly out of step with many of the English people. A serious religious problem disturbed the tranquillity of Charles II's reign. After the restoration of the monarchy, a new Parliament (the Cavalier Parliament) met in 1661 and restored the Anglican Church as the official church of England. In addition, laws were passed to force everyone, particularly Catholics and Puritan Dissenters, to conform to the Anglican Church. Charles, however, was sympathetic to and perhaps even inclined toward Catholicism. Moreover, Charles's brother James, heir to the throne, did not hide the fact that he was a Catholic. Parliament's suspicions were therefore aroused in 1672 when Charles took the audacious step of issuing the Declaration of Indulgence, which suspended the laws that Parliament had passed against Catholics and Puritans. Parliament would have none of it and induced the king to suspend the declaration. Propelled by a strong anti-Catholic sentiment, Parliament then passed the Test Act of 1673, specifying that only Anglicans could hold military and civil offices.

A purported Catholic plot to assassinate King Charles and place his brother James on the throne, though soon exposed as imaginary, inflamed Parliament to attempt to pass a bill that would have barred James from the throne as a professed Catholic. Although these attempts failed, the debate over the bill created two political groupings: the Whigs, who wanted to exclude James and establish a Protestant king with toleration of Dissenters, and the Tories, who supported the king, despite their dislike of James as a Catholic, because they believed that Parliament should not tamper with the lawful succession to the throne. To foil these efforts, Charles dismissed Parliament in 1681, relying on French subsidies to rule alone. When he died in 1685, his Catholic brother came to the throne.

The accession of James II (1685–1688) virtually guaranteed a new constitutional crisis for England. An open and devout Catholic, his attempt to further Catholic interests made religion once more a primary cause of conflict between king and Parliament. Contrary to the Test Act, James named Catholics to high positions in the government, army, navy, and universities. In 1687, he issued a new Declaration of Indulgence, which suspended all laws barring Catholics and Dissenters from office. Parliamentary outcries against James's policies stopped short of rebellion because members knew that he was an old man and that his successors were his Protestant daughters Mary and Anne, born to his first wife. But on June 10, 1688, a son was born to James II's second wife, also a Catholic. Suddenly, the specter of a Catholic hereditary monarchy loomed large.

A Glorious Revolution   A group of seven prominent English noblemen invited William of Orange, husband of James's daughter Mary, to invade England. William and Mary raised an army and invaded England while James, his wife, and their infant son fled to France. With almost no bloodshed, England had embarked on a "Glorious Revolution," not over the issue of whether there would be a monarchy but rather over who would be monarch.

The events of late 1688 set the Glorious Revolution in motion. The far more important part was the Revolution Settlement, which confirmed William and Mary as monarchs. In January 1689, the Convention Parliament asserted that James had tried to subvert the constitution "by breaking the original contract between king and people" and declared the throne of England vacant. It then offered the throne to William and Mary, who accepted it along with the provisions of a declaration of rights, later enacted into law as the Bill of Rights in 1689. The Bill of Rights affirmed Parliament's right to make laws and levy taxes and made it impossible for kings to oppose or do without Parliament by stipulating that standing armies could be raised only with the consent of Parliament. Both elections of members and debates in Parliament had to be free, meaning that the king could not interfere. The rights of citizens to petition the sovereign, keep arms, have a jury trial, and not be subject to excessive bail were also confirmed. The Bill of Rights helped fashion a system of government based on the rule of law and a freely elected Parliament, thus laying the foundation for a constitutional monarchy.

The Bill of Rights did not settle the religious questions that had played such a large role in England's troubles in the seventeenth century. The Toleration Act of 1689 granted Puritan Dissenters the right of free public worship (Catholics were still excluded), although they did not yet have full civil and political equality since the Test Act was not repealed. Although the Toleration Act did not mean complete religious freedom and equality, it marked a departure in English history: few people would ever again be persecuted for religious reasons.

Many historians have viewed the Glorious Revolution as the end of the seventeenth-century struggle between king and Parliament. By deposing one king and establishing another, Parliament had demolished the divine-right theory of kingship (William was, after all, king by grace of Parliament, not God) and confirmed its right to participate in the government. Parliament did not have complete control of the government, but it now had an unquestioned role in affairs of state. Over the next century, it would gradually prove to be the real authority in the English system of constitutional monarchy.

Responses to Revolution   The English revolutions of the seventeenth century prompted very different responses from two English political thinkers—Thomas Hobbes and John Locke. Thomas Hobbes (1588–1679), who lived during the English Civil War, was alarmed by the revolutionary upheavals in his contemporary England. Hobbes's name has since been associated with the state's claim to absolute authority over its subjects, a topic that he elaborated in his major treatise on political thought known as the *Leviathan* (luh-VY-uh-thun), published in 1651.

Hobbes claimed that in the state of nature, before society was organized, human life was "solitary, poor, nasty, brutish, and short." Humans were guided not by reason and moral ideals but by animalistic instincts and a ruthless struggle for self-preservation. To save themselves from destroying each other (the "war of every man against every man"), people contracted to form a commonwealth, which Hobbes called "that great Leviathan (or rather, to speak more reverently, that mortal god) to which we owe our peace and defense." This commonwealth placed its collective power into the hands of a sovereign authority, preferably a single ruler, who served as executor, legislator, and judge. This absolute ruler possessed unlimited power. In Hobbes's view, subjects may not rebel; if they do, they must be suppressed.

John Locke (1632–1704) viewed the exercise of political power quite differently from Hobbes and argued against the absolute rule of one man. Locke's

The Bill of Rights

In 1688, the English experienced yet another revolution, a bloodless one in which the Stuart king James II was replaced by Mary, James's daughter, and her husband, William of Orange. After William and Mary had assumed power, Parliament passed the Bill of Rights, which specified the rights of Parliament and laid the foundation for a constitutional monarchy.

The Bill of Rights

Whereas the said late King James II having abdicated the government, and the throne being thereby vacant, his Highness the prince of Orange (whom it has pleased Almighty God to make the glorious instrument of delivering this kingdom from popery and arbitrary power) did (by the device of the lords spiritual and temporal, and diverse principal persons of the Commons) cause letters to be written to the lords spiritual and temporal, being Protestants, and other letters to the several counties, cities, universities, boroughs, and Cinque Ports, for the choosing of such persons to represent

them, as were of right to be sent to parliament, to meet and sit at Westminster upon the two and twentieth day of January, in this year 1689, in order to such an establishment as that their religion, laws, and liberties might not again be in danger of being subverted; upon which letters elections have been accordingly made.

And thereupon the said lords spiritual and temporal and Commons, pursuant to their respective letters and elections, being now assembled in a full and free representation of this nation, taking into their most serious consideration the best means for attaining the ends aforesaid, do in the first place (as their ancestors in like case have usually done), for the vindication and assertion of their ancient rights and liberties, declare:

1. That the pretended power of suspending laws, or the execution of laws, by regal authority, without consent of parliament is illegal.
2. That the pretended power of dispensing with the laws, or the

experience of English politics during the Glorious Revolution was incorporated into a political work called *Two Treatises of Government*. Like Hobbes, Locke began with the state of nature before human existence became organized socially. But unlike Hobbes, Locke believed that humans lived then in a state of equality and freedom rather than a state of war. In this state of nature, humans had certain inalienable natural rights—to life, liberty, and property. Like Hobbes, Locke did not believe all was well in the state of nature. Since there was no impartial judge in the state of nature, people found it difficult to protect these rights. So they mutually agreed to establish a government to ensure the protection of their rights. This agreement established mutual obligations: government would protect the rights of the people while the people would act reasonably toward government. But if a government broke this agreement—for example, if a monarch failed to live up to his obligation to protect the people's rights or claimed absolute authority and made laws without execution of law by regal authority, as it has been assumed and exercised of late, is illegal.

3. That the commission for erecting the late court of commissioners for ecclesiastical causes, and all other commissions and courts of like nature, are illegal and pernicious.

4. That levying money for or to the use of the crown by pretense of prerogative, without grant of parliament, for longer time or in other manner than the same is or shall be granted, is illegal.

5. That it is the right of the subjects to petition the king, and all commitments and prosecutions for such petitioning are illegal.

6. That the raising or keeping a standing army within the kingdom in time of peace, unless it be with consent of parliament, is against law.

7. That the subjects which are Protestants may have arms for their defense suitable to their conditions, and as allowed by law.

8. That election of members of parliament ought to be free.

9. That the freedom of speech, and debates or proceedings in parliament, ought not to be impeached or questioned in any court or place out of parliament.

10. That excessive bail ought not to be required, nor excessive fines imposed, nor cruel and unusual punishments inflicted.

11. That jurors ought to be duly impaneled and returned, and jurors which pass upon men in trials for high treason ought to be freeholders.

12. That all grants and promises of fines and forfeitures of particular persons before conviction are illegal and void.

13. And that for redress of all grievances, and for the amending, strengthening, and preserving of the laws, parliament ought to be held frequently.

Q *How did the Bill of Rights lay the foundation for a constitutional monarchy? What key aspects of this document testify to the exceptional nature of English state politics in the seventeenth century?*

Source: From *The Statutes: Revised Edition* (London: Eyre and Spottiswoode, 1871), Vol. 2, pp. 10–12.

the consent of the community—the people might form a new government. For Locke, however, the community of people was primarily the landholding aristocracy who were represented in Parliament, not the landless masses. Locke was hardly an advocate of political democracy, but his ideas proved important to both the Americans and the French in the eighteenth century and were used to support demands for constitutional government, the rule of law, and the protection of rights.

THE FLOURISHING OF EUROPEAN CULTURE

In the midst of religious wars and the growth of absolutism, European culture continued to flourish. The era was blessed with a number of prominent artists and writers.

The Changing Faces of Art   After the Renaissance, European art passed through a number of stylistic stages. The artistic Renaissance came to an end when a new movement called Mannerism emerged in Italy in the 1520s and 1530s.

Mannerism   The Reformation's revival of religious values brought much political turmoil. Especially in Italy, the worldly enthusiasm of the Renaissance gave way to anxiety, uncertainty, suffering, and a yearning for spiritual experience. **Mannerism** reflected this environment in its deliberate attempt to break down the High Renaissance principles of balance, harmony, and moderation (the term *Mannerism* derives from critics who considered their contemporary artists to be second-rate imitators, painting "in the manner of" Michelangelo's late style). Italian Mannerist painters deliberately distorted the rules of proportion by portraying elongated figures that conveyed a sense of suffering and a strong emotional atmosphere filled with anxiety and confusion.

Mannerism spread from Italy to other parts of Europe and perhaps reached its apogee in the work of El Greco (1541–1614). Doménikos Theotocópoulos (called "the Greek"—El Greco) was from Crete, but after studying in Venice and Rome, he moved in the 1570s to Spain, where he became a church painter in Toledo. El Greco's elongated and contorted figures, portrayed in unusual shades of yellow and green against an eerie background of turbulent grays, reflect the artist's desire to create a world of intense emotion.

The Baroque Period   A new movement—the **Baroque** (buh-ROHK)—eventually replaced Mannerism. The Baroque began in Italy in the last quarter of the sixteenth century and spread to the rest of Europe, where it was most wholeheartedly embraced by the Catholic reform movement, and especially at the Catholic courts of the Habsburgs in Madrid, Prague, Vienna, and Brussels. Although it was resisted in France, England, and the Netherlands, eventually the Baroque style spread to all of Europe and to Latin America.

Baroque artists sought to bring together the Classical ideals of Renaissance art with the spiritual feelings of the sixteenth-century religious revival. The Baroque painting style was known for its use of dramatic effects to arouse the emotions. In large part, though, Baroque art and architecture reflected the search for power that was so important to the seventeenth-century ethos. Baroque churches and palaces were magnificent and richly detailed. Kings and princes wanted other kings and princes as well as their subjects to be in awe of their power.

Baroque painting was known for its use of dramatic effects to heighten emotional intensity. This style was especially evident in the works of the Flemish master Peter Paul Rubens (1577–1640), a prolific artist and an important figure in the spread of the Baroque from Italy to other parts of Europe. In his artistic masterpieces, bodies in violent motion, heavily fleshed nudes, a dramatic use of light and shadow, and rich, sensuous pigments converge to express intense emotions. The restless forms and constant movement blend together into a dynamic unity.

Perhaps the greatest figure of the Baroque was the Italian architect and sculptor Gian Lorenzo Bernini (ZHAHN loh-RENT-zoh bur-NEE-nee) (1598–1680),

Peter Paul Rubens, *The Landing of Marie de' Medici at Marseilles.* *Peter Paul Rubens played a key role in spreading the Baroque style from Italy to other parts of Europe. In The Landing of Marie de' Medici at Marseilles, Rubens made dramatic use of light and color, bodies in motion, and luxurious nudes to heighten the emotional intensity of the scene. This was one of a cycle of twenty-one paintings dedicated to the queen mother of France.*

who completed Saint Peter's Basilica at the Vatican and designed the vast colonnade enclosing the piazza in front of it. Action, exuberance, profusion, and dramatic effects mark the work of Bernini in the interior of Saint Peter's, where his *Throne of Saint Peter* hovers in midair, held by the hands of the four great doctors of the Catholic Church. Above the chair, rays of golden light drive a mass of clouds and angels toward the spectator. In his most striking sculptural work, the *Ecstasy of Saint Theresa*, Bernini depicts a moment of mystical experience in the life of the sixteenth-century Spanish saint. The elegant draperies and the expression on her face create a sensuously real portrayal of physical ecstasy.

Less well known than the male artists who dominated the art world of seventeenth-century Italy but prominent in her own right was Artemisia Gentileschi (ar-tuh-MEE-zhuh jen-tuh-LESS-kee) (1593–1653). Born in Rome, she studied painting under her father's direction. In 1616, she moved to Florence and began a successful career as a painter. At the age of twenty-three, she became the first woman to be elected to the Florentine Academy of Design. Although she was known internationally in her day as a portrait painter, her fame now rests on a series of pictures of heroines from the Old Testament. Most famous is *Judith Beheading Holofernes*, a dramatic rendering of the biblical scene in which Judith slays the Assyrian general Holofernes to save her besieged town from the Assyrian army.

French Classicism   In the second half of the seventeenth century, France replaced Italy as the cultural leader of Europe. Rejecting the Baroque style as overly showy and impassioned, the French remained committed to the Classical values of the High Renaissance. French late Classicism, with its emphasis on clarity, simplicity, balance, and harmony of design, was a rather austere version of the High Renaissance style. Its triumph reflected the shift in seventeenth-century French society from chaos to order. Though it rejected the emotionalism and high drama of the Baroque, French Classicism continued the Baroque's conception of grandeur in the portrayal of noble subjects, especially those from Classical antiquity. Nicolas Poussin (NEE-koh-lah poo-SANH) (1594–1665) exemplified these principles in his paintings. His choice of scenes from Classical mythology, the orderliness of his landscapes, the postures of his figures copied from the sculptures of antiquity, and his use of brown tones all reflect French Classicism of the late seventeenth century.

Dutch Realism   A brilliant flowering of Dutch painting paralleled the supremacy of Dutch commerce in the seventeenth century. Wealthy patricians and burghers of Dutch urban society commissioned works of art for their guild halls, town halls, and private dwellings. The subject matter of many Dutch paintings reflected the interests of this burgher society: portraits of themselves, group portraits of their military companies and guilds, landscapes, seascapes, genre scenes, still lives, and the interiors of their residences. Neither Classical nor Baroque, Dutch painters were primarily interested in the realistic portrayal of secular everyday life.

This interest in painting scenes of everyday life is evident in the work of Judith Leyster (LESS-tur) (c. 1609–1660), who established her own independent painting career, a remarkable occurrence in seventeenth-century Europe. Leyster became the first female member of the painting Guild of Saint Luke in Haarlem, which enabled her to set up her own workshop and take on three male pupils. Musicians playing their instruments, women sewing, children laughing while playing games, and actors performing all form the subject matter of Leyster's paintings of everyday Dutch life.

The finest product of the golden age of Dutch painting was Rembrandt van Rijn (REM-brant vahn RYN) (1606–1669). During his early career, Rembrandt painted opulent portraits and grandiose scenes that were often quite colorful. He was prolific and successful, but he turned away from materialistic success to follow his own artistic path; in the process, he lost public support and died bankrupt.

Although Rembrandt shared the Dutch predilection for realistic portraits, he became more introspective as he grew older. He refused to follow his contemporaries, whose pictures were largely secular; half of his own paintings depicted scenes from biblical tales. Since the Protestant tradition of hostility to religious pictures had discouraged artistic expression, Rembrandt stands out as the one great Protestant painter of the seventeenth century.

A Wondrous Age of Theater   In England and Spain, writing reached new heights between 1580 and 1640. All of these impressive new works were written in the vernacular. Except for academic fields, such as theology, philosophy, jurisprudence, and the sciences, Latin was no longer a universal literary language. The greatest age of English literature is often called the Elizabethan era because much of the English cultural flowering of the late sixteenth and early seventeenth centuries occurred during the reign of Queen Elizabeth I. Elizabethan literature exhibits the exuberance and pride associated with England's international exploits at the time. Of all the forms of Elizabethan literature, none expressed the energy and intellectual versatility of the era better than drama. And of all the dramatists, none is more famous than William Shakespeare (1564–1616).

William Shakespeare   Shakespeare was the son of a prosperous glovemaker from Stratford-upon-Avon. When he appeared in London in 1592, Elizabethans were already addicted to the stage. In Greater London, as many as six theaters were open six afternoons a week. London theaters ranged from the Globe, which was a circular unroofed structure holding three thousand spectators, to the Blackfriars, which was roofed and held only five hundred. In the former, an admission charge of a penny or two enabled even the lower classes to attend; the higher prices in the latter ensured an audience of the well-to-do. Elizabethan audiences varied greatly, putting pressure on playwrights to write works that pleased nobles, lawyers, merchants, and even vagabonds.

William Shakespeare was a "complete man of the theater." Although best known for writing plays, he was also an actor and shareholder in the chief company of the time, the Lord Chamberlain's Company, which played in theaters as diverse as the Globe and the Blackfriars. Shakespeare has long been recognized as a universal genius. A master of the English language, he was instrumental in codifying a language that was still in transition. His technical proficiency, however, was matched by an incredible insight into human psychology. In tragedies as well as comedies, Shakespeare exhibited a remarkable understanding of the human condition.

Spain's Golden Century   The theater was also one of the most creative forms of expression during Spain's golden century. As in England, actors' companies ran the first professional theaters, which were established in Seville and Madrid in the 1570s. Soon a public playhouse could be found in every large town, including Mexico City in the New World. Touring companies brought the latest Spanish plays to all parts of the Spanish Empire.

Beginning in the 1580s, Lope de Vega (LOH-pay day VAY-guh) (1562–1635) set the agenda for playwrights. Like Shakespeare, he was from a middle-class background. He was an incredibly prolific writer; almost one-third of his fifteen hundred plays survive, which have been characterized as witty, charming, action packed, and realistic. Lope de Vega made no apologies for the fact that he wrote his plays to please his audiences. In a treatise on drama written in 1609, he stated that the foremost duty of the playwright was to satisfy public demand. Shakespeare

William Shakespeare: In Praise of England

William Shakespeare is one of the most famous playwrights of the Western world. He was a universal genius, outclassing all others in his psychological insights, depth of characterization, imaginative skills, and versatility. His historical plays reflected the patriotic enthusiasm of the English in the Elizabethan era, as this excerpt from *Richard II* illustrates.

William Shakespeare, *Richard II*

This royal throne of kings, this
sceptered isle,
This earth of majesty, this seat of
Mars,
This other Eden, demi-Paradise,
This fortress built by Nature for
herself
Against infection and the hand
of war,
This happy breed of men, this
little world,
This precious stone set in the
silver sea,
Which serves it in the office of a
wall
Or as a moat defensive to a house
Against the envy of less happier
lands—
This blessed plot, this earth, this
realm, this England,
This nurse, this teeming womb
of royal kings,
Feared by their breed and
famous by their birth,
Renowned for their deeds as far
from home,
For Christian service and true
chivalry,

As is the sepulcher in stubborn
Jewry [the Holy Sepulcher in
Jerusalem]
Of the world's ransom, blessed
Mary's Son—
This land of such dear souls, this
dear dear land,
Dear for her reputation through
the world,
Is now leased out, I die
pronouncing it,
Like a tenement or pelting
farm.
England, bound in with the
triumphant sea,
Whose rocky shore beats back
the envious siege
Of watery Neptune, is now
bound in with shame,
With inky blots and rotten
parchment bonds.
That England, what was wont to
conquer others,
Hath made a shameful conquest
of itself.
Ah, would the scandal vanish
with my life,
How happy then were my
ensuing death!

Q *Why is William Shakespeare aptly described as not merely a playwright, but a "complete man of the theater"? Which countries might Shakespeare have meant by the phrase "the envy of less happier lands"?*

Source: Excerpt from *Richard II* in *Shakespeare, The Complete Works*, edited by G. B. Harrison (New York: Harcourt Brace & World, 1952).

undoubtedly believed the same thing, since his livelihood depended on public approval, but Lope de Vega was considerably more cynical about it: he remarked that if anyone thought he had written his plays for fame, "undeceive him and tell him that I wrote them for money."

French Drama   As the great age of theater in England and Spain was drawing to a close around 1630, a new dramatic era began to dawn in France that lasted into the 1680s. Unlike Shakespeare in England and Lope de Vega in Spain, French playwrights wrote more for an elite audience and were forced to depend on royal patronage. Louis XIV used theater as he did art and architecture—to attract attention to his monarchy.

French dramatists cultivated a style that emphasized the clever, polished, and correct over the emotional and imaginative. Many of the French works of the period derived both their themes and their plots from Classical Greek and Roman sources, especially evident in the works of Jean-Baptiste Racine (ZHAHNH-bah-TEEST ra-SEEN) (1639–1699). In *Phèdre*, which has been called his best play, Racine followed closely the plot of *Hippolytus* by the Greek tragedian Euripides. Like the ancient tragedians, Racine, who perfected the French neoclassical tragic style, focused on conflicts, such as between love and honor or inclination and duty, that characterized and revealed the tragic dimensions of life.

Jean-Baptiste Molière (ZHAHNH-bah-TEEST mohl-YAYR) (1622–1673) enjoyed the favor of the French court and benefited from the patronage of King Louis XIV. Molière wrote, produced, and acted in a series of comedies that often satirized the religious and social world of his time. In *Tartuffe*, he ridiculed religious hypocrisy. His satires, however, sometimes got him into trouble. The Paris clergy did not find *Tartuffe* funny and had it banned for five years. Only the protection of the king saved Molière from more severe harassment.

CHRONOLOGIES

THE THIRTY YEARS' WAR

1618–1625	Bohemian phase
1625–1629	Danish phase
1630–1635	Swedish phase
1635–1648	Franco-Swedish phase
1648	Peace of Westphalia

ABSOLUTISM IN EUROPE

France

1610–1643	Louis XIII
1643–1715	Louis XIV

Brandenburg-Prussia

1640–1688	Frederick William the Great Elector
1688–1713	Elector Frederick III (King Frederick I)

Austrian Empire

1658–1705	Leopold I

Russia

1613–1645	Michael Romanov
1689–1725	Peter the Great

LIMITED MONARCHY: ENGLAND

1603–1625	James I
1625–1649	Charles I
1649–1653	Commonwealth
1658	Death of Cromwell
1660	Restoration of monarchy
1660–1685	Charles II
1685–1688	James II
1688	Glorious Revolution
1689	Bill of Rights

16

▼

TOWARD A NEW HEAVEN AND A NEW EARTH: THE SCIENTIFIC REVOLUTION AND THE EMERGENCE OF MODERN SCIENCE

A nineteenth-century painting of Galileo before the Holy Office in the Vatican in 1633

Louvre, Paris/© Erich Lessing/Art Resource, NY

CHAPTER OUTLINE

• Background to the Scientific Revolution • Toward a New Heaven:
A Revolution in Astronomy • Advances in Medicine and Chemistry
• Women in the Origins of Modern Science • Toward a New Earth:
Descartes, Rationalism, and a New View of Humankind • The Scientific
Method and the Spread of Scientific Knowledge

Background to the Scientific Revolution

To say that the **Scientific Revolution** brought about a dissolution of the medieval worldview is not to say that the Middle Ages was a period of scientific ignorance. Many educated Europeans took an intense interest in the world around them since it was, after all, "God's handiwork" and therefore an appropriate subject for study. Late medieval scholastic philosophers had advanced mathematical and physical thinking in many ways, but the subjection of these thinkers to a strict theological framework and their unquestioning reliance on a few ancient authorities, especially Aristotle and Galen, limited where they could go. Many "natural philosophers," as medieval scientists were called, preferred refined logical analysis to systematic observations of the natural world. A number of changes and advances in the fifteenth and sixteenth centuries may have played a major role in helping "natural philosophers" abandon their old views and develop new ones.

Ancient Authors and Renaissance Artists
Whereas medieval scholars had made use of Aristotle, Galen, and Ptolemy in Latin translations to develop many of their positions in the fields of physics, medicine, and astronomy, the Renaissance humanists had mastered Greek and made available new works of Galen, Ptolemy, and Archimedes as well as Plato and the pre-Socratics. These writings made it apparent that even the unquestioned authorities of the Middle Ages, Aristotle and Galen, had been contradicted by other thinkers. The desire to discover which school of thought was correct stimulated new scientific work that sometimes led to a complete rejection of the Classical authorities.

Renaissance artists have also been credited with making an impact on scientific study. Their desire to imitate nature led them to a close observation of nature. Their accurate renderings of rocks, plants, animals, and human anatomy established new standards for the study of natural phenomena. At the same time, the "scientific" study of the problems of perspective and correct anatomical proportions led to new insights. "No painter," one Renaissance artist declared, "can paint well without a thorough knowledge of geometry."[1] Renaissance artists were frequently called on to be practicing mathematicians as well. Leonardo da Vinci devised "war machines," and Albrecht Dürer made designs for the fortifications of cities.

Technological Innovations and Mathematics
Technical problems such as accurately calculating the tonnage of ships also stimulated scientific activity because they required careful observation and precise measurements. The relationship between technology and the Scientific Revolution was not a simple one, however, for many technological experts did not believe in abstract or academic learning. Indeed, many of the technical innovations of the Middle Ages and the Renaissance were accomplished outside the universities by people who emphasized practical rather than theoretical knowledge. In any case, the invention of new instruments and machines, such as the telescope and the microscope, often made new scientific discoveries

possible. The printing press had an indirect but crucial role in spreading innovative ideas quickly and easily.

Mathematics, so fundamental to the scientific achievements of the sixteenth and seventeenth centuries, was promoted in the Renaissance by the rediscovery of the works of ancient mathematicians and the influence of Plato, who had emphasized the importance of mathematics in explaining the universe. Applauded as the key to navigation, military science, and geography, mathematics was also regarded as the key to understanding the nature of things. According to Leonardo da Vinci, since God eternally geometrizes, nature is inherently mathematical: "Proportion is not only found in numbers and measurements but also in sounds, weights, times, positions, and in whatsoever power there may be."[2] Moreover, mathematical reasoning was seen as promoting a degree of certainty that was otherwise impossible. In the words of Leonardo da Vinci: "There is no certainty where one can neither apply any of the mathematical sciences nor any of those which are based upon the mathematical sciences."[3] Copernicus, Kepler, Galileo, and Newton were all great mathematicians who believed that the secrets of nature were written in the language of mathematics.

Renaissance Magic

Another factor in the origins of the Scientific Revolution may have been magic. Renaissance magic was the preserve of an intellectual elite from all of Europe. By the end of the sixteenth century, Hermetic magic had become fused with alchemical thought into a single intellectual framework. This tradition believed that the world was a living embodiment of divinity. Humans, who it was believed also had that spark of divinity within, could use magic, especially mathematical magic, to understand and dominate the world of nature or employ the powers of nature for beneficial purposes. Was it Hermeticism, then, that inaugurated the shift in consciousness that made the Scientific Revolution possible, since the desire to control and dominate the natural world was a crucial motivating force in the Scientific Revolution? One scholar has argued:

> It is a movement of the will which really originates an intellectual movement. A new center of interest arises, surrounded by emotional excitement; the mind turns where the will has directed it and new attitudes, new discoveries follow. Behind the emergence of modern science there was a new direction of the will toward the world, its marvels, and mysterious workings, a new longing and determination to understand those workings and to operate with them.[4]

"This time," the author continues, "the return to the occult [Hermetic tradition] stimulates the genuine science."[5] Scholars debate the issue, but histories of the Scientific Revolution frequently overlook the fact that the great names we associate with the revolution in cosmology—Copernicus, Kepler, Galileo, and Newton—all had a serious interest in Hermetic ideas and the fields of astrology and alchemy. The mention of these names also reminds us of one final consideration in the origins of the Scientific Revolution: it largely resulted from the work of a handful of great intellectuals.

Toward a New Heaven:
A Revolution in Astronomy

The greatest achievements in the Scientific Revolution of the sixteenth and seventeenth centuries came in the fields most dominated by the ideas of the Greeks—astronomy, mechanics, and medicine. The cosmological views of the Later Middle Ages had been built on a synthesis of the ideas of Aristotle, Ptolemy (the greatest astronomer of antiquity, who lived in the second century C.E.), and Christian theology. In the resulting Ptolemaic (tahl-uh-MAY-ik) or **geocentric conception**, the universe was seen as a series of concentric spheres with a fixed or motionless earth at its center. Composed of the material substances of earth, air, fire, and water, the earth was imperfect and constantly changing. The spheres that surrounded the earth were made of a crystalline, transparent substance and moved in circular orbits around the earth. Circular movement, according to Aristotle, was the most "perfect" kind of motion and hence appropriate for the "perfect" heavenly bodies thought to consist of a nonmaterial, incorruptible "quintessence." These heavenly bodies, pure orbs of light, were embedded in the moving, concentric spheres, which in 1500 were believed to number ten. Working outward from the earth, eight spheres contained the moon, Mercury, Venus, the sun, Mars, Jupiter, Saturn, and the fixed stars. The ninth sphere imparted to the eighth sphere of the fixed stars its motion, and the tenth sphere was frequently described as the prime mover that moved itself and imparted motion to the other spheres. Beyond the tenth sphere was the Empyrean Heaven—the location of God and all the saved souls. This Christianized Ptolemaic universe, then, was finite. It had a fixed outer boundary in harmony with Christian thought and expectations. God and the saved souls were at one end of the universe, and humans were at the center. They had been given power over the earth, but their real purpose was to achieve salvation.

This conception of the universe, however, did not satisfy professional astronomers, who wished to ascertain the precise paths of the heavenly bodies across the sky. Finding that their observations did not always correspond to the accepted scheme, astronomers tried to "save appearances" by developing an elaborate system of devices. They proposed, for example, that the planetary bodies traveled on epicycles, concentric spheres within spheres, that would enable the paths of the planets to correspond more precisely to observations while adhering to Aristotle's ideas of circular planetary movement.

Copernicus Nicolaus Copernicus (nee-koh-LAU-uss kuh-PURR-nuh-kuss) (1473–1543) had studied both mathematics and astronomy first at Krakow in his native Poland and later at the Italian universities of Bologna and Padua. Before he left Italy in 1506, he had become aware of ancient views that contradicted the Ptolemaic, earth-centered conception of the universe. Between 1506 and 1530, he completed the manuscript of his famous book, *On the Revolutions of the Heavenly Spheres*, but his own timidity and fear of ridicule from fellow astronomers kept him from publishing it until May 1543, shortly before his death.

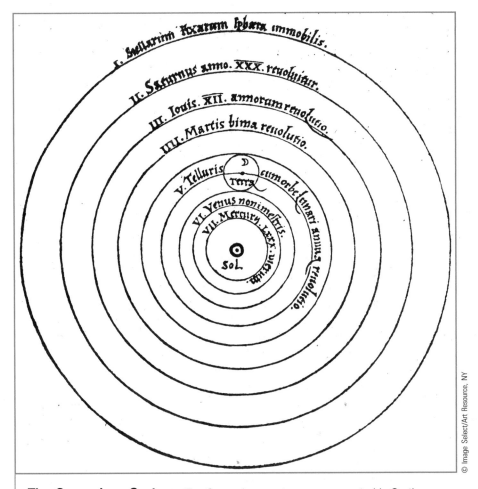

The Copernican System. *The Copernican system was presented in* On the Revolutions of the Heavenly Spheres, *published shortly before Copernicus's death. As shown in this illustration from the first edition of the book, Copernicus maintained that the sun was the center of the universe and that the planets, including the earth, revolved around it. Moreover, the earth rotated daily on its axis. (The circles read, from the inside out: 1. Sun; 2. Mercury, orbit of 80 days; 3. Venus; 4. Earth, with the moon, orbit of one year; 5. Mars, orbit of 2 years; 6. Jupiter, orbit of 12 years; 7. Saturn, orbit of 30 years; 8. Immobile Sphere of the Fixed Stars.)*

Copernicus was not an accomplished observational astronomer and relied for his data on the records of his predecessors. But he was a mathematician who felt that Ptolemy's geocentric system was too complicated and failed to accord with the observed motions of the heavenly bodies. Copernicus hoped that his **heliocentric** or sun-centered **conception** would offer a simpler and more accurate explanation.

Copernicus argued that the universe consisted of eight spheres with the sun motionless at the center and the sphere of the fixed stars at rest in the eighth sphere. The planets revolved around the sun in the order of Mercury, Venus, the earth, Mars, Jupiter, and Saturn. The moon, however, revolved around the earth. Moreover, according to Copernicus, what appeared to be the movement of the sun and the fixed stars around the earth was really explained by the daily rotation of the earth on its axis and the journey of the earth around the sun each year.

Copernicus, however, was basically conservative. He did not reject Aristotle's principle of the existence of heavenly spheres moving in circular orbits. As a result, when he put forth the calculations to prove his new theory, he retained about half of Ptolemy's epicycles and wound up with a system somewhat simpler than that of the Alexandrian astronomer but still extremely complicated.

Nevertheless, the shift from an earth-centered to a sun-centered system was significant and raised serious questions about Aristotle's astronomy and physics despite Copernicus's own adherence to Aristotle. It also seemed to create uncertainty about the human role in the universe as well as God's location. Protestant reformers, adhering to a literal interpretation of Scripture, were the first to attack the new ideas. Martin Luther thundered against "the new astrologer who wants to prove that the earth moves and goes round.... The fool wants to turn the whole art of astronomy upside down. As Holy Scripture tells us, so did Joshua bid the sun stand still and not the earth." Luther's cohort at Wittenberg, Philip Melanchthon, condemned Copernicus as well:

> The eyes are witness that the heavens revolve in the space of twenty-four hours. But certain men, either from the love of novelty, or to make a display of ingenuity, have concluded that the earth moves, and they maintain that neither the eighth sphere [of the fixed stars] nor the sun revolves.... Now it is a want of honesty and decency to assert such notions publicly, and the example is pernicious. It is the part of a good mind to accept the truth as revealed by God and to acquiesce in it.[6]

The Catholic Church remained silent for the time being; it did not denounce Copernicus until the work of Galileo appeared. The denunciation came at a time when an increasing number of astronomers were being attracted to Copernicus's ideas.

Brahe   Copernicus did not have a great impact immediately, but doubts about the Ptolemaic system were growing. The next step in destroying the geocentric conception and supporting the Copernican system was taken by Johannes Kepler. It has been argued, however, that Kepler's work would not have occurred without the material provided by Tycho Brahe (TY-koh BRAH).

A Danish nobleman, Tycho Brahe (1546–1601) was granted possession of an island near Copenhagen by King Frederick II. On it, Brahe built the elaborate Uraniborg Castle, which he outfitted with a library, observatories, and instruments he had designed for more precise astronomical observations. For twenty years, Brahe patiently concentrated on compiling a detailed record of his observations of the positions and movements of the stars and planets, a series of observations described as the most accurate up to that time. This body of data led him to reject the Aristotelian-Ptolemaic system, but at the same time he was unable to accept Copernicus's suggestion that the earth actually moved. Brahe's last years were spent in Prague as imperial mathematician to Emperor Rudolf II, who took a keen interest in astronomy, astrology, and the Hermetic tradition. While he was in Prague, Brahe took on an assistant by the name of Johannes Kepler.

Kepler   Johannes Kepler (yoh-HAHN-us KEP-lur) (1571–1630) had been destined by his parents for a career as a Lutheran minister. While studying theology at the university at Tübingen (TOO-bing-un), however, he fell under the influence of Michael Mästlin (MEST-lin), Germany's best-known astronomer, and spent much time pursuing his real interests, mathematics and astronomy. He abandoned theology and became a teacher of mathematics and astronomy at Graz in Austria.

Kepler's work illustrates well the narrow line that often separated magic and science in the early Scientific Revolution. An avid astrologer, Kepler had a keen interest in Hermetic mathematical magic. In a book written in 1596, he elaborated on his theory that the universe was constructed on the basis of geometric figures, such as the pyramid and the cube. Believing that the harmony of the human soul (a divine attribute) was mirrored in the numerical relationships existing between the planets, he focused much of his attention on discovering the "music of the spheres." Kepler was also a brilliant mathematician and astronomer and, after Brahe's death, succeeded him as imperial mathematician to Rudolf II. There he gained possession of Brahe's detailed astronomical data and, using them, arrived at his three laws of planetary motion. These laws may have confirmed Kepler's interest in the "music of the spheres," but more important, they confirmed Copernicus's heliocentric theory while modifying it in some ways. Above all, they drove another nail into the coffin of the Aristotelian-Ptolemaic system.

Kepler published his first two laws of planetary motion in 1609. Although at Tübingen he had accepted Copernicus's heliocentric ideas, in his first law he rejected Copernicus by showing that the orbits of the planets around the sun were not circular but elliptical, with the sun at one focus of the ellipse rather than at the center. In his second law, he demonstrated that the speed of a planet is greater when it is closer to the sun and decreases as its distance from the sun increases. This proposition destroyed a fundamental Aristotelian tenet that Copernicus had shared—that the motion of the planets was steady and unchanging. Published ten years later, Kepler's third law established that the square of a planet's period of revolution is proportional to the cube of its average distance from the sun. In other words, planets with larger orbits revolve at a slower average velocity than those with smaller orbits.

Kepler's three laws effectively eliminated the idea of uniform circular motion as well as the idea of crystalline spheres revolving in circular orbits. The basic structure of the traditional Ptolemaic system had been disproved, and people had been freed to think in new ways about the actual paths of planets revolving around the sun in elliptical orbits. By the end of Kepler's life, the Ptolemaic system was rapidly losing ground to the new ideas. Important questions remained unanswered, however: What were the planets made of? And how could motion in the universe be explained? It was an Italian scientist who achieved the next important breakthrough to a new cosmology by answering the first question and making important strides toward answering the second.

Galileo   Galileo Galilei (1564–1642) taught mathematics, first at Pisa and later at Padua, one of the most prestigious universities in Europe. Galileo was the first European to make systematic observations of the heavens by means of a telescope, thereby inaugurating a new age in astronomy. He had heard of a Flemish lens grinder who had created a "spyglass" that magnified objects seen at a distance and soon constructed his own after reading about it. Instead of peering at terrestrial objects, Galileo turned his telescope to the skies and made a remarkable series of discoveries: mountains and craters on the moon, four moons revolving around Jupiter, the phases of Venus, and sunspots. Galileo's observations demolished yet another aspect of the traditional cosmology in that the universe seemed to be composed of material substance similar to that of the earth rather than ethereal or perfect and unchanging substance.

Galileo's revelations, published in *The Starry Messenger* in 1610, stunned his contemporaries and probably did more to make Europeans aware of the new picture of the universe than the mathematical theories of Copernicus and Kepler did. The English ambassador in Venice wrote to the chief minister of King James I in 1610:

> I send herewith unto His Majesty the strangest piece of news ... that he has ever yet received from any part of the world; which is the annexed book of the Mathematical Professor at Padua [Galileo], who by the help of an optical instrument ... has discovered four new planets rolling about the sphere of Jupiter.... So upon the whole subject he has first overthrown all former astronomy.... By the next ship your Lordship shall receive from me one of the above instruments [a telescope], as it is bettered by this man.[7]

During a trip to Rome, Galileo was received by scholars as a conquering hero. Grand Duke Cosimo II of Florence offered him a new position as his court mathematician, which Galileo readily accepted. But even in the midst of his newfound acclaim, Galileo found himself increasingly suspect by the authorities of the Catholic Church.

Galileo and the Inquisition In *The Starry Messenger*, Galileo had revealed himself as a firm proponent of Copernicus's heliocentric system. The Roman Inquisition (or Holy Office) of the Catholic Church condemned Copernicanism and ordered Galileo to reject the Copernican thesis. As one cardinal commented, "The intention of the Holy Spirit is to teach us not how the heavens go, but how to go to heaven." The report of the Inquisition ran:

> That the doctrine that the sun was the center of the world and immovable was false and absurd, formally heretical and contrary to Scripture, whereas the doctrine that the earth was not the center of the world but moved, and has further a daily motion, was philosophically false and absurd and theologically at least erroneous.[8]

Galileo was told, however, that he could continue to discuss Copernicanism as long as he maintained that it was not a fact but a mathematical supposition. It is apparent from the Inquisition's response that the church attacked the Copernican system because it threatened not only Scripture but also an entire conception of the universe. The heavens were no longer a spiritual world but a world of matter. Humans were no longer at the center, and God was no longer in a specific place. The new system raised such uncertainties that it seemed prudent simply to condemn it.

Galileo, however, never really accepted his condemnation. In 1632, he published his most famous work, *Dialogue on the Two Chief World Systems: Ptolemaic and Copernican*. Unlike most scholarly treatises, it was written in Italian rather than Latin, making it more widely available to the public, which no doubt alarmed the church authorities. The work took the form of a dialogue among Simplicio, a congenial but somewhat stupid supporter of Aristotle and Ptolemy; Sagredo, an open-minded layman; and Salviati, a proponent of Copernicus's ideas. There is no question who wins the argument, and the *Dialogue* was quickly perceived as a defense of the Copernican system. Galileo was dragged once more before the Inquisition in 1633, found guilty of teaching the condemned Copernican system, and forced to recant his errors. Placed under house arrest on his estate near Florence, he spent the remaining eight years of his life studying mechanics, a field in which he made significant contributions.

Galileo and the Problem of Motion   One of the problems that fell under the heading of mechanics was the principle of motion. The Aristotelian conception, which dominated the late medieval world, held that an object remained at rest unless a force was applied against it. If a force was constantly exerted, then the object moved at a constant rate, but if it was removed, then the object stopped. This conception encountered some difficulties, especially with a projectile thrown out of a cannon. Late medieval theorists had solved this problem by arguing that the rush of air behind the projectile kept it in motion. The Aristotelian principle of motion also raised problems in the new Copernican system. In the Ptolemaic system, the concentric spheres surrounding the earth were weightless, but in the Copernican system, if a constant force had to be applied to objects to cause movement, then what power or force kept the heavy earth and other planets in motion?

Galileo made two contributions to the problem of motion. First, he demonstrated by experiments that if a uniform force was applied to an object, it would move at an accelerated speed rather than a constant speed. Moreover, Galileo discovered the principle of inertia when he argued that a body in motion continues in motion forever unless deflected by an external force. Thus, a state of uniform motion is just as natural as a state of rest. Before Galileo, natural philosophers had tried to explain motion; now their task was to explain changes in motion.

The condemnation of Galileo by the Inquisition, coming at a time of economic decline, seriously undermined further scientific work in Italy, which had been at the forefront of scientific innovation. Leadership in science now passed to the northern countries, especially England, France, and the Dutch

A New Heaven? Faith Versus Reason

In 1614, Galileo wrote a letter to the Grand Duchess Christina of Tuscany in which he explained why his theory that the earth rotated around the sun was not necessarily contrary to Scripture. To Galileo, it made little sense for the church to determine the nature of physical reality on the basis of biblical texts that were subject to different interpretations. One year later, Cardinal Robert Bellarmine, a Jesuit and now a member of the church's Inquisition, wrote a letter to one of Galileo's followers that laid out the Catholic Church's approach to the issue of Galileo's theory.

Galileo, Letter to the Grand Duchess Christina, 1614

Some years ago, as Your Serene Highness well knows, I discovered in the heavens many things that had not been seen before our own age. The novelty of these things, as well as some consequences which followed from them in contradiction to the physical notions commonly held among academic philosophers, stirred up against me no small number of professors—as if I had placed these things in the sky with my own hands in order to upset nature and overturn the sciences....

Contrary to the sense of the Bible and the intention of the holy Fathers, if I am not mistaken, they would extend such authorities until even in purely physical matters—where faith is not involved—they would have us altogether abandon reason and the evidence of our senses in favor of some biblical passage, though under the surface meaning of its words this passage may contain a different sense....

The reason produced for condemning the opinion that the earth moves and the sun stands still is that in many places in the Bible one may read that the sun moves and the earth stands still. Since the Bible cannot err, it follows as a necessary consequence that anyone takes an erroneous and heretical position who maintains that the sun is inherently motionless and the earth movable.

With regard to this argument, I think in the first place that it is very pious to say and prudent to affirm that the holy Bible can never speak untruth—whenever its true meaning is understood. But I believe nobody will deny that it is often very abstruse, and may say things which are quite different from what its bare words signify. Hence, in expounding the Bible if one were always to confine oneself to the unadorned grammatical meaning, one might fall into error. Not only contradictions and propositions far from true might thus be made to appear in the Bible, but even grave heresies and follies. Thus, it would be necessary to assign to God feet, hands, and eyes, as well as corporeal and human affections, such as anger, repentance, hatred, and sometimes even the forgetting of things past and ignorance of those to come. These propositions uttered by the Holy Ghost were set down in that manner by the sacred scribes in order to accommodate them to the capacities of the common people, who are rude and unlearned. For the sake of those who deserve to be separated from the herd, it is necessary that wise expositors should produce the true senses of such passages, together with the special reasons for which they were set down in these words....

This being granted, I think that in discussions of physical problems we ought to begin not from the authority of scriptural passages, but from sense-experiences and necessary demonstrations; for the holy Bible and the phenomena of nature proceed alike from the divine Word.... For that reason it appears that nothing physical which sense-experience sets before our eyes, or which necessary demonstrations prove to us, ought to be called in question (much less condemned) upon the testimony of biblical passages which may have some different meaning beneath their words.

Robert Bellarmine, Letter to Paolo Foscarini, 1615

First. I say that it seems to me that Your Reverence and Galileo did prudently to content yourself with speaking hypothetically, and not absolutely, as I have always believed that Copernicus spoke. For to say that, assuming the earth moves and the sun stands still, all the appearances are saved better than with eccentrics and epicycles, is to speak well; there is no danger in this, and it is sufficient for mathematicians. But to want to affirm that the sun really is fixed in the center of the heavens and only revolves around itself (i.e., turns upon its axis) without traveling from east to west, and that the earth is situated in the third sphere and revolves with great speed around the sun, is a very dangerous thing, not only by irritating all the philosophers and scholastic theologians, but also by injuring our holy faith and rendering the Holy Scriptures false. For Your Reverence has demonstrated many ways of explaining Holy Scripture, but you have not applied them in particular, and without a doubt you would have found it most difficult if you had attempted to explain all the passages which you yourself have cited.

Second. I say that, as you know, the Council [of Trent] prohibits expounding the Scriptures contrary to the common agreement of the holy Fathers. And if Your Reverence would read not only the Fathers but also the commentaries of modern writers on Genesis, Psalms, Ecclesiastes and Josue, you would find that all agree in explaining literally (*ad litteram*) that the sun is in the heavens and moves swiftly around the earth, and that the earth is far from the heavens and stands immobile in the center of the universe. Now consider whether in all prudence the Church could encourage giving to Scripture a sense contrary to the holy Fathers and all the Latin and Greek commentators. Nor may it be answered that this is not a matter of faith, for if it is not a matter of faith from the point of view of the subject matter, it is on the part of the ones who have spoken....

Third. I say that if there were a true demonstration that the sun was in the center of the universe and the earth in the third sphere, and that the sun did not travel around the earth but the earth circled the sun, then it would be necessary to proceed with great caution in explaining the passages of Scripture which seemed contrary, and we would rather have to say that we did not understand them than to say that something was false which has been demonstrated. But I do not believe that there is any such demonstration; none has been shown to me. It is not the same thing to show that the appearances are saved by assuming that the sun really is in the center and the earth in the heavens. I believe that the first demonstration might exist, but I have grave doubts about the second, and in a case of doubt, one may not depart from the Scriptures as explained by the holy Fathers.

Q *What does Galileo think is the difference between knowledge about the natural world and knowledge about the spiritual world? What does Galileo suggest that his opponents should do before dismissing his ideas? In what ways does Cardinal Bellarmine attempt to refute Galileo's ideas? Why did Galileo's ideas represent a threat to the Catholic Church?*

Source: Galileo, Letter to the Grand Duchess Christina, 1614. From *Discoveries and Opinions of Galileo* by Galileo Galilei, translated by Stillman Drake, copyright © 1957 by Stillman Drake. Used by permission of Doubleday, a division of Random House, Inc. Robert Bellarmine, Letter to Paolo Foscarini, 1615. From *Galileo, Science, and the Church* by Jerome J. Langford (New York: Desclee, 1966).

Netherlands. By the 1630s and 1640s, no reasonable astronomer could overlook that Galileo's discoveries, combined with Kepler's mathematical laws, had made nonsense of the Aristotelian-Ptolemaic world system and clearly established the reasonableness of the Copernican model. Nevertheless, the problem of explaining motion in the universe and tying together the ideas of Copernicus, Galileo, and Kepler had not yet been solved. This would be the work of an Englishman who has long been considered the greatest genius of the Scientific Revolution.

Newton   Born in the English village of Woolsthorpe in 1642, Isaac Newton was an unremarkable young man until he attended Cambridge University. His first great burst of creative energy came in 1666, when fear of the plague closed Cambridge and forced him to return to Woolsthorpe for eighteen months. There Newton discovered his creative talents: "In those days I was in the prime of my life for invention and minded mathematics and philosophy more than at any time since."[9] During this period, he invented the calculus, a mathematical means of calculating rates of change; began his investigations into the composition of light; and inaugurated his work on the law of universal gravitation. Two years after his return to Cambridge, in 1669, he accepted a chair in mathematics at the university. During a second intense period of creativity from 1684 to 1686, he wrote his famous *Principia* (prin-SIP-ee-uh). After a nervous breakdown in 1693, he sought and received an administrative post as warden of the royal mint and was advanced to master of the mint by 1699, a post he held until his death in 1727. Made president of the Royal Society (see "The Scientific Societies" later in this chapter) in 1703 and knighted in 1705 for his great achievements, Sir Isaac Newton is to this day the only English scientist to be buried in Westminster Abbey.

Newton and the Occult   Although Newton occupies a very special place in the history of modern science, we need to remember that he, too, remained extremely interested in aspects of the occult world. He left behind hundreds of manuscript pages of his studies of alchemy, and in fact, his alchemical experiments were a major feature of his life until he moved to London in 1696 to become warden of the royal mint. The British economist John Maynard Keynes said of Newton after examining his manuscripts in 1936:

> Newton was not the first of the age of reason. He was the last of the magicians.... He looked on the whole universe and all that is in it as a riddle, as a secret which could be read by applying pure thought to certain evidence, certain mystic clues which God had laid about the world to allow a sort of philosopher's treasure hunt to the esoteric brotherhood. He believed that these clues were to be found partly in the evidence of the heavens and in the constitution of elements,... but also partly in certain papers and traditions handed down by the brethren in an unknown chain back to the original cryptic revelation in Babylonia.[10]

Although Newton may have considered himself a representative of the Hermetic tradition, he chose, it has been recently argued, for both political and psychological reasons to repress that part of his being, and it is as the "symbol of Western science" that he came to be viewed.

Universal Law of Gravitation   Newton's major work, the "hinge point of modern scientific thought," was his *Mathematical Principles of Natural Philosophy*, known simply as the *Principia*, the first word of its Latin title. In this work, the last highly influential book in Europe to be written in Latin, Newton spelled out the mathematical proofs demonstrating his universal law of gravitation. Newton's work was the culmination of the theories of Copernicus, Kepler, and Galileo. Though each had undermined some part of the Aristotelian-Ptolemaic cosmology, until Newton no one had pieced together a coherent synthesis for a new cosmology.

In the first book of the *Principia*, Newton defined the basic concepts of mechanics by elaborating the three laws of motion: every object continues in a state of rest or uniform motion in a straight line unless deflected by a force, the rate of change of motion of an object is proportional to the force acting on it, and to every action there is always an equal and opposite reaction. In book 3, Newton applied his theories of mechanics to the problems of astronomy by demonstrating that these three laws of motion govern the planetary bodies as well as terrestrial objects. Integral to his whole argument was the universal law of gravitation, which explained why the planetary bodies did not go off in straight lines but continued in elliptical orbits about the sun. In mathematical terms, Newton explained that every object in the universe was attracted to every other object with a force (gravity) that is directly proportional to the product of their masses and inversely proportional to the square of the distances between them.

The implications of Newton's universal law of gravitation were enormous, even though another century would pass before they were widely recognized. Newton had demonstrated that one universal law, mathematically proved, could explain all motion in the universe, from the movements of the planets in the celestial world to an apple falling from a tree in the terrestrial world. The secrets of the natural world could be known by human investigations. At the same time, the Newtonian synthesis created a new cosmology in which the world was seen largely in mechanistic terms. The universe was one huge, regulated, and uniform machine that operated according to natural laws in absolute time, space, and motion. Although Newton believed that God was "everywhere present" and acted as the force that moved all bodies on the basis of the laws he had discovered, later generations dropped his spiritual assumptions. Newton's **world-machine**, conceived as operating absolutely in time, space, and motion, dominated the Western worldview until the twentieth century, when the Einsteinian revolution, based on the concept of relativity, superseded the Newtonian mechanistic concept.

Newton's ideas were soon accepted in England, possibly out of national pride and conviction and, as has been argued recently, for political reasons (see "Science and Society" later in this chapter). Natural philosophers on the Continent resisted Newton's ideas, and it took much of the eighteenth century before they were generally accepted everywhere in Europe. They were also reinforced by developments in other fields, especially medicine.

ADVANCES IN MEDICINE AND CHEMISTRY

Although the Scientific Revolution of the sixteenth and seventeenth centuries is associated primarily with the dramatic changes in astronomy and mechanics that precipitated a new perception of the universe, a third field that had been dominated by Greek thought in the Later Middle Ages, that of medicine, also experienced a transformation. Late medieval medicine was dominated not by the teachings of Aristotle but by those of the Greek physician Galen (GAY-len), who had lived in the second century C.E.

Galen's influence on the medieval medical world was pervasive in anatomy, physiology, and disease. Galen had relied on animal, rather than human, dissection to arrive at a picture of human anatomy that was quite inaccurate in many instances. Even when Europeans began to practice human dissection in the Later Middle Ages, instruction in anatomy still relied on Galen. While a professor read a text of Galen, an assistant dissected a cadaver for illustrative purposes. Physiology, or the functioning of the body, was also dominated by Galenic hypotheses, including the belief that there were two separate blood systems. One controlled muscular activities and contained bright red blood moving upward and downward through the arteries; the other governed the digestive functions and contained dark red blood that ebbed and flowed in the veins.

Treatment of disease was highly influenced by Galen's doctrine of four bodily humors: blood, considered warm and moist; yellow bile, warm and dry; phlegm, cold and moist; and black bile, cold and dry. Since disease was supposedly the result of an imbalance of humors that could be discerned from the quantity and color of urine, the examination of a patient's urine became the chief diagnostic tool. Although purging and bleeding to remedy the imbalance were often harmful to patients, treatment with traditional herbal medicines sometimes proved beneficial.

Paracelsus   Three figures are associated with the changes in medicine in the sixteenth and seventeenth centuries: Paracelsus (par-uh-SELL-suss), Andreas Vesalius (ahn-DRAY-uss vuh-SAY-lee-uss), and William Harvey. Philippus Aureolus von Hohenheim (1493–1541), who renamed himself Paracelsus ("greater than Celsus," an ancient physician), traveled widely and may have been awarded a medical degree from the University of Ferrara in Italy. He achieved a moment of glory when he was appointed city physician and professor of medicine at Basel in 1527. But this, like so many other appointments, proved short-lived due to his vanity and quick temper. He could never disguise his contempt for universities and physicians who did not agree with his new ideas:

> I am *monarcha medicorum*, monarch of physicians, and I can prove to you what you cannot prove.... It was not the constellations that made me a physician: God made me.... I need not don a coat of mail or a buckler against you, for you are not learned or experienced enough to refute even one word of mine.... Let me tell you this: every little hair on my neck knows more than you and all your scribes, and my shoebuckles are more learned than your Galen and Avicenna, and my beard has more experience than all your high colleges.[11]

Paracelsus was not easy to get along with, and he was forced to wander from one town to another until his death in 1541.

Paracelsus rejected the work of both Aristotle and Galen and attacked the universities as centers of their moribund philosophy. He and his followers hoped to replace the traditional system with a new chemical philosophy that was based on a new understanding of nature derived from fresh observation and experiment. This chemical philosophy was in turn closely connected to a view of the universe based on the macrocosm-microcosm analogy. According to this view, a human being was a small replica (microcosm) of the larger world (macrocosm). All parts of the universe were represented within each person. As Paracelsus said, "For the sun and the moon and all planets, as well as the stars and the whole chaos, are in man.... For what is outside is also inside; and what is not outside man is not inside. The outer and the inner are one thing."[12] In accordance with the macrocosmic-microcosmic principle, Paracelsus believed that the chemical reactions of the universe as a whole were reproduced in human beings on a smaller scale. Disease, then, was not caused by an imbalance of the four humors, as Galen had argued, but was due to chemical imbalances that were localized in specific organs and could be treated by chemical remedies.

Although others had used chemical remedies, Paracelsus and his followers differed from them in giving careful attention to the proper dosage of their chemically prepared metals and minerals. Paracelsus had turned against the Galenic principle that "contraries cure" in favor of the ancient Germanic folk principle that "like cures like." The poison that caused a disease would be its cure if used in proper form and quantity. Despite the apparent effectiveness of this use of toxic substances as treatment (Paracelsus did have a strong reputation for actually curing his patients), his opponents viewed it as the practice of a "homicide physician." Later generations came to regard Paracelsus more favorably, and historians who have stressed Paracelsus's concept of disease and recognition of "new drugs" for medicine have viewed him as a father of modern medicine. Others have argued that his macrocosmic-microcosmic philosophy and use of "like cures like" drugs make him the forerunner of both homeopathy and the holistic medicine of the postmodern era.

Vesalius   The new anatomy of the sixteenth century was the work of Andreas Vesalius (1514–1564). His study of medicine at Paris involved him in the works of Galen. Especially important to him was a recently discovered text of Galen, *On Anatomical Procedures*, that led Vesalius to emphasize practical research as the principal avenue for understanding human anatomy. After receiving a doctorate in medicine at the University of Padua in 1536, he accepted a position there as professor of surgery. In 1543, he published his masterpiece, *On the Fabric of the Human Body*.

This book was based on his personal dissection of a body to illustrate what he was discussing. Vesalius's anatomical treatise presented a careful examination of the individual organs and general structure of the human body. The book would not have been feasible without both the artistic advances of the Renaissance and technical developments in the art of printing. Together, they made possible the creation of illustrations superior to any done before.

Vesalius's hands-on approach to teaching anatomy enabled him to rectify some of Galen's most glaring errors. He did not hesitate, for example, to correct Galen's assertion that the great blood vessels originated from the liver since his own observations made it apparent that they came from the heart. Nevertheless, Vesalius still clung to a number of Galen's erroneous assertions, including the Greek physician's ideas on the ebb and flow of two kinds of blood in the veins and arteries. It was not until William Harvey's work on the circulation of the blood nearly a century later that this Galenic misperception was corrected.

William Harvey   William Harvey (1578–1657) attended Cambridge University and later Padua, where he received a doctorate in medicine in 1602. His reputation rests on his book *On the Motion of the Heart and Blood*, published in 1628. Although questions had been raised in the sixteenth century about Galen's physiological principles, no major break from his system had occurred. Harvey's work, which was based on meticulous observations and experiments, led him to demolish the ancient Greek's erroneous contentions. Harvey demonstrated that the heart and not the liver was the beginning point of the circulation of blood in the body, that the same blood flows in both veins and arteries, and most important, that the blood makes a complete circuit as it passes through the body. Although Harvey's work dealt a severe blow to Galen's theories, his ideas did not begin to achieve general recognition until the 1660s, when capillaries, which explained how the blood passed from the arteries to the veins, were discovered. Harvey's theory of the circulation of the blood laid the foundation for modern physiology.

Chemistry   Although Paracelsus had proposed a new chemical philosophy in the sixteenth century, it was not until the seventeenth and eighteenth centuries that a science of chemistry arose. Robert Boyle (1627–1691) was one of the first scientists to conduct controlled experiments. His pioneering work on the properties of gases led to Boyle's law, which states that the volume of a gas varies with the pressure exerted on it. Boyle also rejected the medieval belief that all matter consisted of the same components in favor of the view that matter is composed of atoms, which he called "little particles of all shapes and sizes" and which would later be known as the chemical elements.

In the eighteenth century, Antoine Lavoisier (AHN-twahn lah-vwah-ZYAY) (1743–1794) invented a system of naming the chemical elements, much of which is still used today. In helping to show that water is a compound of oxygen and hydrogen, he demonstrated the fundamental rules of chemical combination. He is regarded by many as the founder of modern chemistry. Lavoisier's wife, Marie-Anne, was her husband's scientific collaborator. She learned English in order to translate the work of British chemists for her husband and made engravings to illustrate his scientific experiments. Marie-Anne Lavoisier is a reminder that women too played a role in the Scientific Revolution.

WOMEN IN THE ORIGINS OF MODERN SCIENCE

During the Middle Ages, except for members of religious orders, women who sought a life of learning were severely hampered by the traditional attitude that a woman's proper role was as a daughter, wife, and mother. But in the late fourteenth and early fifteenth centuries, new opportunities for elite women emerged as enthusiasm for the new secular learning called humanism led Europe's privileged and learned men to encourage women to read and study Classical and Christian texts. The ideal of a humanist education for some of the daughters of Europe's elite persisted into the seventeenth century, but only for some privileged women.

Margaret Cavendish   Much as they were drawn to humanism, women were also attracted to the Scientific Revolution. Unlike females educated formally in humanist schools, women interested in science had to obtain a largely informal education. European nobles had the leisure and resources that gave them easy access to the world of learning. This door was also open to noblewomen who could participate in the informal scientific networks of their fathers and brothers. One of the most prominent female scientists of the seventeenth century, Margaret Cavendish (KAV-un-dish) (1623–1673), came from an aristocratic background. Cavendish was not a popularizer of science for women but a participant in the crucial scientific debates of her time. Despite her achievements, however, she was excluded from membership in the Royal Society (see "The Scientific Societies" later in this chapter), although she was once allowed to attend a meeting. She wrote a number of works on scientific matters, including *Observations upon Experimental Philosophy* and *Grounds of Natural Philosophy*, published in 1668. In these works, she did not hesitate to attack what she considered the defects of the rationalist and empiricist approaches to scientific knowledge and was especially critical of the growing belief that through science, humans would be masters of nature: "We have no power at all over natural causes and effects ... for man is but a small part.... His powers are but particular actions of Nature, and he cannot have a supreme and absolute power."[13]

As an aristocrat (she was the duchess of Newcastle), Cavendish was a good example of the women in France and England who worked in science. In Germany, women interested in science came from a different background. There the tradition of female participation in craft production enabled some women to become involved in observational science, especially entomology and astronomy. Between 1650 and 1710, one of every seven German astronomers was a woman.

Maria Merian   A good example of female involvement in the Scientific Revolution stemming from the craft tradition was Maria Sibylla Merian (MAY-ree-un) (1647–1717), who had established a reputation as an important entomologist by the beginning of the eighteenth century. Merian's training came from working in her father's workshop, where she learned the art of illustration, a training of great importance since her exact observation of insects and plants was demonstrated through the superb illustrations she made. In 1699, she undertook an expedition into the wilds of the Dutch colony of Surinam in South America to collect and draw samples of plants and insect life. This led to her major scientific work, the *Metamorphosis of the Insects of Surinam*, in which she used sixty illustrations to show the reproductive and developmental cycles of Surinam's insect life.

Maria Winkelmann   The craft organization of astronomy also gave women opportunities to become involved in science. Those who did worked in family observatories; hence, daughters and wives received training as apprentices to fathers or husbands. The most famous of the female astronomers in Germany was Maria Winkelmann (VINK-ul-mahn) (1670–1720). She was educated by her father and uncle and received advanced training in astronomy from a nearby self-taught astronomer. When she married Gottfried Kirch, Germany's foremost astronomer, she became his assistant at the astronomical observatory operated in Berlin by the Academy of Science. She made some original contributions, including a hitherto undiscovered comet, as her husband related:

> Early in the morning (about 2:00 A.M.) the sky was clear and starry. Some nights before, I had observed a variable star, and my wife (as I slept) wanted to find and see it for herself. In so doing, she found a comet in the sky. At which time she woke me, and I found that it was indeed a comet.... I was surprised that I had not seen it the night before.[14]

Moreover, Winkelmann corresponded with the famous scientist Gottfried Leibniz (who invented the calculus independently of Newton), who praised her effusively as "a most learned woman who could pass as a rarity." When her husband died in 1710, she applied for a position as assistant astronomer for which she was highly qualified. As a woman—with no university degree—she was denied the post by the Berlin Academy, which feared that it would establish a precedent by hiring a woman ("mouths would gape").

Winkelmann's difficulties with the Berlin Academy reflect the obstacles women faced in being accepted in scientific work, which was considered a male preserve. Although no formal statutes excluded women from membership in the new scientific societies, no woman was invited to join either the Royal Society of England or the French Academy of Sciences until the twentieth century. All of these women scientists were exceptional, since a life devoted to any kind of scholarship was still viewed as being at odds with the domestic duties women were expected to perform.

Debates on the Nature of Women   The nature and value of women had been the subject of an ongoing, centuries-long debate known as the **querelles des femmes** (keh-REL day FAHM)—arguments about women. Male opinions in the debate were largely a carryover from medieval times and were not favorable. Women were portrayed as inherently base, prone to vice, easily swayed, and "sexually insatiable." Hence, men needed to control them. Learned women were viewed as having overcome female

Margaret Cavendish: The Education of Women

Margaret Cavendish's husband, who was thirty years her senior, encouraged her to pursue her literary interests. In addition to scientific works, she wrote plays, an autobiography, and a biography of her husband titled *The Life of the Thrice Noble, High and Puissant Prince William Cavendish, Duke, Marquess and Earl of Newcastle*. The autobiography and biography led one male literary critic to call her "a mad, conceited and ridiculous woman." In an essay titled "The Philosophical and Physical Opinions," she discussed the constraints placed upon women, including education.

Margaret Cavendish, "The Philosophical and Physical Opinions"

But to answer those objections that are made against me, as first how should I come by so much experience as I have expressed in my several books to have? I answer: I have had by relation the long and much experience of my lord, who hath lived to see and be in many changes of fortune and to converse with many men of sundry nations, ages, qualities, tempers, capacities, abilities, wits, humours, fashions and customs.

And as many others, especially wives, go from church to church, from ball to ball,... gossiping from house to house, so when my lord admits me to his company I listen with attention to his edifying discourse and I govern myself by his doctrine: I dance a measure with the muses, feast with sciences, or sit and discourse with the arts.

The second is that, since I am no scholar, I cannot know the names and terms of art and the divers and several opinions of several authors. I answer: that I must have been a natural fool if I had not known and learnt them, for they are customarily taught all children from the nurse's breast, being ordinarily discoursed of in every family that is of quality, and the family from whence I sprung are neither natural idiots or ignorant fools, but the contrary, for they were rational, learned, understanding and witty....

But as I have said my head was so full of my own natural fantasies, as it had not room for strangers to board therein, and certainly natural reason is a better tutor than education. For though education doth help natural reason to a more sudden maturity, yet natural reason was the first educator: for natural reason did first compose commonwealths, invented arts and science, and if natural reason hath composed, invented and discovered, I know no reason but natural reason may find out what natural reason hath composed, invented and discovered with the help of education....

Q *What arguments does Cavendish make to defend her right and ability to be an author?*

Source: From Kate Aughterson, *Renaissance Woman: A Sourcebook* (London and New York: Routledge, 1995); pp. 286–288.

liabilities to become like men. One man in praise of a woman scholar remarked that her writings were so good that you "would hardly believe they were done by a woman at all."

In the early modern era, women joined this debate by arguing against these male images of women. They argued that women also had rational minds and

Maria Merian and the Insects of Surinam. *Shown in the engraving is a portrait of Maria Merian, the German naturalist and illustrator, whose study and detailed paintings of plants and insects, especially the transformation of caterpillars into butterflies, attracted scientific attention.*

Iizars sc

© Image Asset Management/age fotostock

could grow from education. Further, since most women were pious, chaste, and temperate, there was no need for male authority over them. These female defenders of women emphasized education as the key to women's ability to move into the world. How, then, did the changes brought by the Scientific Revolution affect this debate over the nature of women? In an era of intellectual revolution in which traditional authorities were being overthrown, we might expect significant change in men's views of women. But by and large, instead of becoming an instrument for liberation, science was used to find new support for the old, stereotypical views about a woman's place in the scheme of things.

An important project in the new anatomy of the sixteenth and seventeenth centuries was the attempt to illustrate the human body and skeleton. For Vesalius, the portrayal of physical differences between males and females was limited to external bodily form (the outlines of the body) and the sexual organs. Vesalius saw no difference in skeletons and portrayed them as the same for men and women. It was not until the eighteenth century, in fact, that a new anatomy finally prevailed. Drawings of female skeletons between 1730 and 1790 varied, but females tended to have a larger pelvic area, and, in some instances, female skulls were portrayed as smaller than those of males. Eighteenth-century studies on the anatomy and physiology of sexual differences provided "scientific evidence" to reaffirm the traditional inferiority of women. The larger pelvic area "proved" that women were meant to be childbearers, and the larger skull "demonstrated" the superiority of the male mind. Male-dominated science had been used to "prove" male social dominance.

At the same time, during the seventeenth and eighteenth centuries, women even lost the traditional spheres of influence they had possessed, especially in the science-related art of midwifery. Women serving as midwives had tradition-ally been responsible for birthing. Similar to barber-surgeons or apothecaries (see Chapter 17), midwives had acquired their skills through apprenticeship. But the impact of the Scientific Revolution caused traditional crafts to be upgraded and then even professionalized as males took over. When medical men entered this arena, they also began to use devices and techniques derived from the study of anatomy. These were increasingly used to justify the male takeover of the traditional role of midwives. By the end of the eighteenth cen-tury, midwives were simply accessories to the art they had once controlled, except among the poor. Since little money was to be made in serving the lower classes, midwives were allowed to continue to practice their traditional art among them.

Overall, the Scientific Revolution reaffirmed traditional ideas about women. Male scientists used the new science to spread the view that women were infe-rior by nature, subordinate to men, and suited by nature to play a domestic role as nurturing mothers. The widespread distribution of books ensured the continuation of these ideas. Jean de La Bruyère (ZHAHNH duh lah broo-YARE), the seventeenth-century French moralist, was typical when he remarked that an educated woman was like a gun that was a collector's item, "which one shows to the curious, but which has no use at all, any more than a carousel horse."[15]

Toward a New Earth: Descartes, Rationalism, and a New View of Humankind

The fundamentally new conception of the universe contained in the cosmological revolution of the sixteenth and seventeenth centuries inevitably had an impact on the Western view of humankind. Nowhere is this more evident than in the work of René Descartes (ruh-NAY day-KART) (1596–1650), an extremely important figure in Western history. Descartes began by reflecting the doubt and uncertainty that seemed pervasive in the confusion of the seventeenth cen-tury and ended with a philosophy that dominated Western thought until the twentieth century.

Descartes was born into a family of the French lower nobility. After a Jesuit education, he studied law at Poitiers but traveled to Paris to study by himself. In 1618, at the beginning of the Thirty Years' War, Descartes volunteered for ser-vice in the army of Maurice of Nassau, but he seems to have been interested less in military action than in traveling and finding leisure time to think. On the night of November 10, 1619, Descartes underwent what one historian has called an experience comparable to the "ecstatic illumination of the mystic." Having perceived in one night the outlines of a new rational-mathematical system, with a sense of divine approval he made a new commitment to mind, mathematics, and a mechanical universe. For the rest of his life, Descartes worked out the details of his vision.

The starting point for Descartes's new system was doubt, as he explained at the beginning of his most famous work, the *Discourse on Method*, written in 1637:

> From my childhood I have been familiar with letters; and as I was given to believe that by their means a clear and assured knowledge can be acquired of all that is useful in life, I was extremely eager for instruction in them. As soon, however, as I had completed the course of study, at the close of which it is customary to be admitted into the order of the learned, I entirely changed my opinion. For I found myself entangled in so many doubts and errors that, as it seemed to me, the endeavor to instruct myself had served only to disclose to me more and more of my ignorance.[16]

Descartes decided to set aside all that he had learned and begin again. One fact seemed beyond doubt—his own existence:

> But I immediately became aware that while I was thus disposed to think that all was false, it was absolutely necessary that I who thus thought should be something; and noting that this truth, *I think, therefore I am*, was so steadfast and so assured that the suppositions of the skeptics, to whatever extreme they might all be carried, could not avail to shake it, I concluded that I might without scruple accept it as being the first principle of the philosophy I was seeking.[17]

With this emphasis on the mind, Descartes asserted that he would accept only those things that his reason said were true.

From his first postulate, Descartes deduced an additional principle, the separation of mind and matter. Descartes argued that since "the mind cannot be doubted but the body and material world can, the two must be radically different." From this came an absolute duality between mind and body that has been called **Cartesian dualism**. Using mind or human reason, the path to certain knowledge, and its best instrument, mathematics, humans can understand the material world because it is pure mechanism, a machine that is governed by its own physical laws because it was created by God, the great geometrician.

Descartes's conclusions about the nature of the universe and human beings had important implications. His separation of mind and matter allowed scientists to view matter as dead or inert, as something that was totally separate from themselves and could be investigated independently by reason. The split between mind and body led Westerners to equate their identity with mind and reason rather than with the whole organism. Descartes has rightly been called the father of modern **rationalism**. His books were placed on the papal Index of Forbidden Books and condemned by many Protestant theologians. The radical Cartesian split between mind and matter, and between mind and body, had devastating implications not only for traditional religious views of the universe but also for how Westerners viewed themselves.

THE SCIENTIFIC METHOD AND
THE SPREAD OF SCIENTIFIC KNOWLEDGE

During the seventeenth century, scientific learning and investigation began to increase dramatically. Major universities in Europe established new chairs of science, especially in medicine. Royal and princely patronage of individual scientists became an international phenomenon.

The Scientific Of great importance to the work of science was establishing
Method   the proper means to examine and understand the physical realm. This development of a **scientific method** was crucial to the evolution of science in the modern world.

Francis Bacon   Curiously enough, it was an Englishman with few scientific credentials who attempted to put forth a new method of acquiring knowledge that made an impact on English scientists in the seventeenth century and other European scientists in the eighteenth century. Francis Bacon (1561–1626), a lawyer and lord chancellor, rejected Copernicus and Kepler and misunderstood Galileo. And yet in his unfinished work, *The Great Instauration*, he called for his contemporaries "to commence a total reconstruction of sciences, arts, and all human knowledge, raised upon the proper foundations." Bacon did not doubt humans' ability to know the natural world, but he believed that they had proceeded incorrectly: "The entire fabric of human reason which we employ in the inquisition of nature is badly put together and built up, and like some magnificent structure without foundation."

Bacon's new foundation—a correct scientific method—was to be built on inductive principles. Rather than beginning with assumed first principles from which logical conclusions could be deduced, he urged scientists to proceed from the particular to the general. From carefully organized experiments and thorough, systematic observations, correct generalizations could be developed.

Bacon was clear about what he believed his method could accomplish. His concern was for practical results rather than for pure science. He stated that "the true and lawful goal of the sciences is none other than this: that human life be endowed with new discoveries and power." He wanted science to contribute to the "mechanical arts" by creating devices that would benefit industry, agriculture, and trade. Bacon was prophetic when he said that he was "laboring to lay the foundation, not of any sect or doctrine, but of human utility and power." And how would this "human power" be used? To "conquer nature in action."[18] The control and domination of nature became a central proposition of modern science and the technology that accompanied it. Only in the twentieth century did some scientists begin to ask whether this assumption might not be at the heart of the earth's ecological crisis.

Descartes   Descartes proposed a different approach to scientific methodology by emphasizing deduction and mathematical logic. As Descartes explained in the *Discourse on Method*, each step in an argument should be as sharp and well founded as a mathematical proof:

Those long chains of reasonings, each step simple and easy, which geometers are wont to employ in arriving even at the most difficult of their demonstrations, have led me to surmise that all the things we human beings are competent to know are interconnected in the same manner, and that none are so remote as to be beyond our reach or so hidden that we cannot discover them—that is, provided we abstain from accepting as true what is not thus related, i.e., keep always to the order required for their deduction one from another.[19]

Descartes believed, then, that one could start with self-evident truths, comparable to geometric axioms, and deduce more complex conclusions. His emphasis on deduction and mathematical order complemented Bacon's stress on experiment and induction. It was Sir Isaac Newton who synthesized them into a single scientific methodology by uniting Bacon's **empiricism** with Descartes's rationalism. This scientific method began with systematic observations and experiments, which were used to arrive at general concepts. New deductions derived from these general concepts could then be tested and verified by precise experiments.

The scientific method, of course, was valuable in answering the question of *how* something works, and its success in doing this gave others much confidence in the method. It did not attempt to deal with the question of *why* something happens or the purpose and meaning behind the world of nature. This allowed religion to retain its central importance in the seventeenth century (see "Science and Religion" later in this chapter).

The Spread of Scientific Knowledge   Also important to the work of science was the emergence of new learned societies and journals that enabled the new scientists to communicate their ideas to each other and to disseminate them to a wider, literate public.

The Scientific Societies   The first of these scientific societies appeared in Italy, but those of England and France were ultimately of greater significance. The English Royal Society evolved out of informal gatherings of scientists at London and Oxford in the 1640s, although it did not receive a formal charter from King Charles II until 1662. The French Royal Academy of Sciences also arose out of informal scientific meetings in Paris during the 1650s. In 1666, Louis XIV formally recognized the group. The French Academy received abundant state support and remained under government control; its members were appointed and paid salaries by the state. In contrast, the Royal Society of England received little government encouragement, and its fellows simply co-opted new members.

Early on, both the English and the French scientific societies formally emphasized the practical value of scientific research. The Royal Society created a committee to investigate technological improvements for industry; the French Academy collected tools and machines. This concern with the practical benefits of science proved short-lived, however, as both societies came to focus their primary interest on theoretical work in mechanics and astronomy. The construction of observatories at Paris in 1667 and at Greenwich, England, in 1675 greatly facilitated research in astronomy by both groups. Although both the English

The Royal Observatory at Greenwich. *To facilitate their astronomical investigations, both the English and the French constructed observatories such as the one pictured here, which was built at Greenwich, England, in 1675. Here the royal astronomer works at the table while his two assistants make observations.*

and the French societies made useful contributions to scientific knowledge in the second half of the seventeenth century, their true significance was that they demonstrated the benefits of science proceeding as a cooperative venture.

Scientific journals furthered this concept of cooperation. The French *Journal des Savants* (zhoor-NAHL day sah-VAHNH), published weekly beginning in 1665, printed results of experiments as well as general scientific knowledge. Its format appealed to both scientists and the educated public interested in the new science. In contrast, the *Philosophical Transactions* of the Royal Society, also initiated in 1665, published papers of its members and learned correspondence and was aimed at practicing scientists. It became a prototype for the scholarly journals of later learned and academic societies and a crucial instrument for circulating news of scientific and academic activities.

Science and Society   The importance of science in the history of modern Western civilization is usually taken for granted. No doubt the Industrial Revolution of the nineteenth century provided tangible proof of the effectiveness of science and ensured its victory over Western minds. But how did science become such an integral part of Western culture in the seventeenth and eighteenth centuries? Recent research has stressed that one cannot simply assert that people perceived that science was a rationally superior system. Several factors, however, might explain the relatively rapid acceptance of the new science.

It has been argued that the literate mercantile and propertied elites of Europe were attracted to the new science because it offered new ways to exploit resources for profit. Some of the early scientists made it easier for these groups to accept the new ideas by showing how they could be applied directly to specific industrial and technological needs. Galileo, for example, consciously sought an alliance between science and the material interests of the educated elite when he assured his listeners that the science of mechanics would be quite useful "when it becomes necessary to build bridges or other structures over water, something occurring mainly in affairs of great importance." At the same time, Galileo stressed that science was fit for the "minds of the wise" and not for "the shallow minds of the common people." This made science part of the high culture of Europe's wealthy elites at a time when that culture was being increasingly separated from the popular culture of the lower classes (see Chapter 17).

It has also been argued that political interests used the new scientific conception of the natural world to bolster social stability. One scholar has argued that "no single event in the history of early modern Europe more profoundly shaped the integration of the new science into Western culture than did the English Revolution (1640–1660)."[20] Fed by their millenarian expectations that the end of the world would come and usher in a thousand-year reign of the saints, Puritan reformers felt it was important to reform and renew their society. They seized on the new science as a socially useful instrument to accomplish this goal. The Puritan Revolution's role in the acceptance of science, however, stemmed even more from the reaction to the radicalism spawned by the revolutionary ferment. The upheavals of the Puritan Revolution gave rise to groups, such as the Levellers, Diggers, and Ranters, who advocated not only radical political ideas but also a new radical science based on Paracelsus and the natural magic associated with the Hermetic tradition. The propertied and educated elites responded vigorously to these challenges to the established order by supporting the new mechanistic science and appealing to the material benefits of science. Hence, the founders of the Royal Society were men who wanted to pursue an experimental science that would remain detached from radical reforms of church and state. Although willing to make changes, they now viewed those changes in terms of an increase in food production and commerce.

At the same time, princes and kings who were providing patronage for scientists were doing so not only for prestige but also for practical reasons, especially the military applications of the mathematical sciences. The use of gunpowder, for example, gave new importance to ballistics and metallurgy. Rulers, especially absolute ones, were also concerned about matters of belief in their realms and recognized the need to control and manage the scientific body of knowledge, as we have seen in the French Academy. In appointing its members and paying their salaries, Louis XIV was also ensuring that the members and their work would be under his control.

Science and Religion   In Galileo's struggle with the inquisitorial Holy Office of the Catholic Church, we see the beginning of the conflict between science and religion that has marked the history of modern Western civilization. Since time immemorial, theology had seemed to be the queen of the sciences. It was natural that the churches would continue to believe that religion was the final measure of all things. The emerging scientists, however, tried to draw lines between the knowledge of religion and the knowledge of "natural philosophy" or nature. Galileo had clearly felt that it was unnecessary to pit science against religion when he wrote:

> In discussions of physical problems we ought to begin not from the authority of scriptural passages, but from sense-experiences and necessary demonstrations; for the holy Bible and the phenomena of nature proceed alike from the divine word, the former as the dictate of the Holy Ghost and the latter as the observant executrix of God's commands. It is necessary for the Bible, in order to be accommodated to the understanding of every man, to speak many things which appear to differ from the absolute truth so far as the bare meaning of the words is concerned. But Nature, on the other hand, is inexorable and immutable; she never transgresses the laws imposed upon her, or cares a whit whether her abstruse reasons and methods of operation are understandable to men.[21]

To Galileo, it made little sense for the church to determine the nature of physical reality on the basis of biblical texts that were subject to radically divergent interpretations. The church, however, decided otherwise in Galileo's case and lent its great authority to one scientific theory, the Aristotelian-Ptolemaic cosmology, no doubt because it fit so well with its own philosophical views of reality. But the church's decision had tremendous consequences, just as the rejection of Darwin's ideas did in the nineteenth century. For educated individuals, it established a dichotomy between scientific investigations and religious beliefs. As the scientific beliefs triumphed, it became almost inevitable that religious beliefs would suffer, leading to a growing secularization in European intellectual life—precisely what the church had hoped to combat by opposing Copernicanism. Many seventeenth-century intellectuals were both religious and scientific and believed that the implications of this split would be tragic. Some believed that the split was largely unnecessary, while others felt the need to combine God, humans, and a mechanistic universe into a new philosophical synthesis. Two individuals—Spinoza and Pascal—illustrate the wide diversity in the response of European intellectuals to the implications of the cosmological revolution of the seventeenth century.

Spinoza   Benedict de Spinoza (spi-NOH-zuh) (1632–1677) was a philosopher who grew up in the relatively tolerant atmosphere of Amsterdam. He was excommunicated from the Amsterdam synagogue at the age of twenty-four for rejecting the tenets of Judaism. Ostracized by the local Jewish community and major Christian churches alike, Spinoza lived a quiet, independent life, earning a living by grinding optical lenses and refusing to accept an academic position in philosophy at the University of Heidelberg for fear of compromising his freedom of thought. Spinoza read a great deal of the new scientific literature and was influenced by Descartes.

Spinoza was unwilling to accept the implications of Descartes's ideas, especially the separation of mind and matter and the apparent separation of an infinite God from the finite world of matter. God was not simply the creator of the universe; he was the universe. All that is is in God, and nothing can be apart from God. This philosophy of pantheism (or monism) was set out in Spinoza's book *Ethics Demonstrated in the Geometrical Manner*, which was not published until after his death.

To Spinoza, human beings are not "situated in nature as a kingdom within a kingdom" but are as much a part of God or nature or the universal order as other natural objects. The failure to understand God had led to many misconceptions—for one, that nature exists only for one's use:

> As they find in themselves and outside themselves many means which assist them not a little in their search for what is useful, for instance, eyes for seeing, teeth for chewing, herbs and animals for yielding food, the sun for giving light, the sea for breeding fish, they come to look on the whole of nature as a means for obtaining such conveniences.[22]

Furthermore, unable to find any other cause for the existence of these things, they attributed them to a creator-God who must be worshiped to gain their ends: "Hence also it follows, that everyone thought out for himself, according to his abilities, a different way of worshiping God, so that God might love him more than his fellows, and direct the whole course of nature for the satisfaction of his blind cupidity and insatiable avarice." Then, when nature appeared unfriendly in the form of storms, earthquakes, and diseases, "they declared that such things happen, because the gods are angry at some wrong done them by men, or at some fault committed in their worship," rather than realizing "that good and evil fortunes fall to the lot of pious and impious alike."[23] Likewise, human beings made moral condemnations of others because they failed to understand that human emotions, "passions of hatred, anger, envy and so, considered in themselves, follow from the same necessity and efficacy of nature" and "nothing comes to pass in nature in contravention to her universal laws." To explain human emotions, like everything else, we need to analyze them as we would the movements of planets: "I shall, therefore, treat of the nature and strength of my emotions according to the same method as I employed heretofore in my investigations concerning God and the mind. I shall consider human actions and desires in exactly the same manner as though I were concerned with lines, planes, and solids."[24] Everything has a rational explanation, and humans are capable of finding it. In using reason, people can find true happiness. Their real freedom comes when they understand the order and necessity of nature and achieve detachment from passing interests.

Pascal   Blaise Pascal (BLEZ pass-KAHL) (1623–1662) was a French scientist who sought to keep science and religion united. An accomplished scientist and a brilliant mathematician, he excelled at both the practical, by inventing a calculating machine, and the abstract, by devising a theory of chance or probability and doing work on conic sections. After a profound mystical vision on the night of November 23, 1654, which assured him that God cared for the human soul, he devoted the rest of his life to religious matters. He planned to write an "apology for the Christian religion" but died before he could do so. He did leave a set of notes for the larger work, however, which in published form became known as the *Pensées* (pahn-SAY) (*Thoughts*).

In the *Pensées*, Pascal tried to convert rationalists to Christianity by appealing to both their reason and their emotions. Humans were, he argued, frail creatures, often deceived by their senses, misled by reason, and battered by their emotions. And yet they were beings whose very nature involved thinking: "Man is but a reed, the weakest in nature; but he is a thinking reed."[25]

Pascal was determined to show that the Christian religion was not contrary to reason: "If we violate the principles of reason, our religion will be absurd, and it will be laughed at." Christianity, he felt, was the only religion that recognized people's true state of being as both vulnerable and great. To a Christian, a human being was both fallen and at the same time God's special creation. But it was not necessary to emphasize one at the expense of the other—to view humans as only rational or only hopeless. Pascal even had an answer for skeptics in his famous wager. God is a reasonable bet; it is worthwhile to assume that God exists. If he does, then we win all; if he does not, we lose nothing.

Despite his own background as a scientist and mathematician, Pascal refused to rely on the scientist's world of order and rationality to attract people to God: "If we submit everything to reason, there will be no mystery and no supernatural element in our religion." In the new cosmology of the seventeenth century, "finite man," Pascal believed, was lost in the new infinite world, a realization that frightened him: "The eternal silence of those infinite spaces strikes me with terror." The world of nature, then, could never reveal God: "Because they have failed to contemplate these infinites, men have rashly plunged into the examination of nature, as though they bore some proportion to her.... Their assumption is as infinite as their object." A Christian could only rely on a God who through Jesus cared for human beings. In the final analysis, after providing reasonable arguments for Christianity, Pascal came to rest on faith. Reason, he believed, could take people only so far: "The heart has its reasons of which the reason knows nothing." As a Christian, faith was the final step: "The heart feels God, not the reason. This is what constitutes faith: God experienced by the heart, not by the reason."[26]

In retrospect, it is obvious that Pascal failed to achieve his goal of uniting Christianity and science. The gap between science and traditional religion grew ever wider as Europe continued along its path of secularization. Of course, traditional religions were not eliminated, nor is there any evidence that churches had yet lost their followers. That would happen later. Nevertheless, more and more of the intellectual, social, and political elites began to act on the basis of secular rather than religious assumptions.

CHRONOLOGY

IMPORTANT WORKS OF THE SCIENTIFIC REVOLUTION

1543	Copernicus, *On the Revolutions of the Heavenly Spheres*
1543	Vesalius, *On the Fabric of the Human Body*
1610	Galileo, *The Starry Messenger*

1620	Bacon, *The Great Instauration*
1628	Harvey, *On the Motion of the Heart and Blood*
1632	Galileo, *Dialogue on the Two Chief World Systems*
1637	Descartes, *Discourse on Method*
1668	Cavendish, *Grounds of Natural Philosophy*
1669	Pascal, *Pensées*
1687	Newton, *Principia*
1677	Spinoza, *Ethics Demonstrated in the Geometrical Manner*

Notes

CHAPTER 1

1. Jean-Marie Chauvet et al., *Dawn of Art: The Chauvet Cave* (New York, 1996), pp. 49–50.
2. Quoted in Amélie Kuhrt, *The Ancient Near East, c. 3000–330 B.C.,* vol. 1 (London, 1995), p. 68.
3. Quoted in Michael Wood, *Legacy: The Search for Ancient Cultures* (New York, 1995), p. 34.
4. Quoted in Marc van de Mieroop, *A History of the Ancient Near East, ca. 3000–323 B.C.* (Oxford, 2004), p. 69.
5. Quoted in ibid., p. 64.
6. Quoted in ibid., p. 106.
7. Quoted in Thorkild Jacobsen, "Mesopotamia," in Henri Frankfort et al., *Before Philosophy* (Baltimore, 1949), p. 139.
8. Quoted in Thorkild Jacobsen, *The Treasures of Darkness: A History of Mesopotamian Religion* (New Haven, Conn., 1976), p. 97.
9. N. K. Sandars, trans. *The Epic of Gilgamesh* (London, 1972), p. 62.
10. James B. Pritchard, *Ancient Near Eastern Texts,* 3rd ed. (Princeton, N.J., 1969), p. 372.
11. Quoted in Angela P. Thomas, *Egyptian Gods and Myths* (London, 1986), p. 25.
12. Pritchard, *Ancient Near Eastern Texts,* p. 445.
13. Quoted in B. G. Trigger, B. J. Kemp, D. O'Connor, and A. B. Lloyd, *Ancient Egypt: A Social History* (Cambridge, 1983), p. 74.
14. Pritchard, *Ancient Near Eastern Texts,* p. 34.
15. Ibid., p. 36.
16. Quoted in Rose-Marie Hagen and Rainer Hagen, *Egypt: People, Gods, Pharaohs* (Cologne, 2002), p. 148.
17. Quoted in Toby Wilkerson, *The Rise and Fall of Ancient Egypt* (New York, 2010), p. 262.
18. Pritchard, *Ancient Near Eastern Texts,* p. 413.
19. Ibid., p. 412.
20. Ibid., p. 413.

CHAPTER 2

1. 2 Samuel 8:2.
2. Psalms 137:1, 4–6.
3. Psalms 145:8–9.
4. Psalms 121:2–3.
5. Exodus 20:13–15.
6. Isaiah 2:4.
7. Proverbs 31:10–20, 24–28.
8. Judges 5:24–27.
9. Quoted in Roland de Vaux, *Ancient Israel: Its Life and Institutions* (New York, 1961), p. 49.
10. Quoted in Marc van de Mieroop, *A History of the Ancient Near East* (Oxford, 2004), p. 242.
11. Quoted in H. W. F. Saggs, *The Might That Was Assyria* (London, 1984), pp. 261–262.
12. John C. Rolfe, trans., *Quintus Curtius I* (Cambridge, Mass., 1971), pp. 337–339.
13. Quoted in John M. Cook, *The Persian Empire* (New York, 1983), p. 32.
14. Herodotus, *The Persian Wars,* trans. George Rawlinson (New York, 1942), p. 257.
15. Isaiah 44:28, 45:1.
16. Quoted in Albert T. Olmstead, *History of the Persian Empire* (Chicago, 1948), p. 168.
17. Quoted in Cook, *The Persian Empire,* p. 76.
18. Yasna 44:3–4, 7, as quoted in A. C. Bouquet, *Sacred Books of the World* (Harmondsworth, England, 1954), pp. 111–112.

CHAPTER 3

1. H. D. F. Kitto, *The Greeks* (Harmondsworth, England, 1951), p. 64.
2. Homer, *Odyssey,* trans. E. V. Rieu (Harmondsworth, England, 1946), p. 337.
3. Xenophon, *Symposium,* trans. O.J. Todd (Cambridge, Mass., 1968), 3.5.
4. Homer, *Odyssey,* pp. 290–291.
5. Quoted in Thomas R. Martin, *Ancient Greece* (New Haven, Conn., 1996), p. 62.
6. Quoted in Victor David Hanson, *The Wars of the Ancient Greeks,* rev. ed. (London, 2006), p. 14.
7. These words from Plutarch are quoted in Elaine Fantham et al., *Women in the Classical World* (New York, 1994), p. 64.
8. Hesiod, *Works and Days,* trans. Dorothea Wender (Harmondsworth, England, 1973), pp. 77, 71, 68.
9. Theognis, *Elegies,* trans. Dorothea Wender (Harmondsworth, England, 1973), pp. 118, 100.
10. Aeschylus, "The Persians," in *The Complete Greek Tragedies,* vol. 1, ed. David Grene and Richmond Lattimore (Chicago, 1959), p. 229.
11. Herodotus, *The Persian Wars,* trans. Robin Waterfield (New York, 1998), p. 3.
12. Thucydides, *History of the Peloponnesian War,* trans. Rex Warner (Harmondsworth, England, 1954), p. 24.
13. Ibid.
14. Ibid.
15. Sophocles, *Oedipus the King,* trans. David Grene (Chicago, 1959), pp. 68–69.
16. Sophocles, *Antigone,* trans. Don Taylor (London, 1986), p. 146.
17. Plato, *The Republic,* trans. F. M. Cornford (New York, 1945), pp. 178–179.
18. Quotations from Aristotle are from Sue Blundell, *Women in Ancient Greece* (London, 1995), pp. 106, 186.

CHAPTER 4

1. Quoted in Sarah B. Pomeroy et al., *Ancient Greece: A Political, Social, and Cultural History* (Oxford, 1999), p. 390.
2. Polybius, *The Histories,* trans. W. R. Paton (Cambridge, Mass., 1960), 18.37.8–18.37.10.
3. Quoted in Graham Shipley, *The Greek World After Alexander, 323–30* B.C. (London, 2000), p. 53.
4. Quoted in ibid., p. 304.
5. Maureen B. Fant and Mary R. Lefkowitz, *Women's Life in Greece and Rome: A Source Book in Translation* (Baltimore, 1992), p. 208.
6. Roger S. Bagnall and Peter Derow, *Greek Historical Documents: The Hellenistic Period* (Chico, Calif., 1981), p. 113.
7. Plutarch, *Life of Marcellus,* trans. John Dryden (New York, n.d.), p. 378.
8. Celsus, *De Medicina,* trans. W. G. Spencer (Cambridge, Mass., 1935), Prooemium 23–24.
9. Cyril Bailey, trans. *Epicurus: The Extant Remains* (Oxford, 1926), pp. 89–90, 115, 101.
10. Diogenes Laertius, *Life of Zeno,* vol. 2, trans. R. D. Hicks (London, 1925), p. 195.
11. Quoted in W. W. Tarn, *Hellenistic Civilization* (London, 1930), p. 324.

CHAPTER 5

1. Polybius. *The Histories,* trans. W. R. Paton (Cambridge, Mass., 1960), Book I, 37.7–37.10.
2. Quoted in Chester Starr, *Past and Future in Ancient History* (Lanham, Md., 1987), pp. 38–39.
3. Cicero, *Laws,* trans. C. W. Keyes (Cambridge, Mass., 1966), 2.12.31.
4. Cato the Censor, *On Farming,* trans. Ernest Brehaut (New York, 1933), 141.
5. Quoted in J. Wright Duff, *A Literary History of Rome* (London, 1960), pp. 136–137.

6. Terence, *The Comedies,* trans. Betty Radice (Harmondsworth, England, 1976), p. 339.

7. Pliny, *Natural History,* trans. W. H. S. Jones (Cambridge, Mass., 1963), 29.7.

8. Mary Beard and Michael Crawford, *Rome in the Late Republic* (London, 1985), p. 3.

9. Quoted in Adrian Goldsworthy, *Caesar: Life of a Colossus* (New Haven, Conn., 2006), p. 235.

10. Quoted in ibid., p. 358.

11. Appian, *Roman History: The Civil Wars,* trans. H. White (Cambridge, Mass., 1961), 4.2.149–4.2.151.

12. Florus, *Epitome of Roman History,* trans. E. S. Forster (Cambridge, Mass., 1960), 2.22.327.

13. Charles Martin, trans., *The Poems of Catullus* (Baltimore, 1990), p. 109.

14. Lucretius, *On the Nature of Things,* trans. Anthony M. Esolen (Baltimore, 1995), 2.115–2.123.

15. Quoted in Anthony Everitt, *Cicero* (New York, 2001), p. 181.

16. Julius Caesar, *The Gallic War and Other Writings,* trans. Moses Hadas (New York, 1957), 2.25.

CHAPTER 6

1. Livy, *The Early History of Rome,* trans. Aubrey de Sélincourt (Harmondsworth, England, 1960), p. 35.

2. Tacitus, *The Annals of Imperial Rome,* trans. Michael Grant (Harmondsworth, England, 1956), p. 30.

3. Velleius Paterculus, *Compendium of Roman History,* trans. Frederick Shipley (Cambridge, Mass., 1967), 2.117.

4. Tacitus, *Annals of Imperial Rome,* p. 37.

5. Virgil, *The Aeneid,* trans. C. Day Lewis (Garden City, N.Y., 1952), p. 154.

6. Horace, "Satires," in *The Complete Works of Horace,* trans. Lord Dunsany and Michael Oakley (London, 1961), 1.1.

7. Ibid., 1.3.

8. Livy, *Early History of Rome,* p. 18.

9. Tacitus, *Annals of Imperial Rome,* p. 31.

10. Tacitus, *The Histories,* trans. Kenneth Wallesley (Harmondsworth, England, 1964), p. 23.

11. Quoted in Martin Goodman, *The Roman World, 44* B.C.–A.D. *180* (London, 1997), p. 67.

12. Quoted in ibid., p. 72.

13. Seneca, *Letters from a Stoic,* trans. Robin Campbell (Harmondsworth, England, 1969), let. 5.

14. Tacitus, *Annals of Imperial Rome,* p. 147.

15. Juvenal, *The Sixteen Satires,* trans. Peter Green (Harmondsworth, England, 1967), satire 7, p. 171.

16. Ibid., satire 10, p. 207.

17. Tacitus, "A Dialogue on Oratory," in *The Complete Works of Tacitus,* trans. Alfred Church and William Brodribb (New York, 1942), no. 29, p. 758.

18. Ovid, *The Amores,* trans. Grant Showerman (Cambridge, Mass., 1963), 2.14.26–2.14.27.

19. Matthew 5:17.

20. Matthew 7:12.

21. Mark 12:30–31.

22. John 18:36.

23. Matthew 26:26–28.

24. *Early Christian Writings* (Harmondsworth, England, 1968), pp. 76–77.

25. These lines and the one by Polycarp are quoted in Colin Wells, *The Roman Empire* (Stanford, Calif., 1984), pp. 263–264.

26. Quotations by Tertullian can be found in David Chidester, *Christianity: A Global History* (New York, 2000), pp. 74, 79, 82.

27. Tertullian, "The Prescriptions Against the Heretics," in *The Library of Christian Classics: Early Latin Theology,* vol. 5, ed. and trans. S. L. Greenslade (Philadelphia, 1956), p. 36.

28. Colossians 3:10–11.

CHAPTER 7

1. Naphtali Lewis and Meyers Reinhold, eds., *Roman Civilization,* vol. 2 (New York, 1955), p. 191.

2. "The Creed of Nicaea," in *Documents of the Christian Church*, ed. Henry Bettenson (London, 1963), p. 35.

3. Charles C. Mierow, trans., *The Gothic History of Jordanes* (Princeton, N.J., 1915), pp. 88–89.

4. Quoted in Chris Wickham, *The Inheritance of Rome: A History of Europe from 400 to 1000* (New York, 2009), p. 82.

5. Quoted in Averil Cameron, *The Mediterranean World in Late Antiquity* (London, 1993), p. 37.

6. Ernest F. Henderson, *Selected Historical Documents of the Middle Ages* (London, 1892), p. 182.

7. Ibid., p. 181.

8. Anne Fremantle, ed., *A Treasury of Early Christianity* (New York, 1953), p. 91.

9. Matthew 16:15–19.

10. R. C. Petry, ed., *A History of Christianity: Readings in the History of Early and Medieval Christianity* (Englewood Cliffs, N.J., 1962), p. 70.

11. Brian Pullan, ed., *Sources for the History of Medieval Europe* (Oxford, 1966), p. 46.

12. Quoted in Sidney Painter and Brian Tierney, *Western Europe in the Middle Ages, 300–1475* (New York, 1983), p. 106.

13. Mark 10:21.

14. Norman F. Cantor, ed., *The Medieval World, 300–1300* (New York, 1963), pp. 104, 101, 108, 103.

15. Bede, *A History of the English Church and People*, trans. Leo Sherley–Price (Harmondsworth, England, 1968), pp. 86–87.

16. Quoted in Peter Brown, *The Rise of Western Christendom: Triumph and Adversity*, A.D. 200–1000 (Oxford, 1997), p. 98.

17. Procopius, *Secret History*, trans. Richard Atwater (Ann Arbor, Mich., 1963), p. 3.

18. H. B. Dewing, trans., *Procopius*, vol. 1 (Cambridge, Mass., 1914), p. 48.

19. Procopius, *Buildings of Justinian* (London, 1897), pp. 9, 6–7, 11.

20. Quoted in Jonathan Harris, *Constantinople: Capital of Byzantium* (New York, 2007), p. 40.

21. Quoted in ibid., p.118.

22. Quoted in Arthur Goldschmidt Jr., *A Concise History of the Middle East*, 7th ed. (Boulder, Colo., 2001), p. 60.

CHAPTER 8

1. Einhard, *The Life of Charlemagne*, trans. Samuel Turner (Ann Arbor, Mich., 1960), p. 30.

2. Ibid., p. 57.

3. Alessandro Barbero, *Charlemagne: Father of a Continent*, trans. Allan Cameron (Berkeley, Calif., 2004), p. 4.

4. Chris Wickham, *The Inheritance of Rome: A History of Europe from 400 to 1000* (New York, 2009), p. 4.

5. Quoted in Pierre Riche, *Daily Life in the World of Charlemagne*, trans. Jo Ann McNamara (Philadelphia, 1978), p. 56.

6. 1 Corinthians 7:1–2, 8–9.

7. Quoted in Derrick Bailey, *Homosexuality and the Western Christian Tradition* (London, 1955), p. 73.

8. Quoted in Paul Veyne, ed., *A History of Private Life: From Pagan Rome to Byzantium*, vol. 1, trans. Arthur Goldhammer (Cambridge, Mass., 1987), p. 440.

9. Stanley Rubin, *Medieval English Medicine* (New York, 1974), p. 136.

10. Quoted in Brian Inglis, *A History of Medicine* (New York, 1965), p. 51.

11. Quoted in Simon Keynes, "The Vikings in England, c. 790–1016," in *The Oxford Illustrated History of the Vikings*, ed. Peter Sawyer (Oxford, 1997), p. 81.

12. Quoted in Oliver Thatcher and Edgar McNeal, *A Source Book for Medieval History* (New York, 1905), p. 363.

13. Simon Keynes and Michael Lapidge, *Alfred the Great: Asser's "Life of King Alfred" and Other Contemporary Sources* (Harmondsworth, England, 1983), pp. 84–85.

14. Quoted in Bernard Lewis, *The Arabs in History* (London, 1958), p. 90.

15. al-Mas'udi, *The Meadows of Gold: The Abbasids*, ed. Paul Lunde and Caroline Stone (London, 1989), p. 151.
16. Quoted in Albert Hourani, *A History of the Arab People* (Cambridge, Mass., 1991), p. 120.

Chapter 9

1. Quoted in Joseph Gies and Frances Gies, *Life in a Medieval Castle* (New York, 1974), p. 175.
2. Quoted in Robert Delort, *Life in the Middle Ages*, trans. Robert Allen (New York, 1972), p. 218.
3. Quoted in Jean Gimpel, *The Medieval Machine* (Harmondsworth, England, 1976), p. 92.
4. Quoted in Charles H. Haskins, *The Rise of Universities* (Ithaca, N.Y., 1957), pp. 77–78.
5. Ibid., pp. 79–80.
6. Quoted in David Herlihy, *Medieval Culture and Society* (New York, 1968), p. 204.
7. Quoted in John H. Mundy, *Europe in the High Middle Ages, 1150–1309* (New York, 1973), pp. 474–475.
8. Helen Waddell, *The Wandering Scholars* (New York, 1961), p. 222.
9. Quoted in John W. Baldwin, *The Scholastic Culture of the Middle Ages, 1000–1300* (Lexington, Mass., 1971), p. 15.

Chapter 10

1. Quoted in John K. Fairbank, Edwin O. Reischauer, and Albert M. Craig, *East Asia: Tradition and Transformation* (Boston, 1973), p. 164.
2. Ernest F. Henderson, ed., *Selected Historical Documents of the Middle Ages* (London, 1892), p. 332.
3. Ibid., p. 365.
4. Oliver J. Thatcher and Edgar H. McNeal, eds., *A Source Book for Medieval History* (New York, 1905), p. 208.
5. Quoted in R. H. C. Davis, *A History of Medieval Europe from Constantine to Saint Louis*, 2nd ed. (New York, 1988), p. 252.
6. Luke 18:23–25.
7. Quoted in Rosalind Brooke and Christopher N. L. Brooke, *Popular Religion in the Middle Ages* (London, 1984), p. 19.
8. Henry T. Riley, ed., *Memorials of London and London Life in the Thirteenth, Fourteenth, and Fifteenth Centuries*, vol. 2 (London, 1868), pp. 148–149.
9. Thatcher and McNeal, *Source Book for Medieval History*, p. 517.
10. Quoted in Thomas Asbridge, *The First Crusade: A New History* (Oxford, 2004), pp. 79–80.
11. Quoted in Hans E. Mayer, *The Crusades*, trans. John Gillingham (New York, 1972), pp. 99–100.

Chapter 11

1. Quoted in H. S. Lucas, "The Great European Famine of 1315, 1316, and 1317," *Speculum* 5 (1930): 359.
2. Quoted in Christos S. Bartsocas, "Two Fourteenth-Century Descriptions of the 'Black Death,'" *Journal of the History of Medicine* (October 1966): 395.
3. Quoted in David Herlihy, *The Black Death and the Transformation of the West*, ed. Samuel K. Cohn Jr. (Cambridge, Mass., 1997), p. 9.
4. Quoted in Rosemary Horrox, ed., *The Black Death* (Manchester, England, 1994), pp. 18–19.
5. Giovanni Boccaccio, *Decameron*, trans. Frances Winwar (New York, 1955), p. xxv.
6. Ibid., p. xxvi.
7. Jean Froissart, *Chronicles*, ed. and trans. Geoffrey Brereton (Harmondsworth, England, 1968), p. 111.
8. Quoted in James B. Ross and Mary M. McLaughlin, *The Portable Medieval Reader* (New York, 1949), pp. 218–219.
9. Quoted in Barbara W. Tuchman, *A Distant Mirror* (New York, 1978), p. 175.
10. Froissart, *Chronicles*, p. 212.
11. Ibid., p. 89.

12. Oliver J. Thatcher and Edgar H. McNeal, eds., *A Source Book for Medieval History* (New York, 1905), p. 288.

13. Quoted in D. S. Chambers, *The Imperial Age of Venice, 1380–1580* (London, 1970), p. 30.

14. Quoted in Robert Coogan, *Babylon on the Rhône: A Translation of Letters by Dante, Petrarch, and Catherine of Siena* (Washington, D.C., 1983), p. 115.

15. Quoted in Caroline Walker Bynum, *Holy Feast and Holy Fast: The Religious Significance of Food to Medieval Women* (Berkeley, Calif., 1987), p. 180.

16. Dante Alighieri, *Divine Comedy*, trans. Dorothy Sayers (New York, 1962), "Paradise," canto 33, line 145.

17. Petrarch, *Sonnets and Songs,* trans. Anna Maria Armi (New York, 1968), no. 74, p. 127.

18. Quoted in Millard Meiss, *Painting in Florence and Siena After the Black Death* (Princeton, N.J., 1951), p. 161.

19. Geoffrey Chaucer, "The Canterbury Tales," in *The Portable Chaucer,* ed. Theodore Morrison (New York, 1949), p. 67.

20. Christine de Pizan, *The Book of the City of Ladies,* trans. E. Jeffrey Richards (New York, 1982), pp. 83–84.

21. Quoted in Susan Mosher Stuard, "The Dominion of Gender, or How Women Fared in the High Middle Ages," in *Becoming Visible: Women in European History*, 3rd ed., eds. Renate Bridenthal, Claudia Koonz, and Susan Stuard (Boston, 1998), p. 147.

22. Quoted in David Herlihy, "Medieval Children," in *Essays on Medieval Civilization*, eds. Bede K. Lackner and Kenneth R. Philp (Austin, Tex., 1978), p. 121.

23. Quoted in Jean Gimpel, *The Medieval Machine* (New York, 1976), p. 168.

CHAPTER 12

1. Quoted in Jacob Burckhardt, *The Civilization of the Renaissance in Italy,* trans. S. G. C. Middlemore (London, 1960), p. 81.

2. Baldassare Castiglione, *The Book of the Courtier,* trans. Charles S. Singleton (Garden City, N.Y., 1959), pp. 288–289.

3. Quoted in De Lamar Jensen, *Renaissance Europe* (Lexington, Mass., 1981), p. 94.

4. Quoted in Iris Origo, "The Domestic Enemy: The Eastern Slaves in Tuscany in the Fourteenth and Fifteenth Centuries," *Speculum* 30 (1955): 333.

5. Quoted in Gene Brucker, ed., *Two Memoirs of Renaissance Florence* (New York, 1967), p. 132.

6. Quoted in Margaret L. King, *Women of the Renaissance* (Chicago, 1991), p. 3.

7. Quoted in Gene Brucker, ed., *The Society of Renaissance Florence* (New York, 1971), p. 190.

8. Quoted in Garrett Mattingly, *Renaissance Diplomacy* (Baltimore, 1964), p. 42.

9. Ibid., p. 95.

10. Niccolo Machiavelli, *The Prince*, trans. David Wootton (Indianapolis, 1995), p. 48.

11. Ibid., p. 55.

12. Ibid., p. 27.

13. Petrarch, "Epistle to Posterity," in *Letters from Petrarch,* trans. Morris Bishop (Bloomington, Ind., 1966), pp. 6–7.

14. Quoted in Frances Yates, *Giordano Bruno and the Hermetic Tradition* (Chicago, 1964), p. 211.

15. Giovanni Pico della Mirandola, "Oration on the Dignity of Man," in *The Renaissance Philosophy of Man*, eds. E. Cassirer, P. O. Kristeller, and J. H. Randall Jr. (Chicago, 1948), p. 225.

16. Ibid., pp. 247, 249.

17. Quoted in W. H. Woodward, *Vittorino da Feltre and Other Humanist Educators* (Cambridge, 1897), p. 102.

18. Quoted in Iris Origo, *The Light of the Past* (New York, 1959), p. 136.

19. Quoted in Elizabeth G. Holt, ed., *A Documentary History of Art*, vol. 1 (Garden City, N.Y., 1957), p. 286.

20. Quoted in Rosa M. Letts, *The Cambridge Introduction to Art: The Renaissance* (Cambridge, 1981), p. 86.

21. Quoted in Johan Huizinga, *The Waning of the Middle Ages* (Garden City, N.Y., 1956), p. 265.

CHAPTER 13

1. Desiderius Erasmus, "The Paraclesis," in *Christian Humanism and the Reformation: Selected Writings of Erasmus,* 3rd ed., John Olin (New York, 1987), p. 101.
2. Thomas More, *Utopia,* trans. Paul Turner (Harmondsworth, England, 1965), p. 76.
3. Quoted in Alister E. McGrath, *Reformation Thought: An Introduction* (Oxford, 1988), p. 72.
4. Quoted in Gordon Rupp, *Luther's Progress to the Diet of Worms* (New York, 1964), p. 82.
5. Martin Luther, "On the Freedom of a Christian Man," in *Martin Luther,* eds. E. G. Rupp and Benjamin Drewery, (New York, 1970), p. 50.
6. Quoted in Roland Bainton, *Here I Stand: A Life of Martin Luther* (New York, 1950), p. 144.
7. Quoted in De Lamar Jensen, *Reformation Europe* (Lexington, Mass., 1981), p. 83.
8. Quoted in Lee Palmer Wandel, *Voracious Idols and Violent Hands: Iconoclasm in Reformation Zurich, Strasbourg, and Basel* (New York, 1995), p. 81.
9. Quoted in A. G. Dickens and Dorothy Carr, eds., *The Reformation in England to the Accession of Elizabeth I* (New York, 1968), p. 72.
10. Quoted in Lewis W. Spitz, *The Renaissance and Reformation Movements* (Chicago, 1971), p. 414.
11. John Calvin, *Institutes of the Christian Religion*, vol. 1, trans. John Allen (Philadelphia, 1936), p. 220.
12. Ibid., vol. 1, p. 228; vol. 2, p. 181.
13. Quoted in Roland Bainton, *Women of the Reformation in Germany and Italy* (Minneapolis, 1971), p. 154.
14. Quoted in Bonnie S. Anderson and Judith P. Zinsser, *A History of Their Own: Women in Europe from Prehistory to the Present,* vol. 1 (New York, 1988), p. 259.
15. Quoted in John A. Phillips, *Eve: The History of an Idea* (New York,1984), p. 105.
16. Quoted in John O'Malley, *The First Jesuits* (Cambridge, Mass., 1993), p. 76.
17. Quoted in R. J. Knecht, *The French Wars of Religion, 1559–1598,* 2nd ed. (New York, 1996), p. 47.
18. Quoted in Mack P. Holt, *The French Wars of Religion, 1562–1629* (Cambridge, 1995), p. 86.
19. Quoted in Garrett Mattingly, *The Armada* (Boston, 1959), pp. 216–217.
20. Quoted in Theodore Schieder, *Handbuch der Europa'ischen Geschichte,* vol. 3 (Stuttgart, 1979), p. 579.

CHAPTER 14

1. Quoted in J. R. Hale, *Renaissance Exploration* (New York, 1968), p. 32.
2. Quoted in J. H. Parry, *The Age of Reconnaissance: Discovery, Exploration, and Settlement, 1450 to 1650* (New York, 1963), p. 33.
3. Quoted in Richard B. Reed, "The Expansion of Europe," in *The Meaning of the Renaissance and Reformation,* ed. Richard De Molen (Boston, 1974), p. 308.
4. Quoted in Ian Cameron, *Explorers and Exploration* (New York, 1991), p. 42.
5. Quoted in J. H. Parry and Robert G. Keith, eds., *New Iberian World,* vol. 2 (New York, 1984), pp. 309–310.
6. Quoted in J. H. Elliott, *Empires of the Atlantic World* (New Haven, Conn., 2006), p. 125.
7. Bernal Diaz, *The Conquest of New Spain* (New York, 1963), pp. 405–406.
8. Quoted in A. Andrea and J. H. Overfield, *The Human Record: Sources of Global History,* 3rd ed. (Boston, 1998), p. 460.
9. Quoted in Basil Davidson, *Africa in History: Themes and Outlines,* rev. ed. (New York, 1991), p. 198.

10. Quoted in Cameron, *Explorers and Exploration*, p. 42.
11. Quoted in Louis J. Gallagher, ed. and trans., *China in the Sixteenth Century: The Journals of Matthew Ricci* (New York, 1953), p. 154.
12. Quoted in G. V. Scammell, *The First Imperial Age: European Overseas Expansion, c. 1400–1715* (London, 1989), p. 62.
13. Miguel Leon-Portilla, ed., *The Broken Spears: The Aztec Account of the Conquest of Mexico* (Boston, 1969), p. 51.

CHAPTER 15

1. Quoted in Joseph Klaits, *Servants of Satan: The Age of the Witch Hunts* (Bloomington, Ind., 1985), p. 68.
2. Quoted in Peter H. Wilson, *The Thirty Years War: Europe's Tragedy* (Cambridge, Mass., 2009), p. 783.
3. Quoted in John B. Wolf, *Louis XIV* (New York, 1968), p. 134.
4. Quoted in James B. Collins, *The State in Early Modern France* (Cambridge, 1995), p. 130.
5. Quoted in Wolf, *Louis XIV*, p. 618.
6. Quoted in D. H. Pennington, *Europe in the Seventeenth Century*, 2nd ed. (New York, 1989), p. 494.
7. Quoted in J. H. Elliot, *Imperial Spain, 1469–1716* (New York, 1963), p. 306.
8. Quoted in B. H. Sumner, *Peter the Great and the Emergence of Russia* (New York, 1962), p. 122.
9. Quoted in Simon Schama, *A History of Britain: The Wars of the British, 1603–1776*, vol. 2 (New York, 2001), pp. 182, 185.

CHAPTER 16

1. Quoted in Alan G. R. Smith, *Science and Society in the Sixteenth and Seventeenth Centuries* (London, 1972), p. 59.
2. Edward MacCurdy, *The Notebooks of Leonardo da Vinci*, vol. 1 (London, 1948), p. 634.
3. Ibid., p. 636.
4. Frances Yates, *Giordano Bruno and the Hermetic Tradition* (New York, 1964), p. 448.
5. Ibid., p. 450.
6. Quoted in Smith, *Science and Society*, p. 97.
7. Logan P. Smith, *Life and Letters of* Sir *Henry Wotton*, vol. 1 (Oxford, 1907), pp. 486–487.
8. Quoted in John H. Randall, *The Making of the Modern Mind* (Boston, 1926), p. 234.
9. Quoted in Smith, *Science and Society*, p. 124.
10. Quoted in Betty J. Dobbs, *The Foundations of Newton's Alchemy* (Cambridge, 1975), pp. 13–14.
11. Jolande Jacobi, ed., *Paracelsus: Selected Writings* (New York, 1965), pp. 5–6.
12. Ibid., p. 21.
13. Quoted in Londa Schiebinger, *The Mind Has No Sex? Women in the Origins of Modern Science* (Cambridge, Mass., 1989), pp. 52–53.
14. Ibid., p. 85.
15. Quoted in Phyllis Stock, *Better Than Rubies: A History of Women's Education* (New York, 1978), p. 16.
16. Rene Descartes, *Philosophical Writings*, ed. and trans. Norman K. Smith (New York, 1958), p. 95.
17. Ibid., pp. 118–119.
18. Francis Bacon, *The Great Instauration*, trans. Jerry Weinberger (Arlington Heights, Ill., 1989), pp. 2, 8, 16, 21.
19. Descartes, *Discourse on Method*, in *Philosophical Writings*, p. 75.
20. Margaret C. Jacob, *The Cultural Meaning of the Scientific Revolution* (New York, 1988), p. 73.
21. Stillman Drake, ed. and trans., *Discoveries and Opinions of Galileo* (New York, 1957), p. 182.
22. Benedict de Spinoza, *Ethics*, trans. R. H. M. Elwes (New York, 1955), pp. 75–76.
23. Ibid., p. 76.
24. Spinoza, *Letters*, quoted in Randall, *The Making of the Modern Mind*, p. 247.

25. Blaise Pascal, *Pensées,* trans. J. M. Cohen (Harmondsworth, England, 1961), p. 100.
26. Ibid., pp. 31, 52–53, 164, 165.

CHAPTER 17

1. Quoted in Paul Hazard, *The European Mind, 1680–1715* (New York, 1963), pp. 304–305.
2. Quoted in Dorinda Outram, *The Enlightenment* (Cambridge, 1995), p. 67.
3. Quoted in Hazard, *The European Mind,* p. 12.
4. John Locke, *An Essay Concerning Human Understanding* (New York, 1964), pp. 89–90.
5. Baron Paul d'Holbach, "Common Sense," in *The Enlightenment,* ed. Frank E. Manuel (Englewood Cliffs, N.J., 1965), p. 62.
6. Jean-Jacques Rousseau, *A Discourse on Inequality,* trans. Maurice Cranston (Harmondsworth, England, 1984), p. 109.
7. Jean-Jacques Rousseau, *The Social Contract,* trans. Maurice Cranston (Harmondsworth, England, 1968), p. 141.
8. Mary Astell, "A Serious Proposal to the Ladies," in *First Feminists: British Women Writers, 1578–1799,* ed. Moira Ferguson (Bloomington, Ind., 1985), p. 190.
9. Mary Astell, "Some Reflections upon Marriage," in ibid., p. 193.
10. Kenneth Clark, *Civilization* (New York, 1969), p. 231.
11. Voltaire, *The Age of Louis XIV,* trans. Martyn P. Pollack (New York, 1961), p. 1.
12. Cesare Beccaria, *An Essay on Crimes and Punishments,* trans. E. D. Ingraham (Philadelphia, 1819), pp. 59–60.
13. Quoted in Rene Sand, *The Advance to Social Medicine* (London, 1952), pp. 86–87.
14. Quoted in Peter Burke, *Popular Culture in Early Modern Europe* (New York, 1978), p. 179.
15. Quoted in ibid., p. 186.
16. Quoted in C. A. Macartney, *The Habsburg and Hohenzollern Dynasties in the Seventeenth and Eighteenth Centuries* (New York, 1970), p. 157.

CHAPTER 18

1. Frederick II, *Forms of Government,* in *The Western Tradition,* ed. Eugen Weber (Lexington, Mass., 1972), pp. 538, 544.
2. Quoted in Reinhold A. Dorwart, *The Administrative Reforms of Frederick William I of Prussia* (Cambridge, Mass., 1953), p. 36.
3. Quoted in Sidney B. Fay, *The Rise of Brandenburg-Prussia to 1786,* rev. ed. by Klaus Epstein (New York, 1964), p. 92.
4. Quoted in Hans Rosenberg, *Bureaucracy, Aristocracy, and Autocracy: The Prussian Experience, 1660–1815* (Cambridge, Mass., 1958), p. 40.
5. Quoted in Fernand Braudel, *Civilization and Capitalism,* vol. 3 (London, 1981–1984), p. 378.
6. Quoted in ibid., p. 245.
7. Quoted in Witold Rybczynski, *Home: A Short History of an Idea* (New York, 1986), p. 105.
8. Quoted in Jonathan Dewald, *The European Nobility, 1400–1800* (Cambridge, 1996), pp. 91–92.
9. Quoted in Peter Gay, *Age of Enlightenment* (New York, 1966), p. 87.
10. Quoted in Paul Hazard, *The European Mind, 1680–1715* (Cleveland, Ohio, 1963), pp. 6–7.
11. Igor Vinogradoff, "Russian Missions to London, 1711–1789: Further Extracts from the Cottrell Papers," *Oxford Slavonic Papers,* New Series 15 (1982): 76.
12. Quoted in Jeffrey Kaplow, *The Names of Kings: The Parisian Laboring Poor in the Eighteenth Century* (New York, 1972), p. 134.

CHAPTER 19

1. Quoted in R. R. Palmer, *The Age of the Democratic Revolutions,* vol. 1 (Princeton, N.J., 1959), p. 239.

2. Quoted in ibid., p. 242.
3. Quoted in O. J. Hufton, "Toward an Understanding of the Poor of Eighteenth-Century France," in *French Government and Society, 1500–1850*, ed. J. F. Bosher (London, 1973), p. 152.
4. Arthur Young, *Travels in France During the Years 1787, 1788, and 1789* (Cambridge, 1929), p. 23.
5. Quoted in D. M. G. Sutherland, *France, 1789–1815: Revolution and Counter-Revolution* (New York, 1986), p. 74.
6. Quoted in William Doyle, *The Oxford History of the French Revolution* (Oxford, 1989), p. 156.
7. Quoted in ibid., p. 184.
8. Quoted in J. Hardman, ed., *French Revolution Documents*, vol. 2 (Oxford, 1973), p. 23.
9. Quoted in W. Scott, *Terror and Repression in Revolutionary Marseilles* (London, 1973), p. 84.
10. Quoted in H. Morse Stephens, *The Principal Speeches of the Statesmen and Orators of the French Revolution*, vol. 2 (Oxford, 1892), p. 189.
11. Quoted in Leo Gershoy, *The Era of the French Revolution* (Princeton, N.J., 1957), p. 157.
12. Quoted in J. M. Thompson, ed., *French Revolution Documents* (Oxford, 1933), pp. 258–259.
13. Quoted in Doyle, *Oxford History of the French Revolution,* p. 254.
14. Quoted in R. R. Palmer, *Twelve Who Ruled* (New York, 1965), p. 75.
15. Quoted in Darline Gay Levy, Harriet Branson Applewhite, and Mary Durham Johnson, eds., *Women in Revolutionary Paris, 1789–1795* (Urbana, Ill., 1979), p. 132.
16. Ibid., pp. 219–220.
17. Quoted in Elizabeth G. Sledziewski, "The French Revolution as the Turning Point," in *A History of Women in the West*, vol. 4, eds. Geneviève Fraisse and Michelle Perrot (Cambridge, 1993), p. 39.
18. Quoted in François Furet and Mona Ozouf, *A Critical Dictionary of the French Revolution*, trans. Arthur Goldhammer (Cambridge, Mass., 1989), p. 545.
19. Quoted in J. Christopher Herold, ed., *The Mind of Napoleon* (New York, 1955), p. 43.
20. Quoted in Felix Markham, *Napoleon* (New York, 1963), pp. 92–93.
21. Quoted in Doyle, *Oxford History of the French Revolution,* p. 381.
22. Quoted in Herold, ed., *The Mind of Napoleon,* pp. 74–75.
23. Quoted in Steven Englund, *Napoleon: A Political Life* (New York, 2004), p. 285.

CHAPTER 20

1. Quoted in W. Gordon Rimmer, *Marshall's of Leeds, Flax-Spinners, 1788–1886* (Cambridge, 1960), p. 40.
2. Daniel Defoe, *A Plan of the English Commerce* (Oxford, 1928), pp. 76–77.
3. Quoted in Albert Tucker, *A History of English Civilization* (New York, 1972), p. 583.
4. Quotations are from Lara Kriegel, *Grand Designs: Labor, Empire, and the Museum in Victorian Culture* (Durham, N.C., 2007), p. 120.
5. Quoted in E. Royston Pike, *Human Documents of the Industrial Revolution in Britain* (London, 1966), p. 320.
6. Ibid., p. 314.
7. Ibid., p. 343.
8. Ibid., p. 315.
9. Charles Dickens, *The Old Curiosity Shop* (New York, 2000), p. 340.
10. Quoted in A. J. Donajgrodzi, ed., *Social Control in Nineteenth-Century Britain* (London, 1977), p. 141.
11. Quoted in Pike, *Human Documents,* pp. 343–344.
12. Quoted in Eric J. Evans, *The Forging of the Modern State: Early Industrial Britain, 1783–1870* (London, 1983), p. 113.
13. Henry Mayhew, *London Labour and the London Poor*, vol. 1 (London, 1851), pp. 342–343.
14. Quoted in Pike, *Human Documents,* pp. 60–61.

15. Quoted in Evans, *Forging of the Modern State*, p. 124.

CHAPTER 21

1. Quoted in Charles Breunig, *The Age of Revolution and Reaction, 1789–1850* (New York, 1970), p. 119.
2. Quoted in M. S. Anderson, *The Ascendancy of Europe, 1815–1914*, 2nd ed. (London, 1985), p. 1.
3. Quotations from Burke can be found in Peter Viereck, *Conservatism* (Princeton, N.J., 1956), pp. 27, 114.
4. Quoted in Rene Albrecht-Carrié, *The Concert of Europe* (New York, 1968), p. 48.
5. Quoted in M. C. Eakin, *The History of Latin America: Collision of Cultures* (New York, 2007), p. 188.
6. Quoted in G. de Berthier de Sauvigny, *Metternich and His Times* (London, 1962), p. 105.
7. Quoted in S. Joan Moon, "Feminism and Socialism: The Utopian Synthesis of Flora Tristan," in *Socialist Women*, eds. Marilyn J. Boxer and Jean H. Quataert (New York, 1978), p. 38.
8. Quoted in Stanley Z. Pech, *The Czech Revolution of 1848* (Chapel Hill, N.C., 1969), p. 82.
9. Quoted in Clive Emsley, *Policing and Its Context, 1750–1870* (New York, 1984), p. 58.
10. Quoted in Clive Emsley, *Crime and Society in England, 1750–1900* (London, 1987), p. 173.
11. Quoted in Emsley, *Policing and Its Context*, p. 66.
12. Quoted in ibid., p. 102.
13. Quoted in Emsley, *Crime and Society in England*, p. 226.
14. William Wordsworth, "The Tables Turned," in *Poems of Wordsworth*, ed. Matthew Arnold (London, 1963), p. 138.
15. William Wordsworth, *The Prelude* (Harmondsworth, England, 1971), p. 109.
16. Quoted in H. G. Schenk, *The Mind of the European Romantics* (Garden City, N.Y., 1969), p. 205.
17. Quoted in Siegbert Prawer, ed., *The Romantic Period in Germany* (London, 1970), p. 285.
18. Quoted in John B. Halsted, ed., *Romanticism* (New York, 1969), p. 156.

CHAPTER 22

1. Quoted in James F. McMillan, *Napoleon III* (New York, 1991), p. 37.
2. Quoted in Robert Gildea, *Barricades and Borders: Europe, 1800–1914*, 2nd ed. (Oxford, 1996), p. 170.
3. Quoted in Otto Pflanze, *Bismarck and the Development of Germany: The Period of Unification, 1815–1871* (Princeton, N.J., 1963), p. 60.
4. Louis L. Snyder, ed., *Documents of German History* (New Brunswick, N.J., 1958), p. 202.
5. Quoted in Pflanze, *Bismarck and the Development of Germany*, p. 327.
6. Quoted in György Szabad, *Hungarian Political Trends Between the Revolution and the Compromise, 1849–1867* (Budapest, 1977), p. 163.
7. Quoted in Rondo Cameron, "Crédit Mobilier and the Economic Development of Europe," *Journal of Political Economy* 61 (1953): 470.
8. Karl Marx and Friedrich Engels, *The Communist Manifesto* (Harmondsworth, England, 1967), p. 79.
9. Ibid., pp. 79, 81, 82.
10. Charles Darwin, *On the Origin of Species*, vol. 1 (New York, 1872), pp. 77, 79.
11. Quoted in Albert Lyons and R. Joseph Petrucelli, *Medicine: An Illustrated History* (New York, 1978), p. 569.

CHAPTER 23

1. Quoted in David Landes, *The Unbound Prometheus: Technological Change and Industrial Development in Western Europe from 1750 to the Present* (Cambridge, 1969), p. 353.
2. Quoted in Barbara Franzoi, "With the Wolf Always at the Door: Women's

Work in Domestic Industry in Britain and Germany," in *Connecting Spheres: Women in the Western World, 1500 to the Present*, eds. Marilyn J. Boxer and Jean H. Quataert (New York, 1987), p. 151.

3. Quoted in W. L. Guttsman, *The German Social Democratic Party, 1875–1933* (London, 1981), p. 63.

4. Quoted in Leslie Derfler, *Socialism Since Marx: A Century of the European Left* (New York, 1973), p. 58.

5. Karl Marx and Friedrich Engels, *The Communist Manifesto* (Harmondsworth, England, 1967), p. 102.

6. Quoted in Paul Avrich, *The Russian Anarchists* (Princeton, N.J., 1971), p. 67.

7. Quoted in Nicholas Bullock and James Read, *The Movement for Housing Reform in Germany and France, 1840–1914* (Cambridge, 1985), p. 42.

8. Quoted in Gary Cross, *A Social History of Leisure Since 1600* (State College, Pa., 1990), pp. 116, 119.

9. Quoted in Sibylle Meyer, "The Tiresome Work of Conspicuous Leisure: On the Domestic Duties of the Wives of Civil Servants in the German Empire (1871–1918)," in *Connecting Spheres*, eds. Boxer and Quataert, p. 161.

10. Quoted in Lenard R. Berlanstein, *The Working People of Paris, 1871–1914* (Baltimore, 1984), p. 141.

11. Quoted in Robert Gildea, *Barricades and Borders: Europe, 1800–1914*, 2nd ed. (Oxford, 1996), pp. 240–241.

12. Quoted in Andrew Lees and Lynn Hollen Lees, *Cities and the Making of Modern Europe, 1750–1914* (Cambridge, 2007), p. 224.

13. Quoted in Cross, *Social History of Leisure*, p. 130.

14. Quoted in Shmuel Galai, *The Liberation Movement in Russia, 1900–1905* (Cambridge, 1973), p. 26.

CHAPTER 24

1. Quoted in Charles Rearick, *Pleasures of the Belle Epoque: Entertainment and Festivity in Turn-of-the-Century France* (New Haven, Conn., 1985), p. 120.

2. Quoted in Arthur E. E. McKenzie, *The Major Achievements of Science*, vol. 1 (New York, 1960), p. 310.

3. Friedrich Nietzsche, *Twilight of the Idols and the Anti-Christ*, trans. R.J. Hollingdale (New York, 1972), pp. 117–118.

4. Friedrich Nietzsche, *Thus Spake Zarathustra*, in *The Philosophy of Nietzsche* (New York, 1954), p. 6.

5. Herbert Spencer, *Social Statics* (New York, 1896), pp. 146, 150.

6. Friedrich von Bernhardi, *Germany and the Next War*, trans. Allen H. Powles (New York, 1914), pp. 18–19.

7. Quoted in Edward R. Tannenbaum, *1900: The Generation Before the Great War* (Garden City, N.Y., 1976), p. 337.

8. William Booth, *In Darkest England and the Way Out* (London, 1890), p. 45.

9. Quoted in John Rewald, *The History of Impressionism* (New York, 1961), pp. 456–458.

10. Quoted in Anne Higonnet, *Berthe Morisot's Images of Women* (Cambridge, Mass., 1992), p. 19.

11. Quoted in Craig Wright, *Listening to Music* (Saint Paul, Minn., 1992), p. 327.

12. Quoted in Catherine M. Prelinger, "Prelude to Consciousness: Amalie Sieveking and the Female Association for the Care of the Poor and the Sick," in *German Women in the Nineteenth Century: A Social History*, ed. John C. Fout (New York, 1984), p. 119.

13. Quoted in Bonnie G. Smith, *Changing Lives: Women in European History Since 1700* (Lexington, Mass., 1989), p. 379.

14. Quoted in Paul Massing, *Rehearsal for Destruction: A Study of Political Anti-Semitism in Imperial Germany* (New York, 1949), p. 147.

15. Quoted in Abba Eban, *Heritage: Civilization and the Jews* (New York, 1984), p. 249.

16. Quoted in John Merriman, *A History of Modern Europe* (New York, 1996), p. 953.

17. Quoted in ibid., p. 965.
18. Karl Pearson, *National Life from the Standpoint of Science* (London, 1905), p. 184.
19. Quoted in John Ellis, *The Social History of the Machine Gun* (New York, 1975), p. 80.
20. Quoted in ibid., p. 86.
21. Quoted in Louis L. Snyder, ed., *The Imperialism Reader* (Princeton, N.J., 1962), p. 220.
22. Quoted in K. M. Panikkar, *Asia and Western Dominance* (London, 1959), p. 116.

CHAPTER 25

1. Martin Gilbert, *The First World War: A Complete History* (New York, 1994), p. 259.
2. Quoted in ibid., p. 264.
3. Arnold Toynbee, *Surviving the Future* (New York, 1971), pp. 106–107.
4. Quoted in Joachim Remak, "1914—The Third Balkan War: Origins Reconsidered," *Journal of Modern History* 43 (1971): 364–365.
5. Quoted in Robert G. L. Waite, *Vanguard of Nazism* (New York, 1969), p. 22.
6. Quoted in J. M. Winter, *The Experience of World War I* (New York, 1989), p. 142.
7. Quoted in ibid., p. 137.
8. Quoted in Hew Strachan, *The First World War* (New York, 2004), pp. 94–95.
9. Quoted in ibid., p. 72.
10. Quoted in Gail Braybon, *Women Workers in the First World War: The British Experience* (London, 1981), p. 79.
11. Quoted in Catherine W. Reilly, ed., *Scars Upon My Heart: Women's Poetry and Verse of the First World War* (London, 1981), p. 90.
12. Quoted in Robert Paxton, *Europe in the Twentieth Century*, 2nd ed. (New York, 1985), p. 110.
13. Quoted in William M. Mandel, *Soviet Women* (Garden City, N.Y., 1975), p. 43.
14. Quoted in Mark D. Steinberg, *Voices of Revolution, 1917* (New Haven, Conn., 2001), p. 55.

CHAPTER 26

1. Quoted in Stéphane Audoin-Rouzeau and Annette Becker, *14–18: Understanding the Great War*, trans. Catherine Temerson (New York, 2002), pp. 212–213.
2. Quoted in ibid., p. 41.
3. Quoted in Robert Paxton, *Europe in the Twentieth Century*, 2nd ed. (New York, 1985), p. 237.
4. Quoted in Denis Mack Smith, *Mussolini* (New York, 1982), p. 51.
5. Benito Mussolini, "The Doctrine of Fascism," in *Italian Fascisms from Pareto to Gentile*, ed. Adrian Lyttleton (London, 1973), p. 42.
6. Quoted in Alexander De Grand, "Women Under Italian Fascism," *Historical Journal* 19 (1976): 958–959.
7. Adolf Hitler, *Mein Kampf*, trans. Ralph Manheim (Boston, 1943), p. 22.
8. Ibid., p. 161.
9. Quoted in Joachim Fest, *Hitler*, trans. Richard Winston and Clara Winston (New York, 1974), p. 241.
10. Quoted in Jeremy Noakes and Geoffrey Pridham, eds., *Nazism, 1919–1945, A Documentary Reader: The Rise to Power 1919–1934*, vol. 1 (Exeter, England, 1983), pp. 50–51.
11. Quoted in Jackson J. Spielvogel and David Redles, *Hitler and Nazi Germany: A History*, 6th ed. (Upper Saddle River, N.J., 2010), p. 83.
12. Irving Howe, ed., *The Basic Writings of Trotsky* (London, 1963), p. 162.
13. Quoted in Sheila Fitzpatrick, *Everyday Stalinism. Ordinary Life in Extraordinary Times: Soviet Russia in the 1930s* (New York, 1999), p. 87.
14. Paul Valéry, *Variety*, trans. Malcolm Cowley (New York, 1927), pp. 27–28.
15. Quoted in Matthis Eberle, *World War I and the Weimar Artists: Dix, Grosz, Beckmann, Schlemmer* (New Haven, Conn., 1985), p. 54.

16. Norman H. Baynes, ed., *The Speeches of Adolf Hitler, 1922–1939*, vol. 1 (Oxford, 1942), p. 591.

CHAPTER 27

1. Adolf Hitler, *Mein Kampf,* trans. Ralph Manheim (Boston, 1971), p. 654.
2. *Documents on German Foreign Policy,* ser. D, vol. 2 (London, 1956), p. 358.
3. Ibid., vol. 7, p. 204.
4. Quoted in Norman Rich, *Hitler's War Aims,* vol. 1 (New York, 1973), p. 129.
5. Quoted in Williamson Murray and Allan Millett, *A War to Be Won: Fighting the Second World War* (Cambridge, Mass., 2000), p. 66.
6. Quoted in ibid., p. 137.
7. Albert Speer, *Spandau,* trans. Richard Winston and Clara Winston (New York, 1976), p. 50.
8. *Nazi Conspiracy and Aggression,* vol. 6 (Washington, D.C., 1946), p. 262.
9. International Military Tribunal, *Trial of the Major War Criminals,* vol. 22 (Nuremberg, 1947–1949), p. 480.
10. Adolf Hitler, *My New Order,* ed. Raoul de Roussy de Sales (New York, 1941), pp. 21–22.
11. Quoted in Lucy Dawidowicz, *The War Against the Jews* (New York, 1975), p. 106.
12. *Nazi Conspiracy and Aggression,* vol. 5, pp. 341–342.
13. Quoted in Raul Hilberg, *The Destruction of the European Jews,* rev. ed., vol. 1 (New York, 1985), pp. 332–333.
14. *Nazi Conspiracy and Aggression,* vol. 6, p. 789.
15. Quoted in Jeremy Noakes and Geoffrey Pridham, eds., *Nazism, 1919–1945: A Documentary Reader: Foreign Policy, War, and Racial Extermination,* vol. 3 (Exeter, England, 1995), p. 1182.
16. Quoted in John Campbell, *The Experience of World War II* (New York, 1989), p. 170.
17. Quoted in Claudia Koonz, "Mothers in the Fatherland: Women in Nazi Germany," in *Becoming Visible:*

Women in European History, eds. Renate Bridenthal and Claudia Koonz (Boston, 1977), p. 466.
18. Quoted in Campbell, *The Experience of World War II,* p. 143.
19. Quoted in ibid., p. 177.
20. Quoted in Robert E. Sherwood, *Roosevelt and Hopkins: An Intimate History* (New York, 1948), p. 870.
21. Quoted in Norman Graebner, *Cold War Diplomacy, 1945–1960* (Princeton, N.J., 1962), p. 117.
22. Quoted in ibid., p. 117.
23. Quoted in Wilfried Loth, *The Division of the World, 1941–1955* (New York, 1988), p. 81.

CHAPTER 28

1. Quoted in Joseph M. Jones, *The Fifteen Weeks (February 21–June 5, 1947),* 2nd ed. (New York, 1964), pp. 140–141.
2. Quoted in Walter Laqueur, *Europe in Our Time* (New York, 1992), p. 111.
3. Quoted in Wilfried Loth, *The Division of the World, 1941–1955* (New York, 1988), pp. 160–161.
4. Quoted in William I. Hitchcock, *The Struggle for Europe: The Turbulent History of a Divided Continent, 1945–2002* (New York, 2003), p. 215.
5. Quoted in Peter Lane, *Europe Since 1945: An Introduction* (Totowa, N.J., 1985), p. 248.
6. Quoted in Robert F. Kennedy, *Thirteen Days: A Memoir of the Cuban Missile Crisis* (New York, 1969), pp. 89–90.
7. Quoted in Larry Collins and Dominique Lapierre, *Freedom at Midnight* (New York, 1975), p. 252.
8. R. Hilton, *Military Attaché in Moscow* (London, 1949), p. 41.
9. Nikita Khrushchev, *Khrushchev Remembers,* trans. Strobe Talbott (Boston, 1970), p. 77.
10. Quoted in Bonnie G. Smith, *Changing Lives: Women in European History Since 1700* (Lexington, Mass., 1989), p. 513.
11. Quoted in Hilda Scott, *Sweden's "Right to Be Human": Sex-Role Equality—The*

Goal and the Reality (London, 1982), p. 125.

12. Simone de Beauvoir, *The Second Sex,* trans. H. M. Parshley (New York, 1961), p. xxviii.

13. Quoted in Henry Grosshans, *The Search for Modern Europe* (Boston, 1970), p. 421.

14. Richard Maltby, ed., *Passing Parade: A History of Popular Culture in the Twentieth Century* (Oxford, 1989), p. 8.

15. Quoted in ibid., p. 11.

Chapter 29

1. Quoted in Marsha Rowe et al., *Spare Rib Reader* (Harmondsworth, England, 1982), p. 574.

2. Betty Friedan, *The Feminine Mystique* (New York, 1963), p. 10.

3. Quoted in Tony Judt, *Postwar: A History of Europe Since 1945* (New York, 2005), p. 390.

4. "To Walk the Moon," *New York Times,* July 20, 1969.

Chapter 30

1. Quoted in Tony Judt, *Postwar: A History of Europe Since 1945* (New York, 2005), p. 585.

2. Mikhail Gorbachev, "Report to the 27th Party Congress," in *Current Soviet Policies* 9 (1986, February 25): 10.

3. Quoted in William I. Hitchcock, *The Struggle for Europe: The Turbulent History of a Divided Continent, 1945–2002* (New York, 2003), pp. 399–400.

4. Quoted in Renate Bridenthal, "Women in the New Europe," in *Becoming Visible: Women in European History,* 3rd eds., Renate Bridenthal, Susan Mosher Stuard, and Merry E. Weisner (Boston, 1998), pp. 564–565.

5. Quoted in Judt, *Postwar Europe,* p. 743.

6. Quoted in Joan W. Scott, *The Politics of the Veil* (Princeton, N.J., 2009), p. 1.

7. Elise Boulding, *Women in the Twentieth-Century World* (New York, 1977), pp. 186–187.

Index

Note: Page numbers in italics indicate illustrations (including captions), maps, and boxed features.